COMPUTER GRAPHICS
THEORY INTO PRACTICE

Jeffrey J. McConnell
Canisius College

JONES AND BARTLETT PUBLISHERS

Sudbury, Massachusetts

BOSTON   TORONTO   LONDON   SINGAPORE

World Headquarters
Jones and Bartlett Publishers
40 Tall Pine Drive
Sudbury, MA 01776
978-443-5000
info@jbpub.com
www.jbpub.com

Jones and Bartlett Publishers
Canada
6339 Ormindale Way
Mississauga, ON L5V 1J2
CANADA

Jones and Bartlett Publishers
International
Barb House, Barb Mews
London W6 7PA
UK

Jones and Bartlett's books and products are available through most bookstores and online booksellers. To contact Jones and Bartlett Publishers directly, call 800-832-0034, fax 978-443-8000, or visit our website www.jbpub.com. Substantial discounts on bulk quantities of Jones and Bartlett's publications are available to corporations, professional associations, and other qualified organizations. For details and specific discount information, contact the special sales department at Jones and Bartlett via the above contact information or send an email to specialsales@jbpub.com.

Cover Images: © Photos.com

ISBN: 0-7637-2250-2

Libary of Congress Cataloging-in-Publication Data
McConnell, Jeffrey J.
  Computer graphics : theory into practice / Jeffrey J. McConnell.
      p. cm.
  Includes bibliographical references and index.
  ISBN 0-7637-2250-2
  1. Computer graphics. I. Title.
  T385.M3779983 2005
  006.6--dc22

                                                2005049289

Production Credits
Acquisitions Editor: Tim Anderson
Production Director: Amy Rose
Production Assistant: Alison Meier
Editorial Assistant: Kate Koch
V.P. of Manufacturing: Therese Connell
Cover Design: Kristin E. Ohlin
Composition: Northeast Compositors, Inc.
Printing and Binding: Malloy, Inc.
Cover Printing: Malloy, Inc.

Printed in the United States of America
09 08 07 06 05   10 9 8 7 6 5 4 3 2 1

To my graphics students through the years, especially Andrea, Claude, Jerry, and Lynda who asked me to teach my first graphics course during the Spring 1984 semester.

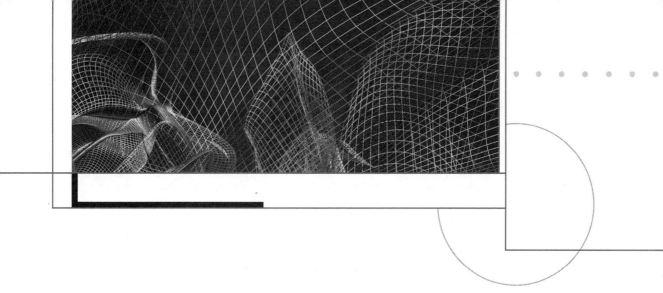

Preface

Computer graphics is a challenging field because it is based on knowledge from many different areas. Properly modeling the interaction of light with objects requires an understanding of how those interactions occur in the real world. There is a wide variety of objects in the world and they behave in many different ways. This book provides an introduction to the process of computer graphics and presents some of the techniques and challenges in creating images using a computer.

This book concentrates on concepts for the production of realistic images in three-dimensional graphics. This is only one component of computer graphics as there are also applications in user interfaces, data visualization, and non-photorealistic rendering to name just three.

To help the flow of presentation, all images are included in gray scale within the body of the text so that the reader can see some image details near the point were they are discussed. For most images, there are color versions in the color plate section of the book that show more details due to being in color.

This book can be used as a textbook for a semester/quarter long course at the upper undergraduate or graduate level. Each chapter of this book could be covered within one week of a semester (approximately three lecture hours), with extra time allocated to longer chapters such as Chapters 1, 2, and 6, and to other course components such as examinations. The last two chapters of the book provide an overview of a number of advanced modeling techniques. The time allocated to these two chapters can be increased as an alternative by expanding on the details discussed. As an alternative, students or student teams could be given a semester project to research more deeply a component of animation or one of the advanced modeling areas discussed in Chapters 11 and 12 and then give classroom presentations on those topics.

There are two ways that a course in computer graphics could be designed. The first way concentrates on the details of the techniques for modeling and expects students to write a rendering program from scratch, directly setting pixel values based on those calculations. The second way discusses the techniques but has students use a graphics API to implement their rendering program. This book is designed to support both of these approaches. The main body of each chapter concentrates on the details behind one component of graphics and then covers the appropriate components of one graphics API, specifically OpenGL, in the last section of the chapter. This organization of the chapters was deliberate to allow flexibility so that the book can be used for either of these two approaches.

People learn better when they are actively involved in doing something with the material they are reading. Project work in computer graphics is a critical component of learning the field. It is expected that students in a graphics course will be involved with implementing a rendering program. The programming exercises at the end of each chapter give examples of the type of programming assignments that could be given to students. For most of the early chapters, these programming assignments add capabilities to the render that has already been developed in earlier assignments. In a course that requires students to create a rendering program from scratch, the students can develop a simple Phong rendering program and then add capabilities such as a z-buffer for obstructions and textures to improve realism. A second project could be a ray tracing program for spheres and planes that includes transparency and shadowing and uses some of the components created for the Phong rendering program. In a course that uses a graphics API such as OpenGL, the students could work on code to read scene descriptions and code to initialize OpenGL and its viewing parameters during the discussion of the first two chapters. As later chapters are covered, students can increase the capabilities of their rendering program. Additional project work could include the use of double buffering to create a smooth rotation of an earlier created scene or could involve a ray tracer that generates the image displayed by OpenGL.

This book assumes that the reader has some prior knowledge of general programming and basic data structures. Algorithms in this text are presented in C/C++ style syntax. This is done for two reasons. First, C and C++ are the most common languages for graphics programming. Second, OpenGL, a component of this text, has a well established language binding for C and C++. Because there is no discussion of class structures within this book, this syntax style will be quite understandable by readers familiar with Java or any of the imperative programming languages.

Graphics is a highly mathematical field. Students with a strong background in mathematics including linear algebra will find the material easier to understand; however, an appendix with additional mathematical details is included for those students who need additional information on the mathematical concepts in the main body of the book. It is highly recommended that any course include where appropriate at least a brief discussion of computer math and round-off error, IEEE floating point numbers, and calculation speed-ups.

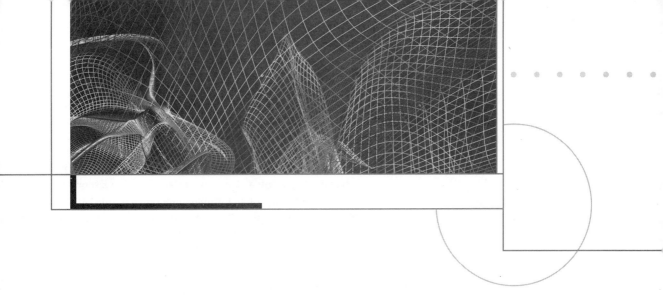

Acknowledgments

I am grateful for those people who provided images for this book. Specifically:

- Erik Svanholm, Allison Ober, and Swapna Sundaram (Zumtobel Staff, Inc.) for Figure 9.2
- Jim Hanan (University of Queensland) for Figures 11.4 and 11.5
- Stéphane Gourgout (Bionatics, Inc.) for Figure 11.8
- Oliver Deussen (University of Constance) and Bernd Lintermann (ZKM Institute for Visual Media) for Figure 11.9
- Ronald Fedkiw (Stanford University) and Douglas Enright (UCLA) for Figure 11.13
- David S. Ebert (Purdue University) for Figures 11.14 and 11.16
- Yoshinori Dobashi (Hokkaido University) for Figure 11.15
- Ronald Fedkiw (Stanford University) and Duc Nguyen (Lockheed Martin Co.) for Figures 11.17 and 11.18
- Robert Bridson (University of British Columbia) for Figure 12.5
- Yanyun Chen (Microsoft Research Asia) for Figures 12.6, 12.12, and 12.13
- Tae Yong Kim and Ulrich Neumann (University of Southern California Computer Graphics and Immersive Technology Laboratory) for Figures 12.7 and 12.8
- Henrik Wann Jensen (University of California, San Deigo) for Figures 12.10 and 12.15
- Michael Gleicher (University of Wisconsin, Madison) for Figure 12.16

The series of images in Figure 10.1 were taken at the Key West Butterfly & Nature Conservatory (www.keywestbutterfly.com). Thanks go to Sam Trophia and George Fernandez for creating this wonderful exhibition.

I am extremely grateful to Adam Zyglis (www.AdamZyglis.com), a talented artist and computer scientist, who drew most of the illustrations in this book. Production of the illustrations was supported in part by a Canisius College Earning Excellence Program grant to Adam and the Computer Science Department at Canisius College.

An early version of this book was reviewed by Nan C. Schaller (Rochester Institute of Technology), Henry L. Welch (Milwaukee School of Engineering), and Ching-Kuang Shene (Michigan Technological University). Their comments helped me to refine the style of presentation in this book and the results are clearly better because of their input.

The students in the Fall 2003 offering of my Computer Graphics class also deserve mention for their high quality feedback on a draft of this book: Brenda Chodkowski, Daniel Hoffman, Brian Kindzierski, Stephen Makula, Daniel McPartlan, Andre Nelson, Hermann Pohl, and Brian Vogt.

I have gotten a great deal of support from many members of the Jones and Bartlett staff: Amy Rose (Production Director), Tim Anderson (Acquisitions Editor), Alison Meier (Production Assistant), and Lesley Chiller (Editorial Assistant). Thanks also go to Lydia Stuart Horton (Copyeditor), Mike Wile (Northeast Compositors), and Donna Marton (Proofreader).

I would like to thank Fred Dansereau for his advice, support, and suggestions throughout this project. Last, but not least, I'd like to thank Barney (6/6/1992–2/19/2005) for the use of his toys for Figures 7.1 and 9.1, for posing for the picture in Figure 12.1, and for providing the type of diversions only a dog can provide.

Though I am grateful for the support from all of the above-mentioned people, any remaining errors in the text are solely the responsibility of the author.

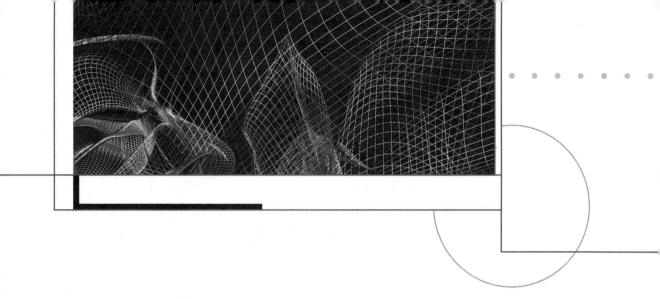

Contents

Computer Graphics Background

In a general sense, computer graphics is the process of producing a picture or image using the computer. At one end of the spectrum, this includes applications that draw simple graphs or line drawings—the sort of capability that is available in most modern word processors and spreadsheets. At the other end are programs that involve complex mathematics and physics in the production of highly accurate images. Added to this is the capability to create a series of images that result in an animation from anywhere along this entire spectrum.

The variety of graphics applications is even more varied than what is perceived as the production of images. Computer interfaces popular on personal computers have a graphical interface that is also influenced by graphics concepts. Drawing and manipulating icons under the control of a pointing device such as a mouse are all graphics involved processes. Research into user interfaces is an active and ongoing area, but is not the concern here.

The production of high-quality documents can now be done entirely on the computer. Desktop publishing software and even today's word processors produce a visually accurate version of the document on the computer screen. Determining how to display such an accurate image is a graphical process, but again is not the concern here.

The purpose of this book is to explore some of the basic ideas of realistic image generation. This means the production of images that give the viewer the impression that he or she is looking at a photograph. The amount of pages that have been written about this topic in specialized graphics books and technical conference papers is considerable. A book of this size, therefore, cannot expect to give all of the details for the simulation of all the possible natural phenomena that can be included in an image. Rather, the intent of this book is to introduce those concepts that are critical components of realistic image generation or are the foundation on which current efforts are built. So, the techniques examined here are used in the necessary steps of creating a model of an object, lighting that object, and rendering that object to simulate a real result. In some cases, these techniques will not be fully explored because of their sheer complexity; instead, solutions for simple situations are presented accompanied by a discussion of more involved approaches.

The goal then is the creation of an image by writing a program instead of taking a picture with a camera. There is some overlap between the two ideas. One of the introductory concepts that will be explored is a model for the camera that can be built into a graphics program. The simplest of cameras is a pinhole camera. Figure 1.1 shows the two parts of a pinhole demonstration camera. The metal plate at the front of the larger section on the left has the pinhole in its center through which light passes. The smaller section on the right is inserted into the back of the larger section so that the light projects onto the frosted glass plate that is mounted at the front of that part. The viewer can look through the back and see the image that is projected onto the glass plate. Altering how much the two pieces are nested allows the viewer to change the size of the projected image. The mechanism that works in a simple pinhole camera serves as the basis for most graphics programs.

We begin this journey by looking at some of the basic terminology and concepts as background for the material in the rest of this book. This chapter explores the graphics pipeline, a camera model, how colors can be specified, and how computer

Figure 1.1 • A pinhole camera

technology actually produces the images on the screen. This is just an introduction to the foundations of graphics, and additional terms and concepts will be introduced in the rest of the book where appropriate.

1.1 Image Terminology

The simplest element in computer graphics is the pixel, which is shorthand for "picture element." A pixel is one location in an image, whether on the computer screen or in a printout. If an image has no colors it is called a gray scale image, and each pixel has one value that indicates where in the range from black to white it is. If an image is color, each pixel will use three values to store the range of intensities for the red, green, and blue (RGB) components. Each of these values, whether for a gray scale or color image, can be expressed as either a floating point number or an integer. In the algorithms in this book, floating point values between 0.0 and 1.0 will be generated for the pixel values, where 0.0 represents black and 1.0 represents the full intensity of the particular color. In some instances, these floating point values might need to be mapped into an integer range that depends on the display system. Most graphics systems use either one or two bytes per value. For a gray scale image, this means a pixel value in the range of zero to 255, or zero to 65,535. For a color system, each of the three RGB values will be in one of these two ranges. Graphics systems typically include an extra value for each pixel, called the alpha-channel. The alpha-channel indicates the transparency of the pixel and is used to blend two pixel values or composite two images.

The pixels of an image are organized into a two-dimensional grid that is called a frame buffer. The frame buffer can be thought of and is frequently used as a two-dimensional array. Graphics hardware has enough memory to store multiple frame buffers, which is useful for animation and game programs. A process called double buffering draws the first image into the first frame buffer and displays that. While the user looks at that image, the next image is drawn into the second frame buffer and then the computer quickly switches to display the second buffer. Now, the next image can be drawn into the first buffer, and then the display is switched back to the first buffer. This process continues to work back and forth between the two buffers, displaying one image while the next image is being drawn in the other.

When programs render an image, that image will typically not fill the entire screen but instead will be drawn in a window[1] opened for that purpose. The pixels within this window are addressed based on their location within the window,

---

[1]Discussions of "windows" in computer graphics do not refer to the PC operating system of the same name. References to the operating system in this book will include the manufacturer and operating system name.

instead of their location on the screen. This way the program can refer to a particular pixel address and that will always access the same place in the image, even if the user moves the window to a different location on the screen.

The goal of realistic image creation is to calculate a collection of pixel values that when viewed creates the impression of a picture. The algorithms in this book will pick those pixel values based on a scene that has been described in a data file. The algorithms will manipulate the objects in the scene and will do calculations that simulate the illumination of the scene. The real-world processes that allow you to see objects are computationally complex. Much of graphics is dedicated to developing algorithms that approximate these processes. Any approximation will not produce accurate results. Graphics algorithms, therefore, attempt to generate as good a result as possible within the time and computation power available. Even with the increase in power and display capabilities, some of the algorithms in use today were developed many decades ago.

1.2 The Graphics Pipeline

There is a wide range of different applications of computer graphics, but there are common elements in all of these applications. They all begin with data, whether it is artistic, medical, or system, and that data is then used to create (or "render") an image, which is then displayed on a computer screen. The process going from data to image is called the graphics pipeline (Figure 1.2), and though there are differences, graphics applications use many of the same steps.

In the case of realistic image generation, the three main stages that are necessary for the production of a computer generated image are modeling, rendering, and display. The modeling stage creates an internal representation of the objects in the scene. The rendering stage converts that scene description into an image of that scene. The display stage shows the image on an output device. Because of the need to have a series of images that work together to convey a story, animation requires additional work beyond these three steps, in order to link the frames of the animation—but every frame follows this pipeline.

The view of computer graphics for this book is as an approximation of what is really happening in the natural world. A simplified view is as follows: Light comes from a number of natural and artificial sources, and reflects off surfaces of many different positions, orientations, and types of materials. It eventually strikes your eyes where it is converted into a signal that your visual system and brain then processes. This requires modeling different types of light sources, including the sun as well as artificial lights in all their variety. Objects can be made of plastic, cloth, metal, or wood to name just a few materials, and they can have rough or polished surfaces. The human visual system processes information differently depending on the amount of light available. Further, there is variation between the visual systems of two individuals. There is a great deal of variety and complexity hidden in those

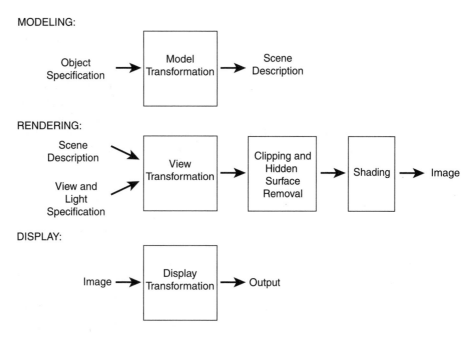

Figure 1.2 • The graphics pipeline

simple descriptions and computers are not fast enough to do the full calculations necessary for every possibility. As computers get faster over time, more actual calculations will be included, meaning fewer approximations will be necessary. The result will be more realistic images.

Early computer graphic images included simple objects and showed very little light interactions. This was an over-simplification of the processes actually involved. As computers got faster, images were not only produced in a shorter amount of time, but more detailed natural phenomena were included. Even with the increasing possibilities with faster computers, another influence on the techniques used is the complexity of the theories behind the techniques. A technique that is simple to implement might be used more than a complex but more accurate one. For example, many rendering programs still rely on simple illumination models developed in the 1970s, even though more complex models are available that produce better results.

1.2.1 Object modeling

Before an image can be created, a model of the scene is developed. The model needs to give the details of each of the objects. This includes not only the shape of the object but also parameters specifying the object's materials that influence how that object appears. This includes the object color, what the object is made of, whether the object is shiny, transparent, or translucent, and whether the object has texture. The choice of which parameters to specify depends in part on the algorithms to be used in the rendering process.

Describing the shape of an object depends on how complex that shape is. For simple geometric objects, the shape can be defined with just a few parameters. To define a sphere, for example, you only need to specify its radius and where its center is located. A complex shape such as a teapot[2] needs many more parameters for the specification of its shape alone. In Chapters 3 and 4, we look at how to specify the shapes of objects and how to scan convert them to determine what pixels they cover in an image.

Whereas Chapters 3 and 4 look at relatively simple shapes, the real world has objects that are much more complex. A tree is complex in both its structure and its bark pattern. Cloth is complex because the way its threads are woven or yarn is knit influences how it drapes and moves. Skin has the complexity of its shape but also requires special illumination and shading methods to create a realistic appearance. These issues will be discussed in Chapters 11 and 12.

The design of a scene or the choices for colors can have a big impact on what is conveyed to the viewer. The objects in a scene or the colors used can be chosen to either enhance or confuse the message being communicated. Issues of clarity of presentation, proper use of contrast, and organization of objects are important, but they are beyond the scope of this book. For readers who are interested in these topics, two good introductory articles are (O'Connell02a) on design and (O'Connell02b) on color.

1.2.2 Rendering

Once the data file has been read and an internal model of the scene has been created, the program now renders that data and produces the image of the scene. The rendering process simulates the flow of light through the scene as it interacts with the objects. Much as there is an internal model for the objects in the scene, there needs to be a model for the light. The presence of light is what lets you see objects in the world.

An illumination model approximates the way that light interacts with the objects in the scene. Illumination models can deal with just the interaction of a light source and an object or they can also look at how light reflects between objects. Illumination models treat light sources, located somewhere in the world being modeled, as single points or as having a size and shape.

---

[2]In the early 1970s, objects with curved surfaces were needed to demonstrate various early algorithms. Ivan Sutherland had his graphics class digitize his Volkswagen Beetle in 1971 for this purpose. In 1975, Martin Newell developed a set of Bézier curved surfaces from a sketch he made of a teapot that he had on his desk (Crow87). The teapot caught on and over the years, this object has been used by many people in the demonstration of their research results. Use of the teapot hit a peak in 1989 when the SIGGRAPH conference was held in Boston—home of the Tea Party tax revolt of 1773.

Some simpler illumination models might not be able to properly illuminate some types of objects. For example, light interacts differently with a metal object than with a plastic object. If an illumination model does not include calculations to account for this difference, objects of two different types can appear the same. Therefore, the final image is influenced by both the illumination model and the object appearance parameters.

Another factor is object visibility. In a complex scene, objects that are far away can be obscured by objects that are closer. The rendering algorithm must account for these obstructions for it to accurately render the scene. Additional rendering issues include the object's texture and the shadows the object casts. Rendering offers the most choices for influencing the final result, so it should not be surprising that most of this book deals with rendering issues.

1.2.3 Image display

With modern computer systems, the issue of displaying the image is less important because there are significant resources available to support this stage. As technology advances, more of the graphics pipeline is handled by firmware and hardware. In the past, all of the processing was handled by software and the graphics board was only responsible for transferring the image data in a form that could be displayed on a monitor. As graphics boards develop, simpler rendering tasks are actually moving to the graphics board. For example, the z-buffer algorithm was included in rendering programs to handle overlapping objects. Today's graphics boards now have z-buffering capabilities built on the board.

One issue with the display of an image is differences with output capability. Each company that manufactures a computer monitor or a color printer uses unique components. Those components differ in how they produce their output, which means that one image can appear differently when displayed on two different monitors or printed on two different printers. Though you might think that a red pixel always looks the same, this is not the case. This issue is more broadly called "color reproduction." This topic is complex and well beyond the scope of this book, but more details can be found in resources such as (Beach99) and (Bruno00).

1.3 A Camera Model

When you mention a camera, most people think of a device with a lens and a shutter that is used to grab pictures in a fraction of a second exposure time. This is a simple, yet good, description of most of the cameras available. There is another class of camera called the pinhole camera that works a bit differently. The picture in Figure 1.1 shows the front of a pinhole demonstration camera and the pinhole is visible on the front of the camera. This demonstration camera has a larger hole than most pinhole cameras so that light can enter more quickly. In this camera, the image projects onto a piece of ground glass inside the box so that you can view the image without having to process film. The larger hole allows more light to enter the camera so that the image is adequately bright. On a regular pinhole camera, the pinhole can be as small as one hundredth of an inch, which requires exposure times of between 20 seconds to as much as a minute and a half. If you search the Web, you will find many sites that give details on how to build your own pinhole camera; in one case, you can use an oatmeal box and aluminum can.

Figure 1.3 is a drawing of a pinhole camera. Light in the environment enters the camera through the pinhole. A location on an object and the pinhole are two points in space that define a straight line. The light coming from that point moves along that line and projects itself into the pinhole camera. Light coming from other objects in the scene also project into the camera, but along different lines. The result as seen in Figure 1.3 is an image in the camera that is upside down and reversed left to right.

Figure 1.4 shows two water lily flowers and how they appear through the pinhole demonstration camera in Figure 1.1. As you can see, the image in the pinhole camera is upside down and reversed. In this example, the pinhole camera image is blurry, but this is because the pinhole demonstration camera uses a ground glass plate for the projection of the image, which causes some blurring. Additionally, the hole in the camera is quite large so as to let enough light enter the demonstration camera. An actual pinhole camera uses film, a much smaller hole, and an extremely long exposure time to get clear and crisp results. The smaller hole also results in a sharper picture. More details on pinhole cameras can be found on pinhole camera Web sites.

To take a picture with a pinhole camera, a piece of film is attached to the inside back of the camera, while in the darkroom, and a shutter is placed over the pinhole

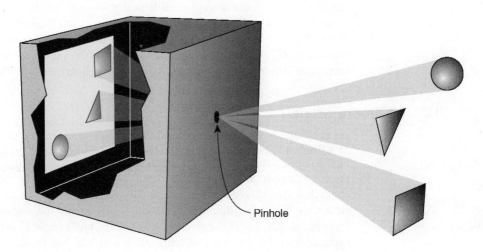

Pinhole

Figure 1.3 • A pinhole camera at work

 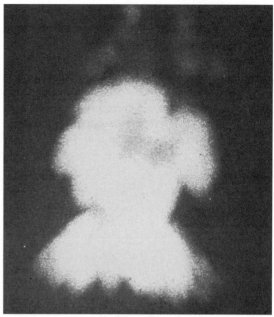

Figure 1.4 • Water lily (Nymphaea Daubeniana) and its image through the pinhole demonstration camera (see Color Plate 1.1)

to block light from entering the camera. The camera would then be positioned with the pinhole facing the scene. The camera is secured in place so that it does not move while the shutter is opened for a span of 20 seconds up to a minute and a half. During this time, the light in the scene flows into the camera through the pinhole, exposing the film at the back. The shutter is then closed and the film is removed and processed in a darkroom as any other film would be. In this process, light reflecting off the objects is projected onto the film causing the exposure that is later developed into a photograph.

A pinhole camera provides the model for the "camera" that is used in computer graphics. Figure 1.5 shows the camera model that is used in computer graphics. The main difference between Figure 1.3 and Figure 1.5 is that the plane where the scene is projected is moved from behind the pinhole to in front of the pinhole. In Figure 1.5, the pinhole is replaced by the location of the viewer of the scene. This location is called the viewpoint. The projection plane is placed between the viewpoint and the scene, and a window in this plane indicates what portion of the scene is in the generated image. The viewing volume is a frustum[3] defined by the viewpoint and

---

[3]A frustum is an area between two parallel planes with sides defined by a cone or a pyramid such as the one created by the viewpoint and the corners of the window.

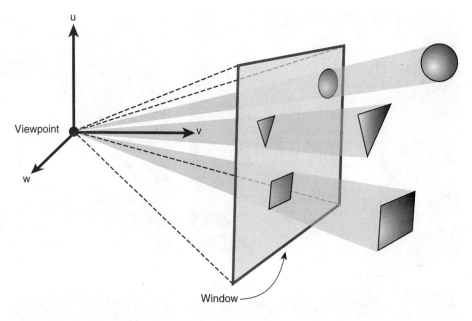

Figure 1.5 • A camera model

the corners of the window. All of the objects in the frustum are projected onto the projection plane and rendered.

The viewpoint gives the location of the viewer and the view direction vector (**v**) gives the direction the viewer is looking. Knowing the direction and location of the viewer is still not enough. A vector also needs to be specified to give the direction of "up" for the viewer. When taking a picture with a camera, the camera can be panned from side to side or tilted up or down. The view vector indicates the direction the camera is pointing to for rendering. A camera can also be rotated, for example, to take a picture horizontally, vertically, or any other angle, so that the scene appears in landscape, portrait, or any other orientation. The view-up vector (**u**) is used to orient the camera model in a similar way by specifying the orientation to be used for rendering the image.

The view vector and the view-up vector should be perpendicular to each other but specifying a view-up vector that is perpendicular can sometimes be difficult. It is possible to calculate a perpendicular view-up vector based on an approximation. If an approximate view-up vector (**u′**) is given, equation (1.1) will calculate a view-up vector that is perpendicular. The dot product of **u′** and **v** will give the cosine of the angle between them. Multiplying this value with the vector **v** results in the amount the vector u′ must be adjusted to make it perpendicular to the vector **v**.

$$\mathbf{u} = \text{normalize}(\mathbf{u'} - (\mathbf{u'} \cdot \mathbf{v}) * \mathbf{v}) \tag{1.1}$$

The third axis of the view coordinate system (**w**) is found by taking the cross product[4] of the view and view-up vectors as in equation (1.2).

$$\mathbf{w} = \mathbf{v} \times \mathbf{u} \tag{1.2}$$

1.4 Coordinate Systems

To be able to describe an object there needs to be a frame of reference for the values specified. That is done with a coordinate system. When working with graphics, there are frequently multiple coordinate systems in use (Figure 1.6). Some of these are completely internal to the software but others relate to the display device. When an object or scene is modeled hierarchically, there can be separate coordinate systems for individual parts of an object, for the entire object, and for the entire scene. There is typically a separate coordinate system based on the location of the viewer of the scene, and there are two-dimensional coordinate systems as the objects are rendered and, therefore, projected onto the two-dimensional screen. Because different graphics books and graphics libraries might use slightly different terminology for various coordinate systems, the most important thing to know is how these

---

[4]The cross-product of two vectors results in a third vector that is perpendicular to the plane containing the first two vectors. Appendix A gives the details for calculating the dot and cross-product.

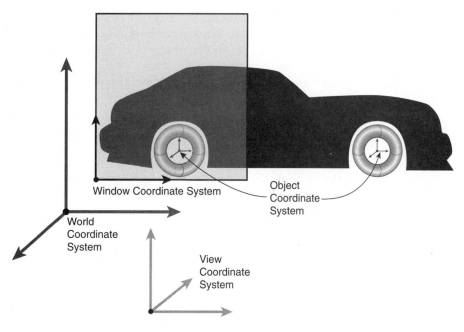

Figure 1.6 • Local or object, world, view, and window coordinate systems

various coordinate systems relate to the tasks in the graphics pipeline. Moving between these coordinate systems is done through a set of transformations that are discussed in Chapter 3. Each of these coordinate systems will now be discussed in greater detail.

In working with computer graphics, a number of different coordinate systems are encountered, especially when scenes are defined hierarchically. The first is the object coordinate system where the shape of an individual object is given. Typically, all objects are specified at the origin of their object coordinate system. For example, a torus, which is shaped like a donut, would always be centered at the origin. These objects can then be positioned relative to other objects in the world, or scene, coordinate system using transformations. It is possible to have duplicates of an object with different transformations to create multiple copies within the scene. Extending the example, a tray of donuts could be created with multiple copies of the torus positioned at different locations and with different orientations. Figure 1.6 shows this relationship. There is one object defined for the tires of the car. This object is defined relative to its own object coordinate system. Four different transformations are used with four copies of this object to position the tires in the correct place in the car object coordinate system. The car object system could then be duplicated and positioned in multiple places in the world coordinate system in the creation of the final scene. Defining a scene hierarchically means that a transformation of the car hierarchy will transform all of the objects that make up that car.

It is possible that the entire scene might not be visible when rendered. The visible area is specified by a clipping window, much as a room's window limits what can be seen outside the room. As objects are rendered, they influence how locations within the window coordinate system appear. The clipping window, also shown in Figure 1.6, helps to identify what part of the world is visible in the scene. Where the window coordinate system defines what is visible, the viewport defines where on a computer screen this scene appears (Figure 1.7). The window and viewport can be of different sizes, in which case the image is squashed or stretched. The viewport location is specified using the normalized device (or display) coordinate system.

This represents many different coordinate systems, but there are only a few that will be of concern. In a hierarchical system, a data file can be defined, for example, with the set of shapes that represent the tire of a car in an object coordinate system. The shapes are typically positioned so the origin of the object coordinate system is at the center of the object. The car data file will then specify four copies of the tire data file with separate transformations to position the copies in their separate locations in the object coordinate system for the car. At the top level, high-level objects are positioned in the scene relative to a world coordinate system. By building up these transformations, all of the low level shapes will be positioned in their proper location within the scene and, therefore, the world coordinate system.

A nonhierarchical view of this process will just create a scene data file that specifies all of the objects directly in the world coordinate system. In the case of the car, the details of the tire shape would be reproduced four times in the car file with the

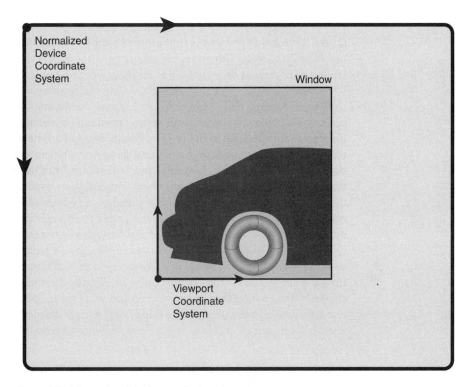

Figure 1.7 • Viewport and display coordinate systems

locations properly adjusted. If the scene is defined in a single, nonhierarchical manner, the object coordinate system is not used.

Another simplification of these coordinate systems is possible if the clipping window and the viewport are the same size. The relationship between these two can be described with a camera analogy. When a picture is taken, the camera settings determine what is transferred onto the film. When the film is processed, a photographic print of many different sizes can be produced from that film. The camera settings are analogous to the clipping window and the print size is analogous to the viewport. Mapping from one size to the other is done with a scaling operation, which is called an enlargement in photographic terms. A similar process is carried out in computer graphics.

If the window and viewport are the same size, no transformation is necessary to map one into the other, but if they are of different sizes, a transformation is needed. A scaling transformation converts the size of the clipping window to the size of the viewport window, but only if they are of the same shape. The aspect ratio is the width divided by the height. If the aspect ratio of the window is different from the aspect ratio of the viewport, the scaling operation will need to be different in the two directions. This distorts the image either stretching it out or squashing it in. Because the

viewport is specified as a set of pixel locations on the screen, it effectively determines the window locations that are sampled in the creation of the image. If the
two aspect ratios are the same, the sampling will occur at the same rate in the horizontal and vertical directions. But if the aspect ratios differ, these sampling rates
will differ as well.

When working with even a limited set of coordinate systems, there are still
options available. The object and scene coordinate systems in this case are three-
dimensional. A three-dimensional system is typically viewed as having the x axis
run with negative values to the left and positive values to the right, and the y axis
run with negative values down and positive values up. Relative to this page, the x
axis runs in the direction of the lines of text and the y axis runs in the direction of
the book binding. The question that remains is, which direction does the z axis
run—with positive values going into the page or coming out of the page? These two
options are called a left-handed and right-handed coordinate system (Figure 1.8),
respectively. In a left-handed coordinate system, if you place your left-hand so that
your fingers are pointing in the positive x direction, and they curl to point in the positive y direction, your thumb will point in the direction of positive z values. In a
right-handed coordinate system, you do the same thing, but with your right-hand.
For the development of ideas in this book,[5] a right-handed coordinate system is
used. This means an increase in x values will move things to the right, an increase

[5]There is no preference between a left-handed and right-handed coordinate system. The
choice between these two has an influence on the rendering software that is developed or is
specified by the graphics API used. For example, OpenGL uses a right-handed coordinate system, which is why this was chosen for the development of this book.

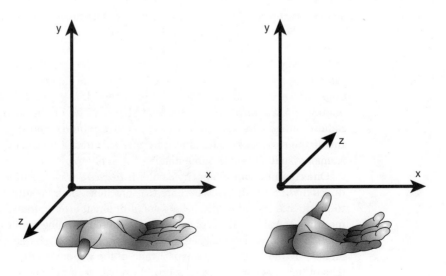

Figure 1.8 • Right- and left-handed coordinate systems

in y values will move things up, and a decrease in z values will move things farther away. This can be remembered by noticing that as objects move away they get smaller, and in a right-handed coordinate system, their z coordinates also get smaller (more negative). Converting between a left-handed and right-handed coordinate system is done by multiplying the z component of every object coordinate by -1.

A two-dimensional coordinate system typically has the x and y values running in the direction given in the three-dimensional system. Relative to this page or a clipping window, the origin is placed at the lower left corner, the positive x axis runs horizontally to the right, and the positive y axis runs up vertically. This is the orientation used for the clipping window coordinate system. Computer systems use a slightly different set up when determining addresses for pixels on the screen. The upper left corner of the screen is the origin (0, 0), and positive y values increase down the screen. On a screen with 1,600 pixels in each of 1,200 rows, the lower-right corner would have a coordinate value of (1599, 1199). Standard routines to render the objects or set pixel values will frequently handle the transformation from window coordinates with the origin at the lower left to computer screen coordinates with the origin at the upper right.

Homogeneous coordinates are typically used when working with three-dimensional coordinates in graphics. In this form, each location is represented by **x**, **y**, **z**, and **w**. In most cases, the value of **w** will be one, but perspective projections have the effect of changing the value of **w**. Because of this, before the **x**, **y**, and **z** values of a homogeneous coordinate are used, each is divided by **w**, if **w** has a value other than one.

1.5 Color Models

There are many ways to specify a color. Each of the models presented here, as well as other available models, have a specific purpose for which they were developed. Though the RGB model is the most commonly used in computer graphics, the other models also play a significant role in various parts of the field. These color models are presented here to give an understanding of color models that might be encountered in graphics work, and also to give the tools used for conversion among these color systems. The RGB model is used for the algorithms in this book.

It should be remembered that these models are just techniques to represent a natural phenomenon. Color is based on perception because it produces a sensation inside the eye that is defined as a particular color. Chapter 2 explores light and the human visual system in more detail.

One common way to specify a color is to give a wavelength for the light that produces that color. Multiple wavelengths or intensities of light can also be combined to produce a color. For example, the RGB model, used in televisions and computer monitors, produces a range of colors through the combination of red, green, and blue light. Though the techniques in this book do calculations using the RGB model, greater accuracy can be achieved by doing calculations at more than just these three wavelengths of light, and then combining the results of all of the wavelength calculations to get the final displayed value.

• 1.5.1 International Commission on Illumination

The International Commission on Illumination (known as CIE from the French "Commission Internationale de l'Éclairage") is an organization responsible for many different facets of lighting and illumination. There are seven active divisions in the organization that set standards in the area of illumination. These divisions are responsible for vision and color; measurement of light and radiation; interior lighting and lighting design; lighting and signaling for transportation and traffic; exterior lighting; photobiology and photochemistry; and image technology. These standards are necessary for accurate communication about issues of illumination and color. There are limitations and differences in the colors that can be accurately printed, so these and other standards allow colors to be specified irrespective of what technology can reproduce.

Experiments with human perception of color allowed an observer to match colors by adjusting a set of three dials that controlled the intensity of light at three wavelengths, namely red (700 nm), green (546.1 nm), and blue (435.8 nm), in the range from +1 to −1, where +1 represented full intensity, and −1 represented the subtraction of the full intensity. The resulting curves (Figure 1.9) showed which

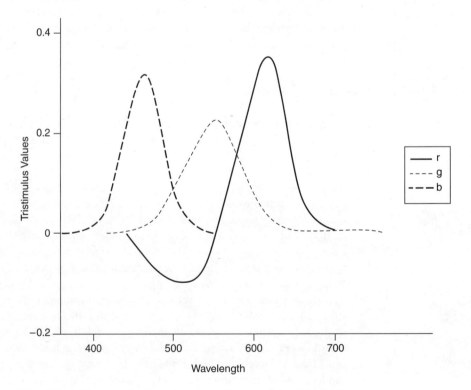

Figure 1.9 • Tristimulus curves for color matching various wavelengths of light

combination of these three intensities would produce the same response as pure wavelengths in the full spectral range. The problem with these curves is that in a portion of the spectrum, it is necessary for the red curve to be negative. This makes these curves difficult to use for technology purposes, because a monitor can only produce positive intensities at each pixel location.

Because of these difficulties, in 1931, CIE defined a set of three hypothetical standard primaries they called X, Y, and Z, and developed a set of curves for them that are positive across the entire spectrum. Thus, these three primaries can be combined in positive amounts so that any color in the visible spectrum can be reproduced. There are differences between what these three hypothetical primaries can produce and what available inks and phosphors can produce. For this reason, even though this system encompasses all colors, there are some colors in the CIE XYZ system that cannot be displayed on computer monitors or be printed. Furthermore, based on the specific materials used for its construction, each device will be able to display a different portion of the CIE XYZ color system.

The CIE XYZ system is a three-dimensional model where locations represent different colors. To get a feeling for this system, one way to look at the CIE XYZ system is to view the CIE chromaticity diagram, which is the cross-section through the full system where X + Y + Z = 1. Figure 1.10 shows this cross-section projected into the xy plane. A series of wavelengths are given along the outer perimeter of the lobed shape representing the approximate location of the associated color. White light occurs at approximately (0.35, 0.35) on this diagram.

The full lobed area in the CIE chromaticity diagram cannot be correctly rendered in color even though you might see other books that show this entire lobed area as color. In fact, CIE has never produced a color rendition of the CIE xy chromaticity diagram or any other because there is no media that can properly reproduce all of these colors, and CIE was unwilling to produce a falsely colored diagram (Makai03). The reason for this is that all devices have a particular color gamut or range of colors that they can display. Figure 1.11 shows the CIE chromaticity diagram with three possible color gamuts. In this figure, the three areas demonstrate how the color ranges for film, a monitor, and printing inks can vary. These areas are not the standards for these three technologies. For example, two different models of computer monitors can have different ranges of color that they can display. This means a color that can be displayed on the first monitor might not be able to be reproduced exactly on the second monitor. Further, there are some colors that can be displayed on a monitor that might not be able to be printed on paper or captured on film, and vice versa. This leads to problems with color reproduction. An image that exists on paper might not be able to be exactly reproduced on a computer monitor, and an image on a monitor might not be the same as what is printed.

A problem with the CIE xy diagram is that the distance between two colors of equal proportional difference is not always the same. For example, the distance between two different shades of green might be longer than the distance between two different shades of red, even though the change in shades appears the same.

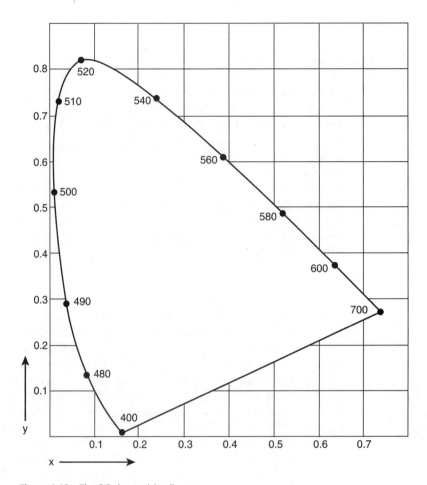

Figure 1.10 • The CIE chromaticity diagram

Expressed another way, for a particular green and red location in the diagram, the first point where a noticeably different color will be found is farther from the green point than from the red point. This difference in lengths caused CIE to develop a new uv diagram in 1960 that attempted to make these lengths more uniform. This was again updated and in 1976 became LUV standard, with the addition of a lightness scale represented by the L. In 1976, CIE also adopted the LAB color system. The LAB system is based on three axes much like an xyz coordinate system. The L axis is in the range[6] [0, 100] and represents the lightness. The A axis ranges from

---

[6]In specifying ranges, a parenthesis represents less than or greater than and a square bracket represents less than or equal or greater than or equal. For example, if x is in the range [2, 4), x has a value that satisfies $2 \leq x < 4$.

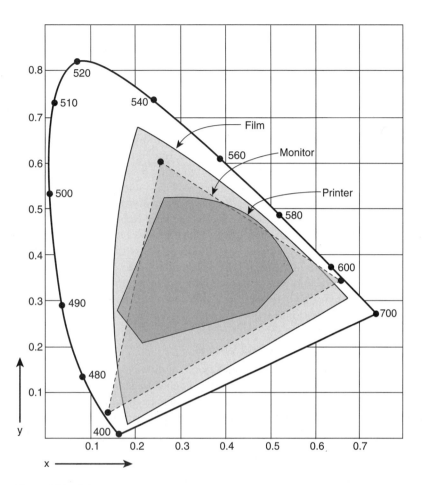

Figure 1.11 • Color gamuts

green on the negative end to red on the positive end. The B axis ranges from blue at the negative end to yellow on the positive end. When the A and B values are both zero, the lightness indicates a shade of gray.

The CIE systems are all independent of any particular technology and, therefore, are much broader than the color models presented next. The following models are used in current graphics software. Computer users are most familiar with the RGB model. The HSV and HLS models are also common in art and design software. The CMYK model is important because it is the standard used for printing. The YUV and YIQ models are used for video signals and broadcast television.

• 1.5.2 RGB

The most common model within computer graphics is the RGB model that specifies the red, green, and blue components of a color. This is an additive color model that creates a range of colors through the addition of various intensities of red, green, and blue light. Fully intense red, green, and blue added together give white. When none of these colors are present, the result is black. If the intensities of red, green, and blue are equal, the result is a shade of gray, somewhere between black and white. The RGB color model is represented with three axes assigned to the colors red, green, and blue as shown in Figure 1.12. The cube represents all of the colors that can be represented in the RGB system. When the value of blue is zero, the bottom face of the cube has varying shades of black, green, red, and yellow. Likewise, when the value of red is one, the front right face has varying shades of red, magenta, yellow, and white. Color Plate 1.2 shows a view of this RGB cube in color.

Figure 1.12 and Color Plate 1.2 show that mixing red and blue will give shades of magenta (purple), mixing red and green will give shades of yellow, and mixing green and blue will give shades of cyan (an aqua blue). Points along the diagonal of this cube between black and white will have equal amount of red, green, and blue and so this is where the shades of gray are found.

• 1.5.3 CMY and CMYK

Where the RGB model is an additive system, the Cyan-Magenta-Yellow (CMY) model is a subtractive color model. In a subtractive model, the more that an element is added, the more that it subtracts from white. So, if none of these are present the result is white, and when all are fully present the result is black. It is still true that

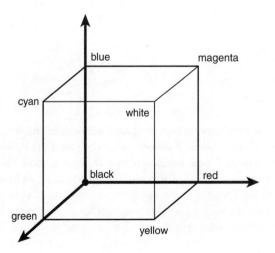

Figure 1.12 • The RGB cube (see Color Plate 1.2)

including equal amounts of each color will produce shades of gray. Each of these primaries subtracts a color from white light. Cyan subtracts red, magenta subtracts green, and yellow subtracts blue. You should notice the relationship between this and the additive RGB system. Figure 1.12 shows that cyan, magenta, and yellow are the remaining three color vertices of the RGB cube. There is a direct relationship between the additive and subtractive systems. In the additive system, yellow is created by mixing red and green light. In the subtractive system, yellow is created because the ink or toner subtracts blue from white light.

Children are told that red, yellow, and blue are the primary colors, and that they create new colors by mixing paints of those primary colors. The difference between that system and the CMY system is that red, yellow, and blue is a good combination of colors for mixing paints or pigments, whereas CMY is a better combination of colors for transparent inks and toners used in printers.

A technical reality is that when full amounts of cyan, magenta, and yellow are mixed, the result is not necessarily a solid black, but is rather a dark muddy color. To get a truer black, a fourth element is included giving the CMYK (Cyan, Magenta, Yellow, and blacK) system. The inclusion of a black component creates a richer output.

It is easy to convert among RGB, CMY, and CMYK. To convert between RGB and CMY, use equations (1.3) and (1.4).

$$C = 1.0 - R, M = 1.0 - G, Y = 1.0 - B \qquad (1.3)$$
$$R = 1.0 - C, G = 1.0 - M, B = 1.0 - Y \qquad (1.4)$$

To convert CMY into CMYK, equations (1.5) are used.

$$K = minimum(C, M, Y), C = C - K, M = M - K, Y = Y - K \qquad (1.5)$$

1.5.4 HSV

The Hue, Saturation, and Value (HSV) color system is based on an artistic viewpoint. The hue specifies the color, the saturation the amount of color, and the value indicates the range of lightness of the color. Said another way, the hue chooses the color, the saturation determines how much white is added to the color, and the value indicates how much black is added to the color.

The hue is specified as an angle with red at 0°, yellow at 60°, green at 120°, cyan at 180°, blue at 240°, and magenta at 300°. A saturation of 1.0 gives the full color and as the saturation gets smaller the result gets closer to white. A saturation of 0.0 gives a shade of gray that depends on what the value (V) is. For example, a hue of red, saturation of 1.0, and value (V) of 1.0 gives a pure red. As the saturation decreases the resulting color goes through lighter shades of red and pink, eventually getting to white. This process moves across the top of the hexcone show in Figure 1.13 from the edge to the center and chooses the "tint." From the same starting point of pure red, as the value (V) decreases the resulting color goes through darker shades of red eventually getting to black. This process moves down the side of the hexcone and chooses the "shade."

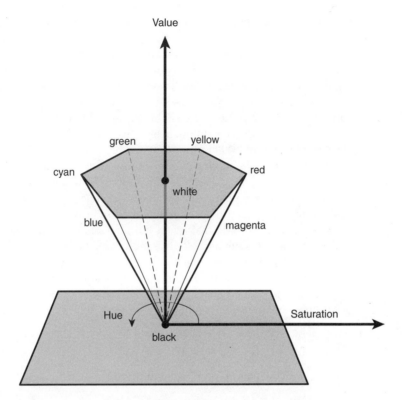

Figure 1.13 • The HSV hexcone (see Color Plate 1.3)

Converting RGB to HSV first requires the determination of the value, which is the largest of the RGB quantities. Next, the saturation is determined. If all of the RGB quantities are zero, the color is black, and so the saturation and value are both zero and the hue does not matter and so is considered undefined. If the RGB quantities are all the same, the color is a shade of grey and so the saturation value is also zero. In all other cases, the saturation is the difference between the largest and smallest RGB quantity divided by the largest one. The last step is to determine the hue. If red is the largest RGB quantity, the color will be somewhere between yellow (60°) and magenta (300°). The hue between yellow and magenta is determined by looking at the relationship between green and blue. Subtracting blue from green and dividing by the difference between the largest and smallest RGB quantity gives a number between +1 and −1. If this number is multiplied by 60 and then 360 is added when the result is negative, the correct hue is found. If the largest RGB quantity is green, a similar result is found subtracting red from blue. In this case, the range will also be between +1 and −1, so 2 is added to bring the result into the range [1, 3]. When this is multiplied by 60, the hue will be between 60° (yellow) and 180° (cyan). Lastly, if the largest RGB quantity is blue, green is subtracted from red and 4 is added to bring the result into the range [3, 5]. When this is multiplied by 60, the hue will be between 180° (cyan) and 300° (magenta). The following algorithm accomplishes this conversion from RGB to HSV.

```
large = maximum( R, G, B )
small = minimum( R, G, B )
V = large
if (large == 0)
    S = 0
else
    S = (large - small) / large
if (S == 0)
    // hue is undefined for 0 saturation
    H = -1
else
{
    range = large - small
    if (R == large)
        // pick a color between yellow and magenta
        H = (G - B) / range
    else if (G == large)
        // pick a color between cyan and yellow
        H = 2 + (B - R) / range
    else if (B == large)
        // pick a color between magenta and cyan
        H = 4 + (R - G) / range
    // convert H to a degree
    H *= 60
    if (H < 0)
        H += 360
}
```

It is also possible to algorithmically convert from HSV to RGB. If the saturation is zero, the color is a shade of gray determined by the value. In the RGB color model, all of the RGB quantities are the same and equal to the HSV value. In all other cases, the hue is divided by 60, which results in a value in the range [0.0, 6.0). The integer part of the division determines which of the six colors shown in Figure 1.13 the hue is between. The fractional part of this result is used with the saturation and value to generate three values that relate to how far along these sections the color lies. The following algorithm handles the conversion from HSV to RGB:

```
if (S == 0)
   R = G = B = V
else
{
   if (H == 360.0)
      H = 0  // which is the same thing
   H /= 60.0
   intPart = trunc( H )
   fractPart = H - intPart
   L = V * (1 - S)
   M = V * (1 - S * fractPart)
   N = V * (1 - S * (1 - fractPart))
   switch (intPart)
   {
      case 0: R = V; G = N; B = L; break;
      case 1: R = M; G = V; B = L; break;
      case 2: R = L; G = V; B = N; break;
      case 3: R = L; G = M; B = V; break;
      case 4: R = N; G = L; B = V; break;
      case 5: R = V; G = L; B = M; break;
   }
}
```

• 1.5.5 HLS

The Hue, Lightness, and Saturation (HLS) color system (Figure 1.14) is very similar to the HSV system. Where HSV is a hexcone, the HLS system is a double hexcone. This means where the pure colors in HSV occur at a value of 1, in the HLS system this occurs at a lightness of 0.5. If you were to take the HSV hexcone and stretch it out by the center of the base, you would get the HLS double hexcone. Intensity of color is still specified by the saturation, which determines the distance from the center of the double hexcone. Lightness ranges from white (1.0) to black (0.0) along the center axis of the double hexcone. Because of the similarity between the HSV and HLS color models, there is also a similarity in the conversion routines.

The algorithm to convert from RGB to HLS is very similar to the one used to convert from RGB to HSV. The difference is in how the lightness and saturation are determined. Because the maximum saturation now occurs at a lightness of 0.5, the lightness is determined by averaging the largest and smallest RGB quantities. If the largest and smallest values are equal, all of the RGB values must be equal and so the result is a gray color, meaning that the saturation is zero and the hue is undefined. In all other cases, the saturation is calculated in one of two ways depending on whether the color

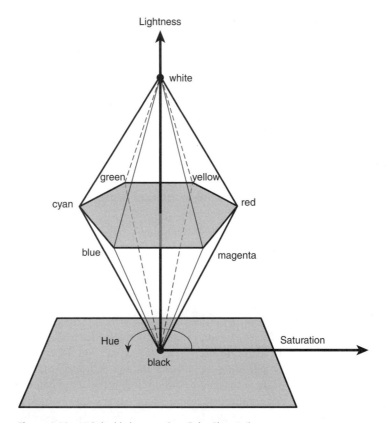

Figure 1.14 • HLS double hexcone (see Color Plate 1.4)

is on the top half or the bottom half of the HLS double hexcone. The following algorithm accomplishes this conversion from RGB to HLS.

```
large = maximum( R, G, B )
small = minimum( R, G, B )
L = (large + small) / 2
if (large == small)
{
    S = 0
    H = -1
}
else
{
    if (L <= 0.5)
        // color is in the bottom half
        S = (large - small) / (large + small)
```

```
else
   // color is in the top half
   S = (large - small) / (2 - large - small)
range = large - small
if (R == large)
   // pick a color between yellow and magenta
   H = (G - B) / range
else if (G == large)
   // pick a color between cyan and yellow
   H = 2 + (B - R) / range
else if (B == large)
   // pick a color between magenta and cyan
   H = 4 + (R - G) / range
// convert H to a degree
H *= 60
if (H < 0)
   H += 360
}
```

Converting from HLS to RGB is similar to that done for the HSV to RGB conversion. If the color is a shade of gray, the three RGB values are the same as the lightness value. In all other cases, two temporary values are calculated one of which depends on whether the color is in the top or bottom half of the double hexcone. These temporary values are based on how intense the color is. The function result uses these two temporary values based on the hue, which indicates where in the double hexcone the color is located. The following algorithm handles the conversion from HLS to RGB.

```
if (S == 0)
   R = G = B = L
else
{
   if (L <= 0.5)
      temp1 = L * (S + 1)
   else
      temp1 = L + S - (L * S)
   temp2 = 2 * L - temp1
   R = result( temp1, temp2, (H + 120) % 360 )
   G = result( temp1, temp2, H )
   B = result( temp1, temp2, (H + 240) % 360 )
}

float result( float t1, float t2, float h )
{
```

```
    if (h < 60)
        return t2 + (t1 - t2) * h/60.0
    if (h < 180)
        return t1
    if (h < 240)
        return t2 + (t1 - t2) * (240 - h)/60.0
    return t2
}
```

1.5.6 Video signal color models

The YUV model is also known as the Y'CbCr model and is used for video applications. The Y component stands for luminance, and the U and V components are color components. The luminance component is a weighted sum of the red, green, and blue values and is the same as the luminance component of the CIE standard. The luminance component of the YUV model is important because it allows one video signal to be used for both color and black and white televisions. A color television uses all three components to display an image, but a black and white television uses only the luminance component. The U component encodes information in the blue range and the V component encodes information in the red range. The full conversion from RGB to YUV is given by the equations (1.6).

$$\mathbf{Y} = 0.299 * \mathbf{R} + 0.587 * \mathbf{G} + 0.114 * \mathbf{B}$$
$$\mathbf{U} = -0.147 * \mathbf{R} - 0289 * \mathbf{G} + 0.437 * \mathbf{B} + 0.5 \qquad (1.6)$$
$$\mathbf{V} = 0.615 * \mathbf{R} - 0.515 * \mathbf{G} - 0.100 * \mathbf{B} + 0.5$$

Converting from the YUV model to the RGB model is given by the equations (1.7).

$$\mathbf{R} = 1.000 * \mathbf{Y} + 0.0004 * (\mathbf{U} - 0.5) + 1.140 * (\mathbf{V} - 0.5)$$
$$\mathbf{G} = 1.000 * \mathbf{Y} - 0.394 * (\mathbf{U} - 0.5) - 0.581 * (\mathbf{V} - 0.5) \qquad (1.7)$$
$$\mathbf{B} = 0.998 * \mathbf{Y} + 2.028 * (\mathbf{U} - 0.5) + 0.0005 * (\mathbf{V} - 0.5)$$

The YIQ color model is used for the NTSC (North American) television broadcast standard. The luminance component is calculated exactly the same as for the YUV model and, so it also provides compatibility with both color and black and white television sets. In the YIQ model, the I stands for in-phase and indicates a range from orange to blue. The Q stands for quadrature represents a range from purple to green. The IQ plane is the UV plane rotated by 33 degrees. This rotation places the I color axis in the region where many flesh tones are found. The original use of this model gave the I signal close to three times the bandwidth of the Q signal because people tend to be more perceptive of incorrect skin tones than other color errors.

The RGB model can be converted to the YIQ model with the matrix multiplication[7] in equation (1.8).

---

[7]Appendix A includes information on matrix multiplication.

$$\begin{bmatrix} Y \\ I \\ Q \end{bmatrix} = \begin{bmatrix} 0.299 & 0.587 & 0.114 \\ 0.596 & -0.275 & -0.321 \\ 0.212 & -0.528 & 0.311 \end{bmatrix} * \begin{bmatrix} R \\ G \\ B \end{bmatrix} \tag{1.8}$$

The YIQ model can be converted to the RGB model with the matrix multiplication in equation (1.9).

$$\begin{bmatrix} R \\ G \\ B \end{bmatrix} = \begin{bmatrix} 1 & 0.956 & 0.621 \\ 1 & -0.272 & -0.647 \\ 1 & -1.105 & 1.702 \end{bmatrix} = \begin{bmatrix} Y \\ I \\ Q \end{bmatrix} \tag{1.9}$$

One of the important points of these two models is in the calculation of the luminance or brightness. In both cases, luminance is given by the equation Y = 0.299 * **R** + 0.587 * **G** + 0.114 * **B**. The color red (an RGB value of (1, 0, 0)) has a luminance of 0.299. The color green has a luminance of 0.587, and blue has a luminance of 0.114. This means that green (an RGB value of (0, 1, 0)) is the brightest color and blue (an RGB value of (0, 0, 1)) is the darkest. Consider an image of three circles with the first being red, the second green, and the third blue. The green circle appears brightest, the red appears about half as bright, and the blue appears the darkest. Another way of expressing this is to say that green component of RGB contributes the most to brightness, while the blue component contributes the least.

1.6 Displaying Images

As previously mentioned, the last step in the creation of an image is its display. This display can be on a computer monitor or printed on a page. Output devices are continually undergoing improvements that increase the capabilities of current technologies, as well as introduce new technologies. This section gives a brief overview of a few of the options available for displaying images.

1.6.1 Monitors

A monitor is the part of a computer system used to display information to the user. The main component of a monitor is the cathode ray tube (CRT). The CRT (see Figure 1.15) receives a signal from the computer that "specifies" the image on the screen. The back of a color CRT contains three electron guns that each creates a very narrow beam of electrons. The electrons go through deflection plates that allow the CRT to alter the path of the electron beams. For example, if the charge on the upper deflection plate is more positive than the lower plate, the beams will be deflected up. If these charges are reversed, the beams will be deflected down. By properly setting the voltages on the deflection plates, the electron beams can be directed to each of the pixel locations on the screen. The signal received from the computer indi-

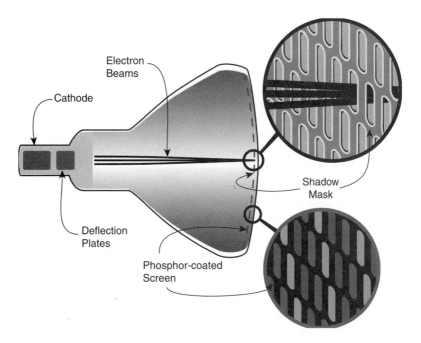

Figure 1.15 • Components of a television monitor (see Color Plate 1.5)

cates how strong the electron beams should be for each of the pixel locations. When the electron beams get near the inside front of the monitor, they pass through a shadow mask that prevents stray electrons from striking the wrong pixel location. Once past the shadow mask, the electron beams strike phosphor dots that coat the inside of the front of the monitor. Each pixel location has three phosphor dots, one for each of the colors of red, green, and blue. The difference between a computer monitor and a television is the shape of the phosphor "dots." Where these are round dots on in a computer monitor, television monitors will use oval phosphor "dots."

Most chemicals, when in an excited state, give off their additional energy through the release of heat. Phosphor, however, releases its extra energy by giving off light. When the electron beam strikes a phosphor dot of a pixel, that phosphor gets excited and begins to glow. The stronger the electron beam, the more energy added and the brighter the phosphor glows. Once the electron beam moves onto the next pixel, the phosphor glow starts to dim. For this reason, a CRT must constantly refresh the image on the screen so the image does not flicker or get dim. Most monitors refresh the image 60 times a second. This means that the intensity of the electron beams have to be changed and deflected to each pixel location 60 times every second.

Different phosphors produce different colors of light and dim at different rates. A color monitor uses a triad with a red, green, and blue phosphor for each pixel. If you look at a television set[8] when it is on with a magnifying glass, you can see these triads. Television sets and computer monitors work in the same way that French Impressionist paintings do. The idea is that if you place two colors next to each other in small quantities, the eye will blend those two colors together to create the appearance of a single color.

The differences between two computer monitors from different manufacturers include different sets of phosphors, among other things. Even though both monitors use a red, green, and blue triad, those colors can be slightly different between the monitors. The two red phosphors can be slightly different shades, or the blue phosphors can have slightly different brightness.

1.6.2 Flat panel displays

Two of the main current technologies for flat panel displays are liquid crystal diodes (LCD) and plasma gas. In an LCD flat panel display, an image is displayed using liquid crystals and polarizing filters (see Figure 1.16). The monitor construction from back to front starts with a fluorescent light with a diffusion plate, then a polarizing filter, then the liquid crystals, and then a second polarizing filter rotated 90° from the first. The two polarizing filters at 90° angles from each other do not normally allow light to pass through, however, the liquid crystals twist the light so that it can pass through the second filter. If there is a current passed through the liquid crystal, it will untwist and then the light will not pass through it. Individual pixels on an LCD display are turned on and off by turning the current on and off through the liquid crystal. The LCD display also has three color filters to produce

---

[8]A television set works better for this than a computer monitor because a television set has larger areas of phosphor than newer high resolution monitors. Also, if you do not have a magnifying glass, you can sometimes see the phosphor triads if you flick a small drop of water on the television screen. The droplet will act like a magnifying glass.

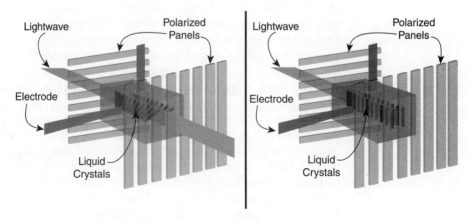

Figure 1.16 • Polarizing light to turn an LCD pixel on (left) or off (right)

red, green, and blue light. For a color display that is 1,000 by 1,000 pixels, there will be three million locations where these currents are applied.

In a plasma gas flat panel display, each pixel location consists of three enclosed cells. The walls of the cell are coated with red, green, or blue phosphor. Wires run horizontally and vertically in front of and behind the cells. The cells are filled with plasma gas, which is a mixture of electrically charged ions and electrons. When at rest, the electrons match up with the ions so that the gas has uncharged particles. Placing a voltage difference across a horizontal and vertical wire pair causes a current of electrons to flow through one cell. These electrons will collide with the gas causing changes in energy that result in the release of ultraviolet photons from the gas. These photons strike the cell walls, which excites the phosphor and causes it to glow as in a CRT. The amount of current flowing through the cell determines the amount of photons, which in turn determines how brightly the cell glows. Because the glow from the cell begins to dim when the voltage difference is moved to light up another cell, plasma displays need to regularly refresh the image being displayed.

1.6.3 Hard copy

Printers create an image by applying an ink or toner to a page in very small dots. Color printers use the CMYK color system. Some color printers place dots of toner very close together in the same way that a computer monitor has the triad for a single pixel close together. Other color printers use transparent inks and actually place the different colors on top of each other in the way that an artist mixes colors. In either case, the quality of the print is based on the size of the dots of color and how closely they are spaced. The smaller the dots and the more closely those are packed, the better the quality of the output.

A more recent type of output is possible from three-dimensional printers. One form of three-dimensional printer uses a starch- or plaster-based powder and a binder. The printer places a thin layer of the powder on a platform and then the binder is applied in the areas where the part is to be printed. The binder solidifies the powder where it is applied. The platform is lowered very slightly (typically less than one hundredth of an inch) and another thin layer of powder is spread on the platform. The binder is again applied where needed. This process repeats until the entire part is printed. The part can then be lifted off the platform, and the excess powder brushed away. Another way to envision this process is to imagine an object being sliced into very thin layers. Each pass of the three-dimensional printer adds one of these slices to the part being printed. The result can be strengthened by applying waxes and resins so that the three-dimensional prototype can be used as part of an engineering design process. A Web search for three-dimensional printers will lead you to company Web sites that typically have animations that demonstrate their printers in action.

1.6.4 Output differences

Each type of output device has a slightly different set of colors that it produces. To accurately reproduce a color on a variety of devices, adjustments are necessary for each particular device. For example, a particular RGB value can produce colors that appear different on two monitors. It is possible to calibrate various devices to try and reduce this difference, but in some instances, a color that can be displayed on one monitor might be outside of the gamut of another one.

Another difference is related to perceived brightness of images. Our perception of changes in brightness is relative not linear. We perceive a change between a brightness of 10 and 20 (an increase of 100 percent) as twice the change in brightness between 40 and 60 (an increase of 50 percent). To see this yourself, look at how much the light changes when you use a 50-100-150-watt three-way light bulb. You will likely get the impression that the amount of additional light is greater when you switch from 50 watts to 100 watts than when you switch from 100 watts to 150 watts, even though the increase in watts is the same in both cases. This perception means that for a monitor to produce 256 different and apparently evenly spaced light levels of output, it cannot simply divide a voltage range of 0.0 to 1.0 into 256 even steps. Rather, the monitor must make sure that the ratio of the change stays the same for each of the 256 steps. Furthermore, you might not be able to perceive it, but black on a monitor is not completely black—there is always an extremely small amount of light produced. The value for this small amount influences the values for all of the 255 other steps. Each monitor has a different small amount of light that represents black and, therefore, a different set of intensities. This set of intensities is determined by what is called the gamma of the monitor, and the process of adjusting one monitor to match another is called gamma correction. Equation (1.10) gives a rough approximation of the relationship between voltage and light intensity. The use of gamma as the exponent is the source of the name "gamma correction."

$$I = k(V - V_0)^{\gamma} \tag{1.10}$$

In this equation, V_0 is the voltage that produces "black" on the screen. The value of gamma can vary among different manufacturers but is typically between 1.7 and 2.7. For example, the standard value for a Macintosh is 1.8 and the standard value for a PC is 2.5. What this means in practice is that an image that looks good on a Macintosh looks dark on a PC, and an image that looks good on a PC looks washed out on a Macintosh. Gamma correction is used to adjust the values before they are used in equation (1.10). For example, to get an image that looks good on a Macintosh to look the same on a PC, a gamma correction of 1/1.8 is applied. Applying a power of 1/1.8 to the values effectively removes the Macintosh gamma from the image before it is displayed on a PC.

1.7 Conclusion

The material in this chapter gives some of the basic building blocks for producing computer graphics images. The basic concepts involved in the production of realistic image generation will be explored in detail in the rest of this book and the reader will come away with many tools for the production of realistic images. For each of the topics discussed, there are additional details that are beyond the scope of this book. For example, a deep and detailed investigation of light and how it interacts with objects requires the study of physics, specifically, optics and material science. An example of this detail can be found in the two-volume series on digital image synthesis by Glassner (Glassner95). Discussions in this textbook will have references to other books and articles that explore these topics in greater detail. The state-of-the-art information can also be found in the proceedings of some of the major conferences in computer graphics.

In reading this book, you will see many references to methods from the early days of computer graphics. These older algorithms still serve as the basis for much of current computer graphics. For example, the shading method used in OpenGL today was first published in 1971. There are other algorithms that might not be used for their original purpose but still have use in other parts of graphics processing.

When writing graphics programs, it is essential that you develop the ability to visualize what a scene should look like. Without this ability, it is difficult to tell if a scene is correctly specified and the rendering algorithm is correctly implemented. You need to be able to create a mental picture of a scene, so that if there are any problems, you can determine whether they are with the way the objects are specified, or the way the rendering algorithms are coded.

1.8 OpenGL Basics

In most of the chapters of this textbook, there is a section called "The OpenGL Way." These sections look at how an application programming interface (API), specifically OpenGL, can be used to accomplish the theories set out in the main body of the chapter. Though OpenGL is a powerful tool in graphics programming, knowledge of the specifics behind any of the graphics APIs available is crucial to the understanding of the API as well as essential to move beyond the capabilities provided. OpenGL is chosen as the API for this textbook because it is available for UNIX, Linux, Microsoft Windows, and MacOS.

1.8.1 What is OpenGL?

Different computers, operating systems, and graphics processors all have a different set of commands to control the output on a computer screen. In the early days of graphics programming, this meant that programs were not very portable. Frequently, programmers developed a set of routines that represented basic graphics operations and hid the details of a particular system in those routines. When the program was moved to a new system, a programmer only had to update those routines. Over time, people realized that having a set of standard routines across platforms would greatly help graphics programmers. A series of different standards has been developed through the years, with OpenGL being one of the more recent standards.

OpenGL is a set of graphics libraries that is available for UNIX, Linux, the X Window System, Microsoft Windows, and Macintosh. These libraries handle different sets of tasks, with the most basic tasks being handled by the core OpenGL library. There is also an OpenGL Utility Library (GLU) that includes more advanced object modeling tasks. There are libraries to handle windowing tasks for most computer systems including the X Window System (GLX), Microsoft Windows (WGL), IBM OS/2 (PGL), and Apple Macintosh (AGL). Kilgard has written a windowing system independent library called the OpenGL Utility Toolkit (GLUT) that sits on top of these and hides some of the complexities of the different windowing systems. This book follows the lead of the *OpenGL Programming Guide* (OpenGL99) and uses calls to GLUT routines to set up the drawing windows, which will make the examples more portable.

OpenGL routines can be called from Ada, C, C++, FORTRAN, Python, Perl, and Java. In this book, code is given in C. C and C++ are the main languages used in computer graphics. For the code samples given here, C will be sufficient.

OpenGL is a state-based system. A number of state variables within OpenGL determine how the objects appear when rendered. For example, the current color is a state variable. When a particular color is set in OpenGL, all objects are drawn using that color until a new color is specified. State variables are used to control how lines are drawn; indicate positions where light sources are located; and specify the material properties of objects, among many others. These state variables and how to set them will be discussed where it is most appropriate to do so.

Most of the chapters of this book will include a section on how these various library routines can be used to accomplish some of the techniques in that chapter. These sections are not meant to be a complete discussion of OpenGL, but rather an introduction to some of its capabilities. Additional details can be found in books such as (OpenGL99), (OpenGL00), (Kilgard96), and (Fosner97), and at the OpenGL web site (www.OpenGL.org).

1.8.2 Naming conventions

Routines in the OpenGL libraries begin with a set of letters that indicate the library that the routine is part of. Table 1.1 shows the beginning letters for each of the OpenGL libraries.

● **TABLE 1.1** OpenGL routine prefixes

core OpenGL library	gl
OpenGL Utility Library	glu
OpenGL Utility Toolkit	glut
X Window System Library	glX
Microsoft Windows Library	wgl
IBM OS/2 Library	pgl
Apple Macintosh Library	agl

The rest of the words in the routine names all begin with an initial capital letter, for example, glClearColor and glutCreateWindow. Some of the OpenGL functions have multiple varieties that differ only in the type of parameters that they take.

OpenGL also has a series of names for constants that are, for example, used to pass options as parameters. These constants are denoted in upper case, with underscore characters to separate the words in the name. For example, a set of vertex locations are given between calls to glBegin and glEnd. The glBegin routine takes a parameter that specifies whether to treat those vertices as individual points by passing the constant GL_POINTS, or as a polygon by passing the constant GL_POLYGON.

The last naming convention has to do with types. In addition to the programming language types, OpenGL has a set of companion types that it uses. So, where C and C++ have a type int, OpenGL has a type GLint. All of these OpenGL types begin with the "GL" and are followed by the standard language type name.

1.8.3 Getting ready to render

Before starting to draw things in OpenGL, GLUT must be initialized. Then GLUT is given details about how things will be specified, and how it should function. After this, the drawing window can be opened. These tasks are done with calls to the routines glutInit, glutInitDisplayMode, and glutCreateWindow, respectively. A size and position for the window can be recommended with the functions glutInitWindowSize and glutInitWindowPosition, but the actual size and position will be determined by the windowing system itself. The following code segment shows the use of these functions:

```
int main(int argc, char **argv)
{
    glutInit( &argc, argv);
    glutInitDisplayMode( GLUT_SINGLE | GLUT_RGB );
    glutInitWindowSize( 300, 300 );
    glutInitWindowPosition( 50, 50 );
    glutCreateWindow( "example" );

        .
        .
        .

}
```

void glutInit(int *argc, char **argv)
The call to glutInit takes two parameters: the first specifying the number of command-line parameters and the second giving those parameters. These are system parameters that are passed into the program. When operating from a command-line operating system, these are parameters that are given when the program is started. Because some of those parameters can be commands to an underlying windowing system such as the X Window System, these need to be passed into GLUT so that

they can be properly handled. If the program also parses these command-line parameters, that can be done either before or after the call to glutInit.

void glutInitDisplayMode(unsigned int mode)
The call to glutInitDisplayMode takes an integer parameter that tells GLUT how colors will be specified, whether there should be one drawing buffer or two, as well as other parameters that will become meaningful later in this book. In the preceding example code, GLUT is initialized to use one drawing buffer and for colors to be specified using a red, green, and blue color model.

void glutInitWindowSize(int width, int height)
The call to glutInitWindowSize takes two integer parameters that specify the width and the height of the window. These are merely suggestions that the windowing system will follow unless other specifications cause these values to be overridden. The default window size is 300 pixels by 300 pixels if there is no call to glutInitWindowSize. The next section discusses how the actual size of the window can be determined.

void glutInitWindowPosition(int xLocation, int yLocation)
The call to glutInitWindowPosition takes two integer parameters that specify the x and y screen location of the upper left corner of the window. As in the case of the size, these values are just suggestions. The initial values for these positions are both −1. A negative value for a position signals that the location is left for the system to decide.

int glutCreateWindow(char *name)
The call to glutCreateWindow takes a string that will be used as the window name, and that will be used in the window title or label. The integer value returned is the window identifier. The identifier is used in programs that open multiple windows so that it can switch between the windows. This allows a program to draw inside two separate windows. For example, one window might hold a draft drawing where the user can make changes. When those changes are accepted, they can then be made in a second window that is used for the final drawing.

The call to this function sets up and creates the window. It also sets the display state of a window to visible; however, the window will not be shown until the main event loop is entered.

1.8.4 Event loops and callback functions

Once the window or windows are set up and the objects are drawn inside those windows, there is still a lot more that can happen. The user can click a mouse button, or can minimize, resize, or close the window. Any of these actions is considered an event and that event needs to be recognized and then processed. The GLUT has the capability to recognize these events and can do some simple work with them, but there are some things that only the program can do. For example, when the user clicks a mouse button, the program needs to decide what that means and how to handle it. If the user resizes the window, the program needs to determine how to handle the ability to draw in this new window. So, how is the interaction between the GLUT and the program handled? It is done through functions that we write, but that the GLUT calls.

Your next question might be, "How does the GLUT know which of my functions to call?" There are a set of routines in the GLUT that register which of the functions are to be used for which tasks. The program functions are called "callback" functions because the GLUT calls back to them when their work is needed. An example of a complete main program that uses a couple of these callback registration functions follows. Details on other callback registration functions can be found in Kilgard (Kilgard96).

```
int main(int argc, char **argv)
{
    glutInit( &argc, argv);
    glutInitDisplayMode( GLUT_SINGLE | GLUT_RGB );
    glutInitWindowSize( 300, 300 );
    glutInitWindowPosition( 50, 50 );
    glutCreateWindow( "example" );
    initialize();
    glutDisplayFunc( drawImage );
    glutReshapeFunc( reshapeWindow );
    glutMouseFunc( handleMouse );
    glutKeyboardFunc( handleKeyboard );
    glutMainLoop();
    return 0;
}
```

```
void initialize( )
```
This is a programmer-written function that does any initialization that is only needed at the start of the program. This function can, for example, set the background color to use when the window is cleared; define the type of shading OpenGL should do when drawing images; and set parameters about lighting. Later chapters will look at various routines that can be called in an initialize function. A very simple initialize function that just sets the color for clearing the window to black is:

```
void initialize( )
{
```

```
   glClearColor( 0.0, 0.0, 0.0, 0.0 );
}
```

void glutDisplayFunc(void (*func)(void))
A function is needed that describes how to display the image. Typically this will be a function that gives the commands to draw the objects in the scene. The display function must not take any parameters and must not return any value. That is what the "void (*func) (void)" means.

The name of the drawing function is passed into the glutDisplayFunc call, so that the GLUT can register that function as being the one to use when the image in the window needs to be redrawn. In the preceding example, the display function is called drawImage, which must be declared somewhere in the program files as void drawImage(). The OpenGL sections in the rest of the book will be concerned with what commands go into this drawImage function to create the scene.

void glutReshapeFunc(void (*func)(int width, int height))
A function is needed that describes what to do if the user changes the size of the window. This is called reshaping because the change in size really changes the overall shape of the window. This function is also called by GLUT when the window is first created. The reshape function has commands that set up the viewing system. The reshape function needs to take two parameters that are the new width and height of the window. In the example code, the reshape function is called reshapeWindow, which must be declared somewhere in the program files as void reshapeWindow(int width, int height).

void glutMouseFunc(void (*func)(int button, int state, int x, int y))
There are a wide variety of things that must be known about a button event on a mouse for it to be processed. The first thing to know is the button that was used, with the options being GLUT_LEFT_BUTTON, GLUT_MIDDLE_BUTTON, and GLUT_RIGHT_BUTTON. If a mouse has just two buttons, the middle option is not available, and if a mouse has just one button, it will generate only the left option. The second thing to know is the button state, with the options being GLUT_DOWN and GLUT_UP, where down occurs when the button is pressed and up occurs when the button is released. The last thing to know is where the mouse was positioned within the window when the event occurred. The action "click the mouse button" refers to a down and up event occurring at the same location, where "dragging" refers to a down event that occurs at the start of the drag and an up event that occurs at the end of the drag. These are the values that are passed into the function that handles mouse clicks. In the example code, the mouse function is called handleMouse, which must be declared somewhere in the program files as:

```
void handleMouse( int button, int state, int x, int y).
void glutKeyboardFunc( void (*func)(unsigned char key,
                              int x, int y)
```

This routine registers a function to handle when keys are pressed on the keyboard. In the example code, the keyboard function is called handleKeyboard, which must be declared somewhere in the program files as void handleKeyboard(unsigned char key, int x, int y), where the key is an ASCII value of the key pressed and x and y gives the location of the mouse when the key was pressed. The location of the mouse can be necessary if the program needs to write the letters pressed into window where the mouse is located.

```
void glutMainLoop( )
```

The glutMainLoop routine call hands control of the program over to the GLUT. The main loop causes windows to be displayed and the contents of those windows to be drawn. This loop then continues to look for events that will cause it to pass control back to one of the callback functions that were registered through the previous routines. The callback functions can change global variables that alter the image and, therefore, change what is displayed. The main loop executes until the user closes the window, at which point the program is finished. Because of this, it is typical for the program to do no work after the call to glutMainLoop.

1.8.5 A simple display function

The example display function draws a square in the center of the window. In the following sample code, the function begins with a call to glClear, which will clear the window of any old images before drawing begins. The parameters provided tell OpenGL to clear out the color buffer, which is where the image displayed on the screen is kept. The next command sets the color of the object as a light gray. The 3f in the routine name indicates that three floating point numbers are being passed as parameters. Next, the identity transformation matrix is loaded and drawing begins. The sample code has calls to the routines glBegin and glEnd. These routines tell OpenGL that the commands between them all relate to one object. The glBegin routine has a parameter that tells it that the set of vertices defines a polygon. The calls between the glBegin and glEnd give the locations of the vertices of the rectangle. The reshape function sets the clipping window to be between −1.0 and 1.0 in the x and y directions, which is the reason for the choice of the x and y vertex values. The z coordinates are given a value of −5.0 to place the object within the viewing area.[9] The glFlush routine is called to tell OpenGL that the command buffer should

---

[9]The z value is negative because OpenGL uses a right-handed coordinate system. In a right-handed coordinate system, positive z values come toward us and negative values move away from us. We will look at coordinate systems again in Chapter 3.

be emptied, which forces OpenGL to render the object. To improve its efficiency, OpenGL can hold the drawing commands waiting for the program to give other commands. The glFlush routine effectively tells OpenGL not to wait.

```
void drawImage( )
{
   glClear( GL_COLOR_BUFFER_BIT );
   glColor3f( 0.75, 0.75, 0.75 );
   glLoadIdentity();
   glBegin( GL_POLYGON );
      glVertex3f( -0.75, -0.75, -5.0 );
      glVertex3f(  0.75, -0.75, -5.0 );
      glVertex3f(  0.75,  0.75, -5.0 );
      glVertex3f( -0.75,  0.75, -5.0 );
   glEnd();
   glFlush();
}
```

• 1.8.6 A simple reshape function

The program needs to specify the portion of the window created by GLUT to be used for the drawing. This portion of the window is called the viewport. Typically, the viewport is the entire window, so the width and height that are passed into the reshape function are used to define the viewport dimensions. It is also possible to divide the window into multiple viewports and draw different images in each one. For example, the program might be required to draw a scene from the front, back, left, and right sides. It could set up the viewport to be the upper left quarter of the window, and draw the scene from the front. Then it could set the viewport to be the upper right quarter and draw the scene from the back, and so on.

In the following sample code, the glViewport command specifies that the lower left corner of the viewport should be at location (0, 0) and the upper right corner should be at location (width, height), which fills the entire window. There is a type cast from integer to GLsizei, which is the type that OpenGL expects for these parameters. Because GLsizei is equivalent to an integer, any constant values specified, such as the zeros, are automatically cast by C/C++. This sort of casting is necessary, however, when a variable of a regular C/C++ type is passed into an OpenGL routine.

Chapter 3 looks at transformations that can be applied to objects to move them around the world. These transformations are implemented as matrix multiplications. OpenGL has a number of stacks to hold these transformations. The two used here are the projection matrix stack and the modelview matrix stack. The projection matrix stack determines how the scene is transformed from the three-dimensional world space to the two-dimensional screen space. The modelview matrix stack is used to position objects in the world. The actual use of these matrix stacks will be explored in later chapters. For now, the program changes to the projection matrix stack; puts the identity matrix on the stack; gives the details of how to do the projection; and then switches back to the modelview matrix stack for any drawing commands that follows.

This sample program uses a simple perspective projection that makes objects look smaller as they move away, much as they do in the real world. A perspective projection is chosen with the call to glFrustum. The parameter values tell OpenGL the range of world coordinates we expect to see on the screen. The range of coordinates in OpenGL and graphics in general has no predefined meaning. A line that runs from coordinates of (0, 0) to (1, 0) can represent a line in the scene with length of one micron, one inch, one meter, one mile, one kilometer, or even one light year. The range of coordinates to be used are chosen based on what seems most natural to the scene described. In the glFrustum call, the first two coordinates give the left to right range of the clipping window, the second two give the bottom to top range of the clipping window, and the last two give the near (the depth of the clipping window) to far distance. Any objects outside of the frustum these values create will not appear in the image on the screen.

Putting all of this together gives a reshape function of:

```
void reshapeWindow( int width, int height )
{
    glViewport( 0, 0, (GLsizei) width, (GLsizei) height );
    glMatrixMode( GL_PROJECTION );
    glLoadIdentity( );
    glFrustum( -1.0, 1.0, -1.0, 1.0, 5.0, 25.0 );
    glMatrixMode( GL_MODELVIEW );
}
```

1.8.7 User input

Two ways for the user to give input to a program are through the mouse and keyboard. In an elaborate graphics program, a user can click locations to indicate object vertices; drag across the screen to select objects; type text to be placed into the scene; or type commands to change the image. Because the purpose of this book is realistic image generation, user input is not a major concern. To illustrate how the mouse and keyboard functions work, consider a simple program where the user can specify the color of an object by typing "r" for red, "g" for green, "b" for blue, and "w" for white. The object will be a triangle that the user can define with three mouse clicks.

Mouse Events
The callback function that handles mouse events is given four pieces of information by the GLUT. The first is the button that was pressed; the second is whether the button was pressed or released; and the third is location of the cursor when the button was pressed. The use of this information will be illustrated by a program that will

allow the user to indicate three points in the window that should be used to draw a triangle.

Each time the user clicks the mouse, there are two events generated. The first event is when the button is depressed and has a state of GLUT_DOWN. The second occurs when the button is released and has the state of GLUT_UP. For this application, either the down or up event can be used, but the function below chooses the release. However, if the application is creating a feature such as a selection, the down and up events have to be handled separately, because the locations at the press and release indicate the bounds of the area selected.

In this case, the callback function only needs to check if the left button was used and if this is the release event. Once the function identifies that the proper event has occurred, it needs to make note of the location of the mouse event. Because the program draws triangles, it needs an array with three locations for the vertices. This array needs to be global to the program so that successive calls to the handleMouse function have access to it, as well as the drawImage function. Additionally, a global counter is needed to keep track of how many times the user has clicked. If this variable, called vertexCount, is three when the button is pressed, this indicates that a new triangle is starting. The counter gets reset and the location gets stored. For the next two vertices, the only action necessary is to store the location. One thing to note about the locations passed to this routine—they are pixel locations as offset from the upper left corner of the window. In this program, the window is 300 by 300 pixels, so a click in the upper left corner returns a location of (0, 0) and a click in the lower right corner returns a location of (299, 299). The y coordinate values increase as they move down the window. But, the drawings are being done using coordinates in the range [–1.0, 1.0], with the y coordinate values increasing as they move up in the scene. The locations need to be transformed into both a different range and a different direction for y. This is done with the equations shown in the code below. It must be noted that the windowWidth and windowHeight variables are global to the program and are set in the reshapeWindow function whenever the user changes the window size.

In looking at this code, you will note that there are two sets of coordinate arrays for the old set of vertices that are currently displayed on the screen and for the new set of vertices that are being entered. Using two sets means that the image will not change until the new set of vertices is completed. Also notice that the function includes a call to the glutPostRedisplay routine. This routine will force OpenGL to redraw the scene so that the new triangle can be seen.

```
void handleMouse( int button, int state, int x, int y)
{
    int i;

    if ((button == GLUT_LEFT_BUTTON) && (state == GLUT_UP))
    {
```

```
    // left button released
    if (vertexCount == 3)
    {
        // start a new triangle
        vertexCount = 0;
    }
    newX[vertexCount] = 2.0*(float)x/windowWidth - 1.0;
    newY[vertexCount] = 1.0 - 2.0*(float)y/windowHeight;
    vertexCount++;
    if (vertexCount == 3)
    {
        // new triangle done
        for (i = 0; i < 3; i++)
        {
            oldX[i] = newX[i];
            oldY[i] = newY[i];
        }
        glutPostRedisplay();
    }
  }
}
```

Keyboard Events

The handleKeyboard callback function is used to set the color of the triangle. This function also uses a set of three global variables that store the color used in the drawImage function. This function needs to examine the key that was pressed to see if it is one of the letters that switches the color. The variables red, green, and blue are global variables so that this function and the drawImage function can both access them. In this case, the location of the mouse is not needed and so the x and y parameters are ignored. As in the case of the handleMouse callback function, the glutPostRedisplay routine needs to be called so the triangle is drawn in the new color.

```
void handleKeyboard( unsigned char key, int x, int y)
{
    switch( key )
    {
        case 'r':
        case 'R': red = 1.0;
                  green = 0.0;
                  blue = 0.0;
                  break;
        case 'g':
        case 'G': red = 0.0;
```

```
                         green = 1.0;
                         blue = 0.0;
                         break;
            case 'b':
            case 'B': red = 0.0;
                         green = 0.0;
                         blue = 1.0;
                         break;
            case 'w':
            case 'W': red = 1.0;
                         green = 1.0;
                         blue = 1.0;
                         break;
        }
      glutPostRedisplay();
}
```

1.8.8 Putting it all together

All of the pieces necessary for a simple OpenGL program that allows the user to select vertices for a triangle, as well as the triangle color, have been discussed. Now all of these are put together into a single program listing so that the reader can see how all of these routines work together.

```
#include <GL/glut.h>
#include <stdlib.h>

// global variables for information entered
// by the user
int   vertexCount;
float  oldX[3], oldY[3];
float  newX[3], newY[3];
float  red, green, blue;
int  windowWidth, windowHeight;

void initialize( )
{
    // clear color is black
    glClearColor( 0.0, 0.0, 0.0, 0.0 );
    // initial color is white
    red = green = blue = 1.0;
    // initial triangle
    oldX[0] =  0.0;  oldY[0] =  0.75;
    oldX[1] = -0.75; oldY[1] = -0.75;
    oldX[2] =  0.75; oldY[2] = -0.75;
```

```
      vertexCount = 3;
}

void drawImage( )
{
   int i;

   glClear( GL_COLOR_BUFFER_BIT );
   glColor3f( red, green, blue );
   glLoadIdentity();
   glBegin( GL_POLYGON );
      // output the triangle vertices
      for (i = 0; i < 3; i++)
         glVertex3f( oldX[i],  oldY[i], -5.0 );
   glEnd();
   glFlush();
}

void reshapeWindow( int width, int height )
{
   glViewport( 0, 0, (GLsizei) width, (GLsizei) height );
   // save the width and height for the handleMouse
   // function to use
   windowWidth = width;
   windowHeight = height;
   glMatrixMode( GL_PROJECTION );
   glLoadIdentity( );
   // set the range for the window.  if these
   // values change the equations in the
   // handleMouse function will have to change
   glFrustum( -1.0, 1.0, -1.0, 1.0, 5.0, 25.0 );
   glMatrixMode( GL_MODELVIEW );
}

void handleMouse( int button, int state, int x, int y)
{
   int i;

   if ((button == GLUT_LEFT_BUTTON) && (state == GLUT_UP))
   {
      // left button released
      if (vertexCount == 3)
      {
```

```
            // start a new triangle
            vertexCount = 0;
        }
        newX[vertexCount] = 2.0*(float)x/windowWidth - 1.0;
        newY[vertexCount] = 1.0 - 2.0*(float)y/windowHeight;
        vertexCount++;
        if (vertexCount == 3)
        {
            // new triangle done
            for (i = 0; i < 3; i++)
            {
                oldX[i] = newX[i];
                oldY[i] = newY[i];
            }
            glutPostRedisplay();
        }
    }
}


void handleKeyboard( unsigned char key, int x, int y)
{
    switch( key )
    {
        case 'r':
        case 'R': red = 1.0;
                  green = 0.0;
                  blue = 0.0;
                  break;
        case 'g':
        case 'G': red = 0.0;
                  green = 1.0;
                  blue = 0.0;
                  break;
        case 'b':
        case 'B': red = 0.0;
                  green = 0.0;
                  blue = 1.0;
                  break;
        case 'w':
        case 'W': red = 1.0;
                  green = 1.0;
                  blue = 1.0;
                  break;
```

```
      }
      glutPostRedisplay();
   }

   int main(int argc, char **argv)
   {
      glutInit( &argc, argv);
      glutInitDisplayMode( GLUT_SINGLE | GLUT_RGB );
      glutInitWindowSize( 300, 300 );
      glutInitWindowPosition( 50, 50 );
      glutCreateWindow( "example" );
      initialize();
      glutDisplayFunc( drawImage );
      glutReshapeFunc( reshapeWindow );
      glutMouseFunc( handleMouse );
      glutKeyboardFunc( handleKeyboard );
      glutMainLoop();
      return 0;
   }
```

1.9 Projects

Get the program given in section 1.8.8 to work on your computer. Then make the following changes:

1) Add the colors magenta, yellow, and cyan to the options recognized by the handleKeyboard function.

2) Add to the handleKeyboard function the recognition of the numbers from three to nine. The number pressed should be the number of vertices that need to be entered for the next image to be drawn. Then update the handleMouse and drawImage functions to incorporate these extra vertices. (Note: You will need new global variables to hold the number of vertices to be entered that is separate from the current vertexCount that keeps track of the number of vertices in the previous object.)

Vision, Light, and Shading

There are a number of stages in and influences on the process of human vision. There are the physical components of light, and how they react with objects in the world. Some objects clearly reflect light, such as mirrors and polished metal surfaces. Others appear to have no light reflection, such as fabrics or walls covered with a flat paint. But for objects in the world to be visible, all objects must give off some light energy.

Once that energy enters the eye, it causes a chemical reaction based on the amount of light and that light's color. Different objects will reflect light onto different parts of the eye. So, there will be many different signals being produced because of the many different objects that can be seen at one time. All of those signals are then processed by our visual system and brain so that we understand what we are seeing. Research into vision finds that different things are processed at different times. For example, the shape of text is processed before the actual words are, which is why it is easier to process a piece of text that is in upper and lower case letters than one that is in all upper case.

To produce images that give the impression of being pictures of real objects, it is important to understand how light and the human visual system work. For example, rendering an image of a mirror with a brushed metal frame requires an understanding of how light interacts with the mirror as well as with the brushed metal surface.

One critical step in working with computer graphics is to begin to look closely at the world around you. If you are going to try and create images that simulate that world, you need to know how that world truly looks. People become so accustomed to looking at everyday objects that they sometimes miss some of the details of what they are seeing. As an example, many people may not be able to say, without looking, whether their analog wristwatch has numbers or just lines for the hours. They might not be able to say which hand the Statue of Liberty holds the book even though they have seen many images of the statue. Others might not be able to identify features of the currency that they use on a regular basis.

So, you need to begin to really look at the objects in your world in a number of different settings. Look at how light reflects off various types of objects. Look for highlights and see where they are, what color they are, and what shape they are. Look for where the light sources creating the highlights are located. Compare how highlights differ on two adjacent objects made of different materials. Watch what happens when light gets dimmer or its color changes. Look at shadows that objects cast and follow shafts of light as they reflect around the room.

Look at the effects of atmosphere as well. Notice how far you can see on a clear versus hazy day. Look at how beams of light can be seen in smoke or haze. Notice the dust or fuzz that floats in the air. Figure 2.1 shows two pictures of Toronto, Ontario. The first picture is on a clear day and the second picture is on a hazy day. In these pictures, the different visibilities of distant buildings in each picture clearly show the impact that atmosphere can have.

All of these factors have an impact on what we see and how we see it. To create a truly realistic image we need to either model these things, or come up with approximations for the same effect.

This chapter looks at how light interacts with objects and at how this interaction can be simulated with various illumination models and shading methods. Some of these shading methods were developed many years ago, but are still in common use. These methods look at only some of the light interaction with objects, in part because they were developed for computers that had limited processing power. More recent illumination models include a greater range of effects and thus are computationally more complex. The models described in this chapter will primarily deal with opaque objects. Though the issue of transparency will be mentioned in the discussion of the Strauss model, refraction of light through an object will not be fully considered until Chapter 8. Because what we see is determined by how light and the human visual system work, this chapter begins with a brief introduction to them, highlighting those components that have an impact on how images are produced.

2.1 How Light Works

Light is a form of energy that bounces around the environment reflecting off and refracting through objects. How light is transferred among objects in the environment depends on the objects that are present. Some objects, such as metals, reflect

Figure 2.1 • Toronto, Ontario on a clear and hazy day (see Color Plate 2.1)

most of the light energy that strikes them. Other objects, such as glass, allow most of the light that strikes them to pass through. Still other objects exhibit a combination of these two possibilities.

How the light is reflected off objects will also vary based on the objects themselves. Plastic objects are very smooth objects that have pigment particles suspended in them. These pigment particles are just chemical compounds that reflect different colors of light. Some of the light that strikes a plastic object reflects off the smooth surface and some of the light penetrates the surface and reflects off the pigment. Different types of paint behave in a similar way. All paint is just pigment particles suspended in an oil or water base. When paint is applied, the water or oil evaporates and the particles are left behind. If the pigment particles are very small, the resulting surface will be smooth and shiny, as in high gloss or enamel paints. If the pigment particles are very large, the resulting surface is dull, as in satin or flat paints. The presence of brush or roller marks, as well as an uneven application, also affects the final appearance. The pigment particles themselves actually absorb part of the light that strikes them, which is what causes the color that is seen.

This discussion treats light as if it was a single thing. Light really has multiple wavelengths. Some of those wavelengths fall into the visible spectrum—those wavelengths that humans can see. In actuality, there is no single visible spectrum because there can be slight variations in the range of visible wavelengths between two different people. What is considered the visible spectrum is really the range of wavelengths that the average person can perceive. The wavelength of light is important because the way that light interacts with an object can depend on the wavelength. Further, some interactions with objects can actually change the wavelength, hence changing the light color.

Light can be composed of many wavelengths at one time. The individual wavelengths are not seen, but rather combine into a single color. When all of the visible wavelengths are present, the result is perceived as white light. A prism can split white light into various wavelengths. The prism works because each of the wavelengths passes through the prism at a different speed, and therefore exits the prism at a different angle. Even though white light can be broken down into the full spectrum, it can be created by combining just a few well-chosen wavelengths. It is this fact that makes it possible for a computer monitor to produce millions of colors, using just red, green, and blue phosphor.

There are other views of light besides as a wavelength. Light can also be treated as energy, and illumination as the transfer of that energy. This is the perspective of radiosity, which is discussed in Chapter 9. But for now, we will discuss light simulated from the wavelength perspective. In the illumination and shading models, light at the red, green, and blue wavelengths can be treated equivalently. This means that an illumination or shading calculation will be done three times for each of the red, green, and blue wavelengths.

2.2 Vision

We see objects through a combination of visual stimulus and the processing of that stimulus. Of primary concern to graphics is the visual stimulus because if that can be duplicated, the normal process will take over and we will believe we are seeing something real. This section will examine the eye and how it works. This will be a simplified overview that will highlight those components of the eye that have an impact on how images are produced.

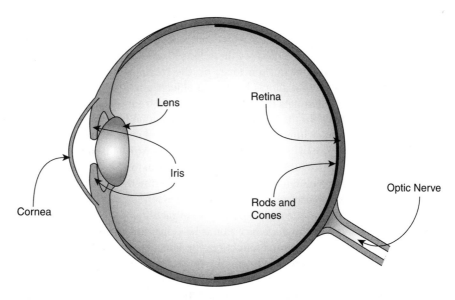

Figure 2.2 • A cross section of the human eye

• 2.2.1 The eye and color vision

In general, light enters the eye (Figure 2.2), is focused by the lens, strikes the retina, and causes a signal to be sent along the optic nerve to the brain. This simple sentence covers a lot of detail.

Light enters the eye through the cornea and the pupil. The eye needs to control how much light enters so that it can be properly handled. If there is too much light, it will overwhelm the retina and particular details will be lost. If there is too little light, there might not be enough for any reaction in the retina. Controlling how much light enters the eye is the responsibility of the iris. At high levels of light, the iris closes, causing the pupil to get small and limiting the amount of light that enters the eye. At low levels of light, the iris opens, causing the pupil to get larger and let in more of the available light. This process controls the amount of light that enters the eye from being too much or too little. Of course, there are limits as to how much the iris can open or close. On extremely bright days, it can be difficult to see without sunglasses that help the retina by darkening the light from the environment. At night, it can also be difficult to see because there is no or very little light around, unless there is artificial illumination from lamps.

Once the iris has controlled the amount of light entering the eye, the light then passes through the lens. Muscles around the lens will change the lens shape, which is what allows us to focus at various distances. When we focus on something close, the muscles push the lens in to make it thick. When we focus on something in the distance, the muscles allow the lens to become thinner. As we age, the lens becomes less elastic, which makes it difficult for us to have a large range where things are clear. This is the reason why people need reading glasses or bifocals as they age—to compensate for a less elastic lens.

The goal of all of these lens shape changes is to get light from the object we are looking at to then focus on the retina at the back of the eye. When the lens gets thick, that allows light from objects close by to be in focus on the retina, and when the lens gets thin, that allows light from distant objects to be in focus. To say that the object is in focus is really to say that light reflecting off the object is striking the proper number and spatially oriented cells in the retina so that the resulting signal is properly processed. An eye test is really just a check to see how well your lens is focusing the light and dark areas from the Snellen eye chart and whether it is focusing well enough for you to see the fine details of the smaller lines of text.

Objects are seen because light is refracted as it passes through the cornea, lens, and fluid in the eye. The index of refraction for the cornea is close to that of water, which is why underwater vision is less clear unless goggles are worn. Much as a prism splits light because of refraction, the lens of the eye does as well. The edges of a white circle are projected onto the retina as a circular rainbow. Each wavelength of light is refracted slightly differently by the lens, so there will be some minor refocusing necessary for different colors. Artists and designers say that warm colors (such as red or orange), move toward you, while cool colors (such as blue and green) move away from you. The need to refocus for these colors suggests one reason for this impression.

The retina is composed of two types of cells—rods and cones—named because of their shape. Rod cells are 10 times more sensitive to levels of light or luminance than cones, and operate at low light levels. Cones take care of color and detail and have three varieties—long, middle, and short. The long cones are most sensitive to longer wavelengths and in the past were called "red" cones for this reason. The middle and short cones are most sensitive to middle and short wavelengths and in the past were called "green" and "blue" cones, respectively. Even though each type of cone has a wavelength where it is most sensitive, the range of reactive wavelengths for each type of cone overlap. Color differentiation is possible because each type of cone has a different level of reaction for every wavelength. About 20 percent of the cones are long cones, 78 percent are middle cones, and 2 percent are short cones.

When light strikes rod or cone cells, it causes a chemical reaction. The amount of light that strikes a rod cell determines the level of reaction. For a cone cell, the wavelength and intensity determine how each of the three types of cones will react. A very oversimplified description is that the light causes a chemical reaction in the rod or cone. The intensity of the light determines the intensity of the chemical reaction. The visual system in the eye will do some processing of these reactions but eventually, a signal travels along the optic nerve to the brain. Additional processing in the brain helps you to understand what you see. The visual system and brain look at the arrangement of rods and cones that are reacting, and the level of reaction to determine the shapes that are being seen. Those shapes are then interpreted to determine the objects being seen. The changes in the reaction of the rods and cones within short periods of time allow the visual system and brain to make determinations about the motion of objects.

Each eye has about 120 million rods and seven million cones. The fovea (center of the retina) is all cones. The density of cones falls off sharply as distance from the fovea increases, which is why more detail is seen in the center of the visual field and less detail is seen in peripheral vision. There is an area in the eye where the optic nerve connects that has no rods or cones and is called the blind spot. Visual processing includes a process called completion that fills in the blind spot based on what is being seen in the surrounding area. If a detail or object is small enough that it falls entirely within the blind spot, it will not be seen because completion cannot fill in that detail.

2.2.2 Light level and vision

The cones need a certain level of light to react. If the light levels are too low, the cones will not produce any chemical reaction. At low levels of light, the rods will still react to the presence of light; therefore, in very dim light you might be able to make out shapes and movement but not color. This makes sense from a protective viewpoint. At night, the color of the animal attacking you is not important, but where it is and what direction it is moving is important. Although you are not typically in situations where you need to worry about being attacked by wild animals, you might notice this effect of being able to see shapes and movement without being able to see color.

At dusk, just after the sun has gone down and it begins to get darker, you are able to make out the shapes of flowers, houses, or cars, but you lose more and more of the color of those objects the darker it gets. The presence of streetlights counteracts this by adding back the light that is lost after sunset. But if you compare objects near a streetlight with objects farther away, the objects near the light show more color than the distant objects.

Rods have a particular set of wavelengths there they are reactive with a peak sensitivity between the middle and short cones. This creates an interesting phenomenon as light levels decrease. Consider two objects—one yellow and the other dark blue. In bright daylight, the yellow object appears brighter than the blue one. As the sun sets and light levels decrease, the reaction in the cones lessens, and the reaction in the rods becomes more dominant. The blue object will cause a greater reaction in the rods and cones than the yellow one does in just the cones. Under moonlight, the blue object will look brighter than the yellow object; even though both will be darker than when in daylight, and might even appear colorless depending on light levels. This change in relative brightness is called the Purkinje shift, which has an impact on how images of low light scenes should be generated. If all colors are treated as washing out of a scene at the same rate, the resulting images will not appear natural.

2.2.3 Depth perception

Relative perception of the depth of two objects occurs for a number of reasons including:

- Binocular eye separation
- Interposition of objects

- Relative size of objects
- Motion of objects

The separation between your two eyes produces a slightly different image in each eye. When these two images are processed, differences help to determine the relative depth of objects. This can be seen by looking along the edge of a table. Close your left eye and align yourself so you are looking down just the right edge of a table. Now, without moving, close your right eye and open your left. You now should not be able to see the right edge of the table. This is because of eye separation.

The amount of difference between what your two eyes see indicates how far away something is. Hold up a piece of paper at arm's length and close your right eye. Notice what objects you can see, and how much of them you can see. Now, without moving the paper, open your right eye and close your left eye. You will be able to see a different amount of the objects that are behind the paper. The amount you can see of the objects near you will change less than those objects that are farther away.

Another cue to relative depth is the interposition of two objects. We know that closer opaque objects will block the view of more distant objects. When one object obscures another one, the blocked object must be further away. This can be combined with the binocular difference to get a good interpretation of the relative distances of what is being seen.

The interpretation of the depth of objects is also based on adaptation to things regularly seen in the world. One of those things is that as objects move away, they get smaller. This is called foreshortening. This can also be seen when looking at a road. The edges of the road are the same distance apart along the length of the road, but in the distance the edges of the road seem to get closer.

Real world perceptions are based on more than just static images. The real world is dynamic. Objects move, we move, and our eyes move. All of this motion also gives feedback as to the relative depth of objects. For example, focus on an object somewhere in the middle of a group of objects. If you move just your head to the left, objects closer than where your vision is fixed will appear to move right and those farther will appear to move left. Processing the relative motions of objects will, therefore, give details about relative distances.

Virtual Reality

There are many applications of computer graphics where it would be helpful to see things in three dimensions. For example, it would be nice to have a three-dimensional image of a molecule to get a good look at how the various atoms are attached. It would be nice to move around all sides of a building that has been designed but not yet built, and even "walk" inside and move through the various rooms. A series of two-dimensional images could be presented with the expectation that the user will construct a mental image that is three-dimensional. A better result is possible by using knowledge of how humans perceive depth and by using some additional technology. This area of research is known as virtual reality—creating the perception of reality by "fooling" the visual system.

One part of virtual reality relies on the binocular nature of the human visual system. A different image is presented to each eye. The images are constructed so as to fool the visual system. If the viewer looks at two images rendered from slightly different viewpoints, called a stereo pair, the illusion of a three-dimensional scene is created.

There are two ways to present separate images to a user. The first is to have a device that allows only one eye at a time to see the monitor, and the second is to have each eye see a separate monitor. In the first, a monitor is connected to glasses that the user wears. The glasses have a mechanism that can alternately black out its left and right lenses, typically using polarizing filters that can change quickly. The software renders two images with the viewpoint location changed by just a few inches to simulate the separation in a human's eyes. When the monitor shows the image rendered from the left viewpoint, the right lens is blacked out so only the left eye can see. When the monitor shows the image rendered from the right viewpoint, the left lens is blacked out so only the right eye can see. This monitor will very rapidly switch between these two images at about 60 times a second. The switching is so rapid that the user does not even notice it. The perception is that both images are being seen at the same time. The user's visual system is fooled into thinking that the two images are real and it properly processes the images to get the depth perceptions.

An alternative is the head-mounted display. In a head-mounted display, there are two very small monitors placed in front of each eye. Instead of having to switch between two images, each monitor can continuously show one of the two images. Head-mounted displays are used in virtual reality applications where there are additional sensors that determine how the user is moving his or her head. These head movements are sent back to the computer, which changes the viewing direction and re-renders the two images. In this way, if the user turns to the left, he or she sees the part of the scene that is to the left. Adding other sensors and output technology can create an immersive environment that can fool users into thinking that they really are in a virtual space created by the computer.

Any additional discussion of virtual reality is beyond the scope of this book. The techniques covered in this book are critical, however, to the generation of scenes that look realistic enough to create the proper sense of these virtual spaces.

2.2.4 Visual illusions

The techniques used in virtual reality work because they fool the visual system into thinking that the two images shown are really just two views of a real world. All visual illusions occur because of the way the visual system processes the images seen by the eyes. In the case of virtual reality, the illusion is created on purpose to cause the perception of a world that might not really exist. There are other visual illusions that influence understanding of what is seen. A few of these illusions are discussed so as to make the reader aware of how elements of scenes might create the wrong impression in the viewer. In some instances, these illusions can purposefully be used to shock or disorient the viewer. An understanding of illusions is still important whether the plan is to use them or avoid them.

One common illusion that could have a great impact on a user is called an after-image. One example of an afterimage is when you have dark spots in your visual field after seeing a bright light. Another case is when you stare at an image for about 15 seconds or more. During that time, the various rods and cones in your eye are stimulated in the same way. The rods and cones get "tired" and produce less of a chemical reaction. The results of this reaction are processed by the visual system in a relative way. Because all of the signals are being reduced, the lesser signals are processed the same as the original. If after staring at the image, you now look away at a white piece of paper, there is a change in the relative amounts of the reaction, which is interpreted as a new image. The colors are re-evaluated based on the levels of signals being produced by the three types of cones. All of the cones should start producing at the same rate because the paper is white. The ones that are tired, however, will still be producing a weaker signal. This weaker signal will be interpreted as the absence of the color you were staring at. You will "see" the reverse color. After some time, all of the cones will produce the correct relative signals and the afterimage will go away.

For example, say that you are staring at a piece of blue paper. This will cause the short cones to become tired. If you now look at a white piece of paper, the long and middle cones will produce a high level of electrical signal, but the short cones will still be producing at a lower rate. This is what occurs when you look at a light yellow piece of paper. This signal combination will be interpreted as combination of high red and green wavelengths and low blue wavelengths, which is yellow, so the white paper will be perceived as being yellow for a short time until the afterimage goes away.

If you are designing software or images that will require intense concentration from the viewer, it is possible that an afterimage could impair later activities. For example, consider a series of screens for a user interface that are predominantly yellow in color. When an error condition occurs that requires quick action, perhaps a screen is presented with a white background, a red "stop" button, and a green "continue" button. Because the user's long and middle cones will be fatigued, the background will look blue and the two buttons will be very dark. This will make it difficult for the user to quickly pick out the appropriate choice. In this example, the afterimage can cause a situation that is potentially dangerous. In less critical situations, a user who has stared at an image for a while will need additional time before he or she can truly see what a follow-up image contains.

The visual system is used to process things from the natural world, and that influences the way it interprets the images that it sees. For example, in Figure 2.3, there are two horizontal lines that appear to be of different lengths but are really the same length. The reason for this difference in appearance is the way the diagonal lines on the ends are interpreted. The upper line appears to be an edge where a wall and the floor meet, whereas the lower line appears to be the closer edge of a box. The diagonal lines at the ends cause the upper image to be interpreted as being part of something farther away than the lower image. Our processing of images has adapted to a world where objects foreshorten. So, if two objects appear to be the same length, but we think that one is farther away, we will interpret the one farther away as being longer. In Figure 2.3, the lines are the same length, but because we

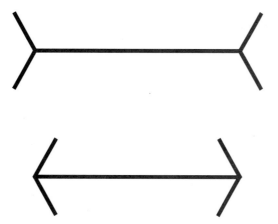

Figure 2.3 • The Müller-Lyon illusion

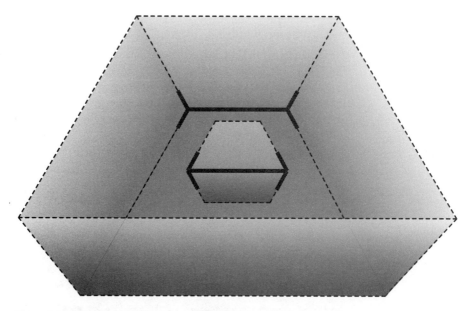

Figure 2.4 • Basis for the interpretation of the Müller-Lyon illusion

interpret the top one as being the corner of a room and the bottom one as an object in the room, the bottom one must be closer as shown in Figure 2.4. This causes us to interpret the top one as being longer.

There are many more illusions that can occur. These few are mentioned to raise awareness of how images could be misinterpreted because of the way that the mind processes what it sees. For this reason, images must be developed with care so that there are no unintended misinterpretations.

2.2.5 Color interactions

When we look at things we see them in a context. That context can influence how what is seen is interpreted. In his book, *The Interaction of Color*, Albers (Albers87) explores the many ways that color and gray scales can interact. One of these effects is called simultaneous contrast. In Figure 2.5, it appears that the two smaller gray boxes are of different shades. They are really the same color it is just that they appear different because of the background that they appear against. Though this is shown in shades of gray, the same thing occurs with the perception of color as can be seen in Color Plate 2.2.

In his book, Albers looks at 25 different color interaction issues. The full set of interactions has subtleties that are beyond the scope of an introductory computer graphics textbook. However, they are important nonetheless for someone working in graphics. Reproducing that discussion here would not be able to give the full depth necessary to do these issues justice, but we encourage you to read Albers's book, which is less than 100 pages long.

2.2.6 Mach bands

Mach bands are the illusion that a smoothly shaded surface, or patches of color, are not uniform in color or color change. Figure 2.6 illustrates this. In the first graphic, the blocks of gray are uniform in intensity, however, each block is perceived as being lighter on the left edge than the right edge. In the second, it appears that there are discontinuities in the shading even though the intensity change is continuous across the entire image.

Figure 2.5 • Simultaneous contrast (see Color Plate 2.2)

Figure 2.6 • Mach band examples

One explanation for the perception of Mach bands is based on ganglion cells in the retina (Schutz90). In this theory, the reaction of a collection of spatially oriented cells is moderated by surrounding cells. Specifically, the signal of the surrounding cells is subtracted from the signal of the central cells. Consider the locations in Figure 2.7 identified as A, B, C, and D. Let's say the light area to the right causes a reaction of 1.0 and the dark area to the left causes a reaction of 0.25. Let's further say that measurements are taken at the center of the inner circle and the amount subtracted is 10 percent of the sum of the measurement taken at four locations in the outer circle (top, bottom, left, and right) at the locations A, B, C, and D. When locations A and C are compared, the amount subtracted from location C is more

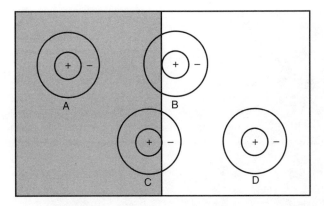

Figure 2.7 • Sample locations that illustrate the cause of Mach banding

than that subtracted from A because part of the outer ring of C falls in a bright area. Specifically, the overall value at location A will be 0.15 (0.25 − 0.1 * (4 * 0.25)) and the overall value at location C will be 0.075 (0.25 − 0.1 * (3 * 0.25 + 1.0)). Thus location C will be interpreted as being darker than location A.

When locations B and D are compared, the amount subtracted from location B is less than that subtracted from D because part of the outer ring of B falls in a dark area. Specifically, the overall value at location B will be 0.675 (1.0 − 0.1 * (3 * 1.0 + 0.25)) and the overall value at location D will be 0.6 (1.0 − 0.1 * (4 * 1.0)). Thus location B will be interpreted as being lighter than location D. Therefore, the area to the left of center will be seen as darker than the left end and the area to the right of center will be seen as lighter than the right end. This is the effect that is seen in the first example of Figure 2.6. The same effect occurs in the second example of Figure 2.6, but this is more subtle because of the smooth transition in gray levels.

2.3 Illumination

Illumination can be classified as global or local. Local illumination is concerned with how objects are directly illuminated by light sources. Global illumination includes how objects are illuminated by light from locations other than light sources, including by reflection of other objects and refraction through objects. This chapter is concerned with local illumination. Global illumination issues are discussed in Chapters 8 and 9.

This section begins by looking at a physical description of how light interacts with objects, known as the bidirectional reflectance distribution function (BRDF). The BRDF is a way to quantify how much light striking an object from a particular direction will be reflected off that object in the direction of the viewer. The discussion of this physical description will be followed by a look at ways to simulate illumination in a much more computationally feasible way. Later sections will apply these illumination concepts to the practical task of calculating the shading of an object.

This discussion will be based on point light sources. A point light source has a location where it is positioned and the light is assumed to emanate from the light source equally in all directions. When considering a location on the object, light is treated as a ray between the light source and the location on the object. A point light source is very much like an incandescent light bulb that has its light project in every direction. There are other methods to describe light sources, including extended light sources that occupy a more than just one point in space, and directed light sources that have their light pointing in a particular direction, such as a spotlight. These will be discussed as part of shadowing and global illumination models.

2.3.1 The bidirectional reflectance distribution function

The bidirectional reflectance distribution function (BRDF) is a way to describe how light reflects off objects. This function is dependent on the relative positions and orientations of the light source, the object, and the viewer. It is called bidirectional because if the location of the light source and the viewer are swapped, the BRDF will still give the same result. It is also called a reflectance distribution because it calculates, based on the light location, the portion of the light that reflects in varying directions.

Figure 2.8 shows an example of BRDF. In this case, the incident light comes along the direction of the gray line to the left and the white vertical line represents the surface normal. The large lobe to the right represents the direction of a mirror reflection and represents the specular reflection of the light. The hemispherical area

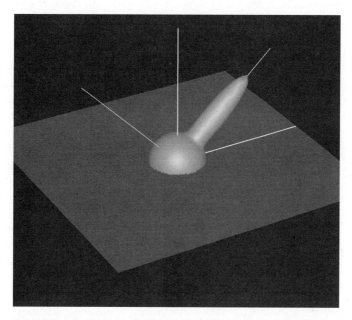

Figure 2.8 • The bidirectional reflectivity function *(Image created with the program bv written by Szymon Rusinkiewicz.)*

near the surface represents the diffuse reflection of the light. This figure graphically represents the value of the BRDF. The interpretation of this figure is that most of the light that arrives along the gray line to the left is reflected to the right, but that a smaller portion is also being reflected in other directions, including back toward the light source. Materials that are highly polished will act like mirrors and so, in a diagram for those, the hemisphere will be small or nonexistent and the lobe to the right will be larger. Materials that are very rough will scatter the light and so, in a diagram for those, the hemisphere will be large and the lobe to the right will be small or nonexistent.

As the incident direction of the light changes, the shape of the BRDF will also change. The BRDF is, therefore, dependent on the direction of the incident light. This change is most pronounced when the light strikes the surface in the direction close to the tangent. In that case, the lobed area will also be close to tangent, and thus the reflected light will be further scattered by the surface.

Materials can be classified as either isotropic or anisotropic. An isotropic material will have the same shape to the BRDF no matter how the incident light direction is rotated around the normal. If the material in Figure 2.8 is isotropic, as the incident light direction rotates about the normal, the size and shape of the lobes would stay the same as long as the angle between the light direction and the normal stays the same. An anisotropic material will reflect light differently as the incident light direction is rotated around the normal.

Another way to demonstrate the difference between isotropic and anisotropic materials is by watching how the reflected light changes as the material is rotated. Consider a flat piece of isotropic material positioned so it is between you and a light source. Rotating the material while keeping the normal direction fixed will not change the reflected light. If the same thing is done with an anisotropic material, the reflected light will get brighter and darker as the material is rotated. This difference is because a grain in the surface of the material creates a distinguishing direction, which is the rotational direction where the light is reflected the most. Examples of anisotropic materials include brushed metals and some fabrics such as satin. Figure 2.9 shows two pictures of a piece of satin rotated at 90° angles from each other. The light and camera positions were not changed but the amount of light reflected is clearly different. Where the shape of the BRDF for an isotropic material depends on the angle between the surface normal and the incident light direction, the shape of the BRDF for an anisotropic material also depends on the rotation around the surface normal.

The shape of the BRDF can also be dependent on the wavelength of the light. Research into reflectance off objects shows that different materials will behave differently as the angle between the light vector and the normal increases. Furthermore, changes in the reflectance as the angle increases can also be different for different wavelengths of light. This can be seen with copper, where the reflected light will shift toward the green end of the spectrum as the incident light direction moves toward the surface tangent.

The bidirectional reflectance distribution function for a material can be measured using a goniometer (Figure 2.10). A goniometer consists of a light source and

Figure 2.9 • Two pictures of satin fabric rotated 90°

detector that are pointing at the same location, which is where the material to be measured is positioned. These devices can be repositioned to any angle relative to the normal and can be rotated around the material for testing anisotropic materials. To measure the BRDF, the light source is positioned at some incident angle. Then the detector is positioned at various angles and rotational positions so that the

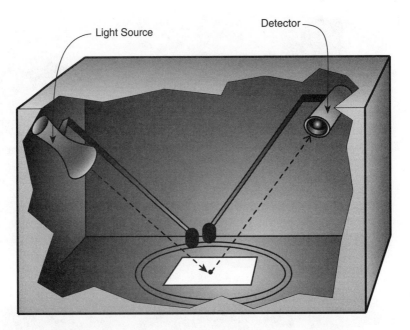

Light Source

Detector

Figure 2.10 • Goniometer

reflectance in that direction could be measured. The goniometer must be in a closed environment so that only the light reflected from the goniometer source is measured by the detector. Varying the wavelength of light emitted by the source allows measurement of the BRDF for different light wavelengths. There is a lot of data that can be produced by this process. If measurements are taken at five degree intervals, there would be about 1,000 samples per incident light direction per wavelength.

The discussion so far implies that light strikes a point on the object from a single direction in an infinitesimally narrow beam from a point light source. In the real world, light reaching a point on an object comes to that point in a conic shape. Additionally, because of minute variations in the surface of the object, the light reaching the viewpoint can get there from a number of very closely spaced locations on the object. The discussion also implies that each object of a particular material behaves in exactly the same way, when minor surface variations can also influence reflectance off an object. This complicates the use of the measured BRDF data.

Material science studies the properties of various materials under ideal conditions. How are the results used to model objects made of these materials under less than ideal conditions? If these measurements are also done using highly refined materials, how does the measured data apply to real objects that are not highly refined; show surface imperfections; or are dirty—none of which is present in the measured materials? Further, the scale of these differences can also have an impact. For example, a small scratch will have less of an influence than a deep gouge. From the perspective of computer graphics the question becomes, "How do these measured results influence illumination calculations?" With the large number of potential materials, measured at many wavelengths and many angles, the amount of data produced can be voluminous. Putting that data in a form that can be useful for a graphics rendering program can therefore be quite difficult.

The result of all of this is: There are a number of different people who have developed shading models that are approximations to the BRDF. Sections 2.4 and 2.5 look at a few of the shading models that have been developed over time. An impact on the complexity of these approximations is when they were developed. Computers in the 1970s were very slow compared to computers today, so very simple approximations were developed back then. Today's computers are much faster, and so recent illumination models use much more accurate and complex calculations. Even though they are very simple, some of those early shading models still play a role in computer graphics today. A shading model that can produce images quickly can be ideal if the application needs many images quickly. Because those images can be on the screen for a very brief time; can be moving quickly; or cannot be the focal point in a real-time animation, the simplistic nature of the approximation might not be as critical.

2.3.2 A simple illumination model

A simple view of local illumination breaks it down into three components: ambient, diffuse, and specular. The specular component produces the bright highlight on an object. This highlight is based on the direction of a true mirror reflection and so will be present when the direction the light reflects is the same or close to the same as the direction of the viewer. For a very smooth object, the viewer needs to be close to the reflection direction to see the specular highlight. However, as the surface becomes rougher, the specular highlight will begin to spread out.

The diffuse component produces a general highlighting of the object and is dependent only on the direction of the light relative to the normal of the surface. The areas where the light direction and the normal are the same will exhibit the highest diffuse component, and as the angle between them increases, the diffuse component will be reduced. If the diffuse component is considered from the viewer's frame of reference, the diffuse reflection will be equal in all directions for a given point on the object. For a point on the object, the diffuse component of the illumination model will depend only on the location of the object and light source. The diffuse reflection will be the same no matter where the viewer is located.

The diffuse and specular components are dependent on direct illumination of the object by the light source. In a room with a single lamp, the diffuse and specular components will only illuminate objects that are not blocked from the light. But objects not directly in the light are visible, which means that light is somehow reaching them. Chapter 9 looks at a global illumination model that will deal with

Figure 2.11 • Spheres showing the ambient, diffuse, specular, and their combined components with different colors (see Color Plate 2.3)

this. For now, the ambient light component is included as a constant added to all objects to approximate this indirect illumination.

Figure 2.11 shows four spheres. The first is rendered with just the ambient component in red. Because there are no highlights, this sphere looks flat. The second is rendered with just the diffuse component in blue. This sphere appears to have some shape, but it appears to be made of a matte material because of the lack of any bright highlights. The third is rendered with just the specular component in green. The center of this area is the location of the mirror reflection of the light source, and at locations away from this point the specular highlight decreases. The fourth is a combination of all of three components. The edge of the last sphere extending out from the lower left is red because this area is not receiving any light and so has just the ambient component. Areas of the sphere that are a shade of purple show areas where there is a mixture of ambient and diffuse components, with the shade indicating the amount of diffuse reflection. Areas of the sphere that are white show where there is a combination of the ambient, diffuse, and specular components. Areas just around this white highlight that are lighter shades of purple show areas where there is some, but not the full, specular component.

The specular, diffuse, and ambient components are linearly combined to get the simplified illumination model shown in equation (2.1).

$$I = k_a * I_a + k_d * I_d + k_s * I_s \tag{2.1}$$

In this equation, k_a is an ambient constant, k_d is a diffuse constant, k_s is a specular constant, and the I terms are the illuminations described. These constants are chosen for each object and are chosen to approximate the actual properties of the individual objects. The choice of constants will influence the color of the object as well as the way that highlights appear. Figure 2.12 shows a series of spheres, where the diffuse constant is increasing across the rows and the specular constant is increasing up the columns.

The diffuse constant impacts the intensity of the diffuse component. Materials with a rough surface would have a larger diffuse constant value than those with a smooth or polished surface. In Figure 2.13, diffuse constant values of 0.1, 0.4, and 0.8 are used. The hemispherical area increases with the increase of this parameter.

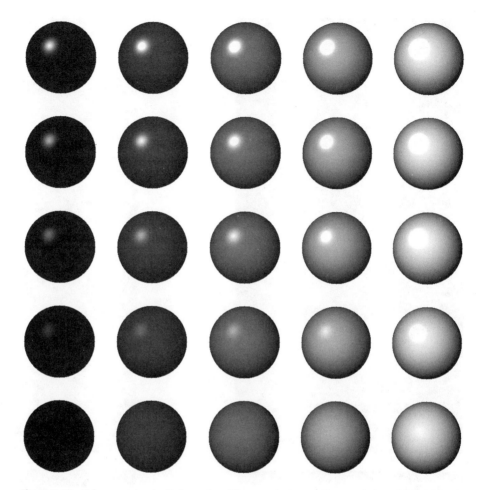

Figure 2.12 • Spheres rendered with increasing diffuse constant across the rows (values of 0.0, 0.25, 0.5, 0.75, and 1.0) and increasing specular constant up the columns (values of 0.0, 0.25, 0.5, 0.75, and 1.0)

It should be noted that the increase in size signifies an increase in intensity at the point at the center of this area. It does not signify an increase in the size of the diffuse highlight. The diffuse highlight will increase in size with an increase in the diffuse constant, but only because the reflection at more locations will be increased so that the reflections are more visible.

The specular constant impacts the intensity of the specular component. Materials with a rough surface would have a smaller specular constant value than those with a smooth or polished surface. In Figure 2.14, specular constant values of 0.2, 0.4, and 0.6

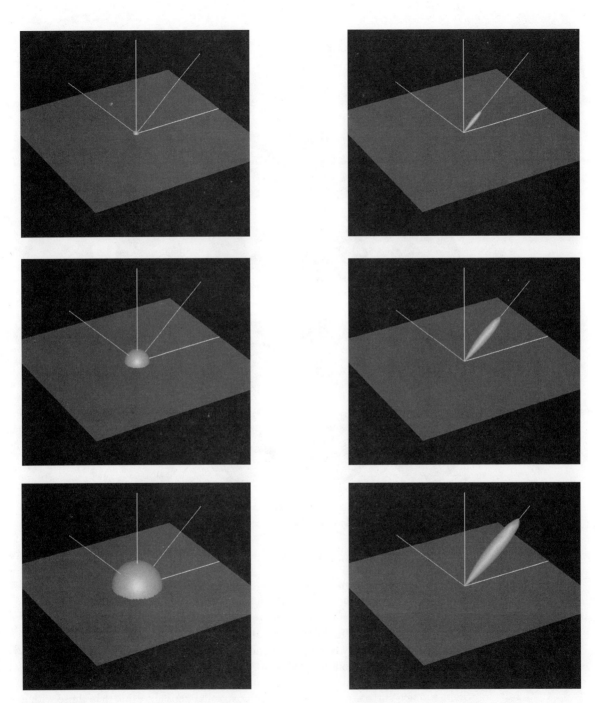

Figure 2.13 • Diffuse constants of 0.1, 0.4, and 0.8 from top to bottom *(Images created with the program bv written by Szymon Rusinkiewicz.)*

Figure 2.14 • Specular constants of 0.2, 0.4, and 0.6 from top to bottom *(Images created with the program bv written by Szymon Rusinkiewicz.)*

are used. This increases the intensity of the specular highlight as indicated by the larger lobe to the right in Figure 2.14. The increase in this parameter will increase the brightness of the specular highlight. The size of the specular highlight will also increase for the same reasons that the diffuse highlight increases with a larger diffuse constant.

The single equation (2.1) is actually calculated for a number of wavelengths. For an RGB color model, this equation is calculated three times for each of red, green, and blue. There will be a separate ambient and diffuse constant for each of the wavelengths. There can be a single specular constant used for all of the wavelengths, or a separate constant could be used for each wavelength.

Ambient Light

Ambient light is modeled by a constant factor added to each object to account for indirect illumination that comes from sources other than lights. Ambient light can be imagined as an amorphous energy that fills the space. This means that ambient light is light without direction. Because it has no direction, it will make objects visible, but it will not cause any highlights or shadows. Ambient light is just an approximation for light that reflects between diffuse objects. For now, a constant ambient component will be used to illuminate all objects equally, but later radiosity will be discussed, which calculates these diffuse-diffuse interactions.

Diffuse Reflections

A diffuse reflection is a distributed reflection of light off of an object. For a perfectly diffuse object, light will reflect equally in all directions. Lambert's model applies to perfectly diffuse objects. The bright spot created by a diffuse reflection will appear the same no matter where the viewer is located. The diffuse reflection will only change if the location or orientation of either the object or the light source changes. Figure 2.15 shows the distribution of light energy off a perfectly diffuse object. This figure shows that the light energy coming in the direction of the gray line to the left is reflected equally in all directions.

A diffuse highlight does not have sharp edges and is influenced by the color of the object. The diffuse reflection component is a simulation of objects with rough surfaces. A rougher surface will have a larger diffuse highlight than a smoother surface.

The diffuse reflection is equal in all directions, meaning that the same amount of light will reflect in every direction. This means that a particular location on an object will have the same diffuse reflection no matter where the viewer is. This does not mean, however, that the diffuse reflection will be the same across the entire object. Each location on the object represents a different combination of surface orientation and light direction. Even on a planar surface, moving across the surface will change the direction of the light. It is the same as when you walk through a room. If you stare at a point as you walk through a room, your head will turn indicating the change in direction to that point. Therefore, the diffuse reflection of a light source will be brightest on the object where the light source is directly above

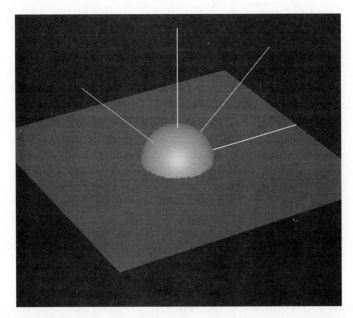

Figure 2.15 • Diffuse reflection *(Image created with the program bv written by Szymon Rusinkiewicz.)*

and will decrease in intensity at points on the object farther and farther away from this location.

Consider how the sun casts its light on the earth (Figure 2.16). When the sun casts its light from directly overhead, the energy is focused directly down. When this energy is cast from an angle, for example at sunrise or sunset, the same amount of energy is spread over a larger area of the earth's surface. So, the energy is not as intense as when the sun is overhead. This, by the way, is also the reason why there is a change in temperature and sun intensity as the seasons change. If you think about what happens at many different angles of light, you should be able to see that as the angle between the horizon and the sunlight direction decreases, the energy is spread out and so the amount of energy at any one point will decrease.

Figure 2.17 shows the object surface, the surface normal,[1] and the direction to the light source at the point under consideration. As θ gets larger, the cosine gets smaller and thus the amount of diffuse reflection will get smaller. Equation (2.2) calculates the illumination from diffuse reflection.[2]

$$I_d = I_L * \cos \theta = I_L * \boldsymbol{L} \cdot \boldsymbol{N} \qquad (2.2)$$

---

[1]The surface normal is a vector that is perpendicular to the surface. A plane has one normal vector, but a sphere has a different normal at each location.

[2]The two vectors need to be of unit length for the dot product to be equal to the cosine of the angle between the vectors.

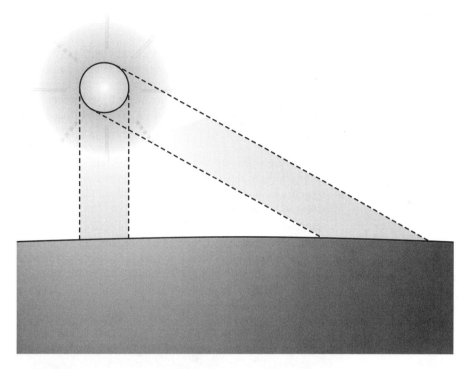

Figure 2.16 • Sunlight casting on the ground

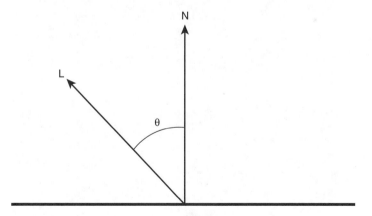

Figure 2.17 • Diffuse reflection

In equation (2.2), I_L is the intensity of the light source, L is the direction of the vector pointing toward the light source location, and N is the normal vector. If the dot product is negative, the angle between the vectors is greater than 90°. This means that the light source must be behind the object, and so there is no diffuse illumination. If the dot product is negative, the diffuse illumination, I_d, should be set to 0 for any further calculations.

The brightest point in a diffuse highlight occurs where the cosine is largest. The largest cosine value is one and will occur when the angle between the vectors is zero. This is a more formal description of what it means for the light source to be directly above the object. At points away from this location, the angle between L and N will increase causing the cosine and the diffuse reflection to decrease.

Specular Reflections

Specular reflections are the bright sharp highlights on an object. The size of the specular highlight is also based on the material the object is made of. An object that is smooth will have a small highlight and as the surface roughness increases, the highlight will spread out.

Specular reflections are the same as reflections off of a mirror. From your experience with mirrors, you probably realize that what you see in a mirror is based on where the mirror is, the direction it is pointing, and the direction you are looking. These are the same factors that influence where the specular highlight will appear on an object. Figure 2.18 shows the distribution of the specular highlight around the mirror reflection direction.

Figure 2.18 • Specular reflection distribution *(Image created with the program bv written by Szymon Rusinkiewicz.)*

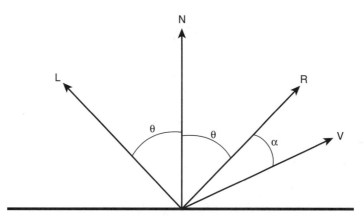

Figure 2.19 • Specular reflection

Figure 2.19 shows that light coming from direction **L** will be reflected in direction **R**. The direction of reflection is calculated with equation (2.3).

$$R = 2 * N * (N \cdot L) - L \qquad (2.3)$$

In Figure 2.19, the vector V represents the direction to the viewer location. If **R** and **V** were pointing in the same direction, the viewer would see the brightest part of the specular highlight. As **R** and **V** separate, the viewer will see less and less of the specular reflection, depending on the object's surface properties. The illumination from the specular reflection is calculated with equation (2.4).

$$I_s = I_L * \cos^n \alpha = I_L * (R \cdot V)^n \qquad (2.4)$$

In this equation, n determines how spread out the specular highlight is, which simulates the surface roughness. As n increases, the size of the highlight will decrease, indicating a smoother surface. In Figure 2.20, increasing the exponent narrows the specular highlight lobe.

2.3.3 Atmospheric attenuation

The atmosphere has many particles in it such as dust, smog, and water vapor among many other things. The quantity and size of these particles determines how far we can see, as shown in Figure 2.1. On a clear day with few particles, you can see farther than on a hazy day. On a hazy day, a distant object may not be visible even though it is on a clear day. The particles in the air get in the way and block our ability to see distant objects. But it is not an all or nothing situation. Looking into the distance, objects get fuzzier until the point at which nothing beyond is visible. Thus, atmospheric attenuation provides an additional cue to the relative depth of objects.

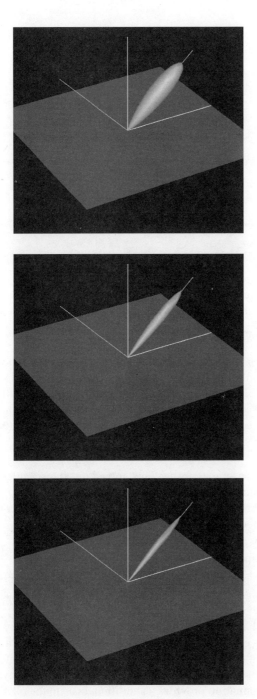

Figure 2.20 • Specular reflection with exponents of 29, 103, and 201 *(Images created with the program bv written by Szymon Rusinkiewicz.)*

When generating an image, atmospheric attenuation can be simulated to give the viewer the feeling of relative depths. First, the color used for the haze (H_R, H_G, H_B), the depth at which the haze starts to appear (z_{start}), and the depth at which the haze obscures all of the objects beyond (z_{end}) need to be chosen. In the range from z_{start} to z_{end}, the resulting color can be linearly interpolated between the object color (O_R, O_G, O_B) and the haze color. The following algorithm is an implementation of a linearly interpolated atmospheric attenuation.

```
calculate the object color as (O_R, O_G, O_B)
if (depth <= z_start)
    (Result_R, Result_G, Result_B) = (O_R, O_G, O_B)
else if (depth >= z_end)
    (Result_R, Result_G, Result_B) = (H_R, H_G, H_B)
else
{
    t = (depth - z_start) / (z_end - z_start)
    (Result_R, Result_G, Result_B) = t * (H_R, H_G, H_B)
                        + (1 - t) * (O_R, O_G, O_B)
}
```

Atmospheric attenuation will also affect light sources. As light travels through the atmosphere, it will be scattered by particles in the air. The farther the light has to travel the more the light will be scattered. A spotlight will get dimmer as objects move farther away. The more haze there is in the atmosphere the faster the light will dim. In the case of light sources, the light intensity can be attenuated based on an object's distance from the light source. This entails multiplying the light by a factor based on distance. Two techniques are linear and quadratic and are given by the equations: $a = 1/d$ and $a = 1/(d + d^2)$. Attenuation constants can be included that will influence the effect of these pieces. Equation (2.5) calculates the full attenuation model, where a_c, a_l, and a_q are the constant, linear, and quadratic attenuation factors, and d is the distance from the light source to the object.

$$a = \frac{1}{a_c + a_l * d + a_q * d^2} \tag{2.5}$$

In equation (2.5), as the distance increases, the attenuation factor decreases. When this factor is multiplied by the light intensity, an increase in distance will cause a decrease in the resulting light intensity used for the illumination calculations.

2.4 Shading

The previous section gave a model to simulate the illumination of objects by point light sources. This section looks at various shading models that use those illumination equations to calculate values used to render an image. For any object, there are an infinite number of locations on the object where these illumination calculations can be done. Each object in the scene will be projected onto some collection of pixels in the drawing window. Depending on the size of the projected object there can be many or few points where the object illumination is calculated. The subsections that follow look at the calculations that are done for the locations to be rendered. Chapters 3 and 4 give algorithms that determine where these object locations are.

Illumination has been discussed as though there is a single light source responsible for all of the illumination. In many instances, a scene can have multiple light sources. If there are multiple light sources, a diffuse and specular component is calculated for each light source for each location on the object. The total illumination for an object location is the sum of the ambient component, the diffuse component for each light source, and the specular component for each light source. The final illumination value should be capped to be in the range [0.0, 1.0].

2.4.1 Flat shading

In flat shading, the illumination calculation is done once for each planar patch, and the entire patch is rendered with this single color value, thus each patch will have a uniform color. There are many ways to specify the shape of complex objects but it is common to break an object into small planar patches for rendering. In that case, an illumination value is calculated for each of the patches that make up an object. Because each of these patches is rendered with a single color, they are clearly visible in the object. The object appears to be faceted as seen in Figure 2.21, which shows an object rendered with flat shading.

Figure 2.21 • Flat shaded pawn (see Color Plate 2.4)

In the illumination model, each object is defined with a set of eight parameters: There is an ambient component for red (k_{ar}), green (k_{ag}), and blue (k_{ab}); a diffuse component for red (k_{dr}), green (k_{dg}), and blue (k_{db}); a specular component (k_s); and a roughness exponent (n). These are used in the color calculations as shown in equations (2.6). In equations (2.6), I_L is the illumination of the light source, L is the direction to the light source, N is the normal for the patch, R is the direction of the light reflection, and V is the direction to the viewer. The relationship to these last four vectors is shown in Figure 2.19.

$$C_r = k_{ar} + I_{Lr} * [k_{dr} * L \cdot N + k_s * (R \cdot V)^n]$$
$$C_g = k_{ag} + I_{Lg} * [k_{dg} * L \cdot N + k_s * (R \cdot V)^n] \qquad (2.6)$$
$$C_b = k_{ab} + I_{Lb} * [k_{db} * L \cdot N + k_s * (R \cdot V)^n]$$

Given a triangular patch, which is guaranteed to be planar, the normal to the plane is found by taking the cross-product of the vectors representing two of the sides of the patch that both start at the same vertex. If this patch is determined from the decomposition of a larger object, it can be possible to have the actual normal vectors for each of the vertices. In that case, the vertex normal vectors can be averaged to get a single normal for the illumination calculations.

This method of rendering will be very fast, because just one illumination calculation is done per patch. The down side is that the image is not very realistic. This technique could, however, be used in a draft mode to check the placement of objects in a scene. This would allow the user to see roughly what the scene will be before doing more complex calculations for final image production.

2.4.2 Gouraud shading

As an improvement on flat shading, Gouraud [Gouraud71] developed an interpolation method for smoothly shading polygonal patches. His method eliminates the discontinuities in illumination values that are obvious in a flat shaded image along the border between two patches. This method calculates an illumination value at each of the patch vertices using equations (2.6). The difference with flat shading is that these calculations are done once for each vertex instead of once for each polygonal patch.

Once the color value at each patch vertex is calculated, linear interpolation[3] between two vertex colors is used to calculate the colors along each of the edges of the patch. Linear interpolation between these edge colors determines the colors within the patch.

If the patches are determined from a complex object, the patch vertices and the original object normal at these vertices can be used in the illumination calculations.

---

[3]Interpolation is basically an average weighted by how close a location is to the individual vertices. Closer vertices have a higher weight in determining the color at a location. Full details on interpolation can be found in Appendix A.

If the object description is just a grouping of adjacent patches, each of the vertex normal vectors can be estimated by averaging the normal vectors of the adjacent patches.

The normal at the vertex is used in the illumination calculations to get a color for each of the patch vertices. These vertex colors are then interpolated across the patch to get the color of the points that are interior to the patch. The result of using a Gouraud shading model can be seen in Figure 2.22. The model is exactly the same as shown in the flat shaded image, but in this case, the edges between the patches cannot be seen. This is because two adjacent patches that share an edge also share the two vertices at the ends of that shared edge. The color at those vertices is used to interpolate along that edge for both patches, so the values along that shared edge will be the same. Moving away from that edge in each of the two patches will change the color values, but linear interpolation will change them smoothly, which causes the visible edges in flat shading to disappear.

Though Gouraud shading produces objects that appear to have curved surfaces and shows no discontinuity of color along patch boundaries, there is still a problem with specular highlights. If a specular highlight falls on a vertex, Gouraud shading will render the highlight, although the highlight shape will depend on the size and shape of the polygons instead of the object properties. If a specular highlight falls on the inside of a polygon or along a polygon edge, that highlight will be missed.

Consider the situation in Figure 2.23. This figure illustrates a patch that has its four vertex normal vectors pointing slightly away from the center of the patch. This would be the situation if this patch was approximating a curved surface similar to a section of a cylinder. There is a "hill" that runs vertically through this patch. The

Figure 2.22 • Gouraud shaded pawn (see Color Plate 2.5)

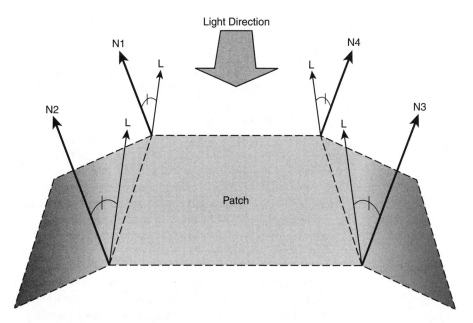

Figure 2.23 • Gouraud shading problem

Figure 2.24 • The patch of Figure 2.23 as it would appear if rendered with Gouraud shading, and if subdivided before rendering

four vertex normal vectors all have the same angle with the direction of the light. If the patch is viewed from directly above the center, the angle between the view vector and each of the vertex normal vectors will also be the same. If these angles are all the same, then the color calculated for each of the vertices will be the same. Doing a linear interpolation with these values will render all patch locations with the same color. This will make the patch look flat, but from experience with real objects, you would expect to see some sort of highlight along the top of the vertical ridge in the patch. The left of Figure 2.24 shows how this patch would appear if rendered with Gouraud shading. The right of Figure 2.24 shows that a more realistic shading of this patch would occur by subdividing it in half vertically.

It is very difficult to predict where Gouraud shading will have problems. If this object were rotated slightly left or right so that a vertex of the patch was below the viewpoint, the highlight would show up. The highlight also shows up if the patch is subdivided, as was shown in the right of Figure 2.24. Therefore, more accurate rendering is possible with Gouraud shading, if many small patches are used instead of fewer large patches.

2.4.3 Phong shading

Consider the problem identified in Figure 2.23. What must have to happen to the normal to have it change from pointing to the left in vectors N_1 and N_2 to have it pointing to the right in vectors N_3 and N_4? For a smooth surface, the normal vector must continuously change direction toward the right as it moves across the patch. As it does so, the normal will eventually point in a direction that picks up the highlight. The problem with Gouraud shading is that interpolating the colors misses the changes in normal vector direction that underlie situations such as this one.

Bui-Tuong Phong[4] (Bui75) improved on Gouraud shading by recognizing this change in normal direction. By interpolating the normal across the patch instead of interpolating the intensities, Phong shading will pick up highlights that Gouraud shading will miss. Phong shading is more computationally complex because equations (2.6) will be calculated for each interpolated normal instead of just for the vertices. Because the normal is interpolated across the object, as the normal approaches the direction of a light source, it will properly capture the diffuse reflection. As the normal approaches the direction that aligns the reflection and view vectors, it will properly capture the specular reflection. An example of the results of Phong shading can be seen in Figure 2.25.

It is computationally expensive to calculate the reflection vector and this is compounded by the number of times this would have to be done across the patch. A speed-up to the Phong shading model was proposed by Blinn (Blinn77). This involved the use of an approximation called the halfway vector (H), which is a vector that is halfway between the light vector (L) and the view vector (V)—see Figure 2.26—and is calculated as in equation (2.7).

$$H = (L + V) / 2 \tag{2.7}$$

Because H should be a unit vector, it will still need to be divided by its length. To save a division, a unit length H vector can be calculated with the single division calculation in equation (2.8). To see the speed-up involved, compare equations (2.3) and (2.8).

$$H = (L + V) / ||L + V|| \tag{2.8}$$

---

[4]Vietnamese names are specified with the family name first, hyphenated with a name that gives the person's generation in the family. The third part of the name is the person's individual name. Calling this shading method "Phong" shading is the equivalent of calling the previous method "Henri" shading instead of Gouraud shading. This shading method should rightfully be called Bui shading, but the term Phong shading is now well established in the graphics literature.

Figure 2.25 • Phong shaded pawn (see Color Plate 2.6)

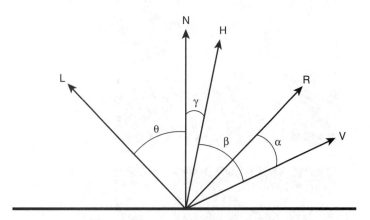

Figure 2.26 • The halfway vector

In the Blinn-Phong shading model, if **R** and **V** point in the same direction, **H** will point in the same direction as the normal. As **R** and **V** diverge, **H** will diverge from the normal. Because of this, **R** · **V** can be approximated with **N** · **H**. This is only an approximation, as can be seen in the specular lobe shape change in Figure 2.27. By increasing the exponent, the lobe of the approximation can be brought closer to shape of the **R** · **V** lobe.

One problem with Phong shading is that the objects in a scene tend to look plastic. A plastic object is made of pigment particles that are suspended in a clear base material. When light reflects off a plastic object, the diffuse reflection is from light

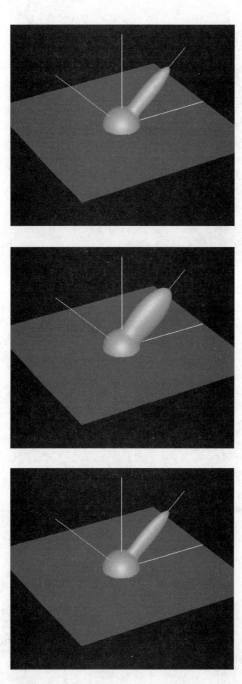

Figure 2.27 • Difference between the reflection and halfway vectors. From top to bottom: $R \cdot V$ (exponent 49), $N \cdot H$ (exponent 49), and $N \cdot H$ (exponent 181) *(Images created with the program bv written by Szymon Rusinkiewicz.)*

that penetrates the surface of the object, bounces around the pigment, and then exits the surface. The specular highlight is just a reflection off the surface of the plastic object and is the color of the light source. In equations (2.6), the diffuse constants are color based, but the specular constant is the same for every wavelength. This is why the diffuse highlight is the color of the object and the specular highlight is the color of the light source. Using a single specular constant, the Phong illumination model renders plastic objects. If a specular constant is specified for each wavelength, a wider range of materials can be simulated.

2.4.4 A more realistic shading: microfacets

Another limitation of Phong shading is that it treats objects as having a perfectly smooth surface. Few objects have perfectly smooth surfaces. Some materials are inherently rough and others have imperfections in their surfaces from when they were created or from when they were used. Chapter 6 discusses objects that have textures, but that handles only part of the limitation—large scale variations in the surface.

Some materials have very small scale variations in their surface. These variations may not be regular or if they are regular are small enough that they are not noticeable when looking at the object. These variations are not seen as a texture or pattern on the object. Instead, these variations are only seen in the way they affect how light reflects off the object. This is especially true of metallic objects.

Consider Figure 2.28, which illustrates a microscopic view of a rough surface. The light that strikes this surface will be scattered in many different directions, but

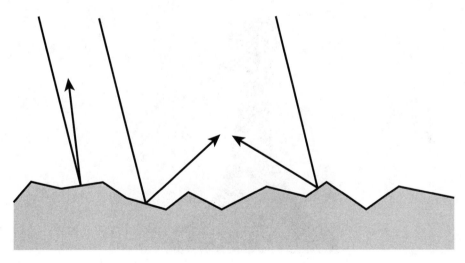

Figure 2.28 • Microfacets and light reflection

the amount scattered in each of these directions in this microscopic view is small relative to the incident light. For rough objects, the surface can be thought of as having a collection of microscopic facets or microfacets. These microfacets will be responsible for the scattering of light that results in highlights with fuzzy edges. The differences in how light reflects off two objects is categorized as a difference in the configuration of microfacet size and orientation.

Microfacets are the basis for the Torrance-Sparrow model (Torrance66 and Torrance67), which is a physical model for how light reflects off of a surface (Figure 2.29). This was adapted to the production of computer graphics images by Blinn (Blinn77), and Cook and Torrance (Cook81). These two applications used slightly different approaches. The following discussion will concentrate on the Cook-Torrance method.

The impact of this model is on the specular component of the shading calculations. The calculation is much more complex and accounts for the impact of the microfacets. The specular component is given by equation (2.9), where F_θ is the Fresnel term that handles the impact of the angle of light incidence, D is the microfacet distribution factor, and G is the microfacet geometry factor. The normal, light, and view vectors are also used in this calculation.

$$S = \frac{F_\theta}{\pi} * \frac{D}{(N \cdot L)} * \frac{G}{(N \cdot V)} \qquad (2.9)$$

Figure 2.29 • Cook-Torrance shaded pawn (see Color Plate 2.7)

The Fresnel term is based on reflection from a perfect mirror surface, so the division by π is to compensate for a rough surface. The distribution factor is based on the orientation of the microfacets and specifically represents the portion of microfacets pointed in the direction of the halfway vector. The microfacet geometry will handle how the position of the microfacets block light as it approaches the surface or leaves the microfacets on its way to the viewer.

The Fresnel Term

The Fresnel term is the equivalent to the specular component in the Phong model. The difference, however, is that the Fresnel term is wavelength and angle dependent. The way that light reflects varies as the angle between the light direction and the normal vector increases. Further, this variation can be different for different wavelengths. The Fresnel term is based on the object material, as different materials will have a different interaction with light. The original Cook-Torrance paper illustrated their results with a copper vase. They showed that with an angle between the normal and the light source of less than 70°, the reflected light would be copper-colored, but at higher values the color shifts through green until becoming white at 90°.

The Fresnel term depends on the object material. The Cook-Torrance paper gives references to physics and material science sources for the Fresnel term for various materials. These measured reflectance values are typically done only in the normal direction at various wavelengths, but these values are needed for many different angles. The key to this is the Fresnel equation (2.10).

$$F = \frac{1}{2} * \frac{(g - c)^2}{(g + c)^2} * \left[1 + \frac{\left(c * (g + c) - 1\right)^2}{\left(c * (g - c) + 1\right)^2} \right] \tag{2.10}$$

In equation (2.10), $c = V \cdot H$, $g = \sqrt{\eta^2 + c^2 - 1}$, and η is the index of refraction for the object material, which would be read from a data file. If the index of refraction is available, the needed values can be calculated, but if the index of refraction is unknown, it can be estimated from the measured normal reflectance (F_0) that would be found in one of the material research sources mentioned. At normal incidence c will have a value of 1, so the Fresnel equation simplifies to:

$$F_0 = \left(\frac{\eta - 1}{\eta + 1} \right)^2 \tag{2.11}$$

$$\eta = \frac{1 + \sqrt{F_0}}{1 - \sqrt{F_0}} \tag{2.12}$$

So, if F_0 has a value of 0.03, the value of η would be calculated as,

$$\eta = \frac{1 + \sqrt{0.03}}{1 - \sqrt{0.03}} \approx \frac{1.173}{0.827} = 1.418$$

This estimated value for η can be used in the original Fresnel equation for various values of c determined from the vectors for the current object location. One thing to note at this point is that when the angle between the view vector and the halfway vector is 90°, c will have a value of 0 and F will have a value of 1. Because the halfway vector is between the light direction and the view direction, the angle between the view vector and the halfway vector will be 90° when the light and view vectors are both tangent to the object. As the angle approaches 90°, the Fresnel factor will approach the color of the light source.

The F_0 values in the Fresnel equation (2.12) are actually wavelength dependent because light of different wavelengths will reflect differently off an object. For this reason, sources for measured data will actually have those measurements for multiple wavelengths. This means that equation (2.12) is calculated for multiple wavelengths. Based on an RGB color model rendering, this calculation would be done three times, using the F_0 value for the red, green, and blue wavelengths to calculate three different indices of refraction. Equation (2.10) would then be calculated three times to get the Fresnel terms for red, green, and blue. This is computationally costly, so Cook and Torrance give an approximation method to save some time.

Based on their approximation method, η_{red}, η_{green}, and η_{blue} would be calculated using equation (2.12) based on the measured reflectance values at those wavelengths. Next, the average of these three η values would be calculated, and this average would be used in equation (2.11) to calculate $F_{0average}$. The intensities (R_0, G_0, and B_0) at a normal incidence are found by multiplying the light intensity for each color by the measured reflectance values from the material science literature. Now $\eta_{average}$ and the angle of interest are used in equation (2.10) to calculate one F value. This one F value, the intensities (R_0, G_0, and B_0), and $F_{0average}$ are used in the linear interpolations shown in equations (2.13).

$$F_{Red} = R_0 + (1 - R_0) * \frac{\max\left(0, F - F_{0average}\right)}{1 - F_{0average}}$$

$$F_{Green} = G_0 + (1 - G_0) * \frac{\max\left(0, F - F_{0average}\right)}{1 - F_{0average}} \qquad (2.13)$$

$$F_{Blue} = B_0 + (1 - B_0) * \frac{\max\left(0, F - F_{0average}\right)}{1 - F_{0average}}$$

For example, consider a measured reflectance for red of 0.007, for green of 0.03, and for blue of 0.01. Equation (2.12) would give calculated indices of refraction of

η_{red} = 1.183, η_{green} = 1.418, and η_{blue} = 1.222, and an average index of refraction of $\eta_{average}$ = 1.274. Equation (2.11) gives an $F_{0average}$ value of 0.0145. A light source with intensity of (0.8, 0.8, 0.8) gives values of R_0 = 0.0056, G_0 = 0.024, and B_0 = 0.008 (the measured value times the intensity). Equation (2.10) would be calculated once using $\eta_{average}$ and the current value of c, and that resulting F would be substituted into the three equations (2.14) to get the three Fresnel factors for red, green, and blue. These three calculations will take less computation time than having to compute equation (2.10) two additional times.

$$F_{Red} = 0.0056 + 0.993 * \frac{\max\left(0, F - 0.0145\right)}{0.9855}$$

$$F_{Green} = 0.024 + 0.97 * \frac{\max\left(0, F - 0.0145\right)}{0.9855} \tag{2.14}$$

$$F_{Blue} = 0.008 + 0.99 * \frac{\max\left(0, F - 0.0145\right)}{0.9855}$$

Schlick (Schlick93) proposed an even quicker approximation for the Fresnel term, which is given in equations (2.15). In these equations, θ represents the angle between the light direction and the normal. Schlick reports that using a normal incidence value of 0.8 for R_0, G_0, and B_0 gives a stainless steel alloy appearance.

$$F_{Red}(\theta) = R_0 + \left(1 - R_0\right) * \left(1 - \cos\theta\right)^5$$

$$F_{Green}(\theta) = G_0 + \left(1 - G_0\right) * \left(1 - \cos\theta\right)^5 \tag{2.15}$$

$$F_{Blue}(\theta) = B_0 + \left(1 - B_0\right) * \left(1 - \cos\theta\right)^5$$

The Distribution Factor

The distribution factor was modeled differently by Torrance-Sparrow, Blinn, and Cook-Torrance. This factor gives an approximation of the portion of the microfacets that point in the direction of the halfway vector. One option is a Gaussian distribution given by equation (2.16), where γ is the angle between the halfway vector and the surface normal, m is based on variation in the orientation of the microfacets (formally called the "root mean square slope" of the microfacets), and k is an arbitrary constant. The parameter m, which indicates the amount of variation in the microfacet directions, would be specified for the object material being modeled.

$$D = k * e^{-\left(\gamma/m\right)^2} \tag{2.16}$$

A drawback of this distribution is that it requires an arbitrary constant. Other distributions have also been developed based on the electromagnetic radiation from either a rough surfaced electrical conductor, metals, or non-metals. Another alternative is the Beckmann distribution, which encompasses all of these types of materials. The Beckman distribution is more computationally complex than the

Gaussian distribution, but it also does not rely on an arbitrary constant as the Gaussian distribution does. The Beckmann distribution used by Cook-Torrance[5] is given by equation (2.17).

$$D = \frac{1}{4 * m^2 * \cos{^4}\gamma} * e^{-(\tan\gamma/m)^2} \tag{2.17}$$

The parameter m is used similarly in both distributions. Specifically, if the microfacets do not vary by much, m (the slope term) will be small and the reflection will be somewhat focused. However, if the microfacets have a great deal of variation, then m will be large and the specular highlight will be distributed. Changing the value of m would change the appearance of the object. Thus, the value of m would be a parameter of the object and would be part of the data file. Figure 2.30 shows the impact of the slope term on the Cook-Torrance reflectance distribution. Increasing values cause the specular reflection to be shifted closer to the surface and below the direction of a mirror reflection.

Some surfaces have a roughness that cannot be categorized by just one slope term. For those cases, Cook-Torrance allows for multiple values of m to account for multiple roughness factors. In that case, a distribution value is calculated for each value of m and then each result is multiplied by its weight and the values are summed. In this case, the total of the weights should be 1. For example, say a surface has $m_1 = 0.1$ with weight $w_1 = 0.25$ and has $m_2 = 0.3$ with weight $w_2 = 0.75$. At an angle of 10°, equation (2.17) gives a value of about 1.186 for m_1 and a value of about 2.091 for m_2. After applying the weights, the final distribution factor would be about 1.865.

Microfacet Geometry
In considering the geometry of the microfacets, Figure 2.31 shows three possibilities. The first is that all of the light striking a microfacet reflects away from the surface in the proper direction. In this first case, the microfacet geometry factor would be 1. The second is that some of the light is blocked by another microfacet as it is leaving the surface. In this second case, the portion that leaves the surface toward the viewer is based on the relationship between the normal and the view vector. The third is that some of the light is blocked by another microfacet before it gets to the surface. In this last case, the portion of light that reaches the surface will depend on the relationship between the light vector and the normal.

The microfacet geometry factor gives the portion of light that will leave the surface based on the microfacet orientation. If there is no light blocked, this factor will

---

[5]The original paper by Cook and Torrance is missing the 4 in the denominator.

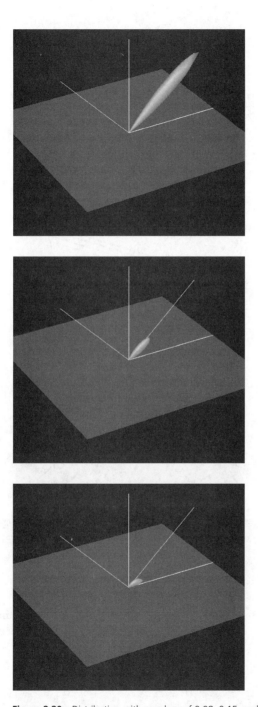

Figure 2.30 • Distribution with *m* values of 0.08, 0.15, and 0.25 *(Images created with the program bv written by Szymon Rusinkiewicz.)*

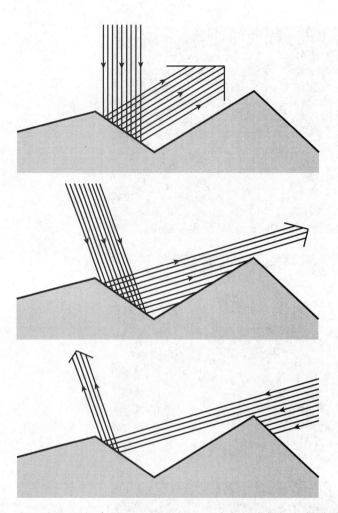

Figure 2.31 • Microfacet geometry. From top to bottom: light is not blocked, light is blocked on the way out, and light is blocked on the way in.

be 1. The full calculation is given by equation (2.18) where the three cases represent, in order, no light blocked, light blocked on the way out, and light blocked on the way in.

$$G = \min\left(1, \frac{2 * (N \cdot H) * (N \cdot V)}{V \cdot H}, \frac{2 * (N \cdot H) * (N \cdot L)}{V \cdot H}\right) \qquad (2.18)$$

A complete derivation of equation (2.18) can be found in (Blinn77).

2.5 Empirical Models

The shading models presented in section 2.4 are a simulation of the physical properties of the object. As such, they produce reasonable results that can be further improved with better simulation methods and increases in the computation time. There are applications where a highly accurate simulation is not required or can be confusing. Without extensive study of illumination models the choice of parameter values is typically ad hoc and can be inconsistent. For example, users of the Phong model can choose inconsistent parameters that result in a small sharp highlight indicative of a very smooth surface and a large diffuse component indicative of a very rough surface.

This section looks at two shading methods that can be used to quickly render images based on more intuitive parameters. These models are called empirical because some of the values used are determined through experimentation until the resulting images represent a reasonably good approximation.

2.5.1 The Strauss model

Strauss (Strauss90) developed a shading model that approximates the Cook-Torrance model. It is based on five parameters: color (c), smoothness (s), metalness (m), transparency (t), and an index of refraction (n). Figure 2.32 shows an object rendered with the Strauss model using values of $s = 0.6$ and $m = 0.5$. Strauss developed this model as an alternative to the Phong and Cook-Torrance models. He wanted a model that would have parameters that are more intuitive than the set of parameters used in those models. He also wanted a model where the parameters

Figure 2.32 • Strauss shaded pawn using $s = 0.6$, $m = 0.5$ (see Color Plate 2.8)

were independent, so that it was impossible for a user to choose a set of parameters that are inconsistent.

In the Strauss model, the color parameter (c) is the underlying color of the object. The equations will treat color as a single value, but these calculations are done for multiple wavelengths in a chromatic system.

The smoothness parameter (s) specifies how rough the surface is. For a perfectly diffuse surface, this parameter will have a value of 0, where for a perfectly specular surface this parameter will be 1. Values between these extremes can be used to specify varying degrees of roughness. This parameter will influence the ratio of diffuse and specular highlight as well as the size and brightness of the specular highlights. If the specular reflections are doubled, the diffuse reflections will be halved and the highlights will become sharper and brighter. In Figure 2.33, moving across the rows of spheres shows the impact of increasing the smoothness parameter.

The metalness parameter (m) will range from a value of 0 for non-metallic surfaces and a value of 1 for metallic surfaces. Values between these extremes can be used to specify varying amounts of metallic content of an object. In Figure 2.33, moving down the columns shows the impact of decreasing the metalness parameter.

The transparency parameter (t) will range between 0 for an opaque surface to 1 for a totally transparent surface. The index of refraction (n) is used to determine how light passes through a non-opaque object. Though Strauss's model includes transparency, Chapter 8 will deal with transparency issues in the context of ray tracing.

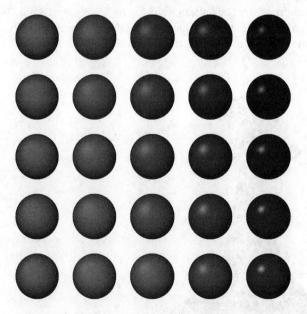

Figure 2.33 • Strauss model spheres with increasing smoothness across the rows (0.0, 0.2, 0.4, 0.6, and 0.8) and decreasing metalness down the columns (1.0, 0.75, 0.5, 0.25, and 0.0)

The Strauss model is similar to the illumination model discussed in section 2.3, with some variations in how the components are calculated. The overall illumination calculation is given by equation (2.19).

$$I = I_L * (r_d * c * I_d + c_s * I_s) \tag{2.19}$$

The calculation of r_d is given by equation (2.20).

$$r_d = (1 - s^3) * (1 - t) \tag{2.20}$$

The exponent of 3 applied to the smoothness parameter was determined empirically by Strauss so as to provide the perception of a linear variation in the diffuse and specular reflectivity for a linear change in the smoothness parameter. The idea is that by using a power of 3, a doubling of the smoothness parameter will appear to double the specular reflections and halve the diffuse reflections. A decrease in the smoothness parameter will result in an increase in r_d. An increase in r_d causes the diffuse component of equation (2.19) to increase. Because r_d also indirectly contributes to the calculation of I_s below, an increase in r_d will result in a decrease in I_s. The opposite is true when the smoothness parameter increases. It is this relationship that keeps the diffuse and specular reflections consistent in the Strauss shading model.

The diffuse illumination is calculated with equation (2.21) where the value of d will attenuate the diffuse reflection based on the smoothness and metalness of the object.

$$I_d = d * \mathbf{L} \cdot \mathbf{N} \tag{2.21}$$

So, an object with low smoothness and metalness will have a high value for d, and the diffuse illumination will be close to the pure Lambertian diffuse value. An object with high smoothness and metalness will have a low value for d, and the diffuse illumination will be minimal. The diffuse attenuation factor is given by equation (2.22).

$$d = 1 - (m * s) \tag{2.22}$$

The specular illumination is calculated with equation (2.23), where the exponent is calculated by $h = 3 / (1 - s)$ and r_j is the adjusted reflectivity.

$$I_s = r_j * (\mathbf{R} \cdot \mathbf{V})^h \tag{2.23}$$

As the smoothness parameter increases, the exponent in equation (2.23) will increase because the denominator in the calculation of h is getting smaller. This has the effect of making more of the smaller values of the cosine of the angle between R and V become zero. This causes the highlights to get smaller as the smoothness increases, the same the way increasing the exponent in the Phong model does. In the Strauss model, however, the exponent is not specified separately but is based on the value of the smoothness, again preventing inconsistent specifications.

The Cook-Torrance model includes a change in the specular reflection based on the angle of the incident light. The adjusted reflectivity (r_j) is an approximation to this change in specular reflection. As such, the calculation of this factor approximates the Fresnel and geometric attenuation components of the Cook-Torrance model. The amount of light that is reflected is the portion of energy left over after part of the light is transmitted through a transparent or semi-transparent object and is diffusely reflected off of the object. The normal reflectance factor, r_n, is calculated with equation (2.24).

$$r_n = 1 - (t + r_d) \tag{2.24}$$

Strauss then calculates the adjusted reflectivity with equation (2.25) where 0.1 is a constant that creates a bright area just off the specular highlight that accounts for very rough surfaces.

$$r_j = \text{minimum}(1, r_n + (r_n + 0.1) * j) \tag{2.25}$$

Strauss has empirically determined that a value of 0.1 produces results that are reasonable, but this value could be changed to get a different effect. Strauss calls j the reflectivity adjustment factor, which is designed to increase the specular reflectivity when the direction of the incident light is near the surface tangent—also called the grazing angle. He includes geometric attenuation as a counteracting factor that deals with angles approaching 90° between the viewing or incident light angle and the surface normal. The reflectivity adjustment factor is given by equation (2.26), where θ is the angle between the incoming light direction and the normal and δ is the angle between the viewing direction and the normal.

$$j = F(\theta * 2 \,/\, \pi) * G(\theta * 2 \,/\, \pi) * G(\delta * 2 \,/\, \pi) \tag{2.26}$$

Because functions F and G require the parameter passed in to be in the range of 0.0 to 1.0, the angles are multiplied by $2 \,/\, \pi$ in the function calls, which shifts the range from $0° - 90°$ (in radians) to the expected range. The functions F and G are defined by equations (2.27) and (2.28) where Strauss empirically determined the constants of 1.12 and 1.01 were values that produced good results but these values could also be changed to get a different effect.

$$F(x) = \frac{\dfrac{1}{(x - 1.12)^2} - \dfrac{1}{1.12^2}}{\dfrac{1}{(1 - 1.12)^2} - \dfrac{1}{1.12^2}} \approx \frac{\dfrac{1}{(x - 1.12)^2} - 0.79719}{68.64725} \tag{2.27}$$

$$G(x) = \frac{\dfrac{1}{(1 - 1.01)^2} - \dfrac{1}{(x - 1.01)^2}}{\dfrac{1}{(1 - 1.01)^2} - \dfrac{1}{1.01^2}} \approx \frac{10000 - \dfrac{1}{(x - 1.01)^2}}{9999.01970} \tag{2.28}$$

For the sake of efficiency, Strauss recommends that these functions can be pre-calculated for a series of angles between 0 and $\pi/2$ and stored in a table for a faster lookup. He indicated (Strauss03) that the following code generates two look up tables that can be indexed with the appropriate cosine value.

```
double fTable[N + 1];
double gTable[N + 1];
for (int i = 0; i <= N; i++)
{
    angle = acos((double) i / N);
    fTable[i] = F(angle);
    gTable[i] = G(angle);
}
```

The arrays fTable and gTable now contain the results of applying the equations (2.27) and (2.28) for a set of N + 1 evenly spaced values. The values passed into the function in this loop are evenly spaced in the range [0, 1] because of the division. Taking the arccosine of these values converts them into angles in the range [0°, 90°] (in radians). Thus, if N = 100, location 45 of these tables would have the values for F(63.3°) and G(63.3°) because arccos(0.45) is approximately 63.3°. Taking the dot product of two vectors that are separated by an angle of 63.3° will result in approximately 0.4493, and multiplying this by N = 100 and rounding gives the location with the result desired.

So, in general, the cosine value calculated by the dot product can be multiplied by the table size and the result rounded to the accuracy of these tables. An alternative is to do a linear interpolation between the two closest table values.

The last component that needs to be determined is c_s, which is the specular color. This component is an approximation of the effect, discussed in section 2.4.4 on the Cook-Torrance model, where the specular highlight color changes as the incident light and normal angle increases. The specular color factor is calculated by equation (2.29), where c_L is the color of the light source.

$$c_S = c_L + m * \left(1 - F\left(\theta * 2 / \pi\right)\right) * \left(c - c_L\right) \tag{2.29}$$

This calculation is just an interpolation between the surface and light color based on the metalness parameter and Fresnel approximation factor.

Strauss points out that this model can be expanded to include global lighting calculations, with the smoothness parameter indicating how much reflections influence the object image and the transparency parameter indicating how much refractions influence the object image. Methods for calculating reflections and refractions are covered in Chapter 8, the discussion of ray tracing. Strauss also talks about how functions or patterns could be substituted for some of these parameters to create texture and spotlight effects.

2.5.2 The Ward model

All of the illumination and shading models discussed up to now have assumed that the object was isotropic. The Ward model (Ward92) can handle isotropic and anisotropic materials.[6] Figure 2.34 shows four objects rendered with the Ward model. The first two objects are isotropic and the second two objects are anisotropic. The change in the parameters for the two anisotropic objects effectively rotates the distinguishing direction by 90°. The anisotropic version of the Ward model is discussed first, followed by how to simplify it to get the isotropic version.

The anisotropic model needs to consider how light reflects off the material in two perpendicular directions. Ideally, the distinguishing direction will be one of these two. These two directions are treated as the X and Y axes of a plane that has the same normal as the object. For these two directions, the root mean square slopes for the microfacets on the surface are needed. These slopes are the same as are used in the Cook-Torrance model. The equation for the anisotropic model is given by equation (2.30), where k_d is the diffuse reflection parameter; k_s is the specular reflection parameter; θ is the angle between the light direction and normal; δ is the angle between the view vector and normal; γ is the angle between the halfway vector and the normal; Φ is the angle between the X direction and the halfway vector

---

[6]Recall that isotropic materials reflect light the same as they are rotated, but that anisotropic materials have a distinguishing direction where the most light reflection will occur as the material is being rotated.

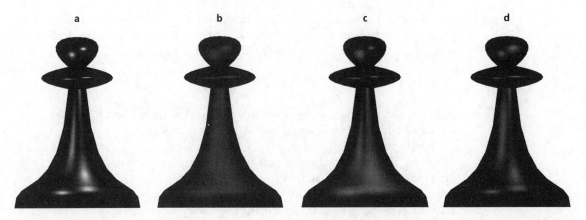

Figure 2.34 • Ward shaded model (a) isotropic with parameter 0.16, (b) isotropic with parameter 0.36, (c) anisotropic with parameters 0.16 and 0.36, and (d) anisotropic with parameters 0.36 and 0.16 (see Color Plate 2.9)

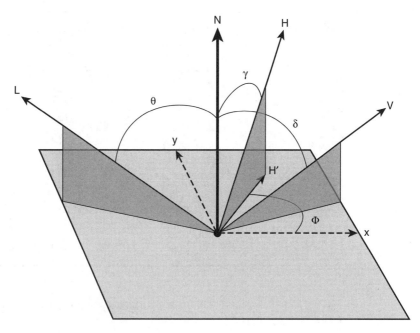

Figure 2.35 • Ward model parameters

projected onto the X-Y plane[7]; m_X is the distribution of microfacets in the X direction; and m_Y is the distribution of microfacets in the Y direction (Figure 2.35).

$$I = \frac{k_d}{\pi} + k_s * \frac{1}{\sqrt{\cos\theta * \cos\delta}} * \frac{e^{-\tan^2\gamma*\left(\cos^2\Phi/m_X^2 + \sin^2\Phi/m_Y^2\right)}}{4 * \pi * m_X * m_Y} \qquad (2.30)$$

Most of these terms will be familiar from the previous discussions, but Φ, m_X, and m_Y are new. The angle between the X direction and the halfway vector projected onto the X-Y plane is used to determine the current orientation relative to the two microfacet distributions. If the projection is in the direction of either the positive or negative X axis, the cosine squared will be one and the sine squared will be zero. This will mean that the tangent is divided by the distribution in the X direction, and the result is something that looks like the Cook-Torrance model. If the projection is in the direction of the positive or negative Y axis, the sine term will now be one and the cosine term will be zero, so that the distribution in the Y direction will be used. At angles between these, a combination of the two distributions will be

---

[7]The X-Y plane is determined by the directions that the two microfacet distributions are oriented and not any object or world coordinate systems.

Material	k_d	k_s	m_X	m_Y
Rolled brass	.1	.33	.05	.16
Rolled aluminum	.1	.21	.04	.09
Lightly brushed aluminum	.15	.19	.088	.13
Varnished plywood	.33	.025	.04	.11
Enamel finished metal	.25	.047	.08	.096
Painted cardboard box	.19	.043	.076	.085
White ceramic tile	.7	.05	.071	
Glossy gray paper	.29	.083	.082	
Ivory computer plastic	.45	.043	.13	
Plastic laminate	.67	.070	.092	

• **TABLE 2.1** Parameters for various materials (from Ward92)

used. The use of two distributions is the way that the Ward model accounts for the fact that the material is anisotropic.

The isotropic version of Ward's model can be easily derived by noting that there is just a single microfacet distribution value for an isotropic material. Because $\sin^2\Phi + \cos^2\Phi$ is equal to 1 for all angles, equation (2.30) simplifies to equation (2.31).

$$
\begin{aligned}
I &= \frac{k_d}{\pi} + k_s * \frac{1}{\sqrt{\cos\theta * \cos\delta}} * \frac{e^{-\tan^2\gamma * \left(\left(\cos^2\Phi + \sin^2\Phi\right)/m^2\right)}}{4 * \pi * m^2} \\
&= \frac{k_d}{\pi} + k_s * \frac{1}{\sqrt{\cos\theta * \cos\delta}} * \frac{e^{-\tan^2\gamma/m^2}}{4 * \pi * m^2}
\end{aligned}
\tag{2.31}
$$

Ward (Ward92) gives a set of parameters that can be used for various materials. Color was not measured so the diffuse reflection parameter is a single value instead of an RGB triple. These values are shown in Table 2.1. The last four items in this table are isotropic, so the simplified equation (2.31) can be used.

Ward (Ward92) also gives the parameters for metal, sheetrock, and wood painted with semi-gloss and gloss latex paint.

2.6 The OpenGL Way

To illustrate the use of OpenGL shading, a simple collection of triangles and spheres will be used in this chapter. More elaborate OpenGL objects will be discussed in the next two chapters.

Drawing a triangular patch begins with a call to the glBegin routine. Then the vertices of the patch are given. The patch is finish with a call to the glEnd routine. For example:

```
glBegin( GL_POLYGON );
    glVertex3f( x1, y1, z1 );
    glVertex3f( x2, y2, z2 );
    glVertex3f( x3, y3, z3 );
glEnd();
```

In this example, the parameter GL_POLYGON tells OpenGL to draw a polygon. There are other options for this parameter that draw points, lines, and other objects. The next three calls specify the vertices of the triangular patch.[8] The specification of the triangular patch is completed with the call to glEnd.

Drawing a sphere requires the specification of the radius of the sphere, and how it should be subdivided for rendering. The sphere will be drawn centered at the origin. For example, the call:

```
glutSolidSphere( 2.0, 36, 10 );
```

will draw a sphere with a radius of 2 units. The other two parameters specify how many slices and stacks to divide the sphere into. This call will divide the sphere into 36 slices, which run from the top to the bottom of the sphere as lines of longitude. The call also divides the sphere into 10 stacks, which divide the sphere horizontally as lines of latitude.

2.6.1 Setting colors

Colors in an RGB model can be specified through the glColor3f, glColor4f, glColor3d, and glColor4d routines. As in the case of the vertex routine, the number in the function name tells OpenGL the number of parameters being specified, the letter f means they are floating point numbers, and the letter d means they are doubles. Colors should be specified in the range of [0.0, 1.0], where 0.0 means that color does not contribute and 1.0 means that it contributes completely. Values outside of this range are acceptable and will be associated with objects, but the values will eventually be clamped to this range before they are used for interpolation or are written into the color buffer.

---

[8]In the vertex routine name, the 3 represents specifying locations in three-dimensions and the f indicates the parameters are of type float. If the f is changed to the letter d, the parameters would need to be of type double. There are additional ways to specify vertices that will be covered in Chapter 3. When we want to generically refer to a routine that may have various types of parameters, we will use a star at the end of the base name, for example, glVertex*.

The routine with four parameters might seem strange, but it relates to the RGBA color model, with A specifying the alpha value. An alpha value specifies how the new object should be blended with whatever is currently displayed, but it can be thought of as indicating how transparent or opaque an object is. An alpha value of 1.0 represents an opaque object, a value of 0.0 represents a transparent object, and other values in this range specify the ratio between the current object and the existing pixel. Remember that this is just a blending function with whatever has already been drawn, so that objects behind a transparent ball will not be properly refracted through the ball. When the alpha value is not specified with the three parameter version, it defaults to a value of one.

The color value can also be passed to OpenGL in an array with the appropriate number of elements by adding a v to the end of the routine name. For example, the routine glColor3fv expects an array of three floating point numbers as a parameter.

Colors can also be set by using values that are bytes (b), unsigned bytes (ub), integers (i), unsigned integers (ui), short integers (s), and unsigned short integers (us). In those cases, the values passed in are scaled into a real number range. For the unsigned options, the values are scaled into the range [0.0, 1.0]. For the signed options, the values are scaled into the range [–1.0, 1.0]. As in the case of floating point values that are out of range, these values will be stored and used for calculations and will only be clamped to the [0, 1] range before interpolation or use in the color buffer.

Recall that OpenGL is a state-based system, so once a color is set, all objects will be drawn with that color until the glColor* routine is called again.

2.6.2 Color interpolation

Where the last section talked about specifying a color for an object, a color can also be specified per vertex. In this case, OpenGL will interpolate between the colors specified for each of the vertices. Color Plate 1.2 shows a sample of this process. For that figure, the RGB cube was drawn as a set of six square planes for each of the sides of the cube. Each vertex of the cube had a different color. For example, the front face for the red-green plane could be specified as:

```
glBegin( GL_POLYGON );
    glColor3f( 0.0, 0.0, 0.0 );
    glVertex3f( -0.5, -0.5, -0.5 );
    glColor3f( 1.0, 0.0, 0.0 );
    glVertex3f(  0.5, -0.5, -0.5 );
    glColor3f( 1.0, 1.0, 0.0 );
    glVertex3f(  0.5,  0.5, -0.5 );
    glColor3f( 0.0, 1.0, 0.0 );
    glVertex3f( -0.5,  0.5, -0.5 );
glEnd();
```

This color interpolation capability could be used to simulate a Gouraud shading model. The program would calculate the color at each of the vertices and then pass those to OpenGL for it to do the interpolation. This is not really necessary, however, because OpenGL has Gouraud shading built-in.

2.6.3 Setting normal vectors

The normal vector can be set once for the entire patch or set separately for each vertex. The routine glNormal3* sets the normal vector, where the star represents the type used for the normal vector. For example the call glNormal3f(0.0, 1.0, 0.0) will set a normal vector that points in the direction of the positive y axis.

If one normal is given followed by the vertices of a patch, that normal will be used for all of the vertices, and will essentially be the normal for the entire patch. To give a unique normal vector for each of the vertices, the glNormal3* routine would be called before each call to glVertex* to set the normal vector for that vertex.

Normal vectors will be transformed by the modelview matrix. When transformations are done on unit vectors, they may no longer be of unit length, especially if scaling transformations are included. There are two options within OpenGL to make sure the vectors are always normalized back to unit vectors. Including the call glEnable(GL_NORMALIZE) tells OpenGL to automatically normalize a vector after transforming it. OpenGL will also normalize vectors when they are specified, freeing the program from having to normalize the vectors. If the call glEnable(GL_RESCALE_NORMAL) is used instead, the vectors must be supplied as unit vectors, and OpenGL will only scale the normal by a value it determines from the modelview matrix. This second option is usually quicker, as long as the vectors are of unit length to begin with.

2.6.4 Light sources and shading

OpenGL uses a Gouraud shading method for rendering objects. The difference between OpenGL and Gouraud shading as discussed here is that the results of the OpenGL shading calculation depends not only on the parameters for the surface, but also on the parameters for the light source. In OpenGL, there are ambient, diffuse, and specular components for both the light sources and the objects, but in addition to these there is a global ambient component. This section looks at how to specify the light source parameters, and the next section looks at specifying parameters for the surface.

To use lighting and shading, lighting is enabled with the call glEnable(GL_LIGHTING) and shading is turned on with the call glShadeModel(GL_SMOOTH). To turn lighting off call glDisable(GL_LIGHTING) and to turn shading off call glShadeModel(GL_FLAT). Standard OpenGL has eight light sources, but different implementations may have more. These light sources are given the constant identifiers of, GL_LIGHT0, GL_LIGHT1, through GL_LIGHT7. Light parameters for each individual source are set through calls to the glLight* routine. There are four varieties of this routine, with two taking integer parameters and the other two taking floating point parameters. These routines will also take in the parameters as either a single value or as an array of values (called a "vector" in OpenGL), depending on which parameters are being set. The parameters set with the vector versions of the glLight* routine are the light source's ambient component (GL_AMBIENT), diffuse component (GL_DIFFUSE), specular component (GL_SPECULAR), and position (GL_POSITION). A typical code segment to set up a light source would be:

```
GLfloat ambient[] = {0.1, 0.1, 0.1, 1.0};
GLfloat diffuse[] = {1.0, 1.0, 1.0, 1.0};
GLfloat specular[] = {1.0, 0.0, 0.0, 1.0};
GLfloat position[] = {1.0, 1.0, 1.0, 0.0};
glLightfv(GL_LIGHT0, GL_AMBIENT, ambient);
glLightfv(GL_LIGHT0, GL_DIFFUSE, diffuse);
glLightfv(GL_LIGHT0, GL_SPECULAR, specular);
glLightfv(GL_LIGHT0, GL_POSITION, position);
```

Notice that the ambient, diffuse, and specular parameters are specified as RGBA, but we will just concentrate on the RGB portion. The alpha component is used when objects are blended. The position for the light will be transformed by the current modelview matrix to place it relative to the objects in the scene. Also notice that four parameters are specified for the light position. The first three are the *x, y,* and *z* values, and the fourth determines what type of light source this is. When the fourth parameter is zero, the light is called a directional light. For a directional light, the *x, y,* and *z* values give the direction the light source is pointed. Directional light sources are assumed to be infinitely far away, which means that OpenGL treats all of the rays of light as traveling parallel into the scene. This means that the light vector will be a constant for the entire scene.

If the fourth parameter for the light position is not zero, the light source is called positional, and the *x, y,* and *z* values specify the position of the light in object coordinates. The light from a positional light source radiates in every direction, so OpenGL calculates a different light vector for each of the vertices of the patches. OpenGL provides a number of other capabilities for positional lights. They can be specified as spotlights and can also be attenuated based on distance to the object.

To specify a spotlight, parameters are specified for the direction of the spotlight (GL_SPOT_DIRECTION), how wide the spotlight beam is (GL_SPOT_CUTOFF), and whether the intensity varies across the spotlight beam (GL_SPOT_EXPONENT). The direction is a vector that points in the direction the light is facing. The direction is also transformed by the modelview matrix. Specifying the width of the beam is how a positional light source is turned into a spotlight. The width should be between 0° and 90°, and represent the radius of the beam. For example, to specify a width of 90° will mean that the light will radiate in 180° much as a ceiling or wall light would. To turn a spotlight back into a positional light that radiates in every direction specify a special beam width of 180°. The GL_SPOT_EXPONENT determines how the light intensity falls off moving away from the center of the light beam. This exponent is used as the exponent of the cosine of the angle between the current direction and the spotlight direction (the center of the beam). If the exponent is increased, the light intensity will decrease more quickly as locations move away from the center of the beam. An example of the use of these parameters is:

```
GLfloat ambient[] = {0.1, 0.1, 0.1, 1.0};
GLfloat diffuse[] = {1.0, 1.0, 1.0, 1.0};
GLfloat specular[] = {1.0, 0.0, 0.0, 1.0};
GLfloat position[] = {5.0, 5.0, 5.0, 1.0};
GLfloat direction[] = {-1.0, -1.0, -1.0};
glLightfv(GL_LIGHT0, GL_AMBIENT, ambient);
glLightfv(GL_LIGHT0, GL_DIFFUSE, diffuse);
glLightfv(GL_LIGHT0, GL_SPECULAR, specular);
glLightfv(GL_LIGHT0, GL_POSITION, position);
glLightfv(GL_LIGHT0, GL_SPOT_DIRECTION, direction);
glLightf(GL_LIGHT0, GL_SPOT_CUTOFF, 30.0);
glLightf(GL_LIGHT0, GL_SPOT_EXPONENT, 3.0);
```

This example places the spotlight in a position roughly over the right shoulder and pointing down to the origin. The spotlight beam is 60° wide (a radius of 30°), and is focused by an exponent of 3.

OpenGL can attenuate positional light sources so the light they cast decreases moving away from the light source. The attenuation factor can have a constant (GL_CONSTANT_ATTENUATION), linear (GL_LINEAR_ATTENUATION), and quadratic (GL_QUADRATIC_ATTENUATION) attenuation parameters. OpenGL calculates the distance from the light source to the object, and then uses these parameters in equation (2.5). These three parameters are specified in calls to glLightf, where the first parameter indicates the light to use, the second parameter is one of the constants given above, and the third parameter is the floating point value that is the attenuation of that term. For example,

```
glLightf(GL_LIGHT0, GL_LINEAR_ATTENUATION, 2.0)
```

would set the linear attenuation constant to 2.0 for the first light source.

2.6.5 Specifying object properties

Where the idea of specifying ambient, diffuse, and specular components for a light source is new relative to the theories discussed in this chapter, specifying the parameters for objects follows some of the theories discussed. When a set of material properties are given, they are in effect for every object drawn until new properties are set. The ambient (GL_AMBIENT), diffuse (GL_DIFFUSE), specular (GL_SPECULAR), and shininess (GL_SHININESS) components for the material can be set. Because it is common for the ambient and diffuse color to be the same for real world objects, OpenGL provides a constant (GL_AMBIENT_AND_DIFFUSE) to set both of these parameters with one routine call.

Polygonal patches in OpenGL have a front and a back face to them. These faces are determined by the order that the vertices are given. If the vertices are specified in a counterclockwise order, you are looking at the front face. If they are specified in a clockwise order, you are looking at the back face. Material properties can be set for the front (GL_FRONT), back (GL_BACK), or both (GL_FRONT_AND_BACK) faces of an object.

Material properties are set with calls to glMaterial*, where the star tells whether the parameters are integers or floats, and whether they are a single value or an array. The glMaterial* routine will take three parameters: the first tells which face or faces to apply the values to, the second tells which values are being set, and the third are the values themselves.

```
GLfloat ambDiff[] = {0.5, 0.0, 0.5, 1.0};
GLfloat specular[] = {0.0, 0.0, 0.8, 1.0};
glMaterialfv(GL_FRONT_AND_BACK, GL_AMBIENT_AND_DIFFUSE,
             ambDiff);
glMaterialfv(GL_FRONT, GL_SPECULAR, specular);
glMaterialf(GL_FRONT, GL_SHININESS, 10.0);
```

This code fragment will set the ambient and diffuse component of the front and back faces as a dark purple, and sets a blue specular component with an exponent of 10 for the front face only.

One additional property that can be set for objects is the emission (GL_EMISSION), which is used to make objects appear to be light sources of the color that has been specified.

```
GLfloat emit[] = {1.0, 0.0, 0.0, 1.0};
glMaterialfv(GL_FRONT, GL_EMISSION, emit);
```

This code, for example, will set the material parameters so that objects will appear to be red light sources. This does not, however, make the objects into light sources. Specifically, these objects will not actually emit light and will not cause highlights on other objects.

Table 2.2 shows a set of parameters from (McReynolds97) that simulate various materials. Figure 2.36 shows a collection of spheres rendered with the values from

● **TABLE 2.2** Material properties (after McReynolds97)

Material	GL_AMBIENT	GL_DIFFUSE	GL_SPECULAR	GL_SHININESS
Black Plastic	0.0, 0.0, 0.0, 1.0	0.01, 0.01, 0.01, 1.0	0.50, 0.50, 0.50, 1.0	32
Brass	0.329412, 0.223529, 0.027451, 1.0	0.780392, 0.568627, 0.113725, 1.0	0.992157, 0.941176, 0.807843, 1.0	27.8974
Bronze	0.2125, 0.1275, 0.054, 1.0	0.714, 0.4284, 0.18144, 1.0	0.393548, 0.271906, 0.166721, 1.0	25.6
Bronze, Polished	0.25, 0.148, 0.06475, 1.0	0.4, 0.2368, 0.1036, 1.0	0.774597, 0.458561, 0.200621, 1.0	76.8
Chrome	0.25, 0.25, 0.25, 1.0	0.4, 0.4, 0.4, 1.0	0.774597, 0.774597, 0.774597, 1.0	76.8
Copper	0.19125, 0.0735, 0.0275, 1.0	0.7038, 0.27048, 0.0828, 1.0	0.256777, 0.137622, 0.086014, 1.0	12.8
Copper, Polished	0.2295, 0.08825, 0.0275, 1.0	0.5508, 0.2118, 0.066, 1.0	0.580594, 0.223257, 0.0695701, 1.0	51.2
Emerald	0.0215, 0.1745, 0.0215, 0.55	0.07568, 0.61424, 0.07568, 0.55	0.633, 0.727811, 0.633, 0.55	76.8
Gold	0.24725, 0.1995, 0.0745, 1.0	0.75164, 0.60648, 0.22648, 1.0	0.628281, 0.555802, 0.366065, 1.0	51.2
Gold, Polished	0.24725, 0.2245, 0.0645, 1.0	0.34615, 0.3143, 0.0903, 1.0	0.797357, 0.723991, 0.208006, 1.0	83.2
Jade	0.135, 0.2225, 0.1575, 0.95	0.54, 0.89, 0.63, 0.95	0.316228, 0.316228, 0.316228, 0.95	12.8
Obsidian	0.05375, 0.05, 0.06625, 0.82	0.18275, 0.17, 0.22525, 0.82	0.332741, 0.328634, 0.346435, 0.82	38.4
Pearl	0.25, 0.20725, 0.20725, 0.922	1.0, 0.829, 0.829, 0.922	0.296648, 0.296648, 0.296648, 0.922	11.264
Pewter	0.105882, 0.058824, 0.113725, 1.0	0.427451, 0.470588, 0.541176, 1.0	0.333333, 0.333333, 0.521569, 1.0	9.84615
Rubber	0.02, 0.02, 0.02, 1.0	0.01, 0.01, 0.01, 1.0	0.4, 0.4, 0.4, 1.0	10
Ruby	0.1745, 0.01175, 0.01175, 0.55	0.61424, 0.04136, 0.04136, 0.55	0.727811, 0.626959, 0.626959, 0.55	76.8
Silver	0.19225, 0.19225, 0.19225, 1.0	0.50754, 0.50754, 0.50754, 1.0	0.508273, 0.508273, 0.508273, 1.0	51.2
Silver, Polished	0.23125, 0.23125, 0.23125, 1.0	0.2775, 0.2775, 0.2775, 1.0	0.773911, 0.773911, 0.773911, 1.0	89.6
Turquoise	0.1, 0.18725, 0.1745, 0.8	0.396, 0.74151, 0.69102, 0.8	0.297254, 0.30829, 0.306678, 0.8	12.8

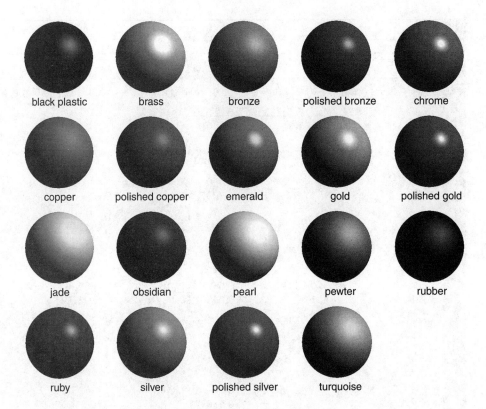

black plastic   **brass**   **bronze**   **polished bronze**   **chrome**

copper   **polished copper**   **emerald**   **gold**   **polished gold**

jade   **obsidian**   **pearl**   **pewter**   **rubber**

ruby   **silver**   **polished silver**   **turquoise**

Figure 2.36 • Spheres using the data from Table 2.2 (see Color Plate 2.10)

Table 2.2. McReynolds also suggests that in general, the ambient and diffuse parameters should be the same, the sum of the diffuse and specular parameters should be close to one, and the shininess should increase as the specular parameter gets closer to one. McReynolds also states, "No promise is made that these relationships or the values in Table [2.2] will provide a perfect imitation of a given material. The empirical model used by OpenGL emphasizes performance, not physical exactness."

2.6.6 Specifying a lighting model

There are a couple of additional items that influence how OpenGL determines the shading of an object. They are a global ambient component (GL_LIGHT_MODEL_AMBIENT), the location of the viewer (GL_LIGHT_MODEL_LOCAL_VIEWER), and whether objects are lit from one or two sides (GL_LIGHT_MODEL_TWO_SIDE).

The global ambient is a color value that is added to all of the objects in the scene, no matter what their properties are or where the light sources are located. Where the ambient component of a light source is considered to be illumination from that light that has bounced around the scene, the global ambient component does not have a specific light source that causes it. If all of the light sources are turned off, the global ambient component will still provide some illumination to all of the objects.

The location of the viewer can be either local or at an infinite location. Choosing infinite uses one view vector for all of the objects in the scene. Choosing local uses a view vector based on the relative location of the viewpoint and the object. Having an infinite viewpoint will result in quicker rendering because the view vector is not recalculated for every vertex; however, the results will not be as good as for a local viewpoint. If this parameter is set as GL_TRUE, the viewpoint will be set at (0, 0, 0) in eye coordinates, and the view vectors will be calculated based on the object's location relative to this point. If this parameter is set as GL_FALSE, the view vector will point in the z direction for all objects.

If the object is properly specified, the front-facing polygons should obscure the back-facing polygons, so highlighting the front-facing polygons is all that should be necessary. If part of or the entire front surface of the object is cut away, the back-facing polygons will become visible. Because their normal vectors will point away from the viewer, those surfaces will not be highlighted. By setting the two sided lighting to GL_TRUE, OpenGL will reverse the normal vectors for the back facing polygons so that they are properly highlighted when visible.

The following sample code shows the use of the glLightModel* routine with these parameters.

```
GLfloat globalAmb[] = {0.1, 0.1, 0.1, 1.0};
glLightModelfv(GL_LIGHT_MODEL_AMBIENT, gloablAmb);
glLightModeli(GL_LIGHT_MODEL_LOCAL_VIEWER, GL_TRUE);
glLightModeli(GL_LIGHT_MODEL_TWO_SIDE, GL_TRUE);
```

2.6.7 Details of OpenGL light calculations

OpenGL uses the Gouraud shading method for determining the color of interior polygon points based on the vertex colors. The color of a vertex in OpenGL is determined by adding together the emission, the global ambient, and the calculated and attenuated ambient, diffuse, and specular components. The results of these calculations are clamped to the range of zero to one.

The emission portion is just the parameters that are specified in the call to glMaterial*. The global ambient portion is the product of the global ambient value multiplied by the material's ambient value. The light source contributions are the sum of the ambient, diffuse, and specular terms, multiplied by both the attenuation factor and the spotlight effect. If there are multiple light sources, this contribution is calculated for each light source and added together. If the object is outside of the spotlight beam, the spotlight effect is zero.

The ambient term is just the product of the light source ambient and the material ambient parameters. The diffuse component is calculated using the dot product in section 2.3.2.2 and the result of the dot product is then multiplied by both the object and light diffuse parameters. The specular component is calculated using the dot product of the normal and the halfway vector, raising that to the shininess parameter of the object, and then multiplying that result by both the object and light source specular parameters.

2.6.8 Fog

OpenGL allows the specification of a fog color and a fog density that adds additional depth cues to a scene. As distance from the viewer increases, the objects fade from their normal shading colors to the fog color. Fog is turned on by making the call `glEnable(GL_FOG)` and is turned off by making the call `glDisable(GL_FOG)`. OpenGL can be set to calculate the fog per pixel or per vertex. A call to `glHint(GL_NICEST)` tells OpenGL to calculate the fog per pixel and `glHint(GL_FASTEST)` tells OpenGL to calculate the fog per vertex. As the constant names indicated, per pixel fog will produce better results than per vertex, but per vertex is faster.

OpenGL interpolates between the object color and the fog color with equation (2.32), where C_{object} is the color from the object (either at a pixel or vertex) and C_{fog} is the color of the fog.

$$Color = factor * C_{object} + (1 - factor) * C_{fog} \tag{2.32}$$

The fog color is set with the call `glFog*v(GL_FOG_COLOR, color)`, where color is a four-element array with the RGBA value for the fog and the star indicates whether this is an array of integers (i) or floats (f). The factor can be calculated with one of the following three equations:

$$factor = e^{-(density*distance)} \tag{2.33}$$

$$factor = e^{-(density*distance)^2} \tag{2.34}$$

$$factor = \frac{end - distance}{end - start} \tag{2.35}$$

In these three equations, distance is the depth of the object relative to the viewpoint. The density in equations (2.33) and (2.34), and the start and end in equation (2.35) are set by calls to the `glFog*` routine. The call `glFog*(GL_FOG_DENSITY, density)` sets the density value, where the star indicates whether the density is an integer (i) or float (f). Setting the start and end is done in the same way, but the first parameter would be GL_START or GL_END.

The choice among these three equations is also set with a call to glFogi(GL_FOG_MODE, mode). To choose equation (2.33), GL_EXP is passed in for mode. To choose equation (2.34), GL_EXP2 is passed in for mode. To choose equation (2.35), GL_LINEAR is passed in for mode.

2.7 Projects

1) Write a program that displays the different faces of the RGB cube. When the user presses a number between one and six, your program should display the face indicated in the following table:

value	face
1	black, red, magenta, blue
2	black, red, yellow, green
3	black, green, cyan, blue
4	white, yellow, red, magenta
5	white, cyan, green, yellow
6	white, cyan, blue, magenta

2) Implement a program that will create a smoothly shaded sphere. Select a group of five colors from Table 2.2, and assign them to the numbers one through five. When the user hits one of those numbers on the keyboard, change the object color appropriately.

3) Implement a program that creates a highlight from a spotlight cast onto a plane. Every time the user hits the "b" key, make the spotlight angle bigger (but never bigger than 75°), and every time the user hits an "s" make the spotlight angle smaller (but never smaller than 15°). Every time the user hits an "m" make the spotlight more concentrated by increasing the exponent, and every time the user hits the letter "l" make the spotlight less concentrated by decreasing the exponent.

4) Write a program that draws seven spheres at varying depths so that they do not overlap. Include fog using white as the fog color. Every time the user hits an "f" make the scene foggier by increasing the density, and every time the user hits a "c" make the scene clearer by decreasing the density. If the user hits a "1," have OpenGL use equation (2.33). For the keys "2" and "3," have OpenGL use equations (2.34) and (2.35), respectively.

 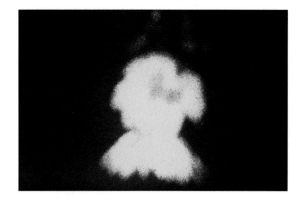

Color Plate 1.1 • Water lily (Nymphaea Daubeniana) and its image through the pinhole demonstration camera (see Figure 1.4)

Color Plate 1.2 • The RGB cube (see Figure 1.12)

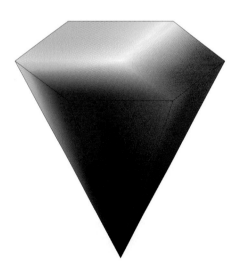

Color Plate 1.3 • The HSV hexcone (see Figure 1.13)

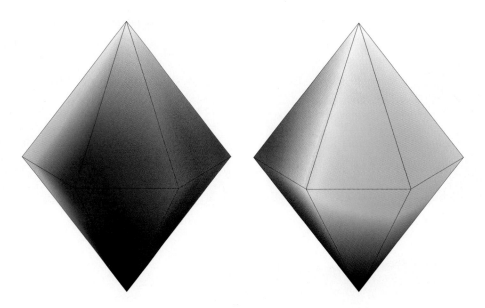

Color Plate 1.4 • Two views of the HLS double hexcone (see Figure 1.14)

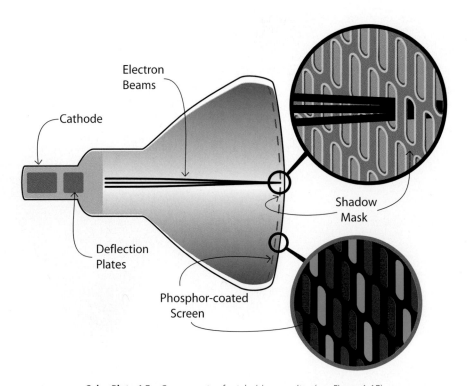

Color Plate 1.5 • Components of a television monitor (see Figure 1.15)

Color Plate 2.1 • Toronto, Ontario on a clear and hazy day (see Figure 2.1)

Color Plate 2.2 • Simultaneous Contrast (see Figure 2.5)

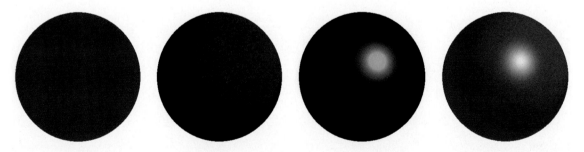

Color Plate 2.3 • Spheres showing the ambient, diffuse, specular, and their combined components with different colors. (see Figure 2.11)

Color Plate 2.4 • Flat shaded pawn (see Figure 2.21)

Color Plate 2.5 • Gouraud shaded pawn (see Figure 2.22)

Color Plate 2.6 • Phong shaded pawn (see Figure 2.25)

Color Plate 2.7 • Cook-Torrance shaded pawn (see Figure 2.29)

Color Plate 2.8 • Strauss shaded pawn using s=0.6, m=0.5 (see Figure 2.32)

(a)

(b)

(c)

(d)

Color Plate 2.9 • Ward shaded model (a) isotropic with parameter 0.16, (b) isotropic with parameter 0.36, (c) anisotropic with parameters 0.16 and 0.36, and (d) anisotropic with parameters 0.36 and 0.16 (see Figure 2.34)

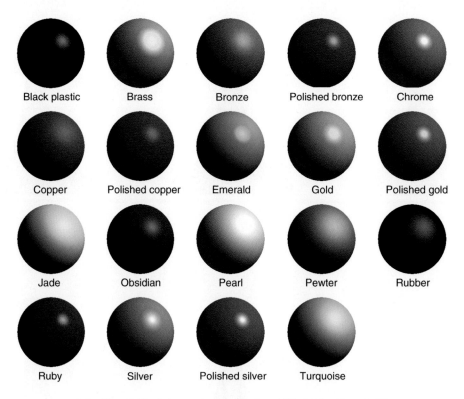

Black plastic Brass Bronze Polished bronze Chrome

Copper Polished copper Emerald Gold Polished gold

Jade Obsidian Pearl Pewter Rubber

Ruby Silver Polished silver Turquoise

Color Plate 2.10 • Spheres using the data from Table 2.2 (see Figure 2.36)

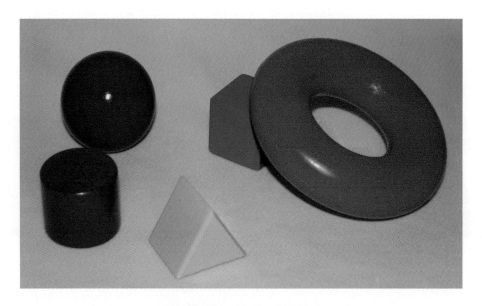

Color Plate 3.1 • Toys (see Figure 3.1)

Color Plate 4.1 • A car front end (see Figure 4.1)

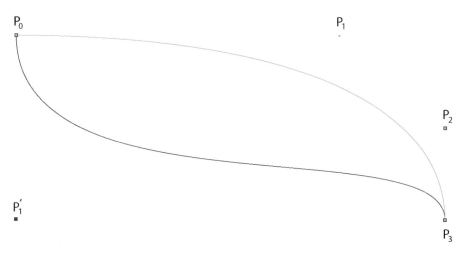

P_0

P_1

P_2

P_1'

P_3

Color Plate 4.2 • Two Bézier curves and their control points—the two curves share three of the four control points. (see Figure 4.3)

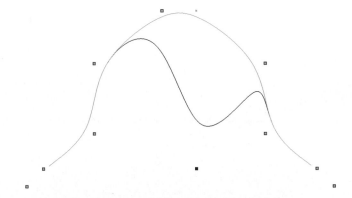

Color Plate 4.3 • B-Splines showing local control (see Figure 4.8)

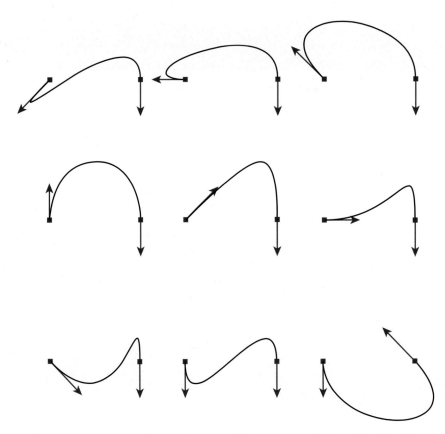

Color Plate 4.4 • Hermite curves showing the impact of the initial vector direction (in red) (see Figure 4.12)

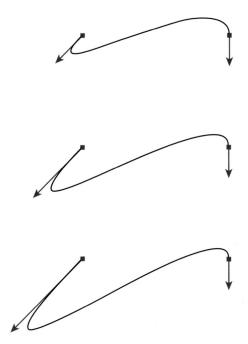

Color Plate 4.5 • Hermite curves with different length initial vectors (in red) (see Figure 4.13)

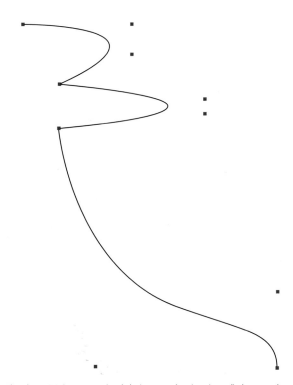

Color Plate 4.6 • The three Bézier curves (and their control points in red) that are the silhouette for the pawn in Chapter 2 (see Figure 4.17)

Color Plate 5.1 • Real windows and obstruction (see Figure 5.1)

Color Plate 6.1 • A section of a brick wall (see Figure 6.1)

Color Plate 6.2 • Textured object with incorrect specular highlighting (see Figure 6.5)

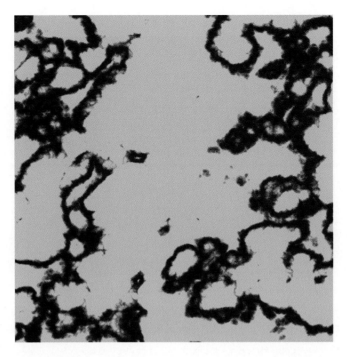

Color Plate 6.3 • A marble texture with frequency in the range [1.0, 256.0] (see Figure 6.17)

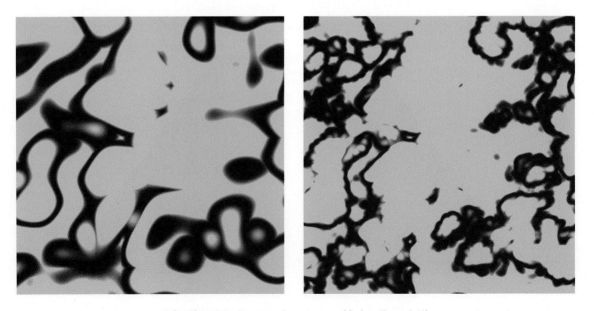

Color Plate 6.4 • Frequency impact on marble (see Figure 6.18)

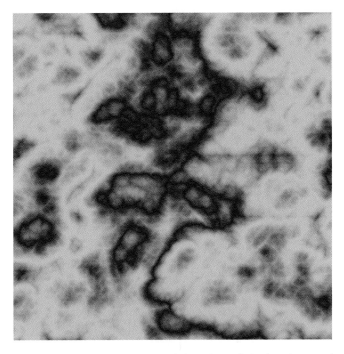

Color Plate 6.5 • Marble sample using Ebert's interpolation (see Figure 6.19)

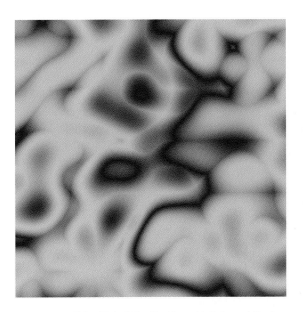 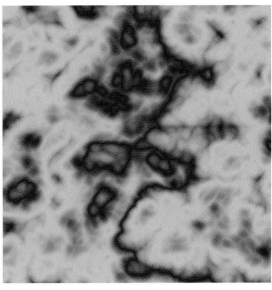

Color Plate 6.6 • Ebert's marbleColor and the frequency ranges [1.0, 4.0] and [1.0, 16.0] (see Figure 6.20)

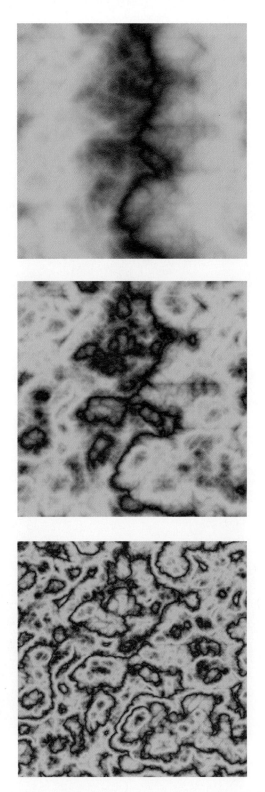

Color Plate 6.7 • Marble using no multiplier and multipliers of 3.0 and 7.0 (see Figure 6.21)

Color Plate 7.1 • A tennis ball resting on the ground and at three different heights (see Figure 7.1)

Color Plate 7.2 • Using a fixed shadow color (see Figure 7.4)

Color Plate 7.3 • Using a percentage reduction (see Figure 7.5)

Color Plate 7.4 • Ignoring the blocked light source (see Figure 7.6)

Color Plate 7.5 • Soft edged shadows using distributed light sources (see Figure 7.14)

Color Plate 8.1 • Refraction through a glass ball (see Figure 8.1)

Color Plate 8.2 • Close-up of the wizard refraction (see Figure 8.9)

Color Plate 8.3 • The wizard without the glass sphere and a ray traced version (see Figure 8.10)

Color Plate 8.4 • Refraction through colored glass (see Figure 8.11)

Color Plate 8.5 • Light refracting through glass objects creating a caustic highlight (see Figure 8.18)

Color Plate 9.1 • Color bleeding (see Figure 9.1)

Color Plate 9.2 • Architectural radiosity images (Image created by Erik Svanholm © 2002 Zumtobel Staff) (see Figure 9.2)

Color Plate 10.1 • A Heliconius sara butterfly in motion (see Figure 10.1)

Color Plate 11.1 • Candle lit flowers (see Figure 11.1)

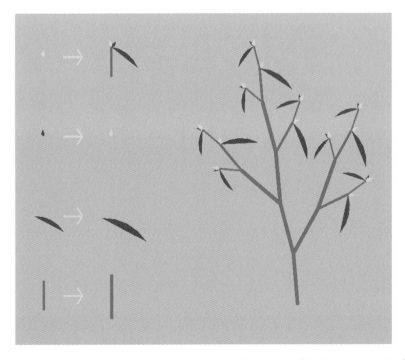

Color Plate 11.2 • Schematic for a bean plant (see Figure 11.4). Courtesy of Jim Hanan, University of Queensland © 2005 Jim Hanan.

Color Plate 11.3 • Four generations of a bean plant (see Figure 11.5). Courtesy of Jim Hanan, University of Queensland © 2005 Jim Hanan.

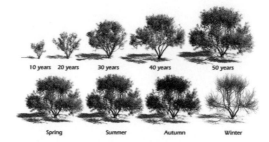

Color Plate 11.4 • Probabilistic model results for a silver willow (see Figure 11.8). Courtesy of Bionatics, Inc. www.bionatics.com © 2004 Bionatics, Inc.

Color Plate 11.5 • A plant ecosystem. Deussen et al., "Realistic modeling and rendering of plant ecosystems," SIGGRAPH 98, © 1998 ACM, Inc. Reprinted by permission. (see Figure 11.9)

Color Plate 11.6 • Water pouring into a glass. Enright et al., "Animation and rendering of complex water surfaces," SIGGRAPH 2002, © 2002 ACM, Inc. Reprinted by permission. (see Figure 11.13)

Color Plate 11.7 • A cumulus cloud created with a texture-based method (see Figure 11.14). Courtesy of David S. Ebert, © 1997 David S. Ebert.

Color Plate 11.8 • Cellular automata-based clouds in the daytime and evening. Dobashi et al., "A simple, efficient method for realistic animation of clouds," SIGGRAPH 2000, © 2000 ACM, Inc. Reprinted by permission. (see Figure 11.15)

Color Plate 11.9 • A steaming teacup produced with a texture-based method (see Figure 11.16). Courtesy of David S. Ebert, © 1997 David S. Ebert.

Color Plate 11.10 • Blowing smoke. Fedkiw et al., "Visual simulation of smoke," SIGGRAPH 2001, © 2001 ACM, Inc. Reprinted by permission. (see Figure 11.17)

Color Plate 11.11 • A campfire. Nguyen et al., "Physically based modeling and animation of fire," SIGGRAPH 2002, © 2002 ACM, Inc. Reprinted by permission. (see Figure 11.18)

Color Plate 12.1 • A golden retriever (see Figure 12.1)

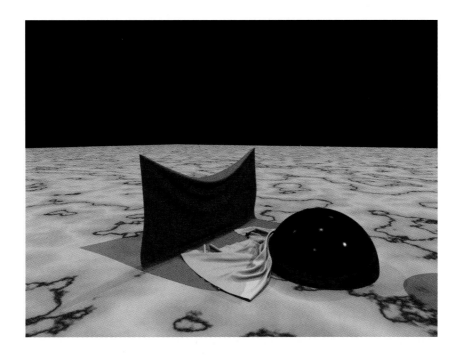

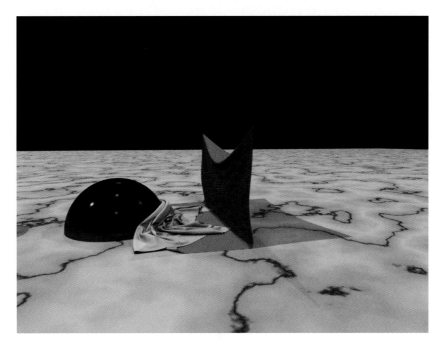

Color Plate 12.2 • Two simulations of cloth showing bending and draping (see Figure 12.5). Courtesy of Robert Bridson © 2004 Robert Bridson.

Color Plate 12.3 • Knitting pattern examples created with the lumislice (see Figure 12.6). Xu et al., "Photorealistic rendering of knitwear using the lumislice," SIGGRAPH 2001, © 2001 ACM, Inc. Reprinted by permission.

Color Plate 12.4 • Different generated hair styles (see Figure 12.7). Kim and Neumann, "Interactive multiresolution hair modeling and editing," SIGGRAPH 2002, © 2002 ACM, Inc. Reprinted by permission.

Color Plate 12.5 • Different generated hair styles (see Figure 12.8). Kim and Neumann, "Interactive multiresolution hair modeling and editing," SIGGRAPH 2002, © 2002 ACM, Inc. Reprinted by permission.

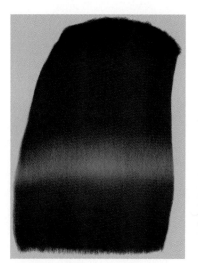 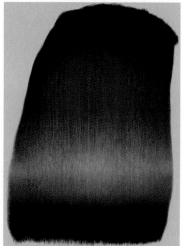 

Color Plate 12.6 • The first image is rendered using the illumination techniques in [Kajiya89], the second image is rendered using the illumination techniques in [Marschner03], and the last image is a photograph of hair (see Figure 12.10) (Marschner et al., "Light scattering from human hair fibers," SIGGRAPH 2003, © 2003 ACM, Inc. Reprinted by permission.)

Color Plate 12.7 • An eagle showing the placement of feathers (see Figure 12.13). Chen, et al., "Modeling and rendering of realistic feathers," SIGGRAPH 2002, © 2002 ACM, Inc. Reprinted by permission.

Color Plate 12.8 • Using measured skin values, the image on the left shows skin rendered with a BRDF model and the image on the right shows skin rendered with a BSSRDF model (see Figure 12.15). Jensen et al., "A practical model for subsurface light transport," SIGGRAPH 2001, © 2001 ACM, Inc. Reprinted by permission.

Color Plate 12.9 • Automatically generated poses showing skin shape deformations (see Figure 12.16). Mohr and Gleicher, "Building efficient, accurate character skins from examples," SIGGRAPH 2003, © 2003 ACM, Inc. Reprinted by permission.

Object Modeling

Let's say that you want to be able to create computer images of the room you're in right now. What would be involved in creating a description of the various objects in that room? Some objects could probably be described as a series of planes, such as tables or desks. Other objects in the room that could be defined as spheres, such as balls or door knobs. Still other objects that have more elaborate curved surfaces, such as lamps or chairs, or may be combinations of these types of shapes. To be able to render this room, you must first be able to describe all of these objects in a way that makes rendering possible.

There is a wide variety to the shapes that objects can take. This chapter looks at techniques to model regular shapes such as lines, planes, spheres, cylinders, cones, ellipsoids, and tori (Figure 3.1). Models for more complex curves and curved surfaces are discussed in the next chapter. These methods merely define the surfaces of the object because the surface is the only concern in the overall look of the object.

Computer-aided design and engineering are applications where objects are modeled as full solids. In this way, objects can be manipulated and tested as part of the design process before a physical prototype is built. These application areas use constructive solid geometry to describe objects. However, constructive solid geometry methods are not necessary to create realistic images, and so those methods will not be discussed here.

Figure 3.1 • Toys (see Color Plate 3.1)

3.1 Transformations

There are a number of transformations that can be performed when working with objects. An object can be translated to move it to a new location. An object can be scaled to change its size. An object can be rotated to face in a different direction. All of these transformations will make modifications to locations on the object to effect these changes.

Transformations are needed for a couple of reasons. First, graphics APIs (application programming interfaces) will typically define objects such as spheres with their center at the origin. Transformations are necessary to move objects into the correct position in the scene. Second, scenes can be described hierarchically with a complex object described in terms of the parts that comprise it. For example, a table can be defined as a top with four legs. Each leg could be described as a cylinder. Transformations would be necessary to get the four legs into the correct place, but transformations could then also be applied to the table as a whole to move it (and thus its legs) into the correct location. Third, transformations are also used to project a three-dimensional scene into two dimensions.

Whereas it might appear that these transformations would need to be applied to every point on the object, only significant locations need to be transformed. For example, a sphere can be transformed by just transforming the center of a sphere (and possibly scaling the radius). Transforming the vertices of a polygon will transform the entire polygon. Specifically, transforming the vertices of a polygon, and then rendering with these new locations, gives the same shape as if all of the interior points of the polygon had been transformed.

Typical transformations include translation, scaling, and rotation around an axis. Transformations can also be used to convert between coordinate systems and to give a scene perspective. These transformations can all be specified as a matrix and then the transformed locations are determined through matrix multiplication[1] as shown in equation (3.1), where T is a 4×4 matrix representing the transformation.

$$\begin{bmatrix} x_n \\ y_n \\ z_n \\ w_n \end{bmatrix} = T * \begin{bmatrix} x \\ y \\ z \\ w \end{bmatrix} \tag{3.1}$$

By representing the transformations as matrices, if a number of different transformations need to be performed, the individual transformation matrices can be multiplied together to get one matrix that includes all of the individual transformations. This means that only one matrix multiplication is necessary to perform multiple transformations on a location.

Equation (3.1) includes not only the x, y, and z coordinates but also a fourth value of w. These are called homogeneous coordinates. As will be seen, representing a three-dimensional translation requires a 4×4 matrix. Using homogeneous coordinates allows translations to be included in composite transformations. Additionally, perspective projection transformations require a 4×4 matrix as well.

The three-dimensional point (x, y, z) is represented as $(x, y, z, 1)$ in homogeneous coordinates. If the last term of the homogeneous coordinate (x, y, z, w) is not one, the coordinates can all be divided by w to produce the three-dimensional point. Thus, $(x/w, y/w, z/w, 1)$ is the three-dimensional point equivalent to (x, y, z, w).

3.1.1 Translation

To move or translate an object, the amount of the translation is added to or subtracted from the x, y, and z coordinates of every point. The amount of the translation can be different in each of these directions. For example, to move the object two units to the right and three units down, two would be added to every x coordinate and three would be subtracted to every y coordinate. This gives the equations $x_n = x + 2$, $y_n = y - 3$, and $z_n = z$. In general, the new location after translating is given by the equations $x_n = x + t_x$, $y_n = y + t_y$, and $z_n = z + t_z$, where the t values are the positive or negative translations in the x, y, and z directions. The matrix form of these three equations is given in equation (3.2).

---

[1] When multiplying a 4 x 4 matrix by a three-dimensional point, the first row of the matrix is multiplied by x, y, z, and w and those results are added to get x_n. Multiplying by the second row gives y_n, and so on. A complete review of matrices and matrix operations can be found in Appendix A.

$$\begin{bmatrix} x_n \\ y_n \\ z_n \\ w \end{bmatrix} = \begin{bmatrix} 1 & 0 & 0 & t_x \\ 0 & 1 & 0 & t_y \\ 0 & 0 & 1 & t_z \\ 0 & 0 & 0 & 1 \end{bmatrix} * \begin{bmatrix} x \\ y \\ z \\ w \end{bmatrix} \tag{3.2}$$

• 3.1.2 Scaling

Much as the translation can have a different value for each of the three directions, the scaling transformation can also have a separate scale factor for x, y, and z. To triple the size in the x direction and halve the size in the z direction, each x coordinate is multiplied by three and each z coordinate is multiplied by 0.5. This gives the equations $x_n = 3 * x$, $y_n = y$, and $z_n = 0.5 * z$. In general, the new location after scaling is given by the equations $x_n = s_x * x$, $y_n = s_y * y$, and $z_n = s_z * z$, where the s values are the scales in the x, y, and z directions. The matrix form of these three equations is given in equation (3.3).

$$\begin{bmatrix} x_n \\ y_n \\ z_n \\ w \end{bmatrix} = \begin{bmatrix} s_x & 0 & 0 & 0 \\ 0 & s_y & 0 & 0 \\ 0 & 0 & s_z & 0 \\ 0 & 0 & 0 & 1 \end{bmatrix} * \begin{bmatrix} x \\ y \\ z \\ w \end{bmatrix} \tag{3.3}$$

Note that the scaling occurs with respect to the origin, not the center of the object. If the object happens to be centered at the origin, the object's center will stay in its current location and the object will expand the appropriate amount out from the origin in all directions. If the origin is outside of the object, the object will expand as well as shift away from the origin. A square with opposite vertices located at (1, 1) and (2, 2) transformed with a scale value of 2 in x and y will wind up with its vertices at (2, 2) and (4, 4). In this example, the square has doubled in size, but also moved farther away from the origin. To have an object scaled with respect to its center, a compound transformation is needed that translates the center of the object to the origin, scales the object, and then translates the center of the object back to its original location. Equation (3.4) shows this three step process for an object that has its center at (c_x, c_y, c_z).

$$\begin{bmatrix} x_n \\ y_n \\ z_n \\ w \end{bmatrix} = \begin{bmatrix} 1 & 0 & 0 & c_x \\ 0 & 1 & 0 & c_y \\ 0 & 0 & 1 & c_z \\ 0 & 0 & 0 & 1 \end{bmatrix} * \begin{bmatrix} s_x & 0 & 0 & 0 \\ 0 & s_y & 0 & 0 \\ 0 & 0 & s_z & 0 \\ 0 & 0 & 0 & 1 \end{bmatrix} * \begin{bmatrix} 1 & 0 & 0 & -c_x \\ 0 & 1 & 0 & -c_y \\ 0 & 0 & 1 & -c_z \\ 0 & 0 & 0 & 1 \end{bmatrix} * \begin{bmatrix} x \\ y \\ z \\ w \end{bmatrix} \tag{3.4}$$

When a sphere is scaled, both the center and the radius must be transformed. If just the center is scaled, the sphere will move but not change size. If different scales are applied to x, y, and z, the sphere will become an ellipsoid. This would then require special processing of the sphere. For example, the sphere could be decomposed into a collection of small patches and then each patch could be transformed to account for the different scales.

• 3.1.3 Rotation

When an object is rotated, you need to identify what that object is being rotated around. A point does not fully define the direction the rotation will occur because there are an infinite number of directions for the rotation. Instead, a line or vector is identified around which the object is to be rotated. In practice, things can be simplified by having the rotations occur around one of the three primary axes. This gives three different rotation matrix forms—one for each of the axes. When rotating around the x axis, none of the x coordinates will change because the object is not moving closer or farther from the origin in the x direction. It follows that when rotating around the y axis none of the y coordinates will change, and when rotating around the z axis none of the z coordinates will change.

In addition to specifying the axis of rotation, the angle for the rotation is also needed. When specifying a rotation angle, a positive angle is treated as representing a counterclockwise direction of rotation when looked at from the positive direction of the axis of rotation. For example, looking down the x axis from the positive direction and rotating an object positioned above the axis by 90° will move the object to the left of the axis. This rotation has affected both the y and z coordinates. The matrix multiplication to rotate by an angle of θ about the x axis is given in equation (3.5). The matrix multiplications for rotations about the y and z axes are given in equations (3.6) and (3.7), respectively.

$$\begin{bmatrix} x \\ y_n \\ z_n \\ w \end{bmatrix} = \begin{bmatrix} 1 & 0 & 0 & 0 \\ 0 & \cos\theta & -\sin\theta & 0 \\ 0 & \sin\theta & \cos\theta & 0 \\ 0 & 0 & 0 & 1 \end{bmatrix} * \begin{bmatrix} x \\ y \\ z \\ w \end{bmatrix} \tag{3.5}$$

$$\begin{bmatrix} x_n \\ y \\ z_n \\ w \end{bmatrix} = \begin{bmatrix} \cos\theta & 0 & \sin\theta & 0 \\ 0 & 1 & 0 & 0 \\ -\sin\theta & 0 & \cos\theta & 0 \\ 0 & 0 & 0 & 1 \end{bmatrix} * \begin{bmatrix} x \\ y \\ z \\ w \end{bmatrix} \tag{3.6}$$

$$\begin{bmatrix} x_n \\ y_n \\ z \\ w \end{bmatrix} = \begin{bmatrix} \cos\theta & -\sin\theta & 0 & 0 \\ \sin\theta & \cos\theta & 0 & 0 \\ 0 & 0 & 1 & 0 \\ 0 & 0 & 0 & 1 \end{bmatrix} * \begin{bmatrix} x \\ y \\ z \\ w \end{bmatrix} \tag{3.7}$$

3.1.4 Order of transformations

The order in which the transformations are performed can be significant. This should not be surprising after the discussion of scaling. Scaling an object by its center involves a translation, the scaling, and then a translation in the opposite direction of the first. Clearly, if the two translations are done consecutively before or after the scaling transformation, they will cancel each other out, and the scaling will be done based on the origin instead of the object center. This should also be expected because matrix multiplication is not commutative, meaning that $A * B$ might not be the same as $B * A$ when A and B are matrices.

In Figure 3.2, the top path shows the result of a translation in the x direction followed by a 90° rotation about the y axis. The bottom path shows the result of a 90° rotation about the y axis followed by a translation in the x direction. This figure shows the difference in the result because the operations are reversed.

3.1.5 Projections

Scenes are defined in three-dimensional space, but they are eventually displayed on a two-dimensional screen. To do this the scene is projected onto a two-dimensional projection plane that is then mapped to the screen. How the projection occurs will depend on the viewpoint and the view direction. This should not be surprising because you see different parts of the objects in a room as you look around (a change in the view direction) or as you move around (a change in the viewpoint).

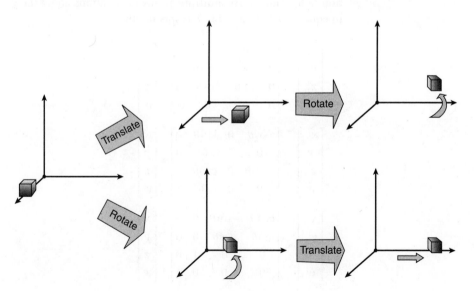

Figure 3.2 • Effect of changing the order of transformations

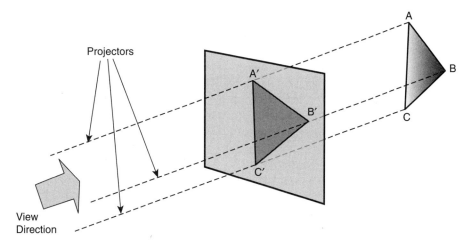

Figure 3.3 • Parallel projection

There are many classifications for projections, but only the two primary ones are discussed here. In a parallel projection, all of the objects are projected along parallel lines onto the projection plane (Figure 3.3).

If the viewpoint is at the origin and the view direction is along the z axis, a parallel projection into the z = 0 plane can be done by setting the z component of the objects to zero. This projection has to be done after shading calculations and visibility determinations, which rely on the actual object z coordinates. Because the projection lines all run parallel to the z axis, the exact location of the projection plane doesn't really matter. If the z = 0 plane is used as the projection plane and the z axis is the view direction, the projection plane normal and the view direction are the same. Other subcategories of parallel projections differ in the relationship between the view direction and the view plane normal. A parallel projection along the z axis into the z = d plane is represented by the matrix multiplication in equation (3.8).

$$\begin{bmatrix} x \\ y \\ d \\ 1 \end{bmatrix} = \begin{bmatrix} 1 & 0 & 0 & 0 \\ 0 & 1 & 0 & 0 \\ 0 & 0 & 0 & d \\ 0 & 0 & 0 & 1 \end{bmatrix} * \begin{bmatrix} x \\ y \\ z \\ 1 \end{bmatrix} \tag{3.8}$$

Parallel projections, although simple, suffer from the loss of visual cues pertaining to distance. In the real world, if two cubes of the same size are placed a foot away and 10 feet away, the closer cube will appear to be larger than the farther cube. This is an effect called foreshortening. The same thing occurs with the edges of a road going off into the distance. Looking along the road into the distance, the edges of the road appear to get closer. In a parallel projection, there is no foreshortening and so both cubes would be rendered the same size and the road edges would always be equidistant. An image gives a more accurate feeling for the relative distances of two objects if a perspective projection is used, because perspective projections give more realistic visual cues of distance.

In a perspective projection, the viewpoint is the center of projection, which is where all lines from all of the objects converge (Figure 3.4). Consider the situation where the viewpoint is at the origin and the projection plane is at $z = d$. A perspective projection determines the intersection of the projection plane and the line between the origin (0, 0, 0) and an object point (x_O, y_O, z_O). Using a proportional approach, the change in the z coordinate is from 0 to z_O and the projection plane is at $z = d$, so the projection plane is d / z_O along the line from the origin to the object point. That makes the complete intersection point $(x_O * d / z_O, y_O * d / z_O, z_O * d / z_O)$. In general, the intersection point can be calculated by the equations (3.9).

$$x_n = x * d / z$$
$$y_n = y * d / z \qquad\qquad (3.9)$$
$$z_n = z * d / z = d$$

To be able to include a perspective projection with the other transformations, these equations need to be put into a matrix form. There is a problem in that the values all require a division by z, which cannot be done with the matrix forms already seen. These matrices can only use multiples of the terms x, y, and z and add translation amounts. To put equations (3.9) into matrix form requires the use of the w term of the homogeneous coordinates. Recall that if w is not one, all of the other components of a homogeneous coordinate are divided by w to get the location to

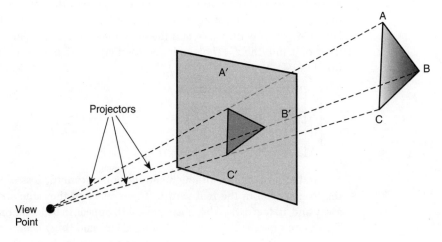

Figure 3.4 • Perspective projection

use. Equations (3.9) can be put in matrix form so that w will be z / d. The final location results when x, y, and z are divided by this value. Therefore, a projection onto the $z = d$ plane with a center of projection at the origin will be accomplished with the matrix multiplication in equation (3.10).

$$\begin{bmatrix} x \\ y \\ z \\ \frac{z}{d} \end{bmatrix} = \begin{bmatrix} 1 & 0 & 0 & 0 \\ 0 & 1 & 0 & 0 \\ 0 & 0 & 1 & 0 \\ 0 & 0 & \frac{1}{d} & 0 \end{bmatrix} * \begin{bmatrix} x \\ y \\ z \\ 1 \end{bmatrix} \tag{3.10}$$

When a perspective projection is done in a sequence of transformations to get the homogeneous coordinate (x_n, y_n, z_n, w), the w term will no longer be 1. Dividing x_n, y_n, and z_n by w gives the location on the projection plane to be used.

For both a parallel and perspective projection, it is possible to have the viewpoint at someplace other than the origin, or to have the view direction other than along the z axis. This is done with a combination of transformations: a translation to move the viewpoint to the origin, and then a rotation to align the view direction with the z axis. After that, a standard projection can be done.

. Because a projection transformation will lose the actual object z values, projections must be done after calculations for depth and visibility. This means that there should be two transformation matrices: a model matrix and a projection matrix. The model matrix can be used to reposition objects to create the scene, and the projection matrix can be used to create the final projection onto the screen.

• 3.1.6 Combining transformations

Transformation and projection matrices can be combined into a single matrix. This section looks at how to order the matrices so that the end result properly accomplishes the task. Matrix transformations can be accomplished by equation (3.11), which multiplies the transformation matrix (T) by a one column matrix with the homogeneous coordinate.

$$\begin{bmatrix} x' \\ y' \\ z' \\ w' \end{bmatrix} = T * \begin{bmatrix} x \\ y \\ z \\ w \end{bmatrix} \tag{3.11}$$

This equation can be viewed as moving a location from the right through the matrix to become the new transformed location on the left. The matrix T can be a combination of transformations that results from an ordering of matrices so that successive steps are placed from right to left. For example, doing a projection from a different viewpoint and direction requires a translation of the viewpoint, a rotation for the view direction, and then the projection. Because the translation needs to be first, it has to be closest to the original point. The entire process is given in equation (3.12).

$$
\begin{bmatrix} x' \\ y' \\ z' \\ w' \end{bmatrix} = Projection * Rotation * Translation * \begin{bmatrix} x \\ y \\ z \\ w \end{bmatrix}
\tag{3.12}
$$

In general, transformations are combined by starting with the identity matrix. The first transformation is multiplied on the left side of the identity matrix. Each additional transformation is also multiplied from the left. To remove transformations from the combined matrix requires a multiplication on the left by the inverse transformation. Removing multiple transformations requires multiplication by the inverses in the opposite order that they were added, much as in a stack data structure, the first thing removed is the last added. For example, to remove the projection and rotation from a combined matrix resulting from the transformation in equation (3.12), the inverse of the projection matrix is multiplied on the left and then the inverse of the rotation matrix is multiplied on the left.

This transformation process can be viewed in another way. The transformation of a point can also be done by multiplying the matrix on the left by a one row matrix with the homogeneous coordinate as in equation (3.13). For this method, the matrices shown in equations (3.2) through (3.7) and (3.10) would have to be transposed[2] and the matrices would be combined by multiplying new transformations on the right.

$$
\begin{bmatrix} x' \\ y' \\ z' \\ w' \end{bmatrix} = \begin{bmatrix} x & y & z & w \end{bmatrix} * T
\tag{3.13}
$$

3.2 Lines

The discussion of object modeling begins with lines. This is not because lines will be a significant component of the models, but because the method discussed for specifying lines lays the foundation for some of the other object algorithms. Additionally, being able to use these forms of a line will be useful in other techniques such as clipping and ray tracing.

One way to specify a line is through the slope-intercept form. In this case, the equation for a line is given as $y = m * x + b$, where m is the slope (the rate of change

---

[2]A matrix is transposed by swapping the rows and columns, so that the first row becomes the first column and the first column becomes the first row. This can also be viewed as reflecting the matrix values along the diagonal that runs from the upper left to the lower right.

in y divided by the rate of change in x) and b is the intercept (the y value where the line crosses the y-axis at $x = 0$). This specifies a line that line is considered infinite in both directions, but graphic applications are interested in just the part of a line between two points. Therefore, it will be simpler to use a parametric form of the equation for a line. This is called a parametric form because points along the line will be specified by a parameter t. The general form for the parametric equation of a line between points P_0 and P_1 is given by equation (3.14), where t is a value between 0.0 and 1.0.

$$L(t) = (1 - t) * P_0 + t * P_1 \qquad\qquad (3.14)$$

Though this is given as one equation, it needs to be calculated for each of the x, y, and z components of the two endpoints. When $t = 0.0$, the result will be P_0, and when $t = 1.0$, the result will be P_1. Other values of t will move along the line connecting these two points.

A second form of the parametric equation for a line can be determined by applying a little algebra on the first form as shown in equation (3.15).

$$L(t) = (1 - t) * P_0 + t * P_1 = P_0 - t * P_0 + t * P_1 = P_0 + t * (P_1 - P_0) \qquad (3.15)$$

Because $P_1 - P_0$ is really a vector along the line, equation (3.15) can be expressed as in equation (3.16), where $v = P_1 - P_0$.

$$L(t) = P_0 + t * v \qquad\qquad (3.16)$$

How can a line be drawn using this parametric form? A series of values for t can be used to create a set of points that can be plotted. For example, values of 0.0, 0.1, 0.2, 0.3, ..., 1.0 can be used to generate 11 points along the line. Unless the line is very short, these 11 points are not likely to be sufficient to give the appearance of a line. So as a first step, the resolution of the line relative to how it will appear on the screen can be determined; specifically how many pixels this line will cross. An increment can be found for t that calculates an x, y, and z value for each of these pixel locations. For example, if the line goes from location (10, 30, 20) to (40, 70, 50), the largest coordinate difference is 40 pixels, which implies that successive t values should differ by 1/40 or 0.025. Calculating a series of locations using values of 0.0, 0.025, 0.05,... is, however, computationally expensive because three additions and multiplications are done for each of those locations. Because the amount of change between each t value is fixed, this can be done faster by just adding the amount of the change each time. If t changes by an increment of d, the multiplications can be eliminated by just adding $d * v$ to the last location to get the next location. In the example, v will be (30, 40, 30) and so 0.025 * v will give an increment of 0.75 for x, 1.0 for y, and 0.75 for z. Now each new point is found by adding (0.75, 1.0, 0.75) to the previous point.

3.3 Planes

Given two points, there is only one line that runs between them. Two points do not define a unique plane but rather can be part of any plane that is rotated around the line between these two points. A third point (not on the line defined by the first two points) is needed to choose among the infinite number of planes that are possible around the line. A plane, therefore, is defined by three points that are not co-linear in three-dimensional space. That plane, however, is assumed by mathematicians to be infinite in all directions but computer graphics uses finite planar patches. Because any three points in space will be on the one plane that they define, a finite triangular patch is guaranteed to be planar. This is one reason triangular patches are preferred in computer graphics.

The full mathematical equation for a plane is given by $A * x + B * y + C * z + D = 0$, where A, B, C, and D are constants that define the plane. All points on the plane have x, y, and z values that make this equation evaluate to 0. The plane equation is determined from the coordinates for three points that are not co-linear, called P_0, P_1, and P_2, in the following way. Two vectors can be created from the three points. The first vector can be $v = P_0 - P_1$ and the second vector can be $w = P_0 - P_2$. The plane normal vector will be given by the cross-product[3] of v and w. The x component of this normal vector is A, the y component is B, and the z component is C. To determine the value of D, any one of the original points is substituted into the plane equation and the equation is solved for D. For example, consider the points $P_0 = (5, 3, 2)$, $P_1 = (4, 6, 5)$, and $P_2 = (2, 3, 6)$. The two vectors would then be $v = [1, -3, -3]$ and $w = [3, 0, -4]$. The cross-product will give a normal of $[12, -12, 9]$, and the plane equation is now $12 * x - 12 * y + 9 * z + D = 0$. Substituting P_0 into the equation gives $12 * 5 - 12 * 3 + 9 * 2 + D = 60 - 36 + 18 + D = 42 + D = 0$. Therefore, D must have a value of -42. This makes the final plane equation:

$$12 * x - 12 * y + 9 * z - 42 = 0$$

A triangular patch can be specified by a parametric form based on the three vertices. The parametric equation of a line depends on one parameter to move along the length of the line, but the parametric equation for a patch needs two parameters to move in two directions on the patch. The parametric form of a triangular patch is given by equation (3.17), where s and t are values in the range [0.0, 1.0].

$$P(s, t) = (1 - s) * ((1 - t) * P_0 + t * P_1) + s * P_2 \tag{3.17}$$

Without the restriction on the range of s and t, equation (3.17) would determine all of the locations on the entire infinite plane defined by these three points. This equation uses the parameter t to interpolate between the points P_0 and P_1. Values of t move along the edge between those two vertices (Figure 3.5). The parameter s then

---

[3]Details on the cross-product can be found in Appendix A.

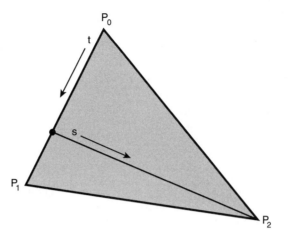

Figure 3.5 • A triangular patch

interpolates between the point along the P_0P_1 edge and the point P_2. The combination of these two parameters in the range [0.0, 1.0] will, therefore, trace out all of the points on the triangular patch that has these three points as its vertices.

The process of determining which locations on an object correspond to pixels on the screen is called scan converting the polygon. Whereas a parametric form can be a nice way to specify the triangular patch, it is not the best way to scan convert the patch for rendering. The problem is determining which values of s and t correspond to pixel locations.

Consider the triangular patch in Figure 3.6. The starting and ending point to render a row of pixels can be determined by looking at the two edges of the patch.

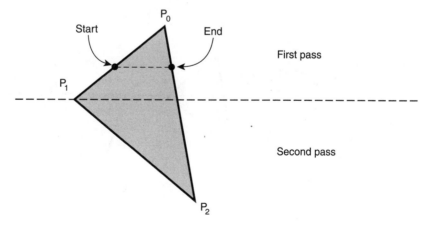

Figure 3.6 • Scan converting a triangular patch

Because the top half of the patch in Figure 3.6 will use the edges P_0P_1 and P_0P_2 and the bottom half will use P_1P_2 and P_0P_2, the scan conversion algorithm will need to have two passes. Within each of these passes, there will be another loop that steps through all of the values of y for that half of the patch. For each of these y values, the range of x values will be determined. This leads to the third nested loop, which steps through these x values from start to end.

Most graphics APIs expect that the vertices for a patch will be specified in a counterclockwise order when looking at the front face of a patch. For this reason, this scan conversion algorithm assumes the same thing. This leads to four general cases for a triangular patch as shown in Figure 3.7. This algorithm also assumes that the first vertex specified has the largest y value as is also shown in Figure 3.7 and it renders down the patch from this largest value. No matter what order the vertices are given in the data file, a simple rotation of the vertex order will bring them into one of the general positions shown without changing the shape of the patch.

The algorithm determines a scale for the change in each of the patch edges. For both Case 1 and 2, the top part of the patch will be rendered between a start that is influenced by the P_0P_1 scale and an end that is influenced by the P_0P_2 scale. The difference between Case 1 and Case 2 is only in the bottom part of the triangle. For the bottom of Case 1, the start is influenced by the P_1P_2 scale and the end is influenced by the P_0P_2 scale. For the bottom of Case 2, the start is influenced by the P_0P_1 scale and the end is influenced by the P_1P_2 scale. To create more compact code the difference is handled by using arrays, where the first elements are assigned the values to be used for the first pass and the second elements are assigned the values to be used for the second pass.

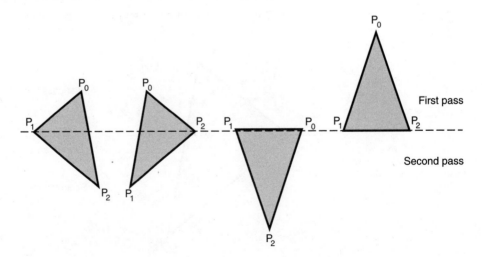

Figure 3.7 • Four general cases for the orientation of a triangular patch

There are two more arrays used to set the starting and ending y values for each pass. The first loop always starts at P_0. In Case 1, the first loop ends at P_1, the second loop starts at $P_1 - 1$, and the second loop ends at P_2. For Case 2, the first loop ends at P_2, the second loop starts at $P_2 - 1$, and the second loop ends at P_1. All of these values are set based on Case 1 and 2. Looking closely at Cases 3 and 4 shows that these are also handled properly if the values are set based on Cases 1 and 2.

Case 3 is actually a special instance of Case 1, so only a few minor adjustments are needed to handle it. First, the scale values for P_0P_1 will not work because of a divide by zero, so they must be set to all zeros. The second adjustment is that the start of the first row of pixels is P_1 but the end is still P_0 as for Cases 1 and 2. Case 4 is actually a special instance of Case 2, but no adjustments are necessary. The scale values for P_1P_2 will not work in this case, but they will never be used because the starting value for the second loop will always be less than the ending value for Case 4.

The algorithm for doing a scan conversion of a triangular patch follows. This algorithm effectively interpolates the x, y, and z values for each pixel location from the coordinates of the vertices. If the shading algorithm determines a color for each of these locations from the colors at the vertices, a similar set of interpolation calculations using the vertex colors are added to the algorithm so that the color can be included in the call to render. If the shading algorithm determines a color using the normal vector at each location, a set of interpolation calculations using the vertex normal vectors are added to the algorithm so that the normal vector can be included in the call to render.

```
// determine how much x and z change
// for each unit change in y
invDiff0 = 1.0 / (P0,y - P1,y);
invDiff1 = 1.0 / (P0,y - P2,y);
invDiff2 = 1.0 / (P1,y - P2,y);
xScale[0] = (P0,x - P1,x) * invDiff0;
zScale[0] = (P0,z - P1,z) * invDiff0;
xScale[1] = (P0,x - P2,x) * invDiff1;
zScale[1] = (P0,z - P2,z) * invDiff1;
xScale[2] = (P1,x - P2,x) * invDiff2;
zScale[2] = (P1,z - P2,z) * invDiff2;
if (invDiff0 == ∞)
{
    // make adjustments for case 3
    xRowStart = P1,x;
    zRowStart = P1,z;
    // fix the scales so they don't
    // mess up the second pass
    xScale[0] = 0.0;
    zScale[0] = 0.0;
```

```
      }
      else
      {
         // these are the other three cases
         xRowStart = P0,x;
         zRowStart = P0,z;
      }
      xRowEnd = P0,x;
      zRowEnd = P0,z;

      loopStart[0] = P0,y;
      xStartRowScale[0] = xScale[0];
      xEndRowScale[0] = xScale[1];
      zStartRowScale[0] = zScale[0];
      zEndRowScale[0] = zScale[1];

      if (P1,y > P2,y)
      {
         // this is cases 1 and 3
         loopEnd[0] = P1,y;
         loopStart[1] = P1,y - 1;
         loopEnd[1] = P2,y;
         xStartRowScale[1] = xScale[2];
         xEndRowScale[1] = xScale[1];
         zStartRowScale[1] = zScale[2];
         zEndRowScale[1] = zScale[1];
      }
      else
      {
         // this is cases 2 and 4
         loopEnd[0] = P2,y;
         loopStart[1] = P2,y - 1;
         loopEnd[1] = P1,y;
         xStartRowScale[1] = xScale[0];
         xEndRowScale[1] = xScale[2];
         zStartRowScale[1] = zScale[0];
         zEndRowScale[1] = zScale[2];
      }

      for (int i = 0; i < 2; i++)
      {

         for (y = loopStart[i]; y >= loopEnd[i]; y--)
         {
```

```
    zLoc = zRowStart;
    // determine how much z changes for
    // each unit change in x
    invRowDiff = 1.0 / (xRowEnd - xRowStart);
    zRowScale = (zRowEnd - zRowStart) * invRowDiff;
    // scan across the row
    for (x = xRowStart; x <= xRowEnd; x++)
    {
        render(x, y, zLoc);
        zLoc = zLoc + zRowScale;
    }
    // determine the starting and ending
    // locations for the current y value
    xRowStart = xRowStart - xStartRowScale[i];
    xRowEnd = xRowEnd - xEndRowScale[i];
    zRowStart = zRowStart - zStartRowScale[i];
    zRowEnd = zRowEnd - zEndRowScale[i];
  }
}
```

There are potential problems with patches that are not triangular, which is why many graphics applications rely on triangular patches. Once more than three vertices are specified, it is difficult to make sure the resulting patch is planar. Any three points are on a single plane defined by those points, so a patch that is specified with just three points is guaranteed to be planar. When a fourth point is specified, the patch can no longer be planar. To guarantee the fourth point is on the same plane as the first three, the plane equation defined by the first three points can be used to calculate the location of the fourth vertex. To determine the fourth vertex in this way might make it hard to get the exact shape desired. A better alternative is to use two triangular patches instead of a single four-sided patch. Additionally, interpolation across nonplanar patches is inaccurate.

There is another problem that occurs with patches that are not triangular. The interpolation of values across a patch can depend on the patch orientation unless the patch is triangular. Cohen and Wallace (Cohen93, pg. 250–251) show that the edges used to interpolate a particular patch location can change as the patch is rotated. Figure 3.8 shows three different orientations for a square patch. (Figure 3.9 shows the shading of these three patch orientations.) In all three, the intensities at the vertices are the same. In the first case where the bright vertices are at the top and the bottom, the interpolation along the edges of the square will decrease the brightness so that it is focused in the corners. Because the interpolation along each of the side edges will produce the same sequence of intensity values, each horizontal row of pixels will have the same value. In the second case, the interpolation process causes the bright intensity at a vertex to be more spread out because each

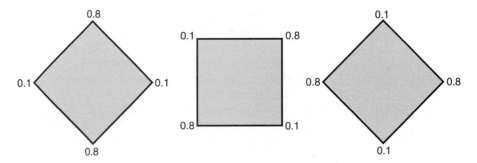

Figure 3.8 • Three patch orientations

Figure 3.9 • Shading of the patches in Figure 3.8

row of pixels is the result of a second interpolation between a light and dark value along the edge. In the third case when the bright vertices are at the sides, the process is similar to the first case, but because the center line will interpolate between the same bright values there is a bright strip across the patch. The third case is almost the photographic negative of the first case. If the patch is triangular, the interpolation will be independent of the orientation of the triangular patch.

A polygon is called convex if a straight line connecting any two points within the polygon lies completely within the polygon. A polygon that is not convex is called concave. Figure 3.10 shows a convex and concave polygon. Another way to view this is that a convex polygon has an internal angle that is less than or equal to 180° between every pair of adjacent polygon sides. A concave polygon will, therefore, have at least one location where the internal angle between two adjacent sides is greater than 180°, which means that the external angle at that vertex will be less than 180°. The concave polygon can be thought of as having a dent at that vertex because the perimeter cuts into the polygon at that vertex. The sum of the internal angles of a triangle is 180°, so none of the individual vertices can have an angle greater than 180°. This means that a triangle is always convex.

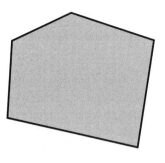 

Figure 3.10 • Convex and concave polygons

Convex polygons are important in computer graphics because algorithms for shading a polygon assume that lines connecting points on the edges of a polygon are entirely within the polygon. This is not always the case for a concave polygon. Triangles are always convex and so they cause no problems for rendering algorithms. Larger and more elaborate polygons might need a check to determine if the polygon is convex. If it is not convex, the polygon can be broken into triangular pieces before rendering. Breaking a complex shape into smaller patches is called tessellation, but if all of the smaller patches are triangular the process can also be called triangulation. Ferguson (Ferguson01) and Schneider and Eberly (Schneider03) are just two of the many sources that have algorithms to triangulate a polygon.

Though triangular patches might not seem very interesting, more complex objects can be broken down into a collection of triangular patches that approximate the overall object. In areas where the object surface is relatively flat, there are fewer large triangular patches. In areas where the object has a high degree of curvature or where the object boundary is irregular, there are more small patches.

3.4 Spheres

Just as there is a neat mathematical description of a line and a patch, there is also a neat mathematical description of a sphere. Given a radius of r and the center of the sphere located at (x_c, y_c, z_c), the mathematical equation $(x - x_c)^2 + (y - y_c)^2 + (z - z_c)^2 = r^2$ can be used to determine points on the surface of the sphere. Any locations (x, y, z) that satisfy this equation are on the surface of the sphere. Locations that result in the left-hand side of the equation being smaller than the right-hand side are inside of the sphere, and when the left-hand side is larger the location is outside of the sphere.

Thus, a sphere can be specified by giving only the location of the center of the sphere and the sphere's radius. This equation, however, does not give an easy way to determine the pixels that are part of the sphere. This can be done with a two part process. Because the sphere projects as a circle onto the two dimensional screen, the *x* and *y* parts of the sphere equation (i.e., the equation for a circle) can be used to determine the range of *x* and *y* values. These values can be used with the full sphere equation to determine the depth or z value. This calculation will actually give two z values. With a view direction that points in the negative z direction, the larger value will be on the front side of the sphere, and the smaller one will be on the back.

Once a location on the sphere surface has been found, the normal vector at that location is found by subtracting the sphere center from the surface point. Specifically, the sphere normal at the surface point (*x, y, z*) is the vector [*x* − x_c, *y* − y_c, *z* − z_c]. An algorithm to scan convert a sphere is:

```
for (y = yc - r; y <= yc + r; y++)
{
    rowSquared = sqr(y - yc);
    temp = sqrt(radiusSquared - rowSquared);
    xStart = xc - temp;
    xEnd = xc + temp;
    for (x = xStart; x <= xEnd; x++)
    {
        z = zc + sqrt(radiusSquared - sqr(x - xc) - rowSquared);
        render(x, y, z);
    }
}
```

This technique is computationally expensive because of the use of square root and squaring. This algorithm takes advantage of the bilateral symmetry of a circle when it calculates the start and end by subtracting and adding temp to the center of the sphere. This means it only calculates the first square root for one half of the circle perimeter. This can be improved by taking advantage of the eight way symmetry of a circle (Figure 3.11) and calculating only one eighth of the circle perimeter. For a circle centered at the origin, when a point (*x, y*) on the sphere is calculated, eight-way symmetry means that the points (−*x, y*), (*y, x*), (−*y, x*), (*y,* −*x*), (−*y,* −*x*), (*x,* −*y*), and (−*x,* −*y*) are also on the circle perimeter. Adding (x_c, y_c) to each of these points gives the eight-way symmetry for a circle centered at that location.

Though this is an improvement, this is still computationally complex. Bresenham (Bresenham77) published an algorithm to determine the points on the perimeter of a circle. This algorithm is notable because it uses increments and addition instead of more costly squaring and square roots. This algorithm also uses eight-way symmetry of a circle.

Bresenham's idea is that moving clockwise along the perimeter of the circle from the topmost point, a decision at each pass is needed to see if the next pixel is to be

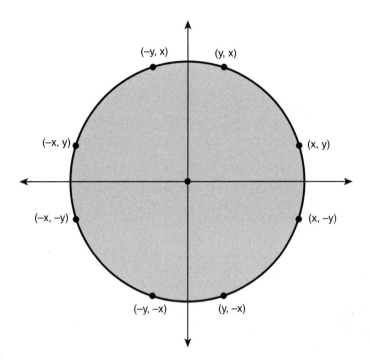

Figure 3.11 • Eight-way symmetry of a circle

directly to the right, or to the right and down one row. In Bresenham's algorithm, the value of the variable d determines if the pixel for the next x value has the same y value (when $d < 0$) or has a y value one smaller (when $d \geq 0$). (See (Bresenham77) for a detailed derivation of the changes to d.) Using Bresenham's method gives the following alternative:

```
x = 0;
y = radius;
d = 5.0 / 4.0 - radius;
// top pixel of the circle
render(x_c, y_c + y, z_c);
// middle row of the circle
rowRender(x_c - y, x_c + y, y_c);
// bottom pixel of the circle
render(x_c, y_c - y, z_c);
while (y > x) do
{
    if (d < 0)
    {
```

```
        d = d + 2 * x + 3;
        x = x + 1;
    }
    else
    {
        d = d + 2 * (x - y) + 5;
        x = x + 1;
        y = y - 1;
    }
    rowRender(x_c - y, x_c + y, y_c + x);
    rowRender(x_c - x, x_c + x, y_c + y);
    rowRender(x_c - x, x_c + x, y_c - y);
    rowRender(x_c - y, x_c + y, y_c - x);
}


void rowRender(xStart, xEnd, row)
{
    x = 0;
    // the radius for this part is one-half
    // the distance between the x start and end
    thisRadius = (xEnd - xStart) / 2.0;
    z = thisRadius;
    d = 5.0 / 4.0 - thisRadius;
    // front pixel of this circle
    render(x_c, row, z_c + z);
    while (z > x) do
    {
        if (d < 0)
        {
            d = d + 2 * x + 3;
            x = x + 1;
        }
        else
        {
            d = d + 2 * (x - z) + 5;
            x = x + 1;
            z = z - 1;
        }
        render(x_c + x, row, z_c + z);
        render(x_c - x, row, z_c + z);
        render(x_c - z, row, z_c + x);
        render(x_c + z, row, z_c + x);
    }
}
```

Bresenham's circle algorithm works in the x-y plane where $z = z_c$. This algorithm can also be applied in the x-z plane where y is equal to the current row being rendered (Porter78). In the preceding algorithm, the function rowRender is just the application of Bresenham's algorithm in an x-z plane. This algorithm allows for rapid calculation of the z values across the sphere because it eliminates square roots and minimizes the number of multiplications. The calls to render all require addition for the z coordinate because in a right-handed coordinate system the z values on the front hemisphere of the sphere will all have values larger than the z coordinate of the center.

3.5 Polygonal Objects

Objects that have curved surfaces can be approximated using planar patches. For example, a sphere could be approximated with a set of six square planar patches, though that would be a cube, which is not a very good approximation. A better approximation is possible, if the patch size is decreased, the patch shape is altered, and the patch count is increased. In the extreme, each patch would be the size of a pixel on the screen or smaller, at which point there would be no visible difference between the approximation and a direct rendering.

If there is an abstract object that should be included in an image, a computer model of it is needed. One option is to develop a surface definition using techniques that are discussed in the next chapter. But what if the model needs to be of a real object? It might be possible to develop a mathematical description of the object shape, but that could be time consuming and there might be inaccuracies in the result. It would be better to identify locations on the object itself, and use those to develop the model.

One way to get locations on an object in order to create the model is through a digitization process. A digitizer allows the capture of surface points in a number of places on the object. Those locations can then be used to create a collection of planar polygon patches that approximate the surface. Manual digitizers have a mechanism that allows the user to touch various places on the object and record that location in three-dimensional space. This is quite time consuming and the results depend on how well the user chooses points on the object. A better solution is an automated laser digitizer. This device scans across the object taking thousands of measurements at equally spaced locations. These locations can be used to create a collection of triangular patches for the object. Software can then analyze these patches to see which can be combined because they are all on the same plane. This is an over-simplification of the process, but the idea is to get a collection of planar patches as the result. A search on the Web will identify companies that have these polygonal models available.

The following chapter will look at techniques for the definition of curves and curved surfaces. These surfaces can be subdivided into polygonal patches for rendering. So, whether an object is digitized or its surfaces are mathematically defined, the result can be a collection of polygons.

3.5.1 Working with polygon meshes

A simple way to store all of the objects in a scene is as an array of polygons that make up all of those objects. Each of these polygons are independent and duplicate any parameters relating to the individual objects. If one of the objects is a cube, it can be stored as six individual square polygons, each of which has a copy of the material parameters necessary to render them. Though this is a simple method, a lot of the data will be duplicated. Even though there are only eight vertices to the cube, this technique would wind up storing 24 vertices—four for each of the six sides. If this was done for a more complex object, there might also be an actual surface normal at each vertex that would also be duplicated for each polygon that meets at that vertex.

In addition to the space needs for all of this duplicated data, all information about how these patches come together to form the entire object is lost. This loss of connectivity makes it more difficult to do texturing across the individual pieces that make up an object. Changing object material parameters in real-time would also be difficult. In radiosity, objects are broken down into polygon meshes, but the result for each polygon in the mesh is needed to properly shade the entire object. Therefore, the ability to relate an object's collection of polygons together is critical.

The balance of this section looks at a few ways that a polygon mesh can be stored. Triangles are used in the discussion. Using polygons with more edges requires a simple modification of these techniques. First is a method for storing a triangular mesh that saves space by limiting duplication of vertices and object parameters. Next is a winged-edge data structure that allows the preservation of information about how triangular patches are connected for an object.

Triangular Meshes

A triangular mesh has two data structures to store the information. The first is a vertex list that stores all of the vertex locations and any parameters related to these vertices or the object as a whole. If an object is modeled with a set of triangular patches that use 50 different vertices, the vertex list will have 50 entries. The triangle list would hold the indexes from the vertex list for the vertices of each triangular patch. Figure 3.12 shows a triangular polygon mesh, the vertex list, and the triangle list. Each entry in the triangle list needs only three integers for the indexes into the vertex list, instead of storing the actual x, y, and z values for each vertex. In Figure 3.12,

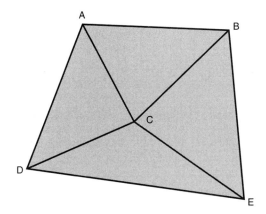

Vertex List	
Material Parameters	k_a, k_d, k_s, exp
Index	
0	(A_x, A_y, A_z)
1	(B_x, B_y, B_z)
2	(C_x, C_y, C_z)
3	(D_x, D_y, D_z)
4	(E_x, E_y, E_z)

Triangle List			
	v_0	v_1	v_2
T_0	0	2	1
T_1	1	2	4
T_2	2	3	4
T_3	0	3	2

Figure 3.12 • Triangular mesh data structures

each vertex is stored just once in the vertex list, instead of storing those values 12 different times for the four triangles.

If there is information stored for each vertex in addition to the vertex location, the savings will be even greater. An actual object normal vector for each of these vertices can be added to the vertex list instead of having multiple copies of it in the triangle list. Additionally, because any parameters needed to render this object are going to be consistent across the triangular mesh, these can be stored once as part of the vertex list. The example in Figure 3.12 shows the inclusion of the ambient, diffuse, and specular coefficients needed to render this object using the Phong shading model. When texturing an object, one technique is to include a texture coordinate for each vertex on an object. These texture coordinates can also be stored with each vertex in the vertex list.

Where a vertex list provides a great space savings by reducing the amount of data that is duplicated, the individual triangles still function independently. The current structure has no way to connect triangles that are adjacent. Identifying adjacent triangles will require searches through the triangle list for matching vertices. For example, to find the triangles adjacent to T_0 in Figure 3.12, the program would have to search the triangle list for other triangles that have edges between (0, 2), (2, 1), or (1, 0), with the vertices in either order. In Figure 3.12, this search identifies T_1 and T_3 as adjacent. Because a complex object can have tens of thousands or hundreds of thousands of triangles, this can become very time consuming.

Winged-Edge Data Structures

While doing research in computer vision, Baumgart (Baumgart74 and Baumgart75) developed a data structure to hold information about the edges found in an image. This data structure has been adapted for use in computer graphics (Glassner 91). When using winged-edge data structures, the edge becomes the primary element on which the representation is built. For each edge, the winged-edge data structure stores the vertices at each end of the edge, the faces to the left and right of the edge, and the edges that leave the vertices for the two adjacent faces. Figure 3.13 shows a polygon mesh and how it would be stored in a winged-edge data structure. As an example, this figure shows that edge r has the vertex C at the start and B at its end. When moving from C to B, face 1 is on the left side of the edge and face 2 is on the right. The next edge encountered around face 1 (the left face) is edge p and the previous edge around that face is q. When traversing around face 2 (the right face), the next edge is t and the previous edge is s.

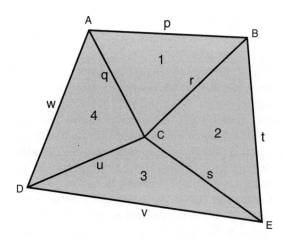

| Edge | Vertices | | Faces | | Left Face Traverse | | Right Face Traverse | |
Name	Start	End	Left	Right	Predecessor	Successor	Predecessor	Successor
p	B	A	1	-	r	q	-	-
q	A	C	1	4	p	r	w	u
r	C	B	1	2	q	p	s	t
s	C	E	2	3	r	t	u	v
t	E	B	2	-	s	r	-	-
u	C	D	3	4	s	v	q	w
v	D	E	3	-	u	s	-	-
w	A	D	4	-	q	u	-	-

Figure 3.13 • A polygon mesh and its winged-edge data structure

The winged-edge data structure is very useful for applications such as radiosity. As will be seen in Chapter 9, large surfaces are broken up into small patches that are used for the radiosity calculation. After the radiosity of each patch is determined, the radiosity of adjacent patches are used to determine the vertex radiosity, which is then used to render the scene. With a winged-edge data structure, it is possible to quickly find all of the patches that are adjacent to the current patch and thus quickly determining the vertex radiosities. Ashdown (Ashdown94) discusses the use of a winged-edge data structure in his radiosity implementation, which relies on this ability to keep information about the relationships between various patches for an object.

The winged-edge data structure can be combined with the vertex table to eliminate duplicate vertex information in each of the edge lists. The vertex table can store for each vertex the name of one of the edges that is connected to that vertex. All of the edges that meet at a vertex can be found by knowing just one edge and then traversing through the predecessor and successor edges for this vertex. There can also be a face table that will give one edge for each polygon in the object. By following along the left or right face edge links, the rest of the edges for a given face can be found. The adjacent faces can be identified by a similar traversal.

The winged-edge data structure gives data that is redundant for the sake of execution speed. Either the predecessor or successor links can be eliminated, because the other can be found by following around the face until returning to the initial edge. This is a classic trade-off between using storage space to store both of the links or using processing time to traverse around the face.

3.5.2 Level of detail

How many polygons are enough to model a surface? It would be nice if there was a single answer to this question, but there is not. There are too many factors involved in this decision. This area of research is known as level of detail (LOD), which is based on human perception research (Luebke03).

Simplification is a common thread in computer graphics. The rendering process simplifies light interactions by doing calculations at just three wavelengths. The range of displayable colors is limited through the capabilities of the hardware used and by expressing these three colors with a limited number of bits each. Positions in three-dimensional space are limited by the precision of the data type used to store them. Shading depends on the complexity of the illumination model used. In each of these cases, better results can be generated by using more colors, bits per pixel, precise data types, or complex illumination models. Though the results will be better, there are also greater costs in compute time and space. Level of detail research goes a step further by looking at the complexity of the models used for the objects.

A simple view of LOD is that objects that are small or far away do not need as complex a model for rendering as objects that are large or close. If an object is small when it appears on the screen, time is wasted by rendering a lot of polygons many of which might only cover a pixel or less of the image. Using larger polygons can produce a suitable result for objects that will be a small part of the scene.

Additionally, when generating a sequence of images in an animation or a game, there can be objects that move fast or that are not the focal point of the scene. For those objects, rendering a highly detailed model will be a waste of time.

Level of detail research is a very active area with algorithms being developed to automatically generate objects at various levels of detail, and to manage those various levels of detail. This work is based on visual perception to determine how much detail is needed to keep the visual fidelity of the scene. The question is, "How much can the mesh of polygons used to model an object be simplified before it will be noticeable to the viewer?" If an object is small or moves fast in an animation, the mesh can be more simplified than if the object is large, stationary, or moving slowly.

Because the focus of this book is the algorithms used in the generation of realistic images, we will not be concerned with level of detail issues. These LOD issues are still critical for real-time and production graphics systems, as well as computer animation and computer games. These topics, though extremely important, are beyond the scope of this book.

3.6 Hierarchical Modeling and Scene Graphs

One way to perceive an object is as a collection of parts. For example, a four-legged table can be broken down into the components of a top and a set of four legs. This creates a hierarchy as shown in Figure 3.14. Hierarchies can be created for all composite objects and those object hierarchies can also be brought together to create an entire scene or world hierarchy. Each component of the hierarchy can have transformations attached to it to bring that part into the correct orientation and size within the next higher level of the hierarchy.

The value of hierarchies of this type is that as a program moves down the hierarchy, it can build the transformations for the next node into the current model transformation matrix. By accumulating these transformations, a change to a transformation higher in the hierarchy will impact all of the components that are below that point when the scene is rendered. For example, if a node in the hierarchy for a scene represents a table and below that node are the components of the table and all of the objects on the table, when the transformation for the table is changed so that the table moves to the left, all of the parts of the table and the objects on the table will automatically move the same amount left. Where hierarchical structures are usually seen as trees, hierarchical models can also be graphs because low level objects can appear as the children of multiple nodes in the hierarchy. For example, all of the legs of the table will be the same so one cylinder object can be used. The "leg" node will then have four different transformations to position the individual leg copies properly, but there would be only one low level cylinder node (Figure 3.15).

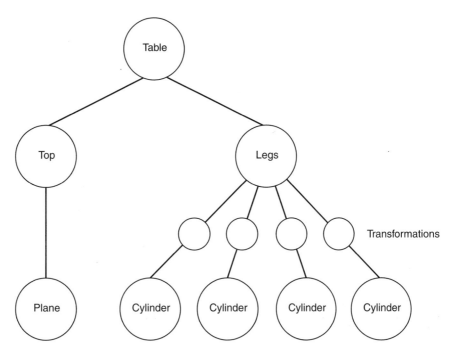

Figure 3.14 • A model hierarchy

The ability to add transformations when moving down the hierarchy and then removing them when moving back up the hierarchy can be handled by creating a stack of transformation matrices. On each move down the hierarchy, a copy of the current transformation is pushed on the stack and then the new transformations are added. When backing up the hierarchy, all the program needs to do is pop the transformation stack to return to the old matrix. Current graphics APIs have built-in capabilities to handle these copy, push, and pop operations.

A version of model hierarchies is the scene graph, which is used in the Java 3D graphical API. Scene graphs in Java 3D are trees built with a collection of objects that are instances of built-in classes. A very simple scene graph (as shown in Figure 3.16) uses the standard set of symbols defined for this task. These scene graph diagrams can be used to design the scene graph but then can also be used in documenting the resulting program.

The top level of the scene graph hierarchy is the *virtual universe*. Off the virtual universe hangs a series of *locales* and each locale has a *content branch* and *view branch*. The content branch has all of the information about objects, and the view branch has information related to how the content should be displayed including the viewpoint location and projection information. The object nodes in a scene graph also have references to nodes that specify the *appearance* and the *geometry* of that object including shading information.

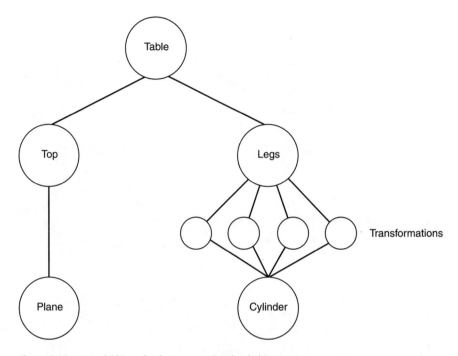

Figure 3.15 • A model hierarchy that reuses a low-level object

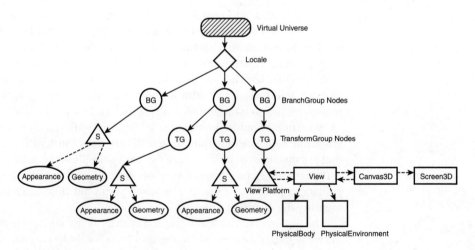

Figure 3.16 • A simple scene graph

Each of the elements shown in Figure 3.16 is an object of a pre-defined class within Java 3D. The solid arrows in this figure indicate parent/child relationships within the scene graph. Each node in the scene graph (except for the virtual universe) should have exactly one parent,[4] which means that objects within the scene must be repeated instead of being reused as in Figure 3.15. The dashed nodes are references that are considered outside of the scene graph. This is significant because it means that there can be multiple references to an appearance or geometry node. For example, even though there needs to be multiple *Shape3D* nodes for the individual legs of a table, those legs could have a common appearance and geometry node that is shared by all. The geometry node will give the details on the shape of the leg and the appearance node will give the material parameters. The positioning of the leg is handled with transformations specified above the Shape3D node in the scene graph.

There are additional nodes within the scene graph that help to group the nodes and specify transformations. The circle nodes represent objects of the *group class*, which have subclasses that allow branches to be grouped and that allow transformations to be specified. The *branch graph* itself has two subclasses: the *view branch graph* and the *content branch graph*. The *transform group* is used to specify a transformation for all nodes under it on the scene graph.

The *view platform* is a node in the scene graph that references, and is referenced, by the view object. The *Canvas3D* and *Screen3D* objects relate to the windowing system that is being used for the graphical user interface (GUI). The *PhysicalBody* and *PhysicalEnvironment* objects can be used to store physical characteristics of the user and the environment where the user is located. These components can be used in virtual reality systems to specify items such as the distance between the viewer's eyes as well as the location of tracking devices in the room. Java 3D includes the ability to create a simple universe that includes basic definitions for the virtual universe, locale, and the view branch group. These objects can then be customized for the application.

This section provides a very brief overview of the capabilities of Java 3D scene graphs. More details on scene graphs can be found in the Java 3D tutorial on the Java Web site as well as in books. See, for example (Palmer01), and (Selman02).

3.7 The OpenGL Way

OpenGL contains a collection of routines that can be used to specify transformations, projections, and object details. This section looks at how this system handles coordinate systems, transformations, and object specification.

---

[4]The class structure defined for Java 3D allows a program to specify scene graphs that are not in the correct form. In these cases, the Java 3D system detects the problem and reports an error as an exception. When that happens, an image will not be rendered.

3.7.1 Coordinate systems

OpenGL uses a right-handed coordinate system. The actual coordinate values themselves have no specific meaning. One model could treat a coordinate of five as five centimeters and another could treat it as five miles. Thus, a range of coordinates that is most appropriate to the application can be used. The range of coordinates used for the scene has an impact on what calls are made to set up OpenGL in the program. The range of values that should be visible in the image is specified with a call to glOrtho or glFrustum. Each of these takes six parameters that specify, in order, the left and right limits, the bottom and top limits, and the near and far limits. The difference between the glOrtho and glFrustum is that the glOrtho routine sets up a parallel projection and the glFrustum routine sets up a perspective projection. In both of these cases, the left, right, bottom, and top values are specified as actual coordinate ranges. The near and far values are set up as distances from the view location, and so both will always be positive. With the viewpoint at the origin and the clipping window at a value of $-d$, the near value is typically set to d, the distance to the clipping window, and the far value is set to indicate the farthest the viewer can "see" beyond that.

For example, the call

```
glOrtho(-20.0, 20.0, -30.0, 30.0, 10.0, 40)
```

sets up a parallel projection with a clipping window that has $(-20.0, -30.0, -10.0)$ as its lower left corner and $(20.0, 30.0, -10.0)$ as its upper right corner. If this call was to glFrustum, the window would be set up to be the same size, but the projection would be perspective with the origin used as the center of the projection. In both cases, the view direction would be along the negative z axis.

The Grand, Fixed Coordinate System

When transformations are applied to an object, those transformations apply to the local coordinate system of the object and are not relative to a grand, fixed coordinate system. See (OpenGL99, pg 143–146) for an example of drawing a sun and planet, where the planet revolves around the sun and rotates on its own axis. Because all objects are drawn at the center of their local coordinate system, calling the glutSolidSphere routine always draws the sphere at the origin. This is fine for the sun, but the planet needs to be some distance away from the sun and at some revolutionary and rotational position.

A rotation of the sphere is needed to account for the rotation of the planet around its axis, a translation is needed to get the planet at the correct distance, and another rotation is needed to get the planet in the proper position in its orbit. When using a grand, fixed coordinate system, this is the order that the transformations will be done. First, the sphere is drawn at the origin of the grand, fixed coordinate system, and then it is rotated around that origin to account for the rotation about the planet's axis. Next a translation along the x axis takes the planet to the proper distance from the center of the planetary system and the origin of the grand, fixed coordinate system. Lastly, a rotation about that origin brings the planet to the correct revolutionary position. Because it is easy to think of things in this way, it is tempting to specify the transformations in this order when setting up the program.

Recall, however, that each transformation occurs relative to the object's local coordinate system. This means that the first rotation will spin the object and the local coordinate system so that the transformation along the x axis away from the sun will depend on this first rotation. So, the first rotation is actually the one to handle the yearly revolution position because it changes where the x axis of the object's coordinate system points. The last rotation will be the one to turn the planet on its axis. It might appear that because of the translation the second rotation moves the object around the sun's center. However, that is not the case because all transformations are done relative to the object's local coordinate system, which moved with the object when it was translated.

There is another way of thinking about this. If the transformations are viewed as occurring relative to a grand, fixed coordinate system, then they should be specified in the reverse order in the program. Going back to the original description in the second paragraph of this section, the planet's movement relative to this grand, fixed coordinate system, it was described as the rotation about the axis, translation to the proper orbit distance, and then rotation in the orbit. This is the reverse order from what is specified as the program order in the previous paragraph.

The reverse order relative to the grand, fixed coordinate system occurs because as the transformations are specified they multiply with the current matrix on the left and the new transformation on the right. When objects are transformed by this matrix, they are also multiplied by the right as shown in equation (3.1), which means the last transformation added to the matrix is the first transformation applied to the object.

3.7.2 Transformations and matrices

OpenGL has built in functions to handle the transformations that were discussed at the start of this chapter. There are a number of transformation matrices—two of which are the modelview matrix and the projection matrix. The modelview matrix is used to hold transformations related to positioning of objects and the projection matrix is used to hold transformations related to the camera or viewing parameters.

OpenGL specifies one of its matrices as the current transformation matrix into which it builds the transformations specified. The call `glMatrixMode (GL_PROJECTION)` specifies that the next set of transformation operations should be applied to the projection matrix, and the call `glMatrixMode(GL_MODELVIEW)` specifies the use of the modelview matrix. Building a new transformation matrix begins with a call to the glLoadIdentity() routine, which as its name indicates sets the current transformation matrix to the identity matrix.

An object is rotated with a call to either the routine glRotatef or the routine glRotated. These two differ only in whether their parameters are of type float or double. The rotate routines take four parameters. The first is the angle (in degrees) for the rotation and the other three are the x, y, and z coordinates of the vector that the rotation will occur around. Rotations will be done using the right-hand rule, which means that if you look at the scene so that the vector specified is pointing at you, the object will rotate in the counterclockwise direction.

An object can be moved with a call to either the routine glTranslatef or the routine glTranslated, which like the rotation routines differ only in the type of parameters. For a translation, three values are provided for the translation in the x, y, and z directions. An object can be scaled with a call to either the routine glScalef or the routine glScaled. These routines also take three parameters that are either type float or double, respectively, and that are the values to scale the object in the x, y, and z directions.

3.7.3 Matrix stacks

OpenGL has a set of matrix stacks that are used to keep track of the current transformations as well as a collection of other transformations. These stacks make it easy to save the current transformation matrix, apply some additional transformations, and then revert to the earlier saved versions. The current transformation matrix of each type is the one at the top of its matrix stack.

Two of the stacks that OpenGL uses to keep transformation matrices are the projection matrix stack and the modelview matrix stack. Transformations for the viewing parameters are put into the matrix at the top of the projection matrix stack. This includes calls to the glOrtho and glFrustum routines. Transformations that move, rotate, or resize objects are put into the matrix at the top of the modelview matrix stack. Because it is common for there to be few view transformations but many object transformations, the projection matrix stack can hold two matrices where as the modelview matrix stack can hold up to 32 matrices. These are the default values for OpenGL and different implementations might have larger limits for these stacks. The current matrix is always kept at the top of the stack. All transformation routines will alter the top element of the active stack. To preserve the current transformation matrix for use in the future, the matrix on the stack can be saved with a call to glPushMatrix. When this routine is called, OpenGL will push the current matrix down on the stack and make a new copy for the top. Then transformations can be added and when glPopMatrix is called, the previous transformation matrix returns to the top of the stack and is used for the next object or objects drawn. OpenGL's modelview matrix stack is used to support the concepts of hierarchical modeling.

Section 1.8.6 shows that the reshapeWindow function makes changes to the projection matrix stack. It loads the identity matrix, which replaces whatever was previously on that stack, sets up a perspective projection, and then switches back to the modelview matrix stack. This is the typical way that the projection matrix stack will be used. Having a second location on the projection matrix stack can be valuable for putting up help or error message windows. To do this, the current projection matrix is pushed, the identity matrix is loaded, a simple parallel projection is specified, the text is displayed, and then the projection matrix stack will be popped to return to the projection needed for the main display window.

3.7.4 Simple objects

The sections on OpenGL in Chapters 1 and 2 showed a couple of examples that used polygons. We now look at the specification of object shapes in more detail. The intent here is not to give all of the details for programming in OpenGL, but rather to show how the ideas discussed in this chapter can be done in OpenGL. For complete description of OpenGL, the reader is directed to (OpenGL00) or (OpenGL99).

Points

The specification of a point or a series of points (Figure 3.17) begins with a call to `glBegin(GL_POINTS)` and ends with a call to `glEnd()`. Between these two calls, the locations of the points or vertices are given with calls to `glVertex*`.

There are 24 different versions of `glVertex*` that vary based on the number and type of parameters. The first option is the number of parameters to provide: two, three, or four. For two-dimensional graphics, only the x and y coordinates are provided with one of the `glVertex2*` routines. Obviously, the `glVertex3*` routines will be used to specify $x, y,$ and z coordinates. The `glVertex4*` routines are also used to

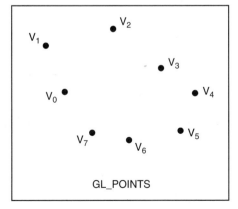

Figure 3.17 • OpenGL points

specify a value for w in homogeneous coordinates.[5] The second option is the type of parameters passed to the `glVertex*` routine. Coordinates can be specified as double (d), float (f), integer (i), or short integer (s). For example, a call the routine `glVertex3d` specifies the *x*, *y*, and *z* coordinates as type double.

The third option is whether to pass the coordinates as individual parameters or in an appropriately sized array. Appending the character "v" to the routine name tells OpenGL that the coordinates are being passed in an array ("v" stands for vector). For example, calling the routine `glVertex4iv` means a single parameter that is an array of four integers will hold the *x*, *y*, *z*, and *w* coordinates of the vertex.

Other properties can be set for a vertex with the appropriate routine call before the vertex location is given. For example, a different color can be set for each vertex by calling `glColor*` before each call to `glVertex*`.

Lines, Line Strips, and Line Loops

There are three different ways to specify a series of lines: individual lines, a set of connected lines, and a loop of lines (Figure 3.18). A set of lines can be drawn by giving pairs of vertices between the calls glBegin(GL_LINES) and glEnd(). Specifically, a line is drawn between the first and second vertex, the third and fourth vertex, and so on. If an odd number of vertices is specified, the last vertex is ignored.

If the first call is to glBegin(GL_LINE_STRIP) a line strip is drawn, which is a set of connected line segments between all consecutive points. Specifically, a line will be drawn between the first and second vertex, the second and third vertex, the third and fourth vertex, and so on. If the first call is to glBegin(GL_LINE_LOOP), a line loop is drawn. The vertices will be connected, as in the case of a line strip, but one additional line will be drawn between the last and first vertices.

Polygons

A polygon is specified by giving its vertices in either clockwise or counterclockwise order around the perimeter of the polygon (Figure 3.19). OpenGL will consider the

---

[5]If you do not specify a z coordinate, it will default to zero. If you do not specify a w coordinate, it will default to one.

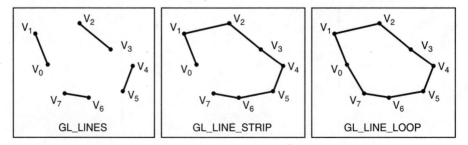

Figure 3.18 • OpenGL line options

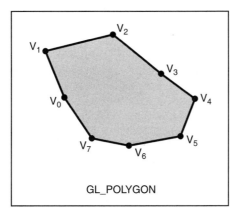

Figure 3.19 • OpenGL polygon

edges of the polygon to be between successive vertices, with the last edge connecting the last and first vertex given. The first vertex does not need to be repeated to create a closed polygon—OpenGL automatically closes the polygon. The difference between a polygon and a line loop is that the interior of a polygon can be filled or shaded by OpenGL.

A polygon is said to have a front and back face. If you specify the vertices in a counterclockwise order, you will be looking at the front face of the polygon, and the other side will be the back face. These are reversed if you specify the vertices in a clockwise order. Recall that object properties can be set differently for the front and back face of a polygon.

A polygon specification begins with a call to glBegin(GL_POLYGON) and ends with a call to glEnd(). Between these two calls, the locations of the vertices are given with calls to glVertex*.

Triangles, Triangle Strips, and Triangle Fans

OpenGL allows triangles to be specified as triangles, triangle strips, or triangle fans (Figure 3.20). Triangles can be specified as individual polygons or can be grouped together into one glBegin/glEnd block. If the block starts with glBegin(GL_TRIANGLES), OpenGL will draw a collection of triangles using groups of three vertices. If three vertices are given in the block, there will be one triangle rendered. If six vertices are given, there will be two triangles rendered. If the number of vertices specified is not a multiple of three, OpenGL will draw as many triangles as possible and the one or two extra vertices will be ignored.

An alternative is to draw a triangle strip. In this case, the block starts with glBegin(GL_TRIANGLE_STRIP). The first triangle is drawn using the first three vertices, but now every new vertex draws a new triangle. If six vertices are given, there will be four triangles drawn using the vertices (v_0, v_1, v_2), (v_2, v_1, v_3), (v_2, v_3, v_4), and

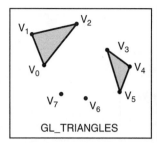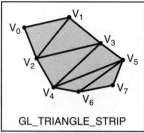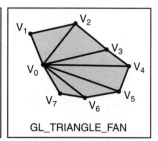

Figure 3.20 • OpenGL triangles, triangle strips, and triangle fans

(v_4, v_3, v_5). The vertices are used in the order shown, so that all of the triangles face in the same direction. If the first triangle is front facing, then all of the others will also be front facing. But if the first triangle is back facing, then the rest will also be back facing.

The last option is a triangle fan, which starts with the call, glBegin(GL_TRIANGLE_FAN). For a triangle fan, the first point is a vertex for all of the triangles and successive pairs of points serve as the other two vertices. If five vertices are supplied, three triangles will be drawn using the vertices (v_0, v_1, v_2), (v_0, v_2, v_3), and (v_0, v_3, v_4).

Quads and Quad Strips

Quads and quad strips (Figure 3.21) function in the same way as triangles and triangle strips, except with four-sided quadrilaterals. These two are drawn in blocks that start with glBegin(GL_QUADS) and glBegin(GL_QUAD_STRIP), respectively. For a collection of quadrilaterals, one will be drawn for groups of four vertices, and if the total number of vertices is not evenly divisible by four, the extra one, two, or three vertices will be ignored. In the case of a quadrilateral strip, the first quadrilateral will be drawn with the first four vertices, and each succeeding quadrilateral will be drawn with the last two vertices and two new vertices. If there are an odd number of vertices, the last one will be ignored. If eight vertices are given, three quadrilat-

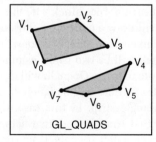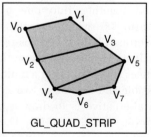

Figure 3.21 • OpenGL quads and quad strips

erals will be drawn in a quad strip with the vertices (v_0, v_1, v_3, v_2), (v_2, v_3, v_5, v_4), and (v_4, v_5, v_7, v_6). As in the case of a triangle strip, the vertices are used in an order that guarantees that all quadrilaterals face in the same direction.

GLUT Objects

GLUT provides nine different objects in both a wire frame and solid form. The wire frame versions are nice for quickly developing draft images to check object layout before doing a shaded rendering of the scene. All of these objects are centered at the origin. Transformations can be used to position them in the correct place within a scene.

The first object is a sphere that is drawn with a call to glutWireSphere or glutSolidSphere. The first of these will draw a sphere as a series of lines in the latitudinal and longitudinal direction, and the second will draw the sphere as a shaded object. Both of these take three parameters, with the first being a double that specifies the radius of the sphere and the other two begin integers that specify the number of slices and stacks into which the sphere should be divided. The slices cut through the sphere as lines of longitude but from the front to the back—parallel to the z axis. The stacks cut through the sphere as lines of latitude but around the z axis. The shading of a solid sphere can be improved to some point by increasing the number of stacks and slices.

The second object is a cube drawn with a call to glutWireCube or glutSolidCube. The first will draw the cube as a wire frame consisting of the cube edges and the second will draw a shaded cube. This routine takes just one double parameter that is the size of the cube centered at the origin.

The third object is a torus (donut) drawn with its axis aligned with the z-axis. When looking down the z-axis, you are looking through the center of the torus. The torus is drawn as either a wire frame or a solid with a call to glutWireTorus or glutSolidTorus, respectively. These routines take four parameters: the inner radius (double), the outer radius (double), the number of sides around the ring of the torus (integer), and the number of radial cuts through the ring of the torus (integer).

The fourth object is a cone drawn with the base in the z = 0 plane, and the top at z = height, meaning that the z-axis runs through the center of the cone with the point toward the positive z direction. The calls to draw a cone are glutWireCone and glutSolidCone. Both take four parameters that are the radius of the base of the cone (double), the height of the cone (double), the number of slices through the cone from the top to the bottom of the cone around the z-axis (integer), and the number stacks through the cone perpendicular to the z-axis (integer).

The next four objects are an icosahedron (20-sided regular solid), a dodecahedron (12-sided regular solid), an octahedron (eight-sided regular solid), and a tetrahedron (four-sided regular solid). These are drawn with calls to the routines glut*Icosahedron, glut*Dodecahedron, glut*Octahedron, and glut*Tetrahedron, respectively, where the * can be either "Wire" or "Solid." The icosahedron and the octahedron are drawn with a radius of 1.0, and the other two are drawn with a radius of $\sqrt{3}$.

The last object is a teapot drawn with the handle on the negative x side and the spout on the positive x side. The routines `glutWireTeapot` and `glutSolidTeapot` take one parameter of type double that is the size of the teapot.

3.8 Projects

1) Add the ability to shade triangular patches to your rendering program.
2) Add the ability to shade a sphere to your rendering program.
3) Add the ability to shade a torus to your rendering program.
4) Add the ability to shade a cone to your rendering program.
5) Add the ability to shade a teapot to your rendering program.

4

Curves and
Curved Surfaces

Though it can be quicker to render simple polygonal surfaces, it can be quite difficult to specify a complex shape by manually listing all of the polygons that are
needed to approximate it. Think about an object with curved surfaces such as a car
(Figure 4.1). Imagine trying to create a collection of polygons and the normal vectors needed for shading that would approximate a general shape. How many polygons will you use? How large will they be? What shape will they be? There are
many decisions that need to be made and many polygons that need to be created.
Once these polygons are specified, it can be a daunting task to modify them to
change the shape of that car or to modify a copy for other similar cars.

The tendency when developing a model for a square table is to use a group of
planar patches, but the result would look artificial. That's because objects are not as
perfect as the result from a mathematical equation. On closer inspection, the edges
of a real square table are not perfectly straight and the top is not perfectly flat. There
is subtle variation in everything. Though the manufacturing process can produce
results that are close to straight or flat, there will be vibrations during fabrication
that cause the results to be imperfect. Furthermore, objects also become worn down
with use. Some of these variations are handled by how the object is specified, and
others are handled with texturing techniques, discussed in Chapter 6.

This chapter introduces a method for the specification of surfaces that are complex but give more and easier control over the object shape. Techniques are

Figure 4.1 • A car front end (see Color Plate 4.1)

explored that can specify complex surface shapes with a small collection of "control points." Surfaces defined in this way can be difficult to render directly. An alternative is to subdivide the surface and then approximate each small patch with a polygon that can be rendered with techniques already discussed. Using these methods, changing the shape of an object can be done by moving the control points and then regenerating the collection of polygons.

A number of different techniques for defining curves and curved surfaces are presented here. There are some techniques that are just briefly discussed, but it is left to the reader to do additional research on those techniques that are needed. A complete coverage of curves and curved surface topics occupies entire books, for example (Bartels87), (Farin90), and (Rogers01) among many others.

Curves are presented first. By the nature of the printed page, these curves will be shown in two dimensions, even though the mathematics for these curves is given for three-dimensional coordinates. By exploring curves first, these techniques can be demonstrated before moving to curved surfaces. An understanding of these curves is also important because they are used in the specification of objects through swept surfaces and for controlling motion in animated sequences.

4.1 Bézier Curves

As an engineer for the Renault car company, Bézier developed a type of parametric polynomial that is now named after him, (Bézier72) and (Bézier74). His application was the specification of car bodies and these curves and surfaces were used in the design process. Bézier curves are parametric in form. The shape of the curve is determined by a collection of control points and blending functions that combine them. The blending functions are polynomials all of the same degree and the number of control points needed is one greater than the degree of the polynomials. The higher the degree of the polynomials is, the greater the flexibility of the shapes that can be created. However, the higher the degree is, the more computationally complex the blending functions are. For the most part, the cubic Bézier curves are sufficient to generate a wide range of shapes and are most commonly used.

Cubic Bézier curves use a set of four control points to determine the shape of the curve. The form of this cubic polynomial determines a number of interesting properties about the resulting curve shape. The polynomial equation for a cubic Bézier curve is given in equation (4.1).

$$C(t) = (1 - t)^3 * P_0 + 3 * t * (1 - t)^2 * P_1 + 3 * t^2 * (1 - t) * P_2 + t^3 * P_3 \qquad (4.1)$$

In equation (4.1), P_0, P_1, P_2, and P_3 are the four control points, and t is a parameter in the range [0.0, 1.0] along the length of the curve. The equation (4.1) is calculated separately for the x, y, and z coordinates of the control points. The coordinates that result from calculating $C(t)$ for t values in this range will trace out the curve. The four polynomials that are multiplied by the control points are called the weight or blending functions. Other types of curves, that will be discussed later, have different blending functions. For a cubic Bézier curve, the blending functions that are part of equation (4.1) are given in equations (4.2).

$$
\begin{aligned}
b_0(t) &= (1 - t)^3 \\
b_1(t) &= 3 * t * (1 - t)^2 \\
b_2(t) &= 3 * t^2 * (1 - t) \\
b_3(t) &= t^3
\end{aligned}
\qquad (4.2)
$$

These blending curves are shown graphically in Figure 4.2. By using the blending function notation in equations (4.2), the equation for a cubic Bézier curve can be given in a more concise manner as in equation (4.3).

$$C(t) = \sum_{i=0}^{3} b_i(t) * P_i \qquad (4.3)$$

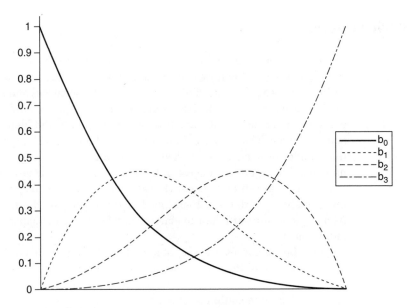

Figure 4.2 • Bézier blending functions

Bézier curves exhibit a number of interesting properties. The first property is that the curve interpolates the first and last control points. This means that the first and last control points will be part of the curve. In equations (4.2), when the parameter t has a value of zero, the first blending function gives a value of one, and all the rest are zero. When the parameter t has a value of one, the last blending function has a value of one, and all the rest are zero. Therefore, a t value of zero results in $C(t)$ returning the first control point, and a t value of one returns the last control point. This is how these control points wind up on the curve. This property can be seen in the curves in Figure 4.3.

The second property is that each control point has influence over the entire curve and, therefore, they are said to have "global control." Figure 4.2 shows the four blending functions are non-zero everywhere except at 0 and 1. This is what gives each control point influence over the shape of the entire curve. In Figure 4.3, the two curves differ in the placement of only one control point. The upper gray curve is defined by the four control points: P_0, P_1, P_2, and P_3. The lower black curve is defined by the four control points: P_0, P'_1, P_2, and P_3. Only the second point is moved, yet the entire shape of the curve has changed.

The third property is that the line or vector from P_0 to P_1 is tangent to the start of the curve and the line or vector from P_3 to P_2 is tangent to the end of the curve.

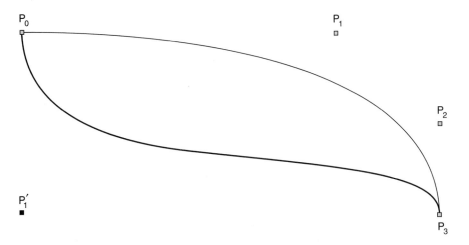

Figure 4.3 • Two Bézier curves and their control points—the two curves share three of the four control points (see Color Plate 4.2)

The length of this vector also indicates the rate of curvature leaving the control point. The longer this vector, the more gentle the change in curvature. This property will be important for continuity at the point where two Bézier curves meet. This property also helps determine the normal vector for Bézier surfaces. This property can be seen in Figure 4.4, which shows the lines between P_0 and P_1 and between P_3 and P_2 are tangent to the start and end of the curve respectively.

The fourth property is that the control points form a convex hull around the resulting curve. This means that the curve will be completely contained in the polygon determined by the four control points. Figure 4.4 shows a Bézier curve with the convex hull shown with dashed lines. This occurs because the blending functions are positive in the entire [0.0, 1.0] range.

Multiple Bézier curves can be connected to create even more complex shapes. For example, a circle cannot be created with a single cubic Bézier curve, but four curves can each trace one quarter of a circle.[1] When curves are put together, there is control over the level of continuity at each of these connections. By the way the control points of two curves are chosen, the two curves can just meet at a point but

---

[1]These four curves do not create a perfect mathematical circle, but this approximation is accurate to within about 0.005%. This is sufficient for many image generation purposes.

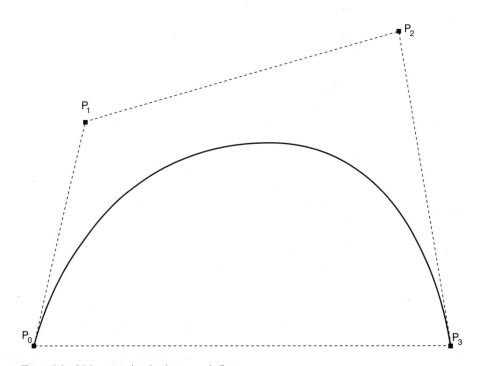

Figure 4.4 • Bézier curve showing its convex hull

change direction, they can be continuous in direction but change the rate of curvature, or they can have the same curvature on both sides of the join point. This is shown in the three pairs of curves in Figure 4.5.

Consider two Bézier curves with the first being specified by control points P_0, P_1, P_2, and P_3, and the second specified by control points P_4, P_5, P_6, and P_7. If the last control point of the first curve is also the first control point of the second curve (i.e., $P_3 = P_4$), the two curves will at least exhibit what is called G^0 continuity (the left-hand curve in Figure 4.5), which means that the curves meet. This is true because of the first property of Bézier curves, namely that they interpolate their endpoints. The first curve interpolates the last point P_3 and the second curve interpolates the first point P_4.

If $P_3 = P_4$, the points P_2, P_3 (P_4), and P_5 are distinct, and all are on the same line with P_3 (P_4) in the middle, the curve at least exhibits what is called G^1 continuity (the middle curve in Figure 4.5), which means that the join point will be smooth because the tangent is in the same direction on both sides of the join point. This occurs because of the third property, which is that the line between the first two and last two control points is tangent to the curve. With the line between P_2 and P_3

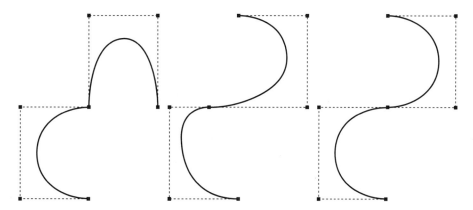

Figure 4.5 • Bézier curves showing from left to right C^0, G^1, and C^1 continuity

and the line between P_3 and P_5 in the same direction, the tangents are the same, which makes the curve continuous at the join point.

If, in addition to these two other conditions, the distance between P_2 and P_3 is the same as the distance between P_3 (P_4) and P_5, the curves will exhibit C^1 continuity (the right-hand curve in Figure 4.5), which means that the join point will be smooth and the rate of curvature coming into the point will be the same as the rate of curvature leaving the point. The distance between these two pairs of points indicates the rates of curvature. When those distances are the same the rate of change in the curvature is the same on both sides of the join point.

Moving one of the internal control points changes the entire shape of the curve, but it will only affect the tangent at the adjacent join point. To preserve the continuity that currently exists there, the control point on the other side of the join must be moved the same amount in the opposite direction. The left-hand curve in Figure 4.6 shows two Bézier curves that have C^1 continuity. In the middle curve in Figure 4.6, only one of the control points is moved and there is now only G^0 continuity at the join location. In the right-hand curve in Figure 4.6, a control point for the other curve is moved in the opposite direction and the join point again has C^1 continuity.

4.1.1 Subdividing Bézier curves

Much as two Bézier curves can be joined with varying degrees of continuity, Bézier curves can also be subdivided into two pieces that are equivalent to the original. When a Bézier curve is subdivided the point where these two sections join will have C^1 continuity, thus the two new Bézier curves are equivalent to the original curve. This section looks at the calculations to subdivide a cubic Bézier curve. The

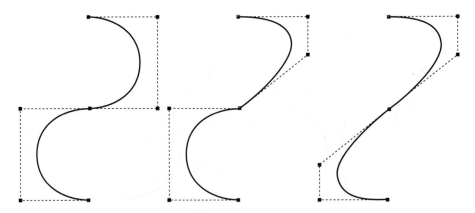

Figure 4.6 • Preserving continuity

subdivision replaces the four control points for the cubic Bézier curve with a collection of seven control points that trace out the two parts. There are only seven control points because the "middle" one is shared by both parts.

Subdivision of a Bézier curve can be used to change the shape of a curve without changing the continuity at a join point. Recall that moving a control point changes the shape of the entire curve. If one of the two interior Bézier curve control points is moved, the entire curve changes shape and the continuity at the join point with an adjacent curve will be changed. Subdividing the curve creates more control points that are effectively internal to this piece. These new internal points can be changed to alter the shape of these curve sections without altering the continuity at the join points at the ends of the original curve. For example, in Figure 4.7, the original curve, defined by control points (P_0, P_1, P_2, P_3), has been subdivided into two curves with control points (Q_0, Q_1, Q_2, Q_3) and (R_0, R_1, R_2, R_3). If point R_1 is moved, the second part of the curve will change shape but the continuity at R_3 will not change. If point Q_2 is also moved in the opposite direction of the R_1 move, the entire original curve will change shape but continuity at both endpoints will be preserved. If the Bézier curve is divided into many pieces, moving control points for the interior pieces will only change the shape of that one piece. The other pieces at the ends of the original curve will not be affected and, therefore, the continuity at the end pieces will also not change.

A Bézier curve is divided into two equivalent pieces with just a few calculations. First, the curve is divided into two pieces by dividing the interval of the parameter t in half. Because this process only involves addition and division by 2, it can be calculated quickly. The subdivision process is shown geometrically in Figure 4.7.

The process begins by dividing the line between the first pair of points (P_0 and P_1) and the last pairs of points (P_2 and P_3) in half, which gives two new control points (Q_1 and R_2). The next step is to divide the line between the second (P_1) and third (P_2) control points in half (H). The next control point on each curve is found by dividing the line between this latest halfway point and the first new control point on each curve in half. Dividing the line between H and Q_1 in half gives the control

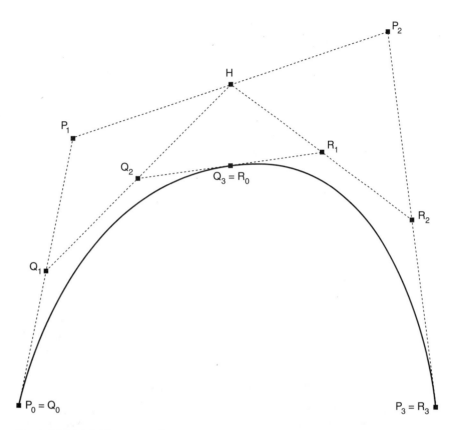

Figure 4.7 • Subdividing a Bézier curve

point Q_2, and dividing the line between H and R_2 in half gives the control point R_1. The final control point for each curve is the midpoint of the line between Q_2 and R_1. This last point calculation guarantees C^1 continuity at the location where the curve is split. Formally, the equations to calculate these new control points are given by:

$$Q_0 = P_0$$
$$R_3 = P_3$$
$$Q_1 = (P_0 + P_1) / 2$$
$$R_2 = (P_2 + P_3) / 2 \qquad (4.4)$$
$$H = (P_1 + P_2) / 2$$
$$Q_2 = (Q_1 + H) / 2$$
$$R_1 = (H + R_1) / 2$$
$$Q_3 = R_0 = (Q_2 + R_1) / 2$$

Where Figure 4.7 and the equations in (4.4) subdivide a curve in half, a Bézier curve can be divided into two pieces of any size. This capability is useful if a large portion of the curve is relatively flat and a small portion has sharp shape changes. In this situation, the curve can be divided into flat and highly curved parts, instead of just in half. The curve can be divided at any point along its length as specified by a t value in the range [0.0, 1.0]. The t value for the split point would be used in the equations (4.5).

$$Q_0 = P_0$$
$$R_3 = P_3$$
$$Q_1 = (1 - t) * P_0 + t * P_1$$
$$R_2 = (1 - t) * P_2 + t * P_3 \qquad\qquad (4.5)$$
$$H = (1 - t) * P_1 + t * P_2$$
$$Q_2 = (1 - t) * Q_1 + t * H$$
$$R_1 = (1 - t) * H + t * R_1$$
$$Q_3 = R_0 = (1 - t) * Q_2 + t * R_1$$

Subdividing the curve in half corresponds to a t value of 0.5. Substituting a value of $t = 0.5$ into equations (4.5) gives the equations (4.4).

Subdividing a Bézier curve gives individual pieces that can be manipulated to fine-tune the overall shape being created. The goal is, however, to produce images using these curves, so the next section looks at how to render a Bézier curve. One method will use this subdivision technique to render these curves.

• 4.1.2 Rendering Bézier curves

One way to render a Bézier curve is to chose an appropriately small increment for the parameter t, and then calculate a series of locations along the curve. If these locations are closely spaced, they might be the actual pixel locations needed to draw the curve. If they are more spaced out than this, these locations can serve as the endpoints of a series of small straight lines that can be drawn to approximate the curve shape. The smaller the increment, the better the approximation of the curve. But using a small increment also increases the number of times that the cubic blending functions need to be calculated. This effort is not always necessary either. An appropriate increment depends on how large the curve will appear in the image and the locations of the control points. If the curve is to be small in the image, big changes in the parameter t will result in small movements on the screen, because the overall curve is small. If the curve is to be large on the screen, large changes in the parameter t might separate points on the curve too far. In this case, a smaller change in t is needed because of the larger distance that has to be covered within the parameter range of 0 to 1. Some of this is also related to the relative positioning of the control points. If the control points are closely spaced, the length of the curve will be short and a large increment for t could be used. If the control points are spread out, the curve length will be longer and a finer increment for t could be used. If a curve has control point spacing that is not uniform, it is better for time and appearance to have the increment change along the length of the curve. For example, if the first two control points are closely spaced, but the other two are widely spaced from the first two and each other, a larger increment might look fine for the beginning of the curve, but not for the end of the curve. A smaller increment looks fine for the end of the curve, but would do extra computations for the beginning. Adaptively altering the increment along the length of the curve can help with this. As points are determined along the curve, the distance between them can be calculated. If the distance between two successive points becomes too large, the increment can be decreased; but if the distance becomes too small, the increment can be increased.

A second method for rendering a Bézier curve is to use the subdivision method that was discussed in the previous section. Figure 4.7 shows that when a curve is subdivided, there are more control points and those control points move closer to the curve. Recursively subdividing the curve creates additional curve sections and moves the new control points for those sections closer and closer to the shape of the overall curve. If the curve is flat enough, it can be approximated by the straight line between the end control points. To determine whether this is the case, the distance of the two interior control points to this line can be calculated.[2] If these distances fall below the threshold chosen for flatness, the straight line can be used. If either is above the threshold, the curve needs to be subdivided again.

4.1.3 Non-cubic Bézier curves

In the discussion so far, all of the Bézier curves have been cubic, because the blending functions had a power of three for the parameter t. Bézier curves, however, can be of any degree greater than two. Cubic curves use four control points. In general, one more control point than the power of the blending functions is used. Three control points are used for a quadratic Bézier curve, and six control points are used for a Bézier curve with blending functions of degree five. In general, the blending functions for an N-degree Bézier curve are given in equation (4.6) where,

$$\binom{N}{i} = \frac{N!}{i! * (N - i)!}$$

is the binomial coefficient.

$$B_i^N(t) = \binom{N}{i} * (1 - t)^{N-i-1} * t^i, \text{ for } 0 \leq i \leq N \tag{4.6}$$

Higher order Bézier curves can represent a wider range of shapes than cubic curves. The penalty is that the blending functions are much more computationally

---

[2]Appendix A gives details on calculating the shortest distance between a point and a line.

complex. Typically cubic Bézier curves are used and more complex shapes are built by using multiple curves joined together.

4.2 B-spline Curves

B-spline curves are another way to specify a curve through control points. Though the process is similar, the blending functions used to calculate points along the curve are different than for Bézier curves, which means that the properties of B-splines are also different.

The first difference is in the number of control points used to specify a B-spline curve. A cubic Bézier curve needs four control points for the first section, and each additional section needs three more control points (assuming that the two sections of curve have at least G^0 continuity). A cubic B-spline begins with four control points, but the curve is extended with the specification of each additional control point. Thus, a single cubic B-spline curve is defined with four or more control points. Each control point beyond the first four adds another piece to the curve. This occurs because of the way that the blending functions are used with the control points. With a Bézier curve, each control point is used with only one of the blending functions. With a B-spline curve, the first four control points are used with the blending functions for the beginning of the curve, but then as more points are added, the blending functions are shifted one control point over to generate the next piece of the curve.

The form of the blending functions and the way they are used with the control points leads to the second difference with Bézier curves. B-splines have "local control." If a curve has many control points, moving one control point only changes a portion of the curve's shape. Each control point only has influence over the part of the entire curve where it is used with one of the blending functions. The first control point only influences the first part of the curve. The second control point influences the first two parts of the curve because in the first part it is used with the second blending function and in the second part it is used with the first blending function. Following this reasoning, the most influence that a control point can have is over four sections of the curve, but that only occurs for one control point, the "center" one, if there are seven control points overall. If there are more than seven control points, all but the three at the start and the three at the end will influence four parts of the curve. Because of local control, a change to the location of a central control point does not influence the start and end of the curve. An example of this can be seen in Figure 4.8, which shows two sets of B-spline curves that differ by only one control point. The points indicted with black and grey represent control points that the two curves share. The only difference in the control points is between the solid grey point and the solid black point.

B-splines do not typically pass through any of their control points. The first and last control points are on a Bézier curve, but Figure 4.8 shows that none of the control points lie on the B-spline curve. More formally, B-splines do not interpolate any

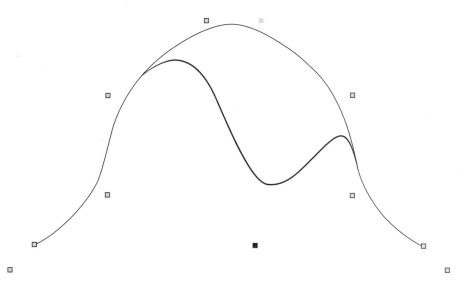

Figure 4.8 • B-Splines showing local control (see Color Plate 4.3)

of their control points. There can be times, however, when a B-spline needs to pass through a control point. One way for a B-spline to do this is by placing multiple control points in that location.

The blending functions for a cubic B-spline curve are:

$$b_3(t) = t^3 / 6$$
$$b_2(t) = (-3 * t^3 + 3 * t^2 + 3 * t + 1) / 6 \tag{4.7}$$
$$b_1(t) = (3 * t^3 - 6 * t^2 + 4) / 6$$
$$b_0(t) = (-t^3 + 3 * t^2 - 3 * t + 1) / 6$$

These blending functions are shown graphically in Figure 4.9. The B-spline blending functions are structured so that they total 1 for any value of t in the range [0.0, 1.0]. Figure 4.9 shows that, except for the first and last blending functions, the value of a blending function at one end of the range [0.0, 1.0] is the same as the next blending function at the other end of the range. For example, the value of $b_2(1.0)$ is the same as $b_1(0.0)$. This is the reason that the curve is continuous as the blending functions shift along the control points.

A B-spline curve can be extended by adding just one more point because of how the blending functions are used. With just four control points for a B-spline curve, the use of the blending functions is the same, as in the case of a Bézier curve. The curve is drawn with $0.0 \leq t \leq 1.0$ by multiplying $b_0(t)$ by the first control point; $b_1(t)$ by the second control point; and so on. When a fifth control point is added, the curve continues by shifting the blending functions over to the next control point and running through the range of the parameter $0.0 \leq t \leq 1.0$ again. For this second

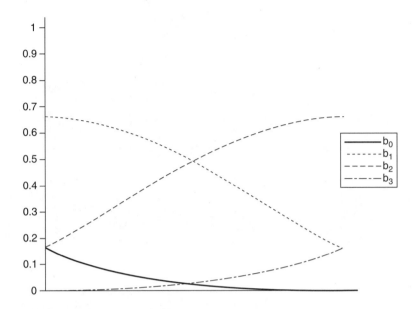

Figure 4.9 • B-spline blending functions

section of the curve, $b_0(t)$ is multiplied by the second control point; $b_1(t)$ is multiplied by the third control point; and so on. Each additional control point added causes the blending functions to be shifted and the parameter t to again run through the range [0.0, 1.0]. The value of b_3 at $t = 1.0$ is the same as b_2 at $t = 0.0$. When the control point P_3 is shifted from $b_3(1.0)$ to $b_2(0.0)$, there is no change in its contribution to the curve. The same thing is true when the control point P_2 shifts from $b_2(1.0)$ to $b_1(0.0)$, and when P_1 shifts from $b_0(1.0)$ to $b_0(0.0)$, because $b_2(1.0) = b_1(0.0)$, and $b_1(1.0) = b_0(0.0)$. Dropping the control point P_0 does not have an impact because $b_0(1.0)$ is zero. Adding the control point P_4 also has no impact because $b_3(0.0)$ is also zero, but as the parameter value increases, P_4 begins to influence the shape of the curve. All of this explains how the curve preserves its continuity as the blending functions change control points.

Having to reset the parameter value and shift the blending functions can lead to a complex algorithm, but there is an alternative way to handle this process. The cubic B-spline parameter range is redefined to be between 3.0 and N, where N is the number of control points. In this expanded range, the first four control points would be used in the range [3.0, 4.0]; the second four control points would be used in the range [4.0, 5.0]; and so on.

The individual blending functions are brought together by a new function $B(T)$ given in equation (4.8).

$$B(T) = \begin{cases} b_3(T) & \text{if } 0.0 \leq T \leq 1.0 \\ b_2(T-1.0) & \text{if } 1.0 \leq T \leq 2.0 \\ b_1(T-2.0) & \text{if } 2.0 \leq T \leq 3.0 \\ b_0(T-3.0) & \text{if } 3.0 \leq T \leq 4.0 \\ 0.0 & \text{otherwise} \end{cases} \tag{4.8}$$

This equation is used to handle the shifting of the blending functions along the control points. Consider the relationship between the parameter T and the blending function that is used. The new function $B(T)$ with T in the range of [3.0, 4.0] returns the value of $b_0(t)$ in the range [0.0, 1.0]. With T in the range of [2.0, 3.0], $B(T)$ returns the value of $b_1(t)$ in the range [0.0, 1.0]. The ranges of [1.0, 2.0] and [0.0, 1.0] return values from $b_2(t)$ and $b_3(t)$, respectively. Over the range of [3.0, 4.0] for the B-spline parameter t, equation (4.8) shows that multiplying the first control point P_0 by $B(t-0)$ is the same as multiplying it by $b_0(t)$. Equation (4.8) also shows that multiplying the second control point P_1 by $B(t-1)$ is the same as multiplying it by $b_1(t)$; multiplying the third control point P_2 by $B(t-2)$ is the same as multiplying it by $b_2(t)$; and multiplying the fourth control point P_3 by $B(t-3)$ is the same as multiplying it by $b_3(t)$. When the blending functions shift to draw the second curve section over a t range of [4.0, 5.0], multiplying P_1 by $B(t-1)$ now uses $b_0(t)$; multiplying P_2 by $B(t-2)$ now uses $b_1(t)$; multiplying P_3 by $B(t-3)$ now uses $b_2(t)$; and multiplying P_4 by $B(t-4)$ now uses $b_3(t)$. In general, over the curve range of [3.0, N] each control point P_i is multiplied by $B(T-i)$ to properly shift the blending functions as needed.

To put this more formally, the B-spline curve is now defined by the equation (4.9) over the range [3.0, N] for the parameter t.

$$C(t) = \sum_{i=0}^{N-1} B(t-i) * P_i \tag{4.9}$$

Consider the first segment of the curve when the parameter ranges is [3.0, 4.0]. At a value just larger than 3.0, the summation values of i between 0 and 3 are used because they are the only ones where $t-i$ is in the range [0.0, 4.0]. Values for i between 0 and 3 will result in $B(t-i)$ having a value from one of the blending functions. Notice that i values between 0 and 3 will use the first four control points. This is true of the entire range up to a value of 4.0. When the curve parameter becomes greater than 4.0, an i value of 0 will give $t-i$ a value greater than 4.0, which is out of range and now produces a zero result for $B(t-i)$. The first control point is no longer used. When the curve parameter becomes larger than 4.0, the second control point (P_1) is now multiplied by the first blending function. The other control points will also shift, and the fifth control point will be multiplied by the fourth blending function. This continues each time the curve parameter passes into the next unit of the range. This formulation of B-spline is called uniform because the segments of the range from 3 to N are all the same length—one unit. Non-uniform B-splines will be discussed in a later section.

A B-spline can be set up to interpolate its endpoints, if the first and last control points are repeated four times each. With the set of control points P_0, P_1, P_2, and P_3, a B-spline does not interpolate the start control point P_0 or the end control point P_3. A B-spline with the 10 control points P_0, P_0, P_0, P_0, P_1, P_2, P_3, P_3, P_3, and P_3 will interpolate both end control points. Notice that having the first four control points the same means that all values in the first segment of the curve evaluates to P_0 because the four blending functions always sum to 1 for any parameter value. This can be generalized to any of the control points along the curve. As any of the control points are duplicated, the curve moves closer to that control point. If four consecutive control points are the same, the curve goes through that control point. Figure 4.10 shows four B-spline curves, with the second, third, and fourth curves having the middle control point duplicated two, three, and four times, respectively. At this resolution, the third and fourth curves appear to be the same. However,

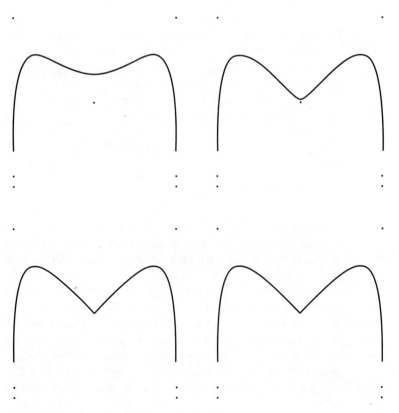

Figure 4.10 • Effect of duplicating a control point

mathematically the third gets near the duplicated control points, whereas the fourth goes through them.

4.2.1 Subdividing B-spline curves

The process of subdividing a B-spline curve is similar to that of a Bézier curve and is done for similar reasons. The lines between the control points are subdivided to identify new control points, but how this happens and how these midpoints relate to the new set of control points are different. Where the Bézier curve subdivision produces two separate curves, the subdivision of a B-spline only adds control points. The subdivision process adds one new control point for each segment of curve. If there are six original control points, there are three curve segments and the subdivision process adds three points, giving nine new control points that produce the same curve as the original six. The new version of the curve has six segments instead of three. Thus, these new control points divide the B-spline curve into twice as many curve segments that trace the same curve. As with Bézier curves, this new set of control points more closely follows the length of the B-spline curve. Thus, the subdivision process can also be used to render the curve.

In the description of this process, the first and last control points are referred to as the "end control points" and the rest of the control points are referred to as "interior control points." The process first takes the midpoint of each of the lines connecting consecutive control points. These midpoints (the Q points with even subscripts in Figure 4.11) will be in the set of new control points. Then the midpoints of the line between these new control points and the old adjacent interior control point are found. These midpoints (the H points in Figure 4.11) are only temporary and are not control points. The last step takes the midpoint of the lines connecting these temporary midpoints and adds those to the set of control points (the Q points with odd subscripts in Figure 4.11). A mathematical formulation of this process for subdividing a B-spline curve with four control points (P_0, P_1, P_2, and P_3) to get an equivalent B-spline curve with five control points (Q_0, Q_1, Q_2, Q_3, and Q_4) is given in equations (4.10).

$$Q_0 = (P_0 + P_1) / 2 \qquad H_0 = (Q_0 + P_1) / 2 \qquad Q_1 = (H_0 + H_1) / 2$$
$$Q_2 = (P_1 + P_2) / 2 \qquad H_1 = (P_1 + Q_2) / 2 \qquad Q_3 = (H_2 + H_3) / 2 \qquad (4.10)$$
$$Q_4 = (P_2 + P_3) / 2 \qquad H_2 = (Q_2 + P_2) / 2$$
$$H_3 = (P_2 + Q_4) / 2$$

The first column of equations finds the midpoint of the existing control points. The second column of equations finds the midpoint of the lines between the new control points and the interior control points. The third column calculates the midpoint of the lines between these halfway points. If there are more than four initial control points, additional equations are needed in each column. The pattern in these equations is clear, so it should be easy to develop loops and arrays to generalize this process for any number of control points.

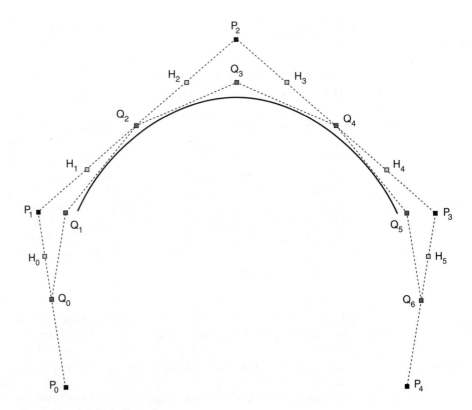

Figure 4.11 • Subdividing a B-spline curve

4.2.2 Rendering B-spline curves

As in the case of Bézier curves, a B-spline can be rendered by choosing an appropriate increment for the curve parameter, generating a series of points along the curve, and then drawing straight lines between these points. A B-spline curve can also be approximately rendered by repeatedly subdividing the curve until it has a fine enough resolution, and then just drawing lines between the control points. As the last subsection mentioned, this is possible because as the curve is subdivided, the increase in the number of control points also means that they will more closely follow the shape of the B-spline.

4.2.3 Non-cubic B-spline curves

Cubic B-spline curves are sufficient for most applications; however, if there is an application that needs a smoother curve, a higher order B-spline is used. We now look at a process that can be used to determine higher order uniform B-splines.

The $b_i(t)$ equations (4.7) for cubic B-splines can be expressed as $b_i^4(t)$. In general, $b_i^N(t)$ defines the ith blending function for an order[3] N uniform B-spline. Each of these blending functions is defined on the range $0 \le t < 1$. The higher order blending functions are defined recursively as in equation (4.11), where $b_D^1(t) = 1$ for $0 \le t < 1$ and $b_i^1(t) = 0$ for all values of t where $i \ne D$.

$$b_i^j(t) = \frac{t + D - (i+1)}{j-1} * b_i^{j-1}(t) + \frac{j+i+1-D-t}{j-1} * b_{i+1}^{j-1}(t) \tag{4.11}$$

When working with a B-spline of degree D, N control points are used and, therefore, N blending functions are needed. This means the functions b_0^N through b_D^N are needed. In all of the resulting equations, the blending function will be the portion of the equation that is multiplied by the b_D^1 term. The recursive form shows that each equation is dependent on two equations of the lower order, but most of those are used twice. The functions b_0^{N-1} through b_{D+1}^{N-1} are the only ones that are really needed for the derivation. With each decrease in order in the recursive process, one additional equation is needed. For example, deriving the blending functions for a degree 4 B-spline would need five equations of degree 4, six equations of degree 3, and seven equations of degree 2.

It is easy, however, to develop the needed blending functions from the lowest degree to the highest. Recreating the cubic B-spline blending functions would first determine b_i^2, then b_i^3, and lastly the blending functions b_i^4 for i in the range [0, 3]. In general, when creating degree D blending functions, only b_D^1 will be non-zero over the range [0, 1]; thus to create the degree 3 blending functions, only b_3^1 will be non-zero. Because of this, only b_2^2 and b_3^2 need to be determined, as they are the only terms that contain b_3^1, and so are the only terms that will be non-zero. Substituting 2 for i and j in equation (4.11) gives a value of $b_2^2(t) = (1 - t) * b_3^1(t)$, because b_2^1 is always zero. Substituting 2 for j and 3 for i in equation (4.11) gives a value of $b_3^2(t) = t * b_3^1(t)$, because b_4^1 is always zero. Next b_1^3, b_2^3, and b_3^3 are determined because they are the only non-zero terms at this level. For example, substituting a value

of 1 for i and 3 for j in equation (4.11) gives $b_1^3(t) = \frac{1-t}{2} * b_2^2(t)$, and when the value

for b_2^2 is substituted in, the result is $b_1^3(t) = \frac{1-t}{2} * \frac{1-t}{2} * b_3^1(t)$. This process is repeated

for b_2^3 and b_3^3 until those two equations are based only on b_3^1. These three equations are then used to calculate b_0^4, b_1^4, b_2^4, and b_3^4, which are the desired blending functions. If you carefully complete this algebraic process, you should get the blending functions given in equation (4.7).

---

[3]The order of a polynomial, N, is one greater than its degree or largest power, D. For example, a cubic B-spline (D = 3) is of order four (N = 4).

The process described here will only work if the B-spline is uniform. The calculations are slightly more involved for non-uniform B-splines. For details on the calculation for non-uniform B-splines, see (Mortenson97), (Farin90), or (Bartels87).

4.3 Other Curve Types

Cubic Bézier and B-spline curves are only two methods for describing a curved shape. This section looks at another way of specifying a curve shape with its endpoints and the tangent vectors at the endpoints, as well as other ways to set up both Bézier curves and B-splines. These other methods provide different ways to specify curves and provide different levels of control over the shape of the curve that are of interest for particular applications. This section is intended as an introduction to the variety of other curve formulations. Further research is left to the reader when use of these curves is need.

4.3.1 Hermite curves

With Bézier curves, the set of control points implicitly specify the tangents at the curve ends. Recall that the line between the first two control points is tangent to the Bézier curve start, and the line between the last two control points is tangent to the Bézier curve end. Hermite curves are specified by the start point and end point, and the tangents at those points. The process then uses a set of blending functions to determine the points on the curve based on these values. A Hermite curve is given by the equation (4.12), where the two endpoints are P_0 and P_1 and their associated tangents are T_0 and T_1, respectively.

$$C(t) = (2*t^3 - 3*t^2 + 1) * P_0 + (-2*t^3 + 3*t^2)$$
$$* P_1 + (t^3 - 2*t^2 + t) * T_0 + (t^3 - t^2) * T_1 \qquad (4.12)$$

The blending functions applied to each of these components behave similarly to those in Bézier and B-spline curves. In this equation, when t has a value of 0.0, the first blending function for P_0 has a value of 1.0 and all the rest will be zero. When t has a value of 1.0, only the blending function for P_1 has a value of 1.0 and all the rest are zero.

Figure 4.12 shows the impact that the direction of the tangent vector can have on the shape of the curve. In each of the curves in this figure, the only thing that changes is the direction of the initial vector. The two curves at the top and bottom of the right column use the same two tangent vectors, but they are reversed—the initial tangent in the top curve becomes the final tangent in the bottom curve, and vice versa. Figure 4.13 shows the impact that the length of the vector can have on the curve. In each of the curves in this figure, the only thing that changes is the length of the initial vector.

Hermite curves are invariant under the transformations of rotation, scale, and translation. Applying these transformations to the endpoints and tangent vectors will effectively apply these transformations to the entire curve.

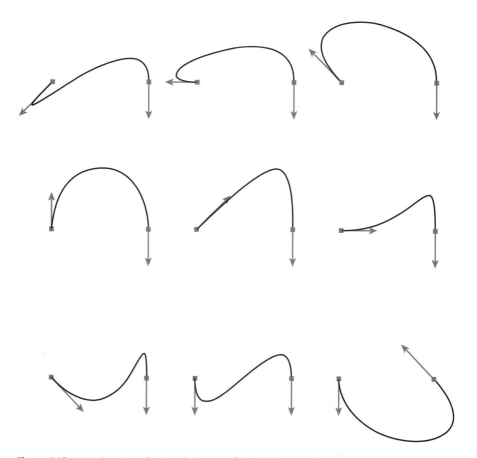

Figure 4.12 • Hermite curves showing the impact of the initial vector direction (see Color Plate 4.4)

• 4.3.2 Rational curves

The Bézier and B-spline curves previously discussed are polynomial curves, because the weighting of the control points is done with polynomial blending functions. Both of these curves also have rational forms where each blending function is not a single polynomial but is instead the ratio of two polynomials. More specifically, a rational Bézier or B-spline curve is a polynomial curve, specified in homogeneous coordinates, that has been projected back into three-dimensional space.

Recall that homogeneous coordinates take the form (x, y, z, w), where w is the weight for the point. When these coordinates are divided by the value of w, the result $(x/w, y/w, z/w, 1)$ is the homogeneous coordinate projected into three-dimensional space. For rational curves, control points are given in homogeneous coordinates, and the blending functions in equations (4.3) and (4.9) are used with all four coordinate

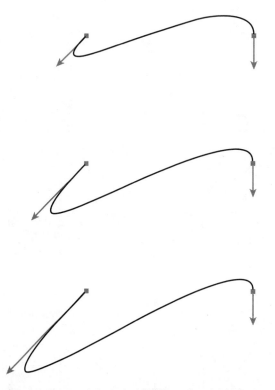

Figure 4.13 • Hermite curves with different length initial vectors (see Color Plate 4.5)

values. Equation (4.13) shows a generic cubic parametric curve where H_i represents the ith homogeneous control point.

$$C^H(t) = \sum_{i=0}^{3} B(t) * H_i \qquad (4.13)$$

If w_i represents the weight (the fourth component) of the ith homogeneous control point, then equation (4.14) gives the weight portion of the homogeneous coordinate that results from equation (4.13).

$$w(t) = \sum_{i=0}^{3} B(t) * w_i \qquad (4.14)$$

When $C^H(t)$ is divided by w(t), the result is the rational cubic parametric equation in three-dimensional space shown in equation (4.15), where P_i is the projection of H_i into three-dimensional space. The term rational comes from the fact that the blending functions applied to the control points P_i are the ratio shown in the last summation of equation (4.15).

$$C(t) = \frac{\sum\limits_{i=0}^{3} B(t) * P_i}{\sum\limits_{i=0}^{3} B(t) * w_i} = \sum\limits_{i=0}^{3} \frac{B(t)}{\sum\limits_{j=0}^{3} B(t) * w_j} * P_i \tag{4.15}$$

It should be noted that if the weight values are 1 for all of the homogeneous control points, the denominator of the fraction will also always be 1, because the blending functions always sum to 1. In this special case, the rational curve degrades to a polynomial curve. In general, if the weight w_i is increased, the resulting curve will be pulled toward the control point P_i.

Another way to view this process is to start with the set of control points P_i and to convert them to homogeneous points (P_i^H) by including a fourth coordinate of 1 for each control point. Each control point is then multiplied by a weight w_i to get the set of homogenous coordinates H_i used in equation (4.13).

The benefit of rational curves is that they can be used to specify a wider variety of curve types than polynomial curves. For example, a circle cannot be represented with a single polynomial Bézier curve, but instead can be very closely approximated with four curves that each trace out one quarter of the circle. A single rational Bézier curve, however, can be used to accurately represent a circle. In general, rational curves are needed to be able to represent any form of conic curve with a single set of control points.

4.3.3 NURBS

The term NURBS stands for Non-Uniform Rational B-Splines. A rational B-spline is a B-spline that has blending functions that are ratios of two polynomials, as described in the previous section. The B-splines discussed in section 4.2 were uniform B-splines because the range of t values for each section of the curve was the same one unit in length. NURBS combine the idea of a rational B-spline with non-uniform ranges of t values for the curve sections.

Equation (4.8) for the function $B(t)$ shows the set of values that define where each of the blending functions is used. These values are more generally called knots, and the collection of them are called a knot vector. In a uniform B-spline, the difference between each of the knot values is a uniform amount. The knot vectors [0 1 2 3 4 5] and [0.0 0.5 1.0 1.5 2.0 2.5] both result in uniform B-splines that differ in the range of values for the parameter t. For the first knot vector and a cubic B-spline, there are five control points, and the first four control points are used over a parameter range of three to four, and the last four control points are used for a range of four to five. With the second knot vector, these ranges would be 1.5 to 2.0, and 2.0 to 2.5, respectively. Though knot vectors only have the restriction that the knot values are in non-decreasing order, typically, knot vectors will begin at zero and for uniform B-splines will increase by one.

The knot values indicate the ranges over which the particular blending function applies. The first example is a standard uniform B-spline, where for the first four control points, the blending functions apply in the ranges (0.0, 1.0], (1.0, 2.0], (2.0, 3.0], and (3.0, 4.0]. For the next group of four control points, the blending functions apply in the ranges (1.0, 2.0], (2.0, 3.0], (3.0, 4.0], and (4.0, 5.0].

In a non-uniform B-spline, the values in a knot vector are not evenly spaced. The only requirement is that the knot values be in non-decreasing order, which means that each knot value must be greater than or equal to the previous knot value. Duplicating a knot value causes the curve to pull closer to the associated control point. Previously, we said that a cubic B-spline interpolates its first control point when that control point is repeated four times. The same thing occurs by just using one copy of the control point, but inserting four copies of the first knot value. For example, the first control point is on the curve when using the control points P_0, P_0, P_0, P_0, P_1, P_2, and P_3 with the knot vector [0 1 2 3 4 5 6 7], or when using the control points P_0, P_1, P_2, and P_3 with the knot vector [0 0 0 0 1 2 3 4]. In the later case, the duplication of the 0 knot means that for the first section of the curve, all blending functions will have a collapsed range, which results in the location P_0 being on the curve.

There is also a connection between Bézier curves and B-splines that can be found by using non-uniform knot vectors. A B-spline with four control points and the knot vector [0 0 0 0 1 1 1 1] will actually draw the Bézier curve that would result from those same four control points.

The value of NURBS is the ability to add an interior control point along with a corresponding knot value, so that the influence of the new control point stays local and does not impact the ends of the curve. NURBS are powerful mechanisms for specifying the shape of objects in computer-aided design and complex characters for animated sequences. A full treatment is beyond the scope of this text, but readers are encouraged to look at books such as (Rogers01) for a complete and approachable look at this topic.

4.4 Surfaces

The discussion of Bézier curves and B-splines was designed to help you understand these methods of specifying complex curves because (1) they are the basis for two methods for specifying curved surfaces, (2) they are useful for sweeping out the shape of objects, and (3) they are useful for specifying motion in animated sequences. This section looks at how to create surfaces from these curve formulations, and the next section looks at using curves to sweep out the shape of objects.

4.4.1 Bézier surfaces

Bézier surfaces merely apply the Bézier curve method in two directions to form the surface. Where a Bézier curve is specified with four control points along the

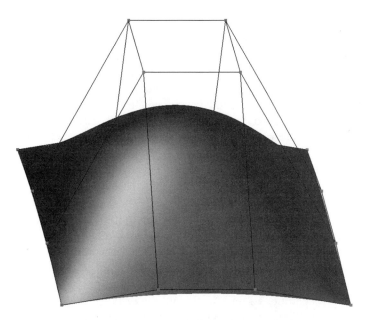

Figure 4.14 • Bézier surface showing grid of control points in black

length of the curve, a Bézier surface is specified by 16 control points in a two-dimensional grid that has four control points on each side. Figure 4.14 shows a Bézier surface with its control points at the intersections of the black lines. When working with this grid of control points, the two perpendicular directions for the control points are referred to as u and v directions, where u is the parameter that moves through the rows of control points and v is the parameter that moves through the columns of control points. Both of these parameters have the range [0, 1].

Bézier surfaces use the same curve blending functions in both the u and v direction. This means that the control point $P_{0,0}$ is used with $b_0(u)$ and $b_0(v)$, and the control point $P_{2,1}$ is used with $b_2(u)$ and $b_1(v)$. In general, $P_{i,j}$ is used with $b_i(u)$ and $b_j(v)$, so that the full surface equation is given by equation (4.16).

$$S(u,v) = \sum_{i=0}^{3} \sum_{j=0}^{3} b_i(u) * b_j(v) * P_{i,j} \qquad (4.16)$$

Because the surface is made up of Bézier curves in two directions, the properties of those curves also apply to the surfaces. First, where a Bézier curve interpolates its end control points, a Bézier surface will interpolate its corner control points. The four corner control points ($P_{0,0}$, $P_{3,0}$, $P_{0,3}$, and $P_{3,3}$) will also be the four corners of the surface itself. Second, the control points exhibit global control over the surface, so moving one control point will change the shape of the entire surface (Figure 4.15). Third, the lines from the corner control points to the adjacent control points in the u and v direction are tangent to the surface in those directions. The lines between $P_{0,0}$ and $P_{1,0}$ and between $P_{0,0}$ and $P_{0,1}$ are both tangent to the surface at $P_{0,0}$. This property is very useful because the cross-product of these two lines or vectors gives the normal to the surface at that corner.

Recall that Bézier curves exhibit varying degrees of continuity:

1. If the last control point of curve C_1 and the first control point of C_2 are the same, the two curves will meet at that point (G^0 continuity).
2. If condition 1 holds, and the line between the last two control points of C_1 is co-linear with the line between the first two control points of C_2, the join point will be continuous though the rate of curvature can be different on the two sides (G^1 continuity).
3. If conditions 1 and 2 hold and the distance between these control points are all the same, the join point will be continuous and the rate of curvature will be the same on the two sides (C^1 continuity).

When dealing with Bézier surfaces, the same conditions along the shared edge of two surfaces lead to the same level of continuity along that edge. These two-dimensional criteria are now imposed along the entire edge of two adjoining Bézier surfaces. If the control points in the v direction along the right edge of surface S_1 are the same as the control points along the left edge of surface S_2, the two surfaces will meet

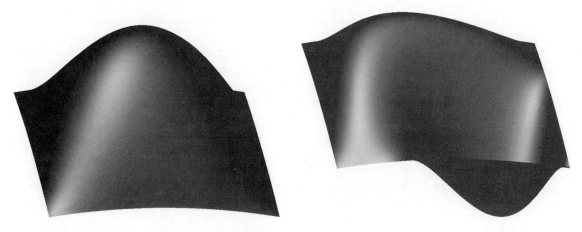

Figure 4.15 • The Bézier surface in Figure 4.14, with one control point moved

along that entire edge with at least G^0 continuity. Now, if the three points in the u direction centered at each of these shared control points are all on the same line, the surfaces will exhibit G^1 continuity along that shared edge. Lastly, if the distance between the control points in each set are the same (though they can be different distances for different sets of three), the shared edge will exhibit C^1 continuity.

Figure 4.6 showed that to preserve continuity across a join point, moving a control point on one side required a move of the control point on the other side in the opposite direction. The same is true of a Bézier surface. In this case, the change occurs with any of the four sets of points along a shared edge. If there are a four surfaces that share a corner point, changes around that corner point will propagate to all three of the other surfaces. To limit the impact of a change, these surfaces can be subdivided, but the subdivision should be done equivalently along all of the shared sides. For example, if a Bézier surface is divided in half "horizontally," any patches that meet along the left and right sides should also be divided horizontally to allow changes to properly propagate across the object.

4.4.2 B-spline surfaces

B-spline surfaces are constructed from curves in the same way that Bézier surfaces are. We again have a two-dimensional grid of control points that determine the shape of the B-spline surface. This grid of points is used with the B-spline blending functions in two directions:

$$S(u, v) = \sum_{i=0}^{N-1} \sum_{j=0}^{N-1} B_i(u - i) * B_j(v - j) * P_{i,j} \tag{4.17}$$

All of the things that were discussed relative to B-spline curves also apply to B-spline surfaces. A surface is extended by adding a control point to each of the curves that run in that direction. Beginning with a grid of control points that is four by four, extending this surface requires four additional points to make the grid four by five control points. To extend the surface in the other direction, an additional five control points are needed so that the grid becomes five by five control points. The B-spline surface will exhibit local control in the u and v directions. Moving one control point will change the surface shape in a small neighborhood around the control point that was moved.

4.5 Sweeping Surfaces

One way to create an object is to sweep or rotate a curve representing the profile of the object. For example, a cylinder can be created by sweeping a circle along a straight line (Figure 4.16). Objects can also be created by sweeping along curves, or changing the size of the object being swept. The act of sweeping the circle is really

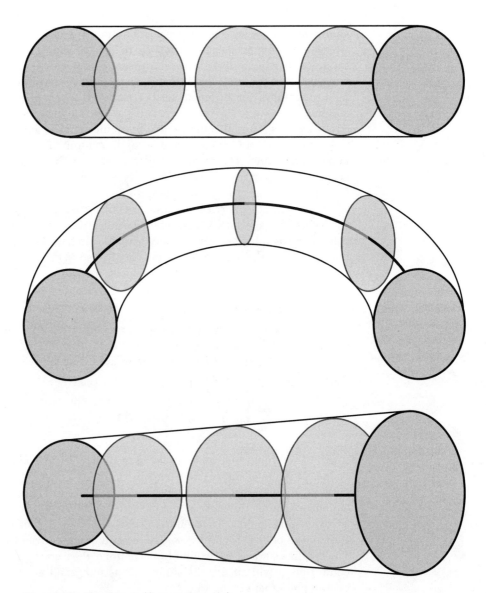

Figure 4.16 • Objects created by sweeping a circle

just translations that move the circle in the direction of the straight line. The pawn in Chapter 2 was produced using this sweeping technique. Figure 4.17 shows the curve that served as the silhouette that was rotated around the y axis to produce this object.

The sweep direction can be determined by a circle, straight line, Bézier curve, or B-spline. In doing all of these sweeps, the definition of the silhouette creates an x, y, and z coordinate system. To sweep the silhouette, the z axis is aligned with the tangent to the curve, and y axis points in the up direction. As the silhouette is moved along the curve, it is actually being transformed so that the z axis and the direction of the tangent continue to be aligned. Rotations around the z axis can also be applied, which will have the effect of changing the direction of "up" (the y axis), thus spinning the silhouette around the curve direction. Scaling operations can also be applied to change the size of the silhouette as it is swept along the curve. For example, a screw could be created by having a silhouette that is a circle with a bump to create the threads. This silhouette will be swept along a straight line while the silhouette is rotated. This causes the threads to wind around the screw along its length. A wood screw is handled similarly, but in this case, a scaling operation is also included because a wood screw tapers to a sharp point.

As the silhouette is swept along the curve, periodic snapshots of the silhouette are taken to be used to build up the object surface. Consider the following simple example. Say that the silhouette is a Bézier curve with four control points, and the sweeping curve is just the z axis. The location of the four control points are captured, which will serve as the first set of control points for the surface. Now, the curve is translated along the z axis about one third the total distance, and the new locations of the silhouette control points are captured. These are the second set of four control points for the surface. This process is repeated two more times to get the rest of the sixteen points needed for the Bézier surface. When you sweep the silhouette a longer distance, snapshots can be taken more frequently to create multiple Bézier patches that together form the object surface.

In the case of the pawn shape in Chapter 2, the silhouette in Figure 4.17 was rotated 30° between each capture. This resulted in 12 surfaces—four each for the top, middle, and bottom sections of the pawn.

4.6 Rendering Surfaces

There are two approaches that can be used to render parametric surfaces (Lane80). The surface can be subdivided into small pieces and each of these pieces is then rendered as a planar patch. A second alternative is to render the surface directly. It might seem that extra work is being done by subdividing the surfaces, but it can be less computationally complex to subdivide and render small planar patches than to render the surfaces directly. All of the shaded pawn images in Chapter 2 used this method. Each Bézier surface was subdivided eight times in each direction, giving 64 patches per Bézier surface. Thus, there were 768 quadrilateral patches that were rendered in each of these images.

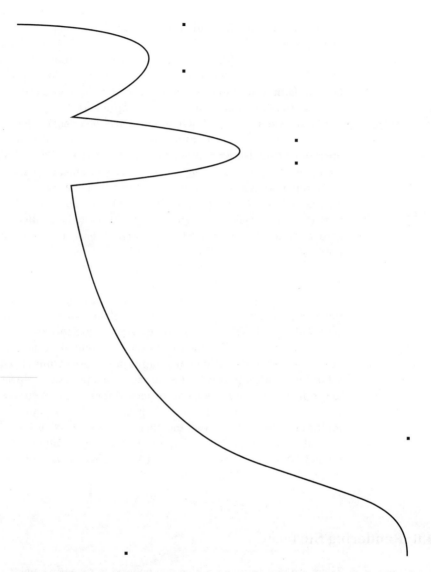

Figure 4.17 • The three Bézier curves (and their control points) that are the silhouette for the pawn in Chapter 2 (see Color Plate 4.6)

4.6.1 Conversion to patches

The discussion of conversion to patches assumes the use of Bézier surfaces. One method for rendering Bézier surfaces is to subdivide until the subsurfaces are of a reasonably small size or are relatively flat. When this occurs, the surface can be approximated by triangular or quadrilateral planes that have vertices located at the corners of the surface. A rendering of the surface is approximated by rendering the set of planes based on the points found in the subdivisions (Lane79 and Lane80). The cross-product of the tangent vectors (the difference between the corner and adjacent control points) at the corners gives the actual surface normal at that location. These actual normal vectors can be used with the shading method to improve the appearance of the approximation.

A test for the size of the patch can look at the distance between the control points in the opposite corners of the surface, and if it is below some threshold, planar patches can be used to approximate the surface. A problem with this technique, however, is that even though the corners of the surface are close together, the other control points can be positioned far away. This creates a large bubble on the surface, making a planar patch defined by the corners a very poor approximation.

A test of the surface curvature provides a better determination to see if it is flat enough for approximation by a plane. In this case, three of the corner control points are used to define a plane. The distance of the other 13 control points to this plane are calculated.[4] If all of these distances fall below some threshold, the corner control points can be used to define planar patches that are a good approximation of the surface. If the distances are above the threshold, the surface still has curvature that is high enough that it needs to be subdivided at least one more time before a planar patch is a reasonable approximation. There are more efficient tests for flatness, for example (Lane79). Once all the distances are below a reasonably chosen threshold, approximating the surface by a quadrilateral patch or two triangular patches, defined from the four corner control points, should produce a reasonable result.

4.6.2 Direct rendering

When scan converting a planar patch, the points along the edge of the object where the current scan line of the image intersected are easily determined. The rest of the values for this scan line are found by linearly interpolating between these values. Linear interpolation works because for a planar patch the path on the surface between two edge points is a straight line. This process is not as simple when it comes to parametrically defined patches because there is not an easy representation of the patch edges, and the curvature of the patch makes it more difficult to determine points along the curve between the edges. Further, a curved surface can either curve back and obstruct itself or have bumps that obscure other parts or even edges of the surface. The edges of these bumps are called silhouette edges and add to the complexity of the process. Because of this we will now only briefly look at some of the issues in direct rendering. Additional details can be found in (Blinn78a) and (Blinn78b). Even this brief discussion will show that direct rendering is so complex

---

[4]See appendix A for equations for this calculation.

that subdividing and approximating curved surfaces is a more common approach to rendering.

Direct rendering of a surface requires the determination of where the surface intersects each scan line. Consider height y_s in the image. A scan conversion algorithm begins by finding where the scan line intersects the edges of the patch. The edges of the patch occur when either of the two parametric parameters u or v is zero or one. Specifically, these are the solutions to the equations $y_s = Y(0, v)$; $y_s = Y(1, v)$; $y_s = Y(u, 0)$; and $y_s = Y(u, 1)$, where $Y(u, v)$ is the y component of the surface equation (4.16) or (4.17). If the scan line does not intersect any of these edges, there will either be no solution to the equation, or the solution will be outside of the range [0.0, 1.0].

The next step is to identify any silhouette edges by solving the equations $y_s = Y(u, v)$ and $N_z(u, v) = 0$, where $N_z(u, v)$ calculates the z component of the normal at the point (u, v) on the patch. This gives two equations with two unknowns, so numeric and algebraic methods can be used to find the values for u and v that satisfy these equations. The first equation identifies those points on the surface that intersect with the current scan line. The second equation narrows down that collection of points to those that have a normal with a z component of zero, which is where the point is on the silhouette.

Envision a point on the front side of a bump in the surface. The normal at that point faces toward the viewer, and in a right-handed coordinate system it has a z component that is positive. Moving along the surface toward the silhouette edge of the bump, the normal will begin to turn away, which means that the z component will become smaller. Imagine points on the back of the bump. Those will have a normal with a negative z component. The point where the z component goes from being positive (front side) to negative (back side) is where the silhouette edge is. This is where the z component of the normal is zero.

Once all locations where the current scan line intersects with the surface are identified, these locations define a collection of spans based on the intersections of the surface edges and silhouette edges. Stepping through these x locations gives points (x_s, y_s). For each one, the equations $x_s = X(u, v)$ and $y_s = Y(u, v)$ are solved. The values determined for u and v from these equations are then used with the surface definition to find the z coordinate and the surface normal to use in the shading calculation.

This process involves a lot of calculations, so it is easier to perform repeated subdivisions of the surface, test them for surface flatness, and then render the appropriate planar patch approximations.

4.7 The OpenGL Way

Bézier curves and surfaces are included in OpenGL, and NURBS are part of the GLU. NURBS routines are really just an interface that uses the OpenGL Bézier curve and surface capabilities. Using this interface requires a good understanding of

NURBS. Because we have not spent much time exploring NURBS, we will not delve into this OpenGL feature. This feature is mentioned so that if your application needs NURBS curves and surfaces, you will be aware that OpenGL supports them.

Bézier curves and surfaces are supported through a capability called an evaluator. These evaluators use the blending functions in equations (4.2). OpenGL supports any order of polynomials up to a maximum that should be at least eight, but is dependent on the particular OpenGL implementation. To determine the maximum order, include the call, `glGetIntegerv(GL_MAX_EVAL_ORDER, &order)`. The second parameter is the address of an integer variable where the answer will be returned.

4.7.1 Bézier curves

The first step is to set up the control points for the Bézier curve by calling the `glMap1f` or `glMap1d` routine. These routines take six parameters. The first is a constant that tells OpenGL the number of coordinates for each control point and can be either `GL_MAP1_VERTEX_3` or `GL_MAP1_VERTEX_4`, depending on whether the control points specify (x, y, z) or (x, y, z, w). The next two parameters are floats (or doubles) that define the range of the curve parameter t. The text has given these in the range [0.0, 1.0], but OpenGL allows a larger or smaller range to be used. The next parameter is an integer called the stride. The stride tells OpenGL how many values there are in the control point array between the start of two consecutive control points. With just one set of control points in the array, the stride will be 3 (or 4 if the w coordinate is included). If the control points are embedded in an array with other data, the stride can be larger. For example, if the array held the x, y, and z coordinates for a control point followed by two additional floating point (or double) values, the stride would have a value of 5, because a new control point starts every five locations in the array. In any case, the three or four coordinates for each control point must be in consecutive locations of the array. The fifth parameter is just the order of the Bézier curve, which is one greater than the degree and is the same as the number of control points specified. The last parameter is the array that contains the control points. This array is copied as part of the call to `glMap1*`, so any changes made to this array after the routine is called will not influence the curve drawn.

Once these parameters have been specified for the evaluator, the evaluator is enabled with the call `glEnable(GL_MAP1_VERTEX_3)` or `glEnable(GL_MAP1_VERTEX_4)`. The last step is to draw the curve, which can be done in two ways. The first makes repeated calls to `glEvalCoord1f` or `glEvalCoord1d` inside a `glBegin/glEnd` pair. The call to `glEvalCoord1*` takes a parameter of type float or double that is the parameter t value for the Bézier curve. This routine calculates the appropriate location on the Bézier curve and issues the proper `glVertex*` command. The following C code fragment shows how these routines are used to draw a Bézier curve using 41 t values spaced evenly in the range [0, 1]:

```
GLfloat controlPoints[4][3];

void init(void)
{
    glClearColor(0.0, 0.0, 0.0, 0.0);
    glShadeModel(GL_SMOOTH);
    glMap1f(GL_MAP1_VERTEX_3, 0.0, 1.0, 3, 4, controlPoints);
    glEnable(GL_MAP1_VERTEX_3);
}

void display(void)
{
    int i;
    glClear(GL_COLOR_BUFFER_BIT);
    glColor3f(1.0, 1.0, 1.0);
    glBegin(GL_LINE_STRIP);
        for (i = 0; i <= 40; i++)
            glEvalCoord1f(i/40.0);
    glEnd();
    glFlush();
}
```

The second way to draw the Bézier curve is to use a map grid, which is a set of evenly spaced parameter values for the curve. The grid is set up with a call to glMapGrid1f or glMapGrid1d. These routines have three parameters: The first is the number of partitions of the interval and the other two are the ranges of the parameter value. The call glMapGrid1f(40, 0.0, 1.0) has the effect of setting up the 41 values that were used in the loop in the preceding code fragment. To render this line, instead of the using the glBegin/glEnd pair and the loop, only a single call glEvalMesh1(GL_LINE, 0, 40) is needed, where the 0 and 40 specify the range of parameter value locations in the grid set up. The call glEvalMesh1(GL_LINE, 0, 20) draws the curve for parameter values in just the range [0, 0.5]. With this alternative method, the code segment becomes:

```
GLfloat controlPoints[4][3];

void init(void)
{
    glClearColor(0.0, 0.0, 0.0, 0.0);
    glShadeModel(GL_SMOOTH);
    glMap1f(GL_MAP1_VERTEX_3, 0.0, 1.0, 3, 4, controlPoints);
    glEnable(GL_MAP1_VERTEX_3);
    glMapGrid1f(40, 0.0, 1.0);
}
```

```
void display(void)
{
   int i;
   glClear(GL_COLOR_BUFFER_BIT);
   glColor3f(1.0, 1.0, 1.0);
   glEvalMesh(GL_LINE, 0, 40);
   glFlush();
}
```

4.7.2 Bézier surfaces

Bézier surfaces work in the same way as Bézier curves, but in two dimensions. A Bézier surface is set up with the glMap2* routine. This routine takes as its first parameter the constant GL_MAP2_VERTEX_*, where '*' is 3 or 4. Next, there are two sets of the four parameters from the curve version, namely, the lower and upper range of the parameter, the stride, and the order. This is included twice—once for the u direction and once for the v direction. The last parameter is the array holding the control point values.

As in the case of a Bézier curve, once the map is set up it needs to be enabled with a call to glEnable(GL_MAP2_VERTEX_*). The surface is rendered by using a collection of calls to the glEvalCoord2 routine as was done in the case of a curve. A code fragment to accomplish this is:

```
GLfloat controlPoints[4][4][3];

void init(void)
{
   glClearColor(0.0, 0.0, 0.0, 0.0);
   glShadeModel(GL_SMOOTH);
   // the first stride is 4 because those points are adjacent
   // the second stride is 12 because there are 12 control
   // points in each "row" of the control point grid.
   glMap2f(GL_MAP2_VERTEX_3, 0.0, 1.0, 3, 4, 0, 1, 12, 4, controlPoints);
   glEnable(GL_MAP2_VERTEX_3);
}

void display(void)
{
   int i, j;
   glClear(GL_COLOR_BUFFER_BIT);
   glColor3f(1.0, 1.0, 1.0);
   for (i = 0; i < 40; i++)
   {
      glBegin(GL_QUAD_STRIP);
```

```
        for (j = 0; j <= 40; j++)
        {
            glEvalCoord2f(i/40.0, j/40.0);
            glEvalCoord2f((i+1)/40.0, j/40.0);
        }
      glEnd();
    }
    glFlush();
}
```

As in the case of a Bézier curve, this process is much easier if OpenGL's mesh evaluation is used. For a surface, a two-dimensional grid of points is set up with a call to the routine glMapGird2*. A call to glEvalMesh2 is used instead of the double loop. This alternative code fragment is:

```
GLfloat controlPoints[4][4][3];

void init(void)
{
    glClearColor(0.0, 0.0, 0.0, 0.0);
    glShadeModel(GL_SMOOTH);
    // the first stride is 4 because those points are adjacent
    // the second stride is 12 because there are 12 control
    // points in each "row" of the control point grid.
    glMap2f(GL_MAP2_VERTEX_3, 0.0, 1.0, 3, 4, 0, 1, 12, 4, controlPoints);
    glEnable(GL_MAP2_VERTEX_3);
    glMapGrid2f(40, 0.0, 1.0, 40, 0.0, 1.0);
}

void display(void)
{
    int i, j;
    glClear(GL_COLOR_BUFFER_BIT);
    glColor3f(1.0, 1.0, 1.0);
    glEvalMesh2(GL_FILL, 0, 40, 0, 40);
    glFlush();
}
```

4.8 Projects

Add the ability to shade Bézier surfaces to your program.

chapter 5

Visibility

There have been two assumptions in previous chapters. The first assumption is that objects are completely within the scene. Objects that are either partially or totally to the left, right, above, or below the viewing volume have not yet been discussed. The second assumption is that all objects are completely visible. Objects that overlap—causing an object that is farther away to be partially or wholly blocked—have also not been discussed. One quick look around and you will realize that you can only see part of the world, and that there are a lot of objects that obscure your view of other things. Consider the two images in Figure 5.1. In the first image, the real window is farther from the camera and so less of the world is visible than the second image where the window is closer to the camera. The perspective inherent in this situation causes the objects in the first image to appear larger. The reason for this is shown graphically in Figure 5.2. When the window is farther from the viewpoint (the top image in Figure 5.2), the angle of the view volume frustum is smaller so each object will project onto a larger area of the window. When the window is closer to the viewpoint (the bottom image in Figure 5.2), the angle of the view volume frustum is wider so each object will project onto a smaller area of the window. The images in Figure 5.1 also show the impact of obstruction, as closer buildings block the view of more distant buildings. These obstructions give cues to the relative depths of the objects.

This chapter looks at some of the techniques that can be used to handle visibility issues for the clipping window and obstruction by other objects. Some of the techniques discussed work in the final image space. This means that the determi-

Figure 5.1 • Real windows and obstruction (see Color Plate 5.1)

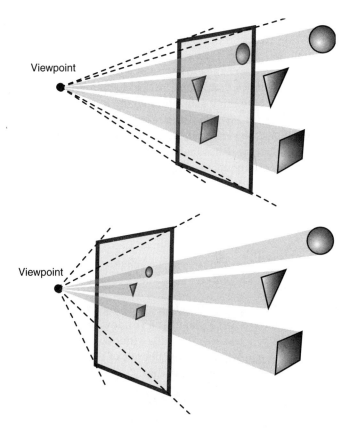

Figure 5.2 • The relationship between the viewpoint and window locations, and how objects project into the window

nation is done once the objects have been projected into two dimensions. Other techniques work in the scene space, which means that clipping and visibility determinations are done in the three-dimensional space where the scene is defined.

Another categorization is based on whether the technique requires additional space or additional compute time. In the early days of computer graphics, this was a real choice because computers typically had much less memory and were much slower than computers today. Today, computers are significantly faster and have significantly more memory. Because of this some of the techniques discussed in this chapter are now built into the rendering firmware on graphics cards. All of these algorithms, however, are still important to graphics programmers because they can have application in other rendering techniques. For example, clipping algorithms have application in radiosity, and hidden surface algorithms have application in shadowing.

The discussion in this chapter assumes that the viewpoint is at the origin, and that the view direction is parallel to the z axis pointing in the negative z direction. These assumptions do not restrict or limit what can be done, because transformations can be used to change to any view location and direction. For example, if the scene is viewed from the right side, the viewpoint might be at the location (100, 0, 0), facing parallel to the x axis, and looking in the negative x direction. A transformation that rotates 90° about the y axis and then translates −100 units in the z direction moves the viewpoint to the origin and the view direction along the negative z axis. Applying that transformation to all of the objects in the scene will move them so that using these clipping, hidden surface, and projection methods will now produce the image of the scene from the right side.

This chapter begins with a look at clipping algorithms that divide objects into pieces that are entirely inside or outside of the viewing area. It then looks at algorithms that can be used to solve the hidden surface problem.

5.1 Clipping

The idea of clipping is that there is a rectangular window that defines the portion of the scene that is visible, much as a window in a wall defines what portion of the outside world can be seen. For this window, there is a minimum and maximum value in both x and y that give the bounds of the window. For a location (x, y) to be visible, it must satisfy the inequalities:

$$x_{min} \leq x \leq x_{max} \quad \text{and} \quad y_{min} \leq y \leq y_{max}$$

It is possible to solve this problem by not worrying about it. Instead all of the points on every object are scan converted and projected, and then those points that project outside of the viewport are ignored. The rendering calculations are only done for those points that are in view. This, however, can be quite time consuming for scenes with many objects that have only a few of them within view because many calculations will be done for objects that do not appear in the result.

This section instead looks at an algorithm that can be used to quickly discard objects and parts of objects that lie outside of the view. The algorithm works on the entire polygon at once, producing a new vertex list for the portion within view.

5.1.1 Sutherland-Hodgeman clipping algorithm

The Sutherland-Hodgeman algorithm (Sutherland74a) was originally designed to clip objects against a two-dimensional window, but it can also be used to clip against a three-dimensional view volume. This algorithm clips the entire polygon against one boundary of the view volume at a time. Each boundary of the view volume divides the space into two parts—the side inside the view volume and the side outside the view volume (Figure 5.3a). By clipping against the left boundary of the view volume, the algorithm eliminates all of the parts of the polygon that fall to the left of this side (Figure 5.3b). Next, the new polygon is clipped against the top boundary and all of the parts of the polygon that are above the top side of the view volume are eliminated. This continues against all of the remaining boundaries and the final result is the visible part of the initial polygon. This algorithm can also be used to clip against a hither and yon plane as well. A hither plane is used to clip objects that are too close to the viewer as well as those behind the viewer. A yon plane is used to clip objects that are too far away to be seen by the viewer.

This algorithm takes as input a sequence of vertices for the polygon and a boundary to clip against, and it outputs a sequence of vertices for the resulting clipped polygon. This algorithm would then be called a number of times for each of the boundaries of the viewing volume, with the polygon that results from one pass being the input polygon for the next pass.

There are four possibilities for each edge of a polygon: It is entirely inside relative to the clip boundary; it is entirely outside relative to the clip boundary; it passes from inside the clip boundary to outside the clip boundary; and it passes from outside the clip boundary to inside the clip boundary. This algorithm moves around the edges of the polygon beginning with the edge between the last and first vertices. On each pass, it checks to see if the ending point of the edge is inside the clip boundary and thus should be part of the new polygon. Additionally, it checks to see if the edge crosses the clip boundary, which means that the intersection point is also a vertex of the new polygon.

The following C code fragment is an implementation of the Sutherland-Hodgeman algorithm. This algorithm clips against one of the boundaries of the view volume.

```c
void polygonClip(int countIn, Vertex verticesIn[],
            int countOut, Vertex verticesOut[], Boundary border)
{
    int j;
    Vertex tempVertex;

    countOut = 0;
    // use the last vertex here to get things started
    firstVertex = verticesIn[countIn-1];
    for (j = 0; j < countIn; j++)
    {
        secondVertex = verticesIn[j];
        if inside(secondVertex, border)
            if inside(firstVertex, border)
                // both vertices are inside so add the second
                // to the new vertex list
                verticesOut[countOut++] = secondVertex;
            else
            {
```

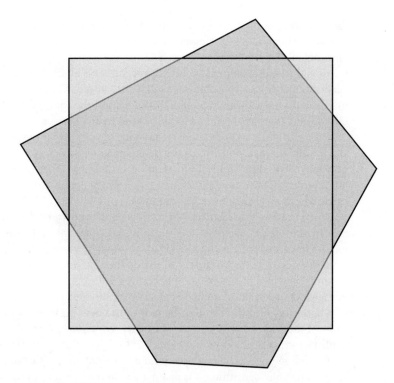

Figure 5.3a • The original polygon and the square clipping window

```
                    // the first vertex is outside but the second is inside
                    // the edge passes from outside to inside the clip border
                    // so find the intersection point and add that and
                    // the second vertex to the new vertex list
                    tempVertex = intersect(firstVertex, secondVertex, border);
                    verticesOut[countOut++] = tempVertex;
                    verticesOut[countOut++] = secondVertex;
                }
            else
                if inside(firstVertex, border)
                {
                    // the first vertex is inside and the second is outside
                    // the edge passes from inside to outside the clip border
                    // so find the intersection point and add only that point
                    // to the new vertex list
                    tempVertex = intersect(firstVertex, secondVertex, border);
                    verticesOut[countOut++] = tempVertex;
                }
```

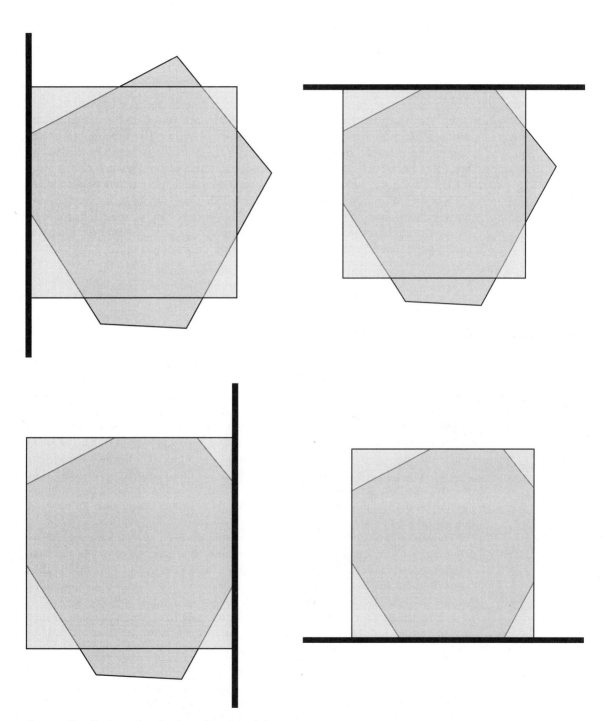

Figure 5.3b • Clipping against the view volume boundaries

```
        // move onto the next vertex
        firstVertex = secondVertex;
    }
}
```

In this algorithm, the function `inside` will return true if the vertex is on the inside of the boundary, and will return false otherwise. The function `intersect` returns the location where the line between the first two parameters crosses the boundary. Recall that the mathematical equation for a plane is given by $A * x + B * y + C * z + D = 0$, where A, B, C, and D are constants that define the plane and (A, B, C) is the unit normal vector of the plane. This plane can be represented by the homogeneous coordinate P = (A, B, C, D). The two vertices, V_0 and V_1, can also be represented in homogeneous coordinates. Once this is done, the intersection point can be determined by the following algorithm:[1]

```
d₀ = V₀ · P
d₁ = V₁ · P
t = d₀ / (d₁ - d₀)
intersect = (1 - t) * V₀ + t * V₁
```

The `polygonClip` algorithm tests each edge of the polygon. If both vertices are outside, nothing is done because that part of the polygon is being clipped off. If the both vertices are inside the boundary, the second vertex is output. If the first vertex is inside the boundary but the second vertex is outside, the point where the edge crosses the boundary is found and outputted. On a later pass, there will be a case where the first vertex is outside but the second vertex is inside. Again the point where the edge crosses the boundary is found and outputted as the next vertex. The second vertex, inside the window, is output as another vertex from this edge. The new intersection point appears in the vertex list immediately following the intersection point from the edge that crossed from the inside to the outside. This creates an edge along the boundary of the view volume.

The Sutherland-Hodgeman clipping algorithm has been discussed as applying to clipping polygons against a regular view volume—but there is nothing in the algorithm that mandates it. In fact, this algorithm can be used to clip a polygon against any polygonal shape. For example, a polygon can be clipped against an octagon by calling `polygonClip` eight times with each of the eight sides of the octagon. This comes in handy because this algorithm can be used to clip one polygon against another for the hidden surface algorithms in the next section.

---

[1]The value of t can also be inspected to determine where the vertices are in relation to the boundary plane. If t is in the range [0, 1], the vertices are on opposite sides of the plane. If t is outside of this range both points are on the same side of the boundary.

5.2 The Hidden Surface Problem

Clipping algorithms will discard objects or parts of objects that are outside of the viewing volume, but that does not solve the problem of one object blocking the view of another object. Instead, hidden surface algorithms deal with this problem. There are a number of different approaches that can be taken to solving the hidden surface problem. Sutherland, Sproull, and Schumacker (Sutherland74b) looked at and classified some of the early solutions to this problem.

One broad classification is between hidden surface removal and visible surface determination. In the first case, the algorithm attempts to determine which surfaces cannot be seen from the viewpoint, and those are not rendered. In the second case, the algorithm attempts to determine which surfaces are visible and should be rendered. The difference between these two approaches is very subtle and so the exact classification is not critical. Back face elimination is an example of hidden surface removal and Warnock's algorithm is an example of visible surface determination.

A second type of classification is based on where the method is applied. There are algorithms that work in the scene space and others that work in the final image space. Algorithms that work in the scene space will classify objects or subdivide the scene space to distinguish the relative depth of the objects. These algorithms work before any viewing transformations or projections and, therefore, can be used for many different views of the scene. Other algorithms work in the final image space. Those make the determination of what appears in the final image with the incorporation of a specific set of viewing transformations and a projection. Because a projection converts all depths to that of the clipping window, these image space algorithms preserve the depth in some matter for proper visibility determination. Binary space partitioning trees are an example of a scene space technique and a z buffer is an example of an image space technique.

The rest of this chapter will look at a number of different methods for solving the hidden surface problem. Though these techniques are presented independently, they can also be combined to improve efficiency. For example, back face elimination can be combined with any of the other techniques because it will quickly remove surfaces that cannot be seen. Those removed patches do not need to be processed by the other visibility algorithm, thereby improving the speed with which it completes its work.

5.2.1 Painter's algorithm

The most simple of the hidden surface techniques is the painter's algorithm. This algorithm is attractive because it merely involves sorting the objects according to their depth and then rendering. However, the simplicity in this process means that there are situations that this algorithm will not render properly.

Imagine a painter creating a picture of a landscape. The painter paints all of the objects in the distance and then paints the objects that are closer (Figure 5.4). As

Figure 5.4 • The painter's algorithm

each new object is painted, the paint just applied will cover over the paint used to draw the objects in back. If all objects are painted from the farthest to the closest, the final result is an accurate image of the scene.

The painter's algorithm does the same thing but with pixels instead of paint. The objects are sorted based on the point on the object that is farthest away. In a right-hand coordinate system, the sorting is done in increasing order because a more negative z value indicates an object that is farther away. In a left-handed coordinate system, the sort would be in decreasing order because a more positive z value indicates an object that is farther away.

Once the objects are ordered, they are rendered in the order that they appear in the list. The object most distant is rendered first, and the closest object is rendered last. When objects that partially or totally block earlier objects are reached in the list, they will just be rendered over the more distant objects. This algorithm renders all objects even if they are not visible in the final scene.

The painter's algorithm only considers the most distant point on each object when sorting them, which causes a problem when objects overlap. Consider the three patches shown in Figure 5.5. Looking at the top half of this figure shows, the patch labeled A is behind patch B but in front of patch C, giving a rendering order of C, A, and B. However, the right of the figure indicates an order of A, B, and C and the left indicates an order of B, C, and A. The painter's algorithm chooses one of

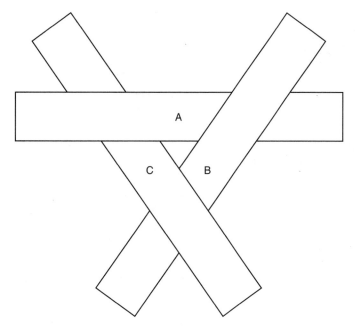

Figure 5.5 • Three overlapping objects

these orderings based on the farthest point on each of these patches, but just rendering the three patches in any one of these orderings will produce the wrong result because of the overlap.

5.2.2 Depth-sort algorithm

The problem identified in Figure 5.5 can be quickly solved by dividing any of the three patches in half. For example, splitting patch A into two parts allows the image to be rendered in the order of A_{right}, B, C, and then A_{left} (Figure 5.6) This problem is quite easily found by looking for instances where two objects have z value ranges that overlap. Then if any of these objects also have x and y coordinate ranges that overlap, the potential for a problem exists. In that case, the objects can be split to resolve any ambiguities. This split can be done using an edge of one polygon to clip the other into two pieces.

The depth-sort algorithm (Newell72) is an improved version of the painter's algorithm that handles the need to split polygons by including a set of five tests. These tests find potential problems that require one or more of the patches to be split.

The depth-sort algorithm first sorts the polygons in order of decreasing distance the same as the painter's algorithm. Comparisons of the polygons are then done to remove problem situations. Specifically, the farthest polygon (P) is compared with

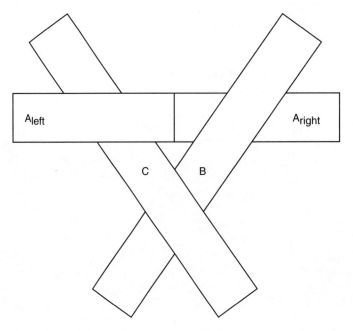

Figure 5.6 • Splitting polygons to remove ambiguity

the next few polygons until all that overlap the z range of P are found. The algorithm will now perform five tests for each polygon T that overlaps z values with P.

1. Do the polygons overlap in x?
2. Do the polygons overlap in y?
3. Are P and the viewpoint on the same side of the plane containing T?
4. Are T and the viewpoint on the opposite sides of the plane containing P?
5. Do the projections of P and T overlap in the z = 0 plane?

If any of these tests returns an answer of "no," P can be rendered before T and the algorithm checks P against the next polygon that overlaps in z. If all of these tests answer "yes," it is possible that P obscures T even though it appears earlier in the sorted list. Tests 3 and 4 are repeated with the roles of P and T reversed. If either of these returns "no," the order of P and T are reversed in the list, and the algorithm begins again trying to render T as the next polygon. If both of these two new tests answer "yes," either P or T needs to be subdivided.

The ordering of these tests is significant. The first two tests can be done with the least amount of work, where later tests are more computationally expensive. Using this ordering means that most insignificant overlaps in z value can be quickly resolved.

The painter's and depth-sort algorithms require additional time for the sorting of the patches; for testing and possibly splitting the patches; and for rendering objects that might not be seen when the entire scene is complete.

5.2.3 Z-buffer

The frame buffer is the place in the hardware where the image being displayed on the screen is written. The frame buffer has one location for each pixel on the screen, and that location will hold values for the red, green, and blue intensities at those points. A z-buffer (Catmull74), also called a depth buffer, is also a block of memory of the same size as the screen (or image being rendered) and it contains a single value related to the depth of the object displayed at each pixel. Specifically, the z-buffer holds the distance to the object is that is being displayed at each pixel in the image. To render the next object, it is scan converted as usual, but before rendering, the distance of each point is checked against the value stored in the z-buffer for that location. This compares the distance of the new object with the distance of the object already displayed at that point. If the new object is closer, the point is rendered, the new color is put into the frame buffer, and the new depth is put into the z-buffer. But if the new object is farther away, one of the objects already rendered is closer and so the current point is skipped. This process needs to be done for each location in the new object, because that object can only be partially blocked.

In the past, computers had limited memory and so the cost of implementing a z-buffer was significant. Today, however, graphics cards come with a built-in z-buffer, and firmware on the card is designed to efficiently use this z-buffer. The z-buffer technique is discussed because it also has application when adding shadows to images.

The comparison of an object's depth with the z-buffer values needs to be done on a pixel by pixel basis because an object can be only partially obscured. Incorporating a z-buffer into the rendering algorithms only requires a small change. Once the location on the object has been determined for a particular pixel location, the z value is compared with the value stored in the z-buffer. If the z value is closer than the z-buffer value, the rendering is done, but if the z value is farther than the z-buffer value, nothing is done and the algorithm moves onto the next point. A general z-buffer algorithm would be:

```
for (i = 0; i < rows; i++)
    for (j = 0; j < columns; j++)
        zBuffer[i, j] = maxDistance;

for every object
    for every pixel in the object
    {
        calculate the (x, y, z) location
        if (z is closer than zBuffer[x, y])
        {
            determine the color of (x, y, z)
            display the color at (x, y)
            zBuffer[x, y] = z;
        }
    }
```

An additional value to the z-buffer algorithm is that it allows the compositing of multiple images with proper obstruction. The objects in the scene can be divided into N groups and different computers can generate an image for each of the N groups. Each computer stores both the image and the z-buffer. Each of the N images will show the proper obstruction among the objects in that group. The images can be quickly combined by comparing z-buffer values for each of the N images. For each location of the final image, the z-buffer that contains the smallest depth is connected with the image that contains the color of the object that is closest. The color in that image is copied to the final image. This produces the same result as doing one rendering with all of the objects but it will be faster because N renderings are being done in parallel.

Space efficiency can still be a concern with z-buffer techniques. Consider a computer screen that is 1,600 by 1,200 pixels. Using an array of floating point numbers for the z-buffer would require 7.5 MB to 15 MB of memory depending on the precision of a floating point number. That much space can easily be declared in the program, but the program might slow down noticeably because of virtual memory swapping done by the operating system. Additionally, the precision available with the floating point number might be greater than necessary for the scene. Where it is natural to declare a z-buffer to be an array of floats or doubles, scaling the depth values into integers might work just as well. For example, if the range of z values is about 600 units, depths can be stored to a precision of 0.01 by multiplying each value by 100 and then truncating to an integer before storing it. With this technique, the precision will be dependent on the size of the range of z values and with a large range there might not be enough precision once a conversion of this type is done. A careful analysis of the particular application would need to be done to see if there is benefit to using this technique.

• 5.2.4 Back face elimination

Consider some opaque object such as a book. When looking at the book, only part of it will be visible because the portion closer to you blocks your view of the part further away. When rendering this book, it is possible to save time by only rendering those portions that are closest to the viewpoint. Back face elimination provides a way to remove the back part of objects that are not visible.

Modeling objects produces descriptions for the entire outer surface of those objects. Part of that outer surface will face toward the viewpoint and part of it will face away from the viewpoint. Any surface that faces away from the viewpoint will not be visible because the surfaces that face toward the viewpoint are obscuring them. These surfaces that face away are called back facing and they can be eliminated because they would not be visible in the final image and they will not obscure any other object that is not already obscured by one of the front facing polygons. Removing these back faces will also not remove all of the obstructions of an object with itself because objects can still have one part obstructing another part. For example, eliminating the back faces of a coffee mug will not solve the obstruction of the cup by the handle.

A back face can be easily identified because it has a surface normal that points away from the viewer. Recall that the view direction is the direction from the view point to the surface. For a back facing polygon, the angle between the view direction and the surface normal will be less than 90°. For a front facing polygon, the angle between the view direction and the surface normal will be greater than 90° (Figure 5.7). One way to identify a back facing polygon is to take the dot product of the view direction and the surface normal and if the result is positive, the polygon is back facing. Because the view vector points in the opposite direction of the view direction, the dot product of the view vector and the surface normal will be negative for back facing polygons.

There is a quicker method than taking a dot product for each surface. This alternative is based on projecting onto a plane parallel to z = 0. In a parallel projection, the direction of projection for a right-handed coordinate system is (0, 0, −1). For the dot product of this vector and the surface normal to be positive, the z component of the surface normal must be negative. A simple comparison to check if the z component is negative will identify all back facing polygons. If using a perspective projection, first apply the projection transformation to the normal and then check to see if the new z component of the normal is negative.

• 5.2.5 Warnock's algorithm

Methods that handle the hidden surface problem through space subdivision exploit the concept of spatial coherence, which is the notion that areas located close

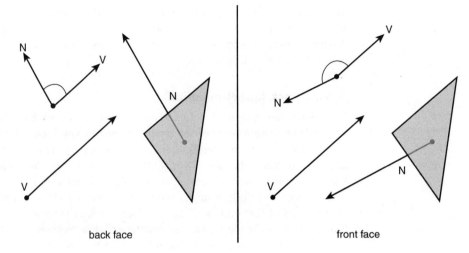

back face   front face

Figure 5.7 • Front and back facing polygons showing the relationship of the surface normal (**N**) and the view direction (**V**)

together in the image are highly likely to show the same object. Space subdivision divides areas until there is no ambiguity among object depths.

Warnock's algorithm (Warnock69) is an image space solution that subdivides the image space until the closest polygonal patch is uniquely identified for each region or until the subdivision reaches the pixel or subpixel level. A polygonal patch can be classified in one of four ways based on its relationship to a region of the image.

- Surrounding—the polygon surrounds the entire region (Figure 5.8a)
- Contained—the entire polygon is contained in the region (Figure 5.8b)
- Intersecting—the polygon partially overlaps the region (Figure 5.8c)
- Disjoint—the polygon does not intersect the region at all (Figure 5.8d)

There are a number of variations of Warnock's algorithm with the difference being how a simple region, one that can be rendered without further subdivision, is defined. One such definition of a simple region is as follows. An empty region is simple (all patches are disjoint), and can be rendered with the background color because there are no objects in that region. A region that has one polygonal patch associated with it (whether surrounding, contained, or intersecting) is also simple and the portion of the patch that overlaps with the region can be rendered. A region that has a patch that is surrounding and closer than all other patches is also simple, so the region can be rendered with the portion of the closer patch that overlaps. All other circumstances would require that the region be subdivided and the process would be repeated for each of the subregions.

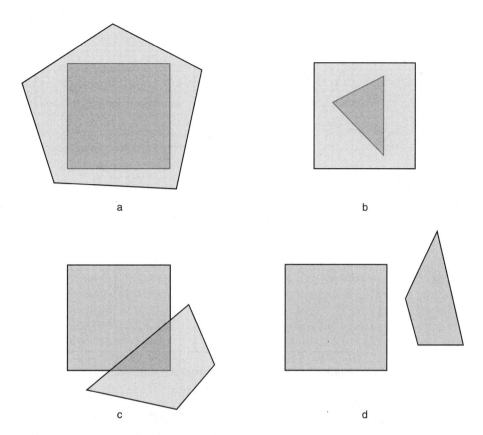

Figure 5.8 • Polygon and region relationships

Another variation is in how the subdivision of the region occurs. One version sub-divides the current space into four equal regions or quadrants. Figure 5.9 shows an example of the subdivision process for a couple of simple polygons using quadrants.

Improvements can be made to this process, if the subdivision creates unequal sized sections. Figure 5.10 shows that by choosing vertices of the polygons to decide on the subdivision, fewer overall regions can result. This can create larger regions that have at most one of the polygons connected with them.

Figures 5.9 and 5.10 are shown with just two polygons, which can give the impression that this method is very simple. If the number of polygons is more typical of a scene to be rendered, this becomes a complex process with a lot of subdivisions because of the large number of polygons present.

5.2.6 Binary space partitioning (BSP) trees

Algorithms that determine the proper obstruction between objects need to be able to quickly determine relative depths of objects or parts of objects. Where the tests

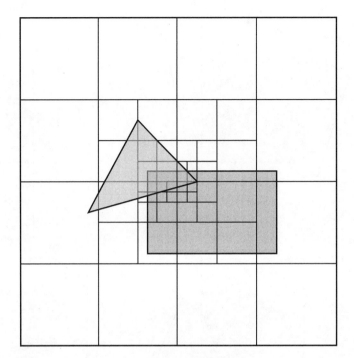

Figure 5.9 • Warnock space subdivision using quadrants

in image space algorithms do this sort of task, if the viewpoint and view direction are changed, the process has to be repeated from scratch. An alternative is to construct a Binary Space Partitioning (BSP) tree for the scene that that is independent of the viewpoint location and thus can be used to render from multiple viewpoints. The BSP tree will break up the scene into regions with the spatial relationship of those regions built into the tree. The space is subdivided until the object in each of the regions is unambiguous in its relationship to the objects in the other regions. For example, in Figure 5.11, the triangular patch T_1 is used to define a plane that divides the space with patch T_0 on one side and T_2 on the other.

The leaf node of the BSP tree where the viewpoint is located also holds the closest object. Moving up one node in the tree and down into the other leaf identifies the second closest object. The other child of each node up the tree will point to the collection of objects that is next farthest away.

BSP trees can also be used to speed up ray tracing and can be used in planning the motion of robots. Research has also been done into combining multiple Level of Detail models with BSP trees (Pan00). This section looks at the application of BSP trees to the problem of hidden surfaces.

The basic idea of BSP trees is that a plane will divide the space into two parts. Objects can be grouped based on whether they are on the positive or negative side

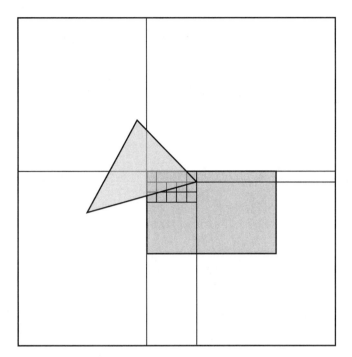

Figure 5.10 • Warnock subdivision based on vertices

of the plane, where the positive side is defined as the direction of the plane normal. These two regions can be further divided by additional planes. Figure 5.12 shows an example of this process. The space is first divided by the plane labeled A that has the normal vector pointing in the direction indicated in the figure. The direction of the normal vector indicates which side of plane A is considered the positive side. Objects 1 and 2 are on the positive side of plane A and so are in the left subtree of node A. Objects 3 and 4 are on the negative sides of plane A and so are in the right subtree of node A. The positive side has been further subdivided by plane C and the negative side has been divided by plane B. Figure 5.12 also shows the binary space partitioning tree that results from this partitioning.

Deciding where to place the planes that subdivide the space can be difficult. Planar faces of objects are an easy place to identify planes that can be used to subdivide the space. So a BSP tree uses planes that are defined by the faces of objects in the scene. In Figure 5.13, the front face of object 0 is used as the first division of space, and the right side face is used for the second division. After subdividing the space by the faces of object 0, one of the faces of object 1 can be used next.

The only remaining problem is that identified in Figure 5.5. If this scene was divided using the planes that the patches lie in, one of these planes would cut through one of the other objects. If that object is split into two parts based on this

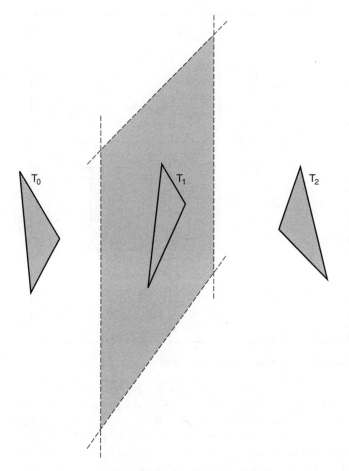

Figure 5.11 • Subdividing space based on one of the polygons

plane, the result could be used for an unambiguous back to front rendering as discussed. Figure 5.14 shows another such situation. In this case, the triangle abc is split along the line AB by the plane. The triangle ABb is on one side of the plane and the quadrilateral aBAc is on the other. To preserve the scene as triangular patches, the quadrilateral can be subdivided into the triangles cBA and aBc.

5.2.7 Polygon clipping

The Warnock algorithms clip polygons into pieces based on rectangular regions of the image, which will not be efficient in cases where polygons do not align nicely with these boundaries. This can be seen in Figures 5.9 and 5.10 where there are a large number of regions along diagonal boundaries of the triangle. The Weiler-Atherton algorithm (Weiler77) improves on this by clipping polygons against each

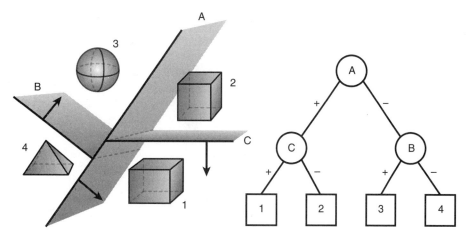

Figure 5.12 • Binary Space Partitioning (BSP)

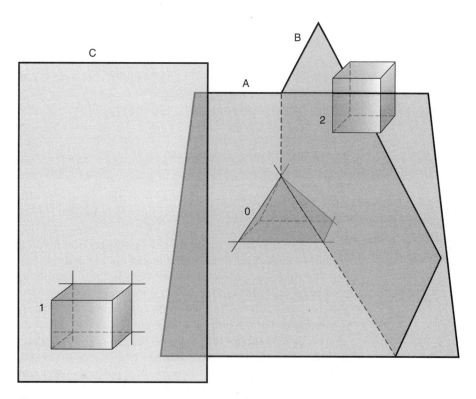

Figure 5.13 • Dividing the space using object faces

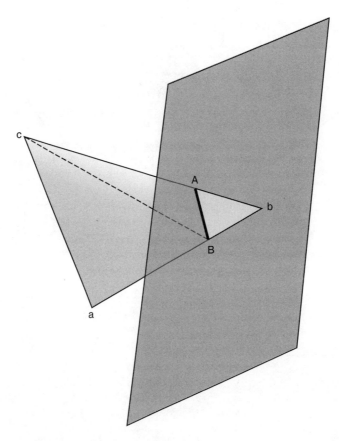

Figure 5.14 • Subdividing a triangular patch

other instead of rectangular regions of image space. The clipping process cuts off parts of distant polygons that are obstructed, in the end leaving only those parts that are completely visible.

The algorithm begins by sorting the polygons in order of increasing depth. This places the closest polygons at the top of the list and the farthest at the end of the list. The algorithm processes the polygons in the order they appear on the list, clipping polygons farther in the list by the current polygon. The portion of each polygon that is behind the first polygon is discarded. Then the second polygon is used to clip the rest of the polygons. This continues until all of the polygons have been clipped by those above it in the list. Once all of the polygons are processed, the list will only have those polygons that are visible and can be rendered.

Figure 5.15 shows this process for three polygons using a parallel projection. The closest polygon is the triangle on the left. The rectangle and the square have the triangle clipped out of them on the first pass. Next the square will be clipped by the

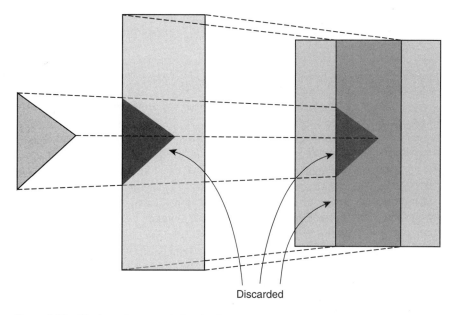

Discarded

Figure 5.15 • Clipping polygons against each other

rectangle. This example also illustrates the potential problems with this algorithm. The rectangle becomes a convex polygon when the triangle is clipped out. The square has a hole in the middle when the triangle is clipped out and then becomes two separate polygons when the rectangle clips out the center on the second pass.

This process is also very time intensive. With a large number of polygons, there are many polygons to compare and clip. For example, 1,000 polygons (not a large number for a complex scene) results in close to 500,000 comparisons to see if objects overlap, and potentially an equal number of polygon clips.

5.3 The OpenGL Way

One of the steps in the OpenGL processing pipeline is called Primitive Assembly. It is during this step that OpenGL clips objects against the boundaries of the viewing volume. This removes portions of objects that are outside of the viewing volume to the left, right, up, or down, as well as being too close or too far away. To handle object obstructions, OpenGL will do back face culling as well as depth-buffer operations. Back face culling is also done during the Primitive Assembly, but the depth-buffer test is done during Fragment Operations in one of the last steps in the OpenGL pipeline. The following sections look at how to specify parameters for each of these operations as well as how to enable OpenGL to perform them.

OpenGL defaults to having the viewpoint at the origin and having the view direction along the negative z axis. This section also looks at how these viewing parameters can be altered.

5.3.1 Setting up clipping

Calls to glOrtho and glFrustum set up the viewing volume based on their parameters. A call to glOrtho(L, R, B, T, N, F) sets six parameters for a parallel or orthographic projection. The first two parameters set the left and right boundaries for the viewing volume. This places clipping planes at x = L and x = R. The next two parameters set the bottom and top boundaries for the viewing volume. This places clipping planes at y = B and y = T. The last two parameters set the near and far locations for hither and yon clipping. These two parameters are different in that they are both positive and give the distance from the viewpoint to these clipping planes. If the viewpoint is located at (x_v, y_v, z_v), this call places the clipping planes at $z = z_v - N$ and $z = z_v - F$ in OpenGL's right-handed coordinate system.

A call to glFrustum(L, R, B, T, N, F) sets six parameters for a perspective projection. Because this is a perspective projection, the viewing volume expands as the distance from the viewpoint increases. The left and right planes of the viewing volume will differ depending on where in space the values of L and R are meant to be. OpenGL will place these values at the location of the near clipping plane. So, if the viewpoint is at (x_v, y_v, z_v), the near clipping plane has opposite corners of $(L, B, z_v - N)$ and $(R, T, z_v - N)$. The four sides of the viewing volume will be determined by the planes that run through the corners of this near clipping plane and the viewpoint. For example, the top clipping plane will be defined by the points (x_v, y_v, z_v), $(L, T, z_v - N)$, and $(R, T, z_v - N)$, and the right clipping plane will be defined by the points (x_v, y_v, z_v), $(R, B, z_v - N)$, and $(R, T, z_v - N)$.

There is another OpenGL routine that can be used to set up a perspective projection. A call to gluPerspective(fovy, aspect, N, F) sets four parameters that OpenGL translates into the parameters for a call to glFrustum. In the case of gluPerspective, the viewing volume will be symmetric about the view direction where a direct call to glFrustum can set up a viewing volume that is not symmetric. The first parameter in this call is the angle of the **Field Of View** in the **Y** direction and should be in the range [0, 180]. The second is the aspect ratio between the width and the height of the frustum. An aspect ratio of 1 means the angle is the same in the x and y directions. An aspect ratio of less than one means the angle in the x direction is less than the angle in the y direction, and a ratio of greater than one is the reverse with the x direction angle being larger. The values of N and F still set the locations of the near and far clipping planes as in the case of the other two calls.

Additional Clipping Planes

OpenGL allows up to six additional clipping planes to be defined, with different OpenGL implementations perhaps allowing more than that. These additional clipping planes can be used to, for example, set up images with cutaway views of the objects. To set up additional clipping planes, call the glClipPlane routine, which takes two parameters. The first parameter is the constant GL_CLIP_PLANEi, where i is a number between 0 and the maximum number of additional clipping planes allowed. The second parameter is an array of four doubles that gives the coefficients of the plane equation Ax + By + Cz + D = 0.

In addition to setting these parameters, the function call

```
glEnable(GL_CLIP_PLANEi)
```

tells OpenGL to perform clipping operations using this plane. The call glDisable(GL_CLIP_PLANEi) stops clipping operations using this plane.

5.3.2 Setting up depth operations

Using the depth buffering capabilities of OpenGL is very easy. The OpenGL depth buffer stores values in the range [0, 1], where the smaller the value the closer the object. The range of depth values from the near to the far clip planes is scaled into this range. This means that the precision of the depth buffer can be increased by limiting the distance between these two clipping planes.

To use the depth buffer, the OpenGL call glEnable(GL_DEPTH_TEST) is needed. Each time an image is rendered, the depth buffer needs to be cleared with a call to glClear(GL_DEPTH_BUFFER_BIT). This sets all of the locations in the depth buffer to a default value of 1.0. To have OpenGL use a different value to clear the depth buffer, call the routine glClearDepth with a parameter value in the range [0, 1]. To turn the depth buffer off, call glDisable(GL_DEPTH_TEST).

5.3.3 Changing viewing parameters

All of the discussions so far have placed the viewpoint at the origin with the view direction along the negative z axis. The routine gluLookAt can be used to change these values. This routine takes nine parameters of type double. The first three parameters give the (x_v, y_v, z_v) location of the viewpoint. The next three parameters give the (x_c, y_c, z_c) location of the center of the scene. This makes the viewing direction $(x_c - x_v, y_c - y_v, z_c - z_v)$. In fact, any point along this viewing direction can be specified for this second set of parameters. The last three parameters specify the vector to consider as "up" in this view. The image created can be spun around the viewing direction by just changing this up vector. The gluLookAt routine is typically called right after initializing the modelview matrix to the identity and before issuing commands for translations and drawing the image.

Depth of Field

Photographs taken with a real camera have some objects that are in focus, and those that are closer or farther away from these objects are blurry. The same thing is true of our vision. When we focus on a particular object, other things that are closer and farther away are blurry. In computer graphics, things will render in focus no matter where they are in the viewing volume because the camera model is equivalent to a pinhole camera.

A depth-of-field effect can be created in OpenGL by rendering the scene from three different but closely spaced locations and combining the results using the accumulation buffer. Full details on this process can be found on pages 458–463 in [OpenGL99].

5.4 Projects

Add a z-buffering to your renderer so that it properly handles obstructions.

Texture

As you look around your world, you will notice that there are very few objects that have a perfectly smooth surface. Even objects that feel smooth have a certain roughness to their surface, which is only obvious when you see that reflection of light is not mirror perfect. Surfaces with very small scale roughness can be modeled through the use of illumination and shading models. For objects with a larger texture, other techniques are needed.

In this chapter, texture is examined from two perspectives: large scale repeated patterns and small scale irregularities. Consider the picture of a brick wall in Figure 6.1. From a large scale perspective, the wall has the regular pattern of the bricks. All of the bricks, except for some along the edges, are of a relatively uniform shape and size. At a small scale perspective, each brick has an irregular pattern to its rough surface that will very likely be different from other bricks. This needs regular patterns that repeat across an object and textures with a bit of randomness to them.

One solution to this problem is to model objects more finely. This is a true model of the shape irregularities caused by the texture. Instead of using one plane for the brick wall, there would be separate planes for each of the bricks and the mortar between them. This would solve the large scale texture, but not the small scale. This would also dramatically increase the number of patches that would be defined, stored, and rendered. For example, a five-foot square wall could need as many as 200 brick patches and 400 mortar patches, instead of just one wall patch. This is an increase of 600-fold for just one wall. To attempt to do this for smaller scale textures creates an even larger problem. For example, a tree bark texture would need to have a series of small patches that followed the irregular up and

Figure 6.1 • A section of a brick wall (see Color Plate 6.1)

down pattern of the bark, which would add thousands of small patches making the impact on the number of patches even greater.

There are techniques that approximate the texture more efficiently than by causing an explosion in the number of patches describing a scene. This chapter explores a number of the techniques that can be used to add this approximation of texture to objects. The shading methods discussed in Chapter 2 dealt with illumination issues. This chapter deals with how those shading methods can be changed to account for objects with texture. These changes must impact the final color determined for various locations on the object. Some methods will change the parameters, for example the diffuse constant, used in the shading method. Another method will simulate the texture by changing the normal vector of the surface before the shading calculations are done. The discussion in this chapter uses examples of how texture changes the Phong shading model, with changes to other models being done in a similar fashion. This chapter also looks at the production of textures using mathematical functions.

6.1 Painted Textures

Early attempts at texture just "painted" a texture onto an object (Catmull74 and Blinn76). After all, if you want to make the walls of your house blue, you just apply blue paint to them. So, if you want a wood grain for the top of a table, why not just paint it with wood grain paint? In the 1970s, there were painting kits with different colors and thicknesses of brown paint that when applied in the correct way created a streaking effect that was a (poor) approximation of wood grain. More recently, craft stores sell similar kits to create marble and mottled textures.

Using a painted texture can be done quickly, though the results might not always be good enough. If an object is small or not a central focus of the scene, a painted texture can add enough detail. But on larger objects, painted textures will likely have incorrect highlighting. The discussion of this simple texturing technique not only introduces this method, it also allows an exploration of mapping concepts that apply to other texture methods as well.

Painted textures use a picture of the texture that could be from any source: a hand drawing, a scanned image, or a digital photograph. The only requirement is that it be in a form that allows access to the various pixel values in the image. The texture is assumed to be stored in a two-dimensional array of size T_u by T_v giving texture coordinate ranges of 0 to $T_u - 1$ for u and 0 to $T_v - 1$ for v. Each of the elements of this texture array is called a texel.

During scan conversion of the object there is a mapping between object and pixel locations. To paint the texture on the object, there needs to be a mapping between locations in the texture and locations on the object. This mapping function is defined from the coordinate space of the object into the texture (Figure 6.2). This function transforms points on the object into the range of coordinates for the texture.

One mapping method is to assign texture locations to each of the vertices of the object. As interior object locations are interpolated, the texture locations will also be interpolated. For example, consider the y value of 3 in the interpolation across the triangle in Figure 6.2. The rendering process determines that the range of object coordinates are from (3, 3) through (20, 3). The first of these coordinates comes from the interpolation along the left edge of the triangle at a parametric t value of 0.3. If

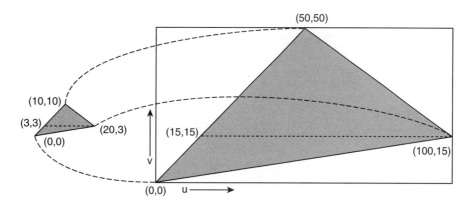

Figure 6.2 • Mapping from the object on the left to the texture on the right

the texture locations for these two vertices are (0, 0) and (50, 50), the texture location for this left edge location would be (15, 15). Because the other end of this row of the triangle is the vertex at (20, 3), the texture location of (100, 15) would be used. So, as the object locations are interpolated from (3, 3) to (20, 3), the texture locations would be interpolated from (15, 15) to (100, 15).

The texture gives a value that will influence the shading process. Specifically, the value from the texture replaces the diffuse constant in the calculation of the diffuse component in the illumination equation. By doing this, the texture values change the object appearance, but shape cues that come from the specular highlights will stay the same. Once the interpolation process has determined the appropriate (u, v) location in the texture, the shading calculations are given in equations (6.1).

$$C_r = k_{ar} + I_L * (\text{texture}[u][v][r] * L \cdot N + k_s * (R \cdot V)^n)$$
$$C_g = k_{ag} + I_L * (\text{texture}[u][v][g] * L \cdot N + k_s * (R \cdot V)^n) \qquad (6.1)$$
$$C_b = k_{ab} + I_L * (\text{texture}[u][v][b] * L \cdot N + k_s * (R \cdot V)^n)$$

The process of interpolation effectively maps locations on the object to locations in the texture. This mapping determines which texture value is used in shading a location on the object. Instead of using interpolation to map from an object location to a texture location, a texture location can be calculated from the object location directly. In general, mapping an object with x coordinates in the range from x_{min} to x_{max} and y coordinates in the range from y_{min} to y_{max} into the texture coordinate range is done with the equations (6.2), where u_{max}, u_{min}, v_{max}, and v_{min} are determined by the range of texture values assigned to the object vertices.

$$u = \frac{u_{max} - u_{min}}{x_{max} - x_{min}} * \left(x - x_{min}\right) \qquad (6.2)$$

$$v = \frac{v_{max} - v_{min}}{y_{max} - y_{min}} * \left(y - y_{min}\right)$$

The calculations in equations (6.2) frequently produce values for u and v that are not integer values. If these values are truncated, this could produce visual artifacts that ruin the appearance of the texture. An alternative is to use the values of u and v to interpolate between the four adjacent values from the texture. For example, if $u = 3.4$ and $v = 5.8$, the four texture values texture[3][5], texture[4][5], texture[3][6], and texture[4][6] are used. First, a value 40 percent of the way between texture[3][5] and texture[4][5] is calculated, as well as another one 40 percent of the way between texture[3][6] and texture[4][6], as shown in equations (6.3).

$$T_1 = 0.6 * \text{texture}[3][5] + 0.4 * \text{texture}[4][5] \qquad (6.3)$$
$$T_2 = 0.6 * \text{texture}[3][6] + 0.4 * \text{texture}[4][6]$$

The texture value to be used is 80 percent of the way between T_1 and T_2, and is calculated similarly to equation (6.3). Equations (6.4) give the general form of this full set of calculations, where trunc gives the integer portion of the number and fract gives the fractional portion of the number.

$$f_1 = \text{fract}(u)$$
$$f_2 = \text{fract}(v)$$
$$T_1 = (1.0 - f_1) * \text{texture}[\text{trunc}(u)][\text{trunc}(v)]$$
$$+ f_1 * \text{texture}[\text{trunc}(u)+1][\text{trunc}(v)] \tag{6.4}$$
$$T_2 = (1.0 - f_1) * \text{texture}[\text{trunc}(u)][\text{trunc}(v)+1]$$
$$+ f_1 * \text{texture}[\text{trunc}(u)+1][\text{trunc}(v)+1]$$
$$\text{result} = (1.0 - f_2) * T_1 + f_2 * T_2$$

This technique will stretch the texture out if the object is larger than the texture or, as in Figure 6.2, shrink the texture if the object is smaller. When the texture is stretched, a larger object coordinate range is mapped into the smaller texture coordinate range. When the texture shrinks, a smaller object range is mapped into the larger texture coordinate range. The only difference between these cases is whether the scaling factor, represented by the fraction in equations (6.2), is less than or greater than one. These divisions can be calculated once for each patch and stored because only x and y will change for different locations on the patch.

An alternative to stretching the texture is to repeat the texture across the surface, called tiling. In this technique, the texture is repeated as many times as needed. To do this, the object coordinates are mapped into the texture coordinates using a scale factor of one. When the location goes out of the bounds of the texture, the start of the texture is used again. This can be implemented through the modulus operator (%) and the equations (6.5).

$$u = (x - x_{\min}) \% T_u$$
$$v = (y - y_{\min}) \% T_v \tag{6.5}$$

When the difference between the object location and the minimum location becomes equal to the size of the texture, the index returns to zero. This cycles through the texture again, which creates the second copy. With each multiple of the texture size, another copy of the texture is used. For example, with tiling, creating the image of a brick wall is possible with a texture showing one brick centered below two half bricks. When this is tiled over a plane, two adjacent copies of the pattern would cause the half bricks to combine into a full brick (Figure 6.3).

The number of times that the pattern will be repeated across a patch using equations (6.5) depends on the relative sizes of the patch and the texture. For example, if the texture is 100 texels wide and the object has an x range of 400 units, the texture will repeat four times in the x direction. A slight modification to equations (6.5) will control the number of times that the texture is tiled. In equations (6.6), the two repeat values determine the number of times the texture will be tiled in the x and y directions.

Figure 6.3 • Brick texture (left) and the results of tiling it three times in each direction (right)

$$u = frac\left(\frac{repeat_x}{x_{max} - x_{min}} * (x - x_{min})\right) * T_u \qquad (6.6)$$

$$v = frac\left(\frac{repeat_y}{y_{max} - y_{min}} * (y - y_{min})\right) * T_v$$

The tiling of the texture in Figure 6.3 works because the left and right edges of the texture are continuous relative to the overall brick wall, as are the top and the bottom. When a texture is tiled, a second copy of the texture in the x direction places the left edge of the texture along the right edge of the texture. If the values along these two edges do not create a "continuous" change across both copies, there will be a clear discontinuity along that edge. The same thing is true for the top and bottom of the texture.

Consider the texture in Figure 6.4. The left and right edges of this texture are not continuous. The right of Figure 6.4 shows this texture tiled across a plane. The edges of this texture are quite obvious where the edges of the texture in the tiling of Figure 6.3 are not.

Painted textures are simple to implement and this process can achieve many different effects. These techniques can also be used to put images into the scenes. For

Figure 6.4 • A non-wrapping texture and a plane tiled with it

example, if you want to render a room that has your picture on the wall, you use your picture as the texture and map it onto a square patch located where the picture will be hanging.

There is a problem, however, when this technique is used for textures that represent highly irregular surfaces such as wood grain or bark. Because the texture value modifies the diffuse component of the illumination model, there is no change to the specular component. Looking at a real object with a wood grain surface or a piece of bark, there are specular highlights at the "top" edges of surface ridges. These highlights will not be there when using a painted surface texture. Because the shape of the object is not changed with a painted texture, the highlighting indicates a smooth surface instead of a textured one.

Figure 6.5 shows a plane rendered using a brick texture from Figure 6.1. Though the plane has the appearance of bricks, the specular highlight down the center is not changed and indicates a smooth surface for the plane. The texture gives the impression of variation in the surface of this plane, but the highlighting is no different from what would appear on a plane without a texture. This figure and other results using painted textures clearly look like a smooth object with a picture of the texture painted on the surface.

Figure 6.5 • Textured object with incorrect specular highlighting (see Color Plate 6.2)

6.2 Bump Mapping

In 1978, Blinn (Blinn78a) developed a technique called bump mapping using textures to modify the specular highlights. The idea is that a real surface with wrinkles has proper highlighting because of the direction that the normal vector points at various locations on the surface. Those changes in normal vector direction need to be simulated to create a similar set of highlights. Instead of modifying the surface, the bump mapping method just modifies the normal vector so that it changes as it would on a wrinkled surface. The Figure 6.6 diagram on the left shows the surface normal vectors for a surface with a curve. If this same set of surface normal vectors is now used with a flat plane in place of its one plane normal, as shown in the diagram on the right, the highlighting on this plane will closely match the highlighting of the curved surface. Modifying the normal of the planar surface before using it in the illumination calculation produces highlighting similar to that of the wrinkled surface. This modification does not alter the planar surface, but does cause the highlighting of the surface to change, because when the normal is modified, there

Figure 6.6 • Wavy surface with its surface normal vectors and a straight line with the same surface normal vectors

will be times when it will move in a direction to increase the highlight and other times it will change in a direction that decreases the highlight.

In the case of painted textures, a texture value is used to modify the diffuse component before calculating the shading for that location. In bump mapping, a texture value is used to determine the displacement of the normal that is used in the shading calculations. The effect is that the specular and diffuse components of the shading formula will change to support the illusion of the texture being real. This changes the Phong shading method by first calculating the displaced normal and then using that normal in the illumination calculations as shown in equations (6.7).

$$N_B = \text{bump}(u, v, N)$$
$$R_B = 2 * N_B * (N_B \cdot V) - V$$
$$C_r = k_{ar} + I_L * [k_{dr} * L \cdot N_B + k_s * (R_B \cdot V)^n]$$
$$C_g = k_{ag} + I_L * [k_{dg} * L \cdot N_B + k_s * (R_B \cdot V)^n]$$
$$C_b = k_{ab} + I_L * [k_{db} * L \cdot N_B + k_s * (R_B \cdot V)^n]$$

$$(6.7)$$

The bump function is based on the gradient of the bump map[1] at location (u, v). The gradient is a measure of how much the bump map values are changing at that location. The change around a location in the bump map determines the change to apply to the surface normal. If the bump map values change from large to small, the normal will move in one direction, but if the values change from small to large, it will move in the opposite direction.

The bump map in Figure 6.7 is 1,024 by 1,024 texels and is based on the sine function. Specifically, the value at location (u, v) is given by $\sin(10 * u * \pi/1024) * \sin(10 * v * \pi/1024)$. Even though the texel values in this texture are determined by a calculation, the result is used the same as other textures that can be drawn or based on photographs. The gradient at location (u, v) would be the difference between the values surrounding this point in the u and v direction. The u gradient would be bumpMap$[u + 1][v]$ − bumpMap$[u - 1][v]$, and the v gradient would be bumpMap$[u][v + 1]$ − bumpMap$[u][v - 1]$. For location (35, 65) in the bump map in Figure 6.7, the u gradient would be $\sin(360 * \pi/1024) * \sin(650 * \pi/1024) - \sin(340 * \pi/1024) * \sin(650 * \pi/1024) \approx 0.81436 - 0.78767 = -0.02669$, and the v gradient would be $\sin(350 * \pi/1024) * \sin(660 * \pi/1024) - \sin(350 * \pi/1024) * \sin(640 * \pi/1024) \approx 0.78995 - 0.81210 = -0.02215$.

The full bump mapping process begins by determining two vectors tangent to the surface at the current object location. These vectors, S_u and S_v, should be perpendicular to each other, and the cross-product of these vectors will give the surface normal at this location. The current x and y values of the object location are transformed into a bump map location using equations (6.2), (6.5), or (6.6). Next, the two bump map gradients are determined for this location. These gradients are used with vectors S_u and S_v to give the modified normal used for the shading calculation. The

---

[1]When used with bump mapping, the texture is called a bump map.

Figure 6.7 • A sine-based texture

results of this process are illustrated in Figure 6.8, which shows a plane with the texture of Figure 6.7 used as a bump map.

Equation (6.8) gives Blinn's formula for calculating the new normal, where B_u and B_v are the gradients in the bump map values and S_u and S_v are the tangents to the surface in the x and y directions.

$$N' = N + \frac{B_u * (N \times S_v) - B_v * (N \times S_u)}{\|N\|} \tag{6.8}$$

The two cross-products in equation (6.8) just produce two vectors in the plane tangent to the surface at the current point. Because S_u and S_v are already tangent, this can be calculated more quickly by equation (6.9). If N, S_u, and S_v are all unit vectors, the two divisions in equations (6.8) and (6.9) are not needed.

$$N' = N + \left(\frac{B_u * S_v}{\|S_v\|} + \frac{B_v * S_u}{\|S_u\|} \right) \tag{6.9}$$

Ferguson (Ferguson01) multiplies the parenthesized expression in equation (6.9) by a parameter h. This additional factor can be used to control the height of the

Figure 6.8 • Bump map applied to a surface patch illuminated with three light sources

bumps. By using a value for h of less than one, the amount of change to the normal will be lessened. While a value for h of greater than one will increase the amount of change to the normal. Figure 6.9 shows the impact of the h parameter.

Blinn gives two potential sources for bump maps: a depth buffer after rendering a scene, and hand-drawn images. If a depth buffer is used, the overall shape and relative depth of the objects in the scene become a texture on the object. A scene can be created with objects representing the texture desired. The depth buffer values for that scene are used for the bump map. Because the only interest is the resulting bump map, none of the shading calculations are done.

With a hand-drawn image, areas of constant intensity will not alter the normal. Only areas that change in intensity will alter the surface normal. For example, in an area where all of the bump map values are 0.5, taking the gradient will produce values of 0.0 for both the u and v directions. When these gradients are plugged into either equation (6.8) or (6.9), the fractions will all be zero, and so the bumped normal will be exactly the same as the original normal.

Using a gray scale bump map that only has black (0.0) and white (1.0) values, the gradient will be 0.0, 1.0, or −1.0. The gradient will be zero in areas of constant value and it will be 1.0 or −1.0 where the bump map changes between black and white. The changes to the normal and hence the appearance of the bumps will be abrupt. Consider the plane y = 0, which has the y axis as its normal (0.0, 1.0, 0.0) and has the x and z axes as its tangent vectors (1.0, 0.0, 0.0) and (0.0, 0.0, 1.0). If the gradient is −1.0 in the u (x) direction and zero in the v (z) direction, the tangent vector in the v direction will be subtracted from the normal giving a modified normal vector of (0.0, 1.0, −1.0), which is about (0, 0.707, −0.707) when of unit length. Thus the normal is now at a 45° angle from the y axis. If both gradients are 1.0, the modified normal vector will be (1.0, 1.0, 1.0), which is about (0.577, 0.577, 0.577) when of unit length. Thus the normal is now at about a 55° angle from the y axis. Thus with a black and white bump map, the normal vector will either be unchanged, or will shift by 45° or 55° in one of eight directions along the tangent vectors or between them.

Figure 6.9 • Two planes bump mapped using *h* values of 0.5 and 2.0

If the bump map is a full gray scale image, the rate that the shade is changing influences the amount the vector will be adjusted. In this case, the changes to the normal will be smoother and the appearance of the bumps will be less abrupt. Consider again the plane at y = 0. If the gradient is 0.2 in the u direction and 0.1 in the v direction, the modified normal will be (0.1, 1.0, 0.2), which is about (0.098, 0.976, 0.195) when of unit length. Thus the normal is now at about a 12° angle from the y axis. Furthermore, because the bump map is a gray scale image, moving one texel over in the bump map will produce gradients that are not likely to be much different from the previous ones, and so the next modified normal will not be radically different from the previous modified normal. This produces bumps with more gradual changes.

There is one problem with the bump mapping that appears on the silhouette of objects and if the objects are animated. Because the actual surface is not altered, if a bump map that produces a ridge is applied so the ridge goes to the edge of the object, the silhouette of the object will not change. The bump appears to abruptly stop or disappear at the profile of the object. Likewise, if bump mapping produces the appearance of a bump in the middle of an object, when that object is rotated the bump will disappear when it reaches the silhouette edge of the object.

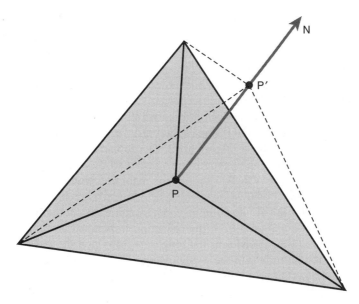

Figure 6.10 • Displacement mapping

An alternative to bump mapping is to use displacement mapping, which will modify the object shape. In displacement mapping, an object is subdivided into many smaller patches. Each of the vertices of these smaller patches is displaced in the direction of the normal vector at that point on the object (Figure 6.10). Texel locations that have a large value result in bigger displacements of the vertices that map to them, than texel locations with smaller values. For this technique to produce bumps that appear to be smooth, the patches used to represent the object must be small relative to the amount of the displacement. So, if the variation in texture values is small, larger patches could be used, but if the variation is larger, smaller patches will produce a better result.

6.3 Environment Mapping

The typical concerns when dealing with textures are objects that have a rough surface, but what about objects that have a reflective surface? A reflective object will have other objects in the scene influence the appearance of the reflective object. The thing influencing a particular location can be found by following the direction of reflection from the reflective object's surface point. A reflective object will bounce the view off in the direction given by equation (6.10), where N is the normal at the surface point and V is the vector pointing back to the viewpoint.

$$R = 2 * N * (N \cdot V) - V \tag{6.10}$$

The vector **R** gives the direction of what is seen in a reflection off the object surface at that point. The ray tracing process discussed in Chapter 8 follows the reflection direction as it bounces around the scene. This is computationally expensive, so an early technique was to follow just one reflection. In 1976, Blinn and Newell (Blinn76) presented a method called reflection or environment mapping to render reflective objects without the cost and overhead of full ray tracing.

Their idea is to project and render all of the objects in the scene (except for the current reflective one) onto a sphere that surrounds the object and that has the same center as the object (Figure 6.11). The projection and rendering uses the center of this sphere as the viewpoint and center of projection. This produces a spherical view of the scene (called a reflection map) as it would appear from inside the reflective object.

The spherical reflection map can be stored in a two-dimensional matrix but this requires a mapping from the reflection direction into the two-dimensional space. This mapping transforms the longitude into the u dimension of the reflection map and the latitude into the v dimension of the reflection map. Thus, the direction of the reflection vector determines the indexes into the reflection map where what is

Figure 6.11 • A teapot in a sphere

seen in the reflected direction can be found. The equations (6.11) will convert the normalized reflection vector into (u, v) coordinates in the range [0.0, 1.0].

$$u = \frac{1}{2}\left(1 + \frac{1}{\pi} * \arctan\left(\frac{R_x}{R_y}\right)\right)$$

$$v = \frac{R_z + 1}{2}$$

(6.11)

In the calculation of the arctangent, the result in the range $[-\pi, \pi]$ is used. There is a problem that occurs at the poles (the top and bottom of the sphere) of a spherical reflection map. In these areas, small changes in the direction of the reflection vector will result in big changes in the (u, v) value.

An alternative to a spherical reflection map is to use a cube that has the same center as the reflective object (Figure 6.12). With a cube, there are six planar sides that can be rendered exactly like the rendering of the full scene but with the cube center as the viewpoint and each of the six sides serving as the projection plane.

Figure 6.12 • A teapot in a cube

The cube is oriented so that its edges are parallel with the axes of the coordinate system as shown in Figure 6.13. When the cube is unfolded, each of the square pieces has its own (u, v) space with the u values running horizontally to the right and the v values running vertically up. The center of each of these square pieces is where the corresponding axis exits the cube. It might seem strange that the negative x axis is pointing to the right in the square labeled as the front face, but this occurs because, in unfolding the cube, the front face swings around the y axis and reverses itself to wind up in its position at the right end of that diagram.

Determining which of the six planes the reflection goes through can be done by just examining the normalized reflection vector. The largest absolute coordinate of the reflection vector will tell which of the cube sides to use. For example, a reflection vector of [0.4, 0.7, 0.59] would intersect the top (positive y) face and a reflection vector of [−0.75, 0.25, 0.433] would intersect the left (negative x) face. The labeling of the faces in Figure 6.13 shows which largest coordinate indicates the use of that side. Once the face has been determined, the (u, v) reflection map location in the range [0.0, 1.0] is calculated by equations (6.12), where a represents the coordinate on the horizontal axis for the face, b represents the coordinate for the vertical axis for the face, and c represents the coordinate for the chosen face.

$$
\begin{aligned}
u &= \frac{a + c}{2c} \\
v &= \frac{b + c}{2c}
\end{aligned}
\tag{6.12}
$$

For the first example that intersects the top face, a would be the x coordinate, b would be the z coordinate, and c would be the y coordinate. This makes the calculation of $u = (0.4 + 0.7) / 1.4 \approx 0.786$ and the calculation of $v = (0.59 + 0.7) / 1.4 \approx 0.921$. For the second example that intersects the left face, a would be the negative of the z coordinate, b would be the y coordinate, and c would be the negative of the x coordinate. This makes the calculation of $u = (−0.433 + 0.75) / 1.5 \approx 0.211$ and the calculation of $v = (0.25 + 0.75) / 1.5 \approx 0.667$.

With reflection mapping, the scene can be rendered from different viewpoints without having to recreate any reflection maps. The only time that the reflection maps need to be regenerated is if any of the objects in the scene have moved. Also, if a reflective object is rotated in any direction around its center, its reflection map will not need to be recreated. But if that object is rotated around any other point or is translated, a new reflection map must be created.

Though reflection mapping can produce somewhat realistic images of reflective objects, there is still a problem. A single projection point is used for the entire reflection map, but the actual points on the surface are in many different places. Each of the locations on the surface of the object is some distance away from the center of the object. The view from that location is somewhat different from the view from the center of the object. The farther away that location is the

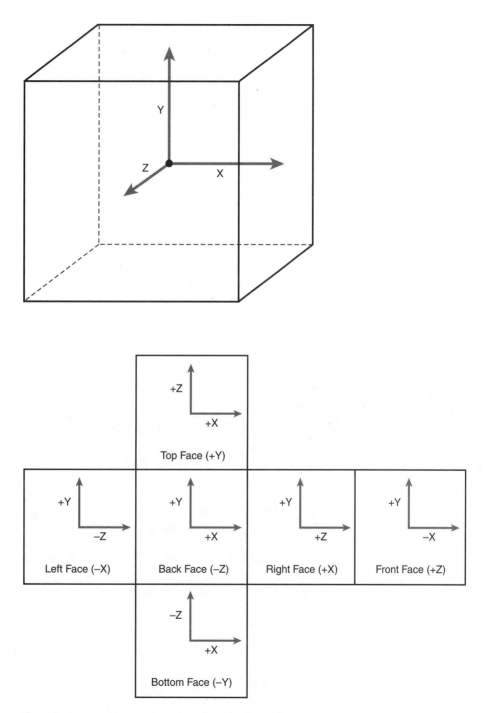

Figure 6.13 • An environment mapping cube and a flattened version

greater the difference. This difference is more pronounced for things that are reflected from some distance away. Therefore, what is seen from the center in the direction of the reflection is different from what is seen from the surface in the direction of the reflection. These variations tend to be minor for small reflective objects, and are typically not noticeable. For larger reflective objects, these errors are more noticeable.

6.4 Three-Dimensional Textures

Continuity issues are important when a texture is tiled across an object. A texture can be specifically designed so that there are no visible seams when it is placed adjacent to itself. If a texture similar to the bricks in Figure 6.3 is wrapped around a cylinder, there is no seam. If the cylinder is tiled instead, the tiling has to be done with an even number of copies of the texture. If a partial piece of the texture is used, there will be a visible seam because it is unlikely that the partial piece will properly line up well with the full texture it winds up next to. When wrapping a square texture around a sphere, things are more complicated. To understand why, try wrapping a square sheet of paper around a ball. When you do so, there will be bumps, wrinkles, and overlaps in the paper representing the parts of the texture that could be skipped over in the texturing process. You will also see the paper come together so that half of each edge can meet up with the other half of the edge. The two-dimensional texturing process that was so neatly described for planar patches becomes much more complex as the object to be textured becomes less planar.

It is difficult if not impossible to create a texture that is unlikely to cause a visible seam when the texture is wrapped or tiled around a complexly shaped object. The problem is in the process of wrapping a flat texture around an object that has curvature. The alternative is to have a three-dimensional texture. Instead of wrapping the texture around the object, the object is placed into the texture space. This eliminates the need to create a texture that has edges that can be brought together in a variety of ways with the result being continuous. Continuity is still an issue if the three-dimensional texture is to be "tiled." A two-dimensional texture must be continuous across its edges, but a three-dimensional texture must be continuous across its planar sides. For a three-dimensional texture, the entire front and back of the texture would have to be continuous along with the left and right sides and the top and bottom.

Where a two-dimensional texture is "painted" on a surface, a three-dimensional texture is a block out of which the object is "carved." The real-world equivalent of this is an object carved out of wood that has a wood grain textured surface. Two-dimensional textures are accessed as an array using a mapping function from the x and y components of the object to the u and v indexes of the texture. For a three-dimensional texture, the process is the same with the addition of a mapping to take the z component of the object to the third index (w) of the texture.

Where the storage needed for a two-dimensional texture is large, the storage requirements for a three-dimensional texture are even greater. A small texture of with 64 texels in each direction will take 64 times the space of an equivalent two-dimensional texture. Doubling the size of the texture in each direction increases by a factor of eight the amount of needed space. Because of these space needs, three-dimensional textures are closely related to functional textures.

6.5 Functional Textures

The textures looked at so far have been calculated, scanned, or drawn and then stored in a file. When creating an image using these textures, the values are read into a two or three-dimensional array for use during rendering. This requires disk and computer memory to store the textures. The benefit of functional textures is that they do not use storage space; however, they are frequently more computationally involved than just looking up a value in an array. This section looks at textures that are not stored but rather are calculated as needed—for example, see (Gardner84), (Peachey85), (Perlin85), and (Ebert03). Functions or procedures have been used to produce textures of marble, stone, bricks, wood, and wallpaper. Procedural techniques to define objects such as smoke, steam, fire, and water will be discussed in Chapter 11.

A functional texture is a mathematical calculation of a texture value based on the x and y, or in the case of a three-dimensional functional texture, on the x, y, and z components of the object point. These calculations could be anything. They could create a texture that runs from dark to light by scaling the object's x and y coordinates with the equation $(x - x_{min}) / (2 * x_{range}) + (y - y_{min}) / (2 * y_{range})$ to get a texture value[2] in the range [0.0, 1.0]. Alternatively, they could use the RGB cube as a three-dimensional texture by scaling the x, y, and z coordinates into the range [0.0, 0.1] and then using them for the red, green, and blue components of the texture. They could also create a checked pattern by just taking the sine of the x and y component, which creates a functional version of the texture in Figure 6.7.

The implementation of functional textures within the shading model is straightforward. Where two-dimensional textures entailed an array lookup, functional textures require a function call that returns, in the case of the Phong model, the texel value as in equations (6.13). The call to the function functionalTexture takes the values of x, y, and z as input and returns an array of three diffuse constants, k_d.

$$k_d = \text{functionalTexture}(x, y, z)$$
$$C_r = k_{ar} + I_L * (k_d[r] * L \cdot N + k_s * (R \cdot V)^n)$$
$$C_g = k_{ag} + I_L * (k_d[g] * L \cdot N + k_s * (R \cdot V)^n)$$
$$C_b = k_{ab} + I_L * (k_d[b] * L \cdot N + k_s * (R \cdot V)^n)$$

$$(6.13)$$

---

[2]Each coordinate contributes up to 0.5 of the final texture value.

Functional textures can also be used as the basis for bump mapping with the function called multiple times to determine the gradient values needed. Functional texture values can also be used for the displacement value needed for displacement mapping. In short, replacing each array access for a static texture with a call to the function that calculates a texture value is all that is needed to make any texture method functional.

Whereas including a functional texture in a shading method is easy, developing the function to create the texture can be quite involved. See (Ebert03), a large book that details the development of functional textures from multiple approaches for many application areas. The next subsections look at a few functional textures and the effects they create.

6.5.1 Noise

Noise is an important part of many functional textures. Noise adds variability to a functional texture to remove a regular or repeating appearance. A true white noise is highly random and can be seen on a television that is tuned to a channel that has no station broadcasting on it. In graphics, it is more important for functional textures to have a pseudo-random noise than a truly random noise, because the noise function has to be repeatable or else the texturing of an object will change between successive frames of an animation.

In 1985, Perlin introduced a noise function (Perlin85) that has served as the basis for many computer generated special effects in Hollywood movies. In 1997, he was given a Technical Achievement Award by the Academy of Motion Picture Arts and Sciences for the noise function that he developed. Perlin bases his work on a noise function, of which he had a number of versions. The noise function is supposed to have three properties: no statistical variance when rotated; no statistical variance when translated; and a narrow range of values.

Perlin improved on his noise function (Perlin02) to solve two problems that existed with the original function: a discontinuity in the second order interpolation, and a gradient computation that was not optimal. The discontinuity was a problem when noise or textures based on noise are used for bump mapping. Second order discontinuity causes abrupt changes in the normal displacement, which causes sharp and visible discontinuities in the shaded object. The new gradient calculation uses 12 fixed directions to the center of the edges of a surrounding cube. Four additional edges are added to bring the total up to 16, which is a power of two allowing multiplications to be replaced with bitwise ands. These changes result in a noise function that produces better-looking results, and does it faster. A C version of Perlin's improved noise function is:

```
#define fade(t) ((t) * (t) * (t) * ((t) * ((t) * 6 - 15) + 10))

#define linearInterp(t, a, b) ((a) + (t) * ((b) - (a)))

int p[512];
//Perlin's permutation of the numbers from 0 to 255
```

```
int permutation[] = {151, 160, 137, 91, 90, 15, 131, 13,
                      201, 95, 96, 53, 194, 233, 7, 225,
                      140, 36, 103, 30, 69, 142, 8, 99,
                      37, 240, 21, 10, 23, 190, 6, 148,
                      247, 120, 234, 75, 0, 26, 197, 62,
                      94, 252, 219, 203, 117, 35, 11, 32,
                      57, 177, 33, 88, 237, 149, 56, 87,
                      174, 20, 125, 136, 171, 168, 68, 175,
                      74, 165, 71, 134, 139, 48, 27, 166,
                      77, 146, 158, 231, 83, 111, 229, 122,
                      60, 211, 133, 230, 220, 105, 92, 41,
                      55, 46, 245, 40, 244, 102, 143, 54,
                      65, 25, 63, 161, 1, 216, 80, 73,
                      209, 76, 132, 187, 208, 89, 18, 169,
                      200, 196, 135, 130, 116, 188, 159, 86,
                      164, 100, 109, 198, 173, 186, 3, 64,
                      52, 217, 226, 250, 124, 123, 5, 202,
                      38, 147, 118, 126, 255, 82, 85, 212,
                      207, 206, 59, 227, 47, 16, 58, 17,
                      182, 189, 28, 42, 223, 183, 170, 213,
                      119, 248, 152, 2, 44, 154, 163, 70,
                      221, 153, 101, 155, 167, 43, 172, 9,
                      129, 22, 39, 253, 19, 98, 108, 110,
                      79, 113, 224, 232, 178, 185, 112, 104,
                      218, 246, 97, 228, 251, 34, 242, 193,
                      238, 210, 144, 12, 191, 179, 162, 241,
                      81, 51, 145, 235, 49, 14, 239, 107,
                      49, 192, 214, 31, 181, 199, 106, 157,
                      184, 84, 204, 176, 115, 121, 50, 45,
                      127, 4, 150, 254, 138, 236, 205, 93,
                      222, 114, 67, 29, 24, 72, 243, 141,
                      128, 195, 78, 66, 215, 61, 156, 180};

void
initializeNoise()
{
   // create two copies of the permutation table
   // to save 3 modulus operators
   for (int i=0; i < 256 ; i++)
      p[256+i] = p[i] = permutation[i];
}


static float grad(int h, float x, float y, float z)
{
```

```
    int hash;
    float u, v;
    float result;

    // calculate the gradient value for the indicated direction
    // get the low four bits which chooses among the 16 directions
    hash = h & 15;
    if ((hash<8)||(hash==12)||(hash==13))
        u = x;
    else
        u = y;
    if ((hash<4)||(hash==12)||(hash==13))
        v = y;
    else
        v = z;
    if ((hash&1) == 0)
        result = u;
    else
        result = -u;
    if ((hash&2) == 0)
        result += v;
    else
        result -= v;
    return result;
}

float noise(float x, float y, float z)
{
    int xInt, yInt, xInt, A, AA, AB, B, BA, BB;
    float u, v, w;
    float grad1, grad2, grad3, grad4, grad5, grad6, grad7, grad8;
    float part1, part2, part3, part4;

    xInt = (int) floor(x) & 255;
    yInt = (int) floor(y) & 255;
    zInt = (int) floor(z) & 255;
    // get the fractional parts of x, y, and z
    x -= floor(x);
    y -= floor(y);
    z -= floor(z);
    u = fade(x);
    v = fade(y);
    w = fade(z);
```

```
A = p[xInt]+yInt;
AA = p[A]+zInt;
AB = p[A+1]+zInt;
B = p[xInt+1]+yInt;
BA = p[B]+zInt;
BB = p[B+1]+zInt;

grad1 = grad(p[AA], x, y, z);
grad2 = grad(p[BA], x-1, y, z);
grad3 = grad(p[AB], x, y-1, z);
grad4 = grad(p[BB], x-1, y-1, z);
grad5 = grad(p[AA+1], x, y, z-1);
grad6 = grad(p[BA+1], x-1, y, z-1);
grad7 = grad(p[AB+1], x, y-1, z-1);
grad8 = grad(p[BB+1], x-1, y-1, z-1);
part1 = linearInterp(u, grad1, grad2);
part2 = linearInterp(u, grad3, grad4);
part3 = linearInterp(u, grad5, grad6);
part4 = linearInterp(u, grad7, grad8);
return linearInterp(w,
                linearInterp(v, part1, part2),
                linearInterp(v, part3, part4));
}
```

This function assumes that the values of x, y, and z will be in the range [0.0, 255.0]. The values in the permutation table are also in the range [0.0, 255.0]. Perlin developed a process that "folds" the three coordinates (equation (6.14)) into a single value that is used as an index into the permutation table.

$$n = p[\text{int}(x) \% 256]$$
$$n = p[\text{int}(n + y) \% 256] \hspace{3cm} (6.14)$$
$$n = p[\text{int}(n + z) \% 256]$$

The values of x, y, z, and those in the permutation table are all between 0 and 255, so the sum of two of these values will be in the range of 0 to 510, which is the reason for the modulus operator. In the previous C code, the permutation table is twice the size necessary and the values are duplicated, which allows Perlin to drop the modulus in the above equations. Figure 6.14 shows the result of using this noise function.

6.5.2 Turbulence

There are many different approaches to using noise to build procedural textures. Many of these first build a turbulence function on top of the noise function. The turbulence function takes multiple samples of the noise function at many different frequencies.

Figure 6.14 • Noise

Peachey has the following simple turbulence function (Ebert03, pg. 86)[3]:

```
float turb(float x, float y, float z,
           float minFreq, float maxFreq)
{
   float result = 0.0;
   for (float freq = minFreq; freq < maxFreq; freq = 2.0*freq)
   {
      result += fabs( noise(x*freq, y*freq, z*freq ) / freq );
   }
   return result;
}
```

The results for Peachey's turbulence function are given in Figure 6.15 for the frequency ranges of [1.0, 4.0], [1.0, 16.0], and [1.0, 256.0].

Perlin also has a turbulence function (Ebert03, pg. 369). In using this function, he sets minFreq to be the lowest frequency component he wants as part of the

---

[3]In this algorithm, fabs is the C/C++ absolute value function for floating point numbers.

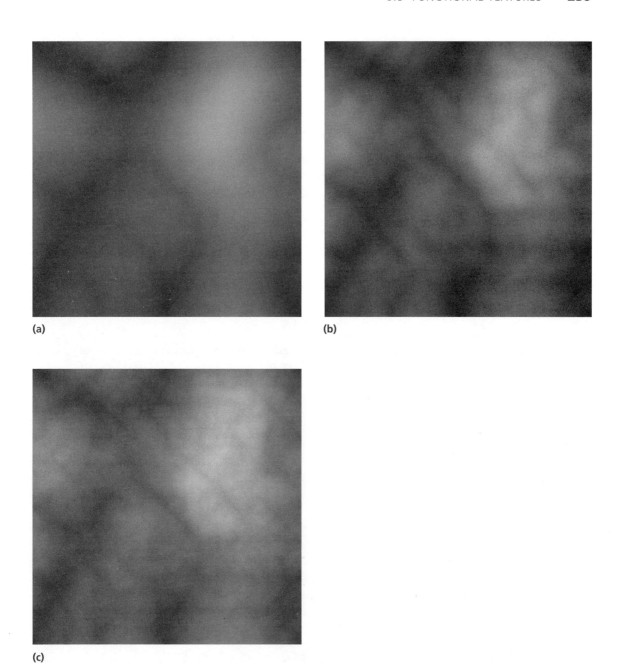

(a)

(b)

(c)

Figure 6.15 • Peachey's turbulence function for the frequency ranges of A, [1.0, 4.0]; B, [1.0, 16.0]; and C [1.0, 256.0]

texture, and he sets maxFreq to be equal to the image resolution so that the turbulence effect goes down to the individual pixel level. Perlin's turbulence function is:

```
float turb(float x, float y, float z,
            float minFreq, float maxFreq)
{
    float result = 0.0;
    x = x + 123.456;
    for (float freq = minFreq; freq < maxFreq; freq = 2.0*freq)
    {
        result += fabs( noise(x, y, z ) ) / freq;
        x *= 2.0;
        y *= 2.0;
        z *= 2.0;
    }
    // return the result adjusted so the mean is 0.0
    return result-0.3;
}
```

Figure 6.16 shows the output of Perlin's turbulence function the frequency ranges of [1.0, 4.0], [1.0, 16.0], and [1.0, 256.0].

Looking at Figures 6.15 and 6.16, the turbulence images almost have a cloud-like appearance. It should not be surprising that this methodology has been used as the basis for a wide range of textures. Perlin's original paper (Perlin85) discussed the use these turbulence functions for the production of images of fire and other functional texture methods for the production of images of waves. Perlin (Perlin89 and Perlin02) and many others have used his noise and a turbulence function to create textures for marble, art glass, waves, and many other objects. Ebert et al. (Ebert03) also examine a wide variety of functional textures.

The next section looks at a marble functional texture. Images in that section will be created using Perlin's turbulence function.

6.5.3 A marble texture

Perlin had a marble function that is the basis for a version by Ebert (Ebert94, pg. 165). Perlin's version (Perlin85) does not have the multiplier of three in the following function. The discussion that follows uses this version of the marble function, but the impact of the multiplier value will be shown later in this section.

```
void marble(float x, float y, float z, float color[3])
{
    float value = x + 3.0 * turb(x, y, z, minFreq, maxFreq);
    marbleColor( sin(π * value), color );
}
```

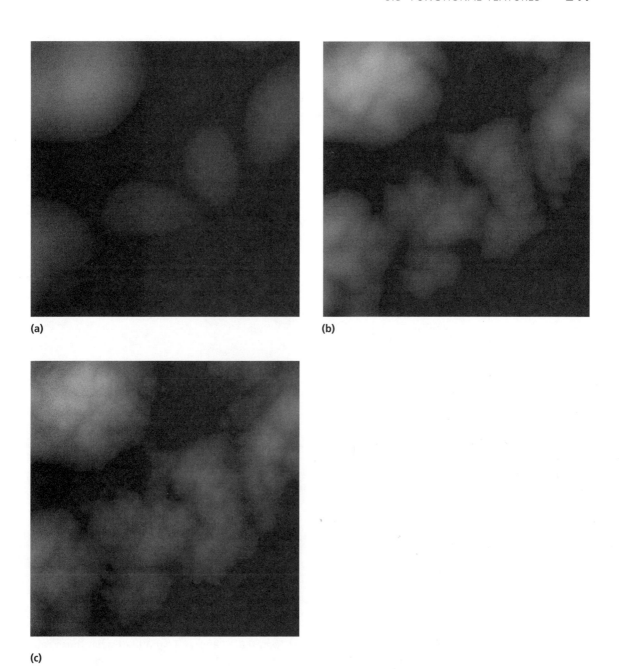

(a)

(b)

(c)

Figure 6.16 • Perlin's turbulence for frequency ranges of A, [1.0, 4.0]; B, [1.0, 16.0]; and C, [1.0, 256.0]

The function marbleColor maps from the range [−1.0, 1.0] into the colors that will be used for the light and dark areas for the marble. A simple version of this marbleColor function would just set thresholds for the light and dark areas and then interpolate between these colors for values between the thresholds. A version of this is:

```
void marbleColor( float value, float color[3] )
{
    float red1 = 0.2, green1 = 0.1, blue1 = 0.0;
    float red2 = 0.9, green2 = 0.8, blue2 = 0.6;
    float diffRed = red2-red1, diffGreen = green2-green1,
        diffBlue = blue2-blue1;
    float lightLimit = 0.6, darkLimit = 0.95;

    if (value < lightLimit)
    {
        color[0] = red2;
        color[1] = green2;
        color[2] = blue2;
    }
    else if (value > darkLimit)
        {
            color[0] = red1;
            color[1] = green1;
            color[2] = blue1;
        }
        else
        {
            float scale = (value - darkLimit)/(lightLimit - darkLimit);
            color[0] = red1 + diffRed * scale;
            color[1] = green1 + diffGreen * scale;
            color[2] = blue1 + diffBlue * scale;
        }
}
```

In this function, results of the sine function that fall in the range [−1.0, 0.6) are mapped to the light color and results that fall in the range (0.95, 1.0] are mapped to the dark color. Results that fall in the range [0.6, 0.95] would be linearly interpolated between these two values. Figure 6.17 shows a sample of what these routines produce. The x and y values used for this image are in the range [0.0, 2.66] with a z value of zero.

Using these routines, there are a number of parameters that can be adjusted to change the result. The appearance of the marble can be altered by changing the colors that are used for the light and dark colored areas. The choices shown will produce light tan and dark brown areas. The lightLimit value indicates the size of the

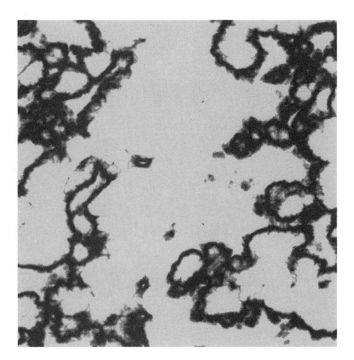

Figure 6.17 • A marble texture with frequency in the range [1.0, 256.0] (see Color Plate 6.3)

light colored areas and the darkLimit value indicates the size of the dark colored areas. If the lightLimit is decreased, the light colored areas decrease in size. If the darkLimit is increased, the dark colored areas decrease in size. The size of the range between the lightLimit and darkLimit determines how sharp the edges are between the dark and light colored areas. If the range is large, there are more values that fall in the interpolation range, so the transition from light to dark is greater and, therefore, fuzzier. If the range is small, the transition will be less and, therefore, sharper.

The samples in Figure 6.18 differ in the range of frequencies used in the turbulence calculation. The sample in Figure 6.17 uses the range of frequencies [1.0, 256.0]. In Figure 6.18, the frequency ranges are [1.0, 4.0] and [1.0, 16.0].

Ebert recommends that a spline should be used for the interpolation between the light and dark values instead of a linear interpolation. Ebert therefore (Ebert03, pg 229) gives the marbleColor function[4]:

```
void marbleColor( float value, float color[3] )
{
    float red1 = 0.2, green1 = 0.1, blue1 = 0.0;
    float red2 = 0.9, green2 = 0.8, blue2 = 0.6;
```

---

[4]Ebert's version uses different colors from what is shown here, and therefore, gets a marble color that is more blue and green.

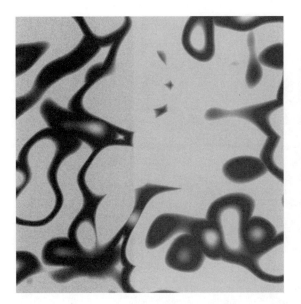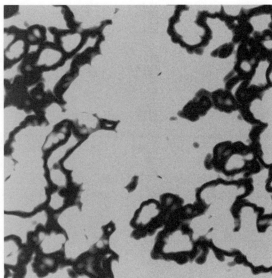

Figure 6.18 • Frequency impact on marble (see Color Plate 6.4)

```
float dr = red2-red1, dg = green2-green1, db = blue2-blue1;

value = sqrt(value+1.0)*0.7071;
color[1] = green1 + dg * value;
value = sqrt(value);
color[0] = red1 + dr * value;
color[2] = blue1 + db * value;
}
```

In this version, the value has one added to it, so that the result of the sine function passed in as value is shifted into the range [0.0, 2.0] before the square root is taken. This is then multiplied by $1/\sqrt{2}$ (approximately 0.7071), which has the effect of bringing the variable value into the range [0.0, 1.0]. The new value is used to interpolate the green value between the light and dark values. Ebert then takes the square root again to get a new value for the interpolation between the light and dark values for red and blue.

Figure 6.19 shows a sample of the marble texture resulting from Ebert's marbleColor function. Figure 6.19 uses a frequency range of [1.0, 256.0]. Figure 6.20 shows the impact that a change in frequency range has. The left-hand image uses a range of [1.0, 4.0] and right-hand image uses a range of [1.0, 16.0].

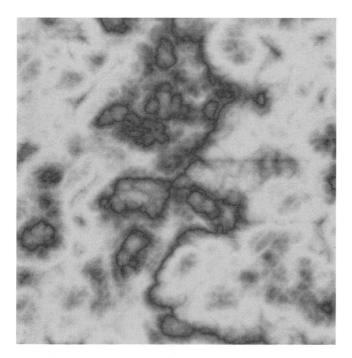

Figure 6.19 • Marble sample using Ebert's interpolation (see Color Plate 6.5)

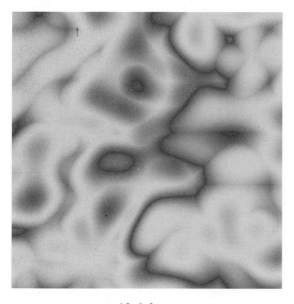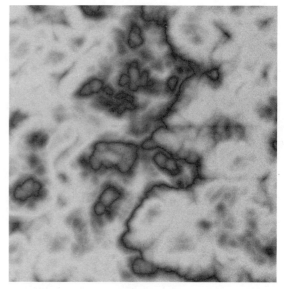

Figure 6.20 • Ebert's `marbleColor` and the frequency ranges [1.0, 4.0] and [1.0, 16.0] (see Color Plate 6.6)

Figure 6.21 shows the effect of the multiplier on the marble texture. This figure shows Perlin's original with no multiplier and two textures with multipliers of three and seven. These results show that the higher the multiplier the more mottled the resulting texture.

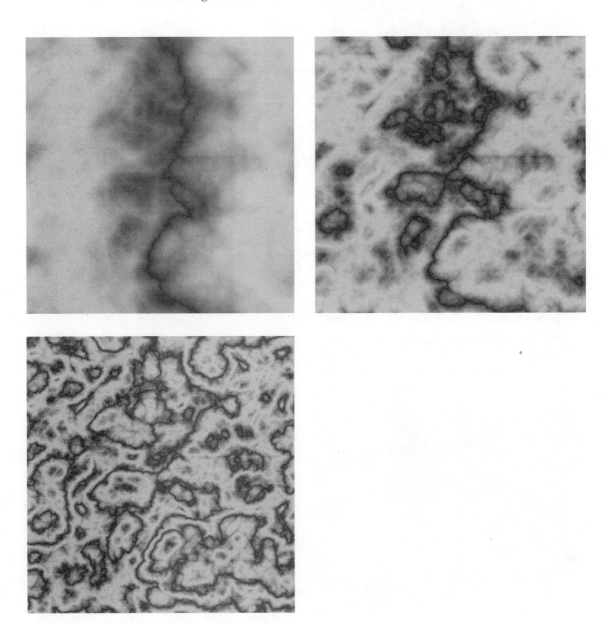

Figure 6.21 • Marble using no multiplier and multipliers of 3.0 and 7.0 (see Color Plate 6.7)

● **6.5.4 Cosine textures**

Another method for generating textures is based on summations of cosine curves instead of noise. Gardner (Gardner84 and Gardner85) developed a functional texture technique that adds a collection of cosine curves with different periods and phases to model textures and components of natural scenes like trees and clouds. The use of this method for natural textures like bark and clouds is explored in this chapter. A later chapter will look at how this method can be used to create images of trees and landscapes.

Gardner has both a two- and three-dimensional version of his functional textures. The difference is a third summation term based on the z component. This adds a third parameter of each of the types now discussed that controls the appearance of the resulting texture in the third direction. The discussion of this method is based on the two-dimensional version because figures on the page are two-dimensional, but the type of control these parameters exhibit in two dimensions translates to the third dimension as well. Gardner's two-dimensional function (equation (6.15)) is a summation of a series of cosines with a collection of nine parameters that control the phase and amplitude.

$$
\begin{aligned}
f(x, y) = & \sum_{i=1}^{N} C_i * \left[\cos\!\left(\omega_{x_i} * \left(x + \Phi_{Gx} \right) + \phi_{x_i} \right) \right. \\
& \left. + A_0 \right] * \sum_{i=1}^{N} C_i * \left[\cos\!\left(\omega_{y_i} * \left(x + \Phi_{Gy} \right) + \phi_{y_i} \right) + A_0 \right]
\end{aligned}
$$

(6.15)

The value of N controls the number of cosine terms used in the function. The constants Φ_{Gx} and Φ_{Gy} are the global phase shifts that move the pattern. The C_i terms are the cosine factors that change the amplitude of the various cosine components. The A_0 are the cosine offsets that also shift the pattern but are related to the cosine factors. The ω_{x_1} and ω_{y_1} are the base period values and determine the number of times that the pattern repeats. Lastly, the ϕ_{x_i} and ϕ_{y_i} are the phase values, which create an interdependence between the base periods of x and y. Each of these factors has an impact on the look of the resulting texture as will be explored in the rest of this section. In general, a set of values for these factors will be determined that produce the desired texture and then are fixed for the texture generation.

The level of complexity of the resulting texture is increased with an increase in the number of cosine terms used as indicated by the value of N. Gardner reports that natural looking patterns are possible with values of N between 4 and 7. Figure 6.22 shows the increasing complexity of the result as the value of N increases. In this and many of the rest of the figures in this section, other parameters are fixed at values that do not influence the result so that the impact of just one of the parameters can be demonstrated. All of these figures are generated on a 1,024 by 1,024 pixel grid.

The global phase shifts are represented by the terms Φ_{Gx} and Φ_{Gy}. These terms are responsible for shifts that move the entire pattern in the x and y directions. These values apply equally to all of the x and y cosine terms, where other parameters that also shift the pattern only apply to one of the individual cosine terms. Figure 6.23 shows the impact of the global phase shift. In this figure, the image on the right has an x phase shift of 150, which causes the bright spots to shift from their position in the image on the left.

There is a cosine factor (C_i) multiplied by each of the cosine terms that modifies that term's amplitude. Gardner defined each succeeding cosine factor as the previous value multiplied by the cosine amplitude ratio (CAR). Therefore, $C_{i+1} = \text{CAR} * C_i$. Gardner felt a cosine amplitude ration of 0.707 gave natural looking results, but other values can also be used. Figure 6.24 uses both double and half this value with four cosine terms to show the impact of the cosine amplitude ratio. Doubling the cosine amplitude ratio produces more consistent light and dark areas, while halving the value gives larger and more frequent dark areas.

The range of values produced by equation (6.15) should be capped at 1.0, but the lower end will not have a limit. Using the cosine factors, there is a fixed maximum value, and larger areas of black can be created wherever the function becomes negative. To get an overall maximum of one, each of the summations of cosine terms in equation (6.15) should be less than or equal to one so that their product will also be less than or equal to one. This requires choosing the proper value for C_1 that creates a sequence of C_i values, which do not allow each summation to become greater than one. Because the cosine function returns a maximum result of one, the series of C values should satisfy the equation (6.16), which is a simplification of each of the summations in equation (6.15).

$$\sum_{i=1}^{N} C_i * \left(1 + A_0\right) \leq 1 \tag{6.16}$$

Dividing both sides of equation (6.16) by $(1 + A_0)$ gives equation (6.17), which gives the limit on the sum of the C_i values.

$$\sum_{i=1}^{N} C_i \leq \frac{1}{\left(1 + A_0\right)} \tag{6.17}$$

Because each C_i value is just the previous value multiplied by the cosine amplitude ratio, the summation in equation (6.17) can be simplified to a summation of a series of powers of the CAR as shown in equation (6.18). This summation is multiplied by C_1 because this is the value at the start of this series.

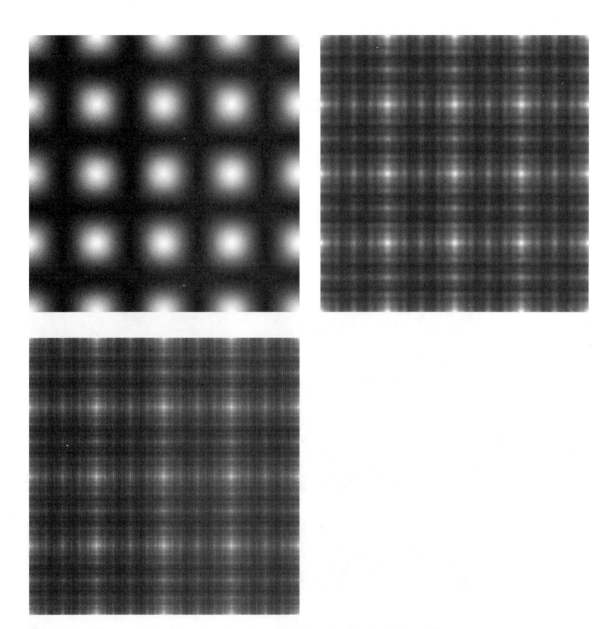

Figure 6.22 • Differences due to the number of cosines summed (number of cosines: 1, 4, and 7)

 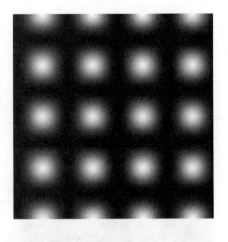

Figure 6.23 • Global phase shifts in x of 0 and 150

Figure 6.24 • Cosine amplitude ratios of 0.3535, 0.7070, and 1.414

$$C_1 * \sum_{i=0}^{N-1} CAR^i \leq \frac{1}{(1 + A_0)} \tag{6.18}$$

By dividing both sides of the inequality of equation (6.18) by the summation, the resulting equation (6.19) shows the relationship between the initial value for C_1 and the values of A_0 and the CAR.

$$C_1 \leq \frac{1}{(1 + A_0) * \left(\sum_{i=0}^{N-1} CAR^i \right)} \tag{6.19}$$

The choice of C_1 is, therefore, dependent on the value of the cosine offset (A_0) and the cosine amplitude ratio (CAR), and will typically be the largest such value that satisfies this inequality. Specifically, values for A_0 and the CAR would be chosen, and then equation (6.19) would be used to calculate the largest possible value for C_1.

If C_1 is chosen to be the largest value that satisfies the inequality in equation (6.19), a cosine offset value (A_0) of 1.0 produces a range of [0.0, 1.0] for the overall function. Using a value of A_0 that is greater than 1.0 increases the lower end of this range, which means that there will be no true black areas of the result. Using a value of A_0 that is less than 1.0 causes the function to sometimes return negative values. These are clamped at zero to create areas of the texture that are pure black. Choosing a value for C_1 as discussed means that the results from equation (6.15) will be in the range [$(A_0 - 1)/(A_0 + 1)$, 1]. Figure 6.25 gives an example of an A_0 value below 1.0, causing an increase in black in the result.

The base period values of ω_x and ω_y are chosen to match the frequency of the feature being modeled. To generate a texture that repeats every 100 texels, the base period would be set at $2\pi/100$. Almost all of the figures in this section have used a base period of 256 for both x and y. Using a base period of 256 texels in these 1024 by 1024 texel images is the reason there are about four repetitions of the pattern. Where the figures presented have used the same base period for x and y, these values can be set differently to stretch out the pattern in the x or y direction. Typically, the base period will be set based on the amount of change in the feature being modeled. Figure 6.26 shows a change in the y base period to 512. This results in about two repetitions of the pattern in the y direction.

Figure 6.26 has just a single cosine term, but when there are more than one terms, successive values of ω_x and ω_y are found by multiplying the previous value by a base period ratio. The base period ratio used so far has been 2.0, but Figure 6.27 shows base period ratios of 1.5, 2.0, and 2.5. The change in base period ratio causes no change to the number of repetitions of a pattern of light and dark areas, but does change the intensity of the brightest areas.

The phase values of $\phi_{x_{i+1}}$ and $\phi_{y_{i+1}}$ are calculated as $\phi_{x_{i+1}} = PSA * \cos(\omega_{y_i} * y)$ and $\phi_{y_{i+1}} = PSA * \cos(\omega_{x_i} * x)$, where PSA is the phase shift amplitude. Thus, the phase

Figure 6.25 • A_0 values of 0.5, 1.0, and 1.5

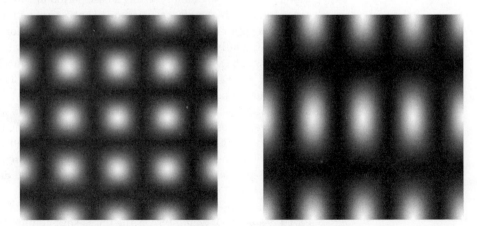

Figure 6.26 • Textures with the same (256) and different base periods for x (256) and y (512)

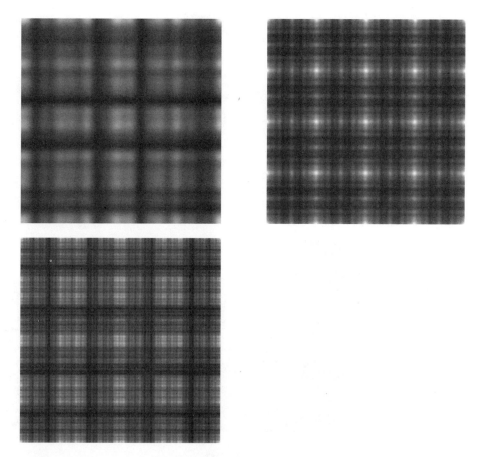

Figure 6.27 • Base period ratios of 1.5, 2.0, and 2.5

for the next x cosine is based on the base period for the last y cosine and vice versa.[5] For the three-dimensional version, the values are cyclically dependent—$\phi_{x_{i+1}}$ is calculated using the z values, $\phi_{y_{i+1}}$ is calculated using the x values, and $\phi_{z_{i+1}}$ is calculated using the y values. Gardner reports that using the base period of one term to set the phase of the other provides a way to create the appearance of randomness using a mechanism that can be controlled. Figure 6.28 uses phase shift amplitudes of 0, $\pi/4$, $\pi/2$, and π.

Putting all of these parameter options together gives a great deal of flexibility in the control of the resulting texture. As an example, Figure 6.29 shows a texture that

---

[5]The initial phase value is the same as the second phase value. Specifically, $\phi_{x_1} = \phi_{x_2}$ and $\phi_{y_1} = \phi_{y_2}$.

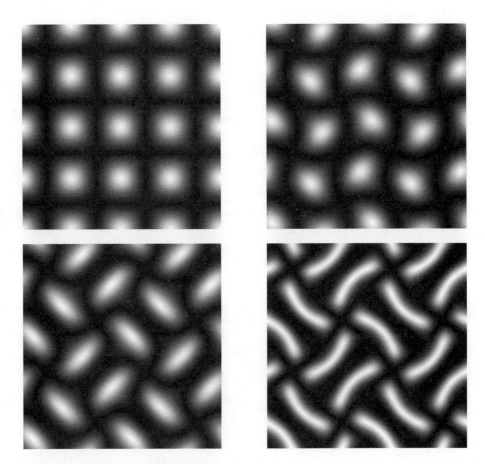

Figure 6.28 • Phase shift amplitudes of 0, π/4, π/2, and π

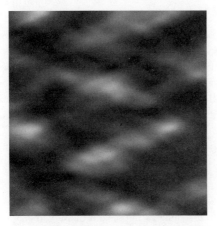

Figure 6.29 • Cloud like texture

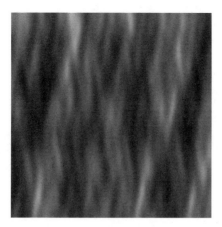

Figure 6.30 • A bark texture

uses 4 cosines, an x global offset of 200, a cosine amplitude ratio of 0.5, a phase shift amplitude of $\pi/2$, a cosine offset of 0.75, a x base period of 655, a y base period of 325, and a base period ratio of 1.7. This texture has the appearance of wispy clouds or the reflection of light off the surface of slightly turbulent water.

Gardner's function can also generate a bark-like texture (Figure 6.30). This figure is generated by 4 cosines and a cosine amplitude ratio of 0.707, a cosine offset of 1.0, an x base period of 256, a y base period of 1216, and a base period ratio of 1.7. In doing research on modeling trees, this author used Gardner's function to model bark but also varied the cosine offset from 0.45 to 1.25 along the length of the y direction. This gives higher variation at one end of the texture than the other to model the difference in the roughness of bark due to age. This changing cosine offset causes the texture to be rougher for the trunk at the base of the tree and smoother for new branches at the outer points of the tree.

The major expense in calculating equation (6.15) is the cosine function, which is typically calculated using a power series. A significant speed up is possible if a table of cosine values is calculated once and is then used to look up individual cosine values instead of calculating each one with a call to the cosine function. Table look-up methods are discussed further in Appendix A.

6.6 Antialiasing Textures

Consider a texture made of alternating red and white stripes, each one texel wide. If the object is half the size of the texture, object locations are mapped into every second texel location. Texturing will, therefore, use texels from only the even locations of the texture. Because the texture is alternating red and white stripes with one texel width, the rendering this object will use either all red or white texels depending on which color is in location 0. This is obviously not a good result for that texture. This problem, called aliasing, is due to a problem with the rate that the texture is sampled. Aliasing causes artifacts to appear in an image. Though addressed with regard to textures, aliasing can also cause problems with objects. Aliasing causes lines and edges of objects to look jagged. The techniques discussed here can also be used when scan converting objects to smooth their silhouettes.

Consider a checkerboard texture that consists of a six by six grid of black and white texels in blocks of three texels each. The texture has six texels on each side, with the lower left and upper right quadrants white, and the upper left and lower right quadrants black (Figure 6.31). Further consider a planar patch in the y = 0 plane that will be tiled with the checkerboard texture. Perspective makes the far edge look smaller than the near edge. At the near end of the patch, each pixel on the screen covers a small portion of the patch, and at the far end of the patch, each pixel covers a larger area of the patch. Suppose that the texel is chosen based on the center of the patch area that the pixel is covering. At the near end, each pixel on the screen can map into one of the locations in the texture, so the texture will appear properly. Moving farther back on the patch, at some point every other texel value will be used because the pixels are mapping onto a larger area of the patch. At this point, some of the checkerboard blocks look wider than others. Because every second texel is used, the block at the lower left is effectively two texels square; the two black blocks are effectively one by two texels; and the upper right block will effectively be just one texel. Continuing to move back, every third texel is used, and then

Figure 6.31 • A checkerboard texture

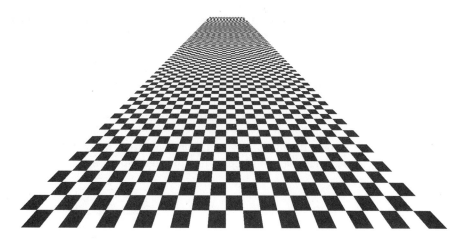

Figure 6.32 • An aliased texture

every fourth texel, and so on. Even further back, every seventh texel will be used producing rows that are either all black or white texture values.

Aliasing manifests itself as visible artifacts that give the impression that the texture is changing. Consider the textured plane in Figure 6.32. The texturing of the beginning of the plane appears reasonable, but about two-thirds of the way back the texture starts to break down. It appears that there are multiple bands of artifacts, including one that gives the appearance of a striped texture.

Aliasing occurs because samples of the texture are taken at a rate that is inconsistent with details in the texture. There are two main ways to deal with this problem: supersampling and inverse mapping. Thus far, the discussion has treated a pixel as a point on the screen, but a pixel can also be treated as a small square area of the screen. It is this view that plays a role in how these two methods work.[6] The process of antialiasing bases the pixel value on what is happening inside this square

---

[6] Viewing the pixel as a square area of the screen can also be used for antialiasing objects. Treating the pixel as a point means that locations along the silhouette of the object are either in the object or in the "background." Treating the pixel as a square area means that part of the pixel will be object, and part will be background, and setting the pixel value based on these proportions will antialias the object.

area. Because it works over a larger area, antialiasing smooths out discontinuities, but it also blurs fine details.

Supersampling

One technique to deal with aliasing is called supersampling because more than one value is taken from the texture for each pixel. For example, four samples can be taken at the "corners" of the pixel area and then these values can be averaged. Another alternative is to take a set of nine samples in a three by three grid centered over the pixel area, and then use a filter (a weighted average) to combine them. A three by three filter for this purpose would be:

1	2	1
2	4	2
1	2	1

The nine samples are multiplied by the values in the associated locations of the filter. The corner ones are multiplied by 1, the side ones by 2, and the center one by 4. All of these are added together and the total is divided by the filter total of 16 in this case.

The weights in the filter are related to how close a sample is to the center of the pixel area. There are larger filters that can be used with more samples. One other thing to note about this filter is that all of the values are powers of two and the total of all of them is also a power of two. If the texture values at these points are integers, this calculation can be done with left and right shifts of the bits instead of doing multiplications. Shifting one bit left is the same as multiplying by two and shifting two bits left is the same as multiplying by four. Shifting the sum of the nine resulting values four bits to the right is the same as an integer division by 16. Figure 6.33 shows the plane in Figure 6.32 rendered using supersampling with the above filter. The aliasing artifacts have been reduced, but are still there. This method is still sampling at a regular rate, but it is just doing so more frequently. A further reduction of aliasing is possible if the sample locations are jittered. Jittering involves using a small random adjustment to the location of the samples. Instead of always taking samples at $(i - 0.5, j - 0.5)$, $(i - 0.5, j)$, $(i - 0.5, j + 0.5)$, $(i, j - 0.5)$, (i, j), $(i, j + 0.5)$, $(i + 0.5, j - 0.5)$, $(i + 0.5, j)$, and $(i + 0.5, j + 0.5)$, there would be a random value in the range $[-0.25, 0.25]$ added to each of these coordinate values. This random value reduces aliasing by disrupting the regular rate of sampling.

Inverse mapping

A second method of antialiasing is called inverse mapping. In this method, the area of a pixel is projected back onto the object, which identifies the part of the object that should contribute to the value of that pixel. In Figure 6.34, this process moves

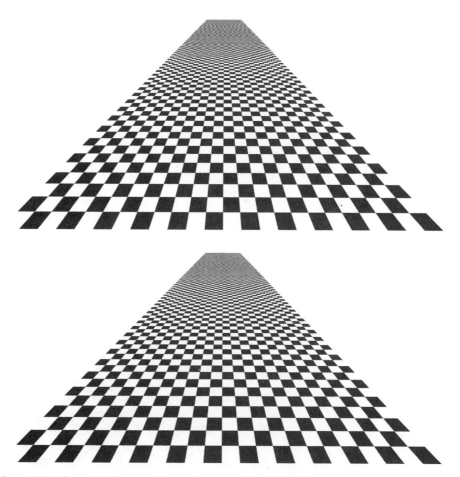

Figure 6.33 • The results of supersampling and supersampling with jittering

from left to right. On the left, the image is shown with the area of one pixel outlined by the square. This square area maps to a section of the patch as shown in the middle of Figure 6.34. The area on the object maps into a collection of u and v values as shown on the texture at the right of the figure. The quadrilateral on the right shows the area of the texture that contributes to the current pixel value. The inverse mapping method then integrates over that area of the texture to determine the texture value to use for the current pixel. An alternative solution to integrating is to simply take the average of the texture values that fall within the area. The results of integrating or averaging is used as the texel value for rendering of the current pixel. In Figure 6.34, the pixel is colored gray to represent the average of the texture values. Figure 6.35 shows the plane in Figure 6.32 rendered by inverse mapping.

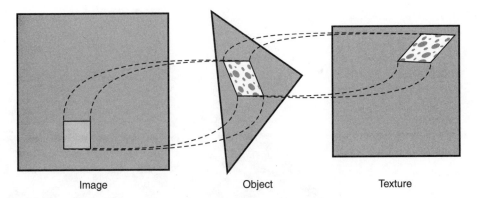

Image   Object   Texture

Figure 6.34 • Mapping from image to object to texture

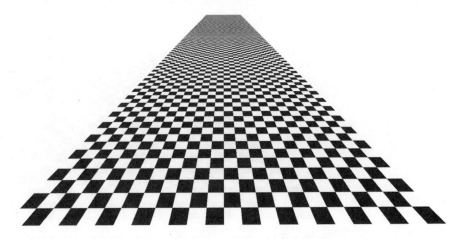

Figure 6.35 • The results of inverse mapping

6.7 The OpenGL Way

There are four steps to using texture in OpenGL: create the texture; enable texturing; indicate how the texture is to be used; and specify the relationship between the object and texture locations. OpenGL has one-, two-, and three-dimensional texture capabilities. A one-dimensional texture is used to, for example, create stripes on an object. A striped object can be created with a one-dimensional texture that has the proper number of texels to specify the width of each stripe. This row of texels can then be repeated down or across the object to produce the stripes. Because the interest here is in more involved textures, this section will concentrate on two- and three-dimensional textures.

6.7.1 Creating the texture

The first step is to create the texture to be used with a call to the glTexImage2D or glTexImage3D routine. The first parameter for each is the target for the texture: GL_TEXTURE_2D, GL_PROXY_TEXTURE_2D, GL_TEXTURE_3D, or GL_PROXY_TEXTURE_3D. Because OpenGL has limited space to store textures, the two proxy options allow a program to check if the parameters will work before transferring the texture itself. The second parameter is the level, which for now will be set as zero, but will be discussed again in section 6.7.5 on advanced OpenGL texturing. The third parameter is the internal format for the data in the texture, which will typically be GL_ALPHA, GL_LUMINANCE,[7] GL_LUMINANCE_ALPHA, GL_INTENSITY, GL_RGB, or GL_RGBA, though there are 32 other options.

The next two parameters (or three for 3D) are the width and height (and depth) of the texture. The next parameter is set at 1 to indicate that there is a one pixel border surrounding the texture or 0, if there is no border. If there is no border, all of the dimensions of the texture must be a power of two. If the texture has a border, the dimensions of the texture must be two greater than a power of two. (Use the gluScaleImage routine to alter the size of a texture to have dimensions that are all powers of two.) For example, a valid texture could be of size 32 by 64 without a border and 34 by 66 with a border. All implementations of OpenGL can handle textures up to 64 texels in each direction, but can also handle larger textures. The maximum size of a texture[8] is returned from a call to the glGetIntegerv routine using the parameter GL_MAX_TEXTURE_SIZE.

The next parameter is the format of the texture array. Options include GL_LUMINANCE, GL_RGB, GL_RGBA, GL_RED, GL_GREEN, and GL_BLUE. The last three indicate that only one of the three color components is present in the texture. These are handy because they save space if only one of the color components is to be affected by the texture. The next parameter is the type of value stored in the array, and includes the choices of GL_BYTE, GL_UNSIGNED_BYTE, GL_INT, and GL_FLOAT. The last parameter is the array holding the texture data.

For example, the call glTextImage2D(GL_TEXTURE_2D, 0, GL_RGBA, 64, 32, 0, GL_RGBA, GL_INT, texture) sets up a two-dimensional texture that is 64 texels wide by 32 texels high with both formats as RGBA and the data in the integer array texture.

---

[7]Luminance in OpenGL is just the sum of the red, green, and blue components. The weighting on these values can be altered by changing the OpenGL values for GL_*_SCALE and GL_*_BIAS, where the * is either RED, GREEN, or BLUE. Details on this can be found in [OpenGL00] and [OpenGL99].

[8]The limit on the size of the texture can also be influenced by the number and size of other textures defined within the program. For this reason, the proxy options show if there really is room available for the texture. If there is room, the width or height value OpenGL returns for the texture will be what was requested. If the space is not available, the width and height values will be zero.

6.7.2 Enabling texture mapping

Texturing is enabled with a call to `glEnable(GL_TEXTURE_2D)` or `glEnable(GL_TEX-TURE_3D)`. If more than one of these dimensions is enabled, texturing will be done using the highest dimension enabled. Texturing can be turned off with a call to `glDisable(GL_TEXTURE_2D)` or `glDisable(GL_TEXTURE_3D)`.

6.7.3 Using the texture

The values in the texture can be used to replace or modify the color that is determined from shading the object. The call `glTexEnvi(GL_TEXTURE_ENV, GL_TEXURE_ENV_MODE, GL_REPLACE)` specifies that the value calculated in the shading process will be replaced by texture values. This replacement is determined by the internal format that was specified in the `glTexImage*D` call. If the internal format was `GL_ALPHA`, `GL_LUMINANCE`, or `GL_RGB`, the texture value would replace the calculated alpha in the first case, and the calculated RGB in the last two. If the internal format was `GL_LUMINANCE_ALPHA` or `GL_RGBA`, the calculated color and alpha values will be replaced by the values for luminance/color and alpha in the texture. If the internal format is `GL_INTENSITY`, the texture intensity value will replace both the calculated color and alpha values.

If the third parameter to the `glTexEnvi` call is `GL_MODULATE`, the texture value will be multiplied by the calculated value in a manner similar to that discussed above. With an internal format of `GL_LUMINANCE`, the texture value is multiplied by the color value, and with an internal format of `GL_RGBA`, the texture red is multiplied by the calculated red, the texture green is multiplied by the calculated green, and so on.

A third parameter of `GL_DECAL` is only available with an internal format of `GL_RGB` or `GL_RGBA`. With the first of these internal formats, the texture color replaces the calculated color as in `GL_REPLACE`. With the second internal format, the texture alpha value is used to linearly interpolate between the calculated color and the texture color. If the texture alpha value is 0, the calculated color is used; and if the texture alpha value is 1, the texture color is used.

The last option for the third parameter to the `glTexEnvi` call is `GL_BLEND`. With this option, the call `glTexEnv*v(GL_TEXTURE_ENV, GL_TEXURE_ENV_COLOR, rgbColor)` is also needed, where the * can be either i if the rgbColor array is of type integer and f if it is of type float. In this mode, the texture value is used to interpolate between the calculated color and the color set with this call.

6.7.4 Specifying texture coordinates

When a texture is set up in OpenGL, there is an (s, t, r, q) coordinate system created for the texture, which corresponds to the (x, y, z, w) homogenous coordinate system used to specify object coordinates. To place an object into the texture space, a texture coordinate is specified for each vertex. Consider the following code fragment:

```
glBegin(GL_QUADS);
    glTexCoord2d(0.0, 0.0); glVertex3d(0.0, 0.0, 0.0);
    glTexCoord2d(0.5, 0.0); glVertex3d(10.0, 0.0, 0.0);
    glTexCoord2d(0.5, 0.5); glVertex3d(10.0, 10.0, 0.0);
    glTexCoord2d(0.0, 0.5); glVertex3d(0.0, 10.0, 0.0);
glEnd();
```

In this example, a square polygonal patch that is 10 units on each side is textured so that only the one quarter of the texture is mapped across the surface of this polygon. Figure 6.36 shows two square patches—the first uses the full range of texture coordinates, and the second uses the range shown in the example above.

By properly choosing the texture coordinates used, a texture can be smoothly mapped along adjacent patches. For example, the following code segment maps a single texture seamlessly across two patches that share a vertical edge.

```
glBegin(GL_QUADS);
    glTexCoord2d(0.0, 0.0); glVertex3d(0.0, 0.0, 0.0);
    glTexCoord2d(0.5, 0.0); glVertex3d(0.5, 0.0, 0.0);
    glTexCoord2d(0.5, 1.0); glVertex3d(0.5, 1.0, 0.0);
    glTexCoord2d(0.0, 1.0); glVertex3d(0.0, 1.0, 0.0);
glEnd();
glBegin(GL_QUADS);
    glTexCoord2d(0.5, 0.0); glVertex3d(0.5, 0.0, 0.0);
    glTexCoord2d(1.0, 0.0); glVertex3d(1.0, 0.0, 0.0);
    glTexCoord2d(1.0, 1.0); glVertex3d(1.0, 1.0, 0.0);
    glTexCoord2d(0.5, 1.0); glVertex3d(0.5, 1.0, 0.0);
glEnd();
```

Figure 6.36 • Two planes mapped using the full texture (left) and one quarter of the texture

Figure 6.37 • Two patches textured seamlessly

In this example, the left half of the texture is mapped onto the left polygonal patch, and the right half of the texture is mapped onto the right polygonal patch. In Figure 6.37, there are two patches, one slightly taller than the other. The left patch is 4 units high and 1.6 units wide, while the right patch is 5 units high and 2.4 units wide. This makes the left patch 40 percent of the entire width, so the texture coordinates are set to be in the range [0.0, 0.4] for u and [0.0, 1.0] for v. For the right patch, the texture coordinates are in the range [0.4, 1.0] for u and [0.0, 1.25] for v. The texture is also set to wrap (tile).

There will be many times when the patch and textures will be of different sizes. In these cases, will the texture be repeated, stretched, or squashed? To have the pattern repeat across the object, use the call glTexParameteri(GL_TEXTURE_2D, GL_TEXTURE_WRAP_S, GL_REPEAT). This will cause the pattern to repeat in a horizontal direction across the object when the first parameter to the glTexCoord* function becomes larger than 1.0. Specifically, with this call, OpenGL ignores the integer portion of the texture coordinate and only uses the fractional portion, which causes the repetition of the texture. glTexParameteri can be called with a second parameter of GL_TEXTURE_WRAP_T to get OpenGL to repeat the texture in the vertical direction as well. The OpenGL default is to repeat the texture.

Using the call glTexParameteri(GL_TEXTURE_2D, GL_TEXTURE_WRAP_S, GL_CLAMP), texture coordinates are clamped within the range [0.0, 1.0]. Any texture coordinates below 0.0 will be set to be 0.0, and any texture coordinates greater than 1.0, will be set to 1.0. This will, for example, repeat the right edge of the texture for all values greater than 1.0.

Textures can also be applied to Bézier surfaces. In addition to all of the preceding steps, a square patch is defined that has the range of coordinates for the Bézier surface. A map is set up for this square texture patch that is associated with the map for the Bézier patch. Now, when OpenGL evaluates the Bézier surface map it also evaluates the texture map to get the texture coordinates it needs. The following code fragment carries this out.

```
GLfloat texturePoints[2][2][2] = {{{0.0, 0.0}, {0.0, 1.0}},
                    {{1.0, 0.0}, {1.0, 1.0}}};

glMap2f(GL_MAP2_VERTEX_3, 0, 1, 3, 4, 0, 1, 12, 4,
                    controlPoints);
glMap2f(GL_MAP2_TEXTURE_COORD_2, 0, 1, 2, 2, 0, 1, 4, 2,
                    texturePoints);
glEnable(GL_MAP2_TEXTURE_COORD_2);
glEnable(GL_MAP2_VERTEX_3);
glMapGrid2f(20, 0.0, 1.0, 20, 0.0, 1.0);
glTexEnvf(GL_TEXTURE_ENV, GL_TEXTURE_ENV_MODE, GL_DECAL);
glTexImage2D(GL_TEXTURE_2D, 0, GL_RGB, imageWidth, imageHeight,
                    0, GL_RGB, GL_UNSIGNED_BYTE, image);
glEnable(GL_TEXTURE_2D);
```

In this example, an array is set up with the texture coordinate ranges. Because a range of points from 0.0 to 1.0 is used, the texture is stretched across the surface. If a wider range is used in this declaration, the texture would then be repeated. For example, if values of 1.0 in the declaration of texturePoints are replaced with the value 4.0, the texture would be repeated four times in both the s and t directions. The second call to glMap2f sets up the texture coordinate map, but the other Bézier surface and texture calls are the same as they would be if these capabilities were not combined. The glEvalMesh* routine is still called to actually draw this textured surface. Figure 6.38 shows the application of these techniques to add a checkerboard texture to a Bézier surface.

◦ 6.7.5 Advanced OpenGL texturing

The shading model of OpenGL calculates the color of the surface, and then the texture is applied. The result is that texturing will also be applied to the specular highlight, which can dim the specular highlight in an inappropriate way. After making the call, glLightModeli(GL_LIGHT_MODEL_COLOR_CONTROL, GL_SEPARATE_SPECULAR_COLOR), OpenGL calculates the illumination as two parts: a primary or nonspecular part and a specular part. The texture is then applied to the primary part before the specular

Figure 6.38 • Texturing a Bézier patch

part is added in. This two-part process results in a specular highlight that is unaffected by the texture operations. To have OpenGL calculate the color as one component again—in other words to restore the default—make the call, glLightModeli(GL_LIGHT_MODEL_COLOR_CONTROL, GL_SINGLE_COLOR). The first object of Figure 6.39 was rendered with GL_SINGLE_COLOR and the second object was rendered with GL_SEPARATE_SPECULAR_COLOR. In the first image, the highlight has been eliminated on the black squares by the texture.

Mipmapping

OpenGL handles antialiasing of textures through the use of mipmaps (Williams83), which are copies of the texture at various resolutions. The idea is that depending on the relationship between the pixel and texel sizes OpenGL chooses the most appropriate copy of the texture to use. To use mipmapping for a texture of size 32 by 8, textures at the resolutions of 16 by 4; 8 by 2; 4 by 1; 2 by 1; and 1 by 1 all need to be provided. If any of the dimensions of the textures becomes one, it stays at one as the other sizes continue to get smaller until all are one. These various texture resolutions are specified by repeatedly calling glTexImage*D with increasing values for level. The biggest texture is always at level 0, and the smallest texture is at the largest level value. In the preceding example, level 0 would be of size 32 by 8; level 1 would be of size 16 by 4; and so on until level 5, which would be of size 1 by 1. More details on how these mipmaps are used can be found in (OpenGL99).

Filtering

The locations on an object do not always correspond directly to texel locations. A method is needed to tell OpenGL how to handle this situation. OpenGL calls this "filtering." OpenGL allows the specification of different filter methods if the pixel maps onto many texel elements (called minified) or if the pixel maps to any area smaller than a texel (called magnified). The option is set with a call to glTexParameteri, where the first parameter is the texture target (e.g., GL_TEXTURE_2D);

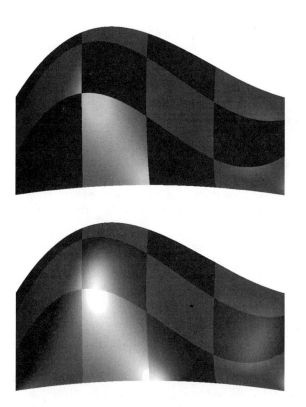

Figure 6.39 • Early and late inclusion of the specular component

the second is either GL_TEXTURE_MIN_FILTER or GL_TEXTURE_MAG_FILTER; and the third parameter indicates the type of filtering to do for that case. The first filter is GL_NEAREST, which chooses the texel nearest to the pixel location in texture space. The second filter is GL_LINEAR, which calculates the weighted average of the four nearest texels. For texels on the edge of the texture, one or two of these nearest texels might fall outside the range of the texture. If GL_REPEAT is specified, the nearest texels will wrap around to the other side of the texture. A texel location that is off the right end of the texture uses a texel from the left edge. When GL_CLAMP is specified, the adjacent border texel is used. The border is, therefore, used to texture two adjacent polygonal patches with different textures. To make sure that the filtering is correct at the edges, the first texture's border is set to be the adjacent edge of the second texture, and vice versa.

The rest of the filtering methods are GL_NEAREST_MIPMAP_NEAREST, GL_NEAREST_MIPMAP_LINEAR, GL_LINEAR_MIPMAP_NEAREST, and GL_LINEAR_MIPMAP_LINEAR. In each of these cases, the first "word" indicates how the choice is made between the two closest mipmaps and the second indicates how these are combined. Specifically, GL_NEAREST_MIPMAP_NEAREST chooses the nearest texel in the nearest mipmap, where GL_LINEAR_MIPMAP_LINEAR uses a linear interpolation of the closest texels in each of the two closest mipmaps and then will do a second linear interpolation between these two mipmap values.

Environment mapping

OpenGL has support for using environment maps, but the environment map still needs to be created before use. OpenGL has an algorithm that finds the point on a sphere that has the same normal vector as the object. That sphere point is used to determine the location in the texture map to use for this object location. To use environment mapping, the texture is set up and then the following code fragment is used.

```
glTexGeni(GL_S, GL_TEXTURE_GEN_MODE, GL_SPHERE_MAP);
glTexGeni(GL_T, GL_TEXTURE_GEN_MODE, GL_SPHERE_MAP);
glEnable(GL_TEXTURE_GEN_S);
glEnable(GL_TEXTURE_GEN_T);
```

Replacing textures

There are high computational costs in setting up a new texture, so it is faster to instead replace all or part of an existing texture. A call to do this is glTexSubImage2D(GL_TEXTURE_2D, level, xOffset, yOffset, width, height, format, type, texture). This call replaces an area of the 2D texture that is width by height texels located at position (xOffset, yOffset). Position (0, 0) of the new texture is considered to be the lower left corner.

Texture objects and binding

In OpenGL, a number of textures can be loaded and each one can be given an internal name. As the image is being drawn, these names are used to rapidly switch between these textures. Of course, the number of textures that can be loaded into OpenGL is limited by the amount of space each needs and the total amount of available space.

OpenGL returns a set of texture names with the call glGenTextures(count, list), where count is the number of textures to be used and list is an array of type GLuint with enough locations to hold the values generated. These texture names are really just unsigned integers.

A call to glBindTexture(GL_TEXTURE_*D, name) does one of two things. If this is the first time that this name is used, a new texture object is created for that name. If this name has been used before, the texture associated with that name becomes the active texture for rendering. After calling glBindTexture, the new active texture is the one that will be changed by successive calls that change the texture or texture parameters.

6.8 Projects

1) Add a texture to your rendering program. Each object now needs a texture attribute that specifies the texture to use. The texture file can be a simple binary file. To have textures of varying size, the first two integers in the file can give the height and width of the texture and the rest of the values can give the RGB triplet values for the texels.

2) Do research to find code to read a JPEG file. One source is the Independent JPEG Group, which distributes free JPEG routines. Use this code to read images and use those images as textures for your scenes.

Shadows

We may not be aware of them all the time, but shadows play an important role in our understanding of the world. Shadows along with highlights provide visual cues as to the location of light sources relative to the objects in the scene. Shadows also help determine the relative position of objects. For example, as one object moves away from another, the shadow it casts changes. Consider how sunlight casts shadows on the ground. An object resting on the ground has a reasonably sharp shadow and that shadow touches the object where the object meets the ground. If an object is above the ground, there is distance between the object and shadow locations, and the shadow has blurry edges. If you pick up an object that is lying on the ground, the shadow edges increases in blurriness as the distance from the ground increases. Figure 7.1 shows one picture of a ball on the ground, and three pictures of a ball at varying heights. The distance increases between the ball and the shadow as the ball is lifted off the ground.

There are two parts to a real shadow: the umbra and the penumbra (Figure 7.2). The umbra and penumbra appear when the light source emits energy from multiple locations even if they are closely spaced. The umbra is the part of the shadow where the light is completely absent because light emanating from all of the locations within the light source is blocked. The penumbra is the part of the shadow where only some of the light from the light source is blocked. Where Figure 7.2 appears to show the penumbra as a uniform area, there is actually a gradation to this part of the shadow from its most dark points right next to the umbra, to no shadowing at all just outside of the penumbra. This occurs because, moving away from the umbra, there are more and more locations within the light source that are casting energy that reaches the penumbra area.

Figure 7.1 • A tennis ball resting on the ground and at three different heights (see Color Plate 7.1)

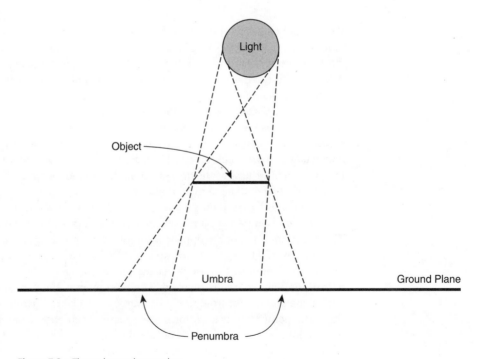

Figure 7.2 • The umbra and penumbra

These two parts of a shadow are dependent on the sizes of the light source and the object, and the relative locations of the light source, object, and where the shadow is being cast. For example, if the location of the light source and the ground plane are fixed, as the object moves toward the light source, the size of the umbra and penumbra will both increase—as can be seen in a comparison of Figure 7.2 and the first drawing of Figure 7.3. Also, if the object location and the ground plane are

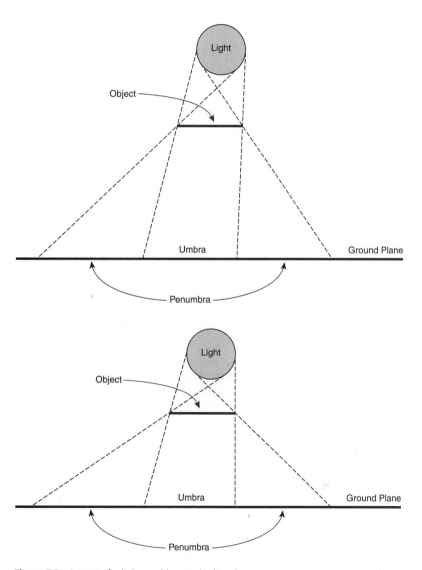

Figure 7.3 • Impact of relative position on shadow size

fixed, as the light source moves toward the object, the size of the umbra and penumbra will both increase—as can be seen in a comparison of Figure 7.2 and the second drawing of Figure 7.3.

Figure 7.2 has multiple lines coming from the light source that show the effect of having many locations that generate light energy. For a point light source, all of the energy comes from a single location. This would change the drawing so that there is just one line from the light source to each end of the object. With a point light source, there is only an umbra part of the shadow. In graphics, some techniques treat light sources as points in space, which means that there will be no penumbra, just umbra. This simplification makes shading calculations easier but produces shadows that look unnaturally sharp.

This chapter presents techniques to add shadows to images. Although adding shadows increases the work that a rendering program must do, the results will be more realistic than images without shadows. The methods presented here can be added to the rendering algorithms that were discussed in previous chapters. This chapter also looks at a technique for distributed light sources that can be used to produce both an umbra and penumbra.

7.1 Coloring Shadows

There are two issues involved with adding shadows to an image: identifying where the shadows are, and altering the illumination calculations to account for the shadows. This section deals with techniques to shade or color areas that are in shadow. Later sections discuss finding where a shadow occurs.

A very simplistic solution to this problem is to use black or dark gray for all of the image locations that are in a shadow. During the rendering of an object or ground plane, this shadow color would be used for locations in shadow instead of the color that would be calculated by the shading model. Though this is a simple solution, it will not lead to very convincing results. If you look around, you will see that shadows will darken an area, but it still retains some of its underlying appearance. In Figure 7.1, the texture of the concrete is still visible in the shadowed areas. If a shadowed area within a generated image has a texture, the texture should still be visible within the shadow. Replacing the calculated value with a constant shadow color will lose any underlying surface detail. Figure 7.4 shows the use of a uniform shadow color of 0.1. This process is quick, but it does not produce very realistic results. In this figure, the shadows on the ground plane are all the same color even though some areas are in the shadow from one light source and others are in the shadow from both. Furthermore, the shadow on the large green sphere is almost black and does not have the same color that occurs at the bottom of the sphere from ambient light.

Because a real shadow does not change the appearance of an object, just darkens it, a second option is to do the shading calculation as usual but then darken the

Figure 7.4 • Using a fixed shadow color (see Color Plate 7.2)

result. This can be done by subtracting some amount from the color or by multiplying the color by some percentage. The amount of the reduction would be determined heuristically so as to produce a reasonably believable result. In this way, the underlying color or texture on the object is partially preserved. If there are multiple light sources, the color can be reduced by this amount or percentage for each light source that is blocked. Therefore, areas that have more than one light source blocked would be darkened a number of times, which would give an approximation to overlapping shadows. A difficulty with this technique is to decide how much to reduce the color by. The reduction is likely to be some empirically chosen and fixed value that does not account for the fact that some light sources are brighter than others. To improve this further, the reduction could be based on the intensity of the light source—dim lights would have a smaller reduction than bright lights. This might seem counterintuitive, but the shadow can be thought of as removing the light source's contribution. A dim light will have a smaller contribution than a bright light and, therefore, the contribution reduction will be less. There is still a problem. Consider an object that normally has a highlight due to a particular light source. If there is an object blocking this light source, this method will still add a highlight to the object, it will just be dimmed. Figure 7.5 shows the shadows cast by a set of three spheres, with the light intensity reduced by 50 percent in the shadowed areas. The shadows on the ground plane now show a variation based on the number of light sources blocked. The large green sphere shows a shadow from the upper right sphere that is now green because of the ambient component. But because this method just reduces the calculated illumination, a highlight caused by the blocked light is still visible in the shadow—it is only reduced in brightness.

Figure 7.5 • Using a percentage reduction (see Color Plate 7.3)

The second alternative moved closer to the situation in the real world, where the amount removed is proportional to the light source that is blocked. A third option does this in an even more realistic way. Instead of reducing the color by an amount based on the blocked light source, the blocked light source is just not included in the calculations. Consider a situation where there are three light sources and, at the current point, the second light source is blocked by some other object. The illumination equation is calculated twice for the first and third light sources. For example, in a Phong shading model, areas not in a shadow have their color determined by the ambient component and the diffuse and specular component from all three light sources. Areas that are blocked from one of the light sources have their color determined by the ambient component and the diffuse and specular component of the remaining two light sources. Overall, this means that the shadows have varying levels of color based on whether one, two, or all three of these light sources are blocked. Figure 7.6 shows the result of using this third technique. Notice that in this figure, the left highlight on the large green sphere does not extend into the shadow. Also the shadows on the ground plane are more realistic because the areas where both light sources are blocked are now black instead of a darker grey as in Figure 7.5.

A high level algorithm for this process is:

```
for each location on the object
   for each light source
      if the light source is not blocked
         color = color + Shade( location, light source )
```

Figure 7.6 • Ignoring the blocked light source (see Color Plate 7.4)

7.2 Simple Shadows

The investigation of shadow location determination begins with a simple solution to this problem. The relative location of an object and its shadow on the ground reveals information about how high above the ground the object is positioned. In a simple scene, with a few widely located objects and a ground plane, a simple projection from the light source can be used to create shadows on the ground plane. This simple shadowing method only creates shadows on the ground plane because the projections onto the ground plane can be calculated quickly as the ground plane is always assumed to be the plane y = 0. Blinn (Blinn88) developed this simple shadowing technique that handles two possibilities: light sources at infinity and locally positioned light sources.

7.2.1 Light sources at infinity

If the light source is at infinity, the rays of light entering the scene are parallel (Figure 7.7). If L represents the vector pointing in the direction the light is traveling, the points on the object cast their shadow onto the ground plane along lines parallel to this direction. The parametric equation of a line[1] between the light source direction (L) and a location on the object (P) is given by $S(t) = P - t * L$. The ground plane location where the object location P casts its shadow is found by setting the equation for the y coordinate to 0 and then solving for t, because when casting shadows onto the ground plane at $y = 0$, the y value for all of the shadow points

---

[1]Recall that this parametric equation actually represents three equations for the x, y, and z components of each point.

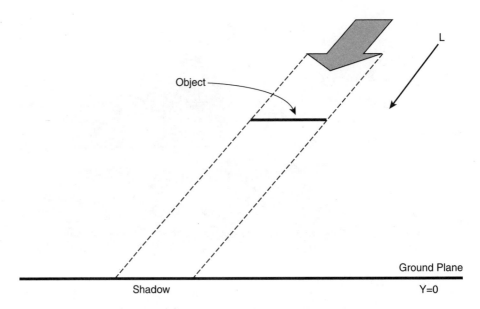

Figure 7.7 • Parallel shadow projection

will be 0. This means that t will have a value of y_P / y_L. If y_L is 0, the light is being cast horizontally, so there is no shadow in the ground plane. The value of t can then be used to calculate the x and z location where the object location P casts its shadow. Equations (7.1) show the complete calculation of the shadow location when the calculation of t is substituted back into the parametric equations.

$$x_s = x_p - \frac{y_P}{y_L} * x_L = x_P - \frac{x_L}{y_L} * y_P$$

$$z_s = z_p - \frac{y_P}{y_L} * z_L = z_P - \frac{z_L}{y_L} * y_P$$

(7.1)

A matrix form of equations (7.1) is given in equation (7.2). This matrix is just a parallel projection matrix into the y = 0 plane.

$$\begin{bmatrix} x_s \\ 0 \\ z_s \\ 1 \end{bmatrix} = \begin{bmatrix} 1 & -x_L / y_L & 0 & 0 \\ 0 & 0 & 0 & 0 \\ 0 & -z_L / y_L & 1 & 0 \\ 0 & 0 & 0 & 1 \end{bmatrix} * \begin{bmatrix} x_P \\ y_P \\ z_P \\ 1 \end{bmatrix}$$

(7.2)

Blinn describes a two-step process. First, the scene is rendered as usual, using the parameters specified for the objects. Next, the shadow matrix is multiplied into the current transformation matrix. The objects are rendered again. This time, because of the shadow matrix, the projection of the objects onto the ground plane is being rendered. On this pass, the area where the projection winds up is filled with the shadow color, or the currently displayed color is reduced appropriately.

This technique can be used with a z-buffer for handling depth. If a plane for the ground has already been drawn, the shadows are rendered when the depth of the projected object is equal to the value stored in the z-buffer. When the values are equal, the image displays the ground plane, which needs to be replaced by the shadow being drawn. Because round-off error might not result in exactly equal values, an alternative is to render the objects and their shadows first, and then render the ground plane only when its depth is strictly farther (by some small amount) than what has already been rendered.

7.2.2 Local light sources

When a light source has a specific location instead of infinity, the process is similar, but in this case the projection onto the ground plane will be a perspective projection (Figure 7.8). A parametric equation for a line is still used but with the light source as a location L instead of a vector. This makes the parametric equation $S(t) = P - t * (P - L)$. Projecting into the $y = 0$ plane and solving for t gives that $t = y_P / (y_P - y_L)$. The values of the projection onto the ground plane are given by equations (7.3).

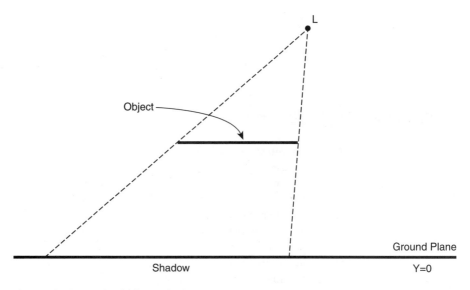

Figure 7.8 • Perspective shadow projection

$$x_s = \frac{x_L * y_P - x_P * y_L}{y_P - y_L}$$

$$z_s = \frac{z_L * y_P - z_P * y_L}{y_P - y_L}$$

(7.3)

A matrix form of equations (7.3) is given in equation (7.4) where x_S and z_S are found by dividing x' and y' by $(y_P - y_L)$. Specifically, $x_S = x' / (y_P - y_L)$ and $z_S = z' / (y_P - y_L)$. The matrix in equation (7.4) is just a perspective projection matrix into the $y = 0$ plane.

$$\begin{bmatrix} x' \\ 0 \\ z' \\ y_P - y_L \end{bmatrix} = \begin{bmatrix} -y_L & x_L & 0 & 0 \\ 0 & 0 & 0 & 0 \\ 0 & z_L & -y_L & 0 \\ 0 & 1 & 0 & -y_L \end{bmatrix} * \begin{bmatrix} x_P \\ y_P \\ z_P \\ 1 \end{bmatrix}$$

(7.4)

Once this matrix is determined, the rest of the process for local light sources is the same as that for light sources at infinity.

When using the simple shadow method, there are two conditions under which false shadows will occur (see Figure 7.9). Placing any light source below the ground plane causes the intersection of the ground plane and the "light rays" to be between the light source and the object. Placing a local light source inside the scene causes some objects to project on the ground plane positioned on other side of the light.

False shadows can be prevented by placing an additional check into the algorithm. Whether the light is at infinity or local, the vertex of the object is along the line at a t value of 0. Negative values of t are positioned farther along the line toward the ground plane. Therefore, positive values of t will be on the "light side" of the object. This means a shadow should only be drawn if the value of t is negative.

7.3 Projection Shadows

So far, simple shadows have only been cast onto the ground plane, but what if one object casts a shadow on another object. This should have an impact on the way the second object is rendered. The simple shadow technique has no way to determine this. In this section and the two that follow, other techniques are explored that determine shadow locations, including shadows cast on other objects.

A shadow occurs because, from the view of the object, something is blocking the light. Another way to look at this is to say that a shadow occurs in places where an object is not visible from the light source. This concept serves as the basis for the rest of the shadow algorithms.

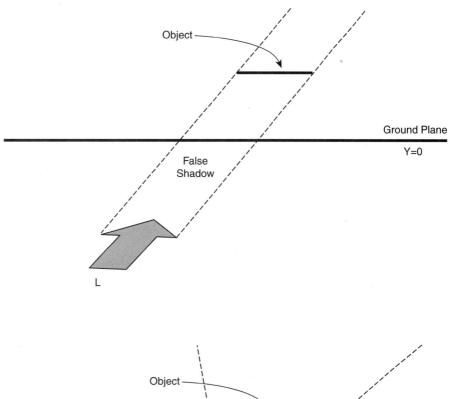

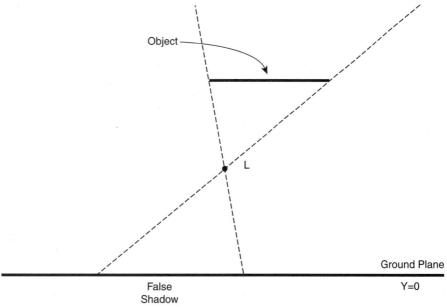

Figure 7.9 • False shadows

7.3.1 Object clipping

Chapter 5 looked at the Weiler-Atherton algorithm for hidden surfaces. That algorithm clips one polygon against another to determine the pieces of each polygon that are visible. This clipping process is done from the perspective of the viewpoint. Atherton, Weiler, and Greenberg (Atherton78) used this idea to determine shadows. They applied the clipping process using the perspective of the light source instead of the viewpoint. The result is two sets of polygons: those visible to the light source and those hidden from the light source. Those polygons flagged as hidden from the light source can have their shading calculations adjusted to account for the fact that they are in a shadow.

If there are multiple light sources, the process is repeated for each of the light sources. In this case, the subdivided polygons of the last pass are used for the next. Each polygon is tagged with a list of light sources that illuminate it or alternatively those that are blocked. Figure 7.10 shows this process for three polygons and two light sources. When clipping for light source L_1, the rectangle on the right is divided into two pieces, where the triangular polygon intersects along one side. On the sec-

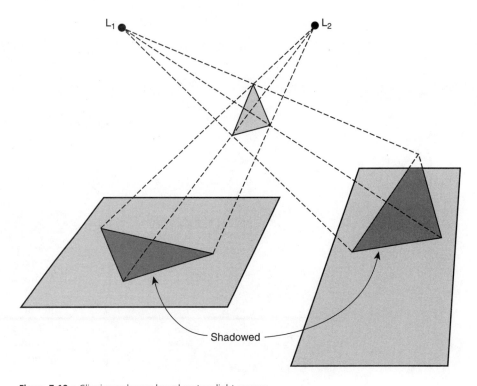

Figure 7.10 • Clipping polygons based on two light sources.

ond pass for light source L_2, the left rectangle is also divided into two pieces, with one of the pieces being in the center of the original rectangle.

The value of this technique is that the shadow determination is done in the object space and has not been influenced by the viewer. As long as none of the objects or light sources is moved, multiple images of this scene can be rendered from various viewpoints without having to repeat the shadow clipping process. Object parameter changes can be distributed to each of the subdivided polygon pieces, if information is kept that relates the new polygons back to the original object.

The problems with this technique are the same as with the original Weiler-Atherton algorithm. Namely, that the clipping process can produce polygons that are concave or that have holes in them as is shown in Figure 7.10. Because of this, additional processing might also be necessary to subdivide these problem polygons into convex pieces.

7.4 Shadow Volumes

When the light strikes an object, this casts a shadow behind the object. Crow (Crow77) used this idea to develop the concept of a shadow volume. A shadow volume is defined for each light source and polygon combination, because a shadow volume is defined by the location of the light source and the location of a polygon. Any polygons or parts of polygons that fall inside the shadow volume are blocked from the light source that created that volume. The task now is to determine the objects in the shadow volumes, so those can be rendered using a shadow coloring method.

A shadow volume for a simple polygon and a local light source can be seen in Figure 7.11. The view volume is the pyramidal area bordered by planes that go through the viewpoint and the edges of the far clipping plane. The shadow volume is defined by the light source (L) and the object. Any other object that falls in the shadow volume behind the object will not be illuminated by the light source. The dark area in Figure 7.11 shows the overlap between the view and shadow volumes. Objects that are located in this area are those that are both visible and shadowed. The sides of the overlap area define the portion of the visible world space that falls inside the shadow.

The sides of the shadow volume are known as shadow polygons. Three of the sides of a shadow polygon are defined by one edge of the object polygon and the two lines that originate at the light source and go through the endpoints of that edge. The fourth edge can be defined by where the two lines from the light source intersect the farthest side of the view volume.

The normal for a shadow polygon is assigned to point out of the shadow volume. Recall from Chapter 5 that a polygon can be classified as either back-facing (when the normal points in the opposite direction of the view vector) or front-facing (when the normal points in the same direction of the view vector). Specifically, if $V \cdot N < 0$, the shadow polygon is back-facing, and if $V \cdot N > 0$, the shadow polygon is front-facing. Once the shadow polygons have been determined, they are added to the

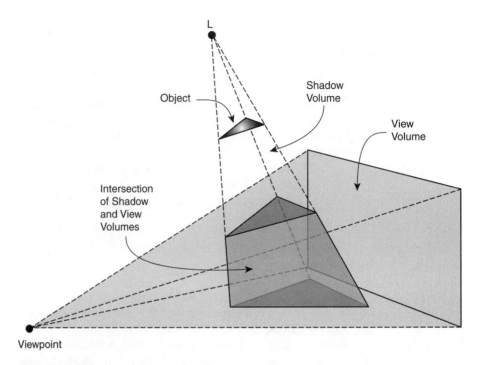

Figure 7.11 • A shadow volume

scene. Each of these shadow polygons will be tagged with an identifier that tells the shadow volume they are a part of. The shadow polygons will not be rendered, but rather will be used to determine if another object is in a shadow or not.

To render a location on an object you determine whether the location is in shadow by using the line from the viewpoint to the object location. Starting with a shadow count of 0, a 1 is added for every front-facing shadow polygon the line passes through, and 1 is subtracted for every back-facing shadow polygon the line passes through. Figure 7.12 shows a top view of one of these lines passing through a series of shadow volumes. The numbers along the line show the shadow count for that portion of the line. When the object location is reached, if the count is positive, the location is in a shadow volume; and the count indicates how many shadow volumes it is in. For example, if the object location is in one of the areas labeled with a 1, that object is within one shadow volume. Likewise, if it is in one of the areas labeled with a 0, it is not in any shadows.

If there are multiple light sources, a list can be kept of the front- and back-facing shadow polygons encountered. This list can then be used to determine which specific light sources are blocked for the illumination calculation. When the list contains both a front- and back-facing polygon for a shadow volume, the object is not

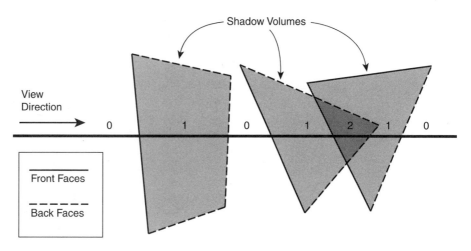

Figure 7.12 • Counting shadow volumes

in that volume, so those pairs of polygons can be removed from the list. Once the list is pared down in this way, the object is known to be shadowed by the volumes for which there is a front-facing polygon left on the list—because there is no matching back-facing one.

The discussion in the previous paragraph assumed that the viewpoint was not in shadow, because the shadow count began at 0. It is possible, however, for the viewpoint to be in the shadow of one or more polygons. So, a first step should be to determine how many and which shadow volumes the viewpoint is within. This information can be found by a process similar to what is used to determine if an object is in a shadow. In this case, a line is followed from the viewpoint to "infinity" in any direction, counting and keeping track of the front and back facing shadow polygons encountered. At "infinity" the line must be outside of all shadow volumes, therefore, if there are more back-facing shadow polygons than front-facing polygons, the start of the line (the viewpoint) must have been inside a shadow volume. As in the case of determining if an object is shadowed, keeping track of which front- and back-facing shadow polygons were intersected can be used to determine the list of shadow volumes the viewpoint is in. When determining if an object is shadowed, the starting viewpoint shadow counter is set to the number of back-facing shadow polygons minus the number of front-facing shadow polygons that are found along the line from the viewpoint to infinity. To determine which shadow volumes the object is in, the intersection list is initialized to the front-facing polygon of each shadow volume the viewpoint is in.

Brotman and Badler (Brotman84) changed Crow's shadow volume process in order to combine it with the z-buffer algorithm. To start, they modified the z-buffer so that it stored not only the depth at each location, but also a pointer to the object displayed there, and a list of shadow polygons that cover that area. In their method, the first step scan converts the objects but will only update the z-buffer and object pointer. The illumination calculations are not yet done—only the object and depth information is updated. At the end of this process, the modified z-buffer has all of the information about which object location needs to be rendered for each pixel of the image, even though the shading calculations have not yet been done. For the second step, each shadow polygon is scan converted, and if it is closer than the current object at a location, it is added to the list for that z-buffer location. Shadow polygons that are further away can be ignored because they are behind the object at that point, and so are not on the line between the viewpoint and the object. At the end of this second step, each z-buffer location holds a pointer to the closest object, the location to render on that object, and a list of the shadow polygons that might be involved. The last step is to go through each location of the z-buffer and do the shading calculation based on the object and shadow polygon list. The list of shadow polygons can be scanned for matching front- and back-facing polygons, and if they all match up, the object is not shadowed and can be rendered as normal. If they do not all match up, the unmatched ones indicated how the location is shadowed, and thus what adjustments are necessary to determine the illumination at that location.

The results of the second step of this process can be made more manageable. The process of matching front- and back-facing shadow polygons can be handled while the shadow polygons are being scan converted. For each shadow volume, the front-facing shadow polygons are scan converted first. Now when a back-facing shadow polygon is scan converted, if it is in front of the object, the algorithm can remove the matching front-facing polygon from the list instead of also adding the back-facing shadow polygon. At the end of this modified second step, each location of the modified z-buffer will have the front-facing polygons for shadow volumes the object is in.

Bergeron (Bergeron86) also made a modification to Crow's shadow volume technique to add atmospheric attenuation to the light source by defining a limit on the size of the shadow volume. Atmospheric attenuation limits how far a source will cast its light, therefore, everything in the shadow volume and everything beyond the attenuation distance in any direction is in "shadow" relative to the light. Bergeron set the shadow volume so that it extended only as far as this attenuation distance, whereas Crow extended it to the far side of the viewing volume. These truncated shadow volumes do not mean that objects beyond them are illuminated, however, because in Bergeron's shadowing method, all objects beyond the attenuation distance are not illuminated under any circumstances. Thus, any objects falling inside these truncated shadow volumes, as well as objects that are beyond the attenuation distance limit in any direction, are rendered without that light source.

7.5 Shadow Z-buffer

One solution to the shadowing problem determines the object locations that are closest to a light source and then all other locations are in shadow. Said another way, locations on an object that are not the closest to a light source are in shadow. The shadow z-buffer[2] technique applies this hidden surface solution to the determination of shadow locations. A z-buffer is used to store the distance from the viewpoint to the object being displayed at each pixel. But if the scene is scan converted (but not rendered to save time) using the light source location as the viewpoint, the resulting z-buffer will have all of the locations that are in the light.

Williams (Williams78) created the idea of a shadow z-buffer—also called a shadow map—that holds the distance from the light source to each location that is not shadowed. A transformation matrix is needed that moves the light source to the viewpoint location and that aligns the direction from the light source to the center of the scene with the view direction. The combination of the light source location and direction could be seen as defining a light source coordinate system, and this transformation would then convert from the light source coordinate system into the viewpoint coordinate system. For example, if the light source is at location $(0, 30, -30)$ and the center of the scene is at $(0, 0, -20)$, a rotation of $135°$ about the x axis would properly align the view direction and would bring the light source location to $(0, 0, 42.4)$. A translation of -42.4 in the z direction would also be needed to bring the light source location to the origin. Applying this combination transformation to all of the objects has the effect of making the viewpoint look at the scene from the light source location and direction. Now, all of the transformed objects are scan converted using the standard algorithms into the shadow z-buffer. This step can be done quickly because there is no need to do the full shading calculation. This step determines the smallest distances of the objects from the light source. If there are multiple light sources, each would have its own transformation and shadow z-buffer. Figure 7.13 shows a simple scene with a shadow z-buffer and the depth z-buffer.

Once the shadow z-buffers have all been determined, the rendering of the image can proceed using the z-buffer algorithm, with one change. In the standard z-buffer algorithm, the rendering process begins by getting a location (x, y, z) on the object. The depth of this location is compared with the z-buffer value and a decision is made about whether this location should be rendered. If the location is to be rendered, the object location is transformed with a transformation that is the inverse of the one used to create the shadow z-buffer. Returning to the previous example, this inverse transformation would first move the object 42.5 in the z direction and then

---

[2]The shadow z-buffer actually holds the object locations that are illuminated by the light source. A better name might be illumination z-buffer; however, the name "shadow z-buffer" is well established in the graphics literature.

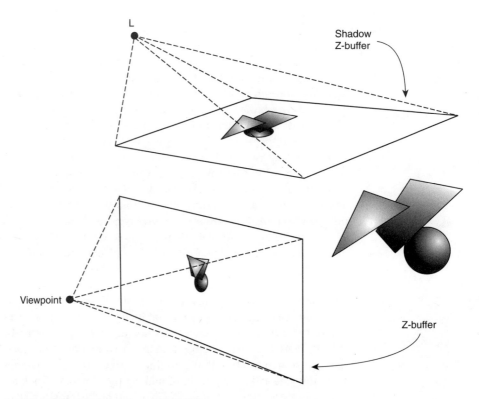

Figure 7.13 • Shadow and regular z-buffers

rotate $-135°$ around the x axis. This inverse transformation has the effect of moving that object location from the viewpoint coordinate system to the light source coordinate system. This inverse transformation converts the point (x, y, z) from the viewpoint coordinate system to the point (x', y', z') in the light source coordinate system. The shadow z-buffer holds the depth of the closest object to the light, so comparing z' with the value in the shadow z-buffer for (x', y') indicates if the object point is in the light or the shadow. Specifically, if the shadow map value for location (x', y') is closer than z', the point (x, y, z) is shadowed relative to this light source and the appropriate adjustment can be made in the rendering process. If the two values are the same, then this point is not shadowed relative to this light source and the illumination calculations can proceed as normal. If there are multiple light sources, each light source will have its own shadow z-buffer and inverse transformation. This process is repeated for each light source to determine which of them actually contribute to the illumination of this object location.

```
calculate the light transformation matrix
transform objects by light matrix
calculate the inverse light transformation matrix
render objects into shadowBuffer

for every object
   for every pixel in the object
   {
      calculate the (x, y, z) location
      // with a right-handed coordinate system
      // values closer are larger than values far away
      if (z > zBuffer[x, y])
      {
         inverseTransform(x, y, z, x', y', z')
         if (z' == shadowBuffer[x', y'])
            determine the color
         else
            determine the shadowed color
         display the color at (x, y)
         zBuffer[x, y] = z;
      }
   }
```

There are two problems with this process. The first is that this is very space intensive because a shadow z-buffer is needed for each of the light sources. The second is that adjustments need to be made to account for round-off error problems.[3] Because of round-off error when doing the transformation multiplications, the value of z' can be slightly greater or less than the distance in the shadow z-buffer even though they both represent the same point. This effectively means that objects can wind up shadowing themselves some of the time because of round-off error. There are two ways to adjust for this. The first way is for the checks against the shadow z-buffer to be done to some tolerance. Specifically, two values are considered the same if they are within some small value, determined by the resolution of the scene. The second way is to incorporate an additional very small translation into the light source transformation. This translation will bring the point z' just a bit closer to the light source, which now allows the check of z' against the shadow buffer to be a less than or equal check, instead of just an equal check.

• 7.5.1 Soft edged shadows

Brotman and Badler (Brotman84) developed a method that can be used to create shadows that include both the umbra and penumbra. Though this was originally

---

[3]See Appendix A for a discussion of round-off error.

published as a modification to Crow's shadow volumes process, a similar technique can be used with any of the shadow rendering methods discussed here, or in ray tracing. This method includes soft shadows produced by non-point light sources.

Figure 7.2 shows the penumbra is caused by light emanating from multiple locations in the light source. To accomplish distributed light sources, Brotman and Badler use a random distribution to locate a collection of point light sources that simulate a larger uniform light source. For example, if the light source is intended to be a sphere, this method locates a number of point light sources inside the area of the sphere. The number of point sources used will depend on the size of the distributed light source—the larger the light source, the more points that should be used. Each of these point light sources is treated as an independent light source, so each gets its own shadow z-buffer or creates its own set of shadow volumes. If the intensity of the distributed light source is equal at all points on the light, each of these individual point light sources has an intensity set at I / n, where I is the overall intensity for the distributed light source, and n is the number of individual points light sources being used to simulate the distributed light. If the intensity of the distributed light source is uneven, the intensity of the randomly distributed points can be set to reflect this unevenness.

For example, Figure 7.14 shows the same set up as in Figure 7.6. However in this case, the light sources are distributed light sources. Using the method of Brotman and Badler, there are 50 light sources uniformly distributed in a spherical shape of radius 100 (about 10 percent of the scene size) around the center of the point light source locations of Figure 7.6. These 50 light sources each have an intensity that is

Figure 7.14 • Soft edged shadows using distributed light sources (see Color Plate 7.5)

1/50th of the light sources in Figure 7.6. The shadows in Figure 7.14 have much softer edges than those of Figure 7.6. These softer edges are not as dark as the centers of the shadows, thus showing both the umbra and penumbra.

7.6 The OpenGL Way

Shadows are not a built-in capability of OpenGL. Where shading and depth tests can be enabled or disabled, there is no equivalent ability to enable or disable shadows. Instead, additional steps are needed to include shadows in images.

There are three techniques that can be used to add shadows in OpenGL. The first two are based on the ideas of Blinn, discussed in section 7.2. One of these uses a simple projection onto the ground plane from the light position and the other uses the OpenGL stencil buffer to identify where on the ground plane shadows occur. The third technique uses the stencil buffer in connection with shadow volume ideas discussed in section 7.4. Additional details on these techniques can be found in Kilgard (Kilgard99).

Some background on the stencil buffer in OpenGL is given in the next section before moving on to the shadowing techniques themselves.

7.6.1 The stencil buffer

The stencil buffer, like the depth buffer, is an area of memory the same size as the frame buffer. Each of these locations applies to one of the pixel locations. Most implementations of OpenGL use 8 or 16 bits for each stencil buffer location, and use those bits as an unsigned integer. Some graphics cards even implement the stencil buffer in hardware.

You are probably familiar with stencils from an art class. A stencil in that context is a card that has a shape cut out of it. You can duplicate that shape by placing the card on a piece of paper and drawing within the cut-out areas. Stencils can be used to create a repeated pattern for a border on paper or on a wall. Many years ago, stencils with cut-out letters were used to create posters and banners.

In OpenGL, the stencil buffer is used as a test to determine whether or not to proceed with the drawing of an object, much like the depth buffer. When using the depth buffer, the depth of the current object is compared to the buffer values in order for OpenGL to make a decision whether to render. Updating the buffer to the new depth is also done in this process. The stencil buffer has a lot more flexibility in how values are set, changed, and used.

For the stencil to be available, include GLUT_STENCIL in the call to glutInitDisplayMode. To have OpenGL use the stencil buffer, a call to glEnable(GL_STENCIL_TEST) is needed. A call to glDisable is used to turn off the stencil buffer.

The stencil buffer has a set of eight tests it can perform to decide whether to continue rendering: GL_NEVER, GL_ALWAYS, GL_LESS, GL_LEQUAL, GL_EQUAL, GL_GREATER,

GL_GEQUAL, and GL_NOTEQUAL. The function is set with a call to the routine glStencilFunc(function, reference, mask), where the function is one of the values just given. The process works as follows: OpenGL gets the stencil buffer value and uses the function to compare it to the reference value. For example, if the function is GL_GREATER, the stencil test will pass if the reference value is greater than the stencil buffer value. The mask parameter is bitwise ANDed with the reference and stencil buffer values before the comparison is done. The mask value is used if you want to use different sets of bits in the stencil buffer for different purposes. The mask value blocks out the bits being used for other purposes before the values are used for the current task.

The stencil buffer value can be updated based on one of three conditions: the stencil test fails; the stencil test passes but the depth test fails; or both the tests pass. The six functions used for updating the stencil buffer are: GL_KEEP, GL_ZERO, GL_REPLACE, GL_INCR, GL_DECR, or GL_INVERT. The routine call glStencilOp(GL_KEEP, GL_INCR, GL_DECR) tells OpenGL that if the stencil test fails, the stencil buffer should not be changed; and if the stencil test passes but the depth test fails, to increment the stencil buffer. If both tests pass, the stencil buffer is decremented. The GL_REPLACE function puts the reference value into the stencil buffer, and the GL_INVERT function will perform a bitwise NOT of the value stored in the stencil buffer. The values in the stencil buffer are kept within the range of integers that can be stored with the stencil buffer resolution. With an eight-bit stencil buffer, the values are always between 0 and $2^8 - 1$. This means that incrementing a location with a value of $2^8 - 1$ will not change it, and decrementing a location with a value of 0 will not change it either.

Portions of the stencil buffer can be used for different purposes. This is accomplished by setting a stencil mask, which is used before any operations that update the stencil buffer including a clear of the stencil buffer. For example, calling glStencilMask(0x0f) sets the mask so that all operations only use the lower four bits of the stencil buffer, and not make any changes to the upper four bits. When using the stencil mask, make sure that you set the mask to 0xff before performing a glClear(GL_STENCIL_BUFFER_BIT) if all of the buffer bits are to be set to 0.

7.6.2 Planar projection shadows

When using simple shadows projected onto a ground plane, the scene is first set up and drawn as usual including the ground plane where the shadows are being cast. A collection of additional steps will then add the shadows to the image. The first of these additional steps is to push the current modelview matrix with the routine glPushMatrix so that any changes made to get the shadows can just be popped off when done. The second step is to create a matrix that moves the light position to the viewpoint and then build it into the modelview matrix. Kilgard (Kilgard99) gives the following function to build the transformation matrix.

```
void shadowMatrix(Glfloat m[4][4], GLfloat plane[4], GLfloat light[4])
{
    GLfloat dot = plane[0]*light[0] + plane[1]*light[1]
                    + plane[2]*light[2] + plane[3]*light[3];
    m[0][0] = dot - light[0] * plane[0];
    m[1][0] = -light[0] * plane[1];
    m[2][0] = -light[0] * plane[2];
    m[3][0] = -light[0] * plane[3];
    m[0][1] = -light[1] * plane[0];
    m[1][1] = dot - light[1] * plane[1];
    m[2][1] = -light[1] * plane[2];
    m[3][1] = -light[1] * plane[3];
    m[0][2] = -light[2] * plane[0];
    m[1][2] = -light[2] * plane[1];
    m[2][2] = dot - light[2] * plane[2];
    m[3][2] = -light[2] * plane[3];
    m[0][3] = -light[3] * plane[0];
    m[1][3] = -light[3] * plane[1];
    m[2][3] = -light[3] * plane[2];
    m[3][3] = dot - light[3] * plane[3];
}
```

In this function, the parameter plane holds the coefficients of the plane equation $(Ax + By + Cz + D = 0)$ and the parameter light holds the position of the light source in homogeneous coordinates. Once the shadow matrix is constructed, it is built into the current modelview matrix with the call glMultMatrixf(shadowMatrix), where the shadowMatrix is the result of the preceding function.

The next step is to render the shadows, but there is a little trick to include first. The shadows will now project directly onto the ground plane, which will give them the same depth as the ground plane. Depending on the resolution of the depth buffer and the amount of round-off error, the shadows can wind up partially in front of and partially behind the ground plane. If the scene is animated, the shadows can also wind up jumping in and out, as position changes influence the amount of round-off error. To get the shadows offset slightly in front of the ground plane, and, therefore, to always be visible, include the code fragment:

```
glEnable(GL_POLYGON_OFFSET_FILL);
glPolygonOffset(1.0, 2.0);
```

The first of these statements enables the offset facility for filled polygons. The second statement sets up how much of an offset OpenGL should use. The first parameter to this call is multiplied by a factor that measures the change in polygon depth relative to the area of the screen it covers. The second parameter is multiplied by a value representing the precision of the depth buffer. The larger these parameters are, the more the shadows will be offset from the ground plane. So if these values are too large, the shadows might begin to look like they are in the wrong location, or might even begin to cover objects where they are not casting shadows.

Now the shadows can be drawn. Because there should be no highlights on the shadows, lighting should be disabled. The current color is set to the shadow color and the objects except for the ground plane are redrawn. This produces a result using the first option discussed in section 7.1 on coloring shadows. As a last step, everything is put back to the way it was before the process was started. A code fragment for all of this is:

```
shadowMatrix( theMatrix, groundPlane, lightLocation );
glMultMatrixf( theMatrix );
glEnable( GL_POLYGON_OFFSET_FILL );
glPolygonOffset(1.0, 2.0);
glDisable( GL_LIGHTING );
glColor3f( shadowRed, shadowGreen, shadowBlue );
drawScene();
glDisable( GL_POLYGON_OFFSET );
glPopMatrix();
glEnable( GL_LIGHTING );
```

7.6.3 Planar stencil buffer shadows

The stencil buffer can improve the results of planar shadows. Replacing the color where a shadow appears does not produce a realistic result because the ground plane details, such as texture or color, are lost. The same is true of the techniques of the previous section. There is a second potential problem. If the ground plane is limited in size (i.e., is not infinite), shadows can be drawn in areas outside of the ground plane. The stencil buffer can be used to get a better result.

The objects in the scene, except for the ground plane, are drawn. Then the stencil buffer is used when drawing the ground plane, so that any pixels displaying the ground plane have their stencil buffer value set. This can be accomplished with the code segment:

```
glEnable( GL_STENCIL_TEST );
glStencilFunc( GL_ALWAYS, groundPlaneValue, 0xff );
glStencilOp( GL_KEEP, GL_KEEP, GL_REPLACE );
drawGroundPlane();
glDisable( GL_STENCIL_TEST );
```

This code sets the stencil buffer to the groundPlaneValue for all pixels where the ground plane appears in the image. The value of groundPlaneValue should be unique[4] relative to any other values used with the stencil buffer. When drawing the shadows, using a stencil test will keep the shadows within the ground plane.

The shadows are added as before, but instead of just replacing the color, OpenGL's blending functions can be used to alter the color displayed in the image. This produces a result using the second shadow coloring option. The stencil buffer prevents the alteration of colors that are not part of the ground plane. This makes the process:

```
glDisable( GL_LIGHTING );
glEnable( GL_BLEND );
glBlendFunc( GL_DST_COLOR, GL_ZERO );
glColor3f( shadowRed, shadowGreen, shadowBlue );
glDisable( GL_DEPTH_TEST );
glEnable( GL_STENCIL_TEST );
glStencilFunc( GL_EQUAL, groundPlaneValue, 0xff );
glStencilOp( GL_KEEP, GL_KEEP, GL_ZERO );
drawScene();
glDisable( GL_BLEND );
glDisable( GL_STENCIL_TEST );
glEnable( GL_DEPTH_TEST );
```

The combination of the glBlendFunc and the glColor3f routine calls means that where the objects are drawn, the current color in the frame buffer is multiplied by the value set in the glColor3f call. Setting the stencil function to GL_EQUAL means pixel values will only be changed where the stencil value is equal to the value set when drawing the ground plane. The stencil operation is set to replace the stencil buffer value with 0 when changing the pixel value for the shadow. This is done so that multiple objects that shadow the same ground plane locations do not cause those pixels to keep getting darker and darker.

This technique is an improvement over the one presented in the previous section, but there are still problems. Because the color already drawn for the ground plane is just being modified, there might be a highlight in an area where there is a shadow. The technique presented here will not remove the highlight, which is what would happen in the real world, but will only darken it. This slightly more complex process will remove the highlight problem.

```
1.    render the objects
2.    render the ground plane and set the stencil buffer
3.    project the objects onto the ground plane
```

---

[4]Unique here means that this value does not require any of the bits used by other values.

4. turn off drawing
5. render the objects to update the stencil buffer
6. turn drawing on and lighting off
7. re-render the ground plane using a stencil test

The process outlined will set the stencil buffer for visible locations of the ground plane and then update the stencil where pixels need to be modified because of shadows. Rendering the ground plane again with the shadowed light turned off will keep all of the ground plane details without any highlighting. Step 4 of this process is done by setting the color mask with the call glColorMask(0, 0, 0, 0). The values of 0 in this call prevent the frame buffer colors from being changed. Step 5 of this process redraws the objects for the sole purpose of incrementing the stencil buffer.[5] To draw images again into the frame buffer, step 6 includes the call glColorMask(1, 1, 1, 1).

After "redrawing" the objects to increment the stencil buffer, it will have the new value in places that are both ground plane and shadow. The ground plane can be re-rendered with the blocked light source disabled, but only where the stencil buffer has this new value. This is the same result as the third of the shadow coloring options. The following code fragment accomplishes this entire shadow rendering process.

```
GLfloat lightLocation[4], groundPlane[4];
glPushMatrix();
// build in the shadow projection matrix
shadowMatrix( shadowMatrix, lightLocation, groundPlane );
glMultMatrixf( shadowMatrix );
glDisable( GL_BLEND );
glDisable( GL_DEPTH_TEST );
// update only if it's the ground plane
glStencilFunc( GL_EQUAL, goundPlaneValue, 0xff );
// increment the stencil value where the shadows are
glStencilOp( GL_KEEP, GL_KEEP, GL_INCR );
// don't change the image yet
glColorMask( 0, 0, 0, 0 );
drawScene();
// later the image will be changed so reset the mask
glColorMask( 1, 1, 1, 1 );
glPopMatrix();
glEnable( GL_LIGHTING );
```

---

[5]When using this technique, the groundPlaneValue and the groundPlaneValue + 1 must be unique relative to any other uses of the stencil buffer.

```
// turn off the blocked light
glDisable( GL_LIGHT0 );
// render only where there is ground plane and shadow
glStencilFunc( GL_EQUAL, groundPlaneValue+1, 0xff );
// decrement so a point isn't double shadowed
glStencilOp( GL_KEEP, GL_KEEP, GL_DECR );
// re-draw the shadowed parts of the ground plane
drawGroundPlane();
```

It is possible to modify this process further so as to throw shadows on multiple planes from multiple sources. For details on this, see (Kilgard99), pages 22–23.

7.6.4 Shadow volume stencil buffer shadows

Doing shadow volumes in OpenGL uses many of the ideas explored in the previous section. A quick description of the process is to (1) render the scene; (2) "render" the shadow volume polygons updating only the stencil buffer; and (3) re-render the scene without the light source for only those pixels in the stencil buffer.

Rendering the scene is done as usual with the light source and depth buffer enabled. The next step turns off lighting but enables the stencil test. Lighting is turned off to save some time in calculations. The color and depth masks are set to 0 because there should be no changes to those. The stencil operation will be GL_INVERT so that a stencil bit is flipped for every shadow volume polygon that is in front of the object. If the stencil bit is 1 at the end, there are an odd number of shadow volume polygons between the viewpoint and the object. If the stencil bit is 0 at the end, there are an even number of shadow volume polygons between the viewpoint and the object. Assuming the viewpoint is outside of a shadow, the stencil bit will be set for every location in the image where there should be a shadow. The following code fragment sets up this situation.

```
glDisable( GL_LIGHTING );
glEnable( GL_STENCIL_TEST );
glDepthMask( 0 );
glColorMask( 0, 0, 0, 0 );
glStencilFunc( GL_ALWAYS, 0, 0 );
// use only one bit of the buffer
glStencilMask( 0x1 );
glStencilOp( GL_KEEP, GL_KEEP, GL_INVERT );
glDisable(GL_CULL_FACE);
drawShadowVolumePolygons();
glEnable(GL_CULL_FACE);
```

It is important to make sure that back-face culling is disabled, because half of the shadow volume polygons will be back-facing. The back-facing polygons are important because they essentially turn off the stencil bit if the object is beyond the shadow volume.

The last step re-renders the scene with the lighting enabled but the blocked light source disabled, and only re-renders where the stencil buffer bit is set. The following code fragment will accomplish this.

```
glEnable( GL_LIGHTING );
glDisable( GL_LIGHT0 );
glStencilFunc( GL_EQUAL, 0x1, 0x1 );
// don't change the stencil while re-rendering
glStencilOp( GL_KEEP, GL_KEEP, GL_KEEP );
glColorMask( 1, 1, 1, 1 );
drawScene();
```

Additional details on using OpenGL facilities to determine the actual shadow volume polygons can be found in (Kilgard99).

7.7 Projects

1) Add the ability to create shadows to your rendering program using one of the techniques discussed in this chapter.
2) Add the ability to handle distributed light sources and soft-edged shadows to your rendering program.

Ray Tracing

In the rendering methods explored so far, points are identified on the object and then the illumination is calculated. This assumes that the appearance of all objects is only influenced by how light strikes the object, which leads to all objects having a solid and nonreflective surface. Objects that are highly polished have a mirror-like reflection off their surface, and objects that are transparent refract things behind them. We are quite familiar with reflections in mirrors and highly polished metals. The canonical example of refraction is the bent appearance of a pencil in a glass of water. Figure 8.1 shows an example of a wizard puppet refracted through a crystal ball. Ray tracing is a different approach to rendering that can handle reflective and refractive objects.

Light can be interpreted as a collection of rays that begin at the light sources and bounce around the world, influenced by the objects the rays encounter. We see the objects because some of that light eventually bounces into our eyes. To render a scene in this way, rays of light are traced as they leave a light source, enter the scene, and bounce around the objects. If the ray reaches the viewpoint through one of the pixel locations, that ray will determine or contribute to that pixel value. A problem with this approach is that many rays are traced for each light source, and most of those rays can wind up leaving the scene and therefore have no influence on the image. The process of tracing a ray from the light source to the viewpoint can be quite computationally complex because a lot of work will be done for rays that leave the scene without reaching the viewpoint.

Figure 8.1 • Refraction through a glass ball (see Color Plate 8.1)

The alternative used for ray tracing is having the rays start at the viewpoint and travel through pixel locations into the scene. These rays are followed as they reflect and refract around the scene gathering information to determine the pixel color. The idea of ray tracing was first proposed by Appel (Appel68) but was popularized by Whitted (Whitted80) to add specular reflections and refractions to the local illumination model. Ray tracing is still a popular tool for rendering as is evidenced by the new book by Pharr and Humphreys (Pharr04), which is a detailed look at a physically based ray tracer, and is an excellent resource for in-depth research into ray tracing.

One of the benefits of ray tracing is that the overall algorithm inherently handles perspective and hidden surfaces. Rays traced from the viewpoint through pixel locations are all within the viewing volume of a perspective transformation. These rays strike the closest object in the scene, thereby properly excluding objects or parts of objects that are obscured. Another benefit is that calculations for shadows are also easy to include because the calculations that determine the intersection of rays and objects are easily adapted to the task of determining if there is an object blocking a ray of light from the light source.

Objects in the scene can be matte objects, reflective objects, refractive objects, or a combination of two or three of these. Therefore, the techniques presented here assume that each object has parameters that indicate how reflective and refractive the object is. There will be (1) a local coefficient that determines the impact of a local illumination model on the object, (2) a reflection coefficient that determines how reflective the object surface is, and (3) a refractive coefficient that determines how transparent the object is. Each of these values will be between 0 and 1, with their sum being exactly 1. The larger a value is, the more that component influences the final appearance of the object. For example, an object with a local coefficient of 1 looks like any object rendered with just a local illumination model, whereas an object with a reflection coefficient of 1 looks like it has a mirror surface.

The first part of this chapter looks at the calculations necessary to determine the intersection of a ray and object. Next the calculations to determine the direction of reflection and refraction as well as the location of shadows are explored. Because the goal of this chapter is the development of a simple ray tracer, the chapter ends with a look at the overall ray tracing process and a brief introduction to some improvements that can be made to it. This chapter assumes a ray data type that includes a starting location and a direction both of which have an x, y, and z component.

8.1 Ray Intersections

The cornerstone of ray tracing is the calculation of intersections between a ray and objects in the scene. Knowing these intersection points is necessary to calculate the local illumination and to determine how the rays reflect and refract. This section will show how to calculate intersections with a few simple objects, as well as how equations for intersections with more complex mathematical objects can be derived.

All of these calculations begin with the parametric equation for a line. For a line (or ray) from point $P_1 = (x_1, y_1, z_1)$ to point $P_2 = (x_2, y_2, z_2)$, the parametric equations are given in equations (8.1), where i, j, and k are short-hand for the three subtractions and are used to make the mathematical derivations below easier to follow. Notice also that P_1 is the starting point of the line and (i, j, k) is the direction the line is going.

$$x(t) = x_1 + (x_2 - x_1) * t = x_1 + i * t$$
$$y(t) = y_1 + (y_2 - y_1) * t = y_1 + j * t \quad (8.1)$$
$$z(t) = z_1 + (z_2 - z_1) * t = z_1 + k * t$$

For an initial ray, P_1 will be the viewpoint location and P_2 will be a pixel location in the image plane. As the value of t goes from 0 to 1, the parametric equations generate locations along the straight line between point P_1 and point P_2. The t value for the intersection point on the initial ray will always be greater than 1 if all of the objects being rendered are beyond where the image plane has been placed in the world space. If the line is considered infinite in both directions, the value of t has no limit. Negative values of t give locations on the line "before" P_1, and values of t greater than 1 give locations on the line "after" P_2. Because locations before P_1 on a ray would be behind the viewing direction, negative t values will not be used in ray tracing.

8.1.1 Plane intersections

Given a plane with the equation $A * x + B * y + C * z + D = 0$, where does the ray with the parametric equation (8.1) intersect this plane? The x, y, and z locations that satisfy the plane equation are all on the plane, and the parametric equations for a line give all of the x, y, and z locations on the line. The intersection point occurs where the x, y, and z values produced by both the plane and parametric equations are the same (Figure 8.2).

To find where the intersection occurs, the parametric equations (8.1) for the ray are substituted into the plane equation and the result is then solved for t. This gives the following derivation:

$$A * (x_1 + i * t) + B * (y_1 + j * t) + C * (z_1 + k * t) + D = 0$$
$$A * x_1 + A * i * t + B * y_1 + B * j * t + C * z_1 + C * k * t + D = 0$$
$$(A * i + B * j + C * k) * t + A * x_1 + B * y_1 + C * z_1 + D = 0$$

$$t = -\frac{A * x_1 + B * y_1 + C * z_1 + D}{A * i + B * j + C * k} \tag{8.2}$$

The value of t that results from equation (8.2) can be substituted back into the original parametric equation for the ray to find the intersection point.

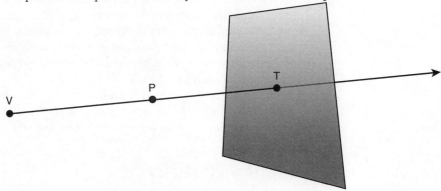

Figure 8.2 • Intersection of a ray and patch

When the denominator of equation (8.2) is 0, there is no value for t, and therefore, no intersection. Recall that (A, B, C) is the vector normal to the plane. Additionally, the denominator is actually the dot product of the plane normal and the ray direction. This dot product is 0 only when the normal and the ray are perpendicular, which means that the ray is parallel to the plane, so no intersection occurs.

The intersection calculations in equation (8.2) are with a mathematical plane that is infinite in all directions. In graphics, however, objects are specified with finite planar patches. To calculate the intersection of a ray with a planar patch requires first calculating the intersection of the ray with the infinite plane containing the patch, and then determining if that intersection is within the bounds of the patch.

A simple way to determine the intersection with the patch is to first project the intersection point and patch into the x, y, or z plane, which is chosen by the largest of the values A, B, and C respectively. The largest value is chosen so that the patch projection is as close to the size of the original patch as possible. Once the patch and intersection point are projected, the number of times patch edges are crossed along any line beginning at the intersection point and going to a point clearly outside the patch is counted. If there are an odd number of crossings, the intersection point is inside the patch. Figure 8.3 shows two intersection points. The lines from intersection I_1 cross the patch edges 0 or 2 times and so intersection I_1 is outside of

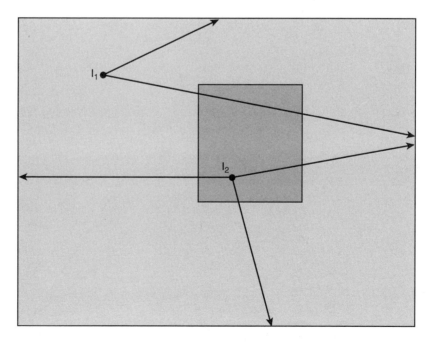

Figure 8.3 • Counting intersections to determine if the intersection is inside or outside the patch

the patch. But all of the lines from intersection I_2 cross the patch edges only once, and so I_2 is inside of the patch.

8.1.2 Triangular patch intersections

Much as there is a parametric equation form of a line, there is a parametric equation for a triangular patch using barycentric coordinates, which is the basis for one method for determining ray and triangular patch intersections. This parametric equation (8.3) is based on the coordinates for the three vertices (P_0, P_1, and P_2) of the patch (Figure 8.4).

$$p(a, b, c) = a * P_0 + b * P_1 + c * P_2 \tag{8.3}$$

In equation (8.3), the values of a, b, and c are all in the range [0.0, 1.0], with their sum being exactly equal to 1. When the values are all in the range (0.0, 1.0), the resulting point is on the interior of the triangular patch. If one of these values is 0, the resulting point is on the edge between the other two coordinates. For example, if b is 0, the points generated with the range of values for a and c will be on the edge between vertex P_0 and vertex P_2. If two of these values are 0, the third must be 1 and the result is the associated vertex. For example, consider the triangular patch with the three vertices of (50, 100, 35), (20, 60, 30), and (70, 80, 40). If $a = 0.5$, $b =$

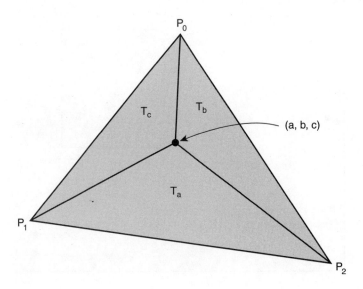

Figure 8.4 • Barycentric coordinates for a triangular patch

0.3, and $c = 0.2$, the location within the patch would be $0.5 * (50, 100, 45) + 0.3 * (20, 60, 35) + 0.2 * (70, 80, 40) = (45, 84, 41)$.

The values of a, b, and c are the ratio of the area of a subtriangle to the area of the entire triangle. For the example shown in Figure 8.4, a would be area(T_a) / area(T), b would be area(T_b) / area(T), and c would be area(T_c) / area(T).

Values of a, b, and c can be calculated for the location of any intersection point between a ray and the plane containing the triangular patch. Intersections of the ray and the patch will produce values of a, b, and c that are all in the range [0, 1] with a sum of exactly 1. If any of the values a, b, or c are not in the range [0, 1] or if their sum is not exactly 1, the intersection of the ray and the plane is outside of the triangular patch.

To simplify things, a can be replaced by $1 - b - c$ because $a + b + c = 1$ for points in the triangular patch. Equation (8.3) becomes equation (8.4) when this substitution is made and the terms are reordered.

$$p(a, b, c) = P_0 + b * (P_1 - P_0) + c * (P_2 - P_0) \tag{8.4}$$

In equation (8.4), b, c, and $b + c$ must be in the range [0, 1].

The ray will intersect the plane containing this triangular patch where the results of the ray parametric equation are the same as the results of this triangular patch equation. The result of setting these equations equal is given in equations (8.5).

$$
\begin{aligned}
x_1 + i * t &= P_{0,x} + b * (P_{1,x} - P_{0,x}) + c * (P_{2,x} - P_{0,x}) \\
y_1 + j * t &= P_{0,y} + b * (P_{1,y} - P_{0,y}) + c * (P_{2,y} - P_{0,y}) \\
z_1 + k * t &= P_{0,z} + b * (P_{1,z} - P_{0,z}) + c * (P_{2,z} - P_{0,z})
\end{aligned}
\tag{8.5}
$$

The equations (8.5) represent three equations with three unknowns (t, b, and c), and can be rewritten as equations (8.6)

$$
\begin{aligned}
b * (P_{0,x} - P_{1,x}) + c * (P_{0,x} - P_{2,x}) + i * t &= P_{0,x} - x_1 \\
b * (P_{0,y} - P_{1,y}) + c * (P_{0,y} - P_{2,y}) + j * t &= P_{0,y} - y_1 \\
b * (P_{0,z} - P_{1,z}) + c * (P_{0,z} - P_{2,z}) + k * t &= P_{0,z} - z_1
\end{aligned}
\tag{8.6}
$$

Equation 8.6 is a 3 x 3 system of linear equations that can be solved using Cramer's Rule. The resulting values of b, c, and t are given by the four equations (8.7), where the vertical bars represent the determinant[1] of the associated matrix. Once equations (8.7) are calculated, the resulting values are checked to see if they are in range and, thus, the intersection is valid.

---

[1]Details on the calculation of the determinant of a matrix can be found in Appendix A.

$$
D = \begin{vmatrix} P_{0,x} - P_{1,x} & P_{0,x} - P_{2,x} & i \\ P_{0,y} - P_{1,y} & P_{0,y} - P_{2,y} & j \\ P_{0,z} - P_{1,z} & P_{0,z} - P_{2,z} & k \end{vmatrix}
$$

$$
b = \frac{\begin{vmatrix} P_{0,x} - x_1 & P_{0,x} - P_{2,x} & i \\ P_{0,y} - y_1 & P_{0,y} - P_{2,y} & j \\ P_{0,z} - z_1 & P_{0,z} - P_{2,z} & k \end{vmatrix}}{D}
$$

$$
c = \frac{\begin{vmatrix} P_{0,x} - P_{1,x} & P_{0,x} - x_1 & i \\ P_{0,y} - P_{1,y} & P_{0,y} - y_1 & j \\ P_{0,z} - P_{1,z} & P_{0,z} - z_1 & k \end{vmatrix}}{D}
$$

$$
t = \frac{\begin{vmatrix} P_{0,x} - P_{1,x} & P_{0,x} - P_{2,x} & P_{0,x} - x_1 \\ P_{0,y} - P_{1,y} & P_{0,y} - P_{2,y} & P_{0,y} - y_1 \\ P_{0,z} - P_{1,z} & P_{0,z} - P_{2,z} & P_{0,z} - z_1 \end{vmatrix}}{D}
$$

(8.7)

For example, consider the triangular patch with the vertices (50, 100, 35), (20, 60, 30), and (70, 80, 40) and the ray from (0, 0, 0) to (25.5, 39.0, 18.0). Substituting these values into the equations (8.7) gives the equations (8.8)

$$
D = \begin{vmatrix} 30 & -20 & 25.5 \\ 40 & 20 & 39.0 \\ 5 & -5 & 18.0 \end{vmatrix} = 19{,}500
$$

$$
b = \frac{\begin{vmatrix} 50 & -20 & 25.5 \\ 100 & 20 & 39.0 \\ 35 & -5 & 18.0 \end{vmatrix}}{19{,}500} = \frac{5{,}850}{19{,}500} = 0.3
$$

(8.8)

$$
c = \frac{\begin{vmatrix} 30 & 50 & 25.5 \\ 40 & 100 & 39.0 \\ 5 & 35 & 18.0 \end{vmatrix}}{19{,}500} = \frac{9{,}750}{19{,}500} = 0.5
$$

$$
t = \frac{\begin{vmatrix} 30 & -20 & 50 \\ 40 & 20 & 100 \\ 5 & -5 & 35 \end{vmatrix}}{19{,}500} = \frac{39{,}000}{19{,}500} = 2.0
$$

The results shown in equations (8.8) indicate a valid intersection because b, c, and their sum are all in the range [0, 1]. Because $a = 1.0 - b - c$, the value of a is

0.2. Using the t value determined by these equations with the ray parametric equation indicates that the intersection point is (51, 78, 36).

The following algorithm will calculate the 3×3 determinants, b, c, and t, and then determine if the intersection is within the triangular patch.

```
term1 = ((P0, y - P2, y) * k) - (j * (P0, z - P2, z))
term2 = (i * (P0, z - P2, z)) - ((P0, x - P2, x) * k)
term3 = ((P0, x - P2, x) * j) - ((P0, y - P2, y) * i)
term4 = ((P0, x - P1, x) * (P0, y - y1)) - ((P0, x - x1) * (P0, y - P1, y))
term5 = ((P0, x - x1) * (P0, z - P1, z)) - ((P0, x - bx) * (P0, z - z1))
term6 = ((P0, x - P1, y) * (P0, z - z1)) - ((P0, y - y1) * (P0, z - P1, z))
denom = ((P0, x - P1, x) * term1) + ((P0, y - P1, y) * term2)
              + ((P0, z - P1, z) * term3)
b = (((P0, x - x1) * term4) + ((P0, y - y1) * term5)
              + ((P0, z - z1) * term6)) / denom
c = ((k * term4) + (j * term5) + (i * term6)) / denom
t = -(((P0, z - P2, z) * term4) + ((P0, y - P2, y) * term5)
              + ((P0, x - P2, x) * term6)) / denom


if ((0 <= b) && (b <= 1) && (0 <= c) && (c <= 1)
        && (0 <= (b + c)) && ((b + c) <= 1))
    // intersection is valid
else
    // intersection is outside the triangular patch
```

8.1.3 Sphere intersections

For a sphere with radius r and centered at location (x_c, y_c, z_c), the equation $(x - x_c)^2 + (y - y_c)^2 + (z - z_c)^2 = r^2$ gives the set of (x, y, z) points on the surface of the sphere. As in the case of a plane, the intersection point or points will occur where the parametric equation for a line and the equation for a sphere give the same x, y, and z values (Figure 8.5). If the ray just grazes the surface of the sphere, there will be only

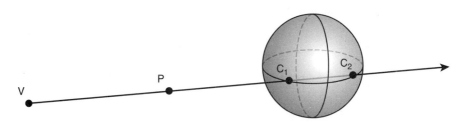

Figure 8.5 • Ray and sphere intersection

one intersection point. All other intersections occur with two points when the ray enters and leaves the sphere.[2]

As in the case of a plane, the parametric equations for a line are substituted into the sphere equation, and the resulting equation is solved for t. The process in this case is a bit more complex because the equation is a quadratic equation. The derivation begins by squaring the terms in the equation for a sphere.

$$(x - x_c)^2 + (y - y_c)^2 + (z - z_c)^2 = r^2$$
$$(x^2 - 2 * x_c * x + x_c^2) + (y^2 - 2 * y_c * y + y_c^2) + (z^2 - 2 * z_c * z + z_c^2) = r^2 \quad (8.9)$$

Next, the parametric equations (8.1) for a line are substituted into the sphere equation (8.9).

$$(x_1 + i * t)^2 - 2 * x_c * (x_1 + i * t) + x_c^2 +$$
$$(y_1 + j * t)^2 - 2 * y_c * (y_1 + j * t) + y_c^2 +$$
$$(z_1 + k * t)^2 - 2 * z_c * (z_1 + k * t) + z_c^2 = r^2 \quad (8.10)$$

The new terms in (8.10) are now squared and the terms are reorganized based on the power of t.

$$x_1^2 + 2 * i * x_1 * t + i^2 * t^2 - 2 * x_c * x_1 - 2 * x_c * i * t + x_c^2 +$$
$$y_1^2 + 2 * j * y_1 * t + j^2 * t^2 - 2 * y_c * y_1 - 2 * y_c * j * t + y_c^2 +$$
$$z_1^2 + 2 * k * z_1 * t + k^2 * t^2 - 2 * z_c * z_1 - 2 * z_c * k * t + z_c^2 = r^2$$

$$i^2 * t^2 + j^2 * t^2 + k^2 * t^2 +$$
$$2 * i * x_1 * t - 2 * x_c * i * t + 2 * j * y_1 * t - 2 * y_c * j * t + 2 * k * z_1 * t - 2 * z_c * k * t +$$
$$x_1^2 - 2 * x_c * x_1 + x_c^2 + y_1^2 - 2 * y_c * y_1 + y_c^2 + z_1^2 + - 2 * z_c * z_1 + z_c^2 = r^2 \quad (8.11)$$

Simplifying equation (8.11) and reordering the terms gives equation (8.12).

$$[i^2 + j^2 + k^2] * t^2 +$$
$$[2 * i * (x_1 - x_c) + 2 * j * (y_1 - y_c) + 2 * k * (z_1 - z_c)] * t +$$
$$x_1^2 + y_1^2 + z_1^2 - 2 * (x_c * x_1 + y_c * y_1 + z_c * z_1) + x_c^2 + y_c^2 + z_c^2 - r^2 = 0 \quad (8.12)$$

This is a quadratic equation in the standard form. From mathematical theory, the quadratic equation $At^2 + Bt + C = 0$ has a solution for t given by equation (8.13), where A, B, and C are found from the coefficients of t^2, t, and 1 in equation (8.12).

$$t = \frac{-B \pm \sqrt{B^2 - 4AC}}{2A} \quad (8.13)$$

---

[2]For now, the discussion assumes the ray begins outside of the object. When the discussion gets to refraction, the ray will sometimes begin inside the sphere, and so both intersection points can be where the ray leaves the sphere. But one of those will be "behind" the direction the ray is pointing.

Specifically, equations (8.14) give the values for A, B, and C to be used with equation (8.13).

$$A = i^2 + j^2 + k^2$$

$$B = 2 * i * (x_1 - x_c) + 2 * j * (y_1 - y_c) + 2 * k * (z_1 - z_c) \qquad (8.14)$$

$$C = x_1^2 + y_1^2 + z_1^2 - 2 * (x_c * x_1 + y_c * y_1 + z_c * z_1) + x_c^2 + y_c^2 + z_c^2 - r^2$$

To determine t, equations (8.14) would be used to calculate the values of A, B, and C, which would be used in equation (8.13). For example, consider a sphere with a radius of 100 that is centered at (120, 150, 70) and a ray that starts at (0, 0, 0) and ends at (50, 65, 25). Equations (8.14) give that $A = 50^2 + 65^2 + 25^2 = 7{,}350$, $B = 2 * 50 * -120 + 2 * 65 * -150 + 2 * 25 * -70 = -35{,}000$, and $C = 120^2 + 150^2 + 70^2 - 100^2 = 31{,}800$. Plugging these values into equation (8.13) gives $t = \dfrac{35{,}000 \pm \sqrt{(-35{,}000)^2 - 4 * 7{,}350 * 31{,}800}}{2 * 7{,}350} \approx \dfrac{35{,}000 \pm 17031.7}{14{,}700}$, which results in approximate t values of 1.222 and 3.540. Thus this ray intersects the sphere at (61.1, 79.4, 30.6) and (177.0, 230.1, 88.5).

This process is computationally complex, but there are some things that in practice can make this calculation more efficient. First, the values of i, j, and k form a vector that represents the direction of the ray. When a vector is normalized, its length, which is the square root of the sum of the squares of the three components, is 1. If this vector associated with the ray is normalized, the A term, which is just the square of the length, will always be 1. Thus, normalizing this ray vector saves three multiplications for the squaring and two additions and allows A to be dropped from the calculation given in equation (8.13), saving two more multiplications.

The calculation of C can also be sped up. The first three terms are the sum of the squares of the initial point of the ray. Because this ray is used to look for intersections against many spheres, this sum of squares can be calculated once and stored as part of the ray data structure. Now for each intersection calculation, instead of calculating this sum the stored value can be used. The last four terms in the calculation of C are dependent on the location and size of the sphere. These values are fixed when the sphere specification is read in from the data file. When the data is input, this sum/subtraction of squares can be calculated and stored as part of the sphere data structure. These two speedups mean that C can be calculated as in equation (8.15) which has four multiplications and four "additions" instead of 11 multiplications and nine "additions" as shown in equation (8.14).

$$C = \text{RaySquared} + \text{SphereSquared} - 2 * (x_c * x_1 + y_c * y_1 + z_c * z_1) \qquad (8.15)$$

Because A is eliminated by normalizing the ray vector, there is no potential for division by 0 in equation (8.13). The only potential problem in the simplified version of equation (8.13) is if the part under the square root (called the discriminant) is negative. If that occurs, this ray does not intersect this sphere. When the discriminant is greater than 0, there are two t values—1 when the square root is added, and the other when it is subtracted. One of these is where the ray goes into the sphere and the other is where the ray leaves the sphere. If the discriminant evaluates to 0, however, that is the case where the ray is tangent to the sphere and so it only grazes the sphere surface at the one intersection point.

Which of these two t values should be used in the ray tracing algorithm? Because the first intersection along the ray occurs at the smallest positive t value, a ray tracer will look for the smallest positive t values among all of the objects intersected. Therefore, any routine that calculates the intersection of a ray and a sphere should return the smallest positive t value, if there is one.

• 8.1.4 Box intersections

Intersections with a box could be done by trying to intersect the ray with the six sides of the box. This involves the application of the plane intersection calculations along with the inside/outside determination six times. There is a faster calculation available if the box is oriented so that its edges are parallel to the x, y, or z axis. This makes the sides parallel to the $x = 0$, $y = 0$, or $z = 0$ plane. In this special case, the ray can be checked to see where it intersects the range of x, y, and z coordinates. The resulting set of t values gives the portion of the ray that is inside the box.

Consider the box that has its close lower left corner at (x_s, y_s, z_s) and its far upper right corner at (x_e, y_e, z_e). This box has the x coordinate range of $[x_s, x_e]$, the y coordinate range of $[y_s, y_e]$, and the z coordinate range of $[z_s, z_e]$. The ray enters and leaves the x coordinate range at t values given by the two equations (8.16), with similar equations for the y and z coordinates.

$$x_s = x_1 + i * t_{x_s}$$
$$x_e = x_1 + i * t_{x_e} \tag{8.16}$$

Solving these six equations gives three pairs of t values, which represent the set of t values where the ray is in the x, y, and z coordinate range of the box.

Figure 8.6 shows a two-dimensional version of this process. In this figure, the two-dimensional box has its lower left corner at $(x_1, y_1) = (10, 5)$ and the upper right corner at $(x_2, y_2) = (20, 10)$. The ray has a starting point of $(0, 2)$ and a direction of $(2, 1)$. In this example, $t_{x_s} = (10 - 0) / 2 = 5$ and $t_{x_e} = (20 - 0) / 2 = 10$. Similarly, $t_{y_s} = (5 - 2) / 1 = 3$ and $t_{y_e} = (10 - 2) / 1 = 8$. This gives a range for t_x of $[5, 10]$ and a range for t_y of $[3, 8]$. The overlap of these two ranges is $[5, 8]$, which is the set of t values where the ray is inside the box. In three dimensions, these calculations would also be performed to get the range of t values for the z coordinate range of the box. The set of t values where all three of these ranges overlap represents the portion of the ray that is inside the three-dimensional box.

In the example, the ray was moving from the left to the right, so that t_{x_s} was less than t_{x_e}. But if the ray is going right to left, the order of these values is reversed. The decision of whether the valid range is $[t_{x_s}, t_{x_e}]$ or $[t_{x_e}, t_{x_s}]$ can be based on the value of i from the ray parametric equation. If i is greater than 0, the first range is valid, but if i is less than 0, the second range is valid. An equivalent set of conditions is true for the y and z coordinate.

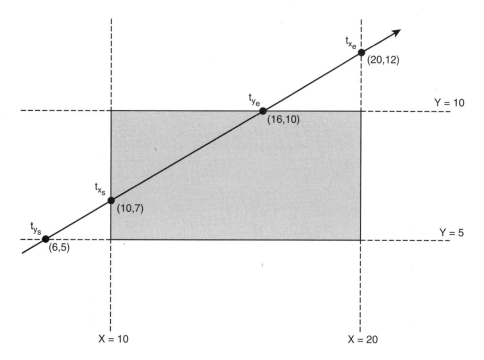

Figure 8.6 • Two-dimensional box intersection

Smits (Smits98) used the IEEE floating point number properties to create an efficient algorithm does not need to test for cases where the divisors are 0. The IEEE floating point properties[3] used are that comparing anything to *NaN* returns false, *infinity* is greater than everything, and *negative infinity* is less than everything. The resulting algorithm is:

```
if i > 0
{
    txs = (xs - x1) / i
    txe = (xe - x1) / i
}
else
{
    txs = (xe - x1) / i
    txe = (xs - x1) / i
}
```

---

[3]A more complete listing of the IEEE floating point properties is discussed in Appendix A.

```
if j > 0
{
    tys = (ys - y1) / j
    tye = (ye - y1) / j
}
else
{
    tys = (ye - y1) / j
    tye = (ys - y1) / j
}
if k > 0
{
    tzs = (zs - z1) / k
    tze = (ze - z1) / k
}
else
{
    tzs = (ze - z1) / k
    tze = (zs - z1) / k
}
// find the largest starting value
if txs > tys
    ts = txs
else
    ts = tys
if tzs > ts
    ts = tzs
// find the smallest ending value
if txe < tye
    te = txe
else
    te = tye
if tze < te
    te = tze
// if the start is less than or equal
// to the end, there is an intersection
return (ts <= te)
```

8.1.5 Other object intersections

The pattern of how the equations are derived to determine the intersection of a ray with a mathematically described object should have become clear in the previous sections. In general, the parametric equations for a line are substituted into the equation for the object, and the result is solved for t. Of course, solving for t can indicate a quite complex process. The end result, however, is a set of equations that can be used to calculate the t value where the intersection between the ray and object occurs.

In the resulting equations, there can be a possible calculation that could lead to a calculation error. In the case of the plane intersection calculations, it was a divide by 0. For the sphere intersection calculations, it was the square root of a negative number. Those are the cases where there is no intersection. A case that leads to a potential error in the intersection calculations for the new object indicates that there is no intersection between the ray and that object.

The complexity of the equations defining the object influences the complexity of the intersection calculations. For example, using one of the cubic parametric polynomial forms presented in Chapter 4 will result in equations that are cubic in the term t and would require determination of the cube root.

8.2 Ray Reflections and Refractions

Ray tracing gives the ability to have objects with mirror reflections or objects with refractions. The first step of the process is to determine where a ray intersects the object. The next step is to determine the direction the ray will travel when it reflects off the surface or refracts through the object. In both of these cases, a new ray direction is calculated based on the incoming ray direction and the surface normal. For refraction, the relative densities of the two materials at the boundary of the object also influence the new direction. This section explores the calculation of the reflection and refraction directions when a ray strikes an object.

8.2.1 Ray reflections

The cornerstone of the reflection calculation is that in a reflection off a smooth surface, such as a mirror, the angle that the incoming ray makes with the surface normal is the same as the angle that the reflected ray makes with the surface normal. Figure 8.7 shows the incoming ray (I), the surface normal (N), and the reflected ray direction (R). That figure also shows a vector labeled I' that is the direction the incoming ray would travel if it did not strike the object. The vectors I and I' are really the same vector, but just drawn in two different locations. This means that I and I' are interchangeable in the following discussion.

The angle that the incoming ray makes with the surface tangent is the same as the angle that the reflected ray makes with the surface tangent. Figure 8.7 shows that the reflected ray direction is just $R = I + 2\,A$. Because the lengths of the incoming ray and reflected ray are the same, the vector A is parallel to the surface normal. If I and I' are unit vectors, the length of the vector A is the sine of the angle between I and the surface tangent. In Figure 8.7, we see that the angle between the directions of I and the surface tangent is ϕ which makes the angle between I and N $90° + \phi$. Trigonometric formulas show that $\cos(90° + \phi) = -\sin(\phi)$. Therefore, the dot product of I and N gives the negative of the length of A. Because A and the normal point

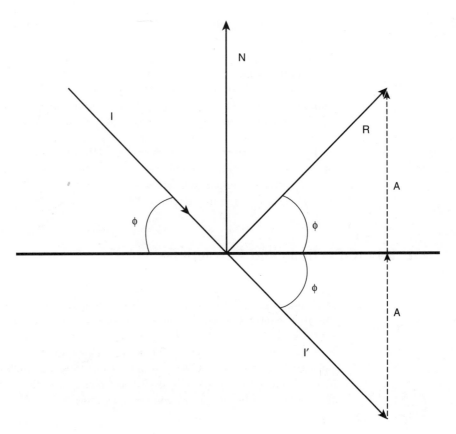

Figure 8.7 • Ray reflection

in the same direction, equation (8.17) is used to calculate the reflection vector when *I* and *N* are unit vectors.[4]

$$R = I - 2 \, (I \cdot N) * N \tag{8.17}$$

An algorithm for the calculation of the reflection vector would be:

```
Ray Reflect( Ray incident, Location intersect, Vector normal )
// incident - the incoming ray
// intersect - the location of the intersection
// normal - the normal to the surface at the intersection point
```

---

[4]This calculation of the reflection direction differs from the one in Chapter 2 because the direction of the incident ray is the opposite of the direction of the light vector used in that equation.

```
Ray result
result.start = intersect
result.direction = incident.direction
                    - 2 * (incident.direction · normal) * normal
// make the direction of unit length
result.direction.Normalize()
return result
```

8.2.2 Ray refractions

When light travels from one transparent medium into another, the direction of the light can change because of the relative densities of the media. Fermat developed a principle that said light traveling from point A to point B will go in the direction or directions that take the least amount of time to travel, even if the distance becomes longer. If light moves through a medium that is consistent in its content, then it will move in a straight line. For example, light moving in a vacuum travels in a straight line. When light goes through two different media to get from point A to point B, the light needs to bend to accomplish this travel in the shortest amount of time. When traveling into denser medium, the light bends toward the normal in an attempt to take the shortest path through the medium since light moves slower in the dense material. When going back into a less dense (also called rarer) medium, the light can now travel farther but at a faster rate than in the dense medium, so it bends away from the normal. This is shown in Figure 8.8. Light moving from a less dense medium to a more dense medium (Figure 8.8b) causes the light direction to bend toward the surface normal orientation. When moving from a more dense medium to

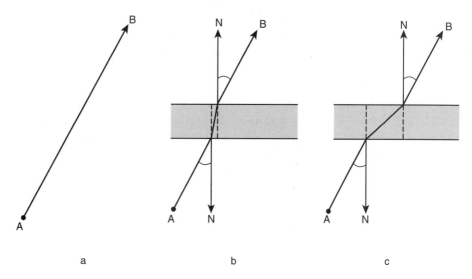

a   b   c

Figure 8.8 • Fastest path for light through a material. Part b shows a material that is more dense and part c shows a material that is less dense.

a less dense medium (Figure 8.8c), the light direction will bend away from the surface normal. In Figure 8.1, the wizard appears upside down in the glass sphere because of the way that the light bends when it enters and leaves this spherical shape (see details in Figure 8.9). The left image in Figure 8.10 shows a picture of the wizard without the glass sphere. That image was used as the background for a sphere in a ray traced version of this situation, shown in the right image in Figure 8.10.

The density of a medium is given through its index of refraction. The denser the medium, the higher its index of refraction with a vacuum at 1.0 and air considered to be close to 1.0. Table 8.1 shows some additional indices of refraction. It should be noted that there is a slight variation in the index of refraction based on the wavelength of light. For some materials the index of refraction decreases by 1 to 3 percent when moving through the visible part of the spectrum. For example, a material with an index of refraction of 1.5 for light at wavelength 400 nm (purple) has an index of refraction of between 1.485 and 1.455 for light at wavelength 700 nm (red).

The color of the transparent object can also influence the apparent color of objects seen. For example, in Figure 8.11, the wizard's white beard appears to be the color of the glass through which it is seen.

Snell's law gives a way to calculate the direction of the refracted vector as shown in equation (8.18), where η_I and η_T are the indices of refraction of the two materials and θ_I and θ_T are the angles relative to the normal for the incident (I) and refracted/transmitted (T) vectors as shown in Figure 8.12.

$$\eta_I * \sin \theta_I = \eta_T * \sin \theta_T \tag{8.18}$$

A problem with equation (8.18) is that it involves the sine function, where the cosine can be calculated more quickly with the dot product. Using trigonometric properties, this equation can be converted to one based on cosines. The derivation of this alternative begins by squaring both sides of the equation to get equation (8.19).

$$\eta_I^2 * \sin^2 \theta_I = \eta_T^2 * \sin^2 \theta_T \tag{8.19}$$

The fact that $\sin^2 \theta + \cos^2 \theta = 1$ gives equation (8.20).

$$\eta_I^2 * (1 - \cos^2 \theta_I) = \eta_T^2 * (1 - \cos^2 \theta_T) \tag{8.20}$$

Because the angle θ_T is of interest, the equation is solved for $\cos \theta_T$ giving equation (8.21).

$$\cos \theta_T = \sqrt{1 - \frac{\eta_I^2 \left(1 - \cos^2 \theta_I\right)}{\eta_T^2}} \tag{8.21}$$

The transmitted ray direction can now be calculated by the equation (8.22).

$$T = \frac{\eta_I}{\eta_T} * I + \left(\frac{\eta_I}{\eta_T} * \cos \theta_T\right) * N \tag{8.22}$$

Figure 8.9 • Close-up of the wizard refraction (see Color Plate 8.2)

In practice, the cos θ_1 would be calculated first by taking the dot product of $-I$ and N. The minus sign on the vector I is necessary because the incident vector points into the surface, and the dot product gives the cosine of the angle between the vectors when their starting points are the same. Without the minus sign, the dot prod-

Figure 8.10 • The wizard without the glass sphere and a ray traced version (see Color Plate 8.3)

● **TABLE 8.1**	Sample indices of refraction
Amber	1.54
Cubic Zirconia	2.15
Diamond	2.417
Emerald	1.57
Fused Quartz	1.46
Garnet	1.73 to 1.89
Glass	1.5
Ice	1.309
Ruby	1.77
Sapphire	1.77
Sodium Cloride	1.53
Water	1.333

Figure 8.11 • Refraction through colored glass (see Color Plate 8.4)

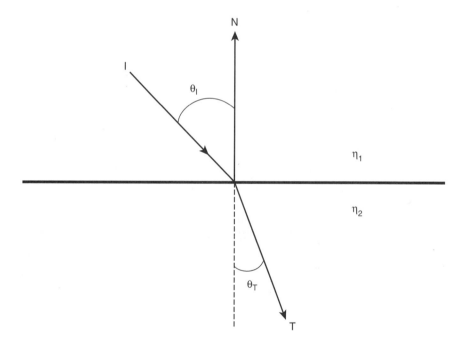

Figure 8.12 • Refraction vector

uct would actually calculate cos $(180° - \theta_I)$. The value of cos θ_I can then be used to calculate cos θ_T, using equation (8.21). The two cosines are then used in the calculation of the transmitted vector using equation (8.22).

There is a potential problem in the calculation of equations (8.21) and (8.22). The divisions of the two indices of refraction should not pose a problem because neither of them will ever be 0, but the square root could be a problem. Looking more closely, there are some conditions where the value inside the square root could be negative. For that to occur, the fraction would need to be greater than 1. The cosine of θ_I will always be less than 1, but could be as small as zero. When the cosine is very small, the ratio of the η values starts to dominate and if η_I is greater than η_T, the value under the radical can be negative. When this occurs, there is no transmitted ray. Rather, the ray reflects internally in the object as though the surface was a reflective one. You can see this effect if you hold up a piece of glass. As the glass is rotated, there will be a point at which you no longer see through the glass but now see objects reflected off of it as though it was a mirror.

The point at which there is no transmitted ray is called the critical angle. The exact value of the critical angle could be calculated, but it is easier to recognize that the angle has been passed when the value under the square root becomes negative. When that occurs, an internal reflection ray should be generated instead of a refraction ray. Figure 8.13 shows three incident rays and the result when they strike the surface. Ray I_1 makes an angle with N that is smaller than the critical angle, so it is refracted into the object along ray T_1. Ray I_2 is at the critical angle, so the resulting ray T_2 is in the direction of the surface tangent. Ray I_3 is at an angle greater than the critical angle, so the resulting ray T_3 is an internal reflection.

Before looking at an algorithm to determine the transmitted ray, consider the relationship between the direction of the incident ray and the normal. First, the surface normal will always point out of the object. If the incident ray is outside of the object, the direction of the normal and the ray will differ by between 90° and 180° when the starting points are co-located. If the incident ray is inside of the object, the direction of the normal and the ray will differ by between 0° and 90°. This means if the dot product of the normal and incident ray is negative, the incident ray is outside of the object and going into it. If the dot product is positive, the incident ray is inside the object and going out. With the assumption that all of the objects are suspended in or surrounded by air,[5] one of the two indices of refraction will always have a value of 1.0. Specifically, if the incident ray is outside the object $\eta_I = 1.0$, and if the incident ray is inside of the object $\eta_T = 1.0$. Putting all of this together with the equations gives the algorithm to calculate the transmitted ray as:

```
Ray Refract( Ray incident, Location intersect, Vector normal)
// incident - the incoming ray
// intersect - the location of the intersection
```

---

[5]A simple modification allows two objects of differing densities to touch. The current index of refraction for the material the incident ray is in can be stored with the ray. The initial value for this incident index of refraction can be 1.0 if the viewpoint is located in air. When the ray is reflected, the index of refraction would not change, but when the ray is refracted, the index of refraction for the material entered would be attached to the new incident ray.

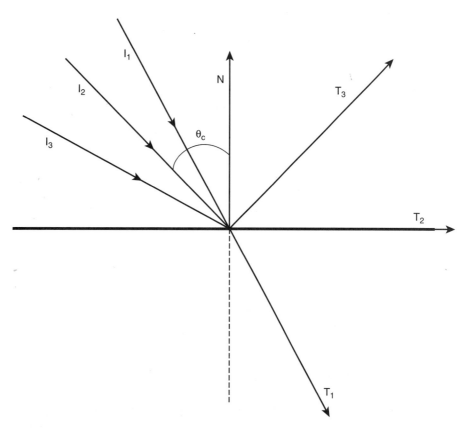

Figure 8.13 • The critical angle

```
// normal - the normal to the surface at the intersection point
Ray result
result.start = intersect
cosThetaI = incident.direction · normal
if (cosThetaI < 0) // outside
{
   norm = - normal
   ni = 1.0
   nt = object.refractCoefficient
   cosThetaI = -cosThetaI
}
else              // inside
{
   norm = normal
   nt = 1.0
```

```
        ni = object.refractCoefficient
    }
    nRatio = ni/nt
    temp = 1 - (square(nRatio) * (1 - square(cosThetaI)))
    if (temp > 0) // there is a valid refraction
    {
        cosThetaT = squareRoot( temp )
        result.direction = nRatio * incident.direction
                        + (nRatio * cosThetaI - cosThetaT) * norm
    }
    else
    {
        // past the critical angle, so there
        // is a total internal reflection
        result = Reflect(incident, intersect, norm)
    }
    return result
```

The algorithm negates the normal direction so that the rest of the calculations are the same whether the incident ray is inside or outside of the object.

8.3 Ray Tracing Shadows

Shadows are a simple addition to a ray tracer because all of the elements necessary to calculate the shadow are part of the ray tracing process. When the point on an object where a ray strikes is identified, whether or not this point is in a shadow, can be determined by the use of a shadow feeler. The shadow feeler is a ray that begins at the surface point and ends at the light source (Figure 8.14). This ray is used with the intersection calculations for each of the objects. If the shadow feeler intersects any object, the object blocks that light source and the light source should not be used in any local illumination calculations. If the full size of the ray from the point to the light is used (in other words, the direction is not normalized), any intersections that block the light will give a t value that is between 0 and 1. If an intersection produces a t value that is less than 0, that object is actually behind the current point relative to the light. If the t value is greater than 1, the object is beyond the light source. In either of these two cases, the object cannot be casting a shadow.

Where simple shadows in this method just ignore a light source that is blocked by any object, a more creative approach is to look at the specification of the blocking object. If that object is transparent, it does not really block the light, it only reduces its intensity. Depending on that object's index of refraction, it might bend the light so that it casts a highlight in a different place, but calculating that effect is discussed later. If an object is not completely transparent but rather translucent,

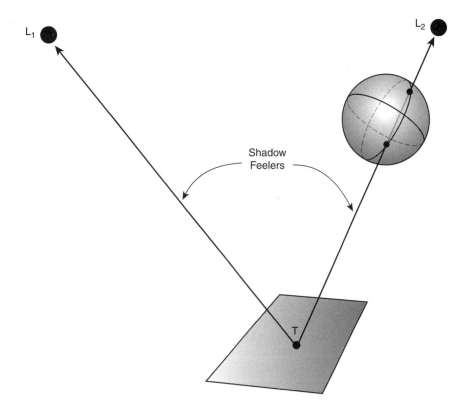

Figure 8.14 • Shadow feelers

only part of the light from the light source will be blocked from the point being shaded. A more sophisticated method is to reduce the light source intensity by the transparency of any objects between the current point and the light source. Specifically, local illumination calculations use a light intensity that is the product of the actual light intensity and the refraction coefficients of every "blocking" object. If an object is transparent, its refraction coefficient will be 1 and all of the light passes though, but if an object has a refraction coefficient of 0.5, only half of the light will pass through. With multiple obstructing objects, all of their refraction coefficients are used in the modification of the intensity.

A shadow feeler needs to be generated for every light source and then tested against every object. As the number of light sources and objects increase this can become a computationally expensive task. The soft shadow technique (as seen in Chapter 7) of representing a single light source as multiple, closely spaced light sources that share the overall intensity can be used here as well. Including this technique greatly expands the number of light sources and obviously greatly increases the processing time. A later section will look at techniques to improve the speed of ray tracing including shadow generation.

8.4 Ray Tracing Process

Ray tracing requires that a viewpoint and screen location be specified (Figure 8.15). An initial ray is determined by the viewpoint and a pixel location. This initial ray is followed into the scene and might strike an object. If the object is reflective, a ray is traced in the direction of reflection. If the object is refractive, a ray is traced in the direction of refraction. These reflected and refracted rays are traced in the same manner as the initial ray; therefore, it is easiest to write a ray tracer as a recursive function. The main program will be responsible for looping through each of the pixel locations, setting up the initial ray, calling the ray trace function, and displaying the result.

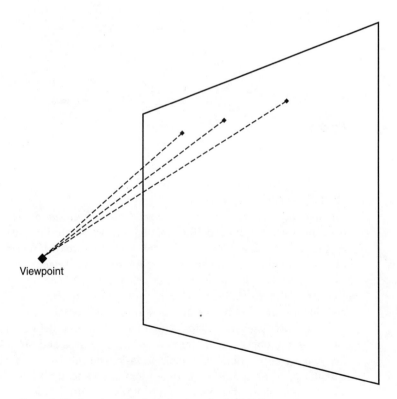

Viewpoint

Figure 8.15 • Rays from the viewpoint through pixel locations

A concern in ray tracing is round-off error. When calculating the closest intersection for a reflected or refracted ray, the point where the ray reflects or refracts should produce a *t* value of 0. Round-off error in the calculations can cause a result that is slightly larger than 0. Additional checks must be done to catch these false intersections. If objects are assumed to be surrounded by air, all object intersections will be some small distance from each other. In this case, one simple way to check it is to do comparisons not with 0, but rather with an epsilon value that is very slightly larger than 0.

8.4.1 Recursive ray tracing

An initial ray starts at the viewpoint and goes through one of the pixel locations in the image. Let's say that the ray travels into the scene and strikes an object that has local, reflective, and refractive components. The local contribution is calculated from a local illumination model such as those discussed in Chapter 2. The reflected and refracted contributions are determined by what is being seen in the reflected and refracted directions. To find those contributions, the reflected and transmitted rays are calculated and followed. The process for calculating the contribution in those two directions is the same as the process for the original ray, which is why the ray trace function can be recursive. A recursive ray tracing algorithm is:

```
Color RayTrace( Ray incident, int depth )
if (depth == MAX_DEPTH)
   return black
else
   determine the t value of the closest intersection
   if there is no intersection
      return background color
   else
      get the intersection point normal
      localColor = Local( incident, normal )
      if the object is reflective
         reflectionRay = Reflect( incident, normal )
         reflectColor = RayTrace( reflectionRay, depth+1 )
      endif
      if the object is refractive
         transmittedRay = Refract( incident, normal )
         refractColor = RayTrace( transmittedRay, depth+1 )
      endif
      return (localColor * localCoefficient)
              + (reflectColor * reflectionCoefficient)
              + (refractColor * refractionCoefficient)
   endif
endif
```

In this algorithm, the functions `Reflect` and `Refract` implement the calculations for finding the reflected and refracted directions discussed in the previous sections. The function `Local` calculates the local illumination color. The recursive process stops when the incident ray either leaves the scene by not striking any objects, or when the incident ray strikes an object that is matte (has no reflective or refractive components). It is possible for the incident ray to bounce among a group of objects for an extremely large number of times. At some point, the recursive process must stop because it is impossible to see any further. One way to do this is through the use of a depth parameter. In the main program the depth parameter is set to 0. On each recursive call it is incremented until it reaches some constant `MAX_DEPTH` value. An equivalent alternative is to set the value to a maximum depth in the main program and decrement with each recursive call until the depth becomes 0.

The ray trace function returns one of three possible colors:

- The color black is returned if the maximum recursive depth was reached
- The background color is returned if the ray strikes no object
- A combination of the local, reflected, and refracted contributions is returned if an object is hit by the ray

The value returned from this function can go back to the main program to be displayed, or can be returned to another call of the ray trace function. In the latter case, this value will represent the color contribution for either the reflected or refracted directions for that ray trace instance. In that case, the value calculated is combined with other contributions as the recursion unfolds until it reaches the main program.

8.5 Improving Ray Tracing Results

Ray tracing can be improved by techniques that decrease the time it takes to generate an image and by techniques that increase the quality of the resulting image. The former topic will be discussed in the next section, while the latter will be discussed here. The improvements discussed will solve the problem of aliasing and light reflection and refraction.

8.5.1 Improving quality

The quality of ray traced images can be improved by removing artifacts that occur because of the regular sampling grid or by including additional calculations that improve the appearance of the object or add secondary highlights. When all objects are solid and matte, they block the path of the light, thus causing shadows. When objects are transparent and reflective, they can reflect and refract beams of light in the scene causing new areas of highlight.

The following sections will briefly look at some of the techniques that can be used to improve the quality of ray traced images.

Supersampling

The problem of aliasing in images was discussed regarding textures, but the same problem exists with ray traced images. One solution is to supersample the image by firing not one but multiple rays into the scene for each pixel, and then combining the results with an appropriate filter.

Firing one ray into the scene treats each pixel as an infinitesimal point in the image. A pixel, however, can be seen as covering a square space of the image. Instead of seeing the pixel as being one point at location (i, j), the pixel can be treated as the square space from location (i − 0.5, j − 0.5) to (i + 0.5, j + 0.5). Supersampling fires a collection of rays in an evenly spaced grid over this area. For example, Figure 8.16 shows the regular grid of rays that result if nine more closely spaced rays were fired for each pixel area. This process does not result in nine times the work because rays fired along the pixel boundaries are shared by the neighboring pixels.

Once the ray tracing returns the color for each of the supersampled locations, they are then combined to get the value that is displayed for the pixel. This combination can be as simple as an average of the individual values, to as complex as a filter that produces a weighted average of the individual values based on how close to the center of the pixel they are.

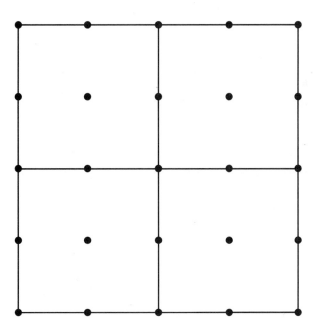

Figure 8.16 • Supersampling nine locations per pixel area

Though supersampling improves the resulting image, there are still some artifacts that can occur. Supersampling still determines color values at a regular interval; it is just that the interval is smaller.

Stochastic Ray Tracing

Stochastic ray tracing is a variety of supersampling that eliminates the regular sampling through the use of a random displacement to the location through which the initial ray is fired. The standard ray tracing algorithm uses an initial ray that begins at the viewpoint and goes through the center of each pixel. A three by three supersample uses nine rays for each pixel in a regular grid across the pixel area. In stochastic ray tracing, those nine rays are randomly distributed across the pixel area and the results of tracing those rays are averaged to get the final pixel value. Because the individual locations used for the rays are no longer in a regular grid, there is no restriction on the number of locations that can be sampled.

As discussed, the pixel at location (i, j) covers the square area with a lower-left coordinate of $(i - 0.5, j - 0.5)$ and upper-right coordinate of $(i + 0.5, j + 0.5)$, which means the coordinates have ranges of $[i - 0.5, i + 0.5]$ and $[j - 0.5, j + 0.5]$. The rays would be fired through a set of locations given by $(i + 0.5 * \text{rand}(), j + 0.5 * \text{rand}())$ where rand() produces a new uniform random number between -1 and $+1$ each time it is called. Using a uniform random number generator creates a different distribution of locations for each pixel area, thus breaking the regular sampling pattern. Figure 8.17 shows an example of this random distribution of locations.

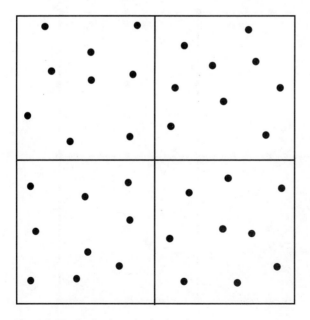

Figure 8.17 • Stochastic ray tracing locations

Ray traced images also have unnaturally sharp reflections and refractions. Real-world objects do not show this perfection. Stochastic ray tracing is one method that can be used to simulate this imperfection. For each reflection and refraction, multiple secondary rays are traced in slightly different directions by making a random adjustment to the ray direction calculated by equations (8.17) and (8.22). The next section looks at an alternative method for handling these imperfections.

Gloss and Translucency

The sharpness with which an object reflects an image is called gloss. An object with high gloss has a sharper reflection than one with a lower gloss. To generate a ray traced image including gloss, secondary rays are fired in an area surrounding the mirror reflection direction. For an object with high gloss, the secondary rays should be close to the mirror direction, and as the gloss reduces, the secondary rays will be fired further away. A specular reflectance function can be used to create the distribution of secondary reflection rays.

The imperfections in a transparent object that cause light to scatter as it moves through the object are referred to as translucency. Much as gloss determines the distribution of the secondary rays about the mirror direction, translucency determines the distribution of the secondary rays about the refracted direction. A specular transmittance function can be used to create the distribution of secondary refraction rays.

Caustic Highlights

Imagine sitting beside a swimming pool while the sun shines. When you look at the pool, you can see a pattern of light dancing along the bottom and sides of the pool, as the sun refracts through the water waves and strikes the bottom and sides of the pool. A similar highlight can be seen when light refracts through a glass object that is sitting on a table. For example, in Figure 8.18, the light refracted through the glass balls creates a bright highlight on the table. The variation in these highlights is due to the imperfections in the glass balls. The pool bottom and sides and the table are all diffuse objects that have this highlight refracted onto them. The same thing is true for light that reaches a diffuse object by reflection off of a shiny surface. Figure 8.19 shows light reaching a surface by reflection off a mirror and refraction through a glass ball. Calculating the highlights on diffuse objects using a local illumination model looks for just the light that strikes the object directly from the light sources. The standard ray tracing process, therefore, does not pick up any highlights that reach an object indirectly.

Bi-directional or two-pass ray tracing (Arvo86) is one method that can be used to include those highlights. On the first pass, rays from the light source are traced through transparent objects and off reflective ones. These rays of light are followed around the scene until they exit the scene or strike a diffuse object. If they strike a diffuse object, the portions of the object that are highlighted are identified. When light from all of the light sources has been traced through refractive objects and off reflective objects into the scene, a standard ray tracer is used for the second pass.

Figure 8.18 • Light refracting through glass objects creating a caustic highlight (see Color Plate 8.5)

The areas where the highlights have been traced can be recorded in an illumination map (similar to a texture map) that records the highlight locations for each of the objects. The illumination map is based only on the relative location of the objects and light sources, so it only needs to be calculated once for a scene, which can then be rendered many times from many different viewpoints.

A second technique that can be used to solve this problem is photon mapping (Pharr04 pg. 769–795), which is a type of particle tracer. Particle tracing follows particles as they leave a light source and are scattered around the scene. As a particle moves around the scene, a list is recorded of the surface locations where it has been. These locations are the basis for determining the transfer of light energy in the scene. Photon mapping is a technique to structure the results of this particle tracing so that those measurements can be used at rendering time to properly illuminate the scene. Photon mapping can be used to handle direct illumination of an

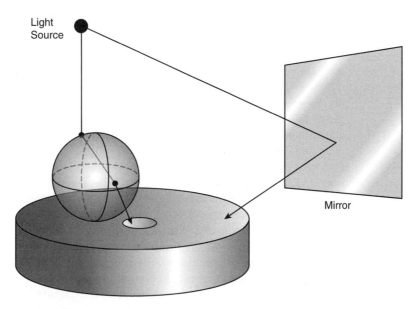

Figure 8.19 • Indirect highlights

object by a light source, caustic illumination caused when light reflects off or refracts through objects, and indirect illumination when light reflects off nonspecular surfaces.

8.5.2 Improving speed

The equations derived for intersection, reflection, and refraction calculations are computationally expensive. When the number of times that some of these calculations are done is factored in, the need for improvements in the general process is obvious. For example, consider a small image with 512 rows of 512 pixels each, and a scene that has three light sources and ten spheres that wind up with about a 50-pixel radius on the screen but have no reflective or refractive components. For each of the 262,144 pixels a ray intersection calculation will be done with every sphere for 2,621,440 such calculations. There will be about 78,540 rays that strike a sphere, and for each of those 78,540 locations intersection calculations will be done between three shadow feelers for each light source and the nine other spheres. That is an additional 2,120,580 intersection calculations for a total of 4,742,020 intersection calculations. If one of the spheres is reflective, the 7,854 rays that strike it will create a reflective ray. This adds an additional 78,540 intersection calculations. If this sphere is partially reflective and partially refractive, the refractive ray will add 86,394 to 157,080 intersection calculations.[6] This can now bring the total up to almost five million intersection calculations. This is not even a complex scene. Once the number of objects is increased, or more objects are reflective or refractive the number of calculations will start to grow exponentially.

One solution is to apply multiple computers to the task. One way is to design the ray tracer to only generate part of the scene. This program can be started on multiple computers giving each a different section of the image to create. In a fully parallel system such as a cluster, the ray tracer can be written to trace just one ray. The head node of the cluster can then tell each of the computers which ray to trace. As each cluster node completes and returns the color, the head node assigns the next ray that needs tracing. In this way, a node that is assigned rays that just leave the scene quickly returns an answer and can then be assigned another ray. This node processes many more rays than a node that is assigned a ray that spawns a lot of reflective and refractive rays that take more time. Though this technique creates the most balanced load across the computers in the cluster, Jensen and Reed (Jensen89) report that the communication overhead of message passing can be such that it is better to assign a bundle of rays instead of just one at a time.

Even with parallel processing, the number of computations is high, and parallel processing might not always be an option. To generate complex images the ray tracing process should be as efficient as possible. Arvo and Kirk (Arvo89) looked at and classified a number of techniques to speed up ray tracing. In their taxonomy, they identified three broad categories: those that have faster calculations; those that have fewer rays; and those that use generalized rays. The category of faster calculations was subdivided into the classes of faster intersection calculations and fewer intersection calculations. The rest of this section will deal with techniques to make the ray tracing process more efficient, looking at adaptive depth control ("fewer rays"); first hit pre-calculation ("fewer intersection calculations"); space subdivision ("fewer intersection calculations"); and bounding objects ("faster intersection calculations").

Adaptive Depth Control

An alternative to using an arbitrary depth limit is to use an attenuation factor (Hall83). The attenuation factor begins with a value of 1 for the initial ray. For each recursive call, the current attenuation factor is multiplied by either the reflection or refraction coefficient, as appropriate. If the attenuation factor falls below some threshold, the recursion is stopped and a color of black is returned. The attenuation factor is a measure of the impact that the ray has on the final pixel color. As the

---

[6]With the assumption that all objects are uniform in material, an inefficient ray tracer checks the refracted rays against all of the other objects, even though the next intersections must be that as the rays leave the object they are inside. So, the inefficient ray tracer will do 78,540 intersection calculations in finding the ways out of the object, and then an additional 78,540 intersection calculations to find where the rays go next. An efficient ray tracer only checks the rays against the current object to find where they leave (7,854 intersection calculations) and then do the additional 78,540 intersection calculations to find where they go next.

attenuation factor decreases, the impact of the ray decreases. If the attenuation factor is 0.5, that ray will contribute half of the final pixel color. If the attenuation factor is 0.1, the ray will contribute only 10 percent of the final color. At some point, the contribution becomes so small that further processing will not noticeably change the image. On a system that displays an image with eight bits per color, an attenuation factor of 0.004 will only change each color value by a maximum of one. With an attenuation factor of 0.001, the contribution of continuing the recursion will be about one quarter of a color unit, so stopping the recursion at this point will have little impact.

For example, consider a scene with four planar patches. If the first two face each other and both have a 0.5 reflective component, a ray will bounce back and forth about ten times before the attenuation factor is below the 0.001 threshold. If the second pair of patches faced each other and both have a 0.75 reflective component, a ray will bounce back and forth about 25 times before reaching the 0.001 threshold.

First Hit Pre-calculation

For a scene consisting of objects that do not have any reflective or refractive components, there is no difference between a z-buffer rendering and a ray traced image that both use the same perspective. When the scene is rendered using a z-buffer, a perspective transformation is applied and the objects are rendered. At the end, the z-buffer holds the depth of the closest object for each pixel location. When ray tracing this scene, if a ray hits an object, the local illumination is calculated and displayed. In both cases, the same object is displayed at each pixel. That fact can help speed up the process of ray tracing (Weghorst84).

As a first step, a perspective transformation is applied that is the same as the perspective produced by the relative location of the viewpoint and the screen in the ray tracer. Next, the objects are scan converted into an expanded z-buffer that holds not only the depth but also the object and location on the object at that depth. This is a similar process to the one used for generating shadows using a shadow z-buffer. Calculating the z-buffer values will be quick because there are no illumination calculations done. The ray tracer uses this expanded z-buffer to eliminate the intersection calculations for the initial ray for each pixel. The initial ray for pixel location (i, j) will intersect the object stored at location (i, j) in the expanded z-buffer. Instead of trying to intersect the initial ray with all of the objects in the scene, the ray tracer only needs to access the proper location in the expanded z-buffer. For the example with 10 spheres at the start of this section, the use of this first-hit pre-calculation saves about 2.6 million intersection calculation.

Space Subdivision

Imagine yourself sitting in a seat of an auditorium, facing the front of the room. You are the viewpoint for the auditorium scene to be rendered. At the top of your visual frame you see the ceiling and lights. Toward the bottom of your visual frame you see the seats in front of you. There are probably many objects in the auditorium that you cannot see because they are behind you but they are still part of the scene.

Now imagine ray tracing that scene. The first ray goes toward the upper-left corner of the scene, yet the standard ray tracer checks to see if it intersects each of the objects in the scene. For the auditorium, the ray tracer still tries to intersect a ray going toward the ceiling with the seats that are closer to the floor; the seats that are behind the ray; and even the floor itself. The ray tracer will try to intersect each ray with all of the objects—even if they are located far from where the ray is pointed.

Space subdivision techniques group the objects in the scene according to their location within the scene (Glassner84). An octree, which is like a binary tree but with eight children for each non-leaf node, is used for this purpose. Imagine the auditorium again, and imagine that the room is divided into eight parts or octants by dividing it in halves from front to back, from side to side, and from top to bottom. One of the pieces is the eighth of the room at the front-left-top, and another is the eighth at the back-right-bottom. Each object in the scene is associated with the octant it is in. If any of the eight sections has too many objects, it can be subdivided into eight additional pieces.

Once the octree is set up, the ray tracing process can quickly determine which of the octree nodes a ray goes through. Intersection calculations are done with the objects associated with just those nodes. In the auditorium example, when a ray is sent toward the upper-left corner of the room, only objects connected to nodes in that upper-left octant are used for the intersection calculations.

This method takes some additional pre-process effort to set up the octree, and there is some additional work necessary to identify the octree nodes through which the ray passes. But the time savings overall can still be significant. Depending on the scene, Glassner reports that using octrees can result in between 1/7 and 1/200 of the intersections that are done without octrees.

Additional details on octrees can be found in Glassner (Glassner84, Glassner89). A grid-based acceleration method can be found in Shirley (Shirley00). Binary Space Partition trees, discussed in Chapter 5, can also be used. These and other methods have as their goal the reduction in the number of expensive intersection calculations even though they are replaced by other (less computationally costly) work.

Bounding Volumes

As the complexity of the mathematical description of an object increases, the complexity of the calculations necessary to find an intersection also increases. For objects that are subdivided into polygonal patches, the number of patches also influences ray tracing time. Often, these calculations will find there was no intersection. One way to increase the overall speed of a ray tracer is to use simpler bounding volumes for complex objects, as in Whitted (Whitted80) and Rubin and Whitted (Rubin80). Consider an object with an elaborately curved surface. A pseudo object (typically a bounding sphere or cube) could be added to the scene so that it completely surrounds the complex object (see Figure 8.20). When attempting to find

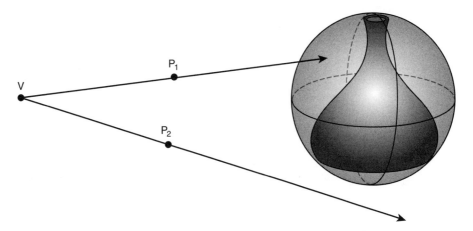

Figure 8.20 • Bounding volumes

intersections with objects, the ray tracer first checks to see if the ray intersects the bounding volume. If the ray misses the bounding volume, the ray must also miss the object contained in it. The simpler intersection calculations with the bounding volume can lead to a savings of the expensive intersection calculations with the complex object or all of the pieces it was subdivided into. The only time object intersections are done is if the ray intersects with the object's bounding volume.

When choosing bounding volumes, the ones that have relatively simple intersection calculations, and that surround the object rather closely are preferred. If the intersection computation for the bounding volume is too complex, the overhead will negate any savings. If the bounding volume does not tightly surround the complex object, there will be too many "hits" on the bounding volume that do not result in an intersection with the complex object. In that case, the ray tracer will actually do more work than without the bounding volume.

Faster Shadows

In the simple sphere scene given earlier, the shadow feeler intersections accounted for almost half of the intersection calculations done. Weghorst, Hooper, and Greenberg (Weghorst84) showed that shadow computations dominate a ray tracer's calculations. Decreasing the time needed to determine if an object is shadowed can dramatically improve ray tracing time.

Haines and Greenberg (Haines86) developed a method to reduce the calculation time for shadows through the use of a light buffer. Each light source is placed at the center of a light buffer cube. Each face of the cube is subdivided into cells. A preprocessing step projects all of the objects onto the faces of the cube, and each cell keeps a record of the object that is closest at that point, much as an expanded z-buffer would do.

During ray tracing, the shadow feeler is intersected with the light buffer cube. The object stored at that location of the light buffer is compared to the current object. If they are the same, the object is not shadowed. If they are different, the object is shadowed. This process is repeated for each of the light sources. In this way, there is only the intersection calculation with the light buffers, instead of intersecting the shadow feeler with each of the objects in the scene.

Haines and Greenberg report a reduction in compute time by a factor of between 2 and 4 when a light buffer is used. An additional benefit of the light buffer is that it only needs to be recalculated if objects in the scene move. The contents of the light buffer are based on the projection of objects in the scene, independent of the location of the viewpoint. Therefore, as long as the objects remain stationary, the light buffer can be re-used to render the scene from multiple viewpoints.

8.6 The OpenGL Way

OpenGL does not have any built-in capability to do ray tracing. All of the ray tracing capability needs to be written by the programmer. OpenGL can, however, be used to display the results of ray tracing.

The first way this can be done is to treat the window as a series of small blocks. For each block, the initial ray is set, the ray tracing calculated, and then the block is drawn as a small rectangle. An algorithm for this would be:

```
for (int i = 0; i < COLUMNS; i += blockSize)
   for (int j = 0; j < ROWS; j += blockSize)
   {
      initialRay = SetDirection( i, j )
      color = RayTrace( initialRay, 0 )
      glColor3f( color.red, color.green, color.blue )
      glRecti( i, j, i + blockSize, j + blockSize )
   }
```

A second way is to set up an array of unsigned bytes (GLubyte) to hold the image generated. The initialization routine calls the ray tracer to generate the image. As the values are generated, they are stored in the array. The array is then loaded into the window with a call to the OpenGL routine glDrawPixels. The following code fragments can accomplish this:

```
GLubyte    image[Height][Width][3];

   ⋮

void initial()
{
```

```
    ⋮
    for (int i = 0; i < ROWS; i++)
        for (int j = 0; j < COLUMNS; j++)
        {
            initialRay = SetDirection( i, j )
            color = RayTrace( initialRay, 0 )
            image[i][j][0] = color.red;
            image[i][j][1] = color.green;
            image[i][j][2] = color.blue;
        }
    // tell OpenGL the pixels are byte aligned
    glPixelStorei(GL_UNPACK_ALIGNMENT, 1);
}

    ⋮

void display()
{
    glClear(GL_COLOR_BUFFER_BIT);
    // set the current position to the lower left corner
    glRasterPos2i(0, 0);
    // draw the image
    glDrawPixels( Width, Height, GL_RGB, GL_UNSIGNED_BYTE, image );
    glFlush();
}
```

It should be noted that the value placed into location image[0][0] will be displayed in the lower left corner of the window.

8.7 Projects

1) Derive the intersection equations for a cone.
2) Derive the intersection equations for a cylinder.
3) Derive the intersection equations for an ellipsoid.
4) Write a simple recursive ray tracer that can handle spheres, and triangular patches.
5) Add shadows to your recursive ray tracer.
6) Add additional shapes to your recursive ray tracer.

Radiosity

The first methods of rendering discussed in this book looked at the local illumination of an object by light sources. In those methods, highlights were created by the direct illumination of an object. In the images produced, all of the objects had a matte appearance. Those methods were then extended to global illumination by tracing rays from the viewpoint that then bounced off the objects. In ray tracing, mirror reflections and transparent and translucent objects are possible. But even with these techniques, there are other effects that are not modeled. In this chapter, the reflection of light between two diffuse surface objects is discussed.

This sort of reflection is more commonly known as color bleeding. Color bleeding occurs when two colored objects are placed next to each other. This is most visible in bright light when one of the objects is brightly colored and the other is white. Figure 9.1 has a red "crab" against a white background. The areas of the background near the crab are tinted a very light red. The tinting is greatest where the crab and background are closest and decreases as the distance increases. Even though the crab and the background are not shiny surfaces, the background picks up some of the tint of the crab. Because of how bright the crab is colored, what is less noticeable is that the crab is more illuminated near the white background. The greater the intensity of the light the more color bleeding can be seen, which is not surprising because the bleeding is caused by the transfer of light energy between these two matte surfaces.

Methods discussed so far cannot model this effect. Ray tracing is the closest, but in that method a transfer of light energy requires that one of the objects is reflective. In Figure 9.1, the object and background have matte surfaces. A technique called radiosity treats light as energy and illuminates the scene through energy transfer

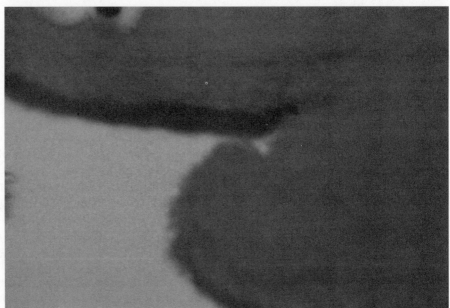

Figure 9.1 • Color bleeding (see Color Plate 9.1)

and can be used for these situations. Radiosity determines how each object in the scene receives and then disperses energy. The final radiosity illumination is a solution to this energy balancing problem.

Radiosity concepts have been used in the illumination and thermal engineering fields for many years. The ideas supporting this concept date back as far as the 1920s, when radiant flux equations were developed for transfer of energy between ideal diffuse surfaces. The first radiosity "image" was produced by Moon and Spencer in 1946 when they calculated the energy transfer in an empty room and then used their calculations to cut out squares of paper from the correct color of the Munsell color chart. In the 1950s, engineers from both the illumination and thermal fields applied the computer to this radiosity research. The issue, however, was how energy was being transferred. It was not until the mid-1980s that these concepts were applied to the production of computer graphics imagery. In today's illumination engineering field, this work is called "radiative transfer theory," while in the thermal engineering and computer graphics fields, this work is called "radiosity theory." The main area of application of radiosity in computer graphics is the production of imagery and animations of architectural designs (see Figure 9.2).

Figure 9.2 • Architectural radiosity images (see Color Plate 9.2)
(Image created by Erik Svanholm © 2002 Zumtobel Staff)

There are three books that are dedicated to radiosity theory for computer graphics by Ashdown (Ashdown94); Cohen and Wallace (Cohen93); and Sillion and Puech (Sillion94). Additionally, Glassner's digital image synthesis two-volume book (Glassner95) also has an in depth treatment of the topic. Radiosity is complex enough to fill entire books, so the presentation here will not be able to address all of the issues. Enough detail will be presented, however, so that the reader will be able to create at least a simplistic radiosity renderer.

9.1 The Radiosity Equation

Frequently when we think of energy, we think of heat. Heat can come from a number of different sources, not all of which are thought of as heat generators. A pan that has just been removed from the stove gives off some of the heat that it picked up during cooking. The exhaust system of a car radiates a lot of heat as well. Even the ground on a sunny day gives off heat built up from the sunlight cast on it. None of these objects produces heat; rather the heat they give off is the result of heat that they receive from other sources. This is a concept called radiative heat transfer and is the basis for radiosity theory.

Light is another form of energy. Things in the world are visible when the energy of the sun and lamps is reflected off and between objects and enters the eye. Nothing in this description seems to depart much from the ray concept used for implementing other graphics algorithms. But the key is that energy can be transferred between objects no matter what their surface characteristics. As the transfer of heat energy between objects can be quantified, the transfer of light energy between objects can also be quantified.

It should come as no surprise that the amount of energy transferred between two objects depends on how much energy each object has, how close the objects are to each other, and how the objects are oriented relative to each other. The more energy that an object has, the more it will give off to other objects. The closer that two objects are positioned, the more energy they will transfer between themselves. And if two objects face each other, they will transfer more energy than if they are partially facing away from each other.

The problem becomes more complex because even though all energy in a scene begins at the sources of energy, as time passes, objects that have absorbed energy will now begin to give off energy. Further, the amount of energy that a non-source object can give off will be dependent on how much energy it receives. This creates an elaborate web of interaction where the amount of energy that each object transfers to the rest of the scene is based in part on how much energy the scene transfers to it.

In the radiosity approach, objects are divided into patches, which can be subdivided further into subpatches in a refinement step. Calculations look at the transfer of energy among these patches. Once the radiosity values are calculated for each of the patches, the values are used in the rendering of the patches. Radiosity theory assumes that each of the objects is a Lambertian reflector and that the light sources are Lambertian emitters. This assumption means that the transfer of energy is independent of the direction it is received. Specifically, the energy reflected or emitted from a Lambertian surface is given by Lambert's cosine law in equation (9.1), where θ is the angle between the normal and the direction the energy is emitted.

$$I_\theta = I * \cos \theta \tag{9.1}$$

Equation (9.1) indicates that the most energy will be emitted in the direction normal to the surface, and as the direction moves away from the normal the energy emitted in that direction will decrease. There will be no energy emitted in the direction tangent to the surface, which is 90° from the normal. Lambert's cosine law is the basis for the diffuse component of the illumination model presented in Chapter 2.

Thus, the amount of energy from patch P_i that reaches patch P_j depends on the angle between the normal of patch P_i and the vector from patch P_i to P_j. Likewise, the amount of energy transferred from patch P_j to patch P_i depends on the normal of patch P_j and the vector from patch P_j to P_i. The transfer of energy between two patches therefore, depends on the angle made by the two normal vectors and the line connecting the center of these two patches. For each pair of patches, P_i and P_j, a form factor F_{ij} will be calculated that indicates the percentage of energy leaving patch P_i that reaches patch P_j.

Formally, radiosity (B) is "radiant exitance," which is the rate of flow of energy ("flux" written Φ) per unit area leaving some location on a surface. The radiosity equation states that the radiosity of a patch is equal to the energy that patch is emitting or producing plus the energy that patch is reflecting from other sources. Equation (9.2) represents the radiosity equation for each of the patches in the scene, where N is the number of patches in the scene, i is in the range [1, N], E_i is the energy emitted by patch P_i, R_i is the surface reflectivity of patch P_i, F_{ij} is the form factor between patches P_i and P_j, and B_j is the radiosity of patch P_j.

$$B_i = E_i + R_i * \sum_{j=1}^{N} \left(B_j * F_{ij} \right) \tag{9.2}$$

In equation (9.2), the values of E_i and R_i are known from the description of the object, and can vary based on wavelength. For example, using an RGB color model, an object that is a red light source would have an E value of (1.0, 0.0, 0.0), where a blue table would have an R value of (0.0, 0.0, 1.0). An object that is a white light source would have an E value of (1.0, 1.0, 1.0). It should be noted that if a light source has a surface reflectivity value other than zero, the final emitted energy will be greater than the initial energy because of the combination of the emission and reflection.

So, if a white light source has a non-zero surface reflectivity value, its final radiosity values will be greater than 1.

Equation (9.2) is repeated for each of the patches in the scene, which gives a set of N linear equations. Because the emittance and surface reflectivity values are known from the objects and the form factors are calculated from the patch orientations, the only values unknown in equation (9.2) are the radiosity values.

The radiosity process described in the rest of this chapter details how this process works.

9.2 Radiosity Pipeline

The radiosity pipeline (Figure 9.3) gives the set of steps to create a scene with this method. The first step is to specify the scene to be rendered. The amount of emitted energy and the surface reflectance values are specified for each object in the scene. The objects need to be subdivided into patches, which can be done by hand or automatically generated. As will be seen, the way the objects are subdivided can influence the final results. The smaller the patches the better the solution will be. But an increase in the number of patches can drastically increase the computation time in this $O(n^2)$ process. Once the patches have been determined, the next step is to calculate the form factors for the scene. The form factors encode the physical relationship between the patches and the energy transfer occurs based on the relative positions. The form factors; emitted energy values; and surface reflectance values are used in a set of linear equations that when solved give the radiosity value for each of the patches. The final step is to use a standard rendering method to render the scene based on the current view. This rendering method can be a simple interpolation method, because all of the highlights and shadows are calculated as part of solving the radiosity equations.

When generating a single image using the radiosity method, the entire radiosity pipeline must be traversed. If there are a series of images to be produced, only part of the pipeline will need to be redone depending on what type of change occurs. In

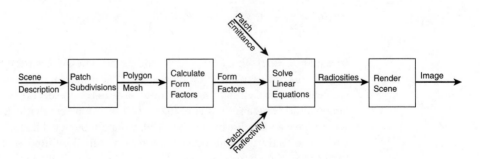

Figure 9.3 • The radiosity pipeline

the worst case, if a new object is added or if an existing object changes shape, patch subdivision will need to be done for this object. In this case, the entire radiosity pipeline will have to be recalculated.

If all of the objects stay the same but one or more objects move, the spatial relationship between the patches will have changed. The patch subdivision will be the same but the form factors no longer represent the new relative orientation of the patches. In this case, the pipeline is re-entered at the stage that recalculates the form factors.

The color or intensity of a light source or the color of an object can also change. The form factors are not influenced by this sort of change, so they do not need to be recalculated. Figure 9.3 shows the emittance and surface reflectivity values coming into play when the linear equations are solved, so the process backs up to solve the linear equations again with the new values, and then renders the scene based on this new solution. The linear equations use the emittance and surface reflectivity as an important part of the solution but these values do not influence the position of the objects, so the existing form factors can still be used.

If the viewpoint or viewing direction for rendering the scene changes, this has no impact on the radiosity values of the patches. A change in viewpoint or viewing direction will only influence how the scene is rendered. Changing where the scene is viewed from will not alter any of the physical relationships between the objects, so there is minimal work that needs to be redone. The quality of the results and the ability to change the view with only the simplest of rendering calculations is the reason that radiosity is used to create real-time architectural walk-throughs of buildings that have been designed but not yet constructed.

9.3 Polygon Meshing

Once the scene has been described, the first step is to decompose that scene into a set of planar patches. Breaking objects into small planar patches is a necessary step if the result is to show variation in the final color of objects. Because the radiosity calculations determine the energy transfer between components of the scene, using entire objects means that the object will have a single radiosity value. In the case of the picture in Figure 9.1, without breaking the background into pieces, the single radiosity value would either be white, which would lose the color bleeding; or light red, which would give a false impression of the background color. When the background is divided into smaller patches, some of the patches will have a radiosity value of white and others will have a light red value. Interpolating with these values creates a gradation of values seen in the picture. Because the radiosity values of these smaller patches need to be brought together for rendering, the decomposition process will need to preserve information that relates patches in the resulting polygon mesh back to the original object. For example, if a wall is subdivided into 25 patches, the spatial relationship of these patches is needed so that the radiosity of the 25 individual patches can be interpolated across the wall.

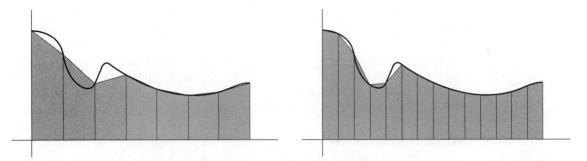

Figure 9.4 • Radiosity sampling for two different patch sizes

The curve in Figure 9.4 is the set of radiosity values that would be measured continuously across the surface of an object. Subdividing that surface into patches and calculating the radiosity value based on those patches results in a sampling of the curve at discrete points shown by the vertical lines. Interpolating between these samples during rendering will create only an approximation of the real radiosity curve. In some cases, for example, at the right end of the curve, the interpolation is reasonably close. In other cases, there can be significant difference between the interpolation and the curve. One solution to this is to use smaller patches, which should improve the approximation by sampling the curve more frequently. This will, however, increase the number of form factors and radiosities that need to be calculated. An advanced solution to this problem, adaptive meshing, will be discussed later.

One heuristic that can be used to determine the size of the patches is the five-times rule. The five-times rule used by illumination engineers states that an emitting patch can be modeled as a point source when the distance to the receiving patch is greater than five times the maximum dimension of the emitting patch. For example, if the distance from patch P_i to patch P_j is 20 units, the maximum dimension of the patch should be no greater than four units. This applies to both patches because each one emits to the other. Though the five-times rule can give a general idea for the size of patches, it is impossible to use the five-times rule when two patches meet, for example, at the corner of a room. When two patches meet, the distance between them will be small, and so the five-times rule requires them to be subdivided. This subdivision creates properly sized sub-patches along the edges that are opposite the coincident edge. The sub-patches along the shared edge will be the same size, but the distance between them will be smaller than the distance between the original patches. Thus the patches along this edge will not meet the five-times rule, and will need to be subdivided again. This process will never end because each subdivision reduces the distance of the smaller and smaller patches along the edge forcing more and more rounds of subdivision.

The requirement that the patches be planar is due to the form factors. If a patch is flat, all of the energy emitted by that patch will move to other patches. But if a patch is curved, one side of the patch can transfer energy to the other side. This means that the form factor F_{ii} will always be 0 for planar patches, but will be greater than 0 for curved patches. Using planar patches will make the resulting system of linear equations easier to solve.

As the details of the radiosity method become clearer, there are many instances where connectivity information between the patches is needed. This information will be necessary as patches are brought back together for rendering and as adjustments are made to the patch mesh to improve the results. It is necessary to quickly determine which patches share a vertex or an edge. A simple radiosity render that uses a regular rectangular surface mesh for simple scenes can store these relationships with arrays and pointers, however, as advanced techniques for surface meshing are added, other structures are needed to store and access this information efficiently. The winged-edge data structure discussed in Chapter 3 is recommended by Ashdown (Ashdown94), Cohen and Wallace (Cohen93), and Sillion and Puech (Sillion94) for storing the patch meshes.

9.4 Form Factors

A form factor indicates the portion of the energy that leaves one patch and strikes another and is based on the relative position and orientation of the two patches. More specifically, F_{ij} is the portion of the energy leaving patch i that strikes patch j. Consider Figure 9.5. In the two patches that face each other, their normal vectors are parallel and face in opposite directions. By Lambert's cosine law, all of the energy leaving each patch travels in the direction of the other patch. Now imagine that one of those patches is turned. As that patch is turned, the angle between the normal and the line between the two patches will increase, and by Lambert's cosine law the amount of energy transferred will decrease. Thus, the form factors will be based on the relative orientation of the two patches.

The proximity to a light source also influences how brightly an object is illuminated. Similarly, the energy transferred between two patches is influenced by the distance between the patches—the greater the distance the less energy that will be transferred.

Overall, each form factor is dependent on the distance between the patches involved and the angles between their normal vectors and the line connecting the patches. Figure 9.6 shows this situation using the center of the two patches, but this figure shows that a different form factor can result from different points on the patches. Furthermore, if the entire patch is emitting energy that is being received by the entire surface of the other patch, the calculation must account for the relationship over the entire area of these patches. The calculation needs to consider how every location on patch P_i interacts with every location on patch P_j. The full

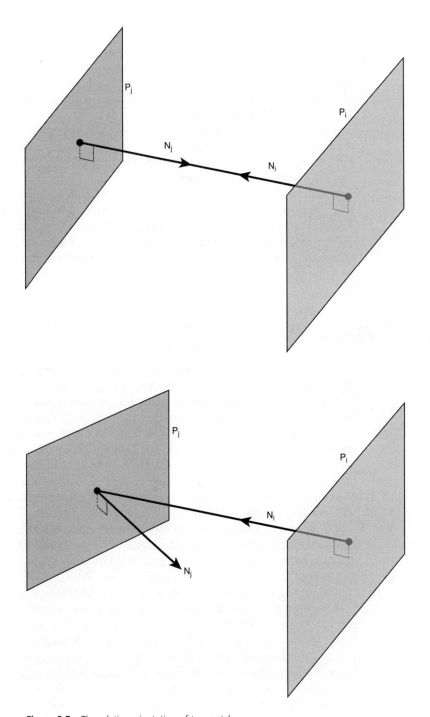

Figure 9.5 • The relative orientation of two patches

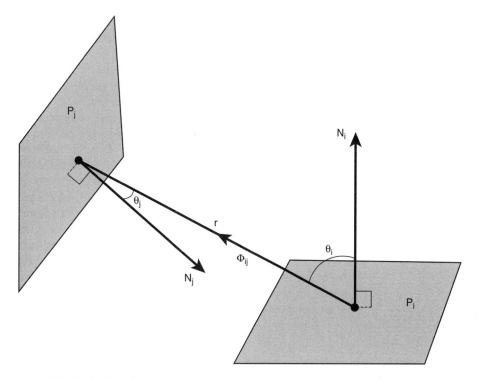

Figure 9.6 • Patch orientation

form factor calculation accomplishes this by equation (9.3), which integrates across the area of both patches.

$$F_{ij} = \frac{1}{A_i} \int_{A_i} \int_{A_j} \frac{\cos \theta_i * \cos \theta_j}{\pi * r^2} * V_{ij} * dA_j * dA_i \qquad (9.3)$$

In equation (9.3), A_i is the area of patch P_i, θ_i and θ_j are the angles between the line connecting the patches and the surface normal vectors, and r is the distance between the patches. The visibility term, V_{ij}, indicates the visibility of these two patches. If patch P_i and P_j are completely visible to each other, V_{ij} will be 1, but if there is something completely blocking the two patches, V_{ij} will be 0.

This double integral is quite complex to solve directly. This can be simplified by using the five-times rule in choosing the patch sizes. When the five-times rule is used to determine the relative patch sizes, the emitting patch P_i can be treated as a point source, and equation (9.3) can be simplified to equation (9.4)

$$F_{ij} = \int_{A_j} \frac{\cos \theta_i * \cos \theta_j}{\pi * r^2} * dA_j \qquad (9.4)$$

Equation (9.4) is still too complex to solve directly, and so early applications of radiosity to computer graphics used a contour-integration approach to this calculation. Equation (9.4) assumes that patch P_j is completely visible from the center of patch P_i. This assumption is not a problem because if the entire patch is not visible, the patch can be subdivided into completely visible and completely hidden parts.

Though the contour-integration approach works, a year after its introduction a simpler form factor approximation method, the hemicube, was developed (Cohen85). Much as a hemisphere is half of a sphere, a hemicube is half of a cube. In the following derivation, (u, v, n) is used for the axes of the hemicube coordinate system instead of (x, y, z). The top surface of the hemicube (Figure 9.7) is two units on a side and has u and v coordinates that range from -1.0 to 1.0 with a constant n coordinate value of 1. The four sides are one unit high and two units wide. The hemicube is positioned so that the normal vector of the patch is aligned with the hemicube n axis, hence that choice of axis label.

The idea behind the hemicube is that the form factor between patch P_i and P_j will be the same as the form factor between the patch P_i and the projection of P_j onto the hemicube (Figure 9.8). Because this projection is a perspective projection, objects further away project onto smaller areas of the hemicube. As a patch rotates, its apparent size will change, and so will its projection on to the hemicube. Thus

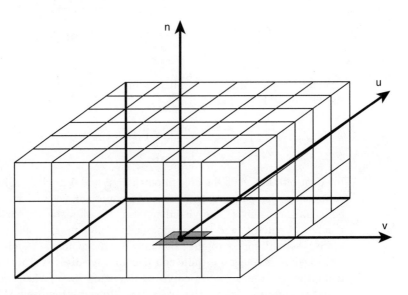

Figure 9.7 • A hemicube

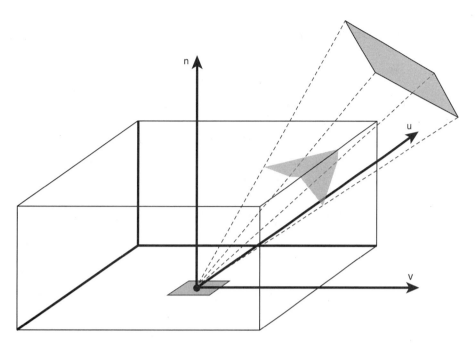

Figure 9.8 • Patch projected onto the hemicube

the location and size of the projection of patch P_j onto the hemicube centered above patch P_i can be used to determine the form factor F_{ij}.

Furthermore, projecting all of the patches onto the hemicube using a hidden surface technique results in the hemicube being "covered" with only those patches (or parts of patches) that can be seen from the center of patch P_i. These are the only patches that actually receive energy from patch P_i.

The hemicube is subdivided into a series of cells for the purpose of determining the form factors. The projection process will associate with each of the hemicube cells, the patch that is closest for that cell. The more cells that are used for the hemicube subdivision, the better the result will be. Increasing the resolution, however, adds computation time to the projection process because there are more cells that each patch can potentially cover. Radiosity researchers have typically subdivided the hemicube so that the top has between 32^2 and 1024^2 hemicube cells. The side faces will be subdivided in a similar way with each side face having half the number of hemicube cells as the top because the sides are only one unit high.

The hemicube approximation associates with each of the hemicube cells the form factor between the patch and that cell area—which is called a delta form factor in the radiosity literature. A delta form factor indicates the portion of the energy leaving the patch that goes through the associated hemicube cell. These delta form

factors can be calculated once during program setup because they are not dependent on any of the individual patches. The patch form factors are then determined
by adding up the delta form factors for all of the cells that patch covers.

When dealing with hemicube cells, equation (9.4) can be further simplified giving equation (9.5), where j refers to a cell in the hemicube.

$$\Delta F_{ij} = \frac{\cos\theta_i * \cos\theta_j}{\pi * r^2} * \Delta A_j \qquad (9.5)$$

In equation (9.5), ΔA_j is the area of the cell relative to the entire face. Because all
cells are the same size, the j subscript can be dropped. For example, with a top face
hemicube resolution of 50 × 50 pixels, ΔA would be $(2 * 2) / (50 * 50) = 0.0016$
because the top face is 2 units square. Figure 9.9 shows the situation for one of the
hemicube cells on the top face. For the top face cell at location (u, v), the distance
r will be given by $r = \sqrt{u^2 + v^2 + 1}$, and $\cos\theta_i$ will be equal to $\cos\theta_j$ because the top
face is parallel to the patch. Further, because the hemicube is one unit high and
the cosine is the length of the adjacent side over the length of the hypotenuse,
these cosine values are both $1 / r$. Substituting these into equation (9.5) gives
equation (9.6).

$$\Delta F_{uv} = \frac{\Delta A}{\pi * r^4} = \frac{\Delta A}{\pi * \left(\sqrt{u^2 + v^2 + 1}\right)^4} = \frac{\Delta A}{\pi * \left(u^2 + v^2 + 1\right)^2} \qquad (9.6)$$

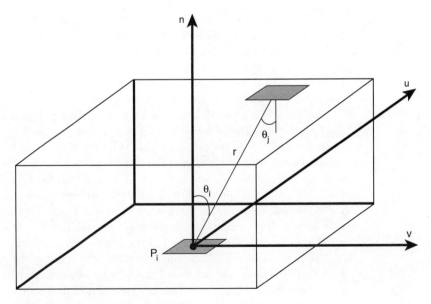

Figure 9.9 • Delta form factor determination for a top face cell

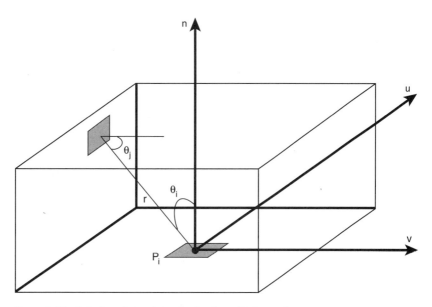

Figure 9.10 • Delta form factor determination for a side face cell

Figure 9.10 shows a hemicube cell on one of the side faces. For a cell on one of the side faces where v is either positive or negative one, the distance to the cell will be given by $r = \sqrt{u^2 + n^2 + 1}$. In this case, the cos θ_j will be the height of the cell location (n) divided by the hypotenuse, but the cos θ_i will be the same as for the top. Substituting into equation (9.5) gives equation (9.7).

$$\Delta F_{un} = \frac{n * \Delta A}{\pi * r^4} = \frac{n * \Delta A}{\pi * \left(\sqrt{u^2 + n^2 + 1}\right)^4} = \frac{n * \Delta A}{\pi * \left(u^2 + n^2 + 1\right)^2} \tag{9.7}$$

The equation for the two faces where u is positive or negative one are similar to equation (9.7), but v is substituted for u.

To determine the form factors from patch P_i to all of the other patches in the scene, the hemicube is moved so that patch P_i is centered at the bottom of the hemicube and so that the patch normal is aligned with the n axis. Another way to approach this is to consider the hemicube to be fixed and the scene transformed so that P_i moved into the proper position in the hemicube. By transforming the scene instead of moving the hemicube, the techniques discussed in other chapters that project and scan convert a polygon are all useable here as well. Figure 9.11 shows a patch that has been scan converted into the cells on the top and side of a hemicube. The form factor is determined by the six cells of the hemicube that are shaded gray in this figure.

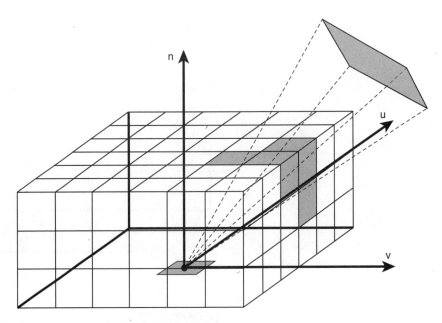

Figure 9.11 • Patch projected onto the hemicube

To use these standard algorithms, the hemicube could be aligned so the n-axis points in the direction of the world coordinate system's negative z axis. This then requires that the patch is transformed so its center is at the origin and its normal vector points in the negative z direction. The transformation developed will then be applied to all of the patches to prepare them for projection onto the hemicube top. The first step of this transformation is to translate the patch. If the patch center is located at (x_c, y_c, z_c), the translation is done by matrix (9.8).

$$\begin{bmatrix} 1 & 0 & 0 & -x_c \\ 0 & 1 & 0 & -y_c \\ 0 & 0 & 1 & -z_c \\ 0 & 0 & 0 & 1 \end{bmatrix} \qquad (9.8)$$

The next step is to rotate the normal direction to align it with the z axis. This can be done with two rotations: the first about the x axis and then the second about the y axis. The following derivation assumes that the normal vector is of unit length. To determine the amount to rotate about the x axis, the normal is parallel projected into the x = 0 plane as shown in Figure 9.12. Because this is a projection, the length of this vector may not be 1. The length of the projected vector is given by $d = \sqrt{N_y^2 + N_z^2}$. If the value of d is 0, the normal points along the x axis, so this rotation can be skipped. From Figure 9.12 and the definition of sine and cosine, it

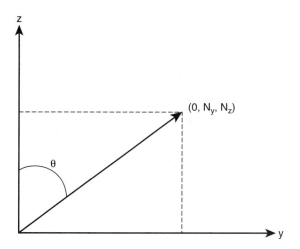

Figure 9.12 • Projection of the patch normal onto the x = 0 plane

can be seen that $\cos \theta = N_z / d$ and $\sin \theta = N_y / d$. Using these values gives the rotation matrix (9.9).

$$
\begin{bmatrix}
1 & 0 & 0 & 0 \\
0 & N_z/d & -N_y/d & 0 \\
0 & N_y/d & N_z/d & 0 \\
0 & 0 & 0 & 1
\end{bmatrix}
\tag{9.9}
$$

The result of transforming with matrix (9.9) is that the normal now lies in the y = 0 plane. Figure 9.13 shows the resulting vector. It should be noted that this vector is the result of a rotation so in this figure the length of the vector will be one. In looking at matrix (9.9), there is no change made to the x coordinate, so in Figure 9.13, x = N_x. From matrix (9.9), the rotated value of z is given by equation (9.10).

$$
\begin{aligned}
z &= N_y * \frac{N_y}{d} + N_z * \frac{N_z}{d} \\
&= \frac{N_y^2 + N_z^2}{\sqrt{N_y^2 + N_z^2}} \\
&= \sqrt{N_y^2 + N_z^2}
\end{aligned}
\tag{9.10}
$$

From Figure 9.13, it can be seen that $\cos \phi = z/1 = d$ and $\sin \phi = x/1 = N_x$. The second rotation matrix is, therefore, given by matrix (9.11).

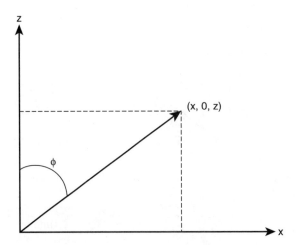

Figure 9.13 • The rotated normal in the y = 0 plane

$$\begin{bmatrix} d & 0 & -N_x & 0 \\ 0 & 1 & 0 & 0 \\ -N_x & 0 & -d & 0 \\ 0 & 0 & 0 & 1 \end{bmatrix} \qquad (9.11)$$

In matrix (9.11), the values in the third column are all negative because the rotation should align with the negative z direction where the angles shown in Figure 9.13 are relative to the positive z direction. Putting all of this together gives the transformation sequence given in equation (9.12).

$$\begin{bmatrix} d & 0 & -N_x & 0 \\ 0 & 1 & 0 & 0 \\ -N_x & 0 & -d & 0 \\ 0 & 0 & 0 & 1 \end{bmatrix} * \begin{bmatrix} 1 & 0 & 0 & 0 \\ 0 & N_z/d & -N_y/d & 0 \\ 0 & N_y/d & N_z/d & 0 \\ 0 & 0 & 0 & 1 \end{bmatrix} * \begin{bmatrix} 1 & 0 & 0 & -x_c \\ 0 & 1 & 0 & -y_c \\ 0 & 0 & 1 & -z_c \\ 0 & 0 & 0 & 1 \end{bmatrix} \qquad (9.12)$$

After being transformed with the matrices in (9.12), the patches are scan converted onto the top hemicube face using a perspective projection. In doing this scan conversion, there is no rendering done. For each hemicube cell, the depth of the patch is determined and compared to the depth of the patch currently associated with the hemicube cell. As in the case of a z-buffer, if a later patch is closer, it replaces what is currently stored. When this process is complete, each hemicube cell has the patch that is closest there. The program can now step through each hemicube cell location and add the delta form factor for that cell to the proper patch form factor. Specifically, if for cell (u, v) patch P_j is closest, the delta form factor for cell (u, v) will be added to F_{ij}.

At this point, the top face of the hemicube has been handled for just one patch. The other faces of the hemicube can be done for this patch with simple transformations to rotate them so their face normal points in the negative z direction. Vilaplana and Pueyo (Vilaplana92) showed that this transformation is a simple matter of swapping and perhaps negating the coordinates. They showed that changing from the top face view to the left face view is possible by having the x coordinate become the z coordinate, the y coordinate become the x coordinate, and the z coordinate become the y coordinate. If this is represented as $(x, y, z) \rightarrow (y, z, x)$, the transformation is $(x, y, z) \rightarrow (-y, z, x)$ for the right face, $(x, y, z) \rightarrow (x, z, -y)$ for the front face, and $(x, y, z) \rightarrow (-x, z, y)$ for the back face. In each case, the hemicube cell distances are reset and then the patches are scan converted again.

All of the work just described calculates the form factors from just one patch. This process is, therefore, repeated for all of the patches that make up the scene. The process of calculating the form factors is very time consuming and research that has shown about 90 percent of the radiosity calculation time is devoted to form factor determination.

There are three assumptions that serve as the basis for the hemicube method for determining the form factors (Baum89). The first is that the distance from patch P_i to the other patches is large relative to the size of patch P_j. To support this assumption, it is necessary to use appropriately small patches. The second assumption is that the visibility of patch P_i does not change relative to the surface of another patch. This means that if the center of patch P_i is visible to patch P_j, all of the points on patch P_i should be visible to patch P_j. This assumption can also be met by using small patches, because with small patches there is less variation between the center and extremes of the patch. The third assumption is that the resolution of the grid of hemicube cells is sufficiently fine to get a good estimate of the projections of the other patches. If the grid resolution is insufficient, patches that project to a small area of the hemicube can cover few if any hemicube cells. This will lead to a low estimate of the actual form factor value. In general, if any of these assumptions do not hold for a particular implementation or data set, the precision of the form factors will be less accurate unless patch sizes are reduced and the hemicube resolution is increased.

9.4.1 Form factor reciprocity

There is a relationship between the form factors between two patches that can be used to speed up the calculation of the full set of form factors. Equation (9.13) shows that the relationship between the two form factors involving patches P_i and P_j is dependent on the relative sizes of the patches.

$$A_i * F_{ij} = A_j * F_{ji} \tag{9.13}$$

Once the form factors are calculated for the energy leaving patch P_j, equation (9.13) can be used to quickly calculate the form factors for the energy arriving at patch P_i from all of the other patches.

9.4.2 Hemicube symmetry

There are symmetries in the hemicube that can reduce the number of delta form factors that need to be calculated and stored. In equations (9.6) and (9.7), because the values of u, v, and n are squared, these delta form factors are symmetric around the various axes. Specifically, $\Delta F_{u,v}$, $\Delta F_{-u,v}$, $\Delta F_{u,-v}$, and $\Delta F_{-u,v}$, all have the same value when u and v are fixed. So the top face has four-way symmetry and the side faces have two-way symmetry.

On closer inspection, however, it can be seen that u and v are used the same in equation (9.6) as are u and n in equation (9.7). Thus, $\Delta F_{u,v}$ will have the same value as $\Delta F_{v,u}$ when u and v are fixed. Therefore, the symmetry is actually eight-way symmetry for the top face and four-way symmetry for the side faces.

The side faces are all equivalent, except for the fact that some use u and n and others use v and n. If $u = v$, the value of $\Delta F_{u,n}$ from the front face will be the same as $\Delta F_{v,n}$ from the side face.

Overall, for a hemicube that has C cells along each side of the top of the hemicube, there will be only $C^2/4$ delta form factors that have to be calculated and stored.

9.4.3 Hemicube aliasing

Another potential problem is hemicube aliasing. As the hemicube is moved from patch to patch along an object, the overall hemicube orientation will only change as the normal changes. For a large flat wall, the hemicube will only move along the length and height of the wall. If there is a patch that projects badly onto the hemicube, in all likelihood it will continue to do so as the hemicube is moved. Wallace, Cohen, and Greenberg (Wallace87) suggest a solution to this problem—randomly rotating the hemicube around the n axis. In this way, each location of the hemicube will be altered so that any problematic alignments between projected patches and hemicube cells will not repeat in successive hemicube locations.

9.5 Solving the Radiosity Equation

Once the form factors have been calculated, all of the components needed to calculate the radiosity values are now available. The radiosity equation in (9.2) represents a set of N equations, one for each of the patches. The radiosity equation can be expressed as a system of linear equations, which is shown in matrix form in equation (9.14), where the B terms are the patch radiosity values, the E terms are the energy emitted by a patch, the R terms are the patch reflectivities, and the F terms are the form factors. In this equation, the emittance and reflectivity values are specified in the data file for the objects in the scene.

$$
\begin{bmatrix} B_1 \\ B_2 \\ B_3 \\ \vdots \\ B_N \end{bmatrix} = \begin{bmatrix} E_1 \\ E_2 \\ E_3 \\ \vdots \\ E_N \end{bmatrix} + \begin{bmatrix} R_1 * B_1 * F_{11} & R_1 * B_2 * F_{12} & R_1 * B_3 * F_{13} & \cdots & R_1 * B_N * F_{1N} \\ R_2 * B_1 * F_{21} & R_2 * B_2 * F_{22} & R_2 * B_3 * F_{13} & \cdots & R_2 * B_N * F_{2N} \\ R_3 * B_1 * F_{31} & R_3 * B_2 * F_{32} & R_3 * B_3 * F_{33} & \cdots & R_3 * B_N * F_{3N} \\ \vdots & \vdots & \vdots & \ddots & \vdots \\ R_N * B_1 * F_{N1} & R_N * B_2 * F_{N2} & R_N * B_3 * F_{N3} & \cdots & R_N * B_N * F_{NN} \end{bmatrix} \quad (9.14)
$$

If the large matrix on the right is subtracted from both sides, the result is equation (9.15).

$$
\begin{bmatrix} B_1 \\ B_2 \\ B_3 \\ \vdots \\ B_N \end{bmatrix} - \begin{bmatrix} R_1 * B_1 * F_{11} & R_1 * B_2 * F_{12} & R_1 * B_3 * F_{13} & \cdots & R_1 * B_N * F_{1N} \\ R_2 * B_1 * F_{21} & R_2 * B_2 * F_{22} & R_2 * B_3 * F_{13} & \cdots & R_2 * B_N * F_{2N} \\ R_3 * B_1 * F_{31} & R_3 * B_2 * F_{32} & R_3 * B_3 * F_{33} & \cdots & R_3 * B_N * F_{3N} \\ \vdots & \vdots & \vdots & \ddots & \vdots \\ R_N * B_1 * F_{N1} & R_N * B_2 * F_{N2} & R_N * B_3 * F_{N3} & \cdots & R_N * B_N * F_{NN} \end{bmatrix} = \begin{bmatrix} E_1 \\ E_2 \\ E_3 \\ \vdots \\ E_N \end{bmatrix} \quad (9.15)
$$

The first column matrix is multiplied by an identity matrix to get it the same size as the large array and the values are subtracted element by element, producing equation (9.16).

$$
\begin{bmatrix} B_1 - R_1 * B_1 * F_{11} & -R_1 * B_2 * F_{12} & -R_1 * B_3 * F_{13} & \cdots & -R_1 * B_N * F_{1N} \\ -R_2 * B_1 * F_{21} & B_2 - R_2 * B_2 * F_{22} & -R_2 * B_3 * F_{13} & \cdots & -R_2 * B_N * F_{2N} \\ R_3 * B_1 * F_{31} & -R_3 * B_2 * F_{32} & B_3 - R_3 * B_3 * F_{33} & \cdots & -R_3 * B_N * F_{3N} \\ \vdots & \vdots & \vdots & \ddots & \vdots \\ -R_N * B_1 * F_{N1} & -R_N * B_2 * F_{N2} & -R_N * B_3 * F_{N3} & \cdots & B_N - R_N * B_N * F_{NN} \end{bmatrix} = \begin{bmatrix} E_1 \\ E_2 \\ E_3 \\ \vdots \\ E_N \end{bmatrix} \quad (9.16)
$$

The radiosity terms can be factored out to give the final matrix form in equation (9.17).

$$
\begin{bmatrix} 1 - R_1 * F_{11} & -R_1 * F_{12} & -R_1 * F_{13} & \cdots & -R_1 * F_{1N} \\ -R_2 * F_{21} & 1 - R_2 * F_{22} & -R_2 * F_{13} & \cdots & -R_2 * F_{2N} \\ -R_3 * F_{31} & -R_3 * F_{32} & 1 - R_3 * F_{33} & \cdots & -R_3 * F_{3N} \\ \vdots & \vdots & \vdots & \ddots & \vdots \\ -R_N * F_{N1} & -R_N * F_{N2} & -R_N * F_{N3} & \cdots & 1 - R_N * F_{NN} \end{bmatrix} * \begin{bmatrix} B_1 \\ B_2 \\ B_3 \\ \vdots \\ B_N \end{bmatrix} = \begin{bmatrix} E_1 \\ E_2 \\ E_3 \\ \vdots \\ E_N \end{bmatrix} \quad (9.17)
$$

All of the terms in the large matrix in equation (9.17) are known. The R values are the surface reflectivities that are associated with each of the patches and come from the object description, and the form factors are calculated with a hemicube or similar technique. The E values are the emittance values for the patches. Though shown as one matrix equation, it is actually multiple equations because the reflectivity and emittance values can be given at multiple wavelengths. This means that equation (9.17) will need to be solved multiple times, once for each of the wavelengths under consideration. For a monochrome image, this is done once, and for an image being rendered in RGB space, this is done for red, green, and blue (three times total). When done for multiple wavelengths, the surface reflectivities would change to represent the different "colors" of the objects in the scene. The emittance values could also change to represent colored light sources.

• 9.5.1 Gauss-Siedel iterative solution

The form of the elements of this matrix makes the Gauss-Siedel method for determining the solution to a set of linear equations a suitable method to apply. Because planar patches are used, the form factors F_{ii} will be 0 for all values of i. Therefore, the diagonal elements of the matrix will all be 1. The rest of the values in each row will be less than or equal to 1 because the sum of the form factors in each row is less than or equal to 1^1 and each of the surface reflectivity values is, at most, 1. This makes the matrix diagonally dominant, because every diagonal element is the largest in its row and column. The Gauss-Siedel iterative method will converge to a solution for a diagonally dominant matrix, which makes this a good option for finding the solution. Cohen and Greenberg (Cohen85) showed that it typically takes between six and eight iterations of the Gauss-Siedel method to solve this equation for each wavelength.

An examination of equation (9.17) shows that the large matrix is just a matrix with the reflectivities and form factors subtracted from the identity matrix as shown in equation (9.18).

$$\left(\begin{bmatrix} 1 & 0 & 0 & \cdots & 0 \\ 0 & 1 & 0 & \cdots & 0 \\ 0 & 0 & 1 & \cdots & 0 \\ \vdots & \vdots & \vdots & \ddots & \vdots \\ 0 & 0 & 0 & \cdots & 1 \end{bmatrix} - \begin{bmatrix} -R_1 * F_{11} & -R_1 * F_{12} & -R_1 * F_{13} & \cdots & -R_1 * F_{1N} \\ -R_2 * F_{21} & -R_2 * F_{22} & -R_2 * F_{13} & \cdots & -R_2 * F_{2N} \\ -R_3 * F_{31} & -R_3 * F_{32} & -R_3 * F_{33} & \cdots & -R_3 * F_{3N} \\ \vdots & \vdots & \vdots & \ddots & \vdots \\ -R_N * F_{N1} & -R_N * F_{N2} & -R_N * F_{N3} & \cdots & -R_N * F_{NN} \end{bmatrix}\right) * \begin{bmatrix} B_1 \\ B_2 \\ B_3 \\ \vdots \\ B_N \end{bmatrix} = \begin{bmatrix} E_1 \\ E_2 \\ E_3 \\ \vdots \\ E_N \end{bmatrix} \quad (9.18)$$

To make the following derivation easier to follow, the identity matrix is represented as I, the square matrix of reflectivities and form factors as RF, the vector of radiosities as B, and the vector of initial emittance values as E. This shorthand makes equation (9.18) into $(I - RF) * B = E$. The goal is to get the values for the elements of B, so multiplying both sides by the inverse of the matrix RF gives equation (9.19).

$$B = (I - RF)^{-1} * E \quad (9.19)$$

Calculating the inverse of this matrix can be time consuming, especially given the size of the matrix for a typical scene with thousands of patches. Instead, there is an

---

[1]Some discussions of radiosity imply that the scene must be a closed world, such as a room, where all of the energy is kept in the room by the walls. This, however, is not a requirement. If the scene does represent a closed world, the sum of the form factors in each row will be exactly 1. If the scene does not represent a closed world, the sum of the form factors will be less than 1, which accounts for the energy that leaves the scene.

approximation of the inverse that is based on a power series expansion as shown in equation (9.20).

$$(I - RF)^{-1} = I + RF + RF^2 + RF^3 + RF^4 + RF^5 + RF^6 + \dots \tag{9.20}$$

Substituting equation (9.20) into equation (9.19) and multiplying out the results gives equation (9.21).

$$B = E + RF * E + RF^2 * E + RF^3 * E + RF^4 * E + RF^5 * E + RF^6 * E + \dots \tag{9.21}$$

Equation (9.21) can be rewritten into an iterative form as shown in equation (9.22).

$$E^{(k)} = RF * E^{(k-1)} + E \tag{9.22}$$

In equation (9.22), $E^{(k)}$ represents the approximate solution after k iterations. A prose description of equation (9.22) is "the kth iterative result is found by taking the k-1st iterative result multiplying it by the matrix RF and then adding the initial emittance values." Because $E^{(k)}$ represents an approximate solution, it is really a representation of the radiosities, therefore, it would be more accurate to write equation (9.22) as:

$$B^{(k)} = RF * B^{(k-1)} + E \tag{9.23}$$

Referring back to equation (9.18) for the definition of the matrix RF, each row of that matrix is the surface reflectivity value for the patch multiplied by each of the form factor values. This means that equation (9.23) can be expanded out into a set of equations for each of the individual patches as in equation (9.24).

$$B_i^{(k)} = E_i + R_i * \sum_{j=1, j \neq i}^{N} F_{ij} * B_j^{(k-i)}, \text{ for } i = 1 \text{ to } N \tag{9.24}$$

If planar patches are used, equation (9.24) can skip the case when j = i because $F_{ii} = 0$.

The Jacobi iterative method implements equation (9.24) and is the basis for the Gauss-Siedel method. In Jacobi iteration, an initial value is chosen for $B^{(0)}$, which is typically just E. That value is used to calculate $B^{(1)}$ using equation (9.24). $B^{(1)}$ is used to calculate $B^{(2)}$, and so on. Each of these results is an approximation, and so the process ends when the difference between two approximations falls below some threshold. For example, using an error threshold of 0.0001, the iteration will stop when each radiosity value in $B^{(k)}$ differs from the corresponding radiosity value in $B^{(k-1)}$ by no more than 0.0001.

A problem with the Jacobi iterative method is that it can take a while to converge on a solution. The Gauss-Siedel method improves on Jacobi iteration by noting that once the calculation of the approximation solutions on pass k has started, those new values can be used in calculating the rest of the kth pass. If each pass is a better approximation than the last, there is no point in waiting until the pass is complete before starting to use the new values already determined. Assuming that the radiosity values are calculated in order, value $B_i^{(k)}$ will be calculated using $B_j^{(k)}$ for values of j that are less than i, and $B_j^{(k-1)}$ for values of j that are greater than i. The Gauss-Siedel version of equation (9.24) is given in equation (9.25).

$$B_i^{(k)} = E_i + R_i * \left(\sum_{j=1}^{i-1} F_{ij} * B_j^{(k)} + \sum_{j=i+1}^{N} F_{ij} * B_j^{(k-i)} \right), \text{ for i } = \text{ 1 to N} \qquad (9.25)$$

An algorithm that implements the Gauss-Siedel iterative method is given in Appendix A.

9.6 Rendering the Image

The radiosity values for the patches in the scene have now been calculated, but there is one more step that needs to be performed before the scene can be rendered. When a scene is rendered, energy from the light sources is distributed around the scene. Typically, a scene can have only a few light sources. The energy from those sources will be shared among the various patches, which will also reflect a portion of that energy around the scene. Overall, it is highly likely that the light sources will have radiosity values that are significantly higher than the radiosity values of the other patches in the scene. Ashdown (Ashdown94) reports that the light sources can have radiosity values that are one hundred times that of the non-light source patches. If the radiosity values are used to directly render the image, the light sources will have full intensity, but the rest of the scene will be too dark, and possibly not even visible. This is generally called the tone reproduction problem.

Ashdown suggests a simple solution to the tone reproduction problem that scales the radiosities based on the value of the largest reflected radiosity. In his implementation, the radiosity due to reflection is kept separate from the emitted radiosity. The maximum of these reflected radiosities is used to linearly scale the full radiosity value for each patch. Ashdown scales each total radiosity (both emitted and reflected) by the value 254 / (255 * maximum_reflected_radiosity) with the result capped at 1.0. This scale value brings the radiosity of light sources to 1.0, and surfaces that are not light sources to below 1.0. This scaling process assures that the light sources will still be the brightest objects in the scene, while increasing the radiosity of the other objects so that they are visible.

Tumblin and Rushmeier (Tumblin93) report that using a linear scaling eliminates the distinction between two images illuminated with different strength light sources. They indicate that while a human observer sees a room quite differently where it is illuminated at two distinctly diverse levels of brightness, the linear scaling approach would render them similarly. Tumblin and Rushmeier solve the tone reproduction problem by developing a calculation that includes the maximum luminance and contrast range of the monitor, as well as the calculated radiosity values. They also use sensitivity and contrast compression constants that approximate how the eye adapts to its surroundings, and a gamma correction along the lines of that discussed in relation to computer monitors. Their solution is based on a more elaborate analysis of the perception of brightness in a real scene versus the display of the scene. Further details on this tone reproduction approach are outside the scope of this book.

After applying a tone reproduction process, the corrected radiosity values are used to render the scene. The radiosity values represent the color of the various patches, and so a simple rendering will just shade each patch using the radiosity value. However, this will create an image with clearly visible patches. A better alternative is to interpolate radiosity values across the patches, along the lines of the Gouraud shading algorithm. In this case, the Gouraud algorithm step of calculating the color at the vertices can be skipped because colors have been determined by the radiosity calculations. The problem is that radiosity values have been calculated for the patch centers and not the vertices. To get smooth shading, the radiosity values need to be transferred to the vertices in a way that allows the interpolation to have continuity across the patch edges and preserve as much as possible the values calculated for the centers.

The radiosity values from the centers will be linearly interpolated to get the vertex radiosities. If the grid of patches is uniform across the object, this becomes a simple averaging process. For vertices on the interior of the object, the radiosity values of the patches adjacent to the vertex are averaged. Vertices on the boundaries have been calculated at least two different ways. Cohen and Greenberg (Cohen85) used the formula $B = B_1 + B_2 - V$, where B_1 and B_2 are the radiosity values of the two adjacent patches and V is the radiosity value calculated for the nearest vertex on the interior of the objects. For vertices at the corner of the object, the formula is $B = 2 * B_c - V$, where B_c is the radiosity of the corner patch. Cohen and Wallace (Cohen93) uses a simple average of the two adjacent patches along the edge. The radiosity value for the corner of the object is directly from the patch in the corner. Figure 9.14 shows the set of four patches and their radiosity values, along with the results that are calculated by these two methods.

9.7 Radiosity Improvements

Improvements in the radiosity process are designed to either improve the speed with which the image can be seen, or to improve the quality of the results. Because of the complexity of the process, improvements should add as little additional work as possible. A simple improvement in quality is possible by making the polygon mesh finer. Doubling the rate at which surfaces are subdivided will increase the number of surfaces by a factor of four. This increases the number of form factors that need to be calculated and increases the number of patches projected onto the hemicube for each form factor. Another improvement is possible with an increase in the resolution of the hemicube. This increases the amount of work done for the

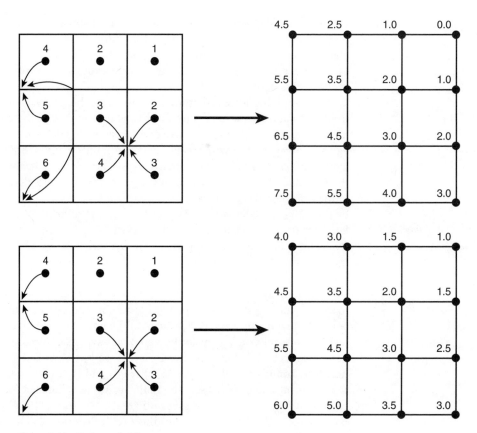

Figure 9.14 • Vertex radiosities

projection of the patches and the calculation of the delta form factors. In both of these cases, there is also an increase in the amount of storage space needed to hold the extra patches or hemicube cells.

This section looks at other techniques to improve radiosity without some of these added costs.

● 9.7.1 Progressive refinement

In the full radiosity pipeline process, the radiosity value for every patch is calculated before rendering the image. Using the Gauss-Siedel method means that the system of linear equations must be completely solved before the image is rendered based on the solution. The image seen is the final result, but the entire process has to complete before the image can be seen. If there are problems with the model, the problems are corrected and then there is another wait while the entire image is regenerated.

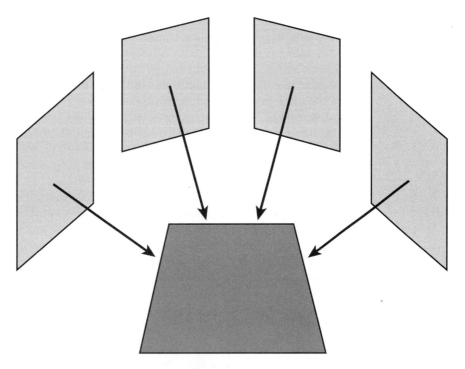

Figure 9.15 • Energy is transferred from the upper patches to the lower patches

The Gauss-Siedel method for calculating the radiosity values can be considered as a gathering process (Figure 9.15). Each new approximate radiosity value for a patch is determined by gathering up all of the light received from the other patches. For example, a new value for B_1 is calculated using the radiosity values of the other patches, which is the equivalent of patch P_1 gathering all of the radiosity it will receive from patches P_2 through P_N. The calculation is repeated because the changes in radiosities during the first iteration will find more light energy reflecting off of other patches, which results in more light energy striking patch P_1. On the second iteration, P_1 gathers more radiosity from these other patches. The process will repeatedly gather light until there are no significant changes in the radiosity values for all of the patches. Because patches are gathering light, the first attempt at rendering cannot occur until the first iteration has been completed for all of the patches. If there are N patches in the scene, equation (9.25) does approximately N multiplications per patch, and N patches per iteration. It will take N^2 multiplications before the first image can be displayed. For example, if there are 25,000 patches, the first image cannot be displayed until equation (9.25) has been calculated 25,000 times doing 625 million multiplications. At that point, the image will only show the first strike of all of the illumination in the scene. Each additional pass of 625 million multiplications will add one bounce of the light. The image can only be updated when an entire iteration is complete.

A patch in the scene that is blocked from receiving light directly from a light source will still be illuminated when light reaches it by bouncing off of other objects. This effect was simulated in the Phong illumination model by the inclusion of the ambient component. In the gathering process of Gauss-Siedel, the blocked patch will not be illuminated until energy has first been transferred to the patches that it receives light from. After the first pass of Gauss-Siedel, this patch and all of the patches blocked from the light sources will still have 0 radiosity. So, 625 million multiplications will result in an image with large areas that are not yet illuminated, meaning that little of the scene will be visible.

It would be nice if draft images could be displayed and updated more quickly. Progressive refinement produces quick draft images by reversing the direction from gathering to shooting (Figure 9.16). In progressive refinement, a record is kept of the amount of unfired radiosity that a patch has. On each pass, the patch with the most unfired radiosity per area is chosen, its light is fired into the scene, and its unfired radiosity is reset to 0. The form factors are used to determine how to distribute this radiosity to the other patches. Each of the other patches has its radiosity and

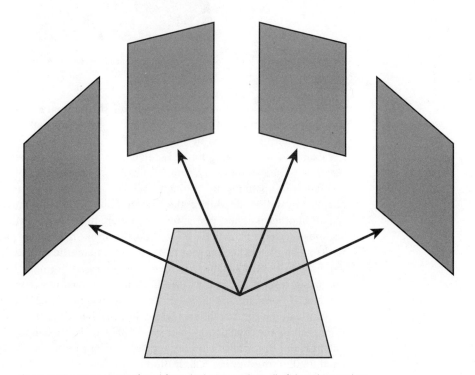

Figure 9.16 • Energy is transferred from the lower patch to all of the other patches

unfired radiosity values updated by the amount received. At each successive step, the patch with the most unfired radiosity is chosen and its radiosity is distributed. This process repeats until all of the unfired radiosity has been distributed.

Each of the passes of the progressive refinement method will multiply the unfired radiosity by the patch reflectivity and the form factor to determine the update to the other patch's radiosity. This calculation is done for each of the patches. Where the Gauss-Siedel method determines radiosities by calculating across the rows of equation (9.14), progressive refinement calculates down the columns.

Using progressive refinement, if there are N patches in the scene, the radiosity of each of the patches is updated after 2N multiplications are done. Under the Gauss-Siedel method, only two radiosity values will have been updated after this amount of work. This means that after just $O(N)$ multiplications, a draft image can be displayed that represents the distribution of the energy of one of the light sources. The Gauss-Siedel method takes $O(N^2)$ of these calculations to get to the draft image stage. For example, with 25,000 patches, progressive refinement will be able to display an image after just 50,000 multiplications, where it will take 625 million multiplications for the first image from Gauss-Siedel.

The progressive refinement process associates with each patch not only its current radiosity value, but also the portion of that radiosity that has not yet been shot into the scene. At the beginning, the radiosity and the unshot radiosity values will both be equal to the energy the patch is emitting. The patch that has the largest product of the unshot radiosity and the patch area is chosen on each pass. The algorithm calculates the updated radiosity and unshot radiosity for all of the other patches, and then sets the chosen patch's unshot radiosity to zero. The process then repeats. An algorithm for progressive refinement is:

```
for (i = 1; i <= N; i++)
   B[i] = E[i]   // initial radiosity estimate
   U[i] = E[i]   // unshot radiosity
end for
done = false
while (not done)
   large = 1
   largeAmount = U[1] * A[1]
   for (i = 2; i <= N; i++)
      if (U[i] * A[i] > largeAmount)
         large = i
         largeAmount = U[i] * A[i]
      end if
   end for
   for (j = 1; j <= N; j++)
      change = U[large] * R_j * F_j large
      U[j] = U[j] + change
```

```
        B[j] = B[j] + change
    end for
    U[large] = 0
    update done
    Display the resulting image
end while
```

Cohen et al. (Cohen88) showed that this algorithm will converge to a good approximation of the complete solution with just a few passes through the while loop. The number of while loop passes will depend on the number of patches, but will be a small fraction of the number of patches. Cohen et al. (Cohen88) demonstrated that with a scene of 7,000 patches, a good approximation can be achieved in just 100 passes.

9.7.2 Adaptive mesh refinement

In Figure 9.4, the mesh locations only sample the radiosity curve. In areas where the curve does not change much, interpolating between the sampled points is sufficient. Where there are rapid changes in radiosity, smaller patches are needed. Just increasing the number of patches throughout the scene significantly increases the computation time and there will be areas of the scene that do not change much with many more small patches. Adaptive mesh refinement increases the number of patches and, therefore, decreases the size of the patches only where needed. Later sections will give the details on two approaches that (1) predict where more patches are needed before doing the calculations—an a priori method, or (2) refine the patch mesh where there are large changes in radiosities after calculating a partial solution—an a posteriori method. Figure 9.17 shows the same curve as in Figure 9.4

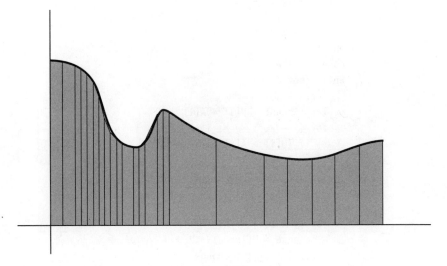

Figure 9.17 • Adaptive mesh and radiosity distribution

after adaptive mesh refinement. In this figure, there are more patches in the areas where there are rapid changes in the radiosity value and fewer patches where the changes are more gradual.

Adaptive mesh refinement is critical for solving problems with a uniform meshing strategy. One such problem is a staircase effect, which is caused when a shadow is cast diagonally across a grid of patches (Figure 9.18a). When this occurs, the patches in the shadow will have a low radiosity value and the others will have a high value. When the patch radiosities are transferred to the vertices, some of the patches will have three vertices in the shadow and will be rendered dark, while adjacent patches may have three vertices in the light and will be rendered light. For

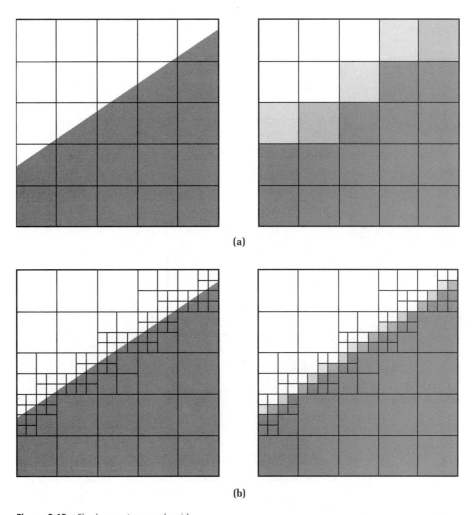

(a)

(b)

Figure 9.18 • Shadow cast on mesh grid

those patches partially in a shadow, the lower radiosity values at the shadowed vertices will be interpolated across the entire patch darkening it. Adjacent patches that are outside of the shadow will have no such darkening, thereby creating the appearance of a shadow staircase. If the number of patches is increased along this shadow border, the shadow boundary will be smoothed out and the staircase effect will be less noticeable (Figure 9.18b).

A second effect is a shadow and light leak under a wall or object that does not align with the patch mesh (Figure 9.19). If a wall does not align with the patch mesh of an adjacent wall, there will be vertices for a single patch that will be on both sides of the adjacent wall. If there is a light source on just one side of the wall, the patches on that side will have a large radiosity value while those on the opposite side will have a low value. When calculating the vertex radiosity values, the values of the adjacent patches are averaged. The vertices of patches split by the adjacent wall will have some vertices on the light source side of the wall and some on the other side. Those vertices on the light source side of the wall will have adjacent patches that have high radiosity values so they will average out to a larger value than those behind the wall, and those vertices behind the wall will average out to a smaller value because of the adjacent shadowed patches. When the values are interpolated across this patch, the vertices on the darker side will spread their value onto the light side of the adjacent wall, causing the shadow to leak under the wall. The vertices on the light source side will also spread their value onto the dark side of the adjacent wall causing the light to leak under the wall in the opposite direc-

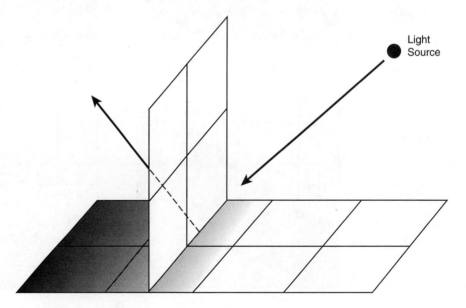

Figure 9.19 • Shadow and light leak

tion. If the number of patches is increased where objects meet, shadow and light leaking can be eliminated or at least reduced.

Implementing an adaptive meshing strategy is complex, and the three books on radiosity spend very little time on the subject. For example, Ashdown (Ashdown94) gives full details, including code, for a simple radiosity program, yet spends just four pages on adaptive subdivision. Because of this complexity, the discussion here will only give an idea of the possibilities for adaptive subdivision, which is commonly used in engineering fields that use finite element analysis. Cohen et al. (Cohen86) were the first to apply adaptive subdivision to radiosity.

An A Priori Approach
The two situations just discussed could be handled before the calculations begin. Shadows occur where an object is blocked from a light source. The positions of the light sources could be used to identify surface areas that fall in the umbra and penumbra of a shadow. Sending projectors from the light source through the vertices of an object indicates the boundaries of the shadow. These boundaries can then be used to determine how the patch mesh should be subdivided. Figure 9.20 shows how one object casts an umbra and penumbra on another. The areas in the umbra and the areas outside of the shadow are somewhat uniformly dark or light, and can use a regular meshing pattern. The areas in the penumbra show a gradation of intensity and the rate at which it changes will depend on the size of the penumbra. To get a good collection of radiosity values that result in a reasonable interpolation of intensities, the area in the penumbra should be subdivided differently and perhaps more finely than the other areas.

Light and shadow leaking occurs because the process of transferring radiosity values from the patches to the vertices can use patches from both sides of the wall. To prevent light and shadow leaking, it is first necessary to identify the areas where

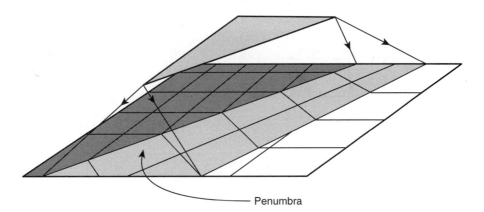

Penumbra

Figure 9.20 • Shadow determination of divisions

two adjacent surfaces meet or intersect. Determining where two planes meet or intersect is straightforward. The details of these calculations can be found in Schneider and Eberly (Schneider03). Once the locations where surfaces come together have been identified, these boundaries are where surfaces are subdivided. In this way, the patches on one side of the boundary will be part of the bright side surface and the patches on the other side will be part of the shadowed surface. Vertices that are created along the boundary are now part of separate surfaces, so their radiosity values are determined from only one side of the wall.

An A Posteriori Approach

A posteriori methods make changes to the patch mesh based on partial results. To use a posteriori methods, a complete or at least partial radiosity solution is generated. A partial solution could be the result of a few passes of the progressive refinement method. Using this solution, if two adjacent patches have a large difference in values, there is a significant change that is not being properly caught by the current subdivision. Subdivisions, therefore, need to occur in areas where there is a large change in the radiosity values of adjacent patches. Adjustments can be of three different types as shown in Figure 9.21. This figure shows the relationship between

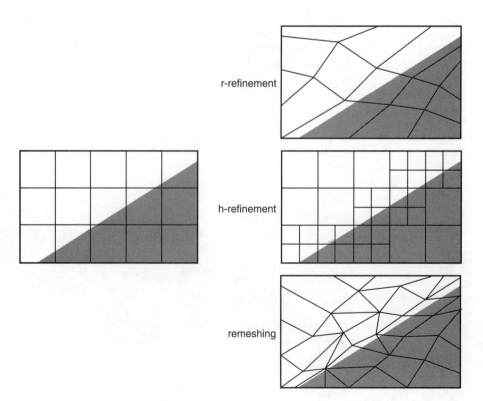

Figure 9.21 • A posteriori mesh improvement

the patches and the boundary between a light and dark area. The left side of Figure 9.21 shows a regular grid of patches that would first be used. The right side of Figure 9.21 shows three alternative patch subdivisions that would be created to improve the results along the boundary between the light and dark areas. The shape and location of the patches in these alternatives are chosen based on differences between the radiosity values of adjacent patches of the regular grid.

The first technique is called r-refinement and involves moving the location of the patch vertices so that some of the edges of the patches are perpendicular with the direction of rapid change. One benefit of this method is that the algorithms and structures that are set up to create the patches and their association with the original object are not modified. Only the vertex locations are changed. The number of patches and their adjacency relationship stays the same in this reorganization. After the vertices are moved, the solution is recalculated with the new patch shapes. A problem with this refinement is that there is a limitation on how much improvement is possible because the number of patches remains the same.

The second technique is called h-refinement and involves increasing the subdivision in areas with rapid change. Having more patches means that the gradation of radiosity can be sampled more regularly in these areas. This is the technique represented in Figure 9.18. The benefit of this method is the subdivision can be quite detailed in areas where the change is greatest and less detailed in areas where the change is least. A difficulty is that the structures and algorithms needed to store a mesh of varying resolution can be complex. Typically, additional layers of hierarchy are added to the data structure. Where the description here has the two levels of surface and patch, it is possible to add an additional level as well that represents the subdivision of a patch. Research has been done that relates the radiosity of a patch and its subpatches. This form factor algebra comes from research in the heat transfer field. This technique is the most commonly implemented method.

The third technique is remeshing. In this case, the results of the partial solution are used to guide the assignment of patches on the surface. This technique completely replaces the patch mesh, and so there is no limitation on the number, size, or placement of the patches that result. The complete replacement of the mesh means that the calculation of form factors must be completely redone.

9.8 Other Issues

When implementing a radiosity solution, there are issues beyond the resolution of the hemicube and the way surfaces are subdivided into patches. Some of these issues arise because of the surface subdivision, and others arise because of the scene.

9.8.1 T-Vertices

When the two patches that share an edge are subdivided in different ways the result is a T-vertex. For example, there are T-vertices in the h-refinement example in Figure 9.21. In that example, a T-vertex occurs on the edges of the larger patches when adjacent to the smaller patches. More formally, a T-vertex occurs where the vertex of one patch is positioned along the edge of another patch instead of at a vertex. A T-vertex poses a problem because the radiosity value determined for that vertex may or may not be the same as the value that will be interpolated along the edge it is coincident with. When that happens, the shading of the larger adjacent patch will not match the shading along the two smaller patches. Consider the situation in Figure 9.22 where a T-vertex occurs at vertex B, which is the midpoint of the adjacent edge between vertices A and C. As values are interpolated along the edge on the side of the large patch between A and C, the interpolated value will be 0.7 at vertex B, yet the value used on the other side of the edge will be 0.75, which is the value at the vertex. So, for the upper half of the edge, the values will range from 0.9 to 0.7 on the left side, and from 0.9 to 0.75 on the right side. For the bottom half of the edge, the values will range from 0.7 to 0.5 on the left side, and from 0.75 to 0.5 on the right side. This creates a visible discontinuity along this edge.

Another difficulty with T-vertices is that round-off error can cause vertex B to be slightly off of the line between vertex A and vertex C. This can create a slight gap between these patches, which will also be visible.

There have been two solutions proposed for this problem. In the first, Cohen and Wallace (Cohen93) use the T-vertex as a slave vertex. It is used for the purposes of meshing, but its radiosity value is determined by interpolation along the adjacent edge. This means that in Figure 9.22 the interpolated value of 0.7 would be used as the radiosity value for vertex B. This solves the interpolation problem, but it does not eliminate any gaps between the edges. The second solution is by Baum et al. (Baum91) and "ziplocks" the T-vertex to the adjoining edge. In this method, the edge between vertices A and C is subdivided into two edges by adding vertex B to the larger patch. Specifically, the edge AC is replaced by the two edges AB and BC.

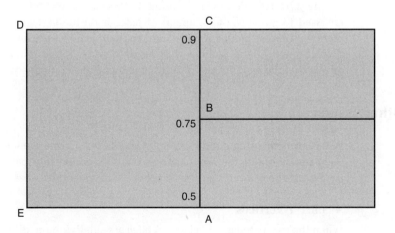

Figure 9.22 • The T-vertex problem

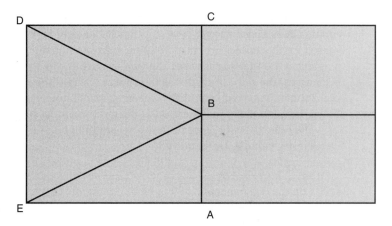

Figure 9.23 • Anchoring the T-vertex

This change gives the square patch five sides, even though two of them are co-linear. Baum et al. also discuss a method to anchor the T-vertex by adding additional edges that subdivide the larger patch. In Figure 9.23, edges are added between the T-vertex and the other two vertices of the larger patch. These edges divide the square patch into three triangular patches ABE, BCD, and BDE.

9.8.2 Coplanar surfaces

Two surfaces are considered coplanar if their positions are, or almost are, identical. This situation could occur if a scene included a sheet of paper lying on a table. The thinness of the sheet of paper means that the position of the paper and the table top are, for all intents and purposes, identical. When the scene is transformed, round-off error can be introduced so that the paper is sometimes above the table top, sometimes below the table top, and other times partially above and below. Baum et al. (Baum91) chose the smaller surface as visible when two surfaces are coplanar. In their approach, the larger surface is modified so as to cut out an area equal to the size, shape, and position of the smaller surface. With this piece of the larger surface removed, they are no longer coplanar. Any slight variations due to round-off error will no longer influence the visibility of the smaller surface.

9.8.3 Textures

As was discussed in Chapter 6, textures are important to realistic image generation. Including textures on objects in images rendered with radiosity will also improve their appearance. There are two ways that textures can be included, depending on whether the texture is a relatively uniform pattern on the object or whether there are larger scale variations.

For a relatively uniform texture such as wood grain, the process begins by calculating an average reflectivity $R_{average}$ for the texture. This average reflectivity will be used for the surface when solving the radiosity equation. This means that all of the patches for that surface will use this average in the solution. When rendering this surface, the radiosity value is interpolated across the surface as usual, but the actual value displayed is modified based on the texture value. The modification is shown in equation (9.26), where B_{xy} is the radiosity at location (x, y) on the surface, T_{xy} is the reflectivity or color at the corresponding point in the texture, and B_{xy}' is the radiosity value to be displayed.

$$B_{xy}' = B_{xy} * \frac{T_{xy}}{R_{average}} \tag{9.26}$$

Some textures show a larger variation. For example, a floor surface can be alternately dark and light marble tiles. Attempting to average these values across the entire floor will not work because there should be a different level of reflection from the light and dark tiles on the adjacent walls. To properly handle this variation, the floor surface will need to be represented as separate dark and light subsurfaces. Each of these subsurfaces will be treated as a separate surface for the purpose of radiosity calculations. This means each tile will be subdivided into patches to be included in the form factor calculation and radiosity solution. Each of these tile surfaces can be treated as in the case of the wood grain texture. In other words, an average reflectivity is calculated to be used as the tile's reflectivity in the radiosity solution. After the radiosity solution is found, the determination of the color to display for each tile will be done with equation (9.26).

9.8.4 Specular highlights

The solution to the radiosity equation gives the diffuse light reflection for the patches that make up a surface. The radiosity solution is a more accurate version of the ambient and diffuse components of the illumination model discussed in Chapter 2. In that discussion of illumination, it was noted that there is also a specular component to light reflection. Including a specular highlight is as simple as calculating the specular component using equation (9.27) and adding it to the interpolated radiosity value.

$$I_s = R_{specular} * I_L * (\boldsymbol{R} \cdot \boldsymbol{V})^n \tag{9.27}$$

In equation (9.27), $\boldsymbol{R}$ is the direction of light reflection, $\boldsymbol{V}$ is the direction of the viewer, and $R_{specular}$ is the specular reflectivity of the object. The specular reflectivity can be the same as or different from the surface reflectivity values used in the radiosity solution. If the specular reflectivity is the same for all of the wavelengths that are part of the calculation, the specular highlight will have the same color as the light, and the object will have a plastic appearance. If the specular reflectivity is the same as the surface reflectivity, the object will have a metallic appearance.

The results of the radiosity calculations can also be used with a ray tracer to add specular highlights as well as reflective and refractive objects.

9.9 The OpenGL Way

OpenGL has no direct support for radiosity; however, OpenGL can be used to display the results of a radiosity calculation in a number of different ways. The first involves the calculation of the image into a two-dimensional array and then displaying that image as discussed in the OpenGL section of Chapter 8. There are also ways to take advantage of the power of OpenGL to progress to a radiosity solution. It should be noted that all of the techniques to be discussed rely on back-face culling. This means that it is critical that patches are specified to have the correct front and back faces. Recall that if the polygon vertices are specified in a counter-clockwise order, the front face of the polygon is seen.

9.9.1 Hardware form factor determination

The process of transforming a patch to the center of the hemicube and then projecting the other patches onto the hemicube surfaces can be facilitated with OpenGL. The general idea is to transform the patch to the origin, and then draw all of the other patches into the frame buffer. If each patch is drawn using flat shading and a unique color, the frame buffer can then be queried to find out the color displayed at each location. These colors are really an index back to the patch. By associating with each pixel location a hemicube cell location, the color indicates which patch form factor that hemicube's delta form factor should be added to. An algorithm for this process is:

```
for each patch
    push the modelview matrix stack
    // handle the top hemicube face
    transform the patch to the origin so its
        normal is pointing in the negative z direction
    draw the patches
    allocate the delta form factors
    clear the frame buffer
    // handle the right face
    rotate the scene 90° around the y axis
    draw the patches
    allocate the delta form factors
    clear the frame buffer
    // handle the front face
    rotate the scene 90° around the x axis
    draw the patches
```

```
allocate the delta form factors
clear the frame buffer
// handle the left face
rotate the scene 90° around the x axis
draw the patches
allocate the delta form factors
clear the frame buffer
// handle the back face
rotate the scene 90° around the x axis
draw the patches
allocate the delta form factors
clear the frame buffer
pop the modelview matrix stack
```

• 9.9.2 Rendering the scene

Once the radiosity values have been scaled and transferred to the vertices of the patches, OpenGL can be used to draw the patches as polygons. The radiosity values will be converted into RGB colors that will be set before the vertex was specified. Rendering in this way makes all of the power of OpenGL available for calculating alternate views, or even rotating the scene. If back-face culling is turned on, as the scene rotates, the walls that are facing away would be culled, allowing the user to see into a closed-world room without the program having to make the decision as to which walls to display and which not to display.

9.10 Projects

Write a radiosity renderer for a simple scene made up of planar patches.

Animation

When you go to see a movie in a theater, what you are shown is a series of individual images projected on the screen at a rapid rate. When the movie is created, the camera takes thousands of pictures during the filming of a scene. A film captures 24 images or frames per second and so a five-minute scene involves 7,200 frames. When these frames are then projected at a rate of 24 frames per second onto a screen, we perceive the same motions that were occurring when the film was created. An afterimage of a frame fills in the gap before the next frame is projected. This persistence of vision causes us to see not a collection of individual images but rather moving objects. The amount that an object's position changes between two frames determines the speed that is perceived. An object that is moving slowly will not change its position very rapidly in $1/24^{th}$ of a second, but one that is moving quickly will. For example, Figure 10.1 shows a set of 18 images taken at regular intervals from a video clip of a butterfly. The difference among these images is in the position of the butterfly. When the butterfly is moving its wings slowly, there is little change in position as can be seen in the fifth through seventh, and ninth through eleventh images in this sequence. When the butterfly moves more quickly, there is a greater change in position, as can be seen in the third and fourth images. When objects move very rapidly, they will not be clear in each image but rather will blur. This motion blur can be seen in the last six images of this sequence.

The impression of motion can be created by drawing objects in slightly different positions and then showing those pictures rapidly. In the late 1800s, kineographs (also called flip books) were invented, using this principle. Each page of a flip book

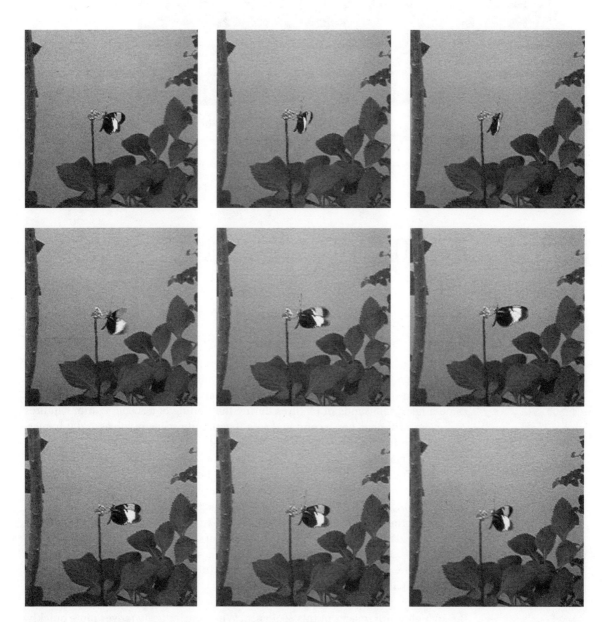

Figure 10.1 • A Heliconius sara butterfly in motion (see Color Plate 10.1)

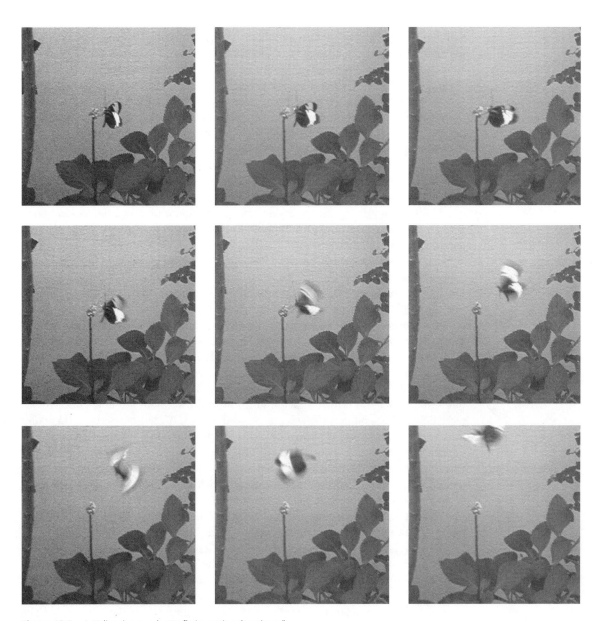

Figure 10.1 • A Heliconius sara butterfly in motion *(continued)*

had a slightly different picture and when a person rapidly flipped the pages with his or her thumb the impression of motion was created. A search of the Web will show many current applications of flip books in education and marketing.

An animated movie is a flip book shown to an audience at movie frame rates of speed. The animation process must, therefore, determine what each individual frame should look like for the impression of motion to be realistic. For a simple object such as a ball, determining the various positions involves acceleration when the ball begins moving, deceleration when the ball stops, and possibly the effect of gravity or other forces while the ball is moving. The movement of more complex objects is complicated because one part influences the motion of another part. For example, animating the motion of a human hand influences the motion of the wrist, elbow, shoulder, and the bones connecting them. In a complex system such as this, there are additional limitations due to restrictions on how some of these parts move and bend.

In an animated movie, this process becomes more involved because there are many objects moving, interacting, and colliding. Thus, there is a lot of work involved in producing an animation. In a 60-minute animated film, there are 86,400 frames, and for a 90-minute film there are 129,600 frames. Video uses a faster rate of 30 frames per second, so there are 108,000 frames needed for a 60-minute video animation and 162,000 frames for a 90-minute video animation. For each of these frames, the proper location of all of the visible objects must be determined, if the result is going to look natural.

All of the issues discussed in the previous chapters of this book apply equally well here. Animation is based on a series of individual images, so modeling and rendering issues are critical, but in addition to those, there are new concerns for realistic motion, character development, and a story. To help cope with this complexity, there are some simplifications that can be made in modeling. The assumption in earlier chapters was that static images were being generated that would, therefore, be viewed for an extended period of time. Because of this, accurate details are needed in all the images created. With an animated sequence, the individual images are shown for a much shorter period of time, and the objects in those images might also be moving. This means that some of the objects modeled and rendered do not need to be as detailed as they would be for a single static image.

The chapter begins with a brief look at conventional animation to provide a background for what is done today. Many of the concepts of conventional animation are equally applicable to computer-based animation. The rest of the chapter discusses the motion of simple objects and complex articulated figures. There are a lot of details that must be mastered to create good quality animation sequences. The material presented in this chapter will give only a brief overview of some of the issues involved in animation. Due to space considerations, a full treatment of these topics cannot be given. There are entire books devoted to animation that serve as the next step for anyone who wants to do further research in animation. For example, see Parent (Parent02), O'Rourke (O'Rourke98), and Parke and Waters (Parke96).

In addition to technical issues, there are artistic issues beyond the scope of this book. Though this chapter looks at the basis for calculating motion, choosing a path for that motion so the result looks natural requires an artistic sense. Facial expressions on characters are another crucial and artistic component of creating believable animations. The artistic issues and technical issues to achieve successful animation is a result of the teamwork between programmers and artists.

10.1 A Brief Look at Conventional Animation

The history of animation is a long one. In the 1800s, flip books and other devices to display a sequence of images were explored. Eadweard Muybridge used a series of cameras to capture sequences of pictures of people and animals in motion. Muybridge also developed a method to project these sequences during his lectures. In 1891, Thomas Edison expanded on Muybridge's work with his invention of the motion picture projector, which made the motion picture industry possible. A few years later, in 1896, Georges Méliès used multiple exposures and stop-motion techniques to create a film with objects that would appear, disappear, and change shape. In 1906, J. Stuart Blackton created the first animated cartoon. The first popular animations were created by Winsor McCay in the 1910s. Early animated sequences were used in vaudeville acts or were combined with film of actors. The beginnings of animation were labor-intensive, as the images that were shown were all hand-drawn. The introduction of the computer to the process decreased the human cost, but increased the complexity of the process.

The epitome of animation has for many years been Disney Studios. Their animated films have stood the test of time and continue to have a sizable following. What makes them so good is a combination of the details put into the images as well as the story line that is developed. When a character walks across the screen, there is a real feeling for that character's weight because of the motions drawn and the shadows that are cast on the ground and nearby objects. But more than just the skills of the artists are involved. These movies are based on stories that are entertaining and captivating.

10.1.1 The storyboard

Creating an animated sequence begins with a storyboard, which is a sequence of hand-drawn images that serve as an outline for the film. The storyboard gives the significant moments in the animation and gives the overall flow of the story. The storyboard serves as the guide during the development of the animation to keep things on track. A production can be described in a hierarchical format (Figure 10.2) by breaking it down into a collection of sequences or scenes. Then, each scene is broken down into a series of shots or camera angles, with each shot made up of a collection of frames.

A storyboard has enough detail for the rest of the animation to be created. In some instances, the elements of the storyboard are put into the animation as placeholders while the overall animation is being created. For example, if one drawing

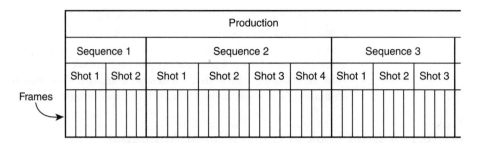

Figure 10.2 • A production hierarchy

in the storyboard represents the action during a 30-second sequence of the movie, those 30 seconds of the animation will be that drawing until that sequence is finished. When the scene is completed, the 30 seconds with the storyboard drawing are removed and the scene takes its place.

The story is a critical component of a successful animation. The story brings the viewers into the movie and helps them to connect with the characters. If done well, at the end of the movie viewers will remember the story and not any special rendering tricks or effects. However, the art of story-telling is not the focus of this book. Instead, this chapter looks at some of the technical issues involved with the creation of realistic motion.

10.1.2 Cel animation

In early animations, in addition to the development of the story, it was necessary to develop a model sheet, which was a set of drawings for each of the characters in a number of different poses. This was important for there to be consistency in how the characters were drawn throughout the entire film because those drawings were likely to be done by many different people. The model sheet served as a guide for all of the animators working on the film.

Additional documents were developed that specified details on sound, camera motion, timing, and the responsibilities for creating the scene. Once all of these elements were prepared, the animators could begin to draw images for the movie. A master animator was at the top of the hierarchy and did not draw the entire movie. Rather, the master animator drew key frames that represented the beginning and ending of movement or action in the scene. The master animator drew enough of the scene so that the next person in the process could complete it.

The associate or assistant animators then took over and filled in the additional frames in a process called in-betweening. Each of these frames represented 1/24th of a second of action, but if the transitions between these images were not smooth it would be noticeable to the viewer. Early animators quickly flipped pages back and forth, looking at the between-frames to assure smooth movement as they were drawn. In computer animation, the key frames can be specified by the animator, and software can perform the task of creating the in-between frames.

Once the frames were drawn, the next step of the process was called inking and entails the transfer of the images to the cels.[1] The cels were then opaqued or painted, which is the process of adding color to the images. The coloring process was done carefully so that objects and characters were a consistent color throughout the scene and between scenes, and so that highlights gave an accurate and consistent feel for the shape of objects and the location of light sources.

The cels were then mounted below a camera, and one picture was taken. Multiple cels were typically stacked for the picture. For example, a background cel contained elements in the room that were static. By using a background cel, these elements only needed to be drawn once.

After the first picture is taken, the next set of cels was loaded and their picture was taken. This process was repeated for the tens to hundreds of thousands of frames for the film. The sound track also needed to be recorded, and for hand-drawn animations, it was frequently easier to have the actors lip-sync to the animation instead of drawing the animation to match the sound track. More recently, software has been developed that actually creates facial animations to match the spoken word.

10.2 Motion

The motion of objects and figures is the most significant component of animation. Without smooth motion, an animated sequence will not look natural to the viewer. Because of our interactions with the world and objects that move within it, we are very aware when the motion in an animation is not natural.

A theme that has run through the discussion of rendering single images has been the approximation of physical properties to produce visual sensations that mimic what happens when people see real objects. There are a number of other properties from physics (for example, gravity, force, and inertia) that have an influence on how objects move. If an object is thrown into the air, gravity will cause that object to stop its upward motion and then fall back to the ground. Likewise, objects thrown horizontally will be pulled to the ground by gravity. The amount of force that is needed for the object to reach a particular height or distance varies based on the object's weight. If the object strikes something else, the change in direction of both objects can also be determined. Animating the action of throwing an object in the air must be faithful to the viewer's expectations. If the object is perceived as being heavy, the force expended must be considerable to get any height to the throw. On the other hand, for an object that is lighter, the force expended will be less to achieve the same height.

This section will look at ways to specify overall motion of simple objects with the special considerations for the motion of articulated figures, to be discussed in a later section.

---

[1]Originally, the cels were made of celluloid, hence their name. Later, cels were made of acetate but kept their original name.

● **10.2.1 Direction and location**

The direction an object is to move can be specified with a curve. This curve could be as simple as a straight line or as complex as a parametric curve. Parametric curves are much more useful because very little motion occurs in a perfectly straight line. It is more typical to want to specify a set of locations for the object to move through. When these points are specified, it is possible to derive the control points for a curve that will smoothly go through those points. See Farin (Farin90) and Rogers (Rogers90).

A problem with using parametric curves for this purpose is that the parameter used to identify points along the curve does not relate to distance along the curve. For example, a parameter value of 0.5 does not necessarily represent a location halfway along the curve. In fact, if the first point is quite some distance from the other three points in a cubic parametric curve, equal steps in the value of the parameter will move big distances along the start of the curve but then smaller distances toward the end of the curve (see Figure 10.3).

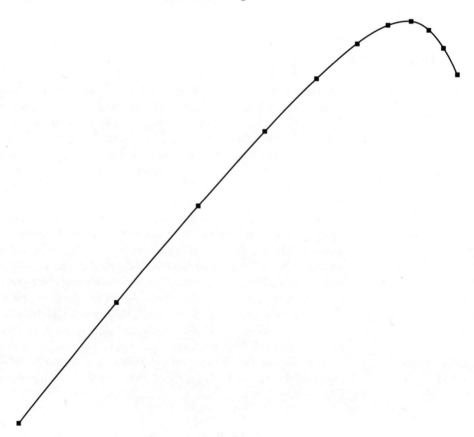

Figure 10.3 • A Bézier curve showing locations for parameter values at a 0.1 step size

Relating distance along the curve to the curve parameter is necessary for motion. For example, when an object begins to move, it goes through a period of acceleration where the speed is increasing but the distance traveled might not be very far. When an object stops, a period of deceleration is needed. The result is that the distance traveled in any unit of time will vary.

How can the distance be related to the parametric parameter? The first way is to create a tabular approximation between the parameter and distance, and the second way is to analytically compute the value. The analytic computation, however, is quite expensive and cannot be done for all curves.

In the tabular method, the (x, y, z) location is calculated for various parameter values along the curve. Typically, a parameter step size of about 0.05 is chosen, which gives 21 values along the curve. Next, the distance between pairs of adjacent points is calculated, and is used to get the cumulative distance from the start of the curve for each parameter value. This table can now be used to find an approximate parameter value for a particular distance along the curve. This is done by looking though the table for the two cumulative distances closest to the distance of interest and interpolating between those to get a parameter value.

For example, consider a two-dimensional example based on the Bézier curve in Figure 10.4, which has the control points (0, 0), (20, 50), (40, 0), and (60, 50). First, the set of points shown in the third column of Table 10.1 is calculated using the parameter values indicated. Then the distance from the previous point is calculated as shown in the fourth column. From there the cumulative distance from the start of the curve can be calculated.

Now, say that motion is desired that places the object at 11 evenly spaced locations along this path. Because the entire length of the path is 85.0 units, this places the locations 8.5 units apart and at distances of 0, 8.5, 17.0, 25.5, 34.0, 42.5, 51.0, 59.5, 68.0, 76.5, and 85.0 from the start of the path. Consider the fourth of these points at 25.5. The last column shows the distance of 25.5 units is somewhere between the fifth and sixth parameter values of 0.2 and 0.25. Doing a linear interpolation between the distances for these two parameters gives:

$$0.2 + \frac{25.5 - 23.2}{27.0 - 23.2} * 0.05 = 0.23 \tag{10.1}$$

In equation (10.1), the 0.2 is the value for the fifth parameter, the denominator of the division is the difference of the fifth and sixth cumulative distances, and the 0.05 is the difference in the parameter values. Equation (10.2) is the general form of this equation, where D is the distance of interest, C_i and C_{i+1} are the two closest cumulative distances, and P_i and P_{i+1} are the parameter values associated with these two cumulative distances.

$$P_i + \frac{D - C_i}{C_{i+1} - C_i} * \left(P_{i+1} - P_i\right) \tag{10.2}$$

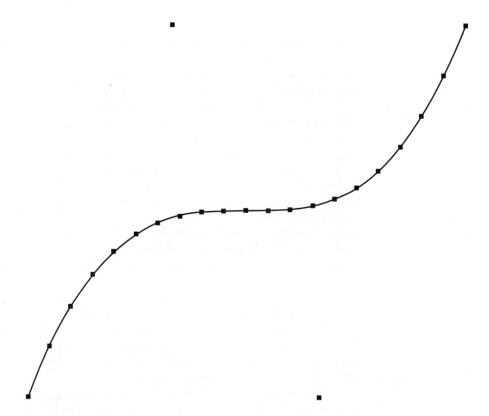

Figure 10.4 • A Bézier curve

If the motion path has a section of high curvature, using evenly spaced points might not be sufficient in those sections because the approximation of distance could be way off. This technique can be improved through the use of an adaptive method for setting the parametric values for the table. The adaptive technique begins with a set of evenly spaced parameter values as in Table 10.1. A new parameter value at the midpoint of each of the ranges is used to calculate another location. The distances to the new point from the two surrounding points are then calculated. If the sum of the two distances is within some small tolerance of the distance between the endpoints, no further subdivisions of the range are needed. But if not, the midpoint is added to the table, and the process is repeated for the two new subsections.

Referring back to Figure 10.4, if the original parameter values were spaced at a range of 0.2, the third point would be at a parameter value of 0.6 and the fourth point at a parameter value of 0.8. The locations associated with these two values are (36, 25.2) and (48, 30.4), respectively, and the distance between them is 13.1. The midpoint of this range is 0.7, which has a location of (42, 26.6). The distances

● TABLE 1 Locations and distances along a Bezier curve (values rounded)

Index	Parameter value	Location	Distance from previous point	Cumulative distance
0	0	(0, 0)	0	0
1	0.05	(3, 6.78)	7.4	7.4
2	0.1	(6, 12.2)	6.2	13.6
3	0.15	(9, 16.43)	5.2	18.8
4	0.2	(12, 19.6)	4.4	23.2
5	0.25	(15, 21.88)	3.8	27.0
6	0.3	(18, 23.4)	3.4	30.4
7	0.35	(21, 24.33)	3.1	33.5
8	0.4	(24, 24.8)	3.0	36.5
9	0.45	(27, 24.98)	3.0	39.5
10	0.5	(30, 25)	3.0	42.5
11	0.55	(33, 25.03)	3.0	45.5
12	0.6	(36, 25.2)	3.0	48.5
13	0.65	(39, 25.68)	3.0	51.5
14	0.7	(42, 26.6)	3.1	54.6
15	0.75	(45, 28.13)	3.4	58.0
16	0.8	(48, 30.4)	3.8	61.8
17	0.85	(51, 33.58)	4.4	66.2
18	0.9	(54, 37.8)	5.2	71.4
19	0.95	(57, 43.23)	6.2	77.6
20	1	(60, 50)	7.4	85.0

between the midpoint and the two endpoints are 6.2 and 7.1, and so the total distance through the midpoint location is 13.3 verses a value of 13.1. For example, if the threshold is 0.075, the difference between the distances is too large, so the midpoint at 0.7 is added to the table, and the two new sections are checked.

● 10.2.2 Speed

For each of the frames of an animation, it is necessary to determine where an object should be. The previous section gave a way to find an approximate relationship between the parameter value and distance along the curve. How far along the curve the object should move with each frame depends on the speed the object is moving. This section looks at how to relate speed to distance so that those distances can then be used to identify locations along the curve.

Adjusting the speed at which the object moves has an impact on the overall distance it covers. The slower an object is moving the less distance it will travel per frame, and likewise, the faster it is moving the more distance it will travel per frame. The speed is not fixed and can vary over the length of the curve. This is especially critical to create natural motion. For example, when objects begin to move, there is a period of acceleration where the speed increases. A similar thing occurs when an object decelerates to a stop. These are referred to as an ease in and ease out. More elaborate changes in speed are also possible.

Figure 10.5 gives a set of curves representing a number of different speed options. These curves plot time on the horizontal axis and the distance along the curve on the vertical axis. In these curves, the slope of the curve indicates velocity and the rate of slope change indicates acceleration. Figure 10.5a gives a typical curve for an ease in and out. At the beginning of this curve, the horizontal section indicates that the object is stopped. The object then increases velocity until the center diagonal section where the velocity (curve slope) is relatively constant. The upper section returns back to the horizontal, representing the deceleration to a stopped position. The beginning and ending sections of this curve can be based on the sine function. Figure 10.5b shows a curve for an abrupt start and stop. Figure 10.5c shows the object slowing down at the first "bump" then backing up before stopping and then continuing forward. In Figure 10.5d, the horizontal section shows the object has stopped for a period of time before starting up again.

10.2.3 Rotation and scaling

The techniques of the last two sections mapped time to distance based on the speed and then mapped distance to location based on the path of motion. This general process can be applied equally well to the rotation and scaling of objects. The curve representing the path of motion is replaced by a curve representing the amount of rotation or scaling. A speed curve is now defined that indicates the rate of rotation or scaling. Thus, six curves could be defined so that two indicate the speed and direction of motion, two indicate the speed and amount of rotation, and two indicate the speed and amount of scaling.

10.2.4 Physically based motion

In some cases, scripting the motion by specifying a path is not sufficient. In those cases, a more accurate animation results from calculating the motion based on physical properties of the object and of natural forces such as gravity.

Animation of a simple rigid body such as a ball or cube is done through a cycle that simulates their motion (Figure 10.6). Each object has a set of properties including its position, velocity, momentum, and mass. Those properties are influenced by forces such as gravity, wind, friction with air or objects in contact, and collisions. When these forces are applied to an object, accelerations or decelerations are applied to the object causing a change in the object properties. Equations from physics are used to determine the motion of objects in time steps equivalent to the

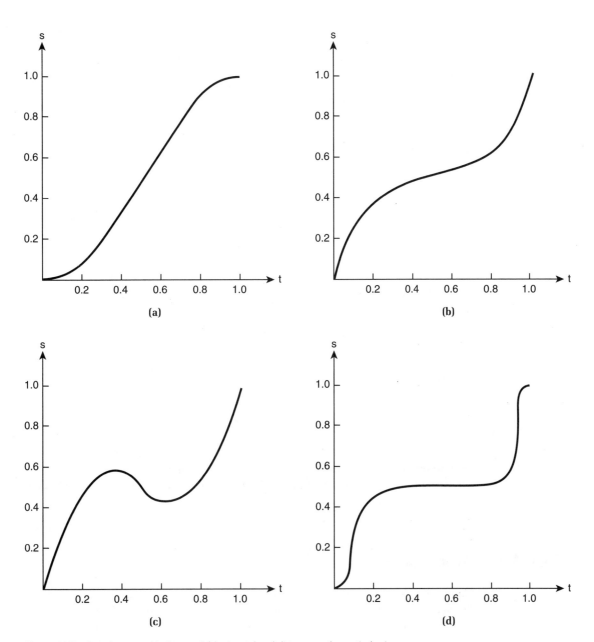

Figure 10.5 • Speed curves with time as the horizontal and distance as the vertical axis

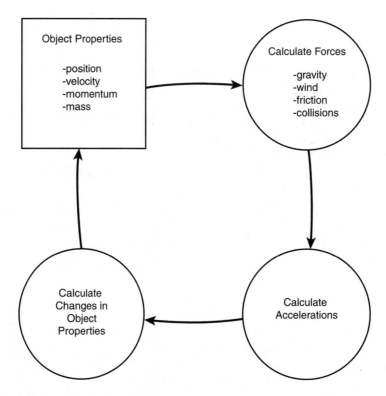

Figure 10.6 • Motion simulation cycle

frames of an animation. Thus, the cycle of Figure 10.6 is executed for every frame to determine the influence of physical forces on the motion.

The application of physical properties can also be used in the creation of single images and is used in animations of particle systems, which are discussed in Chapter 11.

10.3 Articulated Figures

Animating simple objects can be reasonably straightforward but animating humans, animals, or abstract creatures is much more involved. Our experiences create an expectation of how things move. If the movement for a human character is even slightly off, it will be very obvious. This is compounded because of the structure of humans and animals. The skeletal structure is composed of bones connected at joints. The bones determine the lengths of the various parts of the character and the joints have properties that influence how the adjacent bones move relative to each other. On top of this are the muscles and ligaments, which also play a role in this motion.

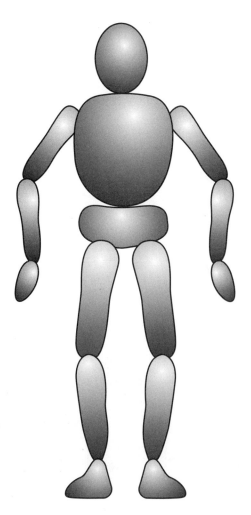

Figure 10.7 • An articulated figure

Articulated figures are models composed of numerous segments connected by joints. Figure 10.7 shows a human form composed of hands, forearms, upper arms, head, torso, pelvis, thighs, calves, and feet. A more detailed model includes fingers, toes, neck, and jaw.

Each of these segments is connected to the adjacent one at a joint. Each joint has a range of possible motions depending on the degrees of freedom. For example, the elbow has one degree of freedom because it can only bend. The shoulder has three degrees of freedom because it can bend, rotate, and twist (Figure 10.8). Overall, the human body has approximately 200 degrees of freedom.

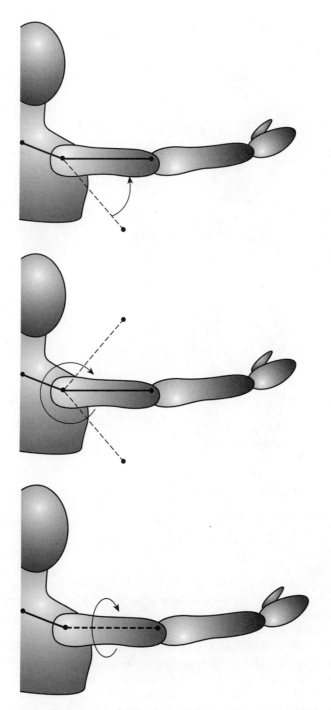

Figure 10.8 • Shoulder motion includes bending, rotating, and twisting

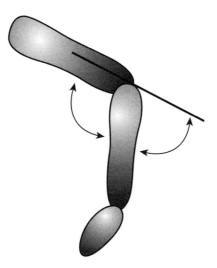

Figure 10.9 • Limitations on joint movement

For some joints, there are limitations on movement. For example, the elbow can bend but in only one direction (Figure 10.9). When reaching for an object, an articulated figure needs to move all of the joints in a way that does not violate limitations and still allows the hand to arrive at the object. When planning this motion, care must also be taken so that not only does the hand avoid any obstacles, but that the arm does as well.

There are additional movements that do not strictly occur at the joints. For example, the hand moves because the wrist can bend, but the hand can also turn. This turn or twist does not occur at either the wrist or the elbow, but rather occurs because of the two bones in the forearm. To model this effect, an additional joint is placed in the forearm (Figure 10.10).

Though this description of articulated figures concentrates on a human figure, the same principles apply to animal models and models of abstract or fantasy figures.

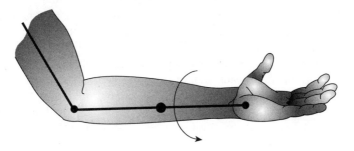

Figure 10.10 • A pseudo-joint in the forearm allows the hand to rotate

The next section introduces some of the basic concepts and issues in modeling the motion of articulated figures. For additional details, the reader is directed to animation books such as Parent (Parent02).

10.3.1 Kinematics

Articulated figures are typically stored in a hierarchy because a movement of the shoulder, for example, influences movements of the arm and hand. For a human figure, the root of this hierarchy is typically the pelvis, as that is the center of gravity for the figure. The relative positioning of the components of the figure are determined by fixed limitations and variable parameters stored within the hierarchy. An example of a fixed limitation is the length of the forearm, which determines the distance that must always exist between the elbow and wrist. An example of a variable parameter is the angle of the elbow bend. Joints in a figure have both parameters and limitations. For example, the knee joint bends in only one direction and has a limit on the range of angles that it can have.

Kinematics deals with motion without concern for the forces that cause that motion. There are two types of kinematics that can be used for computer animation: forward and inverse. Forward kinematics works from the root of the hierarchy to a leaf, making changes to the parameters along the way, to create the necessary motion. Inverse kinematics begins with the movement needed in the leaf and works up the hierarchy setting the parameters as necessary to cause that motion.

Forward kinematics seems simple when considering the movement of a hand waving that just changes the elbow angle. This movement merely requires that the angle of the elbow be changed smoothly. For more complex motion, forward kinematics can become a trial and error process. Consider reaching for an object. This movement causes changes at the shoulder, elbow, wrist, and fingers. One solution to this problem is to change the angle of the shoulder until the upper arm points in the correct direction. Then the elbow angle is changed until the forearm points in the correct direction. Then changes are made to the wrist and fingers to complete the motion. Adjustments might be needed if the object is closer or farther from where the hand winds up by this process. Though this achieves the task of reaching, the resulting motion will not look natural. Natural motion requires that all of these changes occur at the same time—but not necessarily at the same rates.

Inverse kinematics first determines the motion that is necessary, and then calculates how the parameters in the hierarchy should change to cause that movement. Returning to the example of reaching for an object, first the path that the hand takes is determined. For each step of the movement, inverse kinematics determines the change necessary to the wrist, then the elbow, and finally the shoulder. Working in this direction, the natural motion of the hand, and the limitations of the joints and bones determine the positioning of the rest of the arm.

Obstacles provide another challenge when planning motion. When a figure's arm moves in an effort to grasp an object, the motion must assure that the hand and arm avoid any obstacles. In environments that have few objects, simple strategies can be used to determine a path that avoids obstacles. In environments that have many objects, more complex strategies such as gradient fields and genetic algorithms have been used for path planning (see Miller94).

10.3.2 Walking and running

As with other human motions, people are very good at recognizing the details of walking and running. It is often possible to identify a friend in the distance by his or her gait or walking pattern. People can also be identified by the sounds made while walking, due to the variations in individual gait patterns. Given this recognition ability, it should not be surprising that realistic simulation of walking and running is difficult.

Walking and running are different from reaching motions because they are cyclic. But even though there is a cyclic nature to this motion, turning and tripping can disrupt this pattern. Furthermore, walking is dynamically but not statically stable, meaning that a figure in motion will be stable; however, if it suddenly stops it will be unbalanced and will be likely to fall. The walking cycle (Figure 10.11) consists of a stride that is divided into two stances for the left and right leg (Inman81). The left stance begins when the left heel strikes the ground and lasts until the right

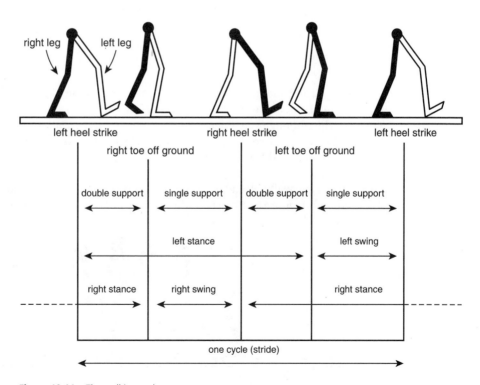

Figure 10.11 • The walking cycle

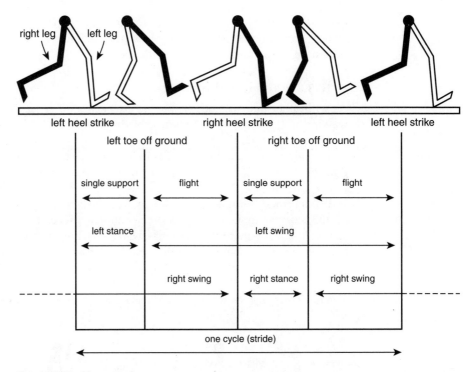

Figure 10.12 • The run cycle

heel strikes the ground. The right stance is defined similarly. The figure is supported by both legs during two parts of the stride.

The running cycle (Figure 10.12) differs from the walking cycle in that the figure is in flight at two times of the cycle. During this flight period, both feet are off the ground. In the walk cycle, the left and right stance overlap, but in the run cycle, the left and right swing overlap during flight.

During walking and running, the pelvis moves up and down relative to the ground (Figure 10.13). In the middle of a stance, both legs are together while the leg

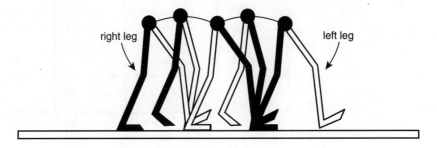

Figure 10.13 • Up and down movement of the pelvis

off the ground swings forward. At this point, the pelvis is at its highest point because the supporting leg is vertical. At the start and end of a stance, the supporting leg is at its greatest angle from vertical, putting the pelvis at its lowest point. The pelvis also rotates during the walk as the swing leg is brought forward.

During this process, the knees flex to both absorb some of the shock when the heel strikes and during the swing so that the foot does not strike the ground. There is also rotation in the ankle and toes during the stance portion of a stride.

The angles of the knee, pelvis, ankle, and toes for various speeds of walking have been measured and appear in a number of sources, see for example Inman, Ralston, and Todd (Inman81). Those graphs could be used to determine the kinematics for walking, however, an artist's skills are necessary to fine-tune this data to create unique walking patterns for different characters. The resulting gait patterns are limited because the data that they are based on assumes a flat ground plane. Thus, this technique cannot be used to simulate a figure walking across a sloped or uneven terrain. There are other techniques that have been used to automatically generate a gait pattern that can also handle a wide variety of ground shapes. Multon et al. (Multon99) give a survey of early methods for gait generation. These methods fall into two broad categories: physically based or kinematics.

One physically based technique is presented in Hodgins et al. (Hodgins95), which discusses a model that was used to automate the movement of human figures as they ran, bicycled, and performed a gymnastic handspring vault. This research uses a state machine to determine which control algorithms will be active. These control algorithms determine the positioning of the hands and feet, and then inverse kinematics are used to position the rest of the arms and legs. The control algorithms in this model are used for balancing, running, bicycling, and vaulting. The user of the system can enter parameters that control the velocity and direction of the figure, and then the control algorithms take over to calculate the velocity and position for the joints based on the system state. These control algorithms use both internal forces and torques for the muscles and joints along with external forces and torques for the ground or other objects such as a bicycle or vaulting horse. Of note in this research is the use of secondary motion to add realism. Whereas many studies of motion use skeletons, Hodgins et al. (Hodgins95) included simulated cloth on the figures and splashing puddle water by the runners. This group also studied platform diving (O'Brien95 and Wooten96), including the secondary motion of a splash when the diver entered the water.

A kinematic model for automatically generating a gait pattern for a walking figure is presented in Sun and Metaxas (Sun01), which uses 14 degrees of freedom in the hips, knees, ankles, and feet to generate a variety of gait patterns on flat as well as uneven terrain. This technique is separated into three modules. A high-level module generates values based on the terrain shape and path direction for use by lower level modules. The lower-level modules use these parameters to calculate the changes in the angles of the joints. When the figure follows a curved path, a lower-level module alters the rotation of the swing leg to move the figure in the new direction. In the case of uneven terrain, a second lower-level module predicts where the foot will strike based on the step length and path. The terrain height at that point is determined and a check is done to verify that the actual step length to this point is acceptable. If it is not acceptable, a new strike prediction is made and the process repeats. Once the lower-level modules have calculated all of the angles for the figure, the next image can be generated. In this technique, these modules are constantly evaluating information about path and terrain so that changes to the gait pattern can occur at any point during the stride.

10.3.3 Facial animation

Whereas people are good at recognizing human motion, facial expressions are such a large part of communication that even small errors in facial animation are easily noticed. This makes realistic facial animation a very difficult process. This section can only present the issues involved in facial animation. For details, the reader is directed to one of the books specifically on facial animation such as Parke and Waters (Parke96).

A first consideration is a model for the shape of a face. This model must not only be of a form that creates a good shape, it must also be controllable in the ways necessary to create different facial expressions. Use of curved surfaces can create a good shape, but there might not be enough control for changing expressions, so polygon meshes are more commonly used. Those meshes must be positioned not only to create a good facial surface, but to be deformable in the proper places so that an eyebrow can be raised, the lips can be narrowed, or the eyes can squint. Adding speech entails movements to the mouth, tongue, jaw, and surrounding areas to match the words that are being spoken. A study by Cosker et al. (Cosker04) showed that if movements of the mouth area are not accurate, the viewer will hear a different word than what is on the sound track.

The source of the mesh can vary depending on the application. If the facial animation is of a fictional character, a physical model can be created out of wood, clay, or plaster. The polygon mesh can be determined by using a low cost three-dimensional digitizer on the model. If the facial animation is of a real person, this digitization process can take too long, unless done with a high-speed laser scanner. An alternative technique takes multiple pictures of the subject and uses image analysis methods to determine points on the face, and thus the polygon mesh.

Parke's approach to facial animation (Parke96) identifies a set of conformational and expressive parameters. The conformational parameters describe the general shape of the face and the expressive parameters are used to control the expression shown on the face. Another specification is the MPEG-4 standard that is used to increase network bandwidth for teleconferencing (Pandzic02). This standard includes a set of 84 Facial Definition Parameters (FDPs) and 68 Facial Animation Parameters (FAPs). The FDPs specify the shape of the face, and the FAPs are used to make changes to animate the face. The locations on the face used for the FDPs are shown by the dots on the face in Figure 10.14. A third specification is the Facial Action Coding System (Ekman78) that was developed to describe facial expressions

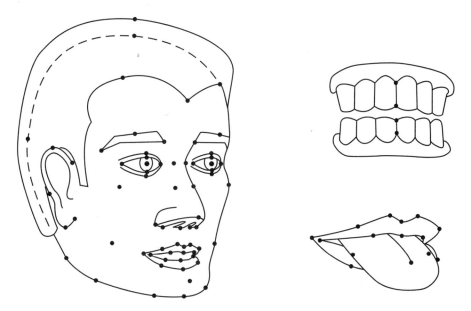

Figure 10.14 • Locations of the MPEG-4 Facial Definition Parameters, shown as dots

through a basic set of facial movements. This system found a collection of 46 Action Units that can be combined to describe all facial expressions. This system can be used as the basis for constructing facial expressions; however, additional movements need to be added for speech because those are not included in the system.

Understanding facial movements is only part of the solution to this problem. The actual movement of the face is done by a collection of muscles under the skin. Different types of facial muscles cause different types of movement. Additionally, the muscles move a muscle layer under the skin, which causes the skin to move. Some researchers attempt to model facial movements by modeling the contraction and relaxation of muscles. However, this method must also incorporate skin elasticity, which can vary and will alter the effect of muscle movements.

10.3.4 Motion capture

For animation applications where there is a set of specific movements to be animated, there is an alternative to calculating movement: motion capture (Menache00). Capturing the motion of a real person is only applicable for situations such as an animated film where the movements of a character are known. If the application is more interactive, such as a character in a computer game, motion capture will not be as helpful.

The basic concept of motion capture is that a person moves the way that the character is supposed to move. The motion of the various parts of the person's body is tracked as the person performs the actions of the character. Those motions are then used to set the position of the character's body parts for each frame of the animation. For example, the character's left hand will move the same way that the person's left hand moved during the motion capture process.

One method of motion capture places large markers on the person's body at significant locations such as the hands, arms, legs, torso, and joints. The person is then filmed performing the needed actions. The locations of these markers are identified on the film using image processing techniques. Multiple camera angles and knowledge about the cameras (e.g., focal length, image center, and aspect ratio) can be used to determine the three-dimensional locations of the points. Tracking the markers from frame to frame captures the motion of that body part.

There are problems with this process. Depending on the complexity of the motion, one or more of the markers can become blocked for a series of frames. Heuristics can be used to fill in the locations of the markers for the frames where they are blocked. Another problem is marker swapping. If two markers pass near enough that they become indistinguishable, the system might swap them when they separate. For example, when marker A and B come together, the path that marker A followed to the point where they joined will be continued by following marker B, and the path that marker B followed to the point where they joined will be continued by following marker A. This could have the effect of moving an elbow marker to a knee and vice versa. This system also has problems with noise caused by markers shifting their position on the person, or interactions between the marker and things in the background. But even with these problems, optical marker tracking is commonly used because it can be done inexpensively, using commercially available video cameras and colored tape for markers. Higher cost versions are also available that use higher quality cameras, more cameras, faster cameras, or even infrared cameras.

A second technique for motion capture uses magnetic sensors. These sensors are placed at the joints. These sensors can transmit a position and orientation back to a central computer either via wires connected to the person or via wireless radio signals. This system has the advantage of having the actual position and orientation relayed to the computer system. However, the readings of these sensors can be thrown-off by any magnetic fields near where the person is moving.

10.4 Flocking

In addition to scripting movement or calculating motion based on physical properties, it is possible to create a collection of autonomous "actors" that will use a set of rules to determine their behavior. This technique is especially helpful for scenes with many individual actors that would take a considerable amount of time to script.

One application of this technique is to model flocking, schooling, and herding behaviors. In Reynolds's (Reynolds87) system, each birdlike object (called a "boid") decides on a direction and velocity by three rules:

1. Collision avoidance—avoid collisions with other boids
2. Velocity matching—travel in the same direction and speed as the other boids
3. Flock centering—travel as near to the center of the flock as possible

These three rules are given in order of precedence, so that avoiding a collision is more important than being at the center of the flock. Further, decisions are made with imperfect knowledge. There is only a limited portion of the flock that can be seen by any one boid, and decisions are made as if the entire flock is being seen.

This technique works equally well to model schools of fish and herds of livestock, though in the latter case all motion is along the ground plane. Hodgins et al. (Hodgins95) used these rules to create a collection of bicycle riders that raced without being scripted or having collisions.

10.5 Motion Blur

Creating an animation of moving objects is nothing more than sampling the scene at regular intervals. When rendering a single image, spatial aliasing can occur because of the regular sampling of objects with continuous changes to their edges or textures. Temporal aliasing will cause fast-moving objects to have erratic or jerky motions, much as the movement of objects illuminated by a strobe light. The problem appears because each image renders the object as sharply as if the object were standing still at that moment in time.

When viewing fast moving objects, limitations in the visual system will result in an integration of the object and the background. Additionally, locations on the object influence a larger portion of the visual field than they would if the object was standing still. Thus, a small portion of the visual field can be influenced by the background and numerous locations on the object. This creates a blurring effect as is seen in the last few images of Figure 10.1.

Consider the same situation with regard to camera technology. When the shutter of a camera is open, light enters the camera lens and is projected onto the film. If the objects are stationary while the shutter is open, each object will be rendered sharply on the portion of the film where it projects. If an object moves while the shutter is open, a portion of the film will be exposed to both object and background. Further, that portion of film will be exposed to many different locations on the object. Just as moving the camera with the shutter open will cause the entire image to be blurry, having an object move while the shutter is open will make just that object blurry.

One solution to spatial aliasing is supersampling, which takes multiple samples for each pixel and combines them with a filter to determine the overall pixel value. In temporal anti-aliasing, the supersampling occurs when the image is rendered multiple times for each frame (Korein83 and Potmesil83). Objects that are stationary are rendered in the same location in each subframe, but objects that move will be rendered in a different location for each subframe. These subframes are then combined with a filter to produce the final frame.

There are two problems with this temporal supersampling. The first is the time involved in creating multiple images for each frame. If the calculations to determine multiple locations are complex, as in the case of articulated figures, the time to generate each subframe can be costly. One solution is to do a simple linear interpolation between the positions at the start and end of the frame for each of the subframes. Additional time can be saved by using a z-buffer approach to first render the stationary objects and then using that result as the starting point for rendering the moving objects in each subframe.

A second problem with temporal supersampling is that for very fast moving objects, instead of creating a blur, there might be faint multiple objects in the result. One solution to this is to create more subframes; but a less costly solution is to have the object also deform in shape to create a stretch in the direction of motion.

10.6 Animation Systems

There are software systems that support the development of an animation. Though there are differences between the way things are specified and specialized capabilities, these animation systems all provide support for the animation process. This section does not attempt to describe the details of each available system, because of their wide variety. Further, these systems are constantly being enhanced to give the user additional capabilities for the creation of more and more elaborate animations.

In general, these systems allow the user to place objects for each of the key frames of an animation and these systems take over the calculation of the rest of the frames. Using the terminology of cel animation, the user is the master animator and the software is the assistant animator that creates the in-between frames.

Animation systems have a timeline for the animation on which the key frames are identified. These timelines can also be used to change the environment. For example, the brightness of a light source or the amount of fog can be changed. Animation systems can also have support to control motion so that it follows straight line or spline based paths. The way that movement occurs around curves can also be controlled.

Animation of hierarchical figures is typically supported. Some systems even allow the user to create a linked skeletal structure and associate a mesh surface with it. Then when the skeleton moves, the mesh surface also moves along with it. There are animation systems with support for modeling some of the phenomena discussed in the next two chapters, such as particle systems and hair.

10.7 The OpenGL Way

OpenGL does not have any facilities for controlling movement or filling in the frames between key frames. OpenGL does support animation through the use of double buffering. A program that generates an animation will take some time to draw each image. During this drawing time, part of the image will be visible. Each frame will be revealed in the order that the objects are drawn. Though this will typically happen quickly, it can cause undesired effects.

In a system with double buffering, there are two frame buffers—one being displayed and the other being rendered. Once the image is complete, the two buffers are "swapped" so that the new image is displayed and the next image is drawn into the other buffer. This process of drawing the new image and then swapping the buffers is repeated for the duration of the animation.

To use double buffering, the constant GLUT_DOUBLE is included in the call to glutInitDisplayMode. For example, a program that uses the RGB color model and double buffering uses the call glutInitDisplayMode(GLUT_RGB | GLUT_DOUBLE). Each time a new image is completed, the buffers are swapped with the call glutSwapBuffers().

There is one concern when using double buffering. Some implementations of OpenGL will not swap buffers until the end of a refresh cycle. On a system that refreshes 60 times a second, there are at most 60 frames that could be displayed in one second. The real concern, however, is when frames of an animation take different amounts of time to render. For example, say that the frames of an animation take slightly more or less than $1/60^{th}$ of a second to render. Those images that take slightly less than $1/60^{th}$ of a second will display almost immediately after the rendering completes. Those images that take slightly longer than $1/60^{th}$ of a second will have to wait almost a full $1/60^{th}$ of a second until the next refresh cycle to be displayed. Though this might not seem like a big deal, there will be a very slight variation in the appearance of motion. Consider a scene with a group of objects that take about $1/20^{th}$ of a second to render. There will be approximately 20 frames displayed per second. If one of the objects leaves the scene so that it now takes $1/30^{th}$ of a second to render an image, there will now be 30 frames displayed per second. If the amount that object locations are changing is consistent between all of these frames, when the object leaves the scene, there will be 50 percent more images displayed per second, so the remaining objects will appear to move 50 percent faster. This can be solved by adding delays so that all frames take the same amount of time to render or by altering the amount object positions change when scene complexity changes.

10.8 Projects

1) Create a simple animation of a bouncing ball that includes the effect of gravity so that the ball goes less high with each bounce.
2) Enhance the bouncing ball program so that the ball exhibits squash and stretch when it hits the ground.

chapter

11

Advanced Object Modeling—Natural Phenomena

Chapters 3 and 4 looked at a variety of ways to model the shape of objects that ranged from simple mathematical shapes to more complex shapes based on Bézier curves and B-splines. Though there is a lot that can be done with these shapes, there are some objects that require something more. For example, mountains have a highly irregular shape and though these could be modeled with a collection of planar or curved patches, the result would require so many patches that the data file would be huge and the specification of all of those patches would be very time consuming. This concern is especially true of natural phenomena because of the complexity that natural objects exhibit.

Consider the picture in Figure 11.1. There is complexity in the arrangement of the petals of the rose, the flowers on the liatris stem, and the shape of the fern frond. The flickering of a candle changes both the shape and coloration of the flame, and the flickering alters the way the flame illuminates nearby objects. Smoke that rises from a flame or steam that rises from a hot cup of coffee, takes a constantly changing shape.

This chapter looks at models for objects that are highly complex and for which the other modeling techniques are not sufficient. In all cases, this is due to the underlying detail or complexity of the objects themselves. There are a number of different techniques that are used to model a wide range of natural phenomena, but only a few are discussed here. Specifically, this chapter looks at a few of the techniques used to model plants, terrain, liquids, clouds, steam, smoke, and fire. Though these topics are discussed individually, there is significant overlap among

Figure 11.1 • Candle lit flowers (see Color Plate 11.1)

them. Modeling the shape of the terrain has an impact on the location of plants and streams, as well as how water flows through those streams. Streams can also cause erosion, which can impact the shape of the terrain.

There are a large number of techniques that are used for the advanced models discussed in this and the next chapter. These two chapters can, therefore, only be a survey of some of the techniques that have been developed. The brief overview of each of these approaches will give the reader an introduction to that methodology, with references that can serve as the starting point for additional research.

11.1 General Techniques

There are two techniques that are common to many of the advanced modeling techniques discussed in this chapter. When dealing with complex models, specifying all of the details of the object will result in extremely large data files. These specifications will likely be difficult to maintain and modify. An alternative is to develop a process that can generate these complex models as needed. For example, instead of creating a data file with all of the surfaces needed for a plant, a process is developed to "grow" the plant when needed. The process can accept a set of input parameters that can be used to modify the output for different situations. Returning to the plant example, the parameters can be used to specify whether to generate an apple tree or a stalk of corn. These parameters will be much more compact than the full object model.

This section discusses both the general process of procedural modeling and the technique of particle systems that can be used in modeling a number of different natural phenomena.

11.1.1 Procedural modeling

A cornerstone of the models in this chapter is the idea of procedural modeling. Instead of specifying all of the details of an object in a scene, the parameters for a procedure that will create the object are specified instead. In a procedural model, the data file only specifies the parameters for the object and the details are then generated by the program. Returning to the mountain example, in a procedural model of a mountain, values for the height of the mountain and the roughness of its surface can be given and then the procedure can create the individual patches needed for the scene.

Multiple procedural models used to create a scene can also communicate information among themselves as they build their objects. Consider three procedures that create a mountain, place a road through that mountain, and position trees on the mountain. As the mountain is being generated, the relative height of the mountain can be communicated to the road process. The road process can communicate to the mountain process the position and width of the road, so that the mountain process assures that path through the mountain is flat. The mountain process can communicate land heights so the tree process can place the trees, and the road process communicates its position so trees are not put in the middle of the road or too close to its edges.

In animation sequences, procedural models can be used to control motion of objects. The discussions in Chapter 10 on motion of articulated figures was really about a procedural model that determined the location of parts of the figure based on constraints placed on those parts. Many of the models discussed in this chapter are also procedural models that can be used to generate a single image or an animation sequence.

11.1.2 Particle systems

Consider a fireworks display. When fireworks explode in the sky, a single charge splits into many smaller pieces. Each piece has its own color and has its own direction of travel. There is a limited lifetime that each piece is visible and some will leave a trail, while others do not. In some cases, smaller pieces will also explode, creating even smaller pieces. The particles in a particle system can behave in a similar way, but can also do much more.

More formally, a particle system—for example, Reeves (Reeves83), Reeves and Blau (Reeves85), and Sims (Sims90)—is a collection of particles that have a set of properties that are updated at discrete times, which creates a dynamic system that evolves over time. At each point in time, a particle can change its attributes; it can split into multiple particles; or it can die. The source of the initial collection of particles can produce one burst of particles that comprise the entire system, or it can continue to produce new particles over the entire simulation time.

Each particle in a particle system has attributes that specify its color, transparency, shape, size, position, speed, direction, and lifetime. These values are assigned at particle creation, but can change over the lifetime of the particle.

To create an animated sequence of a particle system, the initial particles are created and given an initial set of parameters. The first image is then rendered. In preparation for the next image, the process creates any new particles, assigns their attributes, removes any particles that are at their lifetime limit, and moves all of the particles according to their speed and direction attributes. The next image is created and the process repeats. A particle system is rendered using the location, shape, size, transparency, and color attributes of each of the individual particles, as well as any trails those particles might have.

Again consider the fireworks example. When a shell is shot into the air, this is the equivalent of having a single particle moving in an upward direction at a given speed. When that shell explodes, this is the equivalent of a particle splitting into multiple new particles. Each of these new particles has a smaller size than the original, and has a direction and speed determined by the explosion. The color and life of these smaller shells are determined by their composition, much as the color and life of the smaller particles are determined by their attributes.

Fireworks displays are clearly a natural application of particle systems, but particle systems have also been used to model plants (Smith84); fur (Kajiya89); smoke and steam (Holtkämper03); the foam on surf (Peachey86); waterfalls (Sims90); snow (Fearing00); dust (Chen99); fluids (Müller03); cloth (Breen94); and fire (Reeves83).

11.2 Botanical Structures

Plants have a very complex structure that becomes more complex as the plant ages and adds branches, leaves, and flowers. If a model of a plant is created by hand, this results in just one plant, whereas multiple versions of one type of plant will all be different. Creating multiple versions that differ in placement of branches and leaves is very tedious and time consuming. Instead, procedural models can be used to "grow" the plant structure with variety being added by including random variations in the application of those parameters.

Plant structures can be quantified by looking at the range of possibilities for a few plant features. Various plant species can be defined in terms of the value that they exhibit for each of these features. For example, when a new branch appears, it does so at a particular angle from the parent branch and at a particular rotational angle around the parent branch. These angles and the average length of branches differ among plants. Other features that can be quantified include:

- Rhythmic versus continuous growth—does growth occur in distinct bursts or is growth occurring all of the time? Plants in temperate regions exhibit rhythmic growth that is timed with seasonal temperature changes, whereas plants in tropical regions exhibit either rhythmic or continuous growth.
- Orthotropic versus plagiotropic branching—are secondary branches primarily oriented vertically (orthotropic) or horizontally (plagiotropic)?
- Basal versus distal branching—do braches only occur from the base of the plant (basal) or can they appear at any point on the plant (distal)?
- Monopodial versus sympodial branching—do new branches only appear at the primary meristem or growth point (monopodial), or can branches appear at secondary meristems as well (sympodial)?
- Arrangement of leaves—leaf arrangement or phyllotaxis can be spiral, distichous (alternating sides of the branch), or decussate (paired on opposite sides of the branch and rotated 90° from the position of the previous pair).
- Flower location (inflorescence)—flowers can appear at the end of a branch (terminal inflorescence); along the sides of the main branch (cauliflorous inflorescence); or along the sides of the secondary branches (lateral inflorescence).

In Figure 11.2, the plant in part (a) shows basal branching that occurs underground whereas the plants in parts (b) though (e) show distal branching. The plant in part (b) shows rhythmic growth through the tiers of plagiotropic branches. The plant in part (c) shows continues growth, orthotropic branching, and lateral inflorescence. The plant in part (d) shows rhythmic growth and plagiotropic branching. The plant in part (e) shows terminal inflorescence with new branches appearing around the flower locations. Part (f) of Figure 11.2 shows decussate (left) and distichous (right) phyllotaxis. A complete look at the range of combinations that is possible can be found in Hallé, Oldemon, and Tomlinson (Hallé78).

Though this is not a book about plant biology, these few concepts will be helpful in the discussion of various modeling methods.

11.2.1 Grammar-based models

A grammar is a set of rules that generally takes the form A → B, which means that A can be replaced by B, or A can become B. In general, B can actually be a sequence of symbols. So, with the word AAA and the grammar rule A → DE, the word can become DEAA, ADEA, or AADE. Grammars can also be parallel, where rules are

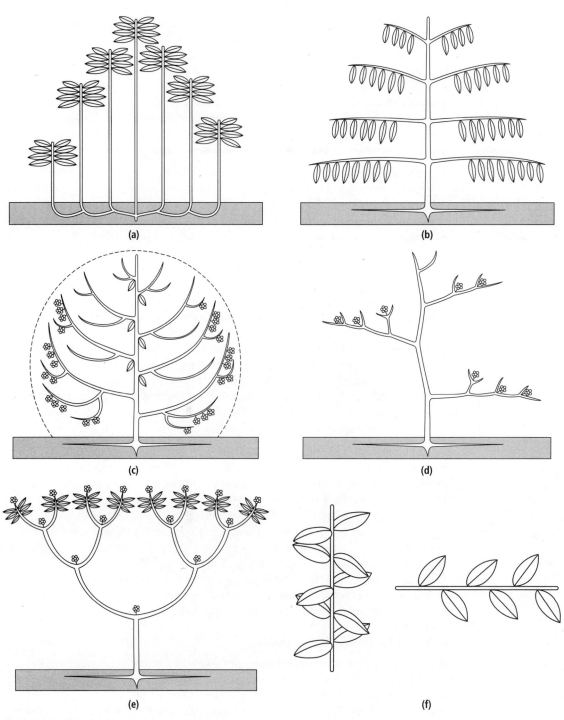

Figure 11.2 • Plant features

applied to all of the symbols at the same time. In a parallel grammar, the preceding example produces the word DEDEDE because the rule is applied to every A symbol at the same time. This is only the briefest of introductions to grammars, and more details can be found in books such as Linz (Linz01).

In 1968, Lindenmayer (Lindenmayer68) developed a set of parallel grammars (now called L-systems) that described the flow of information in filamentous organisms such as algae. In 1984, Smith (Smith84) used these ideas to develop a concept called graftals, which are a parallel grammar that are interpreted to give a graphic representation. The example given in this paper has the rules: 0 → 1[0]1[0]0, 1 → 11, [→ [, and] →]. Beginning with a starting symbol of 0, the next two strings formed would be 1[0]1[0]0 and 11[1[0]1[0]0]11[1[0]1[0]0]1[0]1[0]0. Smith gave these a geometrical representation as follows. For each 0 or 1 symbol, a line of a particular length is drawn. When a "[" symbol is reached, the current location and direction are noted and drawing continues at an angle of 45°. When a "]" symbol is reached, drawing moves back to the most recently noted location and direction. Smith also made note of the direction of the angle change, and would alternate between going to the left and right. The left side of Figure 11.3 shows the graphical representation of the previous two rules with a 0 shown as a gray line and a 1 shown as a black line. The right side of Figure 11.3 shows the graphic representation of the second string.

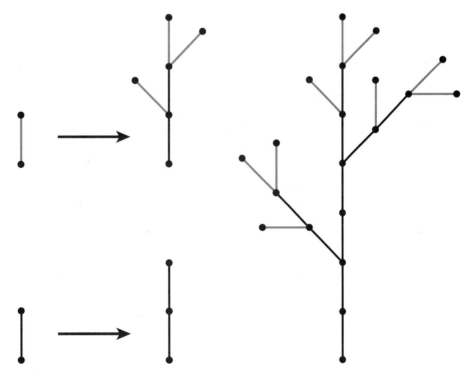

Figure 11.3 • Graftals

L-system based models of plants continue to be researched and the complexity of the grammar rules have increased. Prusinkiewicz and Hanan (Prusinkiewicz88) began their work with Lindenmayer to develop more elaborate grammar rules and a turtle graphics interpretation of the result. Turtle graphics were developed in the 1980s (Abelson86) as a simple line drawing mechanism. The concept is that the "turtle" has a pen attachment that can be down or up. When the turtle moves with the pen down, a line is drawn during the movement. When the turtle moves with the pen up, no line is drawn. In these more recent L-systems, some of the symbols are instructions to the turtle, which draws the plant. This research continues and has resulted in more complex sets of grammar rules and more elaborate graphical renderings of them.

The following is a sample L-system for a bean plant (Hanan04). The axiom represents the starting point for this L-system. The next pair of rules shows how the apex grows. The first of these rules replaces the apex with an internode (branch), a leaf, a secondary bud, and a new apex at the end of this new section of the plant. As in the graftal example, the sections in the square brackets represent branches off the main branch. The values in parentheses before the letter components represent branching and rotational angles for that new section. The values in parentheses immediately following the letter components represent an "age" attribute for that component. The conditional (d < = 0) at the start of the first rule restricts the conditions under which that rule applies—in this case that the age is less than or equal to 0. The star in the second rule indicates that it applies in all other cases. This second rule merely changes the "age" of the apex. The apex added in the brackets of the first rule has an age of 1, so in the next generation the second rule reduces this age to 0 so that it begins to grow another branch section in the next generation. This technique is used to delay a development of, or a change to, a part of the plant. The third and fifth rules increase the age parameter for internodes and branches. The fourth rule removes the leaf from the plant when it reaches an age of 2. Figure 11.4 gives a graphic schematic for these rules, much as Figure 11.3 did so for the graftal example. The schematic shows that as the leaves and branches age they get larger.

```
/* Starting string or axiom */
Axiom: A(0)

/* Morphogenetic rules or productions */
/* apex produces new metamer:
 *              Internode,  Leaf,  axillary Bud  and ongoing Apex */
A(d) : d<=0 --> I(1) [-(10)L(1)] [-(35)A(1)] +(10)/(180)A(0)
A(d) : * --> A(d-1)

I(age) --> I(age+1) /* age internode */

L(a) :a==2 --> %     /* shed leaves when they reach age 2 */
L(a) --> L(a+1)      /* age leaf */
```

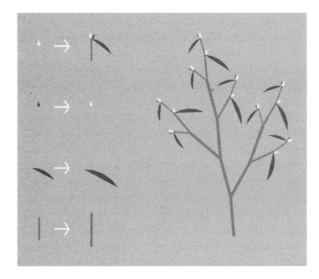

Figure 11.4 • Schematic for a bean plant (see Color Plate 11.2) Courtesy of Jim Hanan, University of Queensland © 2004 Jim Hanan

Figure 11.5 shows a three-dimensional rendering of the plant produced by this L-system. This rendering shows a more elaborate and more realistic interpretation of the leaf and internode symbols.

Figure 11.5 • Four generations of a bean plant (see Color Plate 11.3) Courtesy of Jim Hanan, University of Queensland © 2004 Jim Hanan

Another grammar method for modeling growth in plants was developed by McConnell (McConnell88 and McConnell89). This method uses grammar rules based on three-dimensional graphs instead of text characters that need to be interpreted to render the image. The goal of this research was to develop a method that would specify plant structures in a straightforward way. Because each step of the process produces a three-dimensional structure of the plant, calculations for shadowing and obstruction can be done on the structure without a separate interpretation step.

The structure produced by this method also has attributes attached to the nodes and branches. The rules of the grammar not only change the structure of the tree, they also alter the attributes. These attributes can be used to delay events or communicate information through the structure. Rules are applied in a parallel manner. During each pass, there is a rule chosen for each node in the structure, and then all of these are applied simultaneously to produce the next generation of the plant.

In Figure 11.6, part (a) shows a seed becoming the initial trunk of the plant with the meristem or growth point at the end. Part (b) shows that the meristem becomes another trunk section that has a tier of four branches off of it. Part (c) shows the additional growth of secondary branches. The rule in part (d) shows the change of the branch angle attribute that is used to cause the branches to droop from orthotropic to plagiotropic orientation with age. The plant skeleton in Figure 11.7 results from the use of these rules.

11.2.2 Probabilistic models

Reffye et al. (Reffye88) developed a probabilistic model for growth in plants and trees. This model is based on the activity of a bud on the plant at discrete times: It can become a flower and then die; it can be dormant; it can become a new branch or branches; or it can die. The probability of each of these events is based on the type and variety of the plant to be produced. Further, the result is dependent on the number of branches, their size, and their relative positioning. The complexity of this model is in the determination of the parameters for a particular type of plant. This involved a time-intensive process of measuring many sample plants to determine these parameters. Observations over time are also necessary to determine the time and probability of changes to buds as the plant ages. Once this work is done, however, the results are very good, as can be seen in Figure 11.8.

11.2.3 Plant ecosystems

In addition to the issues of modeling the shape of plants there are the issues of deciding where those plants should be placed. In an early attempt, Gardner (Gardner84) used the functional cosine textures discussed in Chapter 6 to deter-

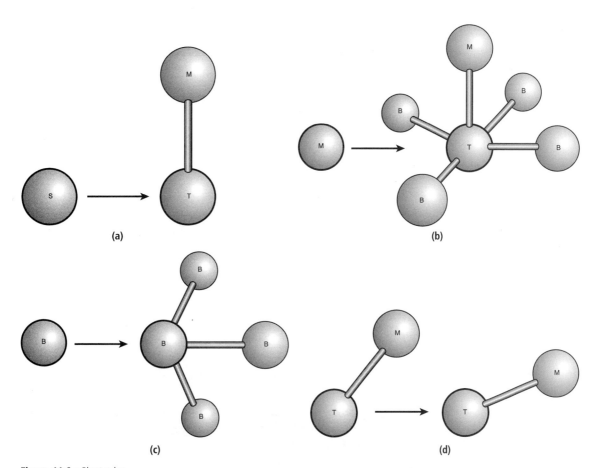

Figure 11.6 • Plant rules

mine the placement of plants. These textures were also used to determine the density of ellipsoids for a crude model of trees. This achieved reasonable results because the application was for flight simulation, in which case the trees would be moving past quickly and thus, a highly detailed rendering was unnecessary.

Deussen et al. (Deussen98) created a four-stage rendering process to solve the problem of plant placement: terrain modeling, plant distribution, individual plant modeling, and scene rendering. Terrain modeling will be discussed in the next section but it must be the first stage in the process because terrain height determines where plants can be placed. The second stage of plant distribution can either be done by hand to create human-designed environments such as gardens and parks, or it can be created though an ecosystem model that includes details on plant

Figure 11.7 • A tree structure

preferences for light level and soil type, as well as the growth and reproduction cycle. After an initial distribution, the growth of plants is simulated and that simulation is influenced by competition among the plants for light, space, water, and nutrients. The resulting plants are quantified to create a collection of plants that can be duplicated for many instances of plants so as to reduce the storage space necessary for the scene. Only the parameters to produce these plants are necessary, because the third stage will actually create the plants that are then the input for the final rendering stage. A result of this process is the forest scene shown in Figure 11.9.

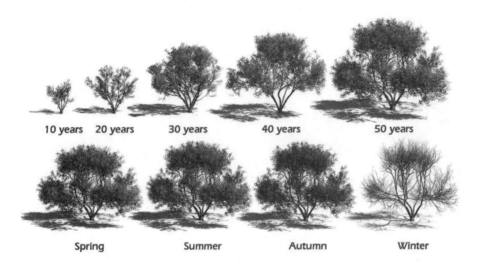

10 years   20 years   30 years   40 years   50 years

Spring   Summer   Autumn   Winter

Figure 11.8 • Probabilistic model results for a silver willow (see Color Plate 11.4) Courtesy of Bionatics www.bionatics.com © 2004 Bionatics, Inc.

11.3 Terrain

There is so much variation in the ground, it cannot be modeled with a simple planar surface. The variation is so great that a collection of planes would be too difficult to specify. This section looks at some of the techniques that can be used instead.

If the scene being created illustrates an actual place, there might be elevation data that has been collected for that area. For example, the United States Geological Survey could be one such source for terrain data within the United States. This data can be used to create a set of triangular patches (Kumler94) for the location being rendered. The rest of this section looks at two techniques that can be used to generate abstract landscapes.

11.3.1 Fractal models

A fractal is an object that exhibits a fractional dimension. For example, a line is a one-dimensional object, but a line in a very tight spiral is close to a two-dimensional plane. This makes the spiral an object that is between one- and two-dimensional.

Another component of a fractal is its self-similarity. The idea of self-similarity is that zooming in or out of the object shows the same patterns repeated at different resolutions. A common example of a fractal is the von Koch snowflake (Figure 11.10). If you look closely at Figure 11.10, you will see that the overall shape of one of the sides is repeated at finer and finer resolutions. Figure 11.11 shows how the von Koch snowflake is constructed by looking at what happens to one of the sides.

Figure 11.9 • A plant ecosystem (see Color Plate 11.5) Deussen et al., "Realistic modeling and rendering of plant ecosystems," SIGGRAPH 98, © 1998 ACM, Inc. Reprinted by permission.

Figure 11.10 • von Koch snowflake

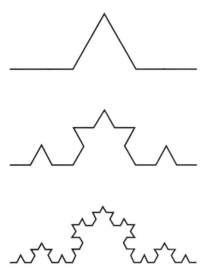

Figure 11.11 • Constructing one side of the von Koch snowflake

The process begins with the first shape in Figure 11.11, and each of the lines of that figure is replaced with a scaled down replica of the original. This process is repeated again in the second and third shapes in this figure. As this process is repeated, the edges of the snowflake get more and more complex, and they get longer and longer. Mathematically, there is no limit to this process because a line, no matter how small, can always be replaced in this manner. From a technical standpoint, this process can be considered finite because it is limited by the resolution of the display or printing process, which makes further replacements invisible.

The fractal dimension of the result can be determined by looking at the piece that is used for the replacement. In Figure 11.11, the replacement has four lines, each of which is one third the size of the original. This gives a fractal dimension of $\log(4)/\log(3) \approx 1.26$. In general, if the replacement has N lines, each of which is $1/M^{th}$ the size of the original, the fractal dimension will be given by $\log(N)/\log(M)$. Thus, changing the pattern used in the replacement will change the fractal dimension of the result.

Irregular surfaces that could be used to model landscapes can be generated through a similar replacement technique called midpoint subdivision (Fournier82). This technique begins with a triangular planar patch. Each of the edges of the patch is divided in half, and the midpoints are randomly displaced to add some irregularity to the surface. After one subdivision, the surface is now a collection of four triangular patches. This process is repeated with each of the new patches creating even more irregularity and more triangular pieces. This can be done infinitely many times, but as in the case of the von Koch snowflake, it makes more sense to limit this by how close the viewer is to the object and the resolution of the display. Figure 11.12 shows a fractal landscape simplistically generated in this manner. The subdivision process can be done by applying the equations (11.1) to the lines that represent the edges of the polygons, where the function S indicates the scale of the change and Rand gives a random number between 0 and 1 based on the value of the new x point.

$$x_{new} = \tfrac{1}{2} * (x_i + x_{i+1})$$
$$y_{new} = \tfrac{1}{2} * (y_i + y_{i+1}) + S(x_{i+1} - x_i) * \text{Rand}(x_{new}) \qquad (11.1)$$
$$z_{new} = \tfrac{1}{2} * (z_i + z_{i+1})$$

The line from (x_i, y_i, z_i) to $(x_{i+1}, y_{i+1}, z_{i+1})$ is replaced by the two lines between (x_i, y_i, z_i) and $(x_{new}, y_{new}, z_{new})$ and between $(x_{new}, y_{new}, z_{new})$ and $(x_{i+1}, y_{i+1}, z_{i+1})$. Additionally, new lines are added for the additional triangular patches that are created in the process of the subdivision. The scale function can vary from simple to more complex. A scale function of $S(d) = d$ produces offsets that are decreasing and related linearly to the size of the x coordinate range. A scale function of $S(d) = 2^{-d}$ produces offsets that start small and increase as the size of the x range decreases.

• 11.3.2 Erosion models

Over time, streams created by water running off adjacent mountains begin to erode the terrain. Likewise, rivers cut through the terrain based on the terrain height and composition. Geomorphology research develops models for stream formation that can serve as the basis for the development of a network of streams and rivers. Kelley, Malin, and Nielson (Kelley88) give one example of terrain modeling using this basis.

A stream convergence model chooses random locations on a grid for the start of streams. It then moves the streams randomly into adjacent grid cells. In this process streams can grow, join, or leave the grid area. Though this process can create a statistically reasonable stream network, it might not be visually appealing.

An alternative is the headward growth model, which produces more realistic stream networks. In this method, the stream network is grown from the end instead of the source. At each step, an adjacent grid cell is randomly chosen and that becomes the next upstream location. When the stream reaches a predetermined length, it splits into two smaller branches that serve as feeders for the main stream. If this upstream growth reaches another stream path, this growth will terminate so that the streams do not cross.

Once the stream network has been set, this also sets the height of the land that it crosses. The shape of the rest of the terrain can be determined by growing the terrain upward from the banks of the streams in the network.

• 11.4 Liquids

The movement of liquids has been studied for some time. Fluid dynamics research has been involved in understanding fluid flow from an engineering perspective. Early attempts at modeling water consisted of attempts to model ocean waves and

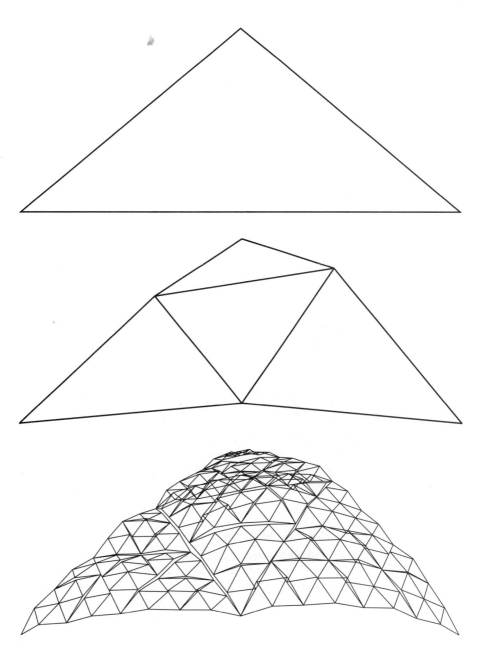

Figure 11.12 • Formation of a simple fractal terrain

surf through the use of simple textures and sine functions. More recently, faster computers make it possible to use the results of fluid dynamics research to create a more accurate model of fluid flow.

Fluids at rest are simple to model because gravity causes the fluid to have a flat surface. The only impact on the fluid's appearance will be the way it is illuminated and how light might refract through it based on its density. Fluids in motion provide a much more complex problem because fluids behave differently based on the properties of each fluid. For example, a more viscous fluid such as syrup moves more slowly than a less viscous one such as water. The properties of the fluid also impact how that fluid interacts with objects. A ball thrown into water creates a much larger splash than one thrown into thick oil. These issues of fluid motion are important whether the goal is an animation or just a snapshot of one instant in the motion of that fluid.

This section begins with a review of some of the early wave efforts and then discusses more recent liquid simulations.

11.4.1 Waves

Early attempts at modeling water concentrated on the waves in large bodies of water (for example: Fournier86, Peachey86, and Ts'o87). These models were concerned with determining the shape of the surface of the water so that the viewer is given the impression of waves crashing on the shore. These methods base the shape of the surface on that of a trochoid.[1]

The depth of the water has an impact on the shape of the wave. That can be seen in the change of wave shapes as water reaches the shore. One solution is to shorten the period and amplitude of the trochoid when the depth becomes smaller than the height of the wave. The curling and crashing of the tops of waves are handled in Fournier and Reeves (Fournier86) by adding a term to the trochoid that is dependent on the height of the wave and that shifts the top of the wave toward the shore. The higher the wave, the greater the shift—which causes the curl at the top of the wave. Spray and foam are simulated by particle systems placed at the crests of the waves.

11.4.2 Height field models

As water flows through streams, the irregular nature of the stream bed and changes in terrain heights influence the rate of water flow and the turbulence of the surface of the water. Additionally, the height of the water and pressure applied by the atmosphere and objects striking the water also influence how the water moves. These are the components of a set of models of water (for example, O'Brien95, Mould97, and Holmberg04).

In these models, the area under consideration is divided into rectangular columns. The fluid in each of these columns can flow into one of the eight adjacent columns through a collection of virtual pipes. The rate of flow in these pipes is

---

[1]More details on the trochoid curves can be found in Appendix A.

determined by the pressure that each of these columns is under. The pressure calculation for the column at position [i, j] is given by equation (11.2) where h_{ij} is the height of fluid, ρ is the density of the fluid, g is the acceleration due to gravity, p_0 is the atmospheric pressure, and E_{ij} is the pressure exerted by an external force.

$$P_{ij} = h_{ij} * \rho * g + p_0 + E_{ij} \tag{11.2}$$

The difference in pressure for two adjacent columns and the size of the pipe are used to determine the flow direction and rate in the pipe. Pipes can be connected to the boundaries of the area under consideration to allow for sources of fluid entering the scene and locations where fluid exits the scene. The flow through the pipes determines how the volume changes in each of the columns, which determines the height of each column. The height of adjacent columns can be used to calculate an average height at the point where four columns join. These heights are used to render the surface of the water.

Sprays of fluid drops are produced when the rate of increase in the height of a column exceeds a set threshold. This simulates the escape of particles of fluid from the surface (a splash) due to rapid changes in fluid location. These drops of fluid are modeled with a particle system, but their volume is also removed from the column, which reduces its height. If those particles leave the scene or strike another object, they are destroyed. But if a particle falls back to the fluid, its volume is added to the column it lands on. In this model, the external pressure term can be used to model objects interacting with fluid such as objects falling into a fluid or the splash created when a character steps into a puddle, which causes water to rush into adjacent columns at a rapid enough rate to cause the escape of fluid drops.

11.4.3 A fluid dynamics model

In the 1800s, Navier and Stokes independently developed a set of equations that describe the forces that act on liquid. In general, the Navier-Stokes equations relate the viscous drag of liquid, momentum, gravity, and pressure to determine changes in velocity and pressure within the liquid. One use of these equations (Foster00 and Foster01) is within a particle-based system. This research divides the space into a grid of cells. Cells are classified as either being empty or filled with some rigid object. Liquid can flow into the empty cells.

Each cell has a pressure value located at the center of the cell, and a set of six velocity values at the center of each of the sides of the cells. The liquid that is being modeled is treated as a collection of particles that flow through this cell grid based on the pressure and velocities connected with each cell. Additionally, the Navier-Stokes equations are used to update the cell velocity values based on changes in pressure.

The shape of the water surface could be modeled as triangular patches with vertices defined by the location of particles at the surface. It is a computationally complex process to determine the appropriate adjacencies for these vertices. Imagine a collection of thousands of points in space and imagine deciding how best to group them to create a surface. Does a set of three points create the optimal water surface, or should these points be combined differently with other adjacent points to create the surface? Because of this complexity, a better alternative is to have each particle be the center of a density field. An implicit surface (Bloomenthal97) is then created by summing these density fields where they overlap and having the surface located at a specific total density within the space. Additional details on implicit surfaces defined in this matter will be discussed in Chapter 12 as they are also used to model the shape of skin.

Enright, Marschner, and Fedkiw (Enright02) enhanced the work of Foster et al. by using particles on both sides of the surface. By using particles on both sides of the implicit surface, Enright et al. can dampen the slashing effects or increase churning effects to increase splashing. Figure 11.13 shows images of water being poured into a glass that results from this method. The use of particles on both sides of the implicit surface allows the method to create the thin sheets of water in the first of these images.

The next development in this technique uses a set of control particles to direct the flow of the liquid. Rasmussen et al. (Rasmussen04) describe control particles that have a control shape, which defines the area where this particle has influence over the fluid. There are soft degrees of control over properties such as viscosity and hard degrees of control over properties such as movement and the visual

Figure 11.13 • Water pouring into a glass (see Color Plate 11.6) Enright et al., "Animation and rendering of complex water surfaces," SIGGRAPH 2002, © 2002 ACM, Inc. Reprinted by permission.

appearance. Directing the movement of the control particles gives control over the movement of the fluid.

11.5 Gaseous Phenomena

Clouds, steam, and smoke represent similar gaseous phenomena, however, there are some distinct differences. Clouds and steam are based on humidity levels whereas smoke is based on the temperature and density of particles produced by fire. Clouds appear high in the atmosphere whereas steam and smoke both rise from a source.

Clouds form when pockets of humid air rise in the atmosphere. As the pocket rises, it becomes less dense and the humidity condenses into small water drops that form the appearance of the clouds. Clouds disappear when the water droplets return to a vapor. Some cloud modeling techniques use temperature gradients to define surface locations between the warm humid air and the colder surrounding air. Whereas this can produce a reasonable surface, it does not incorporate the variation in density of the cloud mass.

Steam and smoke are created in a slightly different way. As humid air rises from a hot liquid, steam is produced. As material combusts, smoke is a by-product. The heat of the liquid/fire causes the steam/smoke to rise and during this rise it mixes with the cooler surrounding air, which causes the curls and vortices that can be seen.

Clouds, steam, and smoke are all influenced by winds that blow from the sides. Wind causes clouds to move in the sky and causes steam and smoke to drift upward at an angle. Because wind is typically faster at higher altitudes, this effect is greater the higher the cloud, steam, or smoke is. Wind also causes clouds, steam, and smoke to disperse.

11.5.1 Texture-based clouds

Schpok et al. (Schpok03) use procedural textures to determine the density of clouds. At the high level of this model, a set of implicit surface ellipsoids are specified to set the general position of the clouds. The clouds form within these ellipsoids. The large scale shape of the clouds is changed through the movement and scaling of these ellipsoids. These ellipsoid changes can be used to create cloud motion through the sky through particle system techniques or user defined curves. Alternatively, a key frame process can be used to specify the evolution of ellipsoid positions and sizes.

At the low level of this model, a procedural texture based on the noise function in Chapter 6 is used to determine the opacity within the ellipsoids. The noise function is used to effectively remove parts of the ellipsoid to create the irregular pattern of a cloud. The color of the cloud at discrete locations on slices through the cloud is determined with a coarse noise function. This noise function sets the density of locations in the cloud and is used to accumulate shadows within the cloud.

Figure 11.14 • A cumulus cloud created with a texture-based method (see Color Plate 11.7) Courtesy of David S. Ebert, © 1997 David S. Ebert

The colors from this process are then modulated by finer noise functions to get the final result.

Schpok et al. (Schpok03) also discuss the use of both software and graphics API capabilities to improve the speed of the rendering process. In this technique, all high-level stages as well as low-level work through the shadow accumulation are done in user written software. Interpolation of colors between the sampled locations and modulation of these colors by the finer noise functions are done using API shading and texturing routines. A sample of the clouds generated using texture-based techniques is given in Figure 11.14.

• 11.5.2 Cellular automata-based clouds

In the cellular automata-based methods for simulating clouds (Nagel92 and Dobashi00), the space is subdivided into a three-dimensional grid of cells. Each cell has three Boolean values associated with it that represent the presence of humidity, clouds, or a phase change. Values for the next time step are determined by the current values within each cell and values in neighboring cells. The transition rules are given in equations (11.3), where *hum* represents the humidity value, *cld* represents the cloud value, and *phs* represents the phase change value. In these equations, *i, j,* and k represent the cell locations and the t values represent successive time steps in the evolution of the clouds.

$$f(i, j, k) = phs(i + 2, j, k, t_i) \vee phs(i + 1, j, k, t_i) \vee phs(i - 1, j, k, t_i)$$
$$\vee phs(i - 2, j, k, t_i) \vee phs(i, j + 1, k, t_i) \vee phs(i, j - 1, k, t_i)$$
$$\vee phs(i, j - 2, k, t_i) \vee phs(i, j, k + 2, t_i) \vee phs(i, j, k + 1, t_i)$$
$$\vee phs(i, j, k - 1, t_i) \vee phs(i, j, k - 2, t_i) \qquad (11.3)$$
$$hum(i, j, k, t_{i+1}) = hum(i, j, k, t_i) \wedge {\sim}phs(i, j, k, t_i)$$
$$cld(i, j, k, t_{i+1}) = cld(i, j, k, t_i) \vee phs(i, j, k, t_i)$$
$$phs(i, j, k, t_{i+1}) = {\sim}phs(i, j, k, t_i) \wedge hum(i, j, k, t_i) \wedge f(i, j, k)$$

The function f relies on the two neighboring cells in the four horizontal directions along x and z, two neighboring cells below, and one neighboring cell above. Only one cell above is used to model the real world where there is more impact from the side and below than from above.

Cloud extinction is modeled though the specification of probabilities for humidity (p_{hum}), clouds (p_{cld}), and phase changes (p_{phs}). At each time step, a random number is generated and if it is less than or equal to p_{cld}, the cld value is set to 0 causing the cloud at that cell to disappear. The humidity and phase change probabilities allows a cloud to form at this location at some point in the future. Random numbers are also generated for the humidity and phase change and if they are less than the associated probability that value is set. This allows the cloud to reform in a later time step. These three probabilities can be set for each cell. The motion of the clouds can then be controlled by how these probabilities are set and changed over time. These extinction transitions are shown in equations (11.4).

$$cld(i, j, k, t_{i+1}) = cld(i, j, k, t_i) \wedge (rnd > p_{cld}(i, j, k, t_i))$$
$$hum(i, j, k, t_{i+1}) = hum(i, j, k, t_i) \vee (rnd < p_{hum}(i, j, k, t_i)) \qquad (11.4)$$
$$phs(i, j, k, t_{i+1}) = phs(i, j, k, t_i) \vee (rnd < p_{phs}(i, j, k, t_i))$$

Dobashi et al. (Dobashi00) use the contents of these cells to determine the location and density of the clouds. The location and density are used with OpenGL blending and texturing functionality to render scenes that not only include realistic clouds but also shadowing and shafts of sunlight coming through breaks in the clouds. Figure 11.15 shows samples of the clouds that this technique can generate. In the daytime image, diagonal streaks show sunlight streaming through gaps in the clouds. The bright spot on the clouds in the evening image shows the intense highlighting of the clouds as the sun sets.

11.5.3 Texture-based steam and smoke

Ebert et al. (for example, Ebert03 and Ebert90) create a volumetric rendering system for steam and smoke that is based on a volumetric density function. This system uses a volume ray tracer that is a modification of the standard technique described

Figure 11.15 • Cellular automata-based clouds in the daytime and evening (see Color Plate 11.8) Dobashi et al., "A simple, efficient method for realistic animation of clouds," SIGGRAPH 2000, © 2000 ACM, Inc. Reprinted by permission.

in Chapter 8. In volume ray tracing, when a ray strikes a volume such as steam, the ray does not stop but rather proceeds through the volume. At a series of steps through this volume, the ray gathers the density or opacity and the color at each of these steps. The process stops following this ray when it accumulates enough opacity so that nothing further is visible. This can happen either because of the density of the cumulative volume being passed through or because it eventually strikes a surface after passing through the volume.

The color components collected along the ray are influenced by the composition of the steam or smoke as well as illumination and self-shadowing factors. Illumination is calculated by treating the gaseous phenomena as its base particles such as water vapor or combustion by-products. Self-shadowing influences this color by attenuating the light source illumination by the density of the gaseous volume that it also passes through.

The density of the gaseous volume is determined by a turbulence function such as the one discussed in Chapter 6. Because steam or smoke dissipates as it rises, the height from the gaseous source influences the density produced by the turbulence function. Figure 11.16 shows steam produced with this technique.

11.5.4 Computational fluid dynamics-based smoke

The field of computational fluid dynamics concerns the development of simulations for the behavior of water and gases. The computations underlying this research can serve as the basis for the creation of images of these phenomena. An earlier section looked at the simulation of liquids using this research. This section looks at the simulation of smoke.

Foster and Metaxas (Foster97) used the Navier-Stokes equations, which describe the changes in a gas based on convection (movement caused by adjacent particles),

Figure 11.16 • A steaming teacup produced with a texture-based method (see Color Plate 11.9) Courtesy of David S. Ebert, © 1997 David S. Ebert

pressure changes, and drag. An additional factor is also included that simulates buoyancy caused by the rise of hot smoke that is surrounded by cooler gasses. As in the case of the Navier-Stokes equations for fluids, the gaseous calculations are done over a three-dimensional grid of cells. The equations determine changes in pressure and velocity for each of the cell locations. The pressure and velocity values determine how the appearance of the smoke changes over time.

Fedkiw, Stam, and Jensen (Fedkiw01) also use research from computational fluid dynamics using the incompressible Euler equations to model the velocity of the smoke. One problem with these techniques is numerical dissipation, which causes a loss of energy from the system. In this technique, the researchers employ vorticity confinement by identifying locations where vortices occur in the smoke. These vortices can be imagined as having paddle wheels that spin the smoke. Numerical dissipation dampens these paddle wheels so the confinement technique adds energy back at these locations to compensate.

The Euler calculations are also done on a three-dimensional grid. Temperature and density are defined at the center of each of the grid cells and velocity values are defined at the center of the grid faces. Grid cells that contain objects are set with values appropriate for that object. The objects will, therefore, influence the smoke motion in the adjacent cells. The result at each time step is a new density value for each of the grid cells. These densities are the basis for illuminating and rendering the smoke. A result from these calculations is shown in Figure 11.17. This image shows both the billowing smoke and shadowing on the ground plane that is caused by the smoke density.

11.6 Fire

Fire is an interesting phenomenon because of its amorphous and chaotic nature. From the gentle flicker of a candle to the dancing flames of a roaring fire, the appearance of fire is dependent on the material that is burning as well as the environment it is burning in. Combustion can be classified as either a low-speed event as in fire or a high-speed event as in an explosion. This section deals with fire. Research into explosions is left to the reader: (Yngve00 and Neff99) are two models for explosions.

The basic elements of a fire are the solid fuel, the gaseous fuel, and the hot gaseous products. Over time, the temperature of the solid fuel increases until it passes into a gaseous state. The temperature of the gaseous fuel continues to increase until it reaches the ignition temperature. At the ignition temperature, the fuel becomes a hot gaseous product that continues to increase in temperature before eventually cooling. In a typical fire, there is a blue-colored core that is at the surface of the gaseous fuel as it ignites. The hot gaseous products produce the yellowish-

Figure 11.17 • Blowing smoke (see Color Plate 11.10) Fedkiw et al., "Visual simulation of smoke," SIGGRAPH 2001, © 2001 ACM, Inc. Reprinted by permission.

orange color of the flame, which is emitted by the carbon soot produced by the fire as that soot cools.

11.6.1 Particle-based fire

Lamorlette and Foster (Lamorlette02) developed a fire model based on particle motion. In their model, they identify three components to a flame: the persistent flame, the intermittent flame, and the buoyant plume. The persistent flame is the more consistent portion of the flame nearest the fuel source. The intermittent flame is the upper portion of the fire that flickers. The buoyant plume represents portions of hot gaseous products that break off from the main flame and then extinguish.

In this model, a series of particles are emitted at the base of the flame and move in an upward direction. The movement of these particles is influenced by Flow Noise (Perlin01) and environmental factors. The series of particles is used to define a B-spline curve that determines the shape of the flame. The movement of particles at the far end of this curve account for the flickering of the flame. A probability-based calculation determines if a portion of the upper flame becomes a buoyant plume. The creation of a buoyant plume breaks the B-spline curve into parts with the plume eventually extinguishing because particles are no longer added to it from the flame.

The flame is based on rotating normalized profiles based on the scale of the fire being modeled. The fire is rendered volumetrically with the color being determined by the type of fuel, oxidation, and temperature of combustion.

11.6.2 Physically-based fire

Nguyen, Fedkiw, and Jensen (Nguyen02) separate the simulation of fire based on its two parts. The blue core is modeled with an implicit surface and the hot gaseous products are modeled with Euler equations. This work is based on a thin flame model where the fuller look of the flame is due to the expansion of the hot gaseous products. The blue core is basically a cone shape with variations possible based on how quickly the gaseous fuel combusts. If the combustion occurs quickly, the blue core is small and compact. If the combustion occurs more slowly, the blue core becomes larger and the implicit surface becomes more turbulent. One set of Euler equations is used to model this blue core, and thus creates the shape of this implicit surface.

A second set of Euler equations is used to model the movement of elements as they pass from the blue core to the hot gaseous products. These elements expand as they move outward, which results in the fullness of the flame. This second set of equations is coupled with the first for the blue core so that mass and momentum are conserved as elements pass from the core to the flame. A result of this model is the campfire shown in Figure 11.18.

Figure 11.18 • A campfire (see Color Plate 11.11) Nguyen et al., "Physically based modeling and animation of fire," SIGGRAPH 2002, © 2002 ACM, Inc. Reprinted by permission.

11.7 Projects

1) Develop a program that models particle systems and use it to create a fireworks simulation.

2) Create a program that randomly creates and displays a stream network created by the stream convergence and headward growth models.

Advanced Object Modeling—Characters

Whereas the previous chapter looked at advanced techniques for modeling natural phenomena, this chapter considers advanced techniques to model characters whether they are human, animal, or abstract in form. Modeling a character involves issues of shape as well as appearance for cloth, hair, fur, feathers, and skin.

The shape and appearance of cloth is determined by the threads (or yarn) that is used to make the cloth and how those threads are interlocked. These elements influence the stiffness of the fabric, which determines how the fabric drapes. Though light illuminates the fabric, it is the interaction of light with the individual threads that gives the overall appearance of the fabric.

Hair, fur, and feathers have a particular shape and a particular arrangement on the skin. The density of these elements determines how they lie but this will also be influenced by external forces such as gravity and wind. In the case of hair, there is the additional influence of styling.

Overall skin shape is determined by the underlying skeleton and muscles. For the purposes of image generation, it is not necessary to specify that level of detail and so techniques have been developed for the creation of reasonable surface shapes around the skeleton. Illumination models for objects typically consider only what happens at the surface of an object. Using a similar technique for skin creates an unnatural appearance. When light interacts with skin, it reflects off a number of layers of the skin, which creates the unique appearance.

The image in Figure 12.1 shows some of these elements. The overall shape of the dog is determined by the dog's skeleton. The density of the fur for the combination of an undercoat and overcoat determines how the fur lies. In this case, the undercoat is

Figure 12.1 • A golden retriever (see Color Plate 12.1)

white whereas the overcoat is a reddish gold and so both contribute to the overall color and texture of the fur. Additionally, there are some sections of fur that are short and straight (for example, on the face) and other areas that are curlier (for example, near the ears). In this image, a small portion of the dog bed and a cloth drape can be seen in the background. The weight of the dog, the foam in the bed, and the fabric covering all contribute to its shape and appearance.

This chapter looks at additional details for each of these elements of characters as well as some of the techniques that have been developed to model them. As was the case in the previous chapter, these discussions will give an overview of some of the techniques that are used, with more detailed research left to the reader.

12.1 Cloth

People are quite familiar with cloth from everyday interactions with it. But unless someone is heavily into fashion design, he or she doesn't typically think of the wide variety of types of cloth. Because of that wide variety there are a number of considerations when rendering it. Rendering of cloth is important for the fashion and textile industries as well as being an important component in animation sequences that include clothing.

This section can only begin to introduce the ideas behind rendering cloth. It starts with a look at some of the types of cloth and then looks at ways to model woven cloth. The special issues for knit cloth are also introduced. Readers interested in a more in-depth look at rendering cloth are referred to the book on cloth modeling edited by House and Breen (House00) or the article by Ng and Grimsdale (Ng96).

12.1.1 Types of cloth

Very broadly, cloth can be classified as either woven or knit. A woven cloth comprises strands of thread or yarn that run perpendicular to each other. The threads in one direction are called the warp threads and the threads in the other direction are called the weft threads. In the simplest of woven fabrics, the threads alternate going over and under the threads that are perpendicular. Figure 12.2 shows a sample of a plain woven cloth. Differences in woven fabrics are based on the type of thread that is used, the pattern of over and under for the threads, and how tightly the threads are woven. The heavier the threads or the tighter they are woven the stiffer the resulting fabric will be. Twill and satin are two other weaving patterns that alter the strict over/under pattern of a plain weave. Modern looms can weave elaborate patterns into the fabric. Complex patterns or images of objects such as a flower, for example, can be woven into the fabric by properly controlling which vertical threads are above and below each horizontal thread. The difference in the pattern as well as the type of thread influences how light reflects off of a fabric.

In a general sense, knitted or crocheted fabrics are the result of many interlocking loops of yarn or thread. Figure 12.3 shows a simple interlocking of yarn that is a generalization of the underlying structure of knit fabrics. There is much more

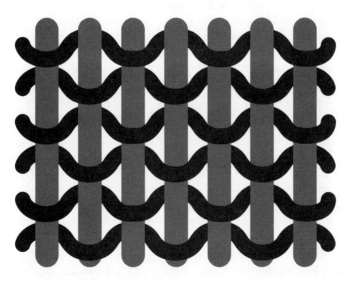

Figure 12.2 • A weaving pattern

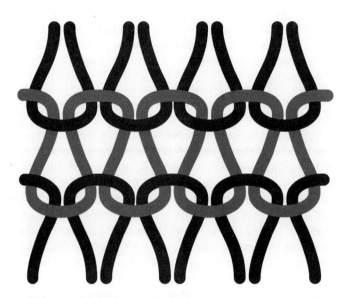

Figure 12.3 • Interlocking loops of knit fabric

"play" in the loops of a knit fabric than there is in the threads of a woven fabric, so knit fabric tends to be stretchy and drapes in a different way than woven fabric. The knitting can be done by hand or by machine. There are many ways to form and interlock these loops, which leads to patterns that can be built into the fabric. The way that the yarn is intertwined determines both the appearance as well as the shape of the fabric. It is also more typical that knitted fabrics are done with heavier yarns, which means that their appearance is also dependent on the look of the yarn itself. Because of this complexity, knit fabrics are only recently being modeled in computer graphics imagery.

12.1.2 Modeling woven cloth

The issue in modeling cloth is not how cloth appears when it is lying flat, but rather how cloth drapes over objects. For example, how would a piece of cloth appear if it was draped over a chair? The discussion in the last section shows this depends on the particulars of how the fabric was created. This is a very complex problem, so this section begins with a highly simplified look at a solution to this situation. Later sections consider more complicated cloth models, efforts to properly model cloth collisions, and woven cloth illumination.

An Early Cloth Model

The first attempt to model cloth using geometrical methods was done by Weil (Weil86). This technique treats the fabric as its individual threads. The fabric is sampled at a set of points along a two-dimensional grid spaced along the horizontal and vertical direction of the fabric. This technique determines the location in the scene's three-dimensional space where each of these points is positioned. It begins by identifying those points of the fabric that are being supported by an object. Those points are fixed by the location of this supporting object. Now these known locations are used with the constraint that the fabric threads lie in a catenary shape (the shape of a rope hanging between two poles) to set the rest of the points on the cloth. Figure 12.4 shows two catenary curves hanging in directions that are perpendicular to each other. This discussion considers the set of fabric points within these fixed locations (for example, the four points at the ends of the curves shown in Figure 12.4) to be interior points and the rest will be considered exterior points.

The stiffness of the fabric can be handled by altering how far apart on the fabric these contact points are located. Fabric that is stiff will have very little drape between the contact points. The stiffer the fabric the straighter it will lie between the contact points. So, a stiffer fabric will have points of contact closer along the distance of the fabric than a limp fabric will have.

Once the contact points are set, a series of triangles are created within the fabric by "connecting" these points. The locations of the points along the triangle boundaries are fixed based on the equations for the catenary curves.[1] If there are more

---

[1] Appendix A gives details on catenary curves.

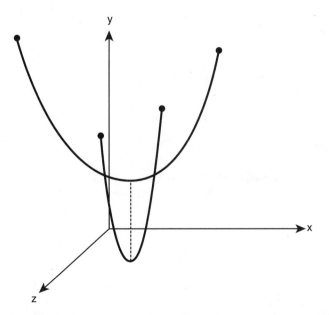

Figure 12.4 • Two crossing catenary curves

than three contact points, there will be cases where the connecting lines will cross. This technique chooses the highest[2] of two crossing curves and discards the other.

The points within the triangles are fixed by repeatedly subdividing each triangle in half. The three catenary curves that connect a vertex with the midpoint of the opposite side are considered, and the highest of the curves is chosen to subdivide the triangle. This process is repeated to fill in all of the interior points on the fabric.

Exterior points on the fabric are handled through a relaxation process. Each of the exterior points is initially placed at negative infinity to simulate the effects of gravity. If the scene has a table or floor that the cloth is assumed to be resting on, that location is chosen as the initial value. Because there are evenly spaced points along the fabric, the distance between adjacent points is known. The technique iterates over the exterior points in the fabric and adjusts their locations so that they are at the proper distance from their neighbors. Adjustments to these points are repeated until the amount of overall change falls below some preset threshold. The issue of fabric stiffness is dealt with in this process by looking at the amount of change along three successive points. With three consecutive points (A, B, and C), if the angle between the lines AB and BC is 180°, the fabric is flat between these points. The smaller this angle is, the more the fabric is bending. If the angle is too small (indicating too much curvature for the stiffness of the fabric), the point locations are adjusted further.

Eventually, the fabric locations are fixed and can be rendered. Depending on the level of detail chosen for the calculations, these points can be used to create small planar patches that can be rendered with any of the techniques discussed in the earlier chapters. Weil's original paper discusses rendering cylinders between each of the points to represent threads within the woven fabric.

Unconstrained Cloth Techniques

Modeling cloth involves complex calculations to determine where the cloth is positioned. Those calculations can result in impossible situations, such as the cloth intersecting with itself. The techniques discussed in this section are called unconstrained because they use simple techniques or applications to try and avoid intersections. The next section will look at more elaborate techniques to deal with cloth/cloth and cloth/object intersections.

Breen et al. (Breen92, House92, and Breen94) present a model for cloth using a particle system. It identifies things that happen to cloth to produce draping and bending where the warp and weft thread directions meet. In this model, a particle is placed at each of these intersections. In these particle systems, the individual particles do not behave independently. Rather, their behavior is determined by a set of energy equations that are in part determined by the position of the neighboring particles.

Specifically, the energy for a particle is a combination of the energy that repels adjacent particles; that stretches the threads; that is due to bending of the fabric;

---

[2]"Higher" is defined relative to the direction of gravitational pull. So, no matter how the world relates to the coordinate systems, if gravity is treated as pulling objects in negative direction of some axis, the higher point will be one that has the larger value.

that is due to shearing of the fabric; and that is due to gravity. All but the last of these are dependent on the location of neighboring particles.

The energy that repels particles is used to keep particles at a minimum distance. This component prevents intersection of the threads and helps to keep the cloth from intersecting itself. The energy from stretching is to prevent the four particles that are adjacent along the thread lines from moving too far away from each other.

The energy from bending is determined by the angles formed by the lines between a particle and its eight nearest neighbors. This energy function decreases as the angles increase. The result is that sharp folds in the cloth are discouraged. Shearing occurs when the two neighboring particles along a thread move in parallel but opposite directions. For a fabric at rest, one of the angles between the warp and weft threads is 90°. As the fabric begins to shear, this angle will decrease. Thus, the shearing energy decreases as this shearing angle decreases.

The final component is the energy due to gravity. This component is simply the product of the mass of the particle, the height of the particle, and the gravitational acceleration constant. The mass for the particle is the mass of the small portion of the fabric that this particle represents. This mass changes depending on the type of cloth that is being simulated.

The modeling of cloth in this method is described as a three-step process that repeats at a series of time steps. The first step calculates changes to the particles as though they are in a free fall influenced only by gravity. This step also deals with particle collisions, and collisions with objects in the world. The second step does an energy minimization calculation to maintain the proper relationship among the particles. The third step corrects the particle velocities due to changes made in the second step.

An interesting component of this research is that the functions that calculate the particle energy can be based on heuristics as was done in the original research, or can be based on measurements of real cloth. Breen et al. (Breen94) specifically discuss the measurement of cloth samples and then the use of those measured results in the calculation of particle energy.

A similar process is used by Baraff and Witkin (Baraff98). In their technique, the cloth is modeled by triangular patches instead of a regular grid of points. Each patch vertex still has a particle associated with it, but where Breen et al. used energy minimization as the basis for particle movement, Baraff and Witkin used an implicit numerical integration method to determine particle movement. This method allows the inclusion of condition equations that control how the cloth moves. Condition equations for stretch, compression, shear, and bending serve the same purpose as the energy calculations in the Breen et al. model. The use of implicit numerical integration allows for larger time steps in the calculation of particle movement, which means there are fewer intermediate positions calculated for the fabric between frames of an animation.

Calculating Cloth Collisions
To be able to model the wrinkling and folding of cloth, it is necessary to deal with cloth/cloth and cloth/object intersections reasonably accurately. This section looks

at two of the techniques that have been used. In the first technique, a history of particle movement is used to keep particles from crossing the boundaries of objects or the cloth itself. In the second technique, parts of the cloth get frozen in place to prevent intersections and also to prevent secondary wiggling due to artifacts in the numerical integration process.

Bridson et al. (Bridson02 and Bridson03) use the velocities of particles in their model of cloth. The location of the cloth is then determined from these particle velocities. By working directly with the particle velocities, they prevent cloth intersections by making sure that the particle velocities do not result in the cloth passing through itself or another object. Thus, this process works based on the history of the cloth—if the cloth does not intersect something, and checks of the velocity prevent the cloth from crossing an object, the cloth will never intersect anything else. To improve the appearance of the resulting cloth, Bridson et al. also limit strain in the cloth by adjusting the velocities so that the distance between two particles does not increase by more than 10 percent of the original length at any time. The value of 10 percent comes from a rule of thumb in computational mechanics. This model also incorporates static and kinetic friction. These two kinds of friction will either stop a moving cloth that is rubbing another object (kinetic friction) or will prevent a cloth from moving because of contact with another object (static friction). Figure 12.5 shows two samples of cloth that are produced by this method.

Baraff et al. (Baraff03) deal with the issue of collisions in a different way. They recognize that even though real objects never interpenetrate, created objects can. They specifically mention that when animated characters move, one part of their body can interpenetrate another. These are typically not noticeable because it will appear that the two surfaces have deformed as the area in question is not visible. For example, when a character squats down its thigh and calf can interpenetrate, but it will appear that they have just squashed together. Baraff et al. solved this problem, and the problem of object and cloth friction, through a technique that they call flypapering. In flypapering, particles at the corners of triangular patches in the fabric can be stuck at a particular place in space or stuck to another object. For the example of the squatting character, the pant legs between the thighs and calves are flypapered to a point in the middle of the overlapped area, which effectively simulates the cloth being in the location of the squashing that occurs in a real person.

Weights can also be applied to the influence of each surface on a particle. If the weight of one surface is close to 100 percent and another surface rubs against the cloth, the cloth will only move a small amount. For example, clothing stays with a person sliding on the floor instead of the clothes sticking to the floor. As this percentage is decreased, the cloth movement will increase. Thus, visual feedback as to the vigorousness of the rubbing can be given through the use of these weights.

The work of Baraff et al. includes a global intersection analysis step that determines where the cloth intersects itself or another object and also determines a process for untangling the cloth. This step is necessary because during the calculations to flypaper the cloth between two objects, the cloth can intersect itself. When the cloth is no longer pinched between two objects, the global intersection analysis

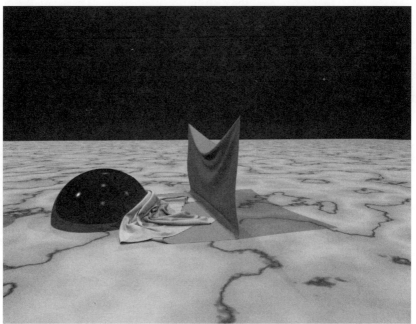

Figure 12.5 • Two simulations of cloth showing bending and draping (see Color Plate 12.2) Courtesy of Robert Bridson © 2004 Robert Bridson

determines that the cloth has self-intersected (or intersected one of the objects) and also determines how to alter the cloth positions so as to remove the intersection.

Woven Cloth Illumination

The weaving pattern can have a number of influences on the appearance of woven fabric. The same threads can be used to create cloth using a plain, twill, or satin weave pattern and each of those cloths reflect light in a different way. More complex weave patterns create a texture on the cloth that also influences the appearance, as does the color combination of threads.

Adabala et al. (Adabala03) created a method to render woven cloth that incorporates these parameters. Their illumination model starts with a Weaving Information File (WIF), which is the textile industry standard for describing how cloth should be woven. This file gives details on the threads including their color, how they should be inserted into the loom, and which warp threads should be raised for each pass of the weft thread. This information is used by Adabala et al. to create a digital version of the weave pattern.

The composition of the threads and how tightly they are wound influences how the weaving pattern appears. This system uses the weaving pattern and thread information to develop a texture for the appearance of the pattern. This texture includes shadowing within the threads as well as in the areas between the threads.

The last component is a bidirectional reflectance distribution function (BRDF) that is based on the distribution of microfacets based on the positioning of the warp and weft threads. It is this BRDF that accounts for the difference in shininess of plain, twill, and satin cloth. Producing a cloth image begins with one of the earlier techniques for cloth positioning and then this model combines the texture and BRDF information to create the proper illumination.

12.1.3 Modeling knit cloth

Most of the work in cloth modeling has been for woven cloth. The stretchiness of knit cloth is one of its unique characteristics, and that can be handled in the woven cloth models through the stretch conditions. There are still rendering issues unique to knit cloth, as it has clearly visible yarn that greatly influences the appearance of the cloth. This section looks at one model for knit cloth.

Knit Cloth Structure

The first influence on the appearance of knit fabric is the way that the yarn is looped together. Simple loop patterns such as the one shown in Figure 12.3 produce a relatively flat fabric, but much more elaborate looping is also possible. When these fabrics are at rest, the looping yarn determines the general shape of the cloth. When a knit fabric is stretched around an object, these loops will deform, changing the appearance and shape of the fabric.

Zhong et al. (Zhong01) present a method to model both the macro and micro structure of knit fabric. This technique models the overall shape of the fabric through a knitwear skeleton that is a parametric surface on which the fabric is created. For a simple stitch pattern, the skeleton is divided into a regular grid and each cell of the grid is the location of one of the stitches. The corners of the grid cell are used to identify six key points on the loop of yarn for that cell. The key points for adjacent cells are then tied together and variations are added to account for the three-dimensional nature of the yarn and over/under pattern in the loops. The key points are used to create a series of spline curves that trace the path of the yarn. Complex stitches have more elaborate looping of the yarn and can involve multiple grid cells.

The knit cloth is stretched around an object by deforming the knitwear skeleton into the proper shape. The process of deforming the skeleton moves the locations of the grid cell corners, which then move the key points for the loops. Because a grid cell corner influences the four loops in the adjoining cells, the interlocking pattern of the yarn loops is preserved and all of the loops deform in the direction of the grid cell corner movements.

Knit Cloth Rendering

The second influence on the appearance of knit cloth is the yarn. Yarn typically has four plies, which means that it has four "sub-threads" in a spiral along its length. Depending on the material used to make the yarn and how it is constructed, yarn can have varying degrees of fuzz/fluff and density. The fuzziness and density of yarn influence how light reflects off the yarn and how light penetrates the yarn.

Xu et al. (Xu01) developed a technique they called the lumislice to efficiently incorporate the qualities of yarn in the rendering process. In this technique, a cross-section of the yarn is created, which indicates the density of the yarn and distribution of the fluff. This cross-section is rotated along the path of the yarn to create the yarn itself in the same way that the swept surfaces discussed in Chapter 4 are created.

The lumislice is a cross-section of the created yarn that is used to pre-compute the illumination of the yarn. The lumislice is subdivided into a collection of cells and each cell has an array of reflectance values. The reflectance value depends on the view and light directions. Each of these directions is specified by two angles: a rotation around the path of the yarn and the angle away from this path direction. These four angles are used as indexes into the reflection array, and the array contains the reflectance value for that particular spatial orientation.

In rendering the knit fabric, the lumislice is rotated along the path of the yarn and the current view and light directions are indexes into the reflectance array to determine how to render various points on the fabric. The rendering reduces to an array lookup instead of repeatedly recalculating the reflectance. There is still one more critical component of a realistic rendering of knitwear—shadows.

Shadow maps were discussed in Chapter 7, and Xu et al. extended this concept to create rough shadows for their knitwear rendering. In their extension, they project the path of the yarn into a special shadow map. When the yarn is being rendered, the object shadow map is first checked to see if an external object is casting a shadow. If not, the yarn shadow map is checked. In this case, the density of any other yarn that might be casting a shadow is used to attenuate the illumination.

Figure 12.6 • Knitting pattern examples created with the lumislice (see Color Plate 12.3) Xu et al., "Photorealistic rendering of knitwear using the lumislice," SIGGRAPH 2001, © 2001 ACM, Inc. Reprinted by permission.

The results of this knitwear research can be seen in Figure 12.6. This figure shows a variety of complex knit patterns that can be modeled. Additionally, these images show the yarn shadowing effects. This is most noticeable along the left side of the figure-eight pattern in the third image.

12.2 Hair and Fur

Hair and fur provide a real challenge in part due to the volume of individual elements. For example, a human head can have between 50,000 and 100,000 hair fibers. Each of these hair fibers has the ability to travel in many different directions and interact with other hair fibers in the area. The individual fibers can be straight, wavy, or curly. Their placement can be altered by combing or by the wind, and their shape can be changed by hair styling. There is an overall appearance to hair as a whole that is dependent on these individual hair fibers but also the placement of the fibers on the scalp. A person's hair has an overall color, but individual hair fibers vary in color.

All of these possibilities lead to a staggering level of complexity for hair and fur. Many commercially available modeling programs include hair and fur capabilities. Additionally, there are programs that specifically deal with the modeling of hair and fur. The following sections will look at some of the techniques used to model the shape, placement, and rendering of hair and fur.

12.2.1 Fur

Kajiya and Kay (Kajiya89) developed an early model for fur that relied on a three-dimensional texture. They created a texture within a cube that they called a texel, which represents a collection of straight fur/hair fibers with a variation in height and color. The fibers in the texel are placed in a Poisson-disk pattern, which can be quickly described as a random distribution where no two locations are closer than some set value. This texture element was rendered through a ray tracing technique that used the density of the fur and the direction of the light source to compute values in the texel. These texel values incorporate both the illumination and the shadowing of the fibers. The texel is "placed" on planar patches that define the object surface that needs fur. Gaps between the texel placements because of patch orientations are removed by joining the outer corners of adjacent texels. These join points are also deformed to create a more natural appearance. This paper by Kajiya and Kay included two very realistic teddy bear images created with their technique.

Goldman (Goldman97) presented a technique to create "fake fur." This model is used for applications where the fine details of the fur will not be visible. The overall impact of the fur will be seen only in the way that a creature is illuminated. The model is used to render creatures that are added to live-action film and so limitations can be placed on lighting to ignore possibilities that are not common in live-action settings. The method begins by calculating a "mean hair geometry" within a sample region of the area to be rendered. The mean hair geometry is used to calculate the illumination and shadowing for the region. The illumination and shadowing includes the impact that the hair has on both the underlying skin as well as other hairs. Images in Goldman's paper show the result of using this technique to model Dalmatians for a feature film.

12.2.2 Hair

An early attempt at modeling hair was proposed by Anjyo, Usami, and Kurihara (Anjyo92). In their model, hairs are modeled by a cantilever beam that bends when the force of gravity was applied. Each hair is treated as a series of segments and bending of the hair occurs at the join points between the segments. Additional forces can also be applied in this system, and those are used to model situations such as hair being blown in the wind. For rendering, each hair is treated as a cylinder and an anisotropic reflection model is used. Due to the use of a cantilever beam for hair, the Anjyo et al. hair model is limited to straight hair.

Watanabe and Suenaga (Watanabe92) proposed a similar model for hair, but segments of the hair fibers are represented by three-sided prisms instead of cylinders. Control over the shape of the hairstyle is handled not on an individual hair basis, but rather on wisps or groups of hair fibers. They have a set of parameters that can be independently set for each wisp. The parameters include the bend, thickness, color, length, density, and color controls. Another component of this technique is the ability to model the shine or glow of hair that is lit from behind. To accomplish this, they keep two z-buffers with the distance to the closest and farthest points in the scene. In areas where there is a small difference between the two buffer values, the objects are not very thick. If that area is the location of hair, back-lighting is added to the illumination calculation to produce these additional highlights.

Kim and Neumann (Kim00) proposed a model of hair based on a thin shell. The first step is to define the shape of the hair with parametric surfaces. The normal to the surface is used as a displacement direction to create surfaces with some thickness. The surfaces are then warped into a rectilinear shape, which is subdivided into a three-dimensional grid. Straight hair fibers are evenly distributed through this grid and particles are placed along each hair. At this point, they now virtually comb the hair by dragging a tooth of a comb through the grid space. As the tooth moves through, it moves the particles. After this has been done some number of times, the particles are used to determine the final curved path of each hair fiber. The rectilinear shape is then warped in the reverse direction to return the hair to the original shape on the head.

Kim and Neumann (Kim02) proposed a second model of hair based on a hierarchy of hair clusters that they called the Multiresolution Hair Model. In this model, a number of strands of hair are distributed across the scalp. Those strands are organized into hair clusters. Each hair cluster can be subdivided into smaller clusters of hair, which creates the hierarchy. The smallest clusters are then composed of a collection of hair strands, each of which is defined by a curve. Transformations can be applied to any of the cylinders in the hierarchy and those transformations can also be duplicated for other clusters. For example, to create a twist of hair, a small cluster can have a rotation applied along the cluster. That rotation can be copied to all of the siblings of this cluster so that they also twist on themselves. Copying this rotation up one level causes the individual twists to wrap around themselves. The effect of this is seen in the twisted hair shown in Figure 12.7. There is a wide range

Figure 12.7 • Different generated hair styles (see Color Plate 12.4) Kim and Neumann, "Interactive multiresolution hair modeling and editing," SIGGRAPH 2002, © 2002 ACM, Inc. Reprinted by permission.

Figure 12.8 • Different generated hair styles (see Color Plate 12.5) Kim and Neumann, "Interactive multiresolution hair modeling and editing," SIGGRAPH 2002, © 2002 ACM, Inc. Reprinted by permission.

of hair styles that can be generated by this method. A few of the possibilities are shown in Figure 12.8.

Bertails et al. (Bertails03) expand the Multiresolution Hair Model by adding an adaptive wisp tree. This tree is used to control changes in the hair clusters for the purpose of animation. For example, the adaptive wisp tree will make changes to the hair clusters to animate hair separating as it moves. Bertails et al. report that their system efficiently models the clustering behavior that occurs in long hair as it moves.

12.2.3 Illumination of hair

Once the positioning of hair has been determined, many groups render hair using a cylinder for each hair. However, the surface of hair is not smooth, but rather has a scaly surface as shown in Figure 12.9. The scales alter the way that light reflects off the hair surface. Additionally, hair is translucent, especially light colored hair such as white, gray, or blond hair.

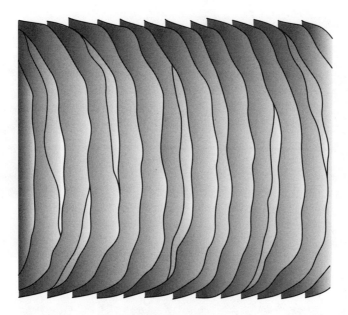

Figure 12.9 • The scaly surface of hair

Marschner et al. (Marschner03) account for these characteristics of hair. In their study of hair's light scattering, they first considered the plane with a normal vector that points in the direction of the hair's path. In that plane, a primary specular highlight appears in every direction around the hair and a secondary highlight appears only on the side of the hair closest to the light source. There are two additional highlights that occur in a direction off of this plane as well. Because hair is not perfectly cylindrical the highlights, especially the secondary highlight, vary based on direction. Additionally, the scales cause the reflection and refraction directions to be different from those of a true cylinder.

Figure 12.10 shows three hair images. The first image was rendered using the illumination methods described by Kajiya and Kay (Kajiya89). The second image was rendered using the illumination methods described by Marschner et al. The final image is an actual photograph of the hair being modeled in the first two images.

12.3 Feathers

A feather has a central shaft or rachis and a set of barbs that branch off from that shaft (Figure 12.11). The barbs have a secondary layer of branching with the barbules that come off the barbs. The barbules have cilium on their ends that allow adjacent barbs to interlock. If all of these parts are properly interlocked, the feather shows a typical shape. If the cilia become separated, gaps appear in the feather. These gaps are not permanent. When a bird preens, it runs its feathers through its

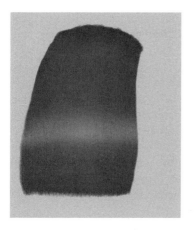

Figure 12.10 • The first image is rendered using the Kajiya illumination techniques, the second image is rendered using the illumination techniques in the Marschner study, and the last image is a photograph of hair (see Color Plate 12.6) Marschner et al., "Light scattering from human hair fibers," SIGGRAPH 2003, © 2003 ACM, Inc. Reprinted by permission.

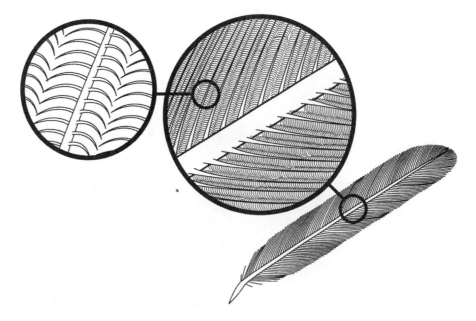

Figure 12.11 • The feather center shaft supports side barbs with barbules that keep the barbs together

beak causing the cilia to reattach and thus, the gaps are removed. Within this general description there are a number of specific types of feathers, each with their own shape and function. Additional details on birds and their feathers can be found in ornithological sources such as Perrins (Perrins03).

Chen et al. (Chen02) recognized that the feathers exhibit a branching pattern much as plants do, and applied L-systems to the modeling of feathers. They developed the following L-system to create a feather. The axiom creates the beginning of the rachis or shaft. The first rule extends the shaft while adding two barbs on either side. The value of N in this rule controls the length of the feather. The last two rules extend the lengths of the barbs, with the values of M_L and M_R controlling their length. The shape of the shaft, the barbs, and the outline of the feather are specified by curves that can be used to create even more variation in the types of feathers that can be generated.

```
Axiom: R(0)
R(i) : i < N → [B_L(i, 0)][B_R(i, 0)]R(i + 1)
B_L(i, j) : j < M_L → B_L(i, j + 1)
B_R(i, j) : j < M_R → B_R(i, j + 1)
```

External forces are also added to this simple L-system to cause the gaps in the feather. Attributes of a total force on the left and on the right are carried along the shaft as it grows. Each application of the first rule adds the left and right force values to these two attributes. When the attribute value exceeds some threshold, a gap is introduced on that side of the feather and that attribute value is set back to zero. The amount of the rotation for the gap is randomly determined so that there is variation among the gaps. Figure 12.12 shows a collection of feathers produced by this method.

Figure 12.12 • Sample feathers created with L-systems Chen, et al., "Modeling and rendering of realistic feathers," SIGGRAPH 2002, © 2002 ACM, Inc. Reprinted by permission.

Feathers on the wings of a bird that can fly have an asymmetric shape with the leading edge of the feather being narrower than the trailing edge.[3] The longer wing feathers are called "primaries" toward the end of the wing, and "secondaries" toward the body. Birds typically have between nine and 11 primary feathers, and between six and 24 secondary feathers. There are additional shorter covert feathers on the wing that fill in the rest of the wing. Birds typically have between eight and 24 tail feathers. There are also contour feathers that cover a bird's body. In the work of Chen et al., the user specifies a small subset of example feathers that the system uses to cover the bird. Their system uses the underlying surface polygons of the bird's skin to place feathers on the bird. The system also alters the growing direction of the feathers so that they do not interpenetrate each other or the skin of the bird.

The rendering of the feathers is done using a bidirectional texture function (Dana99) that is based on the structure of the shaft, barbs, and barbules. A bidirectional texture function (BTF) is analogous to the BRDF. Where the BRDF is used when surface variations are on a microscopic scale, the BTF is used when variations are of a larger scale. In the case of a feather, the pattern or texture of the barb and barbules form just such a surface. Thus, the BTF for a feather allows for the proper rendering of each feather. A result of this technique is shown in the eagle in Figure 12.13.

Figure 12.13 • An eagle showing the placement of feathers (see Color Plate 12.7) Chen, et al., "Modeling and rendering of realistic feathers," SIGGRAPH 2002, © 2002 ACM, Inc. Reprinted by permission.

---

[3]Flightless birds have symmetric feathers.

12.4 Skin

Skin provides an interesting challenge because it is soft, and light penetrates the outer layers. Special techniques are necessary to create a natural look that is dependent on this penetration of light. The softness of skin also requires special modeling techniques that account for the relationship between skeleton and skin positions. This section will deal with the issues of skin rendering and shape.

12.4.1 Rendering

Hanrahan and Krueger (Hanrahan93) presented an early rendering of surfaces including skin that use a subsurface scattering mechanism. Their work is based on research into skin optics done as part of biomedical research. Skin has an epidermal and dermal layer. The outer epidermal layer includes pigments and the inner dermal layer includes blood vessels. When skin is illuminated, some of the light passes into the epidermal and dermal layers and is influenced by pigment and blood as it is scattered before exiting the skin (Figure 12.14). The surface of skin also has a thin layer of oil that causes specular reflections.

Marschner et al. (Marschner99) developed a mechanism for measuring reflectance off objects using a digital camera, a flash, and a scanner to measure objects with an irregular shape. This equipment results in reflectance measurements much like a goniometer does, but this setup makes it also possible to measure a wider range of materials including human skin. Debevec et al. (Debevec00) also present an apparatus for the measurement of reflectance from skin. This research used a "light stage" that is the equivalent of a large scale goniometer. The reflectance values acquired through either of these two methods are then used to render faces. Even though both of these research groups recognize that the appear-

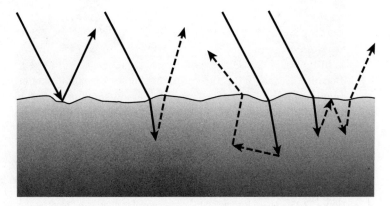

Figure 12.14 • Subsurface scattering in the epidermal and dermal layers of skin

Figure 12.15 • Using measured skin values, the image on the left shows skin rendered with a BRDF model and the image on the right shows skin rendered with a BSSRDF model (see Color Plate 12.8) Jensen et al., "A practical model for subsurface light transport," SIGGRAPH 2001, © 2001 ACM, Inc. Reprinted by permission.

ance of skin is influenced by subsurface scattering, it is not directly included in their rendering methods. Rather, by measuring skin they capture the results of sub-surface scattering and use the measured reflectance for rendering.

Jensen et al. (Jensen01) developed a bidirectional surface scattering reflectance distribution function (BSSRDF). The use of a BSSRDF is necessary to get a realistic rendering of translucent materials such as skin, but also includes foods (milk, bread, cheese, and fruits), plants, fish, and marble. When light illuminates a translucent material, some portion of the light enters the surface, reflects once and leaves the material. This is a single scattering. Some of the light will be scattered multiple times in the object before leaving. This results in a diffuse distribution of the light as it leaves the object. The BSSRDF is a sum of the diffuse term and the single scattering term. Jensen et al. approximate the diffuse term with a dipole light source. A dipole light source replaces the incoming light ray with one light source below the surface of the object at the point where the ray intersects. A second light source is placed above the surface intersection point. The diffuse reflection is deter-mined from this dipole source and Fresnel terms for the incoming light direction and the outgoing radiance direction. Single scattering is calculated using Monte Carlo integration along the direction of the refracted ray. Figure 12.15 shows a com-parison between a BRDF model and a BSSRDF model. Jensen et al. point out that skin typically exhibits a great deal of scattering—often more than 100 per photon. Because of this, the diffuse term dominates the single scattering term for skin. The two images in Figure 12.15 were rendered using the same skin parameters. The first image rendered with a BRDF model has a harder appearance. The image rendered with the BSSRDF model has a softer appearance and color bleeding leads to softer shadows, for example, around the nose.

12.4.2 Shape modeling

The BSSRDF rendering model produces a soft appearance for skin, which is logical because skin is soft. The modeling techniques in the early chapters of this book assumed that objects are hard, thus a different model is necessary for soft objects. These techniques are especially needed when these soft objects are animated. The rest of this section will look at a few of the techniques that can be used to model the shape of skin.

Implicit Surfaces

A unit circle can be specified by the parametric equations (12.1), where the parameter value is in the range $[0, 2\pi]$.

$$S_x(t) = \cos(t)$$
$$S_y(t) = \sin(t) \tag{12.1}$$

The unit circle can also be specified by equation (12.2), where values of x and y that satisfy the equation are on the circle.

$$x^2 + y^2 = 1 \tag{12.2}$$

The equations (12.1) explicitly gives the x and y values of points on the circle. Equation (12.2) does not explicitly give the values for x and y but instead gives the conditions for a point to be on the circle, which implicitly specifies the x and y values.

The implicit equation for a sphere of radius r centered at the origin is given by the function in equation (12.3).

$$f(x, y, z) = x^2 + y^2 + z^2 - r^2 \tag{12.3}$$

The function evaluates to a negative number for points inside the sphere, 0 for points on the surface of the sphere, and a positive number for points outside the sphere. A more complex surface can be created by combining two spheres as in equation (12.4).

$$(x_1^2 + y_1^2 + z_1^2 - r_1^2) * (x_2^2 + y_2^2 + z_2^2 - r_2^2) \tag{12.4}$$

Equation (12.4) evaluates to a negative number at any points that are in just one sphere. It evaluates to a positive number at any points that are either inside or outside of both spheres. It will only evaluate to 0 on the surface of either sphere. The sphere serves as the basis for implicit functions in this section. In these cases, the locations for implicit surfaces are determined relative to the centers of a collection of spheres.

Blinn (Blinn82) used implicit surfaces to create images of blobby molecules. In this application, the density function for an atom with its center at (x_c, y_c, z_c) is given by equations (12.5), where d is the distance to the center of the atom, R is the radius of the atom, and B is blobbiness of the atom.

$$D(x, y, z) = e^{\left(B/R^2\right)*r - B} \tag{12.5}$$

The summation of densities in equation (12.6) gives the density for the entire molecule, where the ith atom is located at (x_i, y_i, z_i).

$$D(x, y, z) = \sum_i e^{\left(B_i/R_i^2\right)*r_i - B_i}. \tag{12.6}$$

The implicit function for the molecule is now defined by subtracting a threshold value (typically 1.0) from the total density. The threshold value determines where the implicit surface will lie in the space.

Using the terminology of parametric surfaces in Chapter 4, the centers of the atoms are essentially control points and the density function is effectively a blending function. As in the case of parametric surfaces, other researchers have developed different blending functions. Nishimura et al. (Nishimura85) used piecewise quadratic blending functions to produce what are called "meta-balls." Wyvill et al. (Wyvill86) used the sixth degree blending polynomial to create what are called "soft objects." Equation (12.7) shows this sixth degree polynomial, where d is the distance from the current point to the center of the sphere, and R is the radius of the sphere (called the radius of influence by Wyvill et al.).

$$B(d) = 1 - \frac{4}{9} * \frac{d^6}{R^6} + \frac{17}{9} * \frac{d^4}{R^4} - \frac{22}{9} * \frac{d^2}{R^2} \tag{12.7}$$

This equation evaluates to one at the center of the sphere and 0 at the radius of influence. Because Wyvill et al. do not allow points to have influence outside of their radius, negative values that occur when the distance is greater than R are never used. The field value for a location in space is the summation of equation (12.7) for each distance that falls within the radius of influence. The location of the implicit surface occurs at some threshold for this field value.

Because the field values are never negative, an interesting effect can be created by placing objects in the space that have negative field values. If an object is placed in the field that has a negative value, it can create dents in the implicit surface. Additionally, if a negative valued plane with a hole is moved through the field, objects will deform their shape so as to appear to squeeze through the hole.

Implicit surfaces can be used to model the shape of skin. Control points are placed along the skeleton of the figure and their radius of influence is used to determine the overall shape. In small areas such as the fingers, the radius of influence is smaller than in larger areas such as the arms, thighs, or torso. The tapering in a finger is handled by increasing radii of influence along the length of the finger. The radii also increase at knuckle joints. In a complex figure, there could easily be many thousand control points. Additional details on implicit surfaces and their applications can be found in Bloomenthal et al. (Bloomenthal97).

Shape Deformation

In the discussion of animating articulated figures, the capability of commercially available animation systems to control skins on figure skeletons was mentioned. In these systems, an artist creates a figure skeleton and places surfaces on the skeleton for the skin. These skin patches are associated with skeleton elements so that changes to the skeleton positions automatically change the associated skin. There are problems with these systems, most notably the skin collapsing at joints. For example, if the hand turns a doorknob, when the rotation reaches 180° the wrist will collapse to a point, much as a twisted paper tube will. Also, when a knee or elbow joint bends, the deformation of the skin in that area folds in an unnatural way. These items can be corrected by the artist adding additional controls to the skeleton that prevent or avoid these problems. Whereas this fine-tuning can be acceptable for animation applications, a more robust system is needed for dynamic systems such as computer games.

Systems have been developed that take sample poses of the character and use data extracted from those poses to generate new figure positions. One of these techniques is called Pose Space Deformation (Lewis00). In this technique, the artist creates a number of poses for the character that are then saved along with information about figure control vertices that have moved. The system then uses the changes among the poses to synthesize new positions for the figure.

Mohr and Gleicher (Mohr03) have developed a system that is also based on multiple poses for the character. In this system, poses that fully exercise each of the joints are sampled and the result is a pairing of skeleton and surface vertex movements. In this process new joints are automatically added to deal with skin collapses. Mohr and Gleicher acknowledge that compared to their own system, systems such as Pose Space Deformation do better with skin deformations based on abstract parameters. But they also state that theirs is better for interactive applications because it is based on a smaller collection of data. Figure 12.16 shows five-

Figure 12.16 • Automatically generated poses showing skin shape deformations (see Color Plate 12.9) Mohr and Gleicher, "Building efficient, accurate character skins from examples," SIGGRAPH 2003, © 2003 ACM, Inc. Reprinted by permission.

system generated positions for a figure from an animation sequence based on an example set of poses.

12.5 Projects

Do additional research on the particle method for cloth simulation, and then develop a program to model the drape of cloth over a cube.

Graphics Math

This appendix reviews mathematical content that is assumed through the text along with some additional topics of interest to people in computer graphics. It is not intended to be a complete review of the math needed for computer graphics as there are other resources available that specifically deal with mathematical issues for graphics. Additional details on these topics as well as other important mathematical concepts can be found in books such as (Lengyel02), (Rogers90), (Schneider03), and (VanVerth04).

A.1 Computer Math Versus Real Math

There is a distinct difference between a mathematical derivation that is done on paper and its implementation on the computer. The difference is not just one of media or of how things are represented, but concerns implementation on a computer. The issue is that a precise real number that can be calculated on paper will in most cases only be approximated on the computer. The amount that the approximation is off will vary based on how much storage space is allocated to the number, but it will still not be exact. For example, some languages have real number data types, in order of increasing precision, of float, double, and quad. It is the case that a quad will be more precise than a float, but the problems still exist with quads.

Consider a set of three real numbers called r, s, and t. When stored on the computer they will have slightly different values of R, S, and T. This difference is sometimes called round-off error because the additional precision in r, s, and t that the computer cannot handle is truncated or rounded-off to get the values R, S, and T. The specific amount of round-off error depends on the type that is used to store the value (i.e., float, double, or quad) and how the computer or language implements that type. The goal here is to identify the problems that can occur so that the appropriate allowances are made when theoretical algorithms are implemented.

Elementary algebra shows that addition and multiplication of real numbers are commutative and associative. This means that $r + s + t = s + t + r = (r + s) + t = r + (s + t)$ and so on. The same is true of multiplication. No matter how these three numbers are added or multiplied, the same answer always results. With addition and multiplication on the computer, the problem of round-off error in storing the numbers becomes compounded. If computer addition is represented by the symbol $\oplus$ and multiplication by the symbol $\otimes$, it will not always be the case that $(R \oplus S) \oplus T$ will be equal to $R \oplus (S \oplus T)$ or that $(R \otimes S) \otimes T$ will be equal to $R \otimes (S \otimes T)$. Consider the case of multiplication. If R and S are extremely small values, multiplying them together can produce a number so small that the computer can only represent it as 0. Then the multiplication by T will also produce a result of 0 no matter what the value of T. If T has an extremely large value—perhaps even $1/S$, and S and T are multiplied together first—the result will be close to 1, making the entire result close to R. Two different orders for the multiplications produce two different results.

This also becomes a problem when doing comparison of real numbers. A mathematical derivation of some property can show a need to handle a special case if two numbers (a and b) are equal. Perhaps the algorithm needs to divide by their difference, so if they are equal, this will be a "divide by 0" error. It is possible that on a computer the values of A and B might be very close to each other but not actually equal. If an equality check is used in the computer program that compared A and B, it will fail and the division will be done. The calculations will proceed as though there was nothing wrong, even though the result would be an extremely large number. As the program continued, it would use this large number and the problems would wind up growing. The solution to this is to not do pure equality checks with real numbers on a computer. One solution is to do checks to see if numbers are extremely close instead of exactly equal. In the previous example, the difference between A and B can be compared with some very small threshold and if it is below that threshold, the two values are considered to be equal for the purpose of the calculation. The value of that threshold will be based on the desired precision of the algorithm and the precision used to store A and B.

A.2   IEEE Floating Point Properties

The Institute of Electrical and Electronics Engineers (IEEE) has a standard for floating point numbers that specifies the format to use when storing floating point numbers on a computer. The details of how that is done are not critical here. What is important are the special values that are added by this standard, because they can be encountered in graphics programming. In some cases, relying on the properties of these special values can lead to more efficient algorithms because some condition checks can be eliminated.

The standard adds a positive and negative infinity, represented as *Inf* and *–Inf*. Positive infinity results from dividing a positive number by 0, and negative infinity results from dividing a negative number by 0. The standard also adds a special value called "not a number," represented as *NaN*. Not a number results from taking the square root of a negative number or dividing 0 by 0. Lastly, the standard has both a positive and negative 0. Even though the standard defines +0 = −0, when they are used in calculations these two 0s can produce different results.

There is also a set of properties for each of these three values:

$+x / 0 = Inf$	$-x / -Inf = +0$	$Inf - Inf = NaN$	$Inf / 0 = NaN$
$-x / 0 = -Inf$	$+x / -Inf = -0$	$Inf * Inf = Inf$	$Inf * 0 = NaN$
$0 / 0 = NaN$	$-x / Inf = -0$	$Inf / Inf = NaN$	$x \% 0 = NaN$
$+x / Inf = +0$	$Inf + Inf = Inf$	$Inf / x = Inf$	$Inf \% x = NaN$

If *NaN* is used in any calculation, the result is always *NaN*. When used in Boolean expressions, *Inf* is greater than all finite numbers, $-Inf$ is less than all finite numbers, $-Inf$ is less than *Inf*, and any expression containing *NaN* is false. These Boolean rules mean that checks to trap conditions that lead to bad results might be able to be eliminated. An example of this is shown in Chapter 8 for intersection calculations with a box.

A.3   Calculation Speedup

The calculations necessary to do advanced modeling and rendering in computer graphics are so complex that there are frequently efforts to speedup the calculations as much as possible. This section will address a few examples of things that can be done to model objects and render scenes more quickly.

The calculation of trigonometric functions on computers is typically done with power series. This means that each call to the sine or cosine function involves a number of multiplications and divisions. A faster alternative is to calculate a table of sine and cosine values for perhaps 1,000 values. Then instead of calling the sine and cosine functions, the value is looked up in the proper table. The closest table value can be returned as the result or, for even better results, a value can be interpolated between the two closest table values. Using a table lookup can be as much as 25 times faster than using the sine and cosine functions directly.

A similar table technique can be used instead of calling the random number generator each time. In this case, the table alternative merely returns successive numbers from the table. When it reaches the end of the table, it just goes back to the first value. If the application is highly complex, the use of a table with just a few hundred numbers is not likely to be visibly different from calling the random number generator each time. Using a random number table can be as much as four times faster than calling the random number generator each time.

The calculation of the length requires a square root. If the calculation of a length is being done for the sake of comparison with another length, the square roots can be saved by doing the comparison between the squares of the lengths. This can be a considerable savings because the square root calculation is computationally expensive.

Another speedup is possible if single-precision floating point numbers are used instead of double-precision numbers. In some cases, single-precision calculations are hardware accelerated where double-precision calculations are done in software. Though the result is of lower precision, there can be a noticeable time speedup. This can be computer dependent as some computers can have double precision calculations hardware accelerated.

A.4   Interpolation

Linear interpolation between two points, P_0 and P_1, can be accomplished with the equation (A.1) where the value of t is in the range [0, 1].

$$C(t) = P_0 + t * (P_1 - P_0) \tag{A.1}$$

If even increments are chosen for the values of t, the resulting points will be evenly spaced along the line from P_0 to P_1.

Linear interpolation can also be used to calculate the range of values of some attribute that changes along the length of that line. In this case, the attributes at points P_0 and P_1 will be used instead of the points themselves. A t value of 0.5, for example, gives the midpoint of the line from equation (A.1) and the attribute at the midpoint of the line from the equation based on the attributes.

If the attribute of a particular point, P', along the line is desired, the equation (A.2) gives the t value needed for the attribute interpolation equation.

$$t = \frac{P' - P_0}{P_1 - P_0} \tag{A.2}$$

A.5   Trigonometry

Trigonometry is used to deal with the angle that occurs between two lines that meet or start at a single point. The angle is measured from the initial side of the angle to the terminal side of the angle. Angles measured counterclockwise are considered positive and those measured clockwise are considered negative. Angle measurements are typically given in either degrees or radians. Where people tend to think in terms of degrees, most computer math routines use radians. The angle between the positive x and positive y axes in a Cartesian coordinate system is 90°, so that a full circle is 360°. A circle is also considered to have 2π radians, which means that conversions between these two measures are given by Radians = Degrees $* \pi$ / 180 and Degrees = Radians $* 180$ / π.

A.5.1 Trigonometric functions

Trigonometric functions can be defined for angles in terms of a right triangle. Figure A.1 shows a labeled right triangle. The equations for sine, cosine, and tangent are:

$$\sin\theta = \frac{opposite\ side}{hypotenuse} = \frac{y}{h}$$

$$\cos\theta = \frac{adjacent\ side}{hypotenuse} = \frac{x}{h}$$

$$\tan\theta = \frac{opposite\ side}{adjacent\ side} = \frac{y}{x}$$

These equations, though shown here for a right triangle, can actually be calculated for any triangle.

The law of sines indicates that the ratio of the sine of an angle to the length of the opposite side of the triangle is constant for all of the vertices and sides of any triangle. For the triangle in Figure A.2, these ratios are given by $\frac{\sin\alpha}{a} = \frac{\sin\beta}{b} = \frac{\sin\gamma}{c}$.

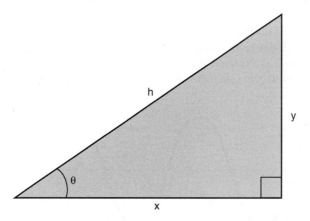

Figure A.1 • A right triangle

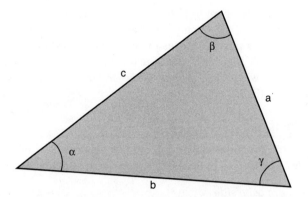

Figure A.2 • A general triangle

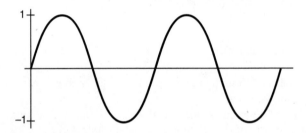

Figure A.3 • A sine curve

The trigonometric functions are periodic, which means that the values of sine and cosine repeat every 2π radians and the values of tangent repeat every π radians. This is seen in the graphs of these three functions shown in Figures A.3 through A.5.

If the sine curve in Figure A.3 is reflected across the y axis, the result will be the negative of the sine curve, so that $\sin(-\theta) = -\sin(\theta)$. Figure A.4 shows that the cosine curve is symmetric across the y axis, so that $\cos(-\theta) = \cos(\theta)$. The tangent curve exhibits the same sort of symmetry across the y axis as the sine curve, thus

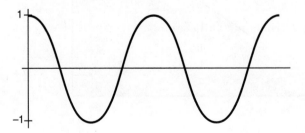

Figure A.4 • A cosine curve

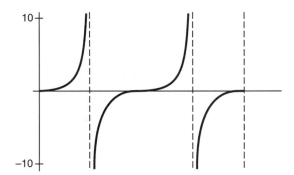

Figure A.5 • A tangent curve

$\tan(-\theta) = -\tan(\theta)$. The full cycle for the sine and cosine curves is 2π radians long, so a distance along these curves of π radians negates the values of sine and cosine. Specifically, $\sin(\theta + \pi) = -\sin(\theta)$ and $\cos(\theta + \pi) = -\cos(\theta)$. The sine and cosine curves can be shifted between each other as well. Examining Figures A.3 and A.4 shows that $\sin(\theta + \pi/2) = \cos(\theta)$ and $\cos(\theta + \pi/2) = -\sin(\theta)$.

A.6   Curves

There are a couple of special curves that are of interest in some of the modeling methods in graphics. This section looks at two of those classes of curves.

A.6.1 Catenary curve

The catenary curve is the curve that results when a rope or chain hangs from two points and is acted on by gravity. The equation for a catenary curve is given by

$y = a * \cosh\left(\dfrac{x}{a}\right)$, where a indicates how quickly the curve opens up. Values of a

close to 0 result in a narrower curve than larger values.

The arc length from the lowest point on the curve is given by $s = a * \sinh\left(\dfrac{x}{a}\right)$.

A.6.2 Trochoids and cycloids

In general, a trochoid is the curve traced by a point at distance b from the center of the circle of radius a as it rolls along a straight line. Figure A.6 shows three possibilities for when $a > b$, $a = b$, and $a < b$. When $a = b$, the curve is also called a cycloid. When $a > b$, the curve is more specifically called a curtate cycloid, and when $a < b$, the curve is more specifically called a prolate cycloid.

The curves for a trochoid are traced by the parametric equations $x(\theta) = a * \theta - b * \sin(\theta)$ and $y(\theta) = a - b * \cos(\theta)$.

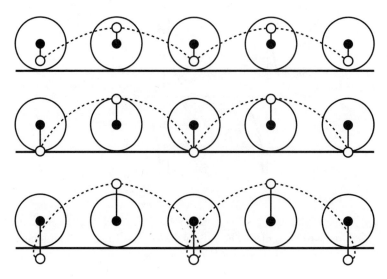

Figure A.6 • Three trochoid curves

A.7 Vectors and Their Properties

A vector has two components to it: a direction and a size. A vector can be drawn as an arrow where the direction of the arrow represents the direction of the vector and the length of the arrow represents its size. Vectors have no fixed position in space, and so no matter where a vector is moved it will be the same as long as its direction or size is not changed. In two dimensions, a vector is a pair of values for the x and y location of where the end of the vector would be, if its beginning is placed at the origin. In three dimensions, a vector also includes a z component. For the sake of simplicity, the following subsections on vectors will show only the equations for three dimensional vectors.

A.7.1 Vector length

The length, size, or magnitude of a vector is given by the square root of the sum of the squares of the components. The notation for the length of a vector is to place double vertical bars[1] around the vector name, $||\boldsymbol{v}||$. So, if $\boldsymbol{v} = [v_x, v_y, v_z]$, $||\boldsymbol{v}|| = \sqrt{v_x^2 + v_y^2 + v_z^2}$.

---

[1]Double vertical bars are used to distinguish the length from absolute value, which uses a single set of vertical bars.

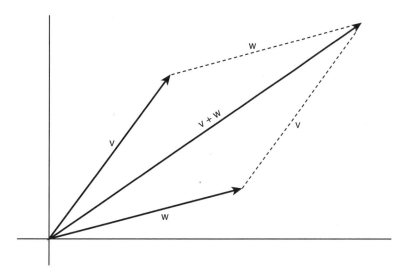

Figure A.7 • Vector addition

• A.7.2 Vector addition

Two vectors can be added by adding their individual components (Figure A.7). So, if $v = [v_x, v_y, v_z]$ and $w = [w_x, w_y, w_z]$, $v + w = [v_x + w_x, v_y + w_y, v_z + w_z]$. Because the individual components of a vector are just numbers, addition of vectors is associative and commutative.

• A.7.3 Scalar multiplication

A vector can be multiplied by a number (called a scalar) by multiplying each of the components of the vector by that scalar number. So, if $v = [v_x, v_y, v_z]$, $s * v = [s * v_x, s * v_y, s * v_z]$. Additionally, multiplying a vector by a scalar, s, produces a vector s times as long as the original (Figure A.8). Specifically, $||s * v|| = s * ||v||$.

• A.7.4 Dot product

For two vectors $v = [v_x, v_y, v_z]$ and $w = [w_x, w_y, w_z]$, the dot product is the value given by the equation $v \bullet w = (v_x * w_x) + (v_y * w_y) + (v_z * w_z)$. The dot product is also defined so that it satisfies the equation $v \bullet w = ||v|| * ||w|| * \cos(\theta)$, where θ is the angle between the two vectors (Figure A.9). If the two vectors are of unit length, $||v||$ and $||w||$ will both have a value of 1 and the dot product will give the cosine of the angle between the two vectors.

• A.7.5 Cross-product

The cross-product of two vectors ($v \times w$) will give a vector that is perpendicular to the plane containing those two vectors. The direction of the cross-product vector is

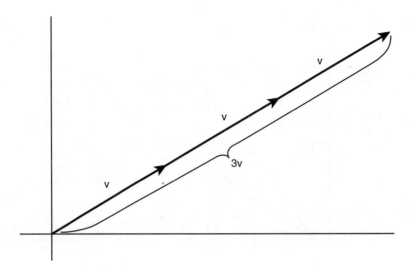

Figure A.8 • Scalar multiplication example

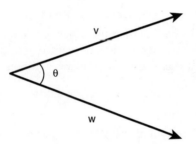

Figure A.9 • The angle between two vectors

determined by the right-hand rule (Figure 1.8). As can be seen in Figure A.10, changing the order of the vectors in the cross-product will reverse the direction of the result. For two vectors $v = [v_x, v_y, v_z]$ and $w = [w_x, w_y, w_z]$, the cross-product is the vector given by the equation $v \times w = [(v_y * w_z) - (v_z * w_y), (v_z * w_x) - (v_x * w_z), (v_x * w_y) - (v_y * w_x)]$. If v and w are of unit length, the length of the vector from the cross-product will be the sine of the angle between v and w.

A.7.6 Vector triple product

The vector triple product is computed by $u \times (v \times w)$. The vector triple product can be used to derive a set of three vectors that are perpendicular to each other. In

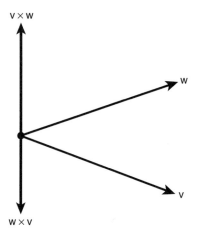

Figure A.10 • The cross-product

Figure A.11, v and w are two initial vectors. The cross-product $v \times w$ gives a vector that is perpendicular to the plane containing v and w and thus is perpendicular to both v and w. The triple product $w \times (v \times w)$ will be a vector perpendicular to the vectors w and $v \times w$, which are themselves perpendicular. If v and w are both of unit length, this makes the vectors w, $v \times w$, and $w \times (v \times w)$ an orthonormal basis (three perpendicular vectors of unit length). The same thing is true of the vectors v, $v \times w$, and $v \times (v \times w)$, though they form a different orthonormal basis.

• A.7.7 Scalar triple product

The scalar triple product is given by the equation $u \cdot (v \times w)$. If the three vectors are the sides of a parallelopiped (Figure A.12), the scalar triple product will give the volume of the parallelopiped. The value of the scalar triple product can also be used to check the shortest rotational direction between the vectors v and w. If the scalar triple product is positive, the shortest rotation of v to w around u is counterclockwise. If the scalar triple product is negative, the shortest rotation is clockwise. This fact can be used to control motion of objects. If u is the up direction for the object, v is the direction the object is going, and w is the desired direction, a positive scalar triple product indicates the object should be turned to the left (counterclockwise) and a negative scalar triple product indicates the object should be turned to the right (clockwise).

The scalar triple product can also be used to determine the handedness of a coordinate system represented by a set of three basis vectors (v_1, v_2, v_3). If the scalar triple product $v_1 \cdot (v_2 \times v_3)$ is positive, the basis is right-handed. If the scalar triple product is negative, the basis is left-handed.

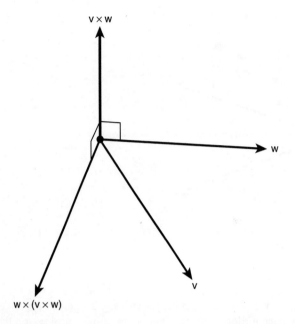

Figure A.11 • Vector triple product

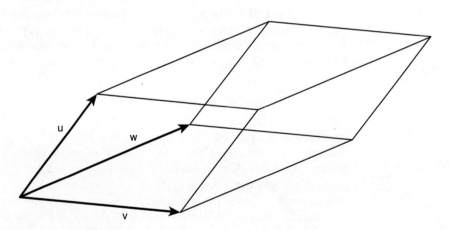

Figure A.12 • A parallelopiped

A.8 Matrices and Their Properties

A matrix is a two-dimensional array of numbers. It can also be viewed as a one-dimensional array of vectors, and as such there are a number of similarities between the vector and matrix operations. A matrix is said to be of size N by M when it has N rows and M columns. A matrix is called a square matrix when it has the same number of rows and columns. Three-dimensional graphics is dominated by square matrices with four rows and columns, with three by three matrices used in two-dimensional graphics.

The main diagonal of a matrix is the set of elements where the row and column number are the same. The main diagonal runs from the upper left down to the lower right of the matrix. An identity matrix is a square matrix that has 0s in every location except for the main diagonal elements which are all ones.

A.8.1 Matrix addition

Two matrices can be added together if they are of the same size. In this case, the individual elements are added together based on their location within the matrix. In other words, the two elements in the first row and column are added together to get the number in the first row and column of the result. More precisely, if

$$A = \begin{bmatrix} a_{1,1} & a_{1,2} & a_{1,3} \\ a_{2,1} & a_{2,2} & a_{2,3} \\ a_{3,1} & a_{3,2} & a_{3,3} \end{bmatrix}$$

and

$$B = \begin{bmatrix} b_{1,1} & b_{1,2} & b_{1,3} \\ b_{2,1} & b_{2,2} & b_{2,3} \\ b_{3,1} & b_{3,2} & b_{3,3} \end{bmatrix},$$

adding these two matrices together gives

$$A + B = \begin{bmatrix} a_{1,1} + b_{1,1} & a_{1,2} + b_{1,2} & a_{1,3} + b_{1,3} \\ a_{2,1} + b_{2,1} & a_{2,2} + b_{2,2} & a_{2,3} + b_{2,3} \\ a_{3,1} + b_{3,1} & a_{3,2} + b_{3,2} & a_{3,3} + b_{3,3} \end{bmatrix}.$$

A.8.2 Scalar multiplication

Like scalar multiplication with vectors, scalar multiplication with a matrix results in the scalar number being multiplied by each of the elements of the matrix. So, if

$$A = \begin{bmatrix} a_{1,1} & a_{1,2} & a_{1,3} \\ a_{2,1} & a_{2,2} & a_{2,3} \\ a_{3,1} & a_{3,2} & a_{3,3} \end{bmatrix},$$

multiplying this matrix by the number s gives

$$s * A = \begin{bmatrix} s * a_{1,1} & s * a_{1,2} & s * a_{1,3} \\ s * a_{2,1} & s * a_{2,2} & s * a_{2,3} \\ s * a_{3,1} & s * a_{3,2} & s * a_{3,3} \end{bmatrix}.$$

A.8.3 Matrix multiplication

When multiplying matrices, it is necessary for the number of columns in the first matrix to be the same as the number of rows in the second matrix. This means a 3×4 matrix can be multiplied by a 4×2 matrix, but they can't be multiplied the other way around. If two matrices are square and the same size, they can be multiplied in either order, however, the two results will not necessarily be the same. This means that matrix multiplication is not commutative, but it is associative.

To multiply two matrices, each row of the first matrix is multiplied by each column of the second, and the results are added. The element in the first row and first column of the result is the dot product of the first row of the first matrix and the first column of the second matrix. The element in the third row and fifth column of the results is the dot product of the third row of the first matrix with the fifth column of the second matrix. More formally, if

$$M_1 = \begin{bmatrix} a & b & c \\ d & e & f \end{bmatrix}$$

and

$$M_2 = \begin{bmatrix} A & B & C & D \\ E & F & G & H \\ I & J & K & L \end{bmatrix},$$

the product of these two matrices is:

$$M_1 * M_2 = \begin{bmatrix} a*A+b*E+c*I & a*B+b*F+c*J & a*C+b*G+c*K & a*D+b*H+c*L \\ d*A+e*E+f*I & d*B+e*F+f*J & d*C+e*G+f*K & d*D+e*H+f*L \end{bmatrix}.$$

A.8.4 Determinant of a matrix

The determinant of a square matrix is a number that acts as a general measure of how a vector's size will change when transformed by the matrix. Additionally, if the columns of a 2×2 matrix are treated as two sides of a parallelogram, the area of the parallelogram is the same as the absolute value of the determinant. For a 3×3 matrix, the parallelopiped formed by the three vectors represented by the columns of the matrix has a volume that is the determinant of the matrix.

The determinant of a 2×2 matrix is given by $\det\left(\begin{bmatrix} a & b \\ c & d \end{bmatrix}\right) = a*d - b*c$. The determinant of larger square matrices can be calculated by either of the recursive equations (A.3), where N is the size of the matrix and $\sim A_{i,j}$ is the $(N-1) \times (N-1)$ square matrix formed by removing row i and column j. Typically, column 1 will be used for the first equation and row 1 will be used for the second.

$$\det(A) = \sum_{i=1}^{N} a_{i,j}(-1)^{i+j} \det\left(\sim A_{i,j}\right)$$

$$\det(A) = \sum_{j=1}^{N} a_{i,j}(-1)^{i+j} \det\left(\sim A_{i,j}\right)$$

(A.3)

For example, the determinant for a 3 $\times$ 3 matrix can be calculated as:

$$\det\left(\begin{bmatrix} a & b & c \\ d & e & f \\ g & h & i \end{bmatrix}\right) = a * \det\left(\begin{bmatrix} e & f \\ h & i \end{bmatrix}\right) - b * \det\left(\begin{bmatrix} d & f \\ g & i \end{bmatrix}\right) + c * \det\left(\begin{bmatrix} d & e \\ g & h \end{bmatrix}\right)$$

$$= a * (e * i - f * h) - b * (d * i - f * g) + c * (d * h - e * g)$$

A.9   Systems of Linear Equations

A system of linear equations is a set of equations that expresses the relationship between a set of variables. Linear equations come up in linear algebra in mathematics and also play a role in computer graphics, for example, in radiosity. These sets of equations can have any number of variables or unknowns, and all of the equations are based on the first power of these variables. In other words, none of the variables are squared or raised to any higher power.

The solution to a system of linear equations is the set of values for each of the variables, which solve all of the linear equations. There are a couple of things that are necessary for a system of linear equations to have a solution. First, there must be at least as many equations as there are unknowns. If there are more, the system of linear equations is over-specified, which can lead to inconsistencies. Second, none of the equations should be linear combinations of any of the others. If they are, the process of determining a solution will eliminate one of the equations completely, which means that an exact solution cannot be found.

A system of linear equations can be represented as a matrix equation. In this form, each variable is "assigned" a column and each equation is assigned a row. Consider the set of equations (A.4), where the x terms are the variables the a terms are the coefficients of the variables and the c terms are the constant results of the equations.

$$a_{1,1} * x_1 + a_{1,2} * x_2 + a_{1,3} * x_3 = c_1$$
$$a_{2,1} * x_1 + a_{2,2} * x_2 + a_{2,3} * x_3 = c_2$$
$$a_{3,1} * x_1 + a_{3,2} * x_2 + a_{3,3} * x_3 = c_3$$

(A.4)

This system of linear equations can be represented as the matrix equation (A.5).

$$
\begin{bmatrix} a_{1,1} & a_{1,2} & a_{1,3} \\ a_{2,1} & a_{2,2} & a_{2,3} \\ a_{3,1} & a_{3,2} & a_{3,3} \end{bmatrix} * \begin{bmatrix} x_1 \\ x_2 \\ x_3 \end{bmatrix} = \begin{bmatrix} c_1 \\ c_2 \\ c_3 \end{bmatrix}
\tag{A.5}
$$

Because this is only intended to be a brief introduction, there are many details omitted here. Additional details can be found in a linear algebra book.

A.9.1 Gaussian elimination

Gaussian elimination can be used to solve a system of linear equations. The description given here is a simplified overview of the process. There are many books and Web-based resources with tested code that implements a process like the one described here.

Gaussian elimination works with a slightly different form of the matrix equation, called an augmented matrix. The augmented matrix contains the coefficients of the variables along with the constant results of the equations. This means that for N equations with N unknowns, the augmented matrix will have N rows and N + 1 columns.

The solution of the system of linear equations is not altered by performing one of three simple operations to the augmented matrix.

- Exchange two rows
- Multiply a row by a scalar value (other than 0)
- Add a multiple of one row to one of the other rows

The process of finding a solution is to apply these operations to try and get the first N rows and columns to have an identity matrix. When that is achieved, the last column of the augmented matrix will have the values of the variables. The basic algorithm is:

```
for each row (i)
   if a_i,i = 0
      find the first row j > i where a_j,i ≠ 0
               and swap rows i and j
   divide row i by the scalar value a_i,i
   for all of the rows (j) except row i
      subtract a_j,i times row i from row j
```

A.9.2 The Gauss-Siedel method

The Gauss-Siedel iterative method can be used to find an approximate solution to a system of linear equations. Code that implements the Gauss-Siedel iterative method follows.

```
int
check(float a1[], float a2[], float epsilon)
{
```

```
      // determines if the two consecutive solutions
      // are close enough to stop the iteration
      for (int i = 0; i < SIZE; i++)
         if (abs(a1[i] - a2[i]) > epsilon)
            return 0;
      return 1;
}

void
gaussSiedel(float A[SIZE][SIZE], float C[SIZE], float X[SIZE])
{
   int i, j;
   int k, k_max;
   float sum, epsilon;
   float old[SIZE];

   // initialize the approximation of X to C
   for (i = 0; i < SIZE; i++)
      X[i] = C[i];

   k_max = 100;        // maximum # of iterations
   epsilon = 0.5e-4;   // maximum change in X values

   for (k = 0; k < k_max; k++)
   {
      // copy the old values to check change later
      for (i = 0; i < SIZE; i++)
         old[i] = X[i];

      for (i = 0; i < SIZE; i++)
      {
         // initialize with the C value
         sum = C[i];

         for (j = 0; j < SIZE; j++)
            if (j!=i)
               sum = sum - A[i][j] * X[j];

         // update X[i] so it is used on the next pass
         X[i] = sum;
      }

      // is the approximation close enough?
      if (check(X, old, epsilon))
```

```
        return;
    }
    return;   // maximum iterations reached
}
```

A.10   Distance and Closest Points in Three Dimensions

This section gives the equations for the distance and closest points for various situations in three dimensions.

Distance between two points

The distance between any two points (x_1, y_1, z_1) and (x_2, y_2, z_2) is given by equation (A.6).

$$d = \sqrt{(x_1 - x_2)^2 + (y_1 - y_2)^2 + (z_1 - z_2)^2}$$

(A.6)

Closest point on a line to a point

Consider the line in the direction of the vector v that goes through point P (Figure A.13). The location, Q', on this line that is closest to a point Q is given by equation (A.7), where $u = Q - P$.

$$Q' = P + \frac{u \cdot v}{\|v\|^2} * v$$

(A.7)

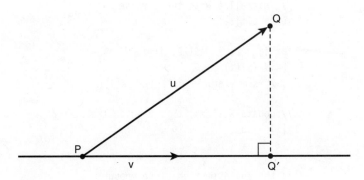

Figure A.13 • The closest point on a line to a point

Shortest distance between a line and a point

The shortest distance between the point Q and the line can be found by first calculating the closest point on the line Q′ using equation (A.7) and then using equation (A.6) with Q and Q′. Equation (A.8) gives a more direct calculation for this shortest distance, where v is the vector along the line and $u = Q − P$.

$$d = \sqrt{u \cdot u - \frac{(u \cdot v)^2}{v \cdot v}} \qquad\qquad (A.8)$$

Closest points on two lines

The parametric equations for two lines (Figure A.14) can be expressed as $L_1(s) = P + s * v$ and $L_2(t) = Q + t * w$. The place where the two lines are closest to each other will occur at some parameter values, s_c and t_c, on the two lines. The vector, u_c, from the closest point on the first line to the closest point on the second line is given by equation (A.9), where $u = Q − P$.

$$u_c = u - s_c * v + t_c * w \qquad\qquad (A.9)$$

At the closest point, the vector u_c will be perpendicular to both lines. This means that $u_c \cdot v = 0$ and $u_c \cdot w = 0$. Taking the dot product of both sides of equation (A.9) by v and w gives the two equations (A.10).

$$0 = u \cdot v - s_c * v \cdot v + t_c * w \cdot v \qquad\qquad (A.10)$$
$$0 = u \cdot w - s_c * v \cdot w + t_c * w \cdot w$$

This is a system of equations with two unknowns, s_c and t_c. Solving these equations gives the following set of calculations.

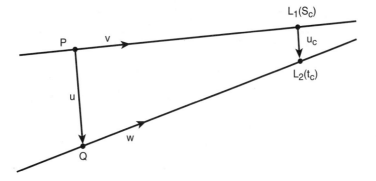

Figure A.14 • The closest points on two lines

$$a = v \cdot v$$

$$b = v \cdot w$$

$$c = w \cdot w$$

$$d = v \cdot u$$

$$e = w \cdot u$$

$$s_c = \frac{b * e - c * d}{a * c - b^2}$$

$$t_c = \frac{a * e - b * d}{a * c - b^2}$$

If the denominator in the calculation of s_c and t_c is 0, the lines are parallel. If the denominator is not 0, s_c and t_c can be calculated and then substituted back into the original parametric equations to find the closest points on the two lines.

Shortest distance between two lines

The shortest distance between two lines can be calculated by doing the previous sequence of calculations to get the values of s_c and t_c. In this case, these two values are substituted into equation (A.9). This gives the vector between the two closest points, and thus the length of this vector is the shortest distance.

Closest point on a plane to a point

Consider the plane $Ax + By + Cz + D = 0$, which has the normal vector $n = (A, B, C)$. The point, Q', on the plane that is closest to a point Q is given by the equation

$$Q' = Q - \frac{Q \cdot n + D}{n \cdot n} * n.$$

Shortest distance between a plane and a point

Consider the plane with a normal vector n with point P on the surface of the plane. The shortest distance between the point Q and the plane is given by equation (A.11), where $u = Q - P$. In this equation, the absolute value in the numerator is necessary to get the positive distance. Without the absolute value, the distance will be negative if the point Q is on the side of the plane opposite the normal direction.

$$d = \frac{|n \cdot u|}{\|n\|} \tag{A.11}$$

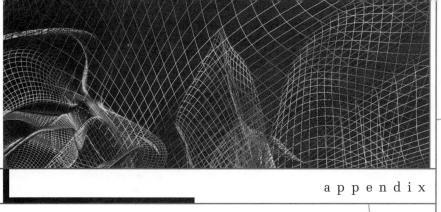

References

SIGGRAPH 2004   *The Proceedings of SIGGRAPH 2004*, August 8–12, 2004, Los Angeles, CA. Also published as *ACM Transactions on Graphics*, 23 (3), August 2004.

SIGGRAPH 2003   *The Proceedings of SIGGRAPH 2003*, July 27–31, 2003, San Diego, CA. Also published as *ACM Transactions on Graphics*, 22 (3), July 2003.

SIGGRAPH 2002   *The Proceedings of SIGGRAPH 2002*, July 21–26, 2002, San Antonio, TX. Also published as *ACM Transactions on Graphics*, 21 (3), July 2002.

SIGGRAPH 2001   *The Proceedings of SIGGRAPH 2001*, August 12–17, 2001, Los Angeles, CA. Also published as *Computer Graphics*, 35 (3), August 2001.

SIGGRAPH 2000   *The Proceedings of SIGGRAPH 2000*, July 23–28, 2000, New Orleans, LA. Also published as *Computer Graphics*, 34 (3), August 2000.

SIGGRAPH 99   *The Proceedings of SIGGRAPH 99*, August 8–13, 1999, Los Angeles, CA. Also published as *Computer Graphics*, 33 (3), August 1999.

SIGGRAPH 98   *The Proceedings of SIGGRAPH 98*, July 19–24, 1998, Orlando, FL. Also published as *Computer Graphics*, 32 (3), August 1998.

SIGGRAPH 97   *The Proceedings of SIGGRAPH 97*, August 3–8, 1997, Los Angeles, CA. Also published as *Computer Graphics*, 31 (3), August 1997.

SIGGRAPH 96   *The Proceedings of SIGGRAPH 96*, August 4–9, 1996, New Orleans, LA. Also published as *Computer Graphics*, Annual Conference Series 1996.

SIGGRAPH 95   *The Proceedings of SIGGRAPH 95*, August 6–11, Los Angeles, CA. Also published as *Computer Graphics*, Annual Conference Series 1995.

SIGGRAPH 94   *The Proceedings of SIGGRAPH 94*, July 24–29, Orlando, FL. Also published as *Computer Graphics*, Annual Conference Series 1994.

SIGGRAPH 93   *The Proceedings of SIGGRAPH 93*, August 1–6, Anaheim, CA. Also published as *Computer Graphics*, Annual Conference Series 1993.

SIGGRAPH 92   *The Proceedings of SIGGRAPH 92*, July 26–31, Chicago, IL. Also published as *Computer Graphics*, 26 (2), July 1992.

SIGGRAPH 91   *The Proceedings of SIGGRAPH 91*, July 28–August 2, Las Vegas, NV. Also published as *Computer Graphics*, 25 (4), July 1991.

SIGGRAPH 90   *The Proceedings of SIGGRAPH 90*, August 6–10, Dallas, TX. Also published as *Computer Graphics*, 24 (4), August 1990.

SIGGRAPH 89   *The Proceedings of SIGGRAPH 89*, July 31–August 4, Boston, MA. Also published as *Computer Graphics*, 23 (4), July 1989.

SIGGRAPH 88   *The Proceedings of SIGGRAPH 88*, August 1–5, Atlanta, GA. Also published as *Computer Graphics*, 22 (4), August 1988.

SIGGRAPH 87   *The Proceedings of SIGGRAPH 87*, July 27–31, Anaheim, CA. Also published as *Computer Graphics*, 21 (4), July 1987.

SIGGRAPH 86   *The Proceedings of SIGGRAPH 86*, August 18–22, Dallas, TX. Also published as *Computer Graphics*, 20 (4), August 1986.

SIGGRAPH 85   *The Proceedings of SIGGRAPH 85*, July 22–26, San Francisco, CA. Also published as *Computer Graphics*, 19 (3), July 1985.

SIGGRAPH 84   *The Proceedings of SIGGRAPH 84*, July 23–27, Minneapolis, MN. Also published as *Computer Graphics*, 18 (3), July 1984.

SIGGRAPH 83   *The Proceedings of SIGGRAPH 83*, July 25–29, Detroit, MI. Also published as *Computer Graphics*, 17 (3), July 1983.

SIGGRAPH 82   *The Proceedings of SIGGRAPH 82*, July 26–30, Boston, MA. Also published as *Computer Graphics*, 16 (3), July 1982.

SIGGRAPH 81   *The Proceedings of SIGGRAPH 81*, August 3–7, Dallas, TX. Also published as *Computer Graphics*, 15 (3), August 1981.

SIGGRAPH 80   *The Proceedings of SIGGRAPH 80*, July 14–18, Seattle, WA. Also published as *Computer Graphics*, 14 (3), July 1980.

SIGGRAPH 79   *The Proceedings of SIGGRAPH 79*, August 8–10, Chicago, IL. Also published as *Computer Graphics*, 13 (2), July 1979.

SIGGRAPH 78   *The Proceedings of SIGGRAPH 78*, August 23–25, Atlanta, GA. Also published as *Computer Graphics*, 12 (3), August 1978.

SIGGRAPH 77   *The Proceedings of SIGGRAPH 77*, July 20–22, San Jose, CA. Also published as *Computer Graphics*, 11 (2), Summer 1977.

SIGGRAPH 76   *The Proceedings of SIGGRAPH 76*, July 14–16, Philadelphia, PA. Also published as *Computer Graphics*, 10 (2), Summer 1976.

SIGGRAPH 75   *The Proceedings of SIGGRAPH 75*, June 25–27, Bowling Green, OH.

SIGGRAPH 74   *The Proceedings of SIGGRAPH 74*, July 15–17, Boulder, CO.

Chapter 1   References

Beach99   Mark Beach and Eric Kenly. *Getting It Printed: How to Work with Printers and Graphic Imaging Services to Assure Quality, Stay on Schedule, and Control Costs*. North Light Books (www.gettingitprinted.com), 1999.

Bruno00   Michael H. Bruno. *Pocket Pal: A Graphic Arts Production Handbook*. GATF Press, 2000.

Crow87   Frank Crow. "The origins of the teapot," *IEEE Computer Graphics and Applications*, 7 (1), January 1987, pp. 8–10.

Fosner97   Ron Fosner. *OpenGL Programming for Windows 95 and Windows NT*, Addison Wesley Longman, Reading, MA, 1997.

Glassner95   Andrew S. Glassner. *Principles of Digital Image Synthesis* (two volumes), Morgan Kauffman Publishers, Inc., San Francisco, CA, 1995.

Kilgard96   Mark J. Kilgard. *OpenGL Programming for the X Window System*, Addison Wesley Longman, Inc., Reading, MA, 1996.

Makai03   János Makai, Technical Manager, CIE Central Bureau. Personal communication, August 2003.

McConnell02   Jeffrey J. McConnell with Anthony Ralston, Edwin D. Reilly, and David Hemmindinger (eds.). *Computer Graphics Companion*, John Wiley & Sons, Inc., New York, NY, 2002.

O'Connell02a   Kenneth R. O'Connell. "Graphic design in new media," in (McConnell02).

O'Connell02b   Kenneth R. O'Connell. "Color as a language of design," in (McConnell02).

OpenGL99   OpenGL Architecture Review Board, Mason Woo, Jackie Neider, Tom Davis, and Dave Shreiner. *OpenGL Programming Guide: The Official Guide to Learning OpenGL* (third edition), Addison Wesley Longman, Inc., Reading, MA, 1999.

OpenGL00   OpenGL Architecture Review Board (Dave Shreiner, ed.). *OpenGL Reference Manual: The Official Reference Document to OpenGL, Version 1.2* (third edition), Addison Wesley Longman, Inc., Reading, MA, 2000.

Chapter 2 References

Albers87   Josef Albers. *Interaction of Color*. Yale University Press, 1987.

Blinn77   James F. Blinn. "Models of light reflection for computer synthesized pictures," SIGGRAPH 77, pp. 192–198.

Bui75   Bui-Tuong Phong. "Illumination for computer generated pictures," *Communications of the ACM*, 18 (6), June 1975, pp. 311–317.

Cook81   Robert Cook and Kenneth Torrance. "A reflectance model for computer graphics," SIGGRAPH 81, pp. 307–316.

Gouraud71   Henri Gouraud. "Continuous shading of curved surfaces," *IEEE Transactions on Computers*, 20 (6), June 1971, pp. 623–629.

McReynolds97   Tom McReynolds, David Blythe, Celeste Fowler, Brad Grantham, Simon Hui, and Paula Womack. *Programming with OpenGL: Advanced Techniques*, SIGGRAPH 97 Course Notes #11 (Tom McReynolds, organizer), 1997.

Schlick93   Christophe Schlick. "A customizable reflectance model for everyday rendering," *Proceedings of the Fourth Eurographics Workshop on Rendering*, June 1993, pp. 73–84.

Schutz90   Bernard F. Schutz. *A First Course in General Relativity*. Cambridge University Press, New York, NY, 1990.

Strauss90   Paul Strauss. "A realistic lighting model for computer animators," *IEEE Computer Graphics and Applications*, 10 (6), November 1990, pp. 56–64.

Strauss03   Paul Strauss. Personal communication, January 2003.

Torrance66   Kenneth E. Torrance and E. M. Sparrow. "Polarization, directional distribution, and off-specular peak phenomena in light reflected from roughened surfaces," *Journal of the Optical Society of America*, 56 (7), July 1966, pp. 916–925.

Torrance67   Kenneth E. Torrance and E. M. Sparrow. "Theory for off-specular reflection from roughened surfaces," *Journal of the Optical Society of America*, 57 (9), September 1967, pp. 1105–1114.

Ward92   Gregory J. Ward. "Measuring and modeling anisotropic reflection," SIGGRAPH 92, pp. 265–272.

Chapter 3 References

Arvo91   James Arvo. *Graphic Gems II*, Academic Press, San Diego, CA, 1991.

Ashdown94   Ian Ashdown. *Radiosity: A Programmer's Perspective*, John Wiley & Sons, Inc., New York, NY, 1994.

Baumgart74   Bruce G. Baumgart. *Geometric Modeling for Computer Vision*, Ph.D. dissertation, Computer Science Department, Stanford University,

Stanford, CA, 1974. Also as Tech. Rep. CS-463, Computer Science Department, Stanford University.

Baumgart75   Bruce G. Baumgart. "A polyhedron representation for computer vision," *National Computer Conference* 1975, pp. 589–596.

Bresenham77   Jack Bresenham. "A linear algorithm for incremental digital display of circular arcs," *Communications of the ACM*, 20 (2), February 1977, pp. 100–106.

Cohen93   Michael F. Cohen and John R. Wallace. *Radiosity and Realistic Image Synthesis*, Academic Press, Cambridge, MA, 1993.

Ferguson01   R. Stuart Ferguson. *Practical Algorithms for 3D Computer Graphics*, A. K. Peters, Ltd., Natick, MA, 2001.

Glassner91   Andrew S. Glassner. "Maintaining winged-edge models," in (Arvo91).

Luebke03   David Luebke, Martin Reddy, Jonathan D. Cohen, Amitabh Varshney, Benjamin Watson, and Robert Huebner. *Level of Detail for 3D Computer Graphics*, Morgan Kaufmann Publishers, San Francisco, CA, 2003.

OpenGL99   OpenGL Architecture Review Board, Mason Woo, Jackie Neider, Tom Davis, and Dave Shreiner. *OpenGL Programming Guide: The Official Guide to Learning OpenGL* (third edition), Addison Wesley Longman, Inc., Reading, MA, 1999.

OpenGL00   OpenGL Architecture Review Board (Dave Shreiner, ed.). *OpenGL Reference Manual: The Official Reference Document to OpenGL, Version 1.2* (third edition), Addison Wesley Longman, Inc., Reading, MA, 2000.

Palmer01   Ian C. Palmer. *Essential Java 3D Fast: Developing 3D Graphics Applications*, Springer-Verlag, London, UK, 2001.

Porter78   Thomas K. Porter. "Spherical shading," SIGGRAPH 78, pp. 282–285.

Selman02   Daniel Selman. *Java 3D Programming*, Manning Publications Co., Greenwich, CT, 2002.

Schneider03   Philip J. Schneider and David H. Eberly. *Geometric Tools for Computer Graphics*, Morgan Kaufmann, San Francisco, CA, 2003.

Chapter 4   References

Bartels87   Richard H. Bartels, John C. Beatty, and Brian A. Barsky. *An Introduction to Splines for Use in Computer Graphics and Geometric Modeling*, Morgan Kaufmann, Los Altos, CA, 1987.

Bézier72   Pierre Bézier. *Numerical Control: Mathematics and Applications*, (trans. A. Robin Forrest and Anne F. Pankhurst), John Wiley and Sons, New York, 1972.

Bézier74	Pierre Bézier. "Mathematical and practical possibilities of UNISURF," in *Computer-Aided Geometric Design*, Robert E. Barnhill and Richard F. Riesenfeld (eds.), Academic Press, New York, 1974, pp. 127–152.
Blinn78a	James F. Blinn. "Simulation of wrinkled surfaces," SIGGRAPH 78, pp. 286–292.
Blinn78b	James F. Blinn. *Computer Display of Curved Surfaces*, Ph.D. thesis, Department of Computer Science, University of Utah, Salt Lake City, UT, December 1978.
Farin90	Gerald Farin. *Curves and Surfaces for Computer-Aided Geometric Design: A Practical Guide*, Academic Press, San Diego, CA, 1990.
Lane79	Jeffrey M. Lane, Loren C. Carpenter. "A generalized scan line algorithm for the computer display of parametrically defined surfaces," *Computer Graphics and Image Processing*, 11 (3), November 1979, pp. 290–297.
Lane80	Jeffrey M. Lane, Loren C. Carpenter, Turner Witted, and James F. Blinn. "Scan line methods for displaying parametrically defined surfaces," *Communications of the ACM*, 23 (1), January 1980, pp. 23–34.
Mortenson97	Michael E. Mortenson. *Geometric Modeling*, (second edition), John Wiley & Sons, New York, NY, 1997.
Rogers01	David F. Rogers. *An Introduction to NURBS with Historical Perspective*, Morgan Kaufmann, San Francisco, CA, 2001.

Chapter 5   References

Catmull74	Edwin Catmull. *A Subdivision Algorithm for Computer Display of Curved Surfaces*, Ph.D. thesis report UTEC-CSc-74-133, Computer Science Department, University of Utah, Salt Lake City, UT, December 1974.
Newell72	Martin E. Newell, R. G. Newell, and T. L. Sancha. "A solution to the hidden surface problem," in the *Proceedings of the ACM National Conference 1972*, pp. 443–450.
OpenGL99	OpenGL Architecture Review Board, Mason Woo, Jackie Neider, Tom Davis, and Dave Shreiner. *OpenGL Programming Guide: the official guide to learning OpenGL* (third edition), Addison Wesley Longman, Inc., Reading, MA, 1999.
Pan00	Zhigeng Pan, Zhiliang Tao, Chiyi Cheng, and Oiaoying Shi. "A New BSP Tree Framework Incorporating Dynamic LoD Models," *Proceedings of the ACM symposium on Virtual Reality Software and Technology*, Seoul, Korea, October 22–25, 2000, pp. 134–141.
Sutherland74a	Ivan E. Sutherland and Gary W. Hodgeman. "Reentrant polygon clipping," *Communication of the ACM*, 17 (1), January 1974, pp. 32–42.

Sutherland74b   Ivan E. Sutherland, Robert F. Sproull, and Robert A. Schumacker. "A characterization of ten hidden-surface algorithms," *Computer Surveys*, 6 (1), March 1974, pp. 1–55.

Warnock69   John Warnock. *A Hidden-Surface Algorithm for Computer Generated Half-Tone Pictures*, Technical Report TR 4-15, NTIS AD-753 671, Computer Science Department, University of Utah, Salt Lake City, UT, June 1969.

Weiler77   Kevin Weiler and Peter Atherton. "Hidden surface removal using polygon area sorting," SIGGRAPH 77, pp. 17–24.

Chapter 6   References

Blinn76   James Blinn and Martin Newell. "Texture and reflection in computer generated images," *Communications of the ACM*, 19 (10), October 1976, pp. 542–547.

Blinn78a   James Blinn. "Simulation of wrinkled surfaces," SIGGRAPH 78, pp. 286–292.

Catmull74   Edwin Catmull. *A Subdivision Algorithm for Computer Display of Curved Surfaces*, Ph. D. thesis report UTEC-CSc-74-133, Computer Science Department, University of Utah, Salt Lake City, UT, December 1974.

Ebert94   David S. Ebert, F. Kenton Musgrave, Darwyn Peachy, Ken Perlin, and Steven Worley. *Texturing and Modeling: A Procedural Approach* (first edition), Academic Press, Chestnut Hill, MA, 1994.

Ebert03   David S. Ebert, F. Kenton Musgrave, Darwyn Peachy, Ken Perlin, and Steven Worley. *Texturing and Modeling: A Procedural Approach* (third edition), Morgan Kaufmann Publishers, San Francisco, CA, 2003.

Ferguson01   R. Stuart Ferguson. *Practical Algorithms for 3D Computer Graphics*, A. K. Peters, Ltd., Natick, MA, 2001.

Gardner84   Geoffrey Y. Gardner. "Simulation of natural scenes using textured quadric surfaces," SIGGRAPH 84, pp. 11–20.

Gardner85   Geoffrey Y. Gardner. "Visual simulation of clouds," SIGGRAPH 85, pp. 297–303.

OpenGL99   OpenGL Architecture Review Board, Mason Woo, Jackie Neider, Tom Davis, and Dave Shreiner. *OpenGL Programming Guide: The Official Guide to Learning OpenGL* (third edition), Addison Wesley Longman, Inc., Reading, MA, 1999.

OpenGL00   OpenGL Architecture Review Board (Dave Shreiner, ed.). *OpenGL Reference Manual: The Official Reference Document to OpenGL, Version 1.2* (third edition), Addison Wesley Longman, Inc., Reading, MA, 2000.

Peachey85   Darwyn Peachey. "Solid texturing of complex surfaces," SIGGRAPH 85, pp. 279–286.

Perlin85   Ken Perlin. "An image synthesizer," SIGGRAPH 85, pp. 287–296.

Perlin89   Ken Perlin and Eric M. Hoffert. "Hypertexture," SIGGRAPH 89, pp. 253–262.

Perlin02   Ken Perlin. "Improving noise," SIGGRAPH 02, pp. 681–682.

Williams83   Lance Williams. "Pyramidal parametrics," SIGGRAPH 83, pp. 1–11.

Chapter 7   References

Atherton78   Peter Atherton, Kevin Weiler, and Donald Greenberg. "Polygon shadow generation," SIGGRAPH 78, pp. 275–281.

Bergeron86   Philippe Bergeron. "A general version of Crow's shadow volumes," *IEEE Computer Graphics and Applications*, 6 (9), September 1986, pp. 17–28.

Blinn88   James Blinn. "Me and my (fake) shadow," *IEEE Computer Graphics and Application*, 8 (1), January 1988, pp. 82-86. Also appearing in *Jim Blinn's Corner: A Trip Down the Graphics Pipeline*, Morgan Kaufmann Publishers, Inc, San Francisco, CA, 1996.

Bouknight70   W. Jack Bouknight and Karl C. Kelly. "An algorithm for producing half-tone computer graphics presentations with shadows and movable light sources," *Proceedings of the Spring Joint Computer Conference 1970*, AFIPS Press, Montvale, NJ, pp. 1–10.

Brotman84   Lynne Shapiro Brotman and Norman I. Badler. "Generating soft shadows with a depth buffer algorithm," *IEEE Computer Graphics and Applications*, 4 (10), October 1984, pp. 5–12.

Crow77   Franklin C. Crow. "Shadow algorithms for computer graphics," SIGGRAPH 77, pp. 242–247.

Kilgard99   Mark J. Kilgard. *Improving Shadows and Reflections via the Stencil Buffer*, NVIDIA Web site, November 1999, (developer.nvidia.com/docs/ IO/1348/ATT/stencil.pdf).

Williams78   Lance Williams. "Casting curved shadows on curved surfaces," SIGGRAPH 78, pp. 270–274.

Chapter 8   References

Appel68   Andrew Appel. "Some techniques for shading machine renderings of solids," *Proceedings of the Spring Joint Computer Conference 1968*, pp. 37–45.

Arvo86   James Arvo. "Backward ray tracing," *SIGGRAPH 86 Developments in Ray Tracing Course Notes*, August 1986.

Arvo89	James Arvo and David Kirk. "A survey of ray tracing acceleration techniques," in (Glassner89), pp. 201–262.
Glassner84	Andrew S. Glassner. "Space subdivision for fast ray tracing," *IEEE Computer Graphics Application*, 4 (10), October 1984, pp. 15–22.
Glassner89	Andrew S. Glassner. *An Introduction to Ray Tracing*, Academic Press, San Diego, CA, 1989.
Haines86	Eric A. Haines and Donald P. Greenberg. "The light buffer: a shadow-testing accelerator," *IEEE Computer Graphics and Applications*, 6 (9), September 1986, pp. 6–16.
Hall83	Roy A. Hall and Donald P. Greenberg. "A testbed for realistic image synthesis," *IEEE Computer Graphics Applications*, 3 (10), November 1983, pp. 10–20.
Jensen89	David E. Jensen and Daniel A. Reed. *Ray Tracing on Distributed Memory Parallel Systems*. University of Illinois at Urbana-Champaign, Department of Computer Science, Report # UIUCDCS-R-89-1551, October 1989.
Pharr04	Matt Pharr and Greg Humphreys. *Physically Based Rendering: From Theory to Implementation*, Morgan Kaufmann Publishers, San Francisco, CA, 2004.
Rubin80	Steven M. Rubin and Turner Whitted. "A three-dimensional representation for fast rendering of complex scenes," SIGGRAPH 80, July 1980, pp. 110–116.
Shirley00	Peter Shirley. *Realistic Ray Tracing*, A. K. Peters, Ltd., Natick, MA, 2000.
Smits98	Brian Smits. "Efficiency issues for ray tracing," *Journal of Graphics Tools*, 3 (2), February 1998, pp. 1–14.
Weghorst84	Hank Weghorst, Gary Hooper, and Donald P. Greenberg. "Improved computational methods for ray tracing," *ACM Transactions on Graphics*, 3 (1), January 1984, pp. 52–69.
Whitted80	Turner Whitted. "An improved illumination model for shaded display," *Communications of the ACM*, 23 (6), June 1980, pp. 343–349.

Chapter 9   References

Ashdown94	Ian Ashdown. *Radiosity: A Programmer's Perspective*, John Wiley & Sons, Inc., New York, NY, 1994.
Baum89	Daniel R. Baum, Holly E. Rushmeier, and James M. Winget. "Improving radiosity solutions through the use of analytically determined form-factors," SIGGRAPH 89, July 1989, pp. 325–334.
Baum91	Daniel R. Baum, Stephen Mann, Kevin P. Smith, and James M. Winget. "Making radiosity usable: automatic preprocessing and meshing

techniques for the generation of accurate radiosity solutions," SIGGRAPH 91, July 1991, pp. 51–60.

Cohen85   Michael Cohen and Donald P. Greenberg. "The hemi-cube: a radiosity solution for complex environments," SIGGRAPH 85, July 1985, pp. 31–40.

Cohen86   Michael F. Cohen, Donald P. Greenberg, David S. Immel, and Philip J. Brock. "An efficient radiosity approach for realisitic image synthesis," *IEEE Computer Graphics and Applications*, 6 (2), March 1986, pp. 26–35.

Cohen88   Michael F. Cohen, Shenchang Eric Chen, John R. Wallace, and Donald P. Greenberg. "A progressive refinement approach to fast radiosity image generation," SIGGRAPH 88, August 1988, pp. 75–84.

Cohen93   Michael F. Cohen and John R. Wallace. *Radiosity and Realistic Image Synthesis*, Academic Press Professional, Cambridge, MA, 1993.

Glassner95   Andrew S. Glassner. *Principles of Digital Image Synthesis* (two vols.), Morgan Kaufmann Publishers, San Francisco, CA, 1995.

Schneider03   Philip J. Schneider and David H. Eberly. *Geometric Tools for Computer Graphics*, Morgan Kaufmann, San Francisco, CA, 2003.

Sillion94   François X. Sillion and Claude Puech. *Radiosity and Global Illumination*, Morgan Kaufmann Publishers, San Francisco, CA, 1994.

Tumblin93   Jack Tumblin and Holly Rushmeier. "Tone reproduction for realistic images," *IEEE Computer Graphics and Applications*, 13 (6), November 1993, pp. 42–48.

Vilaplana92   Joseppe Vilaplana and Xavier Pueyo. "Exploiting coherence for clipping and view transformations in radiosity algorithms," in *Photorealism in Computer Graphics*, Kadi Bouatouch and Christian Bouville (eds.), Springer-Verlag, Berlin, 1992, pp. 137–149.

Wallace87   John R. Wallace, Michael F. Cohen, and Donald P. Greenberg. "A two-pass solution to the rendering equation: a synthesis of ray tracing and radiosity methods," SIGGRAPH 87, pp. 311–320.

Chapter 10   References

Cosker04   Darren Cosker, Susan Paddock, David Marshall, Paul. L. Rosin, and Simon Rushton. "Towards perceptually realistic talking heads: models, methods and McGurk," *Proceedings of the 1st Symposium on Applied perception in graphics and visualization*, Los Angeles, CA, August 7–8, 2004, pp. 151–157.

Ekman78   Paul Ekman and Wallace V. Friesen. *Facial Action Coding System*. Consulting Psychologists Press, Palo Alto, CA, 1978.

Farin90   Gerald Farin. *Curves and Surfaces for Computer-Aided Geometric Design: A Practical Guide*, Academic Press, San Diego, CA, 1990.

Hodgins95   Jessica K. Hodgins, Wayne L. Wooten, David C. Brogan, and James F. O'Brien. "Animating human athletics," SIGGRAPH 95, pp. 71–78.

Inman81   Verne Thompson Inman, Henry Ralston, and Frank Todd. *Human Walking*. Williams & Wilkins, Baltimore, MD, 1981.

Korein83   Jonathan Korein and Norman Badler. "Temporal anti-aliasing in computer generated animation," SIGGRAPH 83, pp. 377–388.

Menache00   Alberto Menache. *Understanding Motion Capture for Computer Animation and Video Games*, Morgan Kaufmann, New York, 2000.

Miller94   Dave Miller and Richard Parent. "An articulated limb motion planner for optimized movement," *The Journal of Visualization and Animation*, 5 (2), April–June 1994, pp. 89–123.

Multon99   Franck Multon, Laure France, Marie-Paule Cani-Gascuel, and Gilles Debunne. "Computer animation of human walking: a survey," *Journal of Visualization and Computer Animation*, 10 (1), January/March 1999, pp. 39–54.

O'Brien95   James F. O'Brien and Jessica K. Hodgins. "Dynamic simulation of splashing fluids," *Proceedings of Computer Animation '95*, pp. 198–205.

O'Rourke98   Michael O'Rourke. *Principles of Three-Dimensional Computer Animation* (revised edition). W. W. Norton & Co., New York, NY, 1998.

Pandzic02   Igor S. Pandzic and Robert Forchheimer (eds.). *MPEG-4 Facial Animation: The Standard, Implementation and Applications*, John Wiley & Sons, New York, NY, 2002.

Parent02   Rick Parent. *Computer Animation: Algorithms and Techniques*. Morgan Kaufmann Publishers, San Francisco, CA, 2002.

Parke96   Frederick Parke and Keith Waters. *Computer Facial Animation*. A. K. Peters, Wellesley, MA, 1996.

Potmesil83   Michael Potmesil and Indranil Chakravarty. "Modeling motion blur in computer-generated images," SIGGRAPH 83, pp. 389–399.

Reynolds87   Craig W. Reynolds. "Flocks, herds and schools: A distributed behavioral model," SIGGRAPH 87, pp. 25–34.

Rogers90   David F. Rogers and J. Alan Adams. *Mathematical Elements for Computer Graphics* (second edition), McGraw-Hill Publishing Company, New York, NY, 1990.

Sun01   Harold C. Sun and Dimitris N. Metaxas. "Automating gait generation," SIGGRAPH 2001, pp. 261–270.

Wooten96   Wayne L. Wooten and Jessica Hodgins. "Animation of human diving," *Computer Graphics Forum*, 15 (1), March 1996, pp. 3–14.

Chapter 11 References

Ableson86   Harold Abelson and Andrea diSessa. *Turtle Geometry: The Computer as a Medium for Exploring Mathematics*, The MIT Press, Cambridge, MA, 1986 (reprint of 1981 edition).

Bloomenthal97   Jules Bloomenthal (ed.), with Chandrajit Bajaj, Jim Blinn, Marie-Paule Cani-Gascuel, Alyn Rockwood, Brian Wyvill, and Geoff Wyvill. *Introduction to Implicit Surfaces*, Morgan Kaufman, San Francisco, CA, 1997.

Breen94   David E. Breen, Donald H. House, and Michael J. Wozny. "Predicting the drape of woven cloth using interacting particles," SIGGRAPH 94, pp. 365–372.

Chen99   Jim X. Chen, Xiadong Fu, and J. Wegman. "Real-time simulation of dust behavior generated by a fast traveling vehicle," *ACM Transactions on Modeling Computer Simulation*, 9 (2), April 1999, pp. 81–104.

Deussen98   Oliver Deussen, Pat Hanrahan, Bernd Lintermann, Radomír Měch, Matt Pharr, and Przemyslaw Prusinkiewicz. "Realistic modeling and rendering of plant ecosystems," SIGGRAPH 98, pp. 275–286.

Dobashi00   Yoshinori Dobashi, Kazufumi Kaneda, Hideo Yamashita, Tsuyoshi Okita, and Tomoyuki Nishita. "A simple, efficient method for realistic animation of clouds," SIGGRAPH 2000, pp. 19–28.

Ebert90   David S. Ebert and Richard E. Parent. "Rendering and animation of gaseous phenomena by combining fast volume and scanline A-buffer techniques," SIGGRAPH 90, pp. 357–366.

Ebert03   David S. Ebert, F. Kenton Musgrave, Darwyn Peachy, Ken Perlin, and Steven Worley. *Texturing and Modeling: A Procedural Approach* (third edition), Morgan Kaufmann Publishers, San Francisco, CA, 2003.

Enright02   Douglas Enright, Stephen Marschner, and Ronald Fedkiw. "Animation and rendering of complex water surfaces," SIGGRAPH 2002, pp. 736–744.

Fearing00   Paul Fearing. "Computer modeling of fallen snow," SIGGRAPH 2000, pp. 37–46.

Fedkiw01   Ronald Fedkiw, Jos Stam, and Henrik Wann Jensen. "Visual simulation of smoke," SIGGRAPH 2001, pp. 15–22.

Foster97   Nick Foster and Dimitris Metaxas. "Modeling the motion of a hot, turbulent gas," SIGGRAPH 97, pp. 181–188.

Foster00   Nick Foster and Dimitris Metaxas. "Modeling water for computer animation," *Communications of the ACM*, 43 (7), July 2000, pp. 61–67.

Foster01   Nick Foster and Ronald Fedkiw. "Practical animation of liquids," SIGGRAPH 2001, pp. 23–30.

Fournier82   Alain Fournier, Don Fussell, and Loren Carpenter. "Computer rendering of stochastic models," *Communications of the ACM*, 25 (6), June 1982, pp. 371–384.

Fournier86   Alain Fournier and William T. Reeves. "A simple model of ocean waves," SIGGRAPH 86, pp. 75–84.

Gardner84   Geoffrey Y. Gardner. "Simulation of natural scenes using textured quadric surfaces," SIGGRAPH 84, pp. 11–20.

Hallé78   Francis Hallé, Roelof A. A. Oldeman, and Philip B. Tomlinson. *Tropical Trees and Forests: An Architectural Analysis*, Springer-Verlag, Berlin, 1978.

Hanan04   Jim Hanan. Personal communication.

Holmberg04   Nathan Holmberg and Burkhard C. Wünsche. "Efficient modeling and rendering of turbulent water over natural terrain," *Proceedings of the 2nd International Conference on Computer Graphics and Interactive Techniques in Australasia and South East Asia*, Singapore 2004, pp. 15–22.

Holtkämper03   Thorsten Holtkämper. "Real-time gaseous phenomena: a phenomenological approach to interactive smoke and steam," *Proceedings of the 2nd International Conference on Computer Graphics, Virtual Reality, Visualisation and Interaction in Africa*, Cape Town, South Africa, February 2003, pp. 25–30.

Kajiya89   James T. Kajiya and Timothy L. Kay. "Rendering fur with three dimensional textures," SIGGRAPH 89, pp. 271–280.

Kelley88   Alex D. Kelley, Michael C. Malin, and Gregory M. Nielson. "Terrain simulation using a model of stream erosion," SIGGRAPH 88, pp. 263–268.

Kumler94   Mark Kumler. "An intensive comparison of triangulated irregular networks (TINs) and digital elevation models (DEMs)," *Cartographica*, 31 (2), June 1994, pp. 1–99.

Lamorlette02   Arnauld Lamorlette and Nick Foster. "Structural modeling of flames for a production environment," SIGGRAPH 2002, pp. 729–735.

Lindenmayer68   Aristid Lindenmayer. "Mathematical models for cellular interactions in development," *Journal of Theoretical Biology*, 18, 1968, pp. 280–315.

Linz01   Peter Linz. *An Introduction to Formal Languages and Automata, (third edition)*. Jones and Bartlett Publishers, Inc., Sudbury, MA, 2001.

McConnell88   Jeffrey J. McConnell. "Three-dimensional tree grammars for the modeling of plants," *Proceedings of the 1988 ACM 16th Annual Computer Science Conference*, Atlanta, GA (February 23–25, 1988), ACM, New York, 1988, pp. 494–499.

McConnell89   Jeffrey J. McConnell. "Botanical models based on three-dimensional attributed graph grammars," *Proceedings of the 20th Annual Pittsburgh Conference on Modeling and Simulation*, Pittsburgh, PA (May 4–5, 1989). ISA, Research Triangle Park, NC, 1989 (also published as *Modeling & Simulation*, 20 (4), pp. 1487–1494).

Mould97   David Mould and Yee-Hong Yang. "Modeling water for computer graphics," *Computer and Graphics*, 21 (6), November/December 1997, pp. 801–814.

Müller03   Matthias Müller, David Charypar, and Markus Gross. "Particle-based fluid simulation for interactive applications," *Proceedings of the 2003 ACM SIGGRAPH/Eurographics Symposium on Computer Animation* (July 2003), San Diego, California, pp. 154–159.

Nagel92   • Kai Nagel and Ehrhard Raschke. "Self-organizing criticality in cloud formation," *Physica A,* 182 (4), April 1992, pp. 519–531.

Neff99   Michael Neff and Eugene Fiume. "A visual model for blast waves and fracture," *Proceedings of Graphics Interface '99*, Kingston, Ontario, Canada, pp. 193–202.

Nguyen02   Duc Quang Nguyen, Ronald Fedkiw, and Henrik Wann Jensen. "Physically based modeling and animation of fire," SIGGRAPH 2002, pp. 721–728.

O'Brien95   James F. O'Brien and Jessica K. Hodgins. "Dynamic simulation of splashing fluids," *Proceedings of Computer Animation '95*, pp. 198–205.

Peachey86   Darwyn R. Peachey. "Modeling waves and surf," SIGGRAPH 86, pp. 65–74.

Perlin01   Ken Perlin and Fabrice Neyret. "Flow noise," SIGGRAPH 2001 *Technical Sketches and Applications*, pp. 187.

Prusinkiewicz88 Przemyslaw Prusinkiewicz, Aristid Lindenmayer, and James Hanan. "Developmental models of herbaceous plants for computer imagery purposes," SIGGRAPH 88, pp. 141–150.

Rasmussen04   Nick Rasmussen, Douglas Enright, Duc Nguyen, Sebastian Marino, N. Sumner, Willi Geiger, S. Hoon, and Ronald Fedkiw. "Directable photorealistic liquids," *SCA '04: Proceedings of the 2004 ACM SIGGRAPH/Eurographics Symposium on Computer Animation*, Grenoble, France, August 27–29, 2004, pp. 193–202.

Reeves83   William T. Reeves. "Particle systems—a technique for modeling a class of fuzzy objects," SIGGRAPH 83, pp. 359–375.

Reeves85   William T. Reeves and Ricki Blau. "Approximate and probabilistic algorithms for shading and rendering structured particle systems," SIGGRAPH 85, pp. 313–322.

Reffye88   Philippe de Reffye, Claude Edelin, Jean Françon, Marc Jaeger, and Claude Puech. "Plant models faithful to botanical structure and development," SIGGRAPH 88, pp. 151–158.

Schpok03   Joshua Schpok, Joseph Simons, David S. Ebert, and Charles Hansen. "A real-time cloud modeling, rendering, and animation system," *Proceedings of the 2003 ACM SIGGRAPH/Eurographics Symposium on Computer Animation*, San Diego, California, 2003, pp. 160–166.

Sims90   Karl Sims. "Particle animation and rendering using data parallel computation," SIGGRAPH 90, pp. 405–413.

Smith84   Alvy Ray Smith. "Plants, fractals, and formal languages," SIGGRAPH 84, pp. 1–10.

Ts'o87   Pauline Y. Ts'o and Brian A. Barsky. "Modeling and rendering waves: wave-tracing using beta-splines and reflective and refractive texture mapping," *ACM Transactions on Graphics*, 6 (3), July 1987, pp. 191–214.

Yngve00   Gary D. Yngve, James F. O'Brien and Jessica K. Hodgins. "Animating explosions," SIGGRAPH 2000, pp. 29–36.

Chapter 12   References

Adabala03   Neeharika Adabala, Nadia Magnenat-Thalmann and Guangzheng Fei. "Real-time rendering of woven clothes," *VRST '03: Proceedings of the ACM Symposium on Virtual Reality Software and Technology*, Osaka, Japan, October 01–03, 2003, pp. 41–47.

Anjyo92   Ken-ichi Anjyo, Yoshiaki Usami, and Tsuneya Kurihara. "A simple method for extracting the natural beauty of hair," SIGGRAPH 92, pp. 111–120.

Baraff98   David Baraff and Andrew Witkin. "Large steps in cloth simulation," SIGGRAPH 98, pp. 43–54.

Baraff03   David Baraff, Andrew Witkin, and Michael Kass. "Untangling cloth," SIGGRAPH 2003, pp. 862–870.

Bertails03   Florence Bertails, Tae-Yong Kim, Marie-Paule Cani, and Ulrich Neumann. "Adaptive Wisp Tree: a multiresolution control structure for simulating dynamic clustering in hair motion," *SCA '03: Proceedings of the 2003 ACM SIGGRAPH/Eurographics Symposium on Computer Animation*, San Diego, CA, July 26–27, 2003, pp. 207–213.

Blinn82   James F. Blinn. "A generalization of algebraic surface drawing," Transactions on Graphics, 1 (3), July 1982, pp. 235–256.

Bloomenthal97   Jules Bloomenthal (ed.), with Chandrajit Bajaj, Jim Blinn, Marie-Paule Cani-Gascuel, Alyn Rockwood, Brian Wyvill, and Geoff Wyvill. *Introduction to Implicit Surfaces*, Morgan Kaufmann Publishers, San Francisco, CA, 1997.

Breen92   David E. Breen, Donald H. House, and Phillip H. Getto. "A physically based particle model of woven cloth," *The Visual Computer*, 8 (5–6), pp. 264–277.

Breen94   David E. Breen, Donald H. House, and Michael J. Wozny. "Predicting the drape of woven cloth using interacting particles," SIGGRAPH 94, pp. 365–372.

Bridson02   Robert Bridson, Ronald Fedkiw, and John Anderson. "Robust treatment of collisions, contact, and friction for cloth animation," SIGGRAPH 2002, pp. 594–603.

Bridson03 — Robert Bridson, Sebastian Marino, and Ronald Fedkiw. "Simulation of clothing with folds and wrinkles," *SCA '03: Proceedings of the 2003 ACM SIGGRAPH/Eurographics Symposium on Computer Animation*, San Diego, CA, July 26–27, 2003, pp. 28–36.

Chen02 — Yanyun Chen, Yingqing Xu, Baining Guo, and Heung-Yeung Shum. "Modeling and rendering of realistic feathers," SIGGRAPH 2002, pp. 630–636.

Dana99 — Kristin J. Dana, Bram van Ginneken, Shree K. Nayar, and Jan J. Koenderink. "Reflectance and texture of real-world surfaces," *ACM Transactions on Graphics*, 18 (1), January 1999, pp. 1–34.

Debevec00 — Paul Debevec, Tim Hawkins, Chris Tchou, Haarm-Pieter Duiker, Westley Sarokin, and Mark Sagar. "Acquiring the reflectance field of a human face," SIGGRAPH 2000, pp. 145–156.

Goldman97 — Dan B. Goldman. "Fake fur rendering," SIGGRAPH 97, pp. 127–134.

Hanrahan93 — Pat Hanrahan and Wolfgang Krueger. "Reflection from layered surfaces due to subsurface scattering," SIGGRAPH 93, pp. 165–174.

House92 — Donald H. House, David E. Breen, and Phillip H. Getto. "On the dynamic simulation of physically based particle-system models," *Proceedings of the Third Eurographics Workshop on Animation and Simulation*, Cambridge, UK, September 7–11, 1992.

House00 — Donald H. House and David E. Breen (eds.). *Cloth Modeling and Animation.* A. K. Peters, Ltd., Natick, MA, 2000.

Jensen01 — Henrik Wann Jensen, Stephen R. Marschner, Marc Levoy, and Pat Hanrahan. "A practical model for subsurface light transport," SIGGRAPH 2001, pp. 511–518.

Kajiya89 — James T. Kajiya and Timothy L. Kay. "Rendering fur with three-dimensional textures," SIGGRAPH 89 pp. 271–280.

Kim00 — Tae-Yong Kim and Ulrich Neumann. "A Thin Shell Volume for Modeling Human Hair," *CA '00: Proceedings of the Computer Animation 2000 Conference*, Philadelphia, PA, May 3–5, 2000, pp. 104–111.

Kim02 — Tae-Yong Kim and Ulrich Neumann. "Interactive multiresolution hair modeling and editing," SIGGRAPH 2002, pp. 620–629.

Lewis00 — J. P. Lewis, Matt Cordner, and Nickson Fong. "Pose space deformation: a unified approach to shape interpolation and skeleton-driven deformation," SIGGRAPH 2000, pp. 165–172.

Marschner99 — Stephen R. Marschner, Stephen H. Westin, Eric P. F. Lafortune, Kenneth E. Torrance, and Donald P. Greenberg. "Image-based BRDF measurements including human skin," *Proceedings of the 10th Eurographics Rendering Workshop*, Granada, Spain, June 21–23, 1999.

Marschner03   Stephen R. Marschner, Henrik Wann Jensen, Mike Cammarano, Steve Worley, and Pat Hanrahan. "Light scattering from human hair fibers," SIGGRAPH 2003, pp. 780–791.

Mohr03   Alex Mohr and Michael Gleicher. "Building efficient, accurate character skins from examples," SIGGRAPH 2003, pp. 562–568.

Ng96   Hing N. Ng and Richard L. Grimsdale. "Computer Graphics Techniques for Modeling Cloth," *IEEE Computer Graphics and Applications*, 16 (5), September 1996, pp. 28–41.

Nishimura85   Hitoshi Nishimura, Makoto Hirai, Toshiyuki Kawai, Tory Kawata, Isao Shirakawa, and Koichi Omura. "Object modeling by distribution function and a method of image generation," *Transactions of the Institute of Electronics and Communications Engineers of Japan*, J68-D (4), 1985, pp. 718–725 (trans. Takao Fujuwara, *Advanced Studies in Computer-Aided Art and Design*, Middlesex Polytenic, UK, 1989).

Perrins03   Christoper M. Perrins (ed.). *Firefly Encyclopedia of Birds.* Firefly Books, Toronto, Ontario, 2003.

Watanabe92   Yasuhiko Watanabe and Yasuhito Suenaga. "A trigonal prism-based method for hair image generation," *IEEE Computer Graphics and Applications*, 12 (1), January 1992, pp. 47–53.

Weil86   Jerry Weil. "The synthesis of cloth objects," SIGGRAPH 86, pp. 49–54.

Wyvill86   Geoff Wyvill, Craig McPheeters, and Brian Wyvill. "Data structure for soft objects," *The Visual Computer*, 2 (4), February 1986, pp. 227–234.

Xu01   Ying-Qing Xu, Yanyun Chen, Stephen Lin, Hua Zhong, Enhua Wu, Baining Guo, and Heung-Yeung Shum. "Photorealistic rendering of knitwear using the lumislice," SIGGRAPH 2001, pp. 391–398.

Zhong01   Hua Zhong, Ying-Qing Xu, Gaining Guo, and Heung-Yeung Shum. "Realistic and efficient rendering of free-form knitwear," *The Journal of Visualization and Computer Animation*, 12 (1), February 2001, pp. 13–22.

Appendix A   References

Lengyel02   Eric Lengyel. *Mathematics for 3D Game Programming and Computer Graphics*, Charles River Media, Hingham, MA, 2002.

Rogers90   David F. Rogers and J. A. Adams. *Mathematical Elements for Computer Graphics*, (second edition), McGraw-Hill, New York, NY, 1990.

Schneider03   Philip J. Schneider and David H. Eberly. *Geometric Tools for Computer Graphics* Morgan Kaufmann, San Francisco, CA, 2003.

VanVerth04   James M. Van Verth and Lars M. Bishop. *Essential Mathematics for Games and Interative Applications: A Programmer's Guide*, Morgan Kaufmann Publishers, San Francisco, CA, 2004.

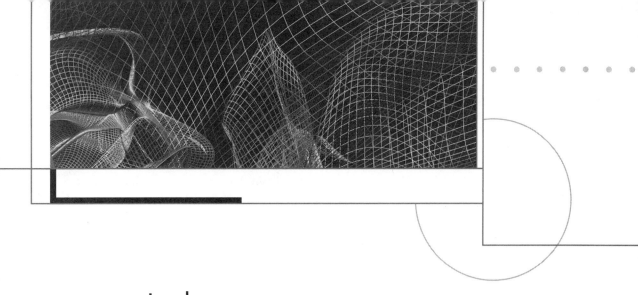

Index

probabilistic models, 416, 419*f*
Bounding volumes, 333–334, 334*f*
Box, ray intersections, 310–312, 311*f*
Branch graph, 143
Branching, plant, 411, 412*f*
Brass, 107*t*, 108*f*
BRDF. *See* Bidirectional reflectance distribution function
Bresenham's algorithm for circle, 132–135
Bricks, perspective of, 215, 216*f*
Brightness (lumination)
    calculation, 28
    perception, 32
    Purkinje shift and, 55
Bright spot, from diffuse reflection, 71, 74
Bronze, 107*t*, 108*f*
B-spline curves, 164–172
    cubic, 164–170
        blending functions, 164, 165–166, 166*f*, 167
        control point duplication, 168–169, 168*f*
        control points, 164–165, 165*f*, 166, 167
        end control points, 169
        endpoint interpolation, 168–169, 168*f*
        equation for, 166–167
        extending, 165–166
        local control, 164, 165*f*
        parameter range, 166–167
        rendering, 170
        subdividing, 169, 170*f*
        uniform formulation, 167–168
    noncubic, 170–172
    non-uniform knot vectors and, 176
    non-uniform rational, 175–176
    for particle-based fire modeling, 433
    sweeping, 181
    vs. Bézier curves, 164
B-spline surfaces, 179
BSP trees (binary space partitioning trees), 205–208, 208*f*, 209*f*, 334
BSSRDF. *See* Bidirectional surface scattering reflectance distribution function
Bump mapping, 222–227, 222*f*, 224*f*–227*f*

C
Calculation speedups, 463–464
Callback functions, 36–39, 41–42
Camera model, 9–11, 10*f*. *See also* Pinhole camera
Canvas3D, 143
Capturing of motion, 401–402
CAR (cosine amplitude ratio), 248, 250*f*, 251
Car, curved surfaces of, 153, 154*f*
Cartesian coordinate system, 465
Catenary curves, 467
Cathode ray tube (CRT), 28–29, 29*f*
Caustic highlights, ray tracing and, 329–331, 330*f*, 331*f*
C^1 continuity
    Bézier curve, 159, 159*f*, 160*f*
    Bézier surface, 178
Cel animation, 384–385
Cellular automata-based method, for clouds, 428–429, 430*f*
Character modeling, 435–459
Checkerboard texture, 256–257, 256*f*
Chrome, 107*t*, 108*f*
CIE LAB color system, 18–19
CIE XYZ color system
    chromaticity diagram, 17, 18*f*
    color gamuts, 17, 19*f*
    LUV standard, 17–18
Circle
    Bresenham's algorithm for, 132–135
    eight-way symmetry of, 132, 133*f*
    radians of, 465
    sweeping, 179–181, 180*f*
Clipping
    applications, 191
    of objects, multiple light sources and, 282–283, 282*f*
    OpenGL, 212–213
    planes, 212–213
    polygon, 208, 210–211, 211*f*
    shadow projection, 282–283, 282*f*
    Sutherland-Hodgeman algorithm for, 192–194, 194*f*, 195*f*, 196